To Cathy, Kirsten, Ingrid, and Sonja
Catherine, Emma, and Aiden

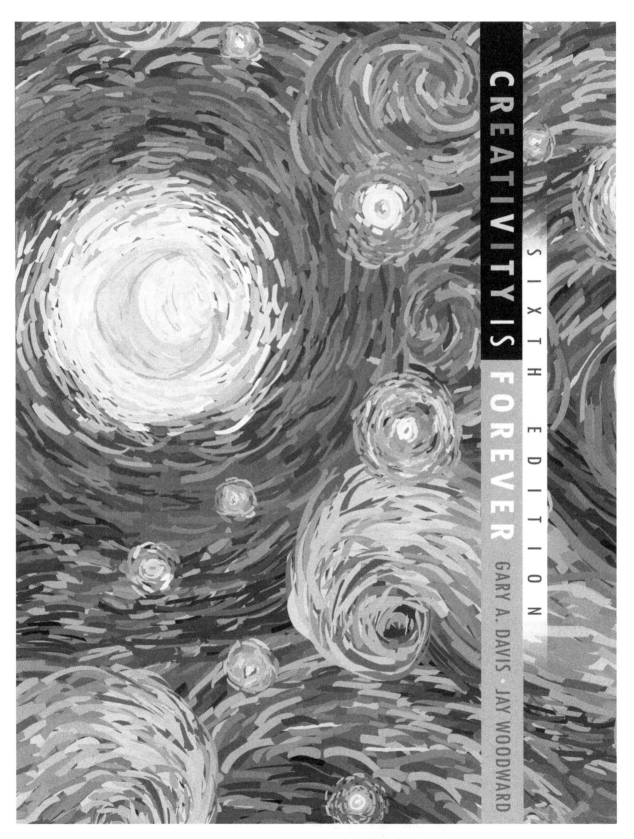

CREATIVITY IS FOREVER

SIXTH EDITION

GARY A. DAVIS · JAY WOODWARD

Kendall Hunt
publishing company

Kendall Hunt
publishing company

www.kendallhunt.com
Send all inquiries to:
4050 Westmark Drive
Dubuque, IA 52004-1840

Contents

Preface   ix

How to Use the Study Guides in This Book   xi

Chapter 1   Creativity Definitions and Theories   1

What Is Creativity?   2

Definitions of Creativity   4

Creative Person   4

Creative Process   6

Creative Product   8

Creative Press   9

Mysterious Mental Happenings   10

Summary   13

Review Exercises   15

Chapter 2   Creativity Approaches   19

Theoretical Approaches   20

Psychoanalytic Theories   20

Behaviorist Theories   21

Cognitive Theories   23

Humanistic Theories   25

Component-Based Theories of Creativity   26

Contemporary Theories of Creativity   28

Summary   33

Review Exercises   35

Chapter 3   Creativity Blocks and Barriers: Impediments to creativity   39

Habit and Learning   40

Rules and Traditions   41

Perceptual Blocks   42

Cultural Blocks   44

Emotional Blocks   46

Resource Barriers   47

Creativity Out of Whack?   47

Idea Squelchers   48

Summary   49

Review Exercises   51

Chapter 4   **The Creative Person: Flexible, funny, and full of energy**   57
Personality Traits, Abilities, Biographical Characteristics   58
Similarities and Differences   59
Creativity and Intelligence: The Threshold Concept   59
Personality Traits   64
Negative Creative Traits   69
Berkeley Studies   70
Creativity and Mental Disturbance   71
Biographical Characteristics   72
Birth Order and Handedness   74
Creative Abilities   76
Information Processing Traits   78
Creativity and Eminence   79
Abraham Tannenbaum: The Star Model   79
Herbert Walberg: Classic Characteristics of Eminence   79
Benjamin Bloom and Lauren Sosniak: Parental Support, Individualized Instruction, Communities of Practice   81
David Feldman: Precocity, Available Knowledge, and Co-Incidence Theory   82
Dean Keith Simonton: Many Factors   82
Cultivating a More Creative Personality   83
Summary   84
Review Exercises   86

Chapter 5   **Creative Process**   93
Where Do Ideas Come from?   94
One Process or Many?   95
Creative Process: Insight, Chance, or Hard Work?   96
Steps and Sequences   97
The Wallas Model   97
Feedback Loops and the Creative Process   99
The Creative Problem-Solving (CPS) Model   100
CPS: The Original Model   101
CPS: An Updated Model (Version 6.1)   105
A Two-Stage Analysis   106
The Creative Process as a Change in Perception   107
The Imagery–Creativity Connection   109
Imagery and the Creative Process   111
Summary   111
Review Exercises   115

Chapter 6   **Creative Inspiration and Analogical Thinking**   121
Importance of Analogical Thinking   122
Is "Borrowing" Ideas Ethical?   123
Analogical Thinking in Creative Innovation   124

Music   124
Cartoons   125
Architecture, Clothes Design   130
Analogical Thinking in Problem Solving   131
Synectics Methods   132
Summary   136
Review Exercises   139

Chapter 7   **Creative Products   143**
Creative Product: A Definition   144
Essential Characteristics of Creative Products   145
Evaluation of Creative Products   149
Creative Product Analysis Matrix (CPAM)   150
Categorization of Creative Contributions   152
Little c Creativity   152
Propulsion Model—Categorizing Creative Contributions   161
Summary   164
Review Exercises   167

Chapter 8   **Creative Applications, Pt. 1—Brainstorming and Creative Problem-Solving   173**
Personal Creative Thinking Techniques   174
Standard Creative Thinking Techniques   177
Brainstorming   178
Variations on Brainstorming   182
Attribute Listing   186
Morphological Synthesis   188
Idea Checklists   191
Summary   195
Review Exercises   199

Chapter 9   **Creativity Applications, Pt. 2—Lateral Thinking and Six Thinking Hats   205**
Lateral Thinking   207
Six Thinking Hats   208
Lateral Thinking Strategies   209
Specific Situations   214
Teaching Thinking Skills to Children   215
Summary   219
Review Exercises   221

Chapter 10   **Creativity Assessment   225**
Psychometrics   226
Uses of Creativity Tests   226
Issues in Measuring Creativity   227
Reliability and Validity in Creativity Assessment   228

Reliability   228
Validity   230
High IQ as an Indicator of Creative Potential   233
Formal Identification: Inventories and Tests   234
Creative Personality Inventories   234
Assessing Past Creative Activities   242
Divergent Thinking Tests   244
Recommendations   257
Summary   257
Review Exercises   261

Chapter 11   Creativity in Education   267
Joyce Junetune   268
Creativity in Gifted Education   269
Definitions of Giftedness   269
Characteristics of Gifted Students   272
Identification of Gifted Students   272
Goals and Curricula of Programs for the Gifted   273
Acceleration, Differentiation, and Enrichment Alternatives   274
Enrichment Triad Model   278
Summary   280
Review Exercises   283

Chapter 12   Creativity Is Forever: Unlocking Your Creative Potential   289
Educating for Creative Thinking and Problem-Solving   290
Issues in Creativity Training   290
This Book So Far   293
Self-Actualization and Creativity   295
Self-Actualized Creativity and Special Talent Creativity   299
Creativity Consciousness and Creative Attitudes   301
Metacognitive Understanding of Creativity   302
Exercising Creative Abilities   302
Creative Thinking Techniques   308
Involvement in Creative Activities   308
Summary   309
Review Exercises   311

References   317
Name Index   341
Subject Index   347

Preface

Creativity leader E. Paul Torrance (1988) once described creativity as:

Wanting to know	Digging deeper
Looking twice	Crossing out mistakes
Listening for smells	Listening to a cat
Getting in	Getting out
Cutting corners	Cutting holes to see through
Building sand castles	Plugging into the sun
Singing in our own key	Shaking hands with tomorrow
Having a ball	

These metaphors translate approximately as looking for what is not there; viewing the commonplace in unconventional ways; imagining the possibilities; experimenting; solving problems; making mistakes; and above all growing personally, professionally, and uniquely to become what you are capable of becoming. Creativity is essential to one's personal growth and success. It also is vital to society.

This book was prepared for anyone interested in better understanding the topic of creativity, becoming a more creative person, or teaching others to think more creatively. It is true that much about human creativity remains—and will remain—an intriguing mystery. It is difficult indeed to untangle the drives, thoughts, images, and inspirations of a Thomas Edison, Georgia O'Keeffe, or Walt Disney. As we will see in the first chapter of this book, extraordinarily creative people have not understood their own creativeness. However, it also is true that we DO understand much about creativity and creative people—their energetic and curious personalities, their idea-finding processes and strategies, and the circumstances that support or squelch their lively imaginations and innovative thinking. It also is true that despite genetic differences in our cognitive and affective gifts, everyone can become a more flexible, imaginative, and productive thinker. This is why we titled the book *Creativity Is Forever*, as we purport that creative ability is on a continuum. The possibilities are endless for expanding your own creativity by exploring this topic in the pages of this book, engaging in the activities, enhancing your appreciation of the topic, and elevating your levels of creativity consciousness through application and reflection.

How to Use the Study Guides in This Book

There are three purposes for the study guides at the end of each chapter:

- To help you master a body of information about creativity
- To provide ideas and strategies for teaching others to understand creativity and develop and use their creativeness
- To help you improve your own creative potential

The first goal is based on the principle that you will learn better if you actively respond to the material, for example, by (1) practicing recalling the information; (2) applying, analyzing, synthesizing, or evaluating the information and skills; (3) thinking about "what's important"; and (4) constructing your own interpretations of the information and skills. These chapters supply much information about the importance and nature of creativity, traits of creative people, elements of creative products, analogical and other creative thinking techniques, testing for creativity, and creativity in education. Chapter 12 focuses entirely on ways to make you a more efficient creative thinker and effective problem-solver.

The second goal will be achieved through completing exercises that will ask you to define or explain important concepts and names and to "think about" the principles and ideas in various ways. You might be asked to: paraphrase a particular issue; take a test that measures an important trait; explain a creativity issue; or expound upon the relevance of the information in each chapter to your own creativity. Real students just like you have done this as part of a college course. If you don't believe me that this helps, take it from them!

After reading the chapter the questions really helped me think about what I read and I would retain more information. The best aspect of the book was the inclusion of small creativity tests at the end of the chapters. This allowed for good analyzation of self and kept me on my toes about what I was lacking.

With that last quote in mind, the third and perhaps most important purpose is helping YOU understand, improve, and use your creative potential. You will be given practice in thinking of creative ideas and applying the concepts in the text to yourself and your own creative development. You might be asked to

- Think of creative ideas and problem solutions,
- Practice using some techniques,
- Think of preposterous ideas,
- Examine the implications of concepts for improving creativeness, or
- Directly apply the ideas (e.g., creative personality traits or barriers to creativity) to your own self-concept and creative disposition.

1 Creativity Definitions and Theories

"I feel such a creative force in me: I am convinced that there will be a time when, let us say, I will make something good every day, on a regular basis . . . I am doing my very best to make every effort because I am longing so much to make beautiful things. But beautiful things mean painstaking work, disappointment, and perseverance."

—*Vincent van Gogh*

Creativity is . . .

Elusive. Transcendent. Genius. The list goes on and on. And depending on who you ask – the scholar or the poet, the inventor or the artist, the professor or the student – the definition varies (and it should). To Van Gogh, it was the pinnacle of his lifetime work – the product of years of trials and tribulation and the result of constant refinement. But to another, creativity might be as simple as a sudden insight on how to speed up their morning routine.

Such is the paradox of defining creativity. How can we provide a single correct, black and white definition to a concept that is, by definition, the antithesis of having a single correct response? In short, we cannot. There is no singular definition of creativity that could possibly encompass what that one word captures across all persons.

Nevertheless, as this chapter will introduce and the following chapters will build upon, there are several varying perspectives on what creativity entails, and the most complete understanding of what truly comprises creativity is obtained when these perspectives are analyzed in complement to one another rather than in competition with one another.

As you read this chapter, keep in mind that each theorist has roots in different domains, and each of their theories will differ accordingly. Just as you likely had a different response to what "creativity is" than the next reader, our creativity theorists did as well.

"Make an empty space in any corner of your mind, and creativity will instantly fill it."

—*Dee Hock*

"You see a child play, and it is so close to seeing an artist paint, for in play a child says things without uttering a word. You can see how he solves his problems. You can also see what's wrong. Young children, especially, have enormous creativity, and whatever's in them rises to the surface in free play."

—*Erik Erikson*

"The creative writer does the same as the child at play. The writer creates a world of phantasy which he or she takes very seriously . . . while separating it sharply from reality."

—*Sigmund Freud*

What Is Creativity?

As we work to *construct* the definition of the term and its many various applications through this textbook, it is important for our framework to consider how creativity can be considered a *construct* itself.

In its verb state, construct means "to make or form by combining or arranging parts or elements" (Merriam-Webster), but as a noun, we can view a construct as being an explanatory variable that is formed through the synthesis of various concepts; typically over a period of time.

So what are these various concepts and how do they combine (or spontaneously combust) to result in the magic elixir that is creativity? Ah, therein lies the rub.

There are *many* definitions and theories of creativity, with the veracity of each challenged by the volume and variety of competing or conflicting explanations. To complicate matters, definitions sometimes are considered theories and some theories are just definitions. Elaborate definitions are especially likely to be called theories.

And then there is the word *model*, which often is used interchangeably with theory. Traditionally, the word model implies an analogical relationship, a point-for-point correspondence between one phenomenon and a different one. For example, we might say an attractive home with a well-manicured yard "looks like a million dollars." The description is analogical. As we will see, the investment theory of creativity is an analogical model. Investment terms and relationships are used to clarify aspects of creativity.

With clarity AND the aspects of creativity in mind, Unsworth (2001) stated that most researchers assume that creativity is a unitary construct, but pointed out that this "belief in homogeneity hinders a finer-grained analysis of the processes and the factors involved in creativity" (p. 289).

This book recognizes that it is a long journey from unitary explanations to united expositions. However, as we navigate the pathway to clarity with regard to creativity, we will shine a light and illuminate many different angles, viewpoints, and approaches to studying creativity. While the terms might differ, the tenets remain the same. The commonality among definitions, theories, and models of creativity is that ALL seek to simplify and explain a complex phenomenon. To impose some structure in this process, this first chapter will briefly review:

- Four categories of definitions of creativity, which focus on the creative person, process, product, and environment (press)—known collectively as the "four Ps."
- Mysterious mental happenings, familiar especially to artists, writers, and composers.

Chapter 2 will continue with definitions and theories by examining:

Three classic theoretical approaches to creativity:

- psychoanalytic
- behavioristic, and
- self-actualization

Seven contemporary "theories" (definitions, ideas):

- Sternberg's three-facet model;
- Amabile's three-part model;
- Csikszentmihalyi's (and Gardner's) person, domain, and field model;
- Simonton's chance-configuration theory;
- Investment theory;
- An interactionist model of creativity that describes interrelationships among everything; and a common sense, almost tongue-in-cheek viewpoint, implicit theories of creativity.
- Finally, we will look briefly at the new field of interdisciplinarity—scientific studies of aesthetic experiences.

As we truly explore the answer to the question "What is Creativity," a good place to begin is with *The Creativity Question* (Rothenberg & Hausman, 1976), a comprehensive collection of interdisciplinary readings and perspectives on creativity. These include: Greek philosopher Plato (divine inspiration of the Muses not named Matt Bellamy); behaviorist B.F. Skinner (who pigeon-holed the reinforcement of creative responses); Paul Torrance (the Godfather of creativity); Frank Barron (creative personality); and Joseph and Glenda Bogen (creativity and brain hemispheres). The book also presents a selection by my favorite classic scholar, Cesare Lombroso, who in 1895 related creativity to insanity—and therefore to brain degeneration—because both the creative and the insane tend to be original!

The Creative Process (Ghiselin, 1952), another anthology, presents original writings by historically creative persons, for example, Einstein, Mozart, van Gogh, Wordsworth, and Neitzsche. A more recent volume by Gardner (2011) describes relevant parts of the lives of seven creatively eminent persons—Freud, Einstein, Picasso, Stravinsky, T.S. Eliot, Martha Graham, and Gandhi. Other books covering creativity theory are by Arieti (1976), Sternberg (1988b), Kaufman & Sternberg (2010), and Runco (2014).

To set the tone, there are about as many definitions, theories, and ideas about creativity as there are people who have set their opinions on paper. As a few pertinent quotes, Freeman, Butcher, and Christie (1968) concluded that "there is no unified psychological theory of creativity" and that we freely use such terms *as imagination, ingenuity, innovation, intuition, invention, discovery,* and *originality* interchangeably with *creativity*. Nicholls (1972) added that "the term creativity is used with something approaching [reckless] abandon by psychologists . . . and people in general."

Tardif and Sternberg (1998b, p. 429), in an attempt to review commonalities and differences among the theoretical explanations in Sternberg's (1988b) anthology on creativity, concluded that "different levels of analysis were used to address the concepts; within levels, different components were put forth; and even when similar components were discussed, differences were seen in how these components are defined and how crucial they were claimed to be for the larger concept of creativity." And after reading these statements, you might conclude that ALL experts have COMPLETELY different ideas about what's important for creativity.

But, while perspectives can differ, as Batey and Furnham (2012) point out, "there have been recent integrative efforts to describe and delineate the field of creativity research," highlighting collaborative efforts to pinpoint personal and intellectual variables that are central to creative thought (Batey & Furnham, 2010) while simultaneously achieving precision in the measurement of creativity (Plucker, Beghetto, & Dow, 2010).

This precision in measurement is key as a main problem in pinning down "creativity" is its complexity and multifaceted nature. We can choose to examine, theorize, or conduct research about any minuscule or global part of creativity, and we do! This is where operational definitions come in; defining the terms of a process that is needed to determine the nature of an item or phenomenon. Just as every creativity test manual must explain what the test purports to measure, we need this surface level of understanding as we speak about the term and seek to unearth the underpinnings of this construct.

And, as far as personal variables go, two traits of creative people are attraction to complexity and tolerance for ambiguity, which also seem to characterize anyone interested in pursuing this topic, so read on all ye creative types as we begin to delineate, deconstruct, and define creativity!

Definitions of Creativity

You do not have to be a Rhodes scholar to try and define creativity! In fact, Rhodes (1961) has already done it for you with his alliterative attempt to conceptualize creativity into its base components. It is both convenient and conventional to organize creativity around the "four Ps." As mentioned in the preceding text, these are the creative person, the creative process, the creative product, and the creative press—the environment. Many people skip the confusing word "press" and just say environment (e.g., Hasirci & Demirkan, 2003), even though it does not begin with "p." (so pfeel pfree to do the same!) After all, there is precedent. For example, sections of Arietti's (1976) classic book are organized around the creative person, process, product, and environment. In the final chapter of their anthology, Tardif and Sternberg (1988b) reviewed each author's chapter in regard to its contributions to clarifying each of the four P areas. Long-time creativity leader Calvin Taylor already had organized his chapter around the four Ps. Person, process, product, and press remain a sensible and popular way to classify creativity research, definitions, theories, and other discussions of the topic (e.g., Hasirci & Demirkan, 2003).

Simonton (1988a, 1990), incidentally, added a fifth P, persuasion, to emphasize the role of leadership in impressing others with one's creativity. "A creator [must] claim appreciators or admirers to be legitimatized as a true creator" (p. 387). This "no-filter" approach has influenced influencers on social media and had an instant impact on Instagram posts. How many times have you looked at someone's feed and liked something you saw, or even tried to copy or emulate it?! We also will see this social-interpersonal part of creativity in the theories of Csikszentmihalyi (1988) and Gardner (1993). For now, we will sample definitions included under the first four Ps—person, product, process, and press.

The four Ps are interrelated in the obvious way: Creative products are the outcome of creative processes engaged in by creative people, all of which are supported by a creative environment. Torrance (1988) relates the creative process, person, product, and press with these words: "I chose a process definition of creativity for research purposes. I thought that if I chose a process as a focus, I could then ask what kind of person one must be to engage in the process successfully, what kinds of environments will facilitate it, and what kinds of products will result from successful operation of the processes" (p. 47).

In addition to the four Ps, this section will include discussions of mysterious mental happenings, a pesky category that cannot be ignored despite the best struggles of contemporary objective thinking.

Creative Person

In Chapter 4, we will review many recurrent personality and biographical traits of creative people, for example, confidence, energy, risk-taking, humor, and a history of creative activities. Definitions with a person orientation respond to the question "What is creativity?" with an answer such as, "Well, a creative person is someone who . . . (possesses particular traits that increase the person's likelihood and level of creativeness)."

While we will "factor" in research findings by Guastello (2009) on personality traits that contribute to creativity in Chapter 4, this section will briefly review three classic and more-or-less amusing definitions (descriptions, theories) regarding the nature of the creative person.

Cesare Lombroso

At the top of our list is Cesare Lombroso's (1895) degenerate brain theory. Naming specific famous and creative people, Lombroso noted that "signs of degeneration in men of genius" include stuttering, short stature, general emaciation, sickly color, rickets (leading to club-footedness, lameness, or being hunchbacked), baldness, amnesia/forgetfulness, sterility, and that awful symptom of brain degeneration—left-handedness! While rating high in entertainment value, the characteristics are not related to creative potential, except possibly the left-handedness.[1]

Otto Rank

While most psychoanalysts of the time assumed artists were neurotic, Otto Rank (1945) described his creative type—also referred to as *the artist* or *the man of will and deed*—as well-adjusted and self-actualized. This is in line with Baer's (1997) conceptualization of creativity as a self-attributed construct, in which creativity is "anything that someone does in a way that is original to the creator and . . . appropriate to their purpose of goal." The creative person has a strong, positive, integrated personality and "is at one with himself . . . what he does, he does fully and completely in harmony with all his powers and ideals." Rank's creative type contrasts with his "average man" and his "conflicted and neurotic man."

Rank also wrote that creating art is "a spontaneous expression of the creative impulse, of which the first manifestation is simply the forming of the personality itself" (Rank, 1932, p. 37). And again, "The creative impulse itself is manifested first and chiefly in the personality" (p. 38). A former glass blower, Rank himself probably was an artist.

Artist or not, his writings left an impression as to personal and personalized nature of creativity. Menaker (1996) describes Rank's viewpoints as being person-centered, emphasizing the nature of human will and surmising that "each individual is unique and carries within him or her the potentiality of creating something new, different and unexpected out of past experience."

Carl Jung

Carl Jung was a colleague of Freud. He was a regular guest at the weekly meetings of Freud's Wednesday Psychological Society. In 1909, Freud and Jung traveled together to Clark University in Massachusetts to promote psychoanalysis, and in 1910 Freud offered Jung the presidency of his new International Psychoanalytic Association (Gardner, 1993).

Jung (1933, 1959, 1976) described the creative works of novelists and poets, particularly Goethe, and identified two types of artistically creative people, the psychological type and the more imaginative visionary type. The psychological type of creator draws from the realm of human consciousness—lessons of life, emotional shocks, and experiences of passion and human crises. For example, said Jung, the poet's work is an interpretation of conscious life that raises the reader to greater clarity and understanding. Novels about love, crime, the family, or society, along with didactic poetry and much drama, also are of the psychological type. According to Jung, the material is understandable, based on experience, and fully explains itself.

More interesting and mystical is his visionary type. "It is a strange something that derives its existence from the hinterland of man's mind. . . . It is a primordial experience which surpasses man's understanding" (Jung, 1933). This "primordial experience" is said to be an activation of one's "archetypes" or "primordial images." Jung claimed that "The archetypal image . . . lies buried and dormant in man's unconscious since the dawn of culture . . . they are activated—one might say 'instinctively'—[in the] visions of artists and seers." When exposed to such archetypes, said Jung, we may be astonished, taken aback, confused, and perhaps even disgusted. They remind us of nothing in everyday life, but they may remind us of dreams, nighttime fears, and "dark recesses of the mind" about which we have misgivings.

The visionary creative person, due to dissatisfaction with current circumstances, is said to reach out to this collective unconscious. "The creative process, in so far as we are able to follow it at all, consists

---

[1] As elaborated slightly in Chapter 4, the suggestion is that left-handers, most of whom are ambidextrous, have superior access to both brain hemispheres, which helps creativity. The jury is still out.

in an unconscious animation of the archetype, and in a development and shaping of this image till the work is completed" (Jung, 1976, pp. 125, 126).

Is there evidence for this eyebrow-raising explanation of the creative person? Said Jung (1976), the assumption that an artist has tapped his collective unconscious for an unfathomable idea can be derived only from a posteriori analysis of the work of art itself, that is, the material seems not to be a reflection of the poet's personality, experience, or psychic disposition. However, noted Jung (1933), "we cannot doubt that the vision is a genuine, primordial experience, regardless of what reason-mongers may say." The critical reader, presumably a reason-monger, might place Jung's archetypes alongside Plato's Muses and the tooth fairy. But tooth be told, research-mongers such as Leveque (2011) have used Jungian theory to construct a model of how talents and traits can be combined with creative personality types to lead to "breakthrough creativity." You be the judge!

Creative Process

E. Paul Torrance

Torrance's (1988, 1995) definition of creativity describes a process that resembles steps in the scientific method: "I have tried to describe creative thinking as taking place in the process of (1) sensing difficulties, problems, gaps in information, or missing elements; (2) making guesses or formulating hypotheses about these deficiencies; (3) testing these guesses and possibly revising and retesting them; and finally (4) communicating the results. I like this definition because it describes such a natural process" (Torrance, 1995, p. 72). Torrance's process definition is unique in including the entire creative episode, from detecting a problem to presenting the results. Other notable contributions are related to his incorporation of creativity tenets related to problem finding and divergent thinking into his systematic approach to inquiry. We will cover those in more detail in future chapters. But, until we get there, take note that Torrance's process definition includes the creative person (someone who can do this), the creative product (the successful result), and the creative press (the environment that facilitates the process).

Graham Wallas

In Chapter 5, we will look at several proposed sets of stages in creativity, each of which has been described as "the creative process." For now, we will mention just briefly Wallas's (1926) ancient-but-still-healthy four steps of preparation, incubation, illumination, and verification. The terms are almost self-defining, but you may peek at Chapter 5 for some more with Graham's cracker of a theory (it is not all just marshmallow fluff!)

Creative Problem-Solving (CPS) Model

The currently most useful set of stages, in the sense of helping one to creatively solve real problems, is the Creative Problem-Solving (CPS) model (e.g., Osborn, 1963; Parnes, 1981; Treffinger, Isaksen, & Dorval, 1994a, 2003). While there have been many adaptations of this model since its inception, for the purpose of this book we will focus on the work coming from Scott Isaksen and Donald Treffinger out of the Center for Creative Learning. The most recent version has seen the theory evolve from its original six-step version (Mess Finding, Fact Finding, Problem Finding, Idea Finding, Solution Finding and Acceptance Finding) to an eight stage model that features four guiding components. The reconceived model has participants engage in (1) Understanding the Challenge (clarifying, formulating, or focusing thinking towards goal); (2) Generating Ideas (coming up with many new possibilities); (3) Preparing for Action (exploring ways to make promising options into workable solutions); and (4) Planning your Approach (metacognitive monitoring of thinking processes during ideational process). Our creativity roots will DEFINITELY be showing when we take a hair-raising look at both old and new versions of this model in Chapters 5 and 8.

Combining Ideas

Many process definitions assume that a creative idea is a combination of previously unrelated ideas, or looking at it another way, a new relationship among existing ideas. The creative process, therefore, is the process of combining the ideas or perceiving the relationships. Thagard's (1997) view of this process is that "conceptual combinations range from the utterly mundane to the sublimely creative . . . and both are essential to our attempts to make sense of the world and people's utterances about it." With utterances in mind, people have been weighing in on this for over half a century, with affirmative statements such as:

"The ability to relate and to connect, sometimes in odd and yet striking fashion, lies at the very heart of any creative use of the mind, no matter in what field or discipline" (Seidel, 1962).

"The intersection of two ideas for the first time" (Keep, cited in Taylor, 1988). "The integration of facts, impressions, or feelings into a new form" (Porshe, 1955).

"That quality of the mind which allows an individual to juggle scraps of knowledge until they fall into new and more useful patterns" (Read, 1955).

"The creative process is the emergence in action of a novel relational product, growing out of the uniqueness of the individual" (Rogers, 1962, p. 65).

"Creativity is a marvelous capacity to grasp two mutually distinct realities without going beyond the field of our experience and to draw a spark from their juxtaposition" (Preface to Max Ernst Exhibition, cited in Fabun, 1968).

David Perkins: Selection, Generation, Preservation

Perkins' (1988) explanation of creativity focused on how one deals with idea combinations. Perkins began by posing the hypothetical question of whether invention is possible: How can something come out of nothing? What is the (literal) Genesis of creativity? Phil Collins might say that we live in a land of confusion on this topic, but Perkins' solution, in brief, includes a process analogous to natural selection—the generation, selection, and preservation of ideas. Unlike natural selection, the generation process is not random. Andreasen (2011) describes it as a primordial soup of thought where "ideas collide until pairs interlock . . . making a stable combination." The potential "combinatorial explosion" of possibilities is "mindfully directed" by creative people, who are motivated, have creative "patterns of deployment" or "personal maneuvers of thought," and have raw ability in a discipline. Such people mentally represent and "operate on" traditional boundaries, producing practical innovations (e.g., the light bulb) and impractical ones (e.g., poetry—his example).

Arthur Koestler: Bisociation

Arthur Koestler's (1964; see also Mudd, 1995) bisociation of ideas theory of creativity is an over-eloquent statement that elaborates the popular notion that creativity involves combining ideas. Said Koestler, "Let me recapitulate the criteria which distinguish bisociative originality from associative routine . . . The first [is] the previous independence of the mental skills or universes of discourse which are transformed and integrated into the novel synthesis of the creative act . . . [Creativity is] the amalgamation of two realms as wholes, and the integration of the laws of both realms into a unified code of greater universality . . . The more unlikely or more 'far-fetched' the [idea combination], the more unexpected and impressive the achievement."

Koestler's broad theory emphasizes the commonality of creativity processes in jokes, artistic representations, and intellectual insights generally. He applied it to genetic codes and amino acids, on one molecular hand, and to aesthetics and organizational behavior, on the other much larger one. If it helps the reader's visualization, a "realm" (domain) is conceived as a two-dimensional plane—a flat matrix containing coded ideas, rules, and action sequences—whose intersection with another plane sparks the creative combination. Said Koestler (1967, p. 36), "The creative act . . . always operates on more than one plane," and "The bisociative act connects previously unconnected matrices of experience" (p. 45).

With Matrices in mind, this is analogous to the red pill or blue pill dilemma that one faces in the creative process. In repurposing a product or refashioning an idea, do you subject yourself to conventional thinking governed by reality OR escape into an illusion of ignorance where rules do not apply. Which would you chose? Do you have a "Neo" view of creativity where you can toss out assumptions and open your mind to new possibilities?

Defining creative ideas as new combinations of existing ideas has strong intuitive appeal. For example, virtually any consumer product, from bread makers and shoes with wheels to Chinese pizza and glowing golf balls, easily can be dissected into the parts that were combined into the innovative wholes. The same usually applies to scientific, medical, technological, and—perhaps with more difficulty—to artistic and literary creations.

Assembling high quality creative combinations normally requires experience, highly developed technical and stylistic skills, high energy, a lively imagination, and a polished aesthetic taste to know when the idea combination is good. The final creation may be complex, such as Beethoven's Ninth, or simple, such as chocolate covered crickets full of protein designed to give you a jump or (many) legs up on the competition!

Creative Product

Some definitions of creativity in the process category are a hair width (or less) from definitions in the creative product category and easily could appear in this section.

Using Guilford's (1950) groundbreaking call to action as an example, Runco and Jaeger (2012) point out that one of the very first attempts to standardize creativity for empirical research "emphasized originality and operationalized it as novelty and, even more precisely, in terms of uncommon behaviors." But with these uncommon behaviors in mind, if the person penning the definition thinks a few seconds longer, he or she usually will include some notion of correctness, appropriateness, value, usefulness, or social worth. Such terms exclude the bizarre, off-the-wall—but unquestionably original—scribblings of a chimpanzee or babblings of a child, a mentally deranged person, or a politician.

Said Briskman (1980), "The novelty of a creative product clearly is only a necessary condition of its creativity, not a sufficient condition; for the man who, in Russell's apt phrase, believes himself to be a poached egg may very well be uttering a novel thought, but few of us, I imagine, would want to say that he was producing a creative one" (p. 95).

With that said, there are definitions that focus on the creative product that emphasize originality, a term closely linked to novelty and often used interchangeably with creativity. Some definitions emphasizing just originality are:

"Creative ability appears simply to be a special class of psychological activity characterized by novelty" (Newell, Shaw, & Simon, 1962).

"Creativity . . . is a noun naming the phenomenon in which a person communicates a new concept (which is the product)" (Rhodes, 1987).

Adding a dash of value, utility, or social worth allows us to align ourselves with the notion that "Originality is vital, but must be balanced with fit and appropriateness" (Runco, 1988, p. 4). Quotes that indicate this, include:

"Creativeness, in the best sense of the word, requires two things: an original concept, or 'idea,' and a benefit to someone" (Mason, 1960).

"To be considered creative, a product or response must be novel . . . and appropriate" (Hennessey & Amabile, 1988).

"Creativity is the occurrence of a composition which is both new and valuable" (Murray, cited in Fabun, 1968).

"A creative person, by definition, . . . more or less regularly produces outcomes in one or more fields that appear both original and appropriate" (Perkins, 1988).

Emphasizing both originality and worth, Barron (1988) wrote that "Creativity is an ability to respond adaptively to the needs for new approaches and new products. It is essentially the ability to bring something new into existence purposefully" (p. 80). Expanding on the purposefulness of innovations, Barron emphasized "their aptness, their validity, their adequacy in meeting a need . . . The emphasis is on whatever is fresh, novel, unusual, ingenious, clever, and apt" (p. 80).

Finally, there are researchers who have tried to bring the conceptualization of the creative product up to "scale," as seen through the Creative Product Semantic Scale (CPSS) of O'Quin and Besemer (1989), which takes a three-factor approach and adds elements of resolution (how well the product functions) and elaboration and synthesis (stylistic components) into the mix.

Creative Press

A fourth category of definitions of creativity emphasizes the creative press, the social and psychological environment.[2] We do not find definitions or theories that are based solely on the presence or absence of a creative environment. We do find continual reference to the role of colleagues, society, or culture in most thoughtful writings on creativity.

We know that the environment may repress imagination and innovation, for example, as described in our cultural barriers section of Chapter 2. In a widely viewed TED talk video, Sir Ken Robinson (2006) purports that educational systems kill creativity; a strong indictment as to the power of societal institutions (a.k.a. schools) have on influencing (or inhibiting) creativity. Beyond this societal institution, we saw that organizations or nations can squelch creativity by stressing conformity, tradition, duty, obedience, role obligations, inflexible rules, and the status quo in general. To anticipate Freud's theory (Chapter 4), he combined virtually all social pressures into his word *superego*, which usually translates social conscience.

We find an emphasis on a favorable creative press in brainstorming, with its defining principle of deferred judgment (no criticism, no evaluation; Chapter 8), in Carl Rogers' (1962) emphasis on psychological safety, and in any classroom or corporate setting where a creative climate *encourages* creative thinking and innovation. Isaksen (1987, p. 14) noted as "necessary conditions for the healthy functioning of the preconscious mental processes which produce creativity: The absence of serious threat to the self, the willingness to risk, . . . [and] openness to the ideas of others."

Rhodes (1987) mentioned two aspects of the environment that are important for creativity. First, many innovations are in response to social needs—the world needed a cotton gin, a telephone, a Xerox machine, wickedly good Broadway shows that can defy gravity, heart transplants, CAT scans, microcomputers, the Internet, and Keurig machines (for those who have a grande-sized need for caffeine but are on a venti-sized budget!) Current highly visible needs—such as a cure for cancer and fewer guns, gangs, and joints in the elementary school—are motivating near-frantic levels of creative problem-solving and innovation. Second, for most creations, especially those based on technology, the environment must offer "a sufficiently advanced state of culture and a proper technical heritage" (Rhodes, 1987, p. 220).

---

[2] Mnemonic device: Think of social pressure as it pertains to the conceptualization of creative press.

In Chapter 7, via the theories of Csikszentmihalyi, Gardner, Van Gundy, and Simonton we will see a perhaps surprising, but to them essential, role of society in the provision of sophisticated judges to decide what products, and therefore what people, truly are creative.

Mysterious Mental Happenings

Lively descriptions of mysterious mental happenings come from people best qualified to examine the process of creativity—eminently creative people themselves. Peanuts cartoonist Shulz, for example, claimed that many of his ideas came from "things that go bump in the night." Despite his own strange suggestion of drawing ideas from one's unconscious, primordial archetypes, Carl Jung (1933) admitted, "Any reaction to a stimulus may be causally explained; but the creative act, which is the absolute antithesis of mere reaction, will forever elude human understanding."

In Art

On a presumably Starry Night, Vincent van Gogh (1952) wrote in a letter to a friend:

> I seldom work from memory. . . . When I have a model who is quiet and steady . . . then I draw repeatedly till there is one drawing that is different from the rest . . . [which] are just studies with less feeling and life in them. . . . The first attempts are absolutely unbearable. . . . I do my best not to put in any detail, as the dream quality would then be lost. (p. 54).

Zervos (1952) wrote the following from a conversation with Picasso. Note Picasso's reactions to people who try to understand his creative processes.

> What misery for a painter who detests apples to have to use them . . . because they harmonize with the table cloth! I put in my pictures everything I like . . . they'll have to get along with one another. . . . The picture is not thought out and determined beforehand, rather while it is being made it follows the mobility of thought . . . A picture comes to me from far off . . . I divined it, I saw it, I made it, and yet the next day I myself don't see what I have done. . . . How can one penetrate my dreams, my instincts, my desires, my thoughts . . . above all seize [understand] in them what I brought about, perhaps against my will? . . . Why is there no attempt to understand the song of birds? (pp. 56–60)

Your textbook "drew" heavily from the influence of Picasso and Van Gogh in shaping the cover of this new edition as well!

In Music

In a letter, Mozart (1952) described unconscious processes in creativity:

> When I am . . . entirely alone and of good cheer—say traveling in a carriage . . . or during the night when I cannot sleep—it is on such occasions that my ideas flow best and most abundantly. Whence and how they come, I know not; nor can I force them. Those ideas that please me I retain in memory, and am accustomed, as I have been told, to hum them to myself. . . . it soon occurs to me how I may turn this . . . to the peculiarities of the various instruments, etc. All this fires my soul, and . . . my subject enlarges itself, becomes methodized and defined, and the whole, though it be long, stands almost complete and finished in my mind, so that I can survey it, like a fine picture or a beautiful statue, at a glance. Nor do I hear in my imagination the parts successively, but I hear them, as it were, all at once . . . All this inventing . . . takes place in a pleasing lively dream . . . the committing to paper is done quickly enough, for everything is . . . already finished; and it rarely differs on paper from what it was in my imagination. (pp. 44–45).

Beethoven, as with Mozart, also heard symphonies in his head. The reader probably knows that Ludwig composed his Ninth Symphony, probably his greatest work, while stone deaf.

In Science

French mathematician Jules Henri Poincaré (1952) wrote:

> One evening, contrary to my custom, I drank black coffee and could not sleep. Ideas rose in crowds; I felt them collide until pairs interlocked, so to speak, making a stable combination. By the next morning I had established the existence of a class of Fuchsian functions. . . . I had only to write out the results. (p. 36)

Albert Einstein (1952) did his remarkable thinking without words, but—curiously—with muscle movements:

> The words in the language, as they are written or spoken, do not seem to play any role in my mechanism of thought. The psychical entities which seem to serve as elements in thought are certain signs and more or less clear images . . . and some of muscular type . . . combinatory play seems to be the essential feature in productive thought. (p. 43)

Finally, in speaking about his developing a "theory of everything" related to the world of theoretical physics, Stephen Hawking stated that

> It is no good getting furious if you get stuck. What I do is keep thinking about the problem but work on something else. Sometimes it is years before I see the way forward. In the case of information loss and black holes, it was 29 years (Brockes 2005).

In Literature

Poet Amy Lowell (1952) wrote:

> In answering the question "How are poems made?" my instinctive answer is a flat "I don't know." It makes not the slightest difference that the question . . . refers solely to my own poems, for I know as little of how they are made as I do of anyone else's. . . . The truth is that there is a little mystery here, and no one is more conscious of it than the poet himself. . . .A common phrase among poets is, "It came to me." So hackneyed has this become that one learns to suppress the expression . . . but really it is the best description I know of the conscious arrival of a poem. (pp. 109, 110)

Playwright Jean Cocteau (1952) suggested that ideas lie within ourselves, and that conscious effort can harness the unconscious inspirations. Easy for him.

> The poet is at the disposal of his night. His role is humble, he must clean house and await its due visitation. [My play] The Knights of the Round Table was a visitation of this sort. I was sick of writing, when one morning, after having slept poorly, I woke with a start and witnessed, as from a seat in a theater, three acts which brought to life an epoch and characters about which I had no documentary information. (p. 82)

In a conversation with John Hyde Preston (1952), author Gertrude Stein said:

> Think of writing in terms of discovery, which is to say that creation must take place between the pen and the paper, not before in thought or afterwards in a recasting . . . It will come if it is there and if you will let it come. . . . you have to know what you want to get; but when you know that, let it take you. (pp. 159, 160)

However, what if you do not have a conventional paper source? J.K. Rowling is famous for crafting the wizarding world of Harry Potter on napkins, barf bags, and any other material that would accept her ink. But, would it have been penned differently if she had a pen when the ideas first started flowing?

> I was traveling back to London on my own on a crowded train, and the idea for Harry Potter simply fell into my head. To my immense frustration, I didn't have a pen that worked, and I was too shy to ask anybody if I could borrow one . . . I simply sat and thought, for four (delayed) train hours, while all the details bubbled up in my brain, and this scrawny, black-haired, bespectacled boy who didn't know he was a wizard became more and more real to me. Perhaps, if I had slowed down the ideas to capture them on paper, I might have stifled some of them (although sometimes I do wonder, idly, how much of what I imagined on that journey I had forgotten by the time I actually got my hands on a pen). I began to write Philosopher's Stone that very evening.
>
> (Frenske, 2008)

Philosopher Friedrich Nietzsche (1952) defined inspiration as when:

> Something profoundly convulsive and disturbing suddenly becomes visible and audible with indescribably definiteness and exactness . . . I have never had any choice about it. . . . There is an ecstasy . . . during which one's progress varies from involuntary impetuosity to involuntary slowness. There is the feeling that one is utterly out of hand. . . . Everything occurs quite without volition. (p. 202)

Inspiration can take many fascinating forms and has led to many fantastic fantasy novels or frightening tales.

Mushens (2015) depicts that

> "C.S. Lewis was 16 years old when he had a bizarre daydream—that a half-man/half-goat creature was hurrying through snowy woods carrying an umbrella and a bundle of parcels. Years later, when he was 40, he started to write about Tumnus the faun in The Lion, the Witch and the Wardrobe"

Mary Shelley (1831) was struck by a dream that came out of her mind like a lightning bolt when revealing the electric jolt that inspired her to write Frankenstein:

> "When I placed my head on my pillow, I did not sleep, nor could I be said to think. My imagination, unbidden, possessed and guided me, gifting the successive images that arose in my mind with a vividness far beyond the usual bound of reverie. I saw—with shut eyes, but acute mental vision—I saw the pale student of unhallowed arts kneeling beside the thing he had put together; I saw the hideous phantasm of a man stretched out; and then, on the working of some powerful engine, show signs of life, and stir with an uneasy, half-vital motion . . . the idea so possessed my mind that a thrill of terror ran through me."

And who knows where George R.R. Martin's (Gilmore, 2014) mind wargs to when he hits a "wall" in the writing process, but in an interview with Rolling Stone he reveals how the world of Westeros began:

> "Suddenly it just came to me, this scene, from what would ultimately be the first chapter of A Game of Thrones. It's from Bran's viewpoint; they see a man beheaded and they find some direwolf pups in the snow. It just came to me so strongly and vividly that I knew I had to write it. I sat down to write, and in, like, three days it just came right out of me, almost in the form you've read."

From White Walkers to a different type of creature, Rudyard Kipling (1952), following Aristotle and others, attributed inspiration to his "Personal Demon":

> I learned to lean upon him and recognize the sign of his approach. If ever I held back . . . I paid for it by missing what I then knew the tale lacked. . . . My Demon was with me in the Jungle Books, Kim, and both Puck books, and good care I took to walk delicately, lest he should withdraw. (pp. 157, 158)

Finally, in an often-cited and colorful description of mental creative processes, John Livingstone Lowes (1927) described Samuel Coleridge's writing of Kubla Khan. Coleridge had reported that he composed over two hundred lines while in a deep opium sleep and published it almost without modification. Lowes proposed that Coleridege's prior readings and writings filled his mind with the ideas and images that combined into the poetic Kubla Khan. Lowes—but not Coleridge himself— wrote:

> Facts which sank at intervals out of conscious recollection drew together beneath the surface through almost chemical affinities of common elements . . . there in the darkness moved phantasms of fishes and animiculae and serpentine forms of his vicarious voyages, thrusting out tentacles of association and interweaving beyond disengagement. Samuel Coleridge probably would have said the same thing.

Summary

Definitions, theories, and models try to clarify complex phenomena. Many attempt to shed light on "creativity."

Most definitions focus on the 4 Ps: the creative person, the creative product, the creative process, or the creative press (environment). They interrelate. Simonton suggested a fifth P, persuasion.

Person definitions emphasize characteristics of creative people. Lombroso proposed that the creative and the insane have mental degeneration in common.

Contrasted with his average man and neurotic man, Rank's creative type is self-actualized. Jung's visionary type of creative person, who contrasts with his psychological type, is said to draw ideas from primordial archetypes, a collective unconscious. Evidence is thin.

Process approaches include Torrance's definition (sensing problems, forming hypotheses, testing them, communicating results); stage approaches such as Wallas' four-step and the CPS four-part models; plus numerous one-sentence definitions based on combining ideas.

Also addressing the creative process, and resembling natural selection, Perkins proposed the generation, selection, and preservation of ideas, with the "combinatorial explosion" of ideas "mindfully directed" by creative people. Koestler referred to the bisociation of ideas—the intersection of two planes (domains) of ideas.

Product definitions emphasize originality ("I am a poached egg"), but usually combined with value, appropriateness, usefulness, or social worth.

Definitions and theories tend not to focus solely on the creative press, but the environment is included in many thoughtful creativity writings. The "press" appears in discussions of barriers, brainstorming, Roger's psychological safety, and the creative climate.

Rhodes noted two aspects of the environment which is important for creativity: Social needs and an appropriate state of technology. "Mysterious mental happenings" emphasizes the complexity of creativity and our frequent inability to explain creative inspiration.

Van Gogh drew the same subject repeatedly until one showed feeling and life.

Picasso questioned why others tried to understand his creative processes when he himself did not.

Mozart described the involuntary mental flow of musical ideas, later developed and quickly written.

Mathematician Poincaré described ideas rising in crowds and interlocking during a sleepless night. In the morning, as with Mozart, Poincaré quickly wrote the results.

Einstein thought not in words, but in signs, images, and muscle movements.

Poet Amy Lowell insisted, "It came to me."

After a sleepless night, playwright Jean Cocteau awoke to witness three acts of a play.

Gertrude Stein emphasized discovery—"creation . . . between the pen and paper."

Nietsche also admitted to an ecstasy during writing, and again ideas were involuntary.

Rudyard Kipling claimed inspiration from a personal demon.

Lowes presented a colorful description of combining ideas.

Finally, tales of fantastic beasts and where to find them in one's mind's eye (or as the three-eyed raven) were revealed!

Review Exercises

Creativity Definitions and Theories

Self-Test: Key Concepts, Terms, and Names

Briefly define or explain each of these:

What is creativity?

_____

_____

_____

What are three terms you would use to describe the construct of creativity at the onset of reading this book?

_____

_____

_____

The four Ps

_____

_____

Simonton's fifth P

_____

_____

Jung's psychological vs. visionary types of creative people

_____

_____

Torrance's systematic and scientific definition of creativity

_____

_____

Koestler's *"bisociation of ideas"*

_____

_____

Elements of the Creative Product

_____

_____

Rhodes (1987) essential environment aspects of the creative press

_____

_____

Mysterious mental happenings

_____

_____

Let's Think about It

1. What is your theory of creativity—your definition, conception, or beliefs? Do you emphasize the creative person? The process? The product? The press (environment)? Some combination of these? Write down three essential terms, characteristics or phrases that YOU believe truly capture the essence of creativity. How can you combine these together to make your VERY OWN unique and fully-formed definition of creativity.

_____

_____

_____

_____

2. Make up a preposterous, totally unbelievable theory of creativity that explains why some people are highly creative and others and not. (If Lombroso and Jung can do it, so can you.)

_____

_____

_____

_____

3. Rhodes (1987) used the letter P to alliteratively distinguish between four different domains of creativity (Person, Process, Product, Press). Pick a different letter of the alphabet and do the same. Can you come up with three to five essential elements, domains, distinctions, etc. of creativity that all start with the same letter? Give it a go below:

_____

_____

_____

_____

4. In the mysterious mental happenings section, we focused on a lot of quotes from artists, poets, authors, scientists, etc. that talked about the unique or inexplainable circumstances that resulted in their notable creative product. Beyond those that are listed, can you find a quote from a famous creator NOT profiled in the chapter that demonstrates the notion of mysterious mental happenings relevant to their idea, invention, or creative contribution? Who were they? What did they create? Expand upon and explain the relevance of their quote below:

_____

_____

_____

_____

2 Creativity Approaches

"... to look at the stars always makes me dream, as simply as I dream over the black dots of a map representing towns and villages. Why, I ask myself, should the shining dots of the sky not be as accessible as the black dots on the map of France?"

—*Vincent van Gogh*

We effortlessly think of creative approaches to be significant life-changing episodes. Yet it can be the simplest technique to spark an idea. It could be the checkmarks on a vision board or even the connection of string between visited places on a map of France. But access to creative application is everywhere; it is the pursuit and it is a field in which we draw from.

Stars are the details in a larger backdrop; dreams are just the same in a creative process and product. Van Gogh may have believed that access was limited to the black dots, but when you change a view and application, you get an infinite amount of potential.

This is an interesting thing to think about. As you read on into creativity approaches, think about the outlining potential you create by a shift of perspective—the pursuit you dream about and the field and environment you pull the creative sparks from.

Chapter foreword contributed by Brandi Gomez. Copyright © Kendall Hunt Publishing Company.

Creativity is paradoxical and complex, and the most steadfast investigator is constantly beset with feelings of awe and a sense of mystery. . . . Creativity encompasses the magical incantations and drawings of primitive man, the appearance of new forms in nature, and the evil genius of Faust.

—Albert Rothenberg and Carl R. Hausman

One takeaway that you will hopefully get from these first two chapters is that while we do understand much about creativity and creative processes, much also remains a mystery—even to highly creative people themselves. We will spend Chapter 2 covering approaches to studying creativity in an attempt to turn the aforementioned magical incantations into incarnate words.

Theoretical Approaches

There are numerous ideas that are considered "theories of creativity," including all of the four Ps definitions in Chapter 1. Many different *principles* of creativity were covered that established a relationship between factors. From there, in this chapter, we will look at how individuals have used these principles to build *theories*, seeking to integrate common terms and tenants and use them to attempt to explain and predict a phenomenon of interest—namely, creativity. Sternberg and Lubart (1999) provide an outline of differing paradigms to approaching the term. We'll follow the lead of these "erudite" scholars, though take a bit of a "Divergent" approach, reviewing three (or should I say "Tris") classic theoretical approaches: the psychoanalytic, behavioristic, and self-actualization views. We then summarize several contemporary theories plus the topics of implicit theories of creativity (what people think creativity is) and interdisciplinarity (the scientific study of aesthetic creativity). Some you might abnegate. Some you might find truth and "candor" in! Let's begin!

Psychoanalytic Theories

There is not a single, unitary, agreed-upon psychoanalytic interpretation of creativity. Rather, there are several. We already saw Otto Rank's theory in Chapter 1, which emphasized his well-adjusted and self-actualized creative type (artist, man of will and deed) as contrasted with his "average man" and "conflicted and neurotic man." We also saw Carl Jung's psychological and visionary types, and perhaps chuckled at his invention of primordial archetypes. Rank and Jung could have appeared in this section.

Sigmund Freud

The best-known psychoanalytic theory of creativity is that of the great man himself, Sigmund Freud. Freud was extremely intelligent and well-read. As a child he topped his school class for many years. His family catered to his talent, giving him his own room and even his own "eating chamber." When his sister's piano practicing annoyed him, the piano was removed from the house! (Gardner, 1993, p. 52). As an adult thinker, dream analysis led him to conclude that sexual themes lay behind the unconscious, and that defense mechanisms, such as repression and sublimation (redirection), would deal with the disturbing sexual notions.

Freud's explanation of creativity focused on the motivation to create. Creative productivity is said to result from an unconscious conflict between the primitive sexual urges (libido) of the id and the repressive influences of our learned social conscience—the superego. Because one cannot freely indulge one's urges, the sexual energy is redirected (sublimated) into acceptable forms—creative fantasies and products. The id is happy, the superego is happy, and the self (ego) has fended off a big-time attack of neurosis from the conflict.

Freud concedes that everyone has the innate sexual urges that must be sublimated, but not everyone is highly or even moderately creative. The solution to this dilemma is that the creative person accepts the libido-stimulated fantasies and elaborates upon them, while the uncreative person represses them.

Freud (1976) described the special case of creative writers, at least novelists, which more or less fits his model of unconscious desires and conflict. He assumed first that common daydreams or fantasies arise from unsatisfied and unacceptable erotic wishes. After all, "the well-brought-up young woman is only allowed a minimum of erotic desire, and the young man [must] suppress the excess of self-regard [?] he brings . . . from childhood" (p. 50). The writer "creates a situation relating to the future which represents a fulfilment of the [erotic] wish." A fantasy thus is created, often including a heroine who, in novels, always falls in love with an invulnerable hero—thus satisfying female erotic fantasies and male egoistic and ambitious ones.

If you were psychoanalyst Sigmund Freud, and had read a few steamy novels, there wouldn't be 50 shades of grey in the interpretation of the novelist's mental life! Only how he came so well-read in a red room. . . .

Freud noted also that fantasy and creative thinking include a regression to more childlike modes of thought—a still-popular idea that relates creativeness to childlike thinking, humor, and a lively imagination. In fact, to Freud creativity is a continuation of and substitute for the free play of childhood.

As a vocabulary lesson, the regression is to primary process thinking. Developmentally, primary process thinking occurs before secondary process thinking. **Primary process thinking** happens during relaxation and includes the chaotic realm of dreams, reveries, free associations, and fantasies—your basic stuff of creativity. **Secondary process thinking** is more "grown up"—more logical, analytical, and realistic.

The Freudian view is a negative one: Creativity is said to be the outcome of an unconscious neurotic conflict. Most of us prefer a more positive explanation of the motivation behind creativity, such as responding to the challenge of a problem; meeting our innate needs to create, construct, achieve success, or improve the lot of humanity; or wanting to make a pile of money, which continues to stimulate high levels of entrepreneurial and corporate creativity.

Ernst Kris

Psychoanalyst Ernst Kris (1976) presented a slight modification of Freud's creativity theory. Creativity is said to be motivated by two main "basic" instincts of the id, the libido (sex drive) and aggressive instincts. Said Kris, "Fantastic, freely wandering thought processes [creativity] tend to discharge libido and aggression." Also, instead of unconscious neurotic conflicts, Kris emphasized preconscious and conscious mental activity. According to Kris, creative fantasies occur in the preconscious mind in the form of idle fantasies and daydreaming, which occur on the fringes of consciousness. The shift of (incubated) creative ideas from the preconscious to the conscious is felt as a sudden "Eureka!" or illuminating experience. As with Freud, Kris also accepts regression to more childlike thought processes—primary process thinking—as part of the preconscious activity.

An important theoretical distinction between Freud and Kris is that, to Freud, creativity is said to "be in the service of the id," since creativity unconsciously relieves libidinal (id) energy. To Kris, however, creativity is said to "be in the service of the ego," since the ego exercises some voluntary control over regression and over the shifting of preconscious ideas to the conscious mind.

Behaviorist Theories

Learning theorists do not agree either. To review your introductory psychology, ancient learning theory emphasized the reinforcement (reward) of correct responses plus the formation of stimulus–stimulus associations. S-R learning and S-S learning. You may recall Skinner's hungry rats who learned to press a bar to earn lunch, and Pavlov's dog who learned the association between bells and food, causing them (the dog) to salivate whenever the bell rang. The approach is called behaviorism because the focus is on the visible behavior itself, rather than the unseen mental events that control the behavior. Useful for training animals (or stimulating appetites), but what is their significance to creativity?

Burrhus F. Skinner

The big gun behaviorist, of course, was B. F. Skinner—a highly creative person who creatively argued that there is no such thing as creativity. In *Beyond Freedom and Dignity* (Skinner, 1971), he argued that we have no freedom, since all of our behavior is controlled by those who dispense reinforcements and punishments (parents, teachers, peers, police, and others who enforce laws, traditions, customs, mores, social expectations, etc.). Nor should we accept the accolades or attention that comes from personal accomplishment, since again those achievements were determined by a series or sequence of rewards and punishments. Succinctly put, this framework holds that external motivations supersede internal drives and, as such, supplant the need for creativity. How does this work? Let's examine the theory in context.

Basically, the behavior of a creative person such as a poet is "merely the product of his genetic and environmental history" (Skinner, 1972). The act of composing a poem out of "bits and pieces" is not an act of creativity, since in the experience of the poet he or she "had to learn how to put them together." In behavioristic terms, "the behavior [response] was . . . triggered by the environment [stimulus] . . . [and] the consequences [reward] may strengthen his tendencies to act in the same way again." According to Skinner, while creating a poem may indeed require exploration and discovery, these are tied to the history of the poet and to trial-and-error learning activities.

Since the poet is not aware of all of his or her history, he or she does not know where the poetic ideas (behavior) come from. Therefore, the poet erroneously attributes his or her own creations to a creative mind, an unconscious mind, or perhaps "to a Muse, . . . whom he has invoked to come and write his poem for him." Even Shakespeare is given little credit for his own works because "Possibly all their parts could be traced by an omniscient scholar to Shakespeare's verbal and nonverbal histories." Shakespeare himself merely put the bits and pieces together in a fashion that produced rewarding consequences (though Othello might beg to differ with heavenly sorrows that strikes where he doth loved!)

Even Shakespeare deserves no dignity. Et tu, Burrhus F. Skinner!

Marching forward a bit (perhaps through the woods of Dunsinane), it's not inane to think that this rigid response to Skinner's position might not have its critics. A publication by Epstein (1991) seeks to clarify Skinner's position on creativity by noting:

> Skinner recognized generative aspects of behavior but did not see generativity per se as a problem worthy of study or analysis. He knew that behavior was fluid, probabilistic, and at least sometimes novel, but he did not know how to advance an analysis of behavior without positing a recurring unit; hence the need to divide up behavior into "lots of little [recurring] responses." In a sense, Skinner took generativity for granted, relying on broad-brush explanations of creativity ("chance," "mutations") or on no explanations at all. (p. 365)

Maybe if you slept on it (or perchance happened to dream) the true answer as to Skinner's actual views might not provide you the toil and trouble that these conflicting statements seem to indicate.

Irving Maltzman

We are now moving to a second and related behavioristic theory of creativity; in a well-known article published in the high-status *Psychological Review*, experimental psychologist Maltzman (1960) argued that we can increase original behavior simply by rewarding it. He reviewed his own laboratory research that substantiated that when original word associations were rewarded, the frequency of original word associations increased. Related research by Pryor, Haag, and O'Reilly (1969) showed that if porpoises were given a dead fish only when they performed a new stunt—but not when they repeated an old one—they quickly learned to put a lot of variety and creativity into their act. Sea World should look into this, especially if their whales take a "bah bah Blackfish" approach to the orca encounter. It's comforting to scientifically confirm that creativity will increase when it is encouraged and rewarded. However, something seems amiss when porpoises are called creative but William Shakespeare is not.

Arthur Staats

A third behavioristic analysis of creative thinking is also straightforward. Staats (1968) described how S-R psychology can explain the production of novel, creative behavior through "complex stimulus control." We begin with the existence of two unrelated stimulus–response (S-R) relationships, each established by previous reinforcement. For example, the stimulus "Berlin Wall" elicits images of the Berlin Wall guarded by East German Soldiers. The stimulus of "people leaving" can elicit the verbal direction "Turn out the lights when you leave." In the fall of 1989, when East Germans were first allowed to leave their country, at least three cartoonists created a cartoon showing exiting East Germans telling a border guard to "Turn out the lights when you leave!"

This theory assumes that creative ideas are new combinations of previously unrelated ideas. The approach simply describes in stimulus–response language how two previously unrelated stimuli, when encountered together, can elicit a creative response combination. The description applies, according to Staats (1968), to any creative act from a child uttering a novel sentence to a scientist creating a theory. Arthur Koestler (1964) agreed, stating that this form of creativity "is the defeat of habit by originality."

Cognitive Theories

As pointed out by Kozbelt, Beghetto, and Runco (2010), cognitive theories of creativity emphasize the "role of mental mechanisms as a basis of creative thought" (p. 31). As you will see, the locus of cognitive theories of creativity are as complex as the human psyche, with shifts in attention and focus that can change at the blink of an eye!

Lawrence Kubie

Lawrence Kubie (1958) ignores ids, egos, libidos, and superegos and emphasizes preconscious mental activity. Imagine a continuum of consciousness. At one end is conscious mental life and conscious symbolic processes (e.g., language). With these conscious symbolic processes, we communicate, think, examine our thinking, and rearrange our experiences into logical categories. Such conscious processes have their roots in learning and experience. Since these processes are anchored in reality, there is little flexibility or imaginative free play, said Kubie.

At the other end of the continuum are unconscious, symbolic processes. According to Kubie, in the unconscious symbolic meanings are hidden, lost, or repressed and can only be made conscious by special techniques, for example, psychoanalysis, hypnosis, or drugs. This unconscious system of symbols, meanings, and relationships is said to be even more fixed and rigid than the conscious system—not flexible or creative at all. This rigidity of the unconscious, said Kubie, leads artists, composers, and poets to repeatedly use the same recognizable style and content in their works.

Creative activity takes place between the conscious and the unconscious, that is, in the preconscious. The preconscious is not tied strictly to the everyday pedestrian realities of the conscious mind, nor is it anchored to the even more rigid symbolic relationships of the unconscious. Rather, the preconscious can engage in free play with ideas, meanings, and relationships, thereby producing the new and unexpected connections, metaphorical relationships, overlapping meanings, puns, and allegories that we call creativity.

On education, Kubie says, "The price we pay for traditional educational methods is that they . . . tie our preconscious symbolic processes prematurely to precise [conscious] realities."

In contrast to the Freud–Kris explanation of creativity that was discussed earlier, Kubie says, "the ad hoc postulate that there is a separate and special mechanism known as the sublimation of unconscious processes may not be needed to explain creativity, and may actually be misleading. . . . Neurosis corrupts, mars, distorts, and blocks creativity in every field" (Kubie, 1958).

Conscious Mind_____[   ]_____Unconscious Mind

Transliminal
Chamber

FIGURE 2.1. Illustration of Harold Rugg's Transliminal Chamber, an area of preconscious, fringe-conscious, or off-conscious creative thinking that draws from the conscious and unconscious minds.

Harold Rugg

Rugg's (1963) formulation of creativity is extremely similar to that of Kubie. The difference, in fact, seems semantic. Rugg emphasized "off-conscious" mental activity or thinking in the **"transliminal chamber,"** which he located midway between the unconscious mind and conscious mental activity (Figure 2.1). The transliminal chamber was called "the center of creative energy." Here, the mind is free to draw from the vast store of experiences in the unconscious and to creatively use these in conscious everyday living.

Both Kubie and Rugg thus emphasize the importance of preconscious, fringe-conscious, or off-conscious thinking in creativity. Perhaps this relates to why creative people have strong needs for privacy, away from the demands of conscious realities, and daydream and incubate—both of which are forms of preconscious activity—as this type of creative cognition can produce creative inspirations.

Skuka (1980) noted that "mathematical solutions and lines of poetry seem to come out of nowhere, gifts from the gods to unwary creators in bed, bus, or bath" (p. 131). So with that in "mind" where do **YOU** get your best ideas? In your *bed*? In the *bath*? Or perhaps just *beyond* your realm of understanding!

Sarnoff Mednick

Waking up a bit (yawn!), let's move from preconscious to conscious thought with a cognitive theory that focuses on mental associations. Mental associations—for example, the word carrot might make you think of rabbit—are assumed to be learned on a stimulus–stimulus contiguity basis. That is, carrots and rabbits are commonly paired together, and so we form a mental association between them. Just like Pavlov's dog Rin-Tin-Tinovich forming the association between the bell and Kibbles and Bits.

According to psychologist Mednick (1962; also Mednick & Andrews, 1967), a highly creative person is one who possesses a large number of verbal and nonverbal mental associations that are available for recombination into creative ideas. A less creative person is one who is able to respond with just a few, highly dominant mental associations. Piers and Kirchner (1971) would term these *"flat associative hierarchies"* as all the words that come to mind exist on the same plane of commonality. For example, in listing unusual uses for a brick, the low-creativity person, with few-but-strong associations, would quickly snap off, "Well, . . . uh . . . you might build a house or a garage with 'em . . . if you had enough. That's all I can think of." In contrast, more creative individuals possess *"steep associative gradients"* whereby one target word can spawn a myriad of terms that might only be tangentially related.

Mednick (1967) published the Remote Associates Test (RAT), which was supposed to measure differences in the availability of verbal associations, that is, differences in creative ability. The test-taker would be given three words (e.g., shopping, washer, picture) and asked to produce a fourth word somehow associated with all three (window). The two main criticisms of the test are that (1) truly imaginative answers—those not on the scoring guide—will lower your score (Say WHAAAT?), and (2) the test correlates too highly with verbal intelligence, .40 to .60 in research by the Mednicks (Mednick, 1962, 1967; Mednick & Andrews, 1967) and .69 in a study by Davis and Belcher (1971). Other tests seem to focus more clearly upon creative potential, separate from intelligence.

The traditional criticism of stimulus–response psychology is that of oversimplification or reductionism. Such complex human behavior as hopes, plans, aspirations, neuroses, speech, reading this book, chuckling at the jokes, or solving chemistry problems, writing poetry, or designing a marketing plan theoretically could be "reduced to" principles of Pavlovian (classical) conditioning or Skinnerian (instrumental) conditioning. But much of the beauty and complexity of learning and mental life is lost in such oversimplification.

Creative Cognition

On the contemporary end, the "creative cognition" uses ideas generated from the realm of cognitive psychology toward an advancement of the knowledge surrounding how individuals use mental processes to generate ideas. The essential notion of this theory is that rather than being an exclusionary trait available to a privileged few, creativity is an inclusionary cognitive skill that is normative in nature; an essential property of human cognition (Finke, Ward, & Smith, 1992). In building this approach, Ward, Smith, and Finke (1996) state that the creative cognition approach has two main goals. "The first is to advance the scientific understanding of creativity by adapting the concepts, theories, methods, and frameworks of mainstream cognitive psychology to the rigorous study and precise characterization of the fundamental cognitive operations that produce creative and non-creative thought. The second is to extend the scientific understanding of cognition in general by conducting experimental operations of the cognitive processes that operate when people are engaged in plainly generative tasks" (p. 189).

Humanistic Theories

The essence of the self-actualization approach to creativity was presented. The central point was that the creative person also is a self-actualized person—a fully functioning, mentally healthy, forward-growing human being who is using his or her talents to become what he or she is capable of becoming (Maslow, 1968, 1970; Rogers, 1962). Some refer to this as a mental health or psychological growth explanation of creativity. To account for creative neurotics, the reader should recall Maslows' distinction between self-actualized creativity, the mentally healthy tendency to approach all aspects of one's life in a creative way, and special talent creativity, having a strong creative talent in a particular area with or without mental health and self-actualization. The reader also should recall Maslow's 15 characteristics of a self-actualized person summarized in Inset 2.1.

INSET 2.1
Maslow's 15 Characteristics of Self-Actualized People

- Perceive reality more accurately and objectively. They are not threatened by the unknown, and tolerate and even like ambiguity.
- Are spontaneous, natural, and genuine.
- Are problem-centered, not self-centered or egotistical. They have a philosophy of life and probably a mission in life.
- Can concentrate intensely. They need more privacy and solitude than others do.
- Are independent, self-sufficient, and autonomous. They have less need for popularity or praise.
- Have the capacity to appreciate again and again simple and common-place experiences. They have a zest in living and an ability to handle stress.
- Have "peak experiences" - moments of intense enjoyment
- Have a high sense of humor, which tends to be thoughtful, philosophical, and constructive.
- Form strong friendship ties with relatively few people, yet are capable of greater love.
- Accept themselves, others, and human nature.
- Are strongly ethical and moral in individual ways. They are benevolent and altruistic.
- Are democratic and unprejudiced in the deepest possible sense. They have deep feelings of brotherhood with all mankind.
- Enjoy the work in achieving a goal as much as the goal itself. They are patient, for the most part.
- Are capable of detachment from their culture and can objectively compare cultures.
- Are creative, original, and inventive, with a fresh, naive, simple, and direct way of looking at life. They tend to do most things creatively, but do not necessarily possess great talent.

Carl Rogers (1962) added additional important conditions for creativity that relate to growth in self-actualization:

1. **Psychological safety**. This is the creative atmosphere, a flexible and receptive environment. It is entirely a matter of attitudes.
2. **Internal locus of evaluation**. This refers to personal characteristics of self-confidence and independence, a tendency to make one's own judgments, and a willingness to accept responsibility for one's successes and failures.
3. **A willingness to toy with ideas and play with possibilities.**
4. **Openness to experience**. This includes a receptiveness to new ideas and an attraction to new interests and experiences. It also includes a willingness to acknowledge internal wants, needs, and habits, some of which could be of questionable social acceptability. For example, a creative male is more willing to accept traditionally feminine interests or behaviors, such as petting a cat, making baby formula, or baking a cake (Bem, 1974).

From Rogers' humanistic point of view, one stimulates creativity by creating a psychologically safe environment, modeling openness to experience and an internal locus of control, and encouraging students to play with possibilities.

Arons (1992) observes that "a major shift of emphasis occurred with the onset of humanistic psychology" (p. 166). Terming this a zeitgeist, it reflected a changing "spirit of the times in the field." He writes:

> First, Maslow (1959) and other humanistic theorists distinguished two major kinds of creativity; one which was talent centered, the other growth centered. The second was more like a creative way of life, a way as one potential realized by those whom Maslow described as self-actualizing individuals. Many of these self-actualizers, unlike the renowned creative genius, could not be recognized by tangible, typically acknowledged, creative products. It was extremely difficult to identify or to study such persons with rigorous scientific methodology. (pp. 166–167)

Component-Based Theories of Creativity

In contrast to process-based theories that highlight specific stages or certain sequences that creative thought must flow through, several theorists have developed component-based theories of creativity that emphasize personal, intellectual, societal, and structural characteristics that must be present for creativity to flourish. Instead of following a precise recipe (add a pinch of this, a dash of this, whisk, stir, and voila—creativity will occur), these theories simply indicate the essential ingredients that are necessary. If not mixed properly then instead of creativity you might have what Gordon Ramsay would call an idiot sandwich. But get the balance just right and BAM! Creativity. Just like personal preferences, not all of these theories might not be to your liking. But who knows, you might find your cup of tea in this section to sip and enjoy!

Sternberg: Intelligence, Cognitive Style, Personality/Motivation

Robert Sternberg's (1988a) three-facet Triarchic model of creativity focuses on characteristics of the creative person. In a summary statement, "creativity is . . . a peculiar intersection between three psychological attributes: intelligence, cognitive style, and personality/motivation. Taken together, these three facets of the mind help us understand what lies behind the creative individual" (p. 126).

Intelligence, from Sternberg's information processing and triarchic theory perspectives, cannot be summarized briefly. Let's just call it intelligence, with an emphasis on verbal ability, fluent thought, knowledge, planning, problem defining, strategy formulation, mental representation, decisional skill, and a general intellectual balance (see Sternberg, 1997, 1988a, 2003, 2006).

The *cognitive style* (or *intellectual style* or *mental self-government*) found in a creative person evolves around low conventionality—a preference for creating one's own rules and doing things one's own way; a liking for problems that are not prestructured; an enjoyment of writing, designing, and creating; and a preference for creative occupations, such as creative writer, scientist, artist, investment banker, or architect. Sternberg included in creative intellectual styles an anarchic form of mental self-government, characterized by a potpourri of needs and goals, a random approach to problems, motivation from "muddle," frequent lack of clear goals, tendencies to simplify, an inability to set priorities, and more. Said Sternberg (1988a), "Anarchics have the ability to remove themselves from existing constraints, ways of seeing things, and ways of doing things. . . . Anarchics are not to the tastes of either teachers or parents, because the anarchics go against the existing grain" (pp. 140–141).

The *personality/motivation* dimension includes creative traits that duplicate those to be described in Chapter 4, for example, tolerance for ambiguity, flexibility, drive for accomplishment, perseverance in the face of obstacles, willingness to grow in creative performance, and moderate risk-taking.

Concluded Sternberg (1988a), "People are creative by virtue of a combination of intellectual, stylistic, and personality attributes" (p. 145).

Amabile: Domain-Relevant Skills, Creativity-Relevant Processes, Task Motivation, and the Environment

Theresa Amabile (1983, 1988, 2012; Conti, Coon, & Amabile, 1996) proposed another comprehensive model of creative productivity. Her "Componential Theory" is a blueprint showing how social and psychological components combine to provide the "foundation" of creativity. Her first component is *domain-relevant skills*—skills that produce competent performance within a domain, for example, writing or drawing. This part of the model includes knowledge about the domain, technical skills, and special domain-relevant talent. *Creativity-relevant processes*, the second component, contribute to one's creative performance across domains. Conti, Coon, and Amabile (1996) mentioned appropriate cognitive styles, favorable working styles, and divergent thinking abilities. The third component is *intrinsic task motivation*, a common feature in descriptions of creative and eminent people. Task motivation includes one's attitude toward the task, motivation for the task, and ability to minimize external constraints. These three components are within the individual. The fourth component is the social environment in which the individual is working. This is an important component as Amabile and Mueller (2008) found that affective state, which is directly influenced by work environment, has a significant impact on an individual's creativity.

The Sternberg and Amabile models are similar in several ways. Both include motivation and thinking styles, although their precise descriptions vary. For example, Sternberg includes creative personality characteristics in his descriptions of both *cognitive style* and *personality/motivation* dimensions and seems to assume the existence of Amabile's *domain-relevant skills*. Amabile substitutes more specific *domain-relevant skills* for Sternberg's *intelligence*.

Csikszentmihalyi: Where Is Creativity? Person, Domain, and Field

Before he invented flow, Csikszentmihalyi (1988, 1990a) assembled a three-part theory of creativity consisting of (1) the creative *person*, (2) the person's *domain* or discipline, and (3) the *field* (institutions, experts, or society). The creative person supplies the necessary ability, talent, and affective traits. He or she receives formal training in the domain, for example, piano or mathematics, which includes exposure to rules, structures, and practices and within which the individual is expected to produce. Society, or the larger field, provides judges who, snobs that they are, pass judgment on the creativeness of the output. All three elements must interact to produce true creativity, defined as an innovation that—if it receives society's blessing—permanently alters the domain.

The model evolves around the question "Where is creativity?" The obvious answers of "in the person's head" or "in the creative product" are unacceptable, said Smith, because without the larger field or society passing judgment ("We hereby stamp this creative"), the person and the product simply are neither recognized nor accepted as "creative." Genuine creativity does not reside in the object itself, said Smith; rather, "the reason we believe that Leonardo or Einstein was creative is that we have read that that is the case" (Csikszentmihalyi, 1988, p. 327). It is the more sophisticated artistic and scientific establishment in which we place great trust that makes such judgments, that decides what is "an adaptive innovation" (p. 326). According to Smith, in regard to the notoriously fickle realm of the arts, the "critics and viewers who have looked . . . closely at Botticelli's work are just as indispensable to Botticelli's creativity as was the painter himself" (p. 328). In math, physics, and chemistry, the attribution of creativity again is a social process that, as in the arts, can be "relative, fallible, and sometimes reversed by posterity" (p. 328).

So that's why van Gogh died poor—the field had not yet made up its mind. In October 1989, one of his paintings was offered for sale at 40 million dollars, which sounds high but the frame and little light were included.

What's wrong? If you have not found it, the flaw in Csikszentmihalyi's thinking is to use *creativity* synonymously with *creative eminence*. Certainly, only a handful of people are sufficiently creative and produce sufficiently creative products such that—as judged by the larger field or society—they permanently impact the domain (e.g., math, chess, art, literature, theater, business, industry, science). But with creative geniuses in mind. . . .

Contemporary Theories of Creativity

The following includes brief summaries of several theoretical explanations of creativity, plus a description of our implicit theories. It is not an exhaustive list. The views represent some of the better-known contemporary speculations about the nature of creativity, creative processes, and creative persons.

Howard Gardner: Person, Domain, and Field

You should recognize the name of Howard Gardner, who has impacted psychology and gifted education by replacing the single IQ number with his eight-part theory of multiple intelligences (Gardner, 1999; von Károlyi, Ramos-Ford, & Gardner, 2003).

In *Creating Minds*, Gardner (1993) presents a case study of the lives of seven creatively eminent persons, Sigmund Freud, Albert Einstein, Pablo Picasso, Igor Stravinsky, T.S. Eliot, Martha Graham, and Mahatma Gandhi, "whose impact on our time has been compelling" (p. 4). Gardner adopts totally the three-part Csikszentmihalyi (1988) definition of true creativity, which requires a talented person, who experiences a period of training, is adventurous, and perhaps even is insubordinate; a domain or discipline within which the individual works; and a field (judges, institutions) that decides the quality of the creations. All three parts of the model appear in Gardner's definition of a creative person:

> The creative individual is a person who regularly solves problems, fashions products, or defines new questions in a domain in a way that is initially considered novel but that ultimately becomes accepted in a particular cultural setting. (p. 35)

As with Csikszentmihalyi, Gardner's conception of creativity is highly restrictive. Perhaps more so: "Of the many individuals and works that undergo scrutiny by the field, only a few are deemed worthy of sustained attention and evaluation. . . . And of the works that are appreciated at a given historical moment, only a small subset are ever deemed to be creative. . . . The works (and the workers) so judged actually cause a refashioning of the domain" (p. 38). In his example, he explains how, out of a 1,000 budding artists at work in Paris, "one or two at most will paint in a manner that becomes so highly valued that their efforts will ultimately exert some effect on the domain—on the structure of knowledge and practice to be mastered by the next generation of painters" (p. 39). The other 24,601 have a "Les Misérables" existence, dreaming a dream of when hope was high and life worth living.

Gardner's definition and assumptions are defensible, but only if the reader accepts his eminence definition of creativity as obviously and extremely restrictive. To use his figures, Gardner's definition eliminates the possibility of being creative for 99.85% of people who, in fact, are doing creative things, specifically, his other Parisian artists. Gardner dismisses the possibility of self-actualized creativeness by arguing that "an individual cannot be creative in the abstract . . . but must make his or her contributions in particular domains" (p. 37). Sayonara, Ciao, and auf Wiedersehen to all efforts of the Creative Education Foundation, most creativity classes and workshops, your creativity class and this text, and all supporters of the CPS model, brainstorming, Synectics, and every other effort to strengthen a general, self-actualized form of creativeness.

Simonton: Chance-Configuration Theory

In Chapter 1, we mentioned Simonton's (1988a) "fifth P," persuasion. Simonton also emphasized that *chance* plays a role in both the production of innovative ideas and in their social acceptance. Persuasion and chance fit together in his *chance-configuration theory* (Simonton, 1988). Like Gardner (1993), Simonton accepts the notion that "individuals become 'creative' only insofar as they impress [persuade] others with their creativity" (p. 386). However, Simonton's chance-configuration theory has different roots, one in his background as a social psychologist interested in personal influence, another in Campbell's (1960) Darwin-inspired *blind variation and selective retention* model of creative thought.

Campbell's three core assumptions, accepted by Simonton, appear in the label of Campbell's model. First, to solve a problem there must be some means of generating ideational variation; second, there must be criteria that select only the adaptively fit ideas; and third, selected idea variations must be preserved and reproduced.

With a seemingly slight alteration of Campbell's basic model, Simonton emphasizes, first, the chance (but not totally random) permutations of mental elements, such as ideas, concepts, recollections, or other aspects of cognitive schemata. We now have ideas or "potential permutations." Second, only the most stable (coherent, sensible) of the permutations are retained for further processing. Stable permutations, or "configurations," take their shape because of experience, rules and conventions, and sensibility. A configuration (solution) is selected based on its apparent usefulness or suitability to the problem.

Following considerable "intrapsychic" development and polishing of the innovation/configuration, the third and final step is the social one. The person now must take a leadership role. He or she must persuade others of the quality—the creativeness—of the final product. The product must be accepted; it must be viewed as having value to the endeavors of sophisticated others within that domain.

For an "aha!" experience, compare Simonton's theory with that of David Perkins.

Investment Theory of Creativity

For a short while, economic and investment terms seemed a profitable way to describe creativity. For example, several scholars described how an investment in the creative development of our youth (involving costs) reaps short- and long-term benefits for society (Rubenson, 1991; Rubenson & Runco, 1992; Walberg & Stariha, 1992). Also using investment terms, Sternberg and Lubart (1992) explained how "investing" in one's own creative research or theory ideas, although risky, can produce greater personal profits (professional prestige, higher visibility) than buying into well-established and popular ideas. Sternberg and Lubart (1996) titled one article "Investing in Creativity" to emphasize society's error in underinvesting in the study of creativity relative to its importance in the world. In a follow-up article Sternberg (2012) went on to add that investment theory helps us understand "creative people as the ones who are willing and able to metaphorically buy low and sell high in the realm of ideas . . . through the confluence of six distinct, but interrelated resources: intellectual abilities, knowledge, styles of thinking, personality, motivation, and environment" (p. 5).

Walberg's (1988) definition of "human capital" included the motivation, skills, and creativity of the person. Said Walberg, people are "capital assets to themselves and others" (p. 342). Their time is valuable and should be allocated efficiently. Also, young people have a choice between working after high school versus investing in enhancing their "personal capital" (e.g., attending college), "which involves risky short- and long-term opportunities, costs, and benefits" (p. 343). The production of talent thus can involve costs (e.g., tuition, books, rent, low income for four, five, or six years—depending on the number of victory laps taken) as well as benefits (higher eventual earnings, prestige, psychological satisfaction).

Gardner (1993) found the vocabulary handy, mentioning that potentially creative children who have opportunities to discover and explore "will accumulate invaluable 'capital of creativity,' on which they can draw in later life" (p. 31).

Analogical models are marvelous theoretical and teaching devices. They simplify complex topics by summarizing large amounts of information in compact, understandable ways. They help illustrate interrelationships among parts. They provide a language and sometimes a visual illustration to aid understanding and prediction.

A popular example is the information processing model, which uses a flow chart—boxes and arrows—to summarize interactions among environmental input, attentional processes, sensory stores, short-term and long-term memories, rehearsal, response modes, and executive control processes. Equating the mind to a computer, they seek to explain and explore how we input, retain, and recall information. Peek ahead at the Interactionist Model of Creative Behavior flowchart summarized in Figure 2.2.

Analogical models are neither right nor wrong, neither valid nor invalid. They either work or do not work in helping us understand point-for-point correspondences. The investment model of creativity plays its simplification and instructional roles nicely. It can even lead to new insights about creativity. For example, bad investments—perhaps in the wrong college major or in the latest pyramid scheme—can cause personal bankruptcy.

Interactionist Model of Creative Behavior

This book tries to present a brief overview of most of the important topics in creativity—self-actualization, barriers, definitions and theories, personality traits, abilities and cognitive styles, stage models of the process, creativity techniques, tests, training, and more. Essentially, everything interacts with everything else.

An interactionist model that attempts to tie much of this together in one picture appears in Figure 2.2 (Woodman & Schoenfeldt, 1990) on the next page. The main emphases are on person and environment. (When you think about it, what else is there?) According to the authors, various theories and research focus sometimes on aspects of the person, sometimes on features of the environment, and "sometimes both plus their reciprocal influences are necessary to even begin to understand what is going on."

The Interactionist Model is conveyed in flowchart form with analogical, but the Interactionist Model is summarized in Figure 2.2—a flowchart with analogical correspondences to aspects of the creative person and environment. The model includes *antecedent conditions* (A), such as one's background, socialization, gender, and other biographical variables; the *"organism"* (O) or person, which includes his or her personality traits (P) as well as abilities, thinking styles, and "openness" (CS); contextual influences (CI), such as the particular task and the organizational climate; social influences (SI), such as expectations and role models; the [solution, creative] behavior (B) itself; and the consequences (C).[1]

Now the fun part. Cognitive explanations of creativity, which emphasize, for example, abilities and thinking styles, would focus on CS-O-B linkages. Social orientations might be found in SI-O-B (with some interest in CI and A). Developmentalists and gifted education folks would look at A-O-B, A-SI-O-B, and A-CIO-B sequences. Scholars with an organizational bent would examine the CI-O-B chain. Stage models of creativity (e.g., Wallas and CPS models) focus on O-B-C-O linkages. Skinner and behaviorism fall in the [A, CI, SI]-B-C chain.

Said Woodman and Schoenfeldt (1990), "the value of the interactionist perspective is . . . to see how various components, elements, and forces come together to result in the behavior of interest, in this case, creativity" (p. 286).

---

[1] Only experimental psychologists would refer to people as organisms, as though paramecia and lab rats could be included in this discussion of creativity.

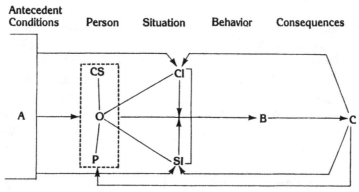

A = Antecedent conditions to current situation. Examples:
    Past reinforcement history, early socialization, biographical
    variables—sex, family position, birth order
B = Creative behavior
C = Consequences
O = "Organism" (person)—gestalt of attitudes, values, intentions
    to behave, motivational orientation, individual differences
CS = Cognitive style/abilities—examples: cognitive complexity,
    divergent thinking, verbal/ideational fluency, problem-solving
    styles/approaches, perceptual openness, field independence/
    dependence
P = Personality dimensions/traits—examples: locus of control
    dogmatism, autonomy, self-esteem, narcissism, intuition
CI = Contextual influences—examples: physical environment,
    culture, group/organization "climate," task and time constraints
SI = social influence—examples: social facilitation, evaluation
    expectation, rewards/punishments, role modeling

FIGURE 2.2. An Interactionist Model of Creative Behavior, R.W. Woodman & L.A. Schoenfeldt, *The Journal of Creative Behavior*, 1990, 24(4), pp. 270–290. Copyright © 2011 John Wiley and Sons. Permission conveyed through Copyright Clearance Center.

Implicit Theories of Creativity

The reader will be delighted to discover that what he or she already thinks about "creativity" has a name: It's an *implicit theory of creativity*. According to Runco (1990, 1999; Plucker & Runco, 1998), an implicit theory of creativity is just that—a theory or conception of creativity that exists in your mind. Such implicit theories serve as mental prototypes that we use to decide if a product, behavior, or person is creative—whether or not we can properly define creativity (Runco, 1999). For example, adults' implicit theories of children's creativity include the adjectives *adventurous, enthusiastic, active, curious, artistic,* and *imaginative* (Lim & Plucker, 2001; Runco, Johnson, & Bear, 1993). In Csikszentmihalyi's (1988, 1990a) and Gardner's (1993) theories, leaders in a field would use their implicit theories to evaluate the creativeness of a contribution.

Runco's (1990) research compared implicit theories of artists and non-artists. As a sample of his results, both groups agreed that artists were imaginative and expressive. Artists added *humorous, open-minded,* and *emotional,* while non-artists endorsed *intelligent, original,* and "draw well." Both groups agreed that scientists were intelligent and curious. Both groups also agreed that "everyday creativity" was characterized by being active. But artists again added *humorous* and *open-minded.* Non-artists added *imaginative, commonsensical,* and "cooks well."

Implicit theories of creativity apparently are similar, but not identical, worldwide. A core consideration is cultural values. In Hong Kong, for example, Chan and Chan (1999) found that teachers listed nonconformity as a creative trait—which was cause for concern in a culture that values social responsibility.

In Korea, Lim and Plucker (2001) managed to convince 478 university students—people waiting for buses or subway trains, supermarket shoppers, high school teachers, and others—to check off, of which 75 descriptors were characteristic of an "ideally creative person" (p. 123). The implicit definitions mostly—not exactly—mirrored Western conceptions. Four categories (factors) of endorsed descriptions were: (1) Personality and General Creativity (e.g., "is passionate about work," "is positive and energetic," "is unique and original," "has lots of ideas"), (2) Perseverance (e.g., "tends to stick to an idea," "is very patient," "must finish if one starts something"), (3) Independence and Deviance (e.g., "is indifferent to others' opinions," "makes conflicts when working in groups," "seems to be abnormal," "is spontaneous"), and (4) Cognition and Motivation (e.g., "solves problems well," "is eager to learn everything," "thinks in a logical and scientific way").

However, the Koreans were negative toward some social behaviors associated with creativity. Especially, viewing creative people as loners and nonconformists was unattractive in a culture "with a strong sense of social responsibility [and] conformity" (p. 127).

Asian research by Yue and Rudowicz (2002) suggested that 489 college students in Beijing, Taipei, Hong Kong, and Guangzhou held mildly confused (implicit) definitions of creativity. The researchers asked the undergraduates to nominate up to three creative people in Chinese history and modern times, and give their reasons for the nominations. Politicians received the most nominations, with scientists and inventors in second place. They rarely nominated artists, musicians, or businessmen. It seems the nominations reflected "social influence or contributions in society . . . [rather than] innovativeness in thinking" (p. 91).

An earlier study by Rudowicz and Hui (1997) indicated that Chinese conceptions of creativity did include the Western characteristics of imagination, innovative ideas, intelligence, independence, and high energy, but not sense of humor or aesthetic taste. As in the Yue and Rudowicz study, the Chinese subjects included "contributing to the progress of society" in their implicit definitions.

Niu and Sternberg (2002) also concluded that "Asians have similar but not identical concepts of creativity to many people in the West" (p. 269). For example, Chinese conceptions include an ethical and moral component quite missing in Western implicit definitions of creativity. (Creativity exercise: Think of possible implications of this conclusion for business, the arts, and social behavior in Western countries.)

In India, Niu and Sternberg (2002) reported that Indian scientists defined creativity as requiring the abilities to synthesize, integrate, and create something new. Scientific creativity, the scientists reported, requires more rules and logic than artistic creativity. The scientists also agreed that all creative persons show curiosity, risk-taking, open-mindedness, motivation, broad interests, and aesthetic taste. But creativity generally is lower in India because "obedience, religion, superstition, and social etiquette required for diverse hierarchical relationships are encouraged more than individual development" (p. 275).

As we know, implicit theories of creativity exist. With the help of Runco, Plucker, Sternberg, Rudowicz and others, such every-day, common-sense "theories" are legitimized.

Interdisciplinarity

One recent seemingly "theoretical" thrust is entitled interdisciplinarity. This perspective examines the ancient contrast between art (and the humanities generally), which focuses on subjectivity and intuition, and science (especially the psychology of cognition), which is rooted in objectivity and quantification (see, for example, the entire 1998, Vol. 11, No. 1 issue of *Creativity Research Journal*). One example of a tie between art and science is experimental aesthetics, the effort to understand and measure human experiences elicited by graphic art, music, and literature. Another example is analyzing various relationships among the age and gender of the artist, aesthetic preferences (e.g., representational vs. abstract), themes (e.g., an "old age" theme), and the quality (e.g., technical skill, creativeness) of art products (Lindauer, 1998). Interdisciplinarity also includes studies of creativity in theater performances, folklore, and ethnomusicology (Sawyer, 1998).

The interdisciplinarity approach to creativity emphasizes a broader focus and greater depth of understanding by objectively examining creativity in a variety of contexts.

Comment

The definitions and theories in this chapter and Chapter 1 help us better understand creative people and their creative processes and products. The variety of approaches is astounding. In Chapter 1, we examined definitions and theories about the creative person, product, process, and press/environment, along with reports of mysterious mental processes that writers and artists themselves do not understand.

This chapter briefly summarized classic psychoanalytic, behavioristic, cognitive, humanistic, the component-based theories of Sternberg, Amabile, and Csikszentmihalyi; contemporary theories of Gardner and Simonton; and three "I" models of creativity, including investment, interactionist, and interdisciplinarity approaches.

Readers may be back where they started—with their own implicit definitions of creativity—but with more ideas and facts about others' conceptions of "creativity." A central message is that we all can be more creative; we all can solve problems with more imagination. A starting place is adopting creative attitudes and a more creative personality, the topic of Chapter 4.

Summary

Freud's psychoanalytic theory focused on an unconscious conflict between the libido (sex drive) and the superego (social conscience), which is resolved in creative fantasies and products. Freud's theory is a negative view of the motivation to create. In the plus column, he stressed regression to childlike thinking (primary process thinking).

Ernst Kris stressed the neurosis-preventing discharge of both libidinal and aggressive energy in creative fantasies. Kris emphasized preconscious and conscious mental activity.

Behaviorist theories focus on the reinforcement of correct responses. Skinner claimed that creative acts are explainable via genetics plus one's history of being rewarded for combining pieces into creative wholes. "We have no freedom and deserve no dignity," said Skinner.

Maltzman simply proposed that originality, like any other behavior, is strengthened through reinforcement. The view was reinforced by cooperative porpoises.

Staats argued that two stimuli, encountered together for the first time, would elicit a novel (creative) combination of responses.

From a cognitive standpoint, Kubie proposed that creative thinking takes place in preconscious mental activity, between conscious and unconscious processes.

Rugg similarly located creative thinking between conscious and unconscious mental activity, in his transliminal chamber.

Mednick suggested that creative people have larger repertoires of mental associations that are available for combination. This capability was said to be measured by their RAT (Remote Associates Test), which means that when I say frog then you think of _____.

As we saw in Chapter 1, humanistic theorists recommend a self-actualization (growth) approach to creativity. Maslow distinguished between self-actualized creativity and special talent creativity. Rogers emphasized psychological safety, internal control, playfulness, and openness to experience.

Component wise, Sternberg's three-facet model includes three dimensions of the creative person—intelligence, cognitive style, and personality/motivation. He mentioned an anarchic style of mental self-government.

Amabile's three components were domain-relevant skills, creativity-relevant processes, and intrinsic task motivation encompassed in the social environment, which was related to ones' affective state.

Mihalhyi asked, "Where is creativity?," leading to a three-part theory including the creative person, the person's domain, and the field of experts who pass judgment.

Contemporary theories included those of Gardner, who used the person, domain, and field approach to elaborate on the highly restrictive group of persons deemed creative. The definition dismisses content-free, self-actualized forms of creativity, which are the focus of many courses, books, and programs.

Simonton combined (nonrandom) chance variation with his fifth P, persuasion, to produce his chance-configuration theory of creativity. The person must persuade sophisticated judges that his or her idea or product (stable permutation, configuration) is creative.

The investment theory of creativity is an analogical model of the creative process. It uses terms from economic theory to explain the value of creativity to society. The analogy seems to work. Is life like a Big Mac?

The Interactionist model uses a flowchart to illustrate the interactions among many components of creativity: antecedent conditions (e.g., biographical variables), the person (e.g., personality), the environmental and social situation, the creative behavior, and consequences.

Like Runco, Plucker, Sternberg, and others, we all have implicit theories of creativity. The theories are similar worldwide, but in Asia and India they are influenced by cultural factors, particularly conformity and social responsibility. Chinese theories included contributions to society.

Interdisciplinarity is using scientific methods to help understand creativity in the arts and humanities.

Review Exercises

Creativity Approaches

Self-Test: Key Concepts, Terms, and Names

Briefly define or explain each of these:

Psychoanalytic approaches of Freud and Kris

_____

_____

Primary process vs. secondary process thinking

_____

_____

Behavioristic approaches of Skinner, Maltzman, and Staats

_____

_____

_____

Cognitive Approaches

_____

_____

Kubie, Rugg, and Transliminal Chamber

_____

_____

Creative Cognition

_____

_____

Humanistic Theories

_____

_____

Carl Rogers factors for self-actualization

_____

_____

Component Based Theories

_____

_____

Sternberg's model

_____

_____

Amabile's model

_____

_____

Csikszentmihalyi's model

_____

_____

Contemporary Theories

_____

_____

Gardner's three-part model

_____

_____

Simonton's Chance-Configuration Theory

_____

_____

Investment theory/model

_____

_____

Interactionist model

_____

_____

Implicit theories

_____

_____

Let's Think about It

1. In exploring the Psychoanalytic approaches of Creativity, Freud states that creativity is said to "be in the service of the id," and that the act of creativity releases libidinal energy. Kris takes the opposite view and argues that creativity is said to "be in the service of the ego," helping to intentionally move preconcious ideas to the forefront of our mind. Distinguish between the ID and the EGO as they relate to Psychoanalytic views and provide your thoughts on which theorist YOU agree with from above.

_____

_____

_____

_____

2. Skinner and Maltzman purported a stimulus-response connection between creativity and behavior. Can you come up with a way to encourage or reinforce creative thoughts or behaviors? What stimuli would you use? What responses are you hoping to elicit? Who is your intended audience? Provide the breakdown of your experimental design here and explain why you think it would work

_____

_____

_____

_____

3. Sarnoff Mednick is known for creating one of the first ever assessments useful for gauging creativity. His Remote Associates Test (RAT) has people find a word that connects three other words together. In the text you were given a sample item. Generate four new ones of your own:

EX: (ROUND / TENNIS / CLOTH)   =   TABLE

(_____ / _____ / _____) = _____

(_____ / _____ / _____) = _____

(_____ / _____ / _____) = _____

(_____ / _____ / _____) = _____

(_____ / _____ / _____) = _____

(_____ / _____ / _____) = _____

(_____ / _____ / _____) = _____

(_____ / _____ / _____) = _____

(_____ / _____ / _____) = _____

(_____ / _____ / _____) = _____

(_____ / _____ / _____) = _____

(_____ / _____ / _____) = _____

4. Look at the list that Maslow generated related to the Characteristics of Self-Actualized People (Inset 2.1). Pick three that you think are the most important to YOU realizing or reaching YOUR creative peak or potential. Describe why you picked the ones you did and how YOU embody those characterisitcs:

_____

_____

_____

_____

3 Creativity Blocks and Barriers
Impediments to creativity

"The heart of man is very much like the sea, it has its storms, it has its tides, and in its depths, it has its pearls too."

—*Vincent van Gogh, The Letters of Vincent van Gogh*

The heart is the most essential thing to creation. It is a creation of love, of passion, and of decisions. Although those are great big treasures in our life, it is at the bottom of the sea, with an obstacle to conquer. The storms and the mental breakdowns, the tides and the challenges, the depths and the discovery. It's all essential to this general idea of creation.

Within this discovery you come upon blocks and barriers to your progress and creativity. But there is an underlying achievement behind a diving effort. The pearls I believe are this discovery, reaching a physical satisfaction and an emotional one. Like a finish line at the end of a long swim. To finish, is the pearl to those blocks and barriers.

We can recall iconic artists and creatives who have shaken society with their ideas and beliefs—from Van Gogh's brilliancy to the music of Beyoncé empowering women. But it was not a leap into fame and adoration. It took temporary strain and invention, it took a trail over harsh waters and personal railings—this is the encouraged journey to your particular pearl, with an open mind to take risks and an open heart to enjoy the challenge.

> The first need is to transcend the old order. Before any new idea can be defined, the absolute power of the established, the hold upon us of what we know and are, must be broken.
>
> —*Brewster Ghiselin (1952)*

All of us would be more creative were it not for internal and external blocks, barriers, and squelchers. But because of well-learned habits, mental heuristics, an unsupportive or repressive environment, or our fears and insecurities, most people do not fully use their creative abilities and imaginations. One argument is that everyone is born creative, but throughout our lives the combined influence of social constraints, educational structures, the societal norms of home, school, and community (respectfully) suppress our lively imaginations and produce dutiful conformers.

This chapter will look more closely at some common barriers to creative thinking and productivity: habit and learning, rules and traditions, perceptual blocks, cultural blocks, emotional blocks, and resource blocks, at least the first four of which are interrelated and stem from lifelong learning. We also will review von Oech's (1983) ten types of mental blocks, which may take a whack on the side of the head to jar loose. Finally, we will itemize probably-too-familiar "idea squelchers," a list that has been growing for half-a-century.

The challenge to anyone wishing to increase his or her personal creativeness is to understand, expect, and be ready to cope with barriers to creativity from the environment or from inside oneself.

Habit and Learning

The first and most obvious barrier to creative thinking and innovation is just habit, our well-learned and customary ways of thinking and responding. It begins when we are munchkins. We learn the "correct" responses, routines, and patterns of behavior (like what to do if someone suddenly "drops in" for a house party in Oz). Akin to what Wertheimer (1959) described as "reproductive thinking," it represents using previous experiences to govern responses to new situations. Could it be that instead of producing novel solutions, we are conditioned to reproduce prior actions? Similarly, using the Piaget's (1970) theory of cognitive development, we build cognitive schemas, which influence how we view new people or objects in our environment. This, in turn, frames our perspectives and shapes how we form and modify the conceptual categories to which things and ideas belong via the processes of accommodation and assimilation. Could it be that we are hardwired

"The hell with natural selection, lets just eat the nice fat young ones"

www.cartoonstock.com

to accommodate than ideate? Finally, we learn "the way things have always been done" and "the way things are supposed to be done." Over the years it becomes more and more difficult to break away from these habits, to see and create new possibilities.

When did you last try something truly new? Deviate from your routine? Order a new food at your favorite restaurant? Change your Starbucks order (GASP!) Enroll in a college course in some intriguing topic? Are your old habits and expectations interfering with new ideas and activities?

Of course, the ability to form habits and expectations is an adaptive and necessary capability for humankind and lower animals. It would be troublesome indeed to open your eyes each morning and wonder what you are supposed to do next. Being a "creature of habit" is a boon and a curse.

Rules and Traditions

Clearly, social groups—from your family to educational, collegiate, corporate, national, and international groups—could not function without the rules, regulations, policies, and traditions that *guide* personal, social, and institutional behavior. Boy Scouts are guided to take an oath to "obey the Scout Law" and anyone who has ever "pledged" allegiance to a sorority knows the hell than is the panhellenic recruitment guide! But before we "rush" to the defense of these two groups, in these contexts, guide often means restrict or inhibit.

Hall (1996), for example, took a few shots at inflexible school systems. He claimed they suffer from a lack of creative flexibility because of top-heavy, bureaucratic structures that cubbyhole people into specialized and rigid roles. Such people focus on everyday minutiae and lose their capability for big-picture, visionary thought. Claimed Ambrose, they seldom have good reason to take risks beyond the confines of established procedures, particularly since "mistakes are routinely punished in our right-answer-fixated bureaucracies" (p. 28). This can also be true for students, not just teachers. Sir Ken Robinson (2006) addressed this in a widely viewed TED talk entitled "Do Schools Kill Creativity" in which he comments that our current education system "stigmatizes mistakes" and cultivates a learning environment where students are "frightened of being wrong." Robinson then points out that it is impossible to come up with anything original if you are not prepared to be wrong. We will discuss this notion more in Chapter 11, but the call to action is simple; we need to do more than flip classrooms instructionally, and we need to structurally transform the way we educate.

In the 1990s, criticizing the rigidity of traditional organizations seemed a common catharsis (e.g., Peters, 1992; Tapscott & Caston, 1993). Ambrose (1995), injured only mildly while hopping on the bandwagon, listed these traits of "dullard . . . brain-damaged bureaucracies . . . inherited from the old industrial era":

- Myopic and coercive leadership that treats employees as automatons
- Premature judgment
- Repressed creativity
- Anger, frustration, and resentment
- Inflexible conformity
- Reflexive ritual
- Habit bound
- Narrow focus
- Poorly integrated subsystems
- Slow

The opposite characterized well-functioning "genius . . . creatively intelligent post-industrial organization":

- Visionary leadership
- Critical analysis and judgment
- Creative thinkers and creative teamwork
- Flexibility
- Excitement
- Pride and purpose
- Sensitivity and responsiveness
- Dynamism

Van Gundy (1987) described additional organizational barriers to creative innovation that also are rooted in rules and traditions. While aimed at corporate organizations, these barriers seem to apply to educational and other organizations as well.

One barrier is the **status hierarchy**. Lower-status persons are reluctant to suggest ideas to those in higher positions due to insecurity and fear of evaluation. With little lower-level participation in decision-making, it is unlikely that new ideas will "trickle up."

Furthermore, if a new idea threatens to reduce status differences ("Hey, we can increase sales if we make everybody a vice-president!"), the idea will be resisted by higher-status persons.

The **formalization** barrier refers to the degree to which following rules and procedures is enforced. Observed Van Gundy in an understatement, *"It is thought that formalization is detrimental to initiation of innovations. . . . If organizational members are expected to behave in prescribed ways, and innovation is not prescribed, fewer idea proposals will be generated"* (p. 361). However, he also observed that after an innovation is accepted, an efficient formal structure expedites its implementation.

Van Gundy's procedural barriers include policies, procedures, and regulations (including unwritten ones) that inhibit creative innovation. Some examples are:

- Promoting administrators based on analytic skills, not on ability to encourage a creative atmosphere.
- Emphasizing short-term (translation: short-sighted) planning.
- Avoiding expenditures that do not produce an immediate payback.
- Overemphasizing external rewards (profit) rather than internal, personal commitment.

Insisting on an orderly advancement with an innovation, with excessive detailed control early in its development.

This is echoed by Hall (1996) who suggests that for a company or organization to thrive instead of just survive, corporate leaders must break paradigms rather than sticking to the status quo. To do so requires foresight (rather than hindsight) along with creative thinking. In direct contrast to the terms identified by Van Gundy (1987), Jones and McFadzean (1997) researched ways that corporations can cultivate a creative climate and encourage creative thinking, including recommendations for ensuring both participative safety (so that people can speak up) AND the ability to challenge assumptions (so that people can speak out). Both should be free of judgment, criticism, retribution, or punishment.

Rules and traditions keep the system working. However, like habits, such predetermined guides can work against creative thinking.

Perceptual Blocks

Perceptual blocks also are based in learning and habit. We become accustomed to perceiving things in familiar ways, and it is difficult to see new meanings, relationships, or applications and uses. Psychologists refer to our predisposition to perceive things in certain ways as perceptual set, mental set, or functional fixedness. We will see in Chapter 9 that de Bono (1992a) teaches several "provocative techniques" designed to combat habits and perceptual sets—and force new ideas and perspectives. For example, he recommends that we deliberately reverse, exaggerate, or distort some part of the given problem, try "wishful thinking," escape from what we take for granted (e.g., that car wheels are round), or use a random word or random object to stimulate new thinking. For example, with the reversal provocation technique, the statement "Customers love big sales" would be reversed to "Big sales love customers" to provoke new views and ideas.

Perceptual sets differ between people because of our unique interests, needs, biases, values, and past learning. Perceptual sets also relate to our tendency to make quick decisions and jump to conclusions, rather than flexibly see alternatives. Perceptual sets can be equated to heuristics; shortcuts we take in analyzing an image or solving a problem that combines old tactics with new information. Heuristics provide us with fast information that we need to make quick judgments. Often they are sufficient, but only provide us with a snapshot of the "big picture," missing many of the important small details.

One old problem-solving experiment demonstrated that when a piece of string was needed to solve a problem, the string would be perceived and used if it were dangling from a nail on the wall—but not if it were hanging a No Smoking sign, mirror, or calendar (Sheerer, 1963). We wouldn't naturally identify it as a separate resource unless it was hanging right in front of our face (literally).

Perceptual blocks lead us to "kick ourselves" for not seeing a solution sooner. Try the following puzzles. The solutions appear after the chapter summary.

1. How do you turn a rabbit into a duck?
   https://www.cnn.com/videos/us/2019/08/22/bird-rabbit-viral-video-sanctuary-orig-js.cnn
2. Consider this puzzle. The police entered the gym containing five wrestlers just as the dying man looked at the ceiling and mumbled the words, "He did it." They immediately arrested one of the wrestlers. How did they know which one?
3. Remove six letters from ASIPXPLETLTERES. What word is left?

Pictures from History/Bridgeman Images

FIGURE 3.1 Rabbit

Perceptual blocks can prevent one from identifying "the real problem." For example, based on symptoms that seem familiar, a physician or auto mechanic may persist in misclassifying a problem and will treat it incorrectly.

Perceptual blocks also prevent us from getting a more complete and accurate picture of the world around us. For example, school teachers who fixate on IQ scores will fail to perceive students who are highly creative, artistic, or gifted in just one area.

A teacher who has successfully used a particular teaching technique for many years will not recognize that another technique is even more effective. A new product developer, who tries to make his or her product exactly right for one purpose, may fail to see other uses or markets for modified versions of the product.

With all the "focus" on perception, you would think that this would be a big research field for creativity theorists. But in reality, the evidence is to the contrary. Flowers and Garbin (1989) noted that "most researchers in the field of perception have not touched upon the topic of creativity, and relatively few researchers in creativity have chosen to integrate their work with perceptual issues" (p. 147). However, those findings aside, that's not to say that there aren't pragmatic ways that creative perception can be enhanced.

Creativity leader William J. J. Gordon (1961) described how making the familiar strange—perceiving common objects and ideas in new ways—is a central creative process. Indeed, it is. Much creativity involves a mental transformation, the perception of new meanings, combinations, and relationships that depend upon overcoming perceptual blocks.

Gruber (1988) advanced an evolving systems approach to creative works and introduced a tactic known as "Deviation Amplification" that involves making small changes to a creative work or theme and exploring how these variations might produce alternative viewpoints or perspectives. Incremental changes that could provide a seismic shift in perspective.

With perspectives shifts in mind, Runco (2014) stated that "one of the most powerful and broadly applicable tactics for creative thinking involves shifts in perspective" (p. 340). Providing visual examples, he demonstrated how looking at a problem from a different vantage point (i.e., turning the situation upside down) forces us to make a 180° turn[1] in not only our assumptions about the problem set but also cognitively confront our perceptual set.

You *see*, we often don't *see* the pathway to Big "See" (or Big C) creativity because of these perceptual block and barriers.

---

[1] A 90° turn might give you an angle to solve a problem on this page!

Cultural Blocks

Cultural blocks amount to social influence, expectations, and conformity pressures, all based on social or institutional norms. Cultural blocks thus include more than learning, habits, rules, and traditions. There are a few dashes of "the way we think others expect us to behave" and several dabs of "fear of being different" (come on, admit it—you KNOW you had a signature dab back when that was cool!). The result is a loss of individuality and creativity.

Torrance (1968, 1977, 1979, 1984) concluded that creativity (fantasy, imagination) drops when children enter kindergarten, an early time when conformity and regimentation suddenly become the rule. Said Torrance (1977), "this drop . . . is a societal or cultural phenomenon rather than a biological or natural one" (p. 21). Further evidence of this notion was provided by a landmark longitudinal study conducted by George Land in 1968 (Land & Jensen, 1993). He conducted a study to test the creativity of 1,600 preschoolers. Using a creativity test designed to select NASA engineers and scientists, he tested kids at the ages of 5, 10, and 15. The results would have halted the space race right in its tracks! The percentage of 5 years old (Kindergarten age) who scored at the creative genius level was 98%. This dropped to 30% when students were assessed with the same instrument 5 years later at the age of 10. Finally, at the age of 15, it had dropped to under 12%. What happened?

There may be an even larger drop in creativity at the fourth-grade level—Torrance's famous fourth-grade slump. Repeated Torrance (1977), "the drop which occurs in the fourth grade is a societal rather than a biological phenomenon" (p. 22). In Korea, Kang (1989) confirmed Torrance's fourth-grade slump with a sample of 1,100 elementary children, but the drop in creativity test scores occurred in the fifth grade rather than fourth.

Perhaps the most visible monkey-see monkey-do conformity pressures exert themselves at adolescence, when new-found abstract thinking abilities (Piaget's formal operational thinking) increase students' self-awareness and self-consciousness. Is it surprising that Torrance (1977) described another drop in creative thinking at the seventh-grade level?

The dynamics of conformity are hardly mysterious. It simply is uncomfortable to be different, to challenge accepted ways of thinking and behaving.[2] We learn that it's good to be correct. But making mistakes, being wrong, or behaving "badly" will elicit disapproval, criticism, or even sarcasm and ridicule. One does not wish to be judged foolish, incompetent, or plain stupid.[3]

Expectations and conformity pressures also work in more subtle ways. The traditionally perceived role of females—overloaded with expectations and stereotypes—is a perennial and slow-changing difficulty that is yet to be overcome (see, for example, Davis & Rimm, 2004). Baer (2008) researched gender differences in creativity after noting that while there was a lack of empirical evidence showing boys outperforming girls on creativity assessments, that there were large gaps in achieving eminence or notoriety for creative contributions to the field for men over women.

There are pressures on all of us to be practical and economical, which can be inconsistent with innovative, creative thinking. We also learn not to be "nosy," not to ask too many questions. However, as Simberg (1978) noted, "By stifling questioning, we are cutting out the very heart of creativity—curiosity" (p. 126). There also is a backstairs belief that fantasy is a waste of time. (Where would creativity be without fantasy?) Moreover, society tells us to have faith in reason and logic, tendencies that can delicately repress imagination and innovation.

Simberg (1978) also noted that, especially in corporate settings, an overemphasis either on cooperation or competition can be a barrier to creativeness. If high cooperation is stressed, a person must temper his or her creative ideas in order to "fit in," to conform and please others. On the other hand,

---

[2] So-called nonconformists—beatniks of the 1960s, hippies of the 1970s, punkers of the 1980s and 1990s, and year 2000 young persons with body piercing and tattoos—may be viewed as conforming to different norms.

[3] However, as we will see in Chapter 4, a creative person sometimes must take risks and even fail. Creativity requires trying new ideas, which sometimes flop.

an overemphasis on competition can orient us toward "beating somebody else to it," rather than toward finding good creative solutions.

Van Gundy (1987) described subtle social/political barriers to creative innovation, which include any organizational norms that reinforce conformity, inhibit innovation, discourage "idea people," or otherwise ban rocking the boat. For example:

- Attitudes of secrecy
- A reluctance to share ideas
- The attitude that creative types do not fit in
- A fear that innovation may change the uniqueness of an organization
- A desire to protect the status quo
- A fear that innovation will reduce jobs

Finally, the greatest cultural barrier to creativity can be the culture itself. Think for a moment about the stark differences in government, religion, individual freedoms (or lack thereof), customs, practices, and traditions that exist worldwide. These factors can make a world of difference (literally) in one's ability to be creative.

Rhodes (1987) purported that for creativity to thrive, two conditions must be present. First, the basic needs of society must be met, noting that "society will not pay attention to developments outside what is pertinent and that which must be immediately satiated" (p. 220). In short, if people are starving or the populous is under strain or civil unrest, creative contributions will be the last thing on their mind. The second factor is existence of technology accompanied with an understanding of how to utilize it. Rhodes stated that the environment must offer "a sufficiently advanced state of culture and a proper technical heritage" (p. 220).

Technology was one of the 3 Ts identified by Florida (2002) in his examination of creative cultures and what must be presented for creativity to flourish. Aside from *technology*, you need people with *talent* (with an education system set up to nurture their gifts) and a culture that is *tolerant* to innovation and inventions. A tolerant society will attract talented people who will create the technology of the future. Makes sense to me! But what is meant by a tolerant society and are there societal and global differences in how creativity is viewed or valued?

Niu and Sternberg (2002) found that while there are many similarities in the conceptions of what creativity is and the common characteristics of creative individuals, there are structural differences in how they view creative contributions. According to their findings, individualistic (Western) cultures reward and value the present contributions of creative individuals while collectivist (Eastern) cultures emphasize how the contribution of a creative individual can benefit society and bridge the gap between past and present.

Khaleefa, Erdos, and Ashria (1996) contrasted Western-oriented individualism, autonomy, self-reliance, and independence with Eastern-oriented obedience, duty, conformity, sacrifice for the group, and low tolerance for deviating from norms. Said the authors, "Conformity to sociocultural institutions and to the expectations of others involves a substantial limitation of one's individuality" (p. 270) and "There is small scope for individuals to be creative" (p. 274). Their research found that in "tight sociocultural systems" females receive less education, experience less freedom and independence, and generally endure more authoritarianism. As a result, girls usually score lower than boys on creativity tests. In their research, males (age 15 to 20) scored higher on a test of creative personality, which measured independence, adventurousness, individuality, activity, curiosity, responsibility, motivation, and freedom. Khaleefa et al. (1996) noted that to be creative—as many wish to be—they must learn how to "attach to the sociocultural system, and at the same time how to detach from it" (p. 278). That is, a creative individual must learn when to conform and how to be creative within the cultural system.

That's just one example of a small study that has global ramifications as to the power of culture in either enhancing or impeding one's ability to fulfill one's true creative potential.

Emotional Blocks

In today's society, our emotions are ALWAYS on display[4] (literally—how many texts with emoji's have YOU sent in the last week). Examining the contribution of emotions to creativity, Averill (2009) notes that "the relation between emotions and creativity is charged with ambivalence. In schools we encourage creativity, and in the arts and sciences, we praise its achievement. A person, it seems, cannot be too creative. By contrast, a person who is too prone to emotion risks being labeled as immature, uncouth, boorish, or worse" (p. 249).

So is there a balance or do emotions simply get in the way? It is clear that emotions have the ability to impede or inhibit clear thinking, but can we harness them to stimulate creative thought? Simberg (1978) imagined a balance scale with emotions on one side and clear thinking on the other; as one side goes up, the other goes down. Some familiar emotional blocks that turn us upside down or "Inside Out" are joy, sadness, fear, anger, and disgust. Some are temporary states, caused perhaps by problems with peers, parents, partners, or preschoolers (the four Ps?), or by pressures at school or work, financial stresses, or poor health. More permanent emotional blocks include such chronic sources of insecurity and anxiety as fear of failure, fear of being different, fear of criticism or ridicule, fear of rejection, fear of supervisors, timidity, or poor self-concept.

To gauge the impact of emotions on the creative state, Averill (1999) created a 30-item Emotional Creativity Inventory that includes subscales on preparedness (understanding emotions), novelty (uniqueness of emotions), and effectiveness (utilization of emotions). While the scale was useful in categorizing those who could harness emotions and use them to enhance creativity, it also pointed to an emotional trait that could block or inhibit the creativity experience—alexithymia. Alexithymia literally means "no words for feelings" and represents a lower capacity for imagination combined with an inability to describe ones' own emotional state or the emotional states of others (Taylor, 1994).

While this book does not deal in psychotherapy, we should note that moderate amounts of tension and anxiety are normal. In fact, some feelings of urgency or motivation are required for creative thinking and problem-solving (Figure 3.2). Van Gundy (1987) noted that some attitudinal barriers, such as fear of taking risks, fear of uncertainty and ambiguity, differences in values, or differences in personal needs, will block either the initial creation of innovations or their adoption and implementation. However, if emotional blocks interfere with thinking, it may help to take a creative problem-solving approach to dealing with them. That is, ask "What is the problem?" and "What can I/we do about it?" Chapter 8 will present the Creative Problem Solving (CPS) model that also may be used with personal problems.

FIGURE 3.2 We'll take a brexit away from creativity to take a quick peak at politicians attempting to make the world better again!.

---

[4] In 2015, Oxford Dictionary declared the "face with tears of joy" emoji to be the 2015 "word of the year!"

Resource Barriers

Van Gundy (1987) described one last type of organizational block to creative innovation, **resource barriers,** which can be a shortage of people, money, time, supplies, or information. Innovation requires such resources, beyond what is needed for routine organizational procedures. Internal conflicts, a type of social/political barrier, are likely if resources are pirated from one department to develop an innovation in another department.

Creativity Out of Whack?

Roger von Oech's (1983) *A Whack on the Side of the Head* explains 10 mental blocks to creative thinking and problem-solving. To von Oech—a successful corporate creativity consultant—stimulating creative thinking is largely a matter of removing mental blocks. As his book title suggests, it can take a whack on the side of the head to jolt us out of our anti-creative mental blocks.

The first of von Oech's mental blocks, *The Right Answer*, is the usual assumption that there is just one right answer. Not so. We should look for a second right answer, a third right answer, and more. A later "right answer" is likely to be more creative than the first right answer. In Chapter 8 we will see that brainstorming, the best known creativity technique, is based squarely on deferring judgment until the person or group produces many possible solutions.

Von Oech's second block, *That's Not Logical*, is based on our culturally rooted assumption that logical thinking is better than illogical thinking. Not necessarily. Illogical thinking can supply the imaginative play and new perspectives necessary for creative breakthroughs. In contrast to logical thinking, von Oech listed other possibilities—speculative thinking, fantasy thinking, analogical thinking, divergent thinking, lyrical thinking, mythical thinking, poetic thinking, visual thinking, symbolic thinking, foolish thinking, ambiguous thinking, surreal thinking, and others. Instead of "getting down to brass tacks" we should consider steel tacks, copper tacks, plastic tacks, sailing tacks, income tax, syntax, or even taxidermy!

A third block to creative thinking is *Follow the Rules*. Following rules includes thinking of things as they are. Instead of following the rules, says von Oech, we should play the revolutionary and challenge the rules. He recommended holding "rule-inspecting and rule-discarding" sessions within one's organization. If NFL coaches get red flags to throw on the field during games, why can't we raise red flags in board room? Failure to do so is just waiving a white flag of surrender.

Be Practical is his fourth block. Instead of being inhibited by pressures toward practicality, we should ask creativity-stimulating "what if?" questions, and encourage "what-iffing" in others. Sometimes preposterous "what-iffing" leads to practical ideas. In von Oech's example, an engineer at a large chemical company asked this question: "What if we put gunpowder in our house paint? . . . [When it got old] we could just blow it right off the house!" This led to adding an inert chemical additive to the paint which, when another additive later was applied, a reaction would take place and the paint would easily strip off.

Earlier we mentioned de Bono's provocative techniques in conjunction with overcoming perceptual blocks. De Bono would like the gunpowder idea—a whacky approach that led to good problem solution.

Avoid Ambiguity is the fifth block. In fact, deliberate ambiguity can stimulate imaginative answers. We will see in Chapter 6 that William J. J. Gordon's compressed conflicts are ambiguous two-word statements deliberately created to provoke new viewpoints. Does the compressed conflict pricey nothing suggest travel ideas? Or free luxury? Actually, whenever one is engaged in creative problem-solving, a period of ambiguity always exists. As Dacey, Lennon, and Fiore (1998) would attest, a tolerance for or even liking of ambiguity is an essential creative trait.

Von Oech's sixth block is *To Err Is Wrong*, which we noted earlier is a well-reinforced habit. A fear of making mistakes inhibits trying new things—but creative innovation necessarily requires making errors and even failing. One story claims that while working on the light bulb, Edison tried nearly 2,000 ideas.

Edison optimistically reported that he now knew 2,000 ways not to build a light bulb! One probably surprising strategy for increasing creative productivity is to deliberately increase your failure rate. Creative person Thomas Watson, founder and president of IBM, claimed that "The way to succeed is to double your failure rate" (von Oech, 1983, p. 93). Observed von Oech, "Errors [serve] as stepping stones. . . . We learn by our failure. A person's errors are the whacks that lead him or her to think something different" (pp. 90–92).

Another block, von Oech's seventh, is the notion that ***Play Is Frivolous***. Playing with ideas has produced countless creative innovations and scientific discoveries. As we will see in Chapter 4, child-like thinking, humor, and playing with ideas are exceedingly common characteristics of creative people. Necessity may be the mother of invention, said von Oech, but play is the father!

Block number eight is ***That's Not My Area***. This block is rich with implications for creative thinking and problem-solving. Especially, it is an excuse for not even trying to solve a problem because of self-proclaimed ignorance. Moreover, such a thinker certainly will not look for ideas and inspiration in other fields. In fact, many innovations are born by adapting ideas from outside of one's own field—as we will see in Chapter 6 on analogical thinking. Von Oech suggested finding ideas in old science magazines, history, want ads, and "studying a subject on a shallow level" (p. 109). Many innovations come from people with little or no background in the problem area.

Don't Be Foolish, block nine, is another cultural barrier rooted in conformity. Says von Oech, you occasionally should play the fool, and you certainly should be aware of when you or others are putting down a creative "fool." Prince's (1968) "get fired" technique, in which you propose an idea so totally foolish that your boss will immediately fire you, helps create the playfulness and craziness that can lead to creative ideas.

Finally, we have the tenth block, the self-squelcher, ***I'm Not Creative***. If you seriously believe this, you will be correct. It is a self-fulfilling prophecy. Do you need an occasional whack on the side of the head?

Idea Squelchers

It is bad enough to be uncreative. It's worse to squelch your own or other people's creative thinking. This list of idea squelchers is based on one created by Warren (1974), who modified a list by Clark (1958) in his book *Brainstorming*, plus a few more from two covers of the *Journal of Creative Behavior* (1974, Issue 2, and 1996, Issue 3), and a couple from Biondi (1980). You never would make any of these comments, would you?

We've never done it before.
We've already tried that before.
It can't be done.
It won't work.
Too blue sky.
No way.
Are you nuts?
It's a waste of time.
I'm telling you, it won't work.
I just know it won't work.
What will the parents think?
Somebody would have suggested it before if it were any good.
Too modern.
Too old-fashioned.
Not that way.
Let's discuss it at some other time.

This is the last try.
You've got to be kidding.
You ask too many questions.
You don't understand our situation.
You don't understand the problem.
We're too small for that.
We're too big for that.
We're too new for that.
Let's not bother.
See? It didn't work!
We haven't the teacher–student ratio.
It's not in the budget.
It has limited possibilities.
We're not ready for it yet.
All right in theory, but can you put it into practice?
Too academic.

Not academic enough; we need supporting theory.
Won't we be held accountable?
Let's form a committee.
Let's put it in writing.
We need more lead time.
Walk, don't run.
You'll never sell it to the union.
Don't forget the chain of command.
Let's not fight city hall.
Stay on their good side.
Don't step on any toes.
Be practical.
Let's wait and see.
I don't see the connection.
It won't work in our neighborhood.
We can't do it under the regulations.
There's no regulations covering it.
We have too many projects now.
It's been the same for 20 years, so it must be good.
This is how it's done. Let's use proven methods.
What bubble head thought that up?
That's trouble.
Don't rock the boat.
I'll bet some professor suggested that.

We have to be practical.
It's not in the plan.
It's not in the curriculum.
We did alright without it.
You can't argue with success.
It'll mean more work.
It's too early.
It's too late.
The Board will faint.
That's not our responsibility.
That's not our department.
That's not our job.
That's not our role.
It's low in our priorities.
It will offend.
What's the use?
Why bother?
It doesn't matter.
Our people won't accept it.
You can't teach an old dog new tricks.
Have you checked with . . . ?
And you stand there saying. . . .
No adolescent is going to tell me how to run this operation!

The main advantage of understanding external barriers to creativity is that it forces you to plan ahead—to anticipate the resistance that may greet your innovative ideas and plans. Understanding internal barriers can help us deal with them in a mentally healthy, creativity-consistent way.

Summary

We all would be more creative if it were not for blocks and barriers to creative thinking.

Habit and learning, which are necessary for humankind, also can be blocks to creative thinking.

Reproductive thinking isn't productive for creativity.

Rules and traditions, too, are essential for society, but can inhibit imagination and innovation. Some recent potshots at traditional, imagination-stifling educational and other organizations emphasized bureaucratic structures, overspecialized roles, punishment for taking risks and making mistakes, near-sighted and coercive leadership, frustration, conformity, ritual, and a narrow focus.

Ken Robinson encouraged us to "bring on the learning revolution" in our schools and encourage critical and creative thinking in our classrooms.

"Creatively intelligent" organizations show visionary leadership, creativity, excitement, flexibility, and dynamism.

Van Gundy's organizational barriers included the status hierarchy, formalization (rule following), and procedural barriers, for example, promotions based on analytic skills, short-term planning, emphasis on external (not personal) rewards, and tight control in developing innovations. Perceptual blocks—mental set, perceptual set, functional fixity—are based in learning. They prevent us from seeing new meanings, relations, applications, and possibilities.

Perceptual blocks are related to "jumping to conclusions," prevent us from "seeing the real problem," and prevent us from getting an accurate picture of our world. De Bono's provocative techniques and Gordon's making-the-familiar-strange procedures help us overcome perceptual blocks.

Cultural blocks are social influence, expectations, and conformity pressures, which combine with our "fear of being different" to squelch creative thinking. Torrance's fourth-grade slump, and his kindergarten and seventh-grade slumps, are due to conformity pressures and expectations.

Regarding dynamics, we simply do not like to be different, make mistakes, be wrong, look stupid, or "ask too many questions." Traditional expectations and stereotypes of females persist.

A traditional belief in reason and logic can repress fantasy and innovation.

Excessive cooperation—fitting in—or competition can stifle creativity.

Van Gundy described such social/political barriers as attitudes of secrecy, dislike for creative types, and protecting the status quo.

The most problematic cultural block is the culture itself, though Rhodes and Florida identified features of a society that would allow creativity to thrive.

Within a culture, traditions, beliefs, authoritarianism, and gender roles can impact one's ability to individually express creative thoughts and fulfill creative potential.

Emotional blocks may be temporary states or more chronic insecurities and fears, particularly fear of failure, ridicule, being different, or taking risks.

One can take a creative problem-solving approach to emotional blocks.

Resource barriers are shortages of people, money, supplies, time, or information.

Von Oech's *Whack on the Side of the Head* approach to increasing creativity amounted to unlocking ten mental blocks: The Right Answer; That's Not Logical; Follow the Rules; Be Practical; Avoid Ambiguity; To Err Is Wrong; Play Is Frivolous; That's Not My Area; Don't Be Foolish; and I'm Not Creative.

Our list of idea squelchers affords an excellent list of suggestions for nipping creativity in its bud.

As a general principle, as one proceeds down the yellow brick road of life, there is a time to conform and a time to be creative.

ANSWERS

1. Turn it 90 degrees! Were you "right" in the angle you took to solve this problem?
2. All of the other wrestlers were female. Did sex-role stereotyping regarding the gender of wrestlers "hold" you back?
3. Removing S-I-X-L-E-T-T-E-R-S leaves you with A-P-P-L-E! Were your efforts fruitful in getting that answer correct?

Chapter 3: Appendix

Pictures from History/Bridgeman Images

FIGURE 3.1 Answer

Review Exercises

Creativity Blocks and Barriers: Impediments to creativity

Self-Test: Key Concepts and Terms

Define each of these terms and then give an example of how each of these barriers can depress YOUR creativity:

Habit and learning

_____

_____

Rules and traditions

_____

_____

Perceptual blocks

_____

_____

Cultural blocks

_____

_____

Emotional blocks

_____

_____

Resource barriers

_____

_____

Idea squelchers

_____

_____

Let's Think about It

1. View Sir Ken Robinson's TED talk on "Do Schools Kill Creativity." Do you think that he is right? Provide your reaction or commentary to the video here. Were there any quotes that resonated with you? Were there any that you disagreed with? Provide some of your own experiences to help accentuate the points you highlight or the position you take. In your commentary, provide a reaction to the notion of Torrance's (1977) fourth grade slump. Do you find that this was true for you with regards to the nature of your experiences after the fourth grade? Why? What about the school structure changed.

_____

_____

_____

_____

_____

2. Look at the terms that Van Gundy (1987) introduced regarding organizational barriers to creativity. Have you seen those stifle creativity in an organization or workplace that YOU are in? Give some examples of how status hierarchy, formalization, policies, procedures, resource barriers and/or regulations inhibit creativity or prevent progress:

_____

_____

_____

Solution as to how you would change the rules at your workplace or in your organization to combat this? What are some bylaw changes that you would suggest to help your organization do more than just get by?

_____

_____

_____

3. Let's play around with your perception a bit. Gordon (1961) says one way to avoid perceptual blocks is to make the "familiar strange" and look at common objects and ideas in new ways. Pick a household object and do just that. Write down three things about that object that you never noticed before:

    1)
    2)
    3)

Now, as a follow-up to that exercise, Gruber (1988) introduced a term called "Deviation Amplification" and looked at how small changes to a creative work or product could have big ramifications. So let's do that with the product you just picked from above.

Change three essential components and replace them with something new and see what that does to the nature, functionality, or use of the product (ex. If you changed the end of a dishwashing brush from a sponge to sandpaper, you'd now have an exfoliator or carpentry tool instead of a kitchen item!)

    1)
    2)
    3)

4. Rhodes (1987) identified two conditions necessary for creativity to thrive in a society. Comment as to whether you believe that both of these exist in the United States today. Do we live in a creative country? If so, why do you think this is the case? What allows creativity to flourish? If not, why not? What is impeding creativity from happening?

_____

_____

_____

5. Make up at least five absolutely ridiculous, preposterous blocks to creativity, i.e., things that STOP you from thinking creatively, or reasons you are not more creative (for example, "EEG says I am brain dead").

    a. _____

    b. _____

    c. _____

    d. _____

    e. _____

6. Which three of von Oech's (1983) ten barriers do you see impacting you the most when it comes to blocks or barriers to your own creativity? Explain and expand upon your answer for each

    a. _____

    b. _____

    c. _____

7. Look over the list of idea squelchers in this chapter. Which do you think are the most common? Which do YOU utilize yourself? Can you add a three more to the list that are not only characteristic of you but could characterize other people?

MOST COMMON

a. _____

b. _____

c. _____

ONES I UTILIZE

a. _____

b. _____

c. _____

THREE MORE IDEA SQUELCHERS

1. _____

2. _____

3. _____

Self-Rating of Creativity

I AM A CREATIVE PERSON

Strongly Disagree		Unsure		Strongly Agree
1	2	3	4	5

Creativity Test

Indicate the degree to which each statement applies to you. Use the following scale:

1 = No
2 = To a small degree
3 = Average
4 = More than average
5 = Definitely

———— 1. I am unconventional in many ways.

———— 2. I am very artistic.

———— 3. I am quite absentminded.

———— 4. I try to use metaphors and analogies in my writing.

———— 5. I am a very active, energetic person.

———— 6. I enjoy thinking of new and better ways of doing things.

———— 7. I am very curious.

———— 8. I am quite original and inventive.

———— 9. Some of my past or present hobbies would be considered "unusual."

———— 10. I like the nonsense forms and bright colors of modern art.

———— 11. My ideas are often considered impractical or even "wild."

———— 12. I would rate myself high on "intuition" or "insightfulness."

———— 13. I like some body smells.

———— 14. I am able to work intensely on a project for many hours.

———— 15. I like trying new ideas and new approaches to problems.

———— 16. I often become totally engrossed in a new idea.

———— 17. Most of my friends are unconventional.

———— 18. The word "quick" describes me.

———— 19. I could be considered a spontaneous person.

———— 20. I have engaged in a lot of creative activities.

———— 21. I would rate myself high in self-confidence.

———— 22. I am always open to new ideas and new activities.

———— 23. Sometimes I get so interested in a new idea that I neglect what I should be doing.

———— 24. I am often inventive or ingenious.

———— 25. I enjoy trying new approaches to problems.

———— 26. I have taken things apart just to find out how they work.

———— 27. I have participated in theatrical productions.

———— 28. I have a great sense of humor.

———— 29. Many stories of mysterious, psychical happenings are true.

———— 30. When I was young, I was always building or making things.

Scoring: Add up your ratings. The following is a guideline for interpretation:

30–55	Low in creative personality traits
56–79	Below average
80–102	Average
103–126	Above average
127–150	High in creative personality traits

Does your test score agree with your initial rating?

Regardless of your score (but especially if it is below about 90), try developing your creative personality traits—see Chapter 4.

4 The Creative Person
Flexible, funny, and full of energy

"I want to touch people with my art. I want them to say *'he feels deeply, he feels tenderly.'*"

—*Vincent van Gogh*

Vincent van Gogh is an individual who is regularly cited as the epitome of the creative person. He longed for a sense of identity, and through his painting and creation he searched for it.

There are many traits that indicate a creative person, and Van Gogh exhibits the positives but also the more negatives, such as his heightened emotionality that is evident in all his paintings.

Vincent's paintings were like a mirror to his internal sense of self and identity, manifesting his turmoil on to the page (Lubetzky, 2019). Van Gogh was searching for his sense of identity after a challenging familial experience, constantly searching to find his place. His work in The Starry Night is an expression of his search for identity and the places he sought it specifically (Stamm, 1971).

The creative person model is an "O.C.E.A.N." of primary traits and characteristics, three of which are openness to experience, conscientiousness, and neuroticism. Van Gogh demonstrated a wide breadth of these traits along each individual scale.

He is most characterized by his openness to experience and his neuroticism, which ultimately were potential causes of his mental illness and his death.

He famously said that "normalcy was a road that was comfortable to walk, but no flowers grow on it." His life was certainly uncomfortable, and marked with hurt and loss and suffering, but he painted the flowers and beauty along the path of his life.

Art and creativity were his expression of his identity and the way that he found the flowers along the road of his life, instead of strolling along the paved road of normality.

Psychologists and educators have taken many long looks at creative people in a continuing effort to understand the traits, characteristics, and abilities that underlie and exemplify creativeness. The purpose of this chapter is to examine commonalities—characteristics that have recurred again and again in studies of creative people. Dozens of research studies, buttressed by informed opinions, point to one conclusion: *Creative people may be nonconformist, but they certainly have a lot in common.*

An awareness of characteristics of creativity will help us understand creative people and how they think. It also will help us recognize creative children and adults. We will not become perfect in our recognition of creative talent, however. Consider these examples of creative persons who were *not* recognized by their teachers, professors, or supervisors:

Thomas Edison was told by his teachers that he was too stupid to learn anything.

Albert Einstein was 4 years old before he could speak and 7 before he could read.

Pablo Picasso could barely read and write by age 10. His father hired a tutor, who gave up and quit.

Walt Disney was fired by a newspaper editor because he had "no good ideas."

Louisa May Alcott was told by an editor that she could never write anything popular.

Enrico Caruso's music teacher told him, "You can't sing, you have no voice at all!"

Oprah Winfrey was fired from one of her first TV jobs because a producer declared that she was "unfit for television"

Colonel Sanders had $105 in his pocket when he pitched his chicken recipe to investors and was rejected by over 1,000 people before finding success with a restaurant in Utah (surprisingly not Kentucky!)

Harrison Ford (Indiana Jones) flunked out of Ripon College in Wisconsin.

Leo Tolstoy also flunked out of college.

Abraham Lincoln entered the Black Hawk War as a Captain and came out a private.

Winston Churchill failed sixth grade. He also was at the bottom of his class in one school, and twice failed the entrance exams for another.

Werner von Braun failed ninth-grade algebra.

Louis Pasteur was rated mediocre in chemistry at the Royal College.

Charles Darwin did poorly in the early grades and failed a university medical course.

F. W. Woolworth worked in a dry goods store when he was 21, but his employers would not let him wait on customers because he "didn't have enough sense."

Charles Dickens, Claude Monet, Isadora Duncan, and *Mark Twain* never finished grade school.

George Gershwin, Will Rogers, both *Wilbur* and *Orville Wright,* and newscaster *Peter Jennings* dropped out of high school.

A 1938 letter found in 1991 said that western movie star *Gene Autry* "needed to improve his acting," that an acting course was "evidently wasted," and that "he needed darker make-up to give him the appearance of virility." Replied 83-year-old Autry, "A lot of that is true."

Such facts are amusing. They also emphasize the complexity, subtlety, and sometimes obscurity of creative talent.

Personality Traits, Abilities, Biographical Characteristics

Three types of characteristics combine to produce creativeness: *Personality traits* (including motivation), *cognitive abilities* (including information processing styles), and *biographical traits* (experiences). The distinction between affect (personality), cognition (mental abilities), and learning (biographical traits, experiences) is an ancient one.

In the creativity area, the three categories of traits interweave tightly, and each will influence the development of the other two. As easy illustrations, *learning* and experiences help determine the development of one's personality, intelligence, and thinking styles. *Intelligence* relates closely to such personality traits as ethics, confidence, self-esteem, articulateness, and tendencies to be analytical, as well as to the type of learning experiences one selects—for example, dropping out of high school or attending medical school. The *cognitive style* of internal control—the feeling of mastery over one's environment and destiny—includes such personality traits as high motivation, independence, self-esteem, social sensitivity and warmth, and even likability. Personality traits, mental abilities, and learning/experiences do indeed interrelate and influence each other. However, there are limitations in solely using these traits, characteristics, and abilities to define creative persons. This was pointed out by Glăveanu (2013), who in his Five As framework preferred to refer the creative person as an **actor**. "Referring to actors acknowledges people as socialized selves, as beings that are shaped by a sociocultural context and act from within it, in coordination with others, to change and mold this context in suitable ways" (p. 72). He continues to state that "making a list of traits or cognitive factors, for as comprehensive as it may be, tells us nothing about how people come to acquire (them)" (p. 72).

But if we did make a list of traits, some traits of creativity could fit into one category as well as another. For example, *humor, independence, originality*, and *perceptiveness* could be viewed as personality traits, cognitive abilities, or both.

Similarities and Differences

There are then, commonalities among creative persons in different areas. A creative scientific researcher, a creative artist, and a creative business entrepreneur—by virtue of being creative—will have many personality traits and abilities in common. However, as one might guess, there also is wide variation in personality patterns, abilities, and experiences not only between persons in different areas but also among persons within the same area (e.g., two artists). For example, in Runco's research on implicit theories mentioned in Chapter 2, artists were judged (by themselves or non-artists) to be *expressive, imaginative, humorous, original, emotional, open-minded*, and *exciting*, while scientists were seen as *intelligent, logical, curious, perfectionistic, patient*, and *thorough*.

In Chapter 12 we will see that some persons with a great creative talent—Maslow's *special-talent creativity*—are well-adjusted in the self-actualization sense and some are not. As we will see later, some highly creative people are fair-to-middling in neuroses, schizophrenia, or sociopathy.

Most special-talent creative people are creative in their own area, but typically not in another. A creative chemist, for example, may be an unimaginative artist, writer, or cook. On the other hand, a few gifted personages have been creative in many areas—Leonardo Da Vinci, Thomas Jefferson, Benjamin Franklin (best known for trying to electrocute himself with a kite), Howard Hughes, and Orson Welles.

For now, the perhaps obvious message is that even among the single category of people judged "creative" there will be large differences in personality, mental traits, experiences, and capabilities.

Creativity and Intelligence: The Threshold Concept

Before turning to personality, cognitive, and biographical traits, let's look at a longstanding issue in creativity: the relationship between creativity and intelligence. On one hand, some research recognizes creativity and intelligence as two separate constructs. Landmark research by Getzels and Jackson (1962) and Wallach and Kogan (1965) identified and contrasted highly intelligent versus highly creative students, confirming that the two traits are indeed not the same. Furthermore, developers of creativity tests take pride in demonstrating very low correlations between scores on their creativity test and IQ scores on intelligence tests. They wish to argue that their test measures creative potential and not just components of intelligence, such as verbal ability, logical thinking, or decision-making.

On the other hand, it also is known that creativity and intelligence very clearly *are* related. There are findings that dispute the landmarks studies mentioned above. Silvia (2008) researched the relationship between creativity and intelligence variables via latent variable analysis and found, in contrast to Wallach and Kogan's assertions, that the relationship was stronger than originally reported. Some descriptions of creative people that reflect high intelligence appear in Table 4.1. In the creative eminence area, summarized later in this chapter, we will find total agreement that intelligence is needed for high creativity. For example, after reviewing the biographies of creatively eminent men and creatively eminent women, Walberg and Zeiser (1997) concluded that "the most common psychological trait of eminent women . . . was the same as that shown by eminent American and European men of previous centuries—intelligence" (p. 332). Walberg also compared high school students who had won competitive awards in science or art with control students who were not award winners. Said Walberg (1988), "They [the award winners] indicated they were brighter than their friends and quicker to understand" (p. 256).

TABLE 4.1 Categories of Recurrent Personality Traits of Creative People

1. Aware of Creativeness	
Creativity-conscious	Values originality and creativity
Values own creativity	
2. Original	
Adapts, and is adaptable	A dreamer
Alert to novelty	Avoids perceptual sets
Avoids entrenched ways of thinking	Bored by the routine and obvious
Builds and rebuilds	Clever
Constructs	Does things differently
Enjoys pretending	Fantasizes
Flexible in ideas and thought	Full of ideas
Imaginative	Improves
Innovative	Inventive
Is a "What if?" person	Manipulates ideas
Modifies (objects, systems, institutions)	Nonconforming
Odd habits	Radical
Resourceful	Sees things in new ways
Selects the more unusual solutions	Unconventional in behavior
Unique	Uses analogies, metaphors
Uses imagery, visualization	Uses wide categories
Versatile	Visionary
3. Independent	
Aloof	Assertive
Capable	Confident, believes in oneself
Critically examines authoritarian	Does not fear being different
Pronouncements	Dissatisfied with the status quo
Dresses differently	Egotistical
Freedom of spirit	Individualistic

TABLE 4.1 Continued

Rejects limits	Independent in judgments
Informal	Intense independence
Internally controlled, inner-directed	May not fit environment
May have conflict between self-confidence and self-criticism	May need to maintain distance from peers
May resist societal demands	Outspoken
Prefers working alone	Questions norms, conventions, assumptions
Radical and spirited in disagreement	Self-aware
Self-accepting	Self-directed
Self-confident	Self-organized
Self-esteem high	Sets own rules
Self-sufficient	Unconcerned with impressing others
Strong-willed	Uninhibited
Unconventional	
4. Risk-Taking	
Courageous	Does not mind consequences of being different
Not afraid to try something new	Optimistic
Little regard for social conventions, mores, rules, or laws	Opportunistic
Rejects limits imposed by others	Speculative
Willing to cope with failure	Willing to cope with hostility
5. High Energy	
Action-oriented	Active
Adventurous	Alert
Ambitious	Blazing drive
Capable of concentrating	Devotion to study or work
Drive for accomplishment and recognition	Drive to produce
Enjoys telling about discoveries/inventions	Driving absorption
Excitable	Enthusiastic
Expressive in gestures, body language	Exciting
Goes beyond assigned tasks	Gets lost in a problem
High commitment	Hard working
High need for competence in meeting challenges	High intrinsic motivation
	Hurried
Impulsive	Industrious
Joy in work	Overactive, hyperactive
Persevering	Persistent
Persuasive	Problem-centered
Quick	Restless
Seeks interesting situations	Sensation-seeking
Serious	Spontaneous
Unwilling to give up vitality	Vision and sense of destiny

(continued)

TABLE 4.1 Continued

6. Curious	
Asks many questions	Asks "Why?"
Distractible	Enjoys taking things apart
Experiments	Inquisitive
Likes to hear other people's ideas	Open to the irrational
Seeks interesting situations	Wide interests
7. Sense of Humor	
Childlike freshness in thinking	Playful
Plays with ideas	Sharp-witted
8. Capacity for Fantasy	
Animistic and magical thinking Had imaginary playmate(s) as a child	Believes in psychical phenomena and flying saucers
Mixes truth and fantasy/fiction	Theatrical interests
9. Attracted to Complexity, Ambiguity	
Attracted to novelty	Attracted to the mysterious, asymmetrical
Is a complex person	
Tolerant of ambiguity	Tolerant of disorder
Tolerant of incongruity	
10. Artistic	
Artistic interests	Aesthetic interests
Enjoys art, music, creative dramatics	Expressive
Good designer	Sensitive to aesthetic characteristics
Sensitive to beauty	
11. Open-minded	
Liberal	Open to new experiences and growth
Open to impulses	Receptive to new ideas
Receptive to other viewpoints	
12. Thorough	
Disciplined, committed to one's work	Organized Perfectionistic
13. Needs Alone Time	
Internally preoccupied	Introspective
Reflective	Reserved
14. Perceptive	
Discerning	Good at problem finding
Heightened sensitivity to details, patterns, other phenomena	Insightful Observant
Intuitive	Sees relationships
Sees implications	Uses all senses in observing
Senses what should follow the solution	
15. Emotional	
Can express feelings and emotions	Desires attention, praise, and support
Experiences deep emotions	Experiences soaring highs and deep lows

Immature	Impulsive
Introverted	Irresponsible
Low frustration tolerance	Moody
Selfish	Sensitive
Withdrawn	
16. Ethical	
Altruistic	Empathic
Helpful	Honest and courageousness
Idealistic	Philosophic
Sensitive to the needs of others	

In Simonton's (1988; see also Simonton, 1994, 1997) review of factors contributing to creativity he concluded that "creative individuals are noticeably more intelligent than average" (p. 399). He noted that intelligence fills the brain with images, sounds, phrases, and abstract concepts and the highly intelligent person has a greater chance of forming the novel combinations of ideas, images, and symbols that constitute a masterpiece than does someone with just a "starter set." In a *Newsweek* article about genius, Begley (1993) wrote "Ph.D.'s have a vast, complicated neural web, but high-school dropouts only a sparse, inefficient one " (p. 49). (This could explain why geniuses are more adept at bringing together disparate images, thoughts and phrases: Their brains look like Ma Bell's network).

There is compelling YET competing research evidence of a correlation between creativity and intelligence. From research by himself and others, Frank Barron (1961) reported a modest correlation of about .40 between IQ scores and measures of creativity. However, a meta-analysis by Kim (2005) found a weak correlation of only about .17 (mild to say the least!). Another set of findings by Silvia (2008) suggests that the relationship between creativity and intelligence could be underestimated, but could also be statistically masked by confounding variables.

A response to this question—whether or not creativity is related to intelligence—was put forth in the *threshold* concept. The cornerstone research was Donald MacKinnon's (1961, 1978a) studies of creative architects at the University of California at Berkeley. MacKinnon's creative architects scored higher on intelligence tests than did undergraduate students. However, when the architects were rank-ordered according to peer-rated degree of creativity, the correlation between their IQ scores and their rated creativity was nil, zip, nada ($-.08$).

MacKinnon's research illustrated that *a base level of intellectual ability is essential for creative productivity; above that threshold, however, there is virtually no relationship between measured intelligence and creativeness.*

From his study of deceased eminent persons, Walberg (1988) concluded that the linkage between intelligence and creative eminence is by no means tight: "The brightest . . . are not necessarily the best" (p. 355). His research on contemporary writers, scientists, and those adolescents who won art or science awards suggests that outstanding performance does indeed require a base level of moderately superior intelligence. However, higher levels of intelligence are less important than the presence of other psychological traits and conditions (Walberg, 1988; Walberg, Williams, & Zeiser, 2003).

These other psychological traits, particularly the personality ones, are the focus of this chapter.

In sum, creativity and intelligence are separate constructs. A highly intelligent person may or may not be highly creative. A highly creative person may or may not be highly intelligent. At the same time, over the wide range of intelligence there is a moderate correlation. The threshold concept assumes a minimal required level of intelligence, about IQ = 120, above which there is little correlation between intelligence and creativity.

Personality Traits

In the previous edition of this textbook, Davis (2004) sorted over 200 adjectives and brief descriptions of creative personality traits into 16 categories. These exclude both negative traits—consisting of seven categories—and a group of pathological characteristics, both of which are discussed later. Sources of creative personality traits and descriptions were Barron (1961, 1969, 1978, 1988), MacKinnon (1976, 1978a, 1978b), Torrance (1962, 1979, 1981a, 1984a, 1984b, 1987a, 1987b, 1995; see also Millar, 1995), Gough (1979), Walberg (1988; Stariha & Walberg, 1995; Walberg et al., 1996, 2003), Lim and Plucker (2001), Plucker and Runco (1998), Simonton (1988a, 1988b, 1990, 1994, 1997, 2003), Sternberg (1988a; Tardiff & Sternberg, 1988), Solomon and Winslow (1988, 1993; Winslow & Solomon, 1989), Davis (1975, 1995, 1999, 2003; Davis & Bull, 1978; Davis & Rimm, 1982; Davis & Subkoviak, 1978; Rimm & Davis, 1980), Runco (1990, 1999; Runco, Johnson, & Bear, 1993), Renzulli (2003), Albert (1990), Gardner (1993), and Csikszentmihalyi (1988, 1990a, 1990b).

The characteristics extracted from these sources were sorted into 16 categories via the carefully controlled question: "Now where the heck should this go?" A theory with narrower categories could produce many more groupings; one with wider categories would use fewer. There are examples of both in the literature. Feist (1998) used the five-factor model of personality to examine the relationship between personality and creativity, honing in on openness to experience as a key trait among creative individuals. Martinsen (2011) started with a group of 38 constructs related to creativity and then narrowed that list down to seven in his development of a creative person profile, a broad listing of pertinent traits that ranged from ambition to the need for originality.

While not as formal as the studies above, the "sweet" 16 listed below appeared appropriate and seemed to summarize the main, recurrent traits of creative people found in literature. The 16 categories of traits are:

1. Aware of creativeness
2. Original
3. Independent
4. Risk-taking
5. High energy
6. Curious
7. Sense of humor
8. Capacity for fantasy
9. Attraced to complexity & ambiguity
10. Artistic
11. Open-minded
12. Thorough
13. Needs alone time
14. Perceptive
15. Emotional
16. Ethical

The categories are interrelated because all are part of the creative personality. Such interrelatedness sometimes made it difficult to decide, for example, whether *nonconformity* best fit under *originality* or *independence*, or whether *adventurous* belonged under *risk-taking* or *energetic*.

If these seem familiar, you are right! The 16 categories and approximate synonyms or close descriptions appeared in Table 4.1. Of course, not all traits will apply to all creative persons. There simply are too many forms of creativity and creative people to make such a generalization. Besides, some traits are contradictory, for example, *receptive to new ideas* versus *sarcastic*. Also, there is a subtype of artistic/poetic creative people who are shy and withdrawn —not at all high in the confidence, energy, and humor that characterize the stereotyped creative nut.

While virtually all traits are self-defining, we will comment briefly on each to insure exposure to some sources and to sometimes surprising elaborations and implications.

Aware of Creativeness. Most highly creative people are quite aware of their creativeness. They are in the habit of doing creative things and they like being creative. Walberg's (1988) high school art and science award winners were consciously interested in creativity and were confident of their own creativity. "The creative groups felt more creative, imaginative, curious, and expressive and . . . felt that it is important to be creative" (p. 356). They attached great importance to money, but when choosing the "best characteristic to develop in life" they selected "creativity" more often than "wealth and power."

Creativity consciousness is a common and important trait among creative people. *In improving our own creativity and in teaching creativity to others, it is the number one trait to develop.*

Originality. In a memorable understatement, Tardiff and Sternberg (1988) noted that originality and a good imagination "are commonly said to be associated with creative individuals" (p. 434). We suspect also that comedians are reputed to be funny and thieves lean toward dishonesty. Originality obviously is a core characteristic, and dictionaries often use *originality* interchangeably with *creativity*. We noted earlier that *originality* is both a creative ability and a personality trait, in the sense of being unconventional, flexible, habitually looking for new ways of doing things, and being a "what if?" person. It is also, as Runco and Jaeger (2012) point out, part of the standard definition of creativity, an essential trait of someone (or something) who is creative. But originality by itself is not sufficient; there must be other traits that are present for the creative person to flourish. The rest of the traits on this list are features and facets that can help creativity flourish in an individual.

Independence, Risk-Taking. The creative person must dare to differ, make changes, stand out, challenge traditions, make a few waves, and bend a few rules. Creative people tend to have an internal locus of evaluation, rather than being swayed too easily by external influences and opinions. Because of their independence and innovativeness, creative people expose themselves to (a) failure, (b) criticism, (c) embarrassment, (d) the distinct possibility of making idiots of themselves, or (e) all of the above. In regard to creatively eminent people, Simonton (1997, p. 340) mentioned that "even after notable achievers establish their reputations . . . failures will accompany successes throughout their lives" (p. 340).

Sandra Bem's (1974, 1981) *Bem Sex-Role Inventory* classifies persons—of either gender—as having a gender-role orientation of either masculinity (instrumental, assertive, independent), femininity (expressive, understanding, gentle), androgyny (both), or—for lack of a suitable name—"undifferentiated," "unclassifiable," or "nonandrogynous" (neither). Generally, androgynous persons (e.g., women in executive positions) are less influenced by gender-based stereotypes (translation: they are more *independent*) and are more flexible and creative than others (e.g., Bem, 1974; Hittner & Daniels, 2002; Norlander, Erixon, & Archer, 2000).

High Energy. Creative people typically have a high energy level—a certain enthusiastic zest and a habit of spontaneous action. The creative person may get caught up in seemingly simple problems, perhaps working well into the night on an exciting project. "Driving absorption," "high commitment," "passionate interest," "blazing drive," and "unwilling to give up" are phrases used to describe the energy and motivation of highly creative persons. The creative artist, writer, researcher, business person, engineer, or advertising executive becomes totally immersed in his or her ideas and creations, literally unable to rest until the work is complete. According to Taylor (1988), "One fellow scientist described his colleague by saying that the only way one could stop him from working on his problem would be to shoot him" (p. 99).

Author Schawlow, Nobel Prize Winner in physics, stated that "The labor of love is important. The successful scientists are often not the most talented, but the ones who are just impelled by curiosity—they've got to know what the answer is" (Amabile, 1987, p. 224). Amabile reported that General Motors' most successful locomotive was designed by a small team of scientists and technicians who had been told four times to "cease and desist from building a locomotive" (p. 224).

A related motivational trait has been called *sensation-seeking, arousal-seeking,* or *thrill-seeking* (Farley, 1986), which combines traits of high energy, adventurousness, and risk-taking. A personality test called the *Sensation Seeking Scale* (Zuckerman, 1975) is a better measure of creative tendencies than some creativity tests, according to a study by Davis, Peterson, and Farley (1973). In their research with college students, creative individuals were much more likely than the average to say "yes," they would like to:

- Take up skiing
- Ride motorcycles

- Parachute jump from an airplane
- Try mountain climbing
- Be hypnotized
- Work in a foreign country
- Explore strange cities without a guide

They preferred:

- Camping to a good motel
- To jump right into a cold pool instead of dipping a toe first
- Bright colors in loud modern art over subdued traditional paintings
- They liked:
- Some body odors

More recently, de Vries, de Vries, and Feij (2009) analyzed sensation-seeking in relation to the HEXACO model of personality, with the construct of creativity highly correlated to the variables of experience-seeking and boredom susceptibility. Now it makes sense why creative individuals do as they do (or "Do the Dew"), as their drive for thrill-seeking can either create a sugar rush of ideas or cause one to crash and burn (after the natural energy OR caffeine wears off!)

Is this creative couple carrying the traits of originality, self-confidence, and sensation-seeking too far? Giving up a "free solo" life for the ball and chain (or carabiner and ropes) requires risk-taking and might not be for the faint of heart. Before you take "the plunge" of saying "I Do," you might want to gain a perspective of how some couples are going to extremes (literally) to pull off the perfect wedding photos.

Curiosity. The creative person also has strong curiosity, a childlike sense of wonder and intrigue. He or she may have a history of taking things apart to see how they work, exploring attics, libraries, or museums, and have a generally strong urge to understand the world about him or her. The curiosity produces wide interests, unusual hobbies, and an experimenting nature. More than one creative person has muddled college graduation requirements by taking intriguing courses that do not meet graduation requirements.

High curiosity has been identified as a natural characteristic of creative individuals (Schmidhuber, 2006). And in describing this trait in relation to creativity, Kashdan and Silvia (2009) stated that "curiosity motivates people to act and think in new ways and investigate, be immersed, and learn about whatever is the immediate interesting target of their attention" (p. 368).

Humor. Another frequent creative trait is a good sense of humor, which is first cousin to the ability to take a fresh, childlike, and playful approach to a problem. Many discoveries, inventions, problem solutions, and artistic creations are the result of "fooling around" with ideas, playing with strange possibilities, or turning things upside down or backward. A favorite quote is that "The creative adult is essentially a perpetual child—the tragedy is that most of us grow up" (Fabun, 1968, p. 5). Both Sigmund Freud and Carl Rogers agreed that regression to a more childlike, fanciful, playful state of mind is an important feature of creative thinking and creative thinkers. Empirically, O'Quin and Derks (1997) were able to substantiate a hearty relationship between humor and creativity, and that's no laughing matter!

Attraction to Complexity, Ambiguity, Fantasy, and Novelty. The creative person is attracted to complexity, ambiguity, fantasy, and the mysterious, a proclivity that may reflect the creative person's own complexity. One creativity test, the *Barron Welsh Art Scale* (Welsh & Barron, 1963; see Chapter 10), has shown repeatedly that creative persons prefer smudgy, complex, asymmetrical drawings over simple and balanced ones (Barron, 1969).

Martindale (1975) made a relevant observation:

> Confronted with novelty, whether in design, music, or ideas, creative people get excited and involved . . . and overlook defects or problems. . . . Less creative students do the opposite. They find fault . . . and start analyzing defects rather than exploring potential.

Sternberg (1988a) reviewed the critical role of tolerance for ambiguity, dubbing it "almost a *sine qua non* of creative performance" (p. 143), an observation also made by others (e.g., Barron, 1968; Dacey, 1989; MacKinnon, 1978b; Vernon, 1970). Creative ideas normally require some amount of elaboration and development. It follows that the creative person must work with ideas that are incomplete and ambiguous: Relevant facts are missing, rules are unclear, and "correct" procedures do not exist (MacKinnon, 1978b). Whether writing a novel, creating a work of art, or solving an engineering problem, the ideas will evolve from the original insight or "big idea" through a series of modifications, approximations, and improvements—which requires coping with uncertainty and ambiguity.

An attraction to complexity and fantasy includes a probably surprising twist: Creative persons tend to be stronger believers in such psychical and mysterious matters as extrasensory perception (ESP), mental telepathy, precognition, astral projection (out-of-body experience), flying saucers, and spirits and ghosts (Davis, 1975; Davis et al., 1973; Schuldberg et al., 1988). They also are more likely to have psychical experiences (Torrance, 1962). Many creative persons have reported mystical experiences, for example, Mark Twain. Another example is the late Orson Welles, creator of the 1938 radio show *The War of the Worlds*, which scared the daylights out of millions of Americans, and the movie *Citizen Kane*, often rated the best movie ever made. Welles frequently demonstrated his psychical abilities on TV shows, but he also was an accomplished magician, suspiciously enough.

Thalbourne (1991, 2000) coined the term *transliminality* to describe persons who are said to have "experiences that we variously know . . . as psychic, mystical and creative, and at higher, more overwhelming intensities, as psychotic" (p. 194). Persons low in transliminality are "lacking in experiences of the psychic, the mystical, the creative, and the psychotic" (p. 194). Thalbourne's research duplicated that of Davis (1975) and Davis et al. (1973). College students who scored high on a transliminality scale (e.g., "I am convinced that I am psychic") also scored high on a measure of creative personality.

There are at least four possibly interrelated explanations for this belief in paranormal happenings by many creative people. First, such beliefs simply may reflect the creative person's livelier imagination and openness to fantastic possibilities. Second, such beliefs might reflect a mild psychopathology, as noted by Thalbourne (2000). Thalbourne et al. (1997) found "schizotypy" (not in your dictionary) to be a correlate of claimed transliminal ability. Third, as we will shortly see in the *Emotional* description, extremely intelligent persons may experience *emotional giftedness*, which includes—among many other characteristics—paranormal thinking. The fourth possibility is that highly creative people *do* have mystical and psychic experiences that escape the rest of us.

What do you think? "Stranger Things" have happened than people living in an upside-down world?!.

Artistic, Aesthetic Interests. The creative person usually will rate himself or herself high in being "artistic," whether or not he or she can draw. The creative person thus tends to be more conscious of artistic considerations and also has aesthetic interests— interests in music and dance concerts, plays, art galleries, photo exhibits, antique shows, Masterpiece Theatre, a good sunset, scenic views from the freeway, and so on. On the *How Do You Think* test (Davis, 1991a; Chapter 10), an inventory for assessing creative personality traits, a high self-rating on *artistic* is one of the single best items on the test (Davis & Subkoviak, 1978).

One obvious reason for above-average artistic and aesthetic interests is that creative people are more likely to be, or to have been, involved in artistic and aesthetic enterprises—music, dance, theater, art, handicrafts, or others. With those outlets in mind, when discussing artistic creativity, John Hospers (1985) stated that "creation . . . is always out of preexistent materials, from which the created product is made, and creation consists not in bringing these materials into existence but in arranging them in an order which did not exist before" (p. 245)

Thorough. The common traits of risk-taking and high energy of the creatively productive person do not present a complete picture of work habits. He or she must finish the work, and therefore has been described as thorough, organized, disciplined, committed to the work, and sometimes even perfectionistic.

Open-minded. Open-mindedness is a prime creative attitude. It includes receptiveness to new ideas and a willingness to look at a problem or situation from other points of view. It includes not fearing the new, different, or unknown, and not making up your mind in advance (Dacey, 1989). Open-mindedness includes a dash of adventurousness and leads to personal growth.

The reader is encouraged to look again at von Oech's 10 whack-on-the-side-of-the-head guides in Chapter 3. Barriers to creativity—such as looking for just one right answer; being practical and logical; and avoiding ambiguity, frivolity, mistakes, and foolishness—are quite inconsistent with creative open-mindedness.

Need for Alone Time. Creative children and adults need some privacy and alone time. The urge to create demands time for thinking, for reflection, for solving problems, for creating. Creative children and adults may prefer to work alone, which reflects their creative independence. In the recent book, *Wired to Create*, Kaufman and Gregoire (2016) highlight the aspect of solitude and its role in creativity, noting that "solitude is a means of intellectually separating oneself from the crowd and forging a unique perspective" (p. 42). They go on to state that "reflection (in solitude) can give rise to our most profound personal and creative insights" (p. 47). Take some alone time yourself to let that sink in!

Perceptive. As described by the adjectives in Table 4.2, perceptiveness and intuitiveness include a creative person's higher sensitivity to details, patterns, implications, and "what should follow." Creative people are quicker to see relationships and make "mental leaps." Such perceptiveness and intuition relate to the insightfulness and problem-finding ability of creative people.

Emotional. A literature exists on *emotional giftedness* or *overexcitability* (e.g., Piechowski, 1997, 2003). Some gifted persons with extremely high intelligence show high creativity in the sense of "free play of imagination, with vivid imagery, fantasy . . . paranormal thinking, metaphorical thought, inventions, and poetic and dramatic perceptions" (Davis & Rimm, 2004, p. 437). The syndrome includes

TABLE 4.2 Descriptions Reflecting Intelligence

Analytical	Alert to gaps in knowledge
Articulate	Cannot write fast enough to keep up with ideas
Capable	Clear thinking
Competent	Complicated
Commonsensical	Finds order in chaos
Ingenious	Knowledgeable
Likes complicated ideas	Logical
Precocious	Rational
Skilled in decision-making	Well read
Well informed	

having deep emotions, experiencing emotional highs and lows, as well as moodiness and emotional sensitivity. Other traits of the emotionally gifted include high psychomotor activity (e.g., high energy, fast-talking), a high concern for right-and-wrong (moral thinking), and an aliveness of sensual experiences. But can we harness the power of emotions for creativity? Averill (2005) states that "emotions are related to creativity in many ways—as facilitators, inhibitors, and simply as adventitious by-products" (p. 225). With products in mind, Averill and Thomas-Knowles (1991) put forth the notion of Emotional Creativity (EC), which relates to one's ability to experience or express unique, appropriate, and authentic combinations of emotions. So with that in mind, how do you "feel" you would score on an Emotional Creativity Inventory?

Ethical. Another trait related to high mental ability and creativity is a tendency toward idealism, altruism, sensitivity to others' needs, and just plain helpfulness. Perhaps a lively imagination and the ability to see outcomes strengthen one's empathic understanding of others' difficulties and problems. Renzulli (2003) recommended that sensitivity to human concerns—not just college success and consumerism—should be a central part of educating intellectually and creatively gifted students.

Negative Creative Traits

So far, with few exceptions, the creative person looks pretty good—intelligent, independent, energetic, good sense of humor, artistic, open-minded, perceptive, and so on. However, creative children and adults are quite capable of showing habits and dispositions that can upset a normal supervisor, parent, teacher, or other students. Table 4.3 lists some not-uncommon characteristics of creative individuals, most of which were found in Torrance (1962, 1981a), Smith (1966), and Domino (1970). The items were intuitively placed into the seven categories of *egotistical, impulsive, argumentative, childish, absentminded, neurotic,* and *hyperactive.* Some may be rooted in a creative students' general unconventionality, independence, persistence, high energy and activity, and perhaps curiosity and humor.

TABLE 4.3 Common "Negative" Traits of Some Creative Persons Sometimes

1. Egotistical	
Claims rest of the parade is out of step	Intolerant
Self-centered	Selfish
Snobbish	
2. Impulsive	
Acts without planning	Capricious
Compulsive	Disorderly
Disorganized with unimportant matters	Impatient
Irresponsible	Tactless
Uninterested in details	
3. Argumentative	
Autocratic	Cynical
Defiant	Demanding
Intolerant	Rebellious
Refuses to participate in class activities	Resists domination
Sarcastic	Stubborn
Tactless	Uncooperative
Questions rules, conventions, law, authority	

(continued)

TABLE 4.3 Continued

4. Childish	
Immature	Silly
Sloppy	
5. Absentminded	
Careless	Forgetful
Mind wanders	Watches windows
6. Neurotic	
Aloof	Low frustration tolerance
Moody	Sociopathic, mildly
Temperamental	Unable to control emotions
Uncommunicative	
7. Hyperactive	
Overactive physically or mentally	Restless

Many are likely to cause personal or social adjustment problems, for example, *egotistical* ("I know more than anyone here"), *argumentativeness* and *sarcasm* ("I'm always right"), and being *capricious, disorderly,* and *careless* ("and I'll do what I want").

In discussing business entrepreneurs—who seem like a creative bunch—Solomon and Winslow (1988) described negative traits of being *mildly sociopathic* (or being a *social deviate*), partly because they cannot work for someone else; *clannish,* because they seek out people like themselves; and *outspoken, impatient,* and *stubborn.* On the positive side, the authors noted that entrepreneurs are "confident and optimistic . . . [and are] independent and self-reliant" (p. 170).

When Stubborn Sammy or Independent Elissa show some of the upsetting characteristics in Table 4.3, the teacher might consider the possibility that the symptoms are part of a larger picture of energetic creativeness that may need rechanneling into constructive outlets. In the business or professional setting: patience and understanding.

Berkeley Studies

The single most extensive examination of traits of creative people took place at the University of California, Berkeley, in the 1950s. Psychologists Frank Barron (1969, 1978, 1988), Donald MacKinnon (1976, 1978a), and others studied nationally recognized creative architects, writers, and men and women mathematicians. The names were selected by nominations from faculty in Berkeley's Departments of Architecture, English, and Mathematics. The creative persons were observed informally over a three-day weekend and took intelligence tests and a variety of personality tests and self-descriptive inventories (e.g., the *Minnesota Multiphasic Personality Inventory,* MMPI; *California Psychological Inventory,* CPI; *Adjective Check List,* ACL; *Myers–Briggs Type Indicator,* MBTI). Barron also went to Ireland to study innovators in business management, using many of the same tests. Many of the personality traits described in this chapter originated from or were confirmed by this research. For example, their creative people tended to be original, imaginative, independent, verbally fluent, flexible, energetic, productive, artistic, emotional, unconventional, nonconforming, and generally had aesthetic interests and wide interests.

Creativity and Mental Disturbance

The Berkeley group also uncovered an interesting trend among high-level creative people, reminiscent of Maslow's sometimes-disturbed *special-talent* creative persons (Chapter 12). The research indicated that some traits of these very talented people would not be considered mentally healthy. Compared with representative women mathematicians, creative women mathematicians were more likely to be self-centered, rebellious, and have fluctuating moods, and they tended to be undependable, irresponsible, and/or inconsiderate. Looking at successful creative writers, "the *average* creative writer, in fact, is in the upper 15 percent of the general population on *all* measures of psychopathology furnished by this test!" (MMPI; Barron, 1965, p. 62): *hypochondriasis, depression, hysteria,*[1] *psychopathic deviation, paranoia, psychasthenia,*[2] *schizophrenia,* and *hypomania.* Critically, they also scored high on *ego strength,* a measure of mental health and stability. Barron (1969) summed up his findings as follows: "they are both sicker and healthier psychologically than people in general . . . they are more troubled psychologically, but they also have far greater resources with which to deal with their troubles."

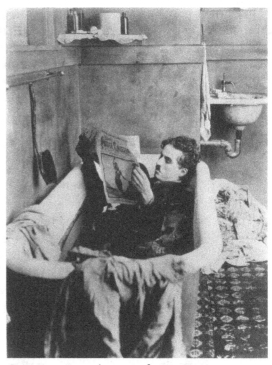

Creative people may forget unimportant details. (Charlie Chaplin in "Pay Day," 1922. Courtesy of PhotoFest.)

This interesting tendency of highly creative people to show mental disorders has a continuing history (see, for example, Andreason, 1978; Jamison, 1989; Richards, 1981; Schuldberg et al., 1988). Wrote Schuldberg et al.: "research has noted affective disorders, schizophrenia, unconventional or antisocial behavior, and alcohol and substance abuse in eminent and creative individuals and sometimes in their relatives" (p. 648). The research of Schuldberg et al. showed that normal (?) garden-variety male and female college students who scored high on a creative personality inventory (*How Do You Think,* HDYT; Davis, 1975, 1991a) also scored high on a combined measure of psychopathology: *perceptual aberration* (e.g., ordinary sounds are reported as sometimes uncomfortable) and *magical ideation* (having superstitious and supernatural beliefs). Shields (1988) found that the best group of items in the HDYT creativity test were those that measured belief in paranormal phenomena (ESP, precognition, flying saucers, etc.), which relates closely to Schuldberg's magical ideation.

In Walberg's (1988; Walberg & Herbig, 1991) study of historically eminent people, about a quarter to a third showed definite introversion or neuroses. The business manager of Yves St. Laurent said in a TV interview that, despite his fame and success, the genius of fashion design actually is withdrawn and somewhat neurotic.

We noted Solomon and Winslow's (1988) conclusion that their sample of entrepreneurs showed mild sociopathy and/or were social deviates. Characteristics described as "not necessarily mentally ill but aberrant" included *immature, irresponsible, impulsive, selfish, little anxiety or guilt about immediate acts, little ability to control emotions, low frustration tolerance,* and *little regard for societal conventions, mores, rules,* or *laws.* The description seems to qualify as mild sociopathy.

A study by Walker, Koestner, and Hum (1995; see also Runco, 1998) explored the personalities of 48 eminent creative achievers (25 men, 23 women), finding that the "creative achievers were rated significantly higher than controls on general neuroticism, as well as on depressive style and impulsivity" (p. 75).

---

[1] Excitability, anxiety, uncontrolled behavior.
[2] Neuroses characterized by fear, anxiety, and phobias.

They noted that creative artists and writers Sylvia Plath, Jack London, Virginia Woolf, Jackson Pollock, and Vincent van Gogh experienced sufficient depression to commit suicide. Jamison (1989) asked 47 award-winning British artists and writers about any history of affective disorders, and 38% reported psychiatric treatment for depression. Andreason (1987) found that in a sample of creative writers, a full 80% had an affective illness at some time and 43% had some type of bipolar (manic-depressive) illness.

Creative writers apparently are the most troubled group. Andreason (1987; Andreason & Cantor, 1974; Andreason & Glick, 1988) compared creative writers with matched controls. The writers were more likely to be manic-depressive, and, remarkably, so were the writers' close relatives. Ludwig (1994) also compared writers with controls, again finding higher mental illness with the writers. Post (1994), looking at biographies, concluded that artists and writers showed higher rates of mental illness, compared with persons in other groups. Writers were more likely than artists to show depression.

If we compare categories of writers—for example, poets, fiction writers, nonfiction writers, and playwrights—we find that poets win hands down. Or lose. Jamison (1993) discovered that suicide rates were higher than average among the eighteenth-century British poets. Jamison suggested that intervals of clear and logical thinking—characteristic of manic depression—could aid their writing. In an earlier study of British writers and artists, Jamison (1989) found higher-than-expected rates of mental illness, especially affective (emotional) disorders. Poets showed the highest rates of bipolar disorder. Ludwig (1995) studied biographies written between 1960 and 1990 of over 1,000 eminent persons. He found higher mental illness among writers, artists, and theater people, compared with persons in business, politics, and science. Poets had the highest rates of psychosis and depression. However, to use an oft-quoted piece of poetry, it's unclear whether if two roads diverged in the woods, which would lead to madness and which would lead to creativity. Or would they merge together?

Silvia and Kaufman (2010) addressed this in a recent publication in the *The Cambridge Handbook on Creativity* on creativity and mental illness. They set forth several notions about the nature of the relationship. The first argument is that mental illness causes creativity as "some disorders foster, enable, or provoke creative thought and accomplishment" (p. 384) feeding the "mad genius" stereotype. A second argument flips the mad hatter notion upside down. What if creativity causes mental illness, perhaps due to "an accumulation of risk factors as a result of a creative lifestyle" (p. 384). Finally, the third possibility they offer up is that creativity and mental illness symbiotically feed off each other. Whether they coexist OR one is a host for the other, the end result still can lead to the creative individual consuming himself or herself with aberrant thoughts or abhorrent actions.

Biographical Characteristics

Recurrent biographical traits of creative people may be of two sorts, *subtle* and the *not-so-subtle*. Not-so-subtle biographical factors are simply the person's history of creative activities and creative behaviors. It is hardly surprising that, beginning in childhood, most creative people accumulate a history of building and making things and of literary, artistic, and scientific involvement. One list of "things done on your own," from Torrance (1962), appears in Table 4.4. A list of creative behaviors from Renzulli and Reis (1991) is in Table 4.5.

If the person has been creative in the past, there is a strong likelihood he or she will be creative in the future. Involvement in creative activities can be used as a predictor of creative behavior—a predictor that may have more validity than some creativity tests.

Subtle biographical correlates of creativity include background facts that are a bit more surprising. Schaefer (1969, 1970) found that creative high school students were more likely to have friends younger and older than themselves, rather than the same age. The creatives also were more likely to have lived in more than one state and may have traveled outside the United States. High school girls who were creative writers were more likely to personally own a cat. Definitely subtle. Schaefer, confirmed in studies reviewed by Somers and Yawkey (1984), also found that creative students more often reported having an imaginary childhood playmate. Said Somers and Yawkey, imaginary companions contribute to creativity by developing originality and elaboration and by fostering sensitivity in relationships.

TABLE 4.4 A Sample of Creative Activities

• Wrote a poem (story, play)
• Produced a puppet show
• Acted in, directed, organized, or designed stage settings for a play or skit
• Made up a song (dance, musical composition, new game)
• Explored a cave
• Read a science magazine
• Printed photographs
• Made an electric motor (musical instrument, ink, leaf prints)
• Planned an experiment, dissected an animal
• Grafted a plant or rooted one from a cutting
• Collected insects (rocks, stamps, postmarks, wild flowers)
• Kept a daily record of weather
• Organized or helped to organize a club
• Figured out a way of improving the way we do something at home (or school)
• Found out how some government agency (post office, court, etc.) operates
• Made a poster for a club, school, or other event
• Organized or helped organize paper drive, rummage sale, and so on
• Sketched a landscape, designed jewelry
• Illustrated a story, drew cartoons
• Made linoleum cuts (watercolor, oil painting)
• Made a toy for a child (or a wood or soap carving, ornamental basket)
• Drew up plans for (or constructed) an invention or apparatus
• Made up a recipe

Source: Adapted from Torrance's (1962) *Things Done On Your Own Inventory.*

In your author's opinion, two biographical traits *each* are accurate as predictors of creativity: participation in theater or having had an imaginary playmate as a child. Creative secondary students and adults may laughingly concede, "I still have an imaginary playmate." Typically, the young child will talk to and play with the imaginary companion, have tea parties, blame things on the playmate ("I didn't break it, Yoohoo did!"), and require mom—or the waitress in a restaurant—to set an extra place at the table. Sometimes there are many imaginary friends and sometimes they are animals. Some creative children do a continuous ventriloquist act, talking back and forth with a stuffed animal or doll. The imaginary friend usually, not always, disappears after children enter kindergarten (Somers & Yawkey, 1984). Persons who claim a background in theater or having had an imaginary playmate (or both, which is common) invariably show the typical creative personality traits described in this chapter. They also will report present or past involvement in creative activities.

TABLE 4.5 Examples of Renzulli's Action Information

• Goes "above and beyond the call of duty" in completing, for example, an art, writing, or science project that shows superlative quality.
• Is obsessed with a particular topic or area of study.
• Is sought out by others because he or she is an expert in a particular area.
• Is labeled by others (not always in complimentary ways) as the "math marvel," "computer whiz kid," "poet in residence," or "mad scientist."
• Wants to "get something going," for example, a class newspaper, money-raising project, field trip, or action on a social problem.
• Has extracurricular activities that are more important than regular school work.
• May start a club, interest group, or project (e.g., film making) on his or her own.
• Typically is the class clown or lackadaisical, but becomes very serious and immersed in a particular topic area.
• Voluntarily visits museums, laboratories, power plants, and so on, on his or her own.
• Forgets to come back to class or is always late when returning from a particular course or special interest area, for example, the computer, art, or industrial arts room.
• Is a clever humorist—sees whimsical implications of otherwise serious situations.
• Has set up a laboratory, photography darkroom, or other special interest area at home on his or her own.
• Feels compulsion to begin work on a topic ("I have to write it down before I go nuts").

Source: From Renzulli and Reis (1997). Reprinted by permission of Creative Learning Press.

The Buckets © 1997 Greg Cravens. Reprinted by permission of Andrews McMeel Syndication. All rights reserved.

Birth Order and Handedness

Birth order and handedness are two traits that occasionally are mentioned as possibly related to creativity.

Birth-Order Effects. The birth-order effect has been studied for some decades, beginning with Galton's (1876) study of eminent British scientists. There seems little doubt that firstborn and only children tend to be more studious, higher achievers, and more likely to be National Merit scholars or even prodigies. They are likely to be better educated and have higher-level careers (Hilgard, Atkinson, & Atkinson, 1979). Firstborns predominate among doctors, lawyers, professors, and other professionals (Simonton, 1997, 2003). Most U.S. presidents are first or only children (e.g., Schubert, Wagner, & Schubert, 1977), as are about 93% of U.S. astronauts. Firstborn and only children were overrepresented in Terman's sample of 1,528 gifted children, most of whom scored above IQ 140.

Speculations on the cause of the birth-order effect are amusing. Briefly, one view was that first and only children somehow have a more favorable prenatal environment, which produces less "fetal stress." Another explanation proposed that later-born children experience repeated and unexpected intrusions by the older sibling, resulting in an altered brain limbic system that makes the younger child more sensitive, anxious, and withdrawn.

Social explanations seem more on target. One argument is simply that first and only children receive more attention, are read to more, and receive more educational encouragement and assistance. Another points out that a new baby requires older children to be more grown-up, responsible, and to depend less on mother for assistance. For example, older children are expected to help with and sometimes care for the new arrival. Firstborns thus may develop a personality and learning style that aids their informal and formal education and ultimate achievement. For example, in school they tend to work hard, impress teachers, and try hard on IQ tests. This portrait may be compared with the reported tendency of later-borns to not work hard in school or on IQ tests, not try to impress teachers, and not necessarily assume the existence of one right answer (e.g., on an intelligence test; Simonton, 1997).

While education and achievement favor first and only children, some have argued that later-borns generally are more creative. According to Hetherington and Parke (1979), first and only children are more anxious, conforming, passive, and worried about failure—traits that favor academic accomplishment, but not creative thought. Eisenman's (1964) research with 20 art students seemed to confirm that, sure enough, firstborns were less creative than middle or youngest children. But in a different study, Eisenman and Schussel (1970) found a contrary result in a sample of 450 undergraduates at Temple University (go Owls!). Their data showed that firstborn males outperformed later-born males on all creativity measures (though there were no differences between firstborn and later-born female students in the same sample). And to muddy the empirical waters even further, Szobiová (2008) found that second-born adolescents outperformed all other classifications of siblings (oldest, middle child, youngest, only child) on a divergent thinking test. So what to make of this hazy sibling constellation of creativity results? Is the fault truly in the stars? Sulloway (1999) sums it up by saying "birth order provides one important source of personality differences, which in turn underlie differences in creative achievement" (p. 202).

Simonton (1997, 2003) expanded upon this view relating birth order to creativity. Based on a literature review, he concluded that "the overall tendency is for firstborns to achieve eminence in prestigious positions that are well integrated with the Establishment, whereas the later-borns are more likely to succeed as rebellious agents of a new order or even as advocates of disorder" (p. 342). For example, he noted that our scholarly firstborns are more likely to attain distinction in scientific areas, but the more creative later-borns are likely to distinguish themselves in artistic areas—as artists, writers, or others who conform less to societal expectations. An exception is that classic composers are more aligned with the scientists—they tend to be first- or only-borns (Schubert et al., 1977). The reference is a real one.

Simonton (1997) reached a similar conclusion regarding leadership: "First-borns provide the politicians, while the last-borns populate the revolutionaries" (p. 342). Interestingly, said Simonton, later-borns who do go into science are more apt to become "scientific revolutionaries" who might overthrow established models and standards.

Handedness. While Simonton's conclusions regarding birth order are suggestive, research on the relation of handedness to creativity remains ambiguous (or is the term ambidextrous).

There has been speculation that lefthanders are more creative. The main—but weak—evidence is that many historically creative people were left-handed, for example, Leonardo Da Vinci, Michelangelo, and Benjamin Franklin. The argument is that left-handed people, most of whom in fact are ambidextrous, have better access to both hemispheres of their brains. That is, with normal right-handed people the left side of the brain controls speech, writing, sequential, and analytical functions; the right side controls spatial, wholistic, intuitive, and creative functions (Springer & Deutsch, 1985). The left-handed person's more integrated access to both hemispheres should aid creative thinking and problem-solving; at least that's the logic.

Peterson and Lansky (1980), in fact, discovered that in a sample of 17 architecture faculty, five were left-handed (29.4%), and two more were left-handed as children but were "cured," for a total of 7 of 17 (41.2%). Dacey (1989) reported that 65% of the students in a major art school were left-handed. These figures are substantially above the universe-wide average of 10% left-handedness. On the other hand (sorry), with a group of 100 twenty-year-olds Katz (1980) found absolutely no relationship between handedness and scores on three different creativity tests.

Though the association of left-handedness with higher creativity is inconclusive, research conducted by Shobe, Ross, and Fleck (2009) shows that mixed-handed individuals perform better than strong-handed individuals (right- or left-dominant) on five creativity dimensions based on higher levels of interhemispheric interaction (meaning that they aren't simply right-minded folks)

Creative Abilities

In addition to personality (or affective) traits and biographical characteristics, there also are *cognitive* abilities that are important for creative thinking—abilities that are well-developed and often used by creative people. Such abilities are partly genetic and partly learned. Long-time creativity expert Frank Barron (1988) listed just six "ingredients" of creativity that intermix affective and cognitive traits:

1. Recognizing patterns
2. Making connections
3. Taking risks
4. Challenging assumptions
5. Taking advantage of chance
6. Seeing in new ways

Barron's six ingredients certainly are central traits of a creative person. However, there are many more intellectual and stylistic abilities that contribute in one way or another to creative capability. Actually, it would be difficult to isolate mental abilities that have absolutely *nothing* to do with creativeness. We also noted that the line between "abilities" and "personality characteristics" sometimes is very thin, for example, in the cases of originality, humor, or perceptiveness.

A short list of abilities that seem especially important to creativity appears in Table 4.6.

Fluency is the ability to produce many ideas, verbal or nonverbal, for an open-ended problem or question. Pseudonyms include *associational fluency* and *ideational fluency*.

TABLE 4.6 Creative Abilities

Fluency	Able to predict outcomes, consequences
Flexibility	Analysis
Originality	Synthesis
Elaboration	Evaluation
Transformation	Logical thinking
Sensitivity to problems	Able to regress
Able to define problems	Intuition
Visualization, imagination	Concentration
Analogical/metaphorical thinking	

Flexibility is the ability to take different approaches to a problem, think of ideas in different categories, or view a problem from different perspectives.

Originality is just that—uniqueness, nonconformity in thought and action. Dictionary synonyms include creativity, novelty, rarity, singularity, and innovativeness.

Elaboration is the important ability to add details to an idea, which includes developing, embellishing, improving, and implementing the idea.[3]

Transformation is a subtle term that could be used interchangeably with *creative thinking* itself. Every creative idea involves a transformation—changing one object or idea into another by modifying, combining, or substituting. Transformation also is "seeing" new meanings, implications, or applications or adopting something to a new use. For nearly four decades, J. P. Guilford (e.g., 1986) emphasized the significance of transformation abilities for creative thinking. We will see in Chapter 5 that *perceptual change*—looking at one thing and seeing another—is a creative process that is approximately identical in meaning to *transformation*.

Sensitivity to problems reflects the ability to find problems, detect difficulties, detect missing information, and ask good questions. Many writers, including Albert Einstein, have stressed that creative people generally are excellent "problem finders" (e.g., Getzels & Csikszentmihalyi, 1976; Okuda, Runco, & Berger, 1991; Subotnik, 1988). Creative people can locate problems worth working on, and they always assume their own work can be improved.

The related complex ability of *problem defining* includes at least the abilities to (1) identify the "real" problem, (2) isolate important (and unimportant) aspects of a problem, (3) clarify and simplify a problem, (4) identify sub-problems, (5) propose alternative problem definitions, and (6) define a problem more broadly; that is, to ask "What is (or are) the broader, underlying problem(s)?" (e.g., with not having enough money). Abilities 5 and 6 open the door to a wider variety of problem solutions. Note that one's logical thinking ability would be involved throughout "problem defining" as described here.

Note also that both *sensitivity to problems* and *problem defining* seem to require a certain *perceptiveness* and *intuitiveness*, described earlier as personality traits. Once again the distinction between abilities and personality traits is clearly blurred.

Visualization is the ability to fantasize, to see things in the "mind's eye," to mentally manipulate images and ideas. The term is used interchangeably with *imagination* itself and is an essential creative ability. It also is a complex one. Creative writing, for example, has been described as a recursive process of moving back and forth between mental images (based on novel syntheses of memories and current experiences) and the prose itself (Flower & Hayes, 1984). Imagery actually takes place in all senses, not just the visual one, as when Beethoven and Mozart imagined their compositions. *Synesthesia* is cross-modal imagery, as in "the murmur of gray twilight" and "the sound of coming darkness" (Poe) and "the dawn comes up like thunder" (Kipling; see Daniels-McGhee & Davis, 1994).

Analogical/metaphorical thinking is the ability to borrow ideas from one context and use them in another, borrow a solution from a related problem, or otherwise "see a connection" between one situation and another. Analogical thinking is sufficiently important to justify a relatively substantial chapter in this book (Chapter 6).

Predicting outcomes or consequences is the ability to foresee the results of different solution alternatives and actions. It is related to *evaluation* ability.

Analysis is the ability to separate details, break down a whole into its parts.

Synthesis is the ability to see relationships, to combine parts into a workable, perhaps creative whole. *Creativity* sometime is called *synthetic thinking*.

Evaluation is the important ability to separate the relevant from the irrelevant, to think critically, and to evaluate the "goodness" or appropriateness of an idea, product, or solution.[4]

---

[3] Fluency, flexibility, originality, and elaboration are four scores derived from the popular *Torrance Tests of Creative Thinking* (Chapter 10). They are important and well-known creative abilities, but not the only creative abilities.

[4] The reader with a background in education might recognize *analysis, synthesis,* and *evaluation* as higher-order thinking skills in Bloom's taxonomy of educational objectives, cognitive domain.

Logical thinking is the ability to make reasonable decisions and deduce reasonable conclusions. It permeates all aspects of creative thinking and problem-solving and, logically, would be part of every other ability in this list.

The *ability to regress* includes a facility for "thinking like a child," whose mind is less cluttered by habits, traditions, rules, conformity pressures, and so on—the barriers we explored in Chapter 3. The ability to regress is related to playfulness and humor.

Intuition is a little-understood capability to make "mental leaps" or "intuitive leaps"; to see relationships based upon little, perhaps-insufficient, information, and to "read between the lines." It relates to *perceptiveness*, described earlier in the personality list.

Concentration is the ability to focus one's attention. It relates to the task orientation or even "driving absorption" of creatively productive people.

Information Processing Traits

A list of dynamic information processing characteristics related to creative thinking, modified from Tardiff and Sternberg (1988), and which they extracted from numerous chapters in the Sternberg (1988b) book, appears in Table 4.7. Because these seem self-defining, and in fact overlap with the personality traits and cognitive abilities presented in Tables 4.2 and 4.6, we will bypass a tedious definition of each.

TABLE 4.7 Information Processing Traits

• Using existing knowledge as a basis for new ideas
• Building new structures, instead of using existing ones
• Using wide categories, seeing "forest" instead of "trees"
• Avoiding perceptual sets and entrenched ways of thinking
• Questioning norms and assumptions
• Recognizing gaps in knowledge
• Finding problems
• Thinking logically
• Thinking with flexibility
• Thinking metaphorically
• Using internal visualization
• Skill and flexibility in decision-making
• Making independent judgments
• Using novelty
• Finding order in chaos
• Using nonverbal communication

Source: Partly adapted from Tardif and Sternberg (1998).

Creativity and Eminence

In Chapter 2 we summarized briefly the Csikszentmihalyi (1988) and Gardner (1993) theories of creativity, both of which emphasized the components of *person*, *domain*, and *field* (society). Their restrictive definition of *creative* applied only to persons who were evaluated by the field/society as "creative" and whose ideas permanently altered the domain. Since creative eminence was their focus, both theories could have been included in this section. Simonton's chance-configuration theory, which also noted the importance of outside judges to decide which products are eminently creative, also would fit well in this section.

In recent years, many other scholars also have focused on persons who achieve creative eminence. In this section, we will look briefly at contributions by Abraham Tannenbaum, Herbert Walberg, Benjamin Bloom and Lauren Sosniak, David Feldman, and some additional ideas and traits proposed by Simonton.

Abraham Tannenbaum: The Star Model

Tannenbaum's (1997, 2003) five-point star model reviews factors needed to achieve creative excellence (Figure 4.1). Each factor, or point on the star, includes *static* and *dynamic* dimensions ("subfactors"). Static dimensions are stable characteristics of the person or situation. Dynamic dimensions are variable and situation specific; they reflect "how well [a person] interacts with their surroundings" (Tannenbaum, 1997, p. 40).

Point 1 of the star is *general ability*, consisting of basic intelligence (static) as well as relevant thinking styles such as those presented in Table 4.7 (dynamic). Star point 2 is *special aptitude* in an area such as mathematics, art, moviemaking, or politics (static), plus favorable situational work styles such as problem finding and strategy finding (dynamic). Point 3 is *nonintellective requisites*, including personality variables such as independence, flexibility, and, most importantly, achievement motivation (static), along with, for example, external rewards and level of overexcitability (described earlier; dynamic). Point 4 is *environmental factors*, whose static dimension includes the Csikszentmihalyi/Gardner domain of activity (e.g., moviemaking) and the judges who evaluate the creative goodness (e.g., with 0 to 4 stars). As dynamic environmental factors Tannenbaum cited the home educational environment, which may or may not stress language development, general learning, and high achievement.

Finally, star point 5 is *chance* itself, an ignored yet critical feature in achieving eminence—people's best efforts can be "affected by circumstances over which they have no control . . . accidents and exigencies" (Tannenbaum, 1997, pp. 38–39). Serendipity! Static factors include one's heredity and formative environment. Dynamic factors include the good (or bad) luck to be in the right (or wrong) place at the right (or wrong) time. Tannenbaum noted that luck may improve by "setting the mind and body into constant motion . . . [and] stirring the pot of random ideas constantly so that a few will connect in unanticipated combinations" (p. 39).

Somebody once mentioned that "The harder you work, the luckier you get" (Davis, 2004c). Agreed Tannenbaum (2003), "One truism seems irrefutable: Luck interacts with perspiration in a mutually dependent way" (p. 56).

Tannenbaum's five factors of general ability, special aptitude, nonintellective factors (personality, motivation), environment, and chance all must be favorable to maximize the likelihood of creative excellence and recognition.

Herbert Walberg: Classic Characteristics of Eminence

The research and findings of Walberg have been mentioned several times in conjunction with the threshold concept of intelligence, one's awareness of creativity, and mental disturbance. In his eminence research, Walberg (1988; Walberg & Herbig, 1991; Walberg & Stariha, 1992; Walberg et al., 2003; Walberg & Zeiser, 1997) reviewed biographical information of 282 historically eminent men, for example, Wolfgang Mozart, Abraham Lincoln, Martin Luther King, Johann Wolfgang Goethe, George Washington, Rembrandt, Leonardo Da Vinci, Ludwig Van Beethoven, Charles Dickens, Galileo, and

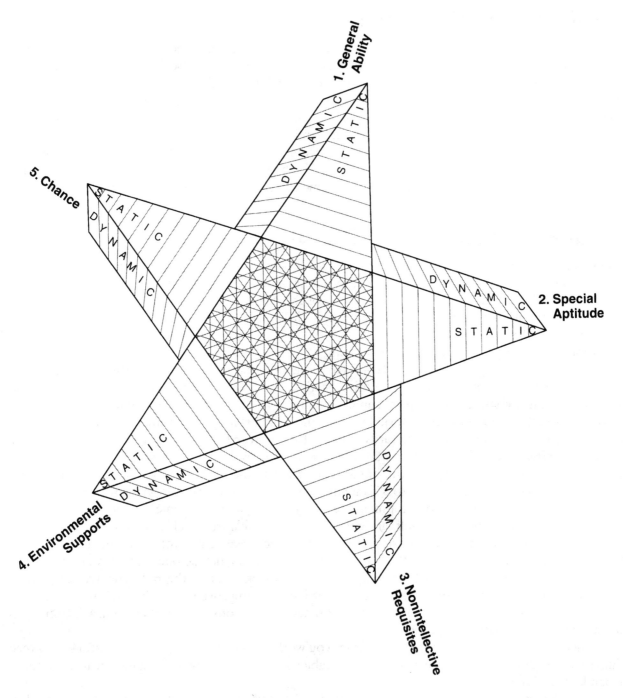

FIGURE 4.1. Tannenbaum's (1997, 2003) star model of factors influencing creative excellence.

Chuck Darwin. He also examined traits of 256 eminent women, for example, Sonia Henie, Ethel Barrymore, Mahalia Jackson, Babe Didrikson Zaharias, Helena Rubinstein, Helen Keller, Grandma Moses, Eleanor Roosevelt, civil rights leader Mary McLeod Bethune, and scientist Rachel Carson.

A central conclusion was that traits of eminent men and of eminent women essentially were identical: All were more intelligent, curious, and expressive than the average, and all were open-minded, self-confident, and versatile. Of relevance, noted Walberg and Zeiser (1997), they were sufficiently inquisitive, original, and imaginative to question current conventions. Furthermore, motivation—in the form of high energy, concentrated effort, and unusual perseverance and ambition—was an essential factor in distinguished accomplishment. Most showed "psychological wholesomeness" in the sense of being ethical, sensitive, solid, magnetic, optimistic, and popular. However, as noted earlier, about a fourth to a third showed introversion or neuroses. Many experienced stimulating family, educational, and cultural conditions during childhood. About 70% had clear parental expectations for their conduct, but 90% had opportunities for exploration on their own—emphasizing the importance of autonomy in the development of eminence. More than half were encouraged in their educational and professional development by parents, and a larger majority were encouraged by teachers and other adults at an early age. Most were stimulated by the availability of both cultural materials and teachers in their field of eminence. One surprising finding was that about 60% of the eminent males were exposed to eminent persons during childhood.

At least moderately high intelligence was important, but only if one possessed the needed creative personality dispositions. Said Walberg and Herbig (1991), "There is no doubt that IQ and eminence are linked. . . . [However] higher levels of intelligence seem less important than other psychological traits and conditions" (p. 251). School grades showed little relation to adult success. Indeed, among eminent women about 70% were not particularly successful in school.

Again, the main traits of creatively eminent women and creatively eminent men were identical: Persons in both groups were intelligent, creative, worked hard, persevered, and were thorough (Walberg & Zeiser, 1997). They benefited from encouragement, stimulation, and teaching by parents, teachers, and other adults. Many had tutors and received recognition for early accomplishments. Luck and opportunity also played a part.

Benjamin Bloom and Lauren Sosniak: Parental Support, Individualized Instruction, Communities of Practice

Bloom and Sosniak (1981; Sosniak, 2003) examined the home environment and early training of accomplished pianists, sculptors, swimmers, tennis players, mathematicians, and research neurologists. Note the three areas of artistic, motoric, and cognitive achievement. They discovered that the person's parents were almost entirely responsible for nurturing early interests and helping develop the child's skills.

Typically, one or both parents were interested in the area, and usually were skilled and experienced themselves. In every case, the parents encouraged and rewarded the children's interests, talents, and efforts. The parents usually served as role models; they were living illustrations of the personality and lifestyle of experts in the domain. The children essentially could not resist exploring and participating in the particular talent area—it was expected and accepted as proper. As understated by Sosniak (2003), "pianists were not likely to come from [Olympic] swimmers' homes, swimmers were not likely to come from the pianists' homes, and so on" (p. 250).[5]

While parents provided the initial training and supervision of practice, at some point each child switched to a professional instructor. Sometimes, family support was so strong they would move to another location to be nearer an outstanding teacher or better facilities. The student often would be the single focus of the devoted instructor. During this time, the youth's dedication to the talent area grows strong—which explains the willingness to spend about 15 hours per week in lessons and practice.

Importantly, the students learned to handle failures constructively. Failures were learning experiences that pinpointed problems to be solved and skills to be learned. In contrast, according to Bloom (1985), among "talent dropouts, failures led to feelings of inadequacy and quitting."

In contrast with today's schooling, Bloom and Sosniak's talent development is totally individualized, highly specialized, more informal (and may resemble play), and has clear purposes and goals.

Sosniak (2003) strongly emphasized the importance of *communities of practice*. Early on, this included parents and the home environment, as we have seen. Later, the budding experts joined peers in the same talent area. For example, Sosniak's young pianists got together for recitals and music competitions;

---

[5] When watching Olympics on TV, listen for the announcer to comment on how the athlete's parents had excelled in the same sport. Tiger Woods' father had his son hitting golf balls at about age 3. The phenomenon is common.

swimmers joined swim clubs; artists displayed their work in art shows; and young scientists joined like-minded friends in basement experiments with science sets. They participated in after-school and summer programs and camps in music, art, math, or science. They participated in school science fairs, community art shows, and swim club competitions. They watched performances by more advanced students in their fields. They were exposed to books, magazines, and other media in their talent area. Communities of practice supplied strong and essential support.

A fascinating, thought-provoking, and often-repeated finding by Bloom and Sosniak is that—presumably within limits—high-level talent is made, not born. Bloom (1985) emphasized that they began by looking for exceptional talent; what they found was exceptional environmental circumstances that allowed creativity to bloom (couldn't resist)

David Feldman: Precocity, Available Knowledge, and Co-Incidence Theory

Morelock and Feldman (1997, 2003) reviewed biographies of such persons as Wolfie Mozart and Bobby Fischer, who performed at the level of adult professionals before age 10. They attributed such amazing accomplishments to a coincidence of *individual, environmental,* and *historical* forces, which Feldman (1994) had dubbed the *Co-Incidence Theory.*

The *individual* component is the prodigies themselves, who are described as highly intelligent, developmentally advanced, and remarkably "preorganized." A biological propensity toward the talent (imagine a violin player or Sumo wrestler) as well as family support in the area are needed. Physical, social, and emotional development factors—such as manual dexterity and peer influence—determine a prodigy's receptiveness to, for example, violin playing or Sumo wrestling.

Environmental factors emphasize the existence of a highly evolved domain of knowledge that can be taught to the precocious child, for example, sophisticated literatures and instruction in math, chess, or music.

The main *historical* factor is the value society attaches to a domain, which affects opportunities for learning. Perhaps this is one reason the Jamaican bobsled team did not excel.

Many of the conclusions itemized by Morelock and Feldman (1997) resemble those of Bloom and Sosniak:

- The children possessed extraordinary ability.
- They were born into families that valued and supported that ability.
- They received instruction from master teachers in ways that engaged interest and commitment.
- The children were passionately committed to their field and found great joy in their achievements.

Finally, in an unpublished report Feldman noted that many theories of creative eminence (e.g., Tannenbaum's *star* model, above, and Simonton's *multiplicative* notion, below) assume that *all* of the theorist's important factors must be present. Feldman described 17 high-achieving women who were exceptions. Their extraordinary "personal inner strength"—perseverance, independence, and originality—permitted them to overcome a non-supportive environment.

Dean Keith Simonton: Many Factors

Simonton (1997; see also Simonton, 2003) described a number of factors that contribute to creative eminence. A noteworthy assumption is the *multiplicative* nature of necessary components. All must have an above-threshold value. A too-low value of any one component eliminates the possibility of creative eminence, since zero times anything is zero. Simonton (2010) also noted that "specific factors tend to direct creativity toward particular domains of achievement" (p. 176). Labeling these dispositional and developmental correlates, he explores how two states of mind can interact with biological, social, and cognitive factors to impact creative potential.

But what are these factors? Many of Simonton's components of exceptional achievement can be summarized quickly.

Intelligence, important as usual, sometimes requires a middle rather than a high level, particularly in leadership areas. Noted Simonton, talking over the head of your audience does not persuade listeners of the value of your ideas.

Personality is critical, including traits of high motivation, persistence, and willingness to occasionally fail.

Developmental considerations include one's natural ability plus training and practice: "Genius is not just born; it is also made" (p. 341).

Education is relevant, although many recognized geniuses were miserable scholars. According to Simonton, peak creative eminence is most likely to happen at a *middle* level of education, at about the bachelor's degree elevation, rather than at lower or higher levels.

A touch of mental disorder may stimulate "bizarre thoughts, crazy associations, or offbeat metaphors or analogies" that lead to insights, said Simonton. "Genius level talents probably reside at the delicate boundary between a healthy and an unhealthy personality" (p. 341).

Regarding *birth order*, we have seen Simonton's suggestion that firstborn and only children are more likely to realize creative eminence in science, politics, or other socially valued area. Later-borns may excel in artistic or other nonconformist areas.

Traumatic events, with accompanying unhappy childhoods, may contribute. Parental loss runs high among distinguished scientists. As possible explanations, Simonton suggested that, first, such events may make it difficult to conform to social expectations, since parents are not there to teach norms and values. Second, a "bereavement reaction"—namely, attaining fame and fortune—may reduce the emotional stress caused by the traumatic event. Third, the unpleasant event may strengthen one's ability to handle disappointment and frustration.

The matter is complicated, noted Simonton, and includes such matters as bright children who do not realize their potential, late-blooming adults who showed no early promise, gender considerations, "spirit of the times" (*Zeitgeist*) factors, crystallizing experiences (that confirm the talent and direction), socioeconomic class, religious affiliation, interactions among the variables, change, and nonlinear relationships in which a mid-level is optimal.

Cultivating a More Creative Personality

This chapter should make it clear that creativity—both general self-actualized creativity and special-talent creativity—is tied closely to personality. Based upon outcomes of creativity training programs and courses (e.g., Davis & Bull, 1978; Edwards, 1968; Torrance, 1987a, 1995), there is every reason to believe that attitudes and personality can be changed to produce a more flexible, creative, and self-actualized person. Simple exposure to the topic of creativity, as in reading this book, can raise *creativity consciousness*—the single most important step in becoming a more creative individual.

One source of evidence for environmental (learning) influences on creativity, including both affective and cognitive components, comes from the eminence literature. Many creatively eminent persons were exposed to stimulating family, educational, and cultural conditions during childhood. Most important—and common—was a trait of strong drive and perseverance. The harder they worked, the more productive (and luckier) they became.

Many of the traits discussed in this chapter probably can be channeled in a more creative direction—if a person is motivated to do so. Increases in creativeness, incidentally, frequently are accompanied by increases in self-confidence and independence (Parnes, 1978), although it is a chicken–egg problem—which causes which? One might consciously try to strengthen curiosity and widen interests. One also might cultivate artistic and aesthetic interests via exposure to creative domains—attending concerts and plays and visiting art galleries, museums, and scientific exhibits. One's adventurousness can be exercised by exploring new places and trying new activities. Most likely, one's sense of humor can be sharpened. Of critical importance, becoming involved in creative activities is guaranteed to increase one's creativity consciousness and other creative personality characteristics, as well as strengthen some creative abilities and visibly increase creative productivity.

Summary

Studies of creative people indicate that despite their unconventionality and individualism, they have a lot of traits in common.

Three relevant types of characteristics are personality traits, cognitive abilities (including information processing styles), and biographical characteristics. The distinction between personality traits and cognitive abilities sometimes is blurred.

There are common traits among creative people in different areas, such as art and science, but also differences in characteristics between areas and between individuals within the same general area.

Most special-talent creative people are creative in a single area. Over the wide range of intelligence, creativity and intelligence are moderately related. The threshold concept states that above an IQ of about 120 there is no relationship between creativity and intelligence. Other factors, particularly personality and motivation, determine creative productivity.

Feist has an O.C.E.A.N. of evidence regarding the relationship between creativity and the "Big Five Factors" of Openness, Conscientiousness, Extraversion, Agreeableness, and Neuroticism.

Over 200 creative personality traits were reduced to 16 categories: aware of own creativeness (creativity-conscious), original, independent (perhaps androgynous), risk-taking, high energy (even thrill-seeking), curious, sense of humor, capacity for fantasy, attraction to complexity and ambiguity (including a belief in paranormal phenomena; Thalbourne's transliminality), artistic (including aesthetic interests), open-minded, thorough, needs alone time, perceptive, emotional, and ethical.

Negative personality traits—those likely to disturb others—fell into the seven categories of egotistical, impulsive, argumentative, childish, absentminded, neurotic (including sociopathic), and hyperactive.

Much information on the creative personality came from research by Frank Barron and Donald MacKinnon at Berkeley, where they studied creative architects, writers, and mathematicians.

Many showed neuroses or psychoses, especially the creative writers. However, writers also scored high on MMPI ego strength, indicating they were psychologically "sicker and healthier" than the average.

Much research indicates mental disorders among highly creative and historically eminent people, particularly writers and poets—and their close relatives.

Non-subtle biographical traits include one's background of creative interests, hobbies, and activities, for example, as in the lists provided by Torrance and Renzulli and Reis. More subtle biographical traits include traveling, owning a cat, having an imaginary childhood playmate, and participating in theater.

Firstborn and only children are likely to be higher achievers in school and careers, probably because of social reasons—they receive more attention, encouragement, and responsibility. Simonton proposed that first and only children tend to achieve eminence in establishment areas, such as science; later-borns tend to achieve eminence in less-conforming artistic areas.

The relationship between hand preference and creativity is mixed, but mixed-handed individuals have a leg up on their strong-handed counterparts.

Barron listed "six ingredients" of creativity that mixed personality and cognitive traits: recognizing patterns, making connections, taking risks, challenging assumptions, taking advantage of chance, and seeing in new ways.

Many (or all) abilities can contribute to creativity. Some seemingly important factors include fluency, flexibility, originality, elaboration, transformation, sensitivity to problems, problem defining, visualization, analogical/metaphorical thinking, predicting outcomes, analyses, synthesis, evaluation, logical thinking, ability to regress, intuition, and concentration.

Examples of information processing traits that aid creativity include using existing knowledge as a basis for new ideas, using wide categories, avoiding perceptual sets, questioning norms and assumptions, finding problems, thinking logically and flexibly, thinking metaphorically, using internal visualization, and others.

The topic of creative eminence would include the theories of Csikszentmihalyi and Gardner, plus Simonton's chance-configuration theory, presented in Chapter 2. Tannenbaum's star model included the five points of intelligence, special aptitude, nonintellective factors (personality, motivation), environment, and chance.

Walberg reviewed characteristics of eminent men and women, finding common characteristics of high motivation and perseverance, thoroughness, intelligence, open-mindedness, confidence, curiosity, versatility, and supportive environments (parents and tutors). Some showed introversion or neuroses.

Bloom and Sosniak are known for emphasizing the critical early role of parents as both teachers and supporters of talent development. Students later switched to high-quality teachers. Individualized, specialized, and informal talent development with clear purposes and goals, contrasts with typical education. Sosniak described supportive communities of practice. Bloom and Sosniak emphasize that high-level talent is made, not born.

Feldman's coincidence theory stemmed from the study of prodigies. Three necessary components for creative eminence are the capable individual; his or her environment, which includes a specialized domain of knowledge; and history, which stressed the cultural value placed on a creative skill.

Simonton identified how dispositional and developmental factors can influence and interact with variables and life experiences such as intelligence, personality, development (ability and training), education, mental disorder, birth order, traumatic events, and others to impact creative eminence

Creative attitudes and personality traits can be strengthened. Especially recommended is involvement in creative activities.

Review Exercises

The Creative Person: Flexible, Funny, and Full of Energy

Self-Test: Key Concepts, Terms, and Names

Briefly define or explain each of these:

Three types of characteristics that combine to produce creative people:

_____

_____

_____

Glăveanu (2013)

_____

_____

Threshold concept (MacKinnon)

_____

_____

Sensation seeking (arousal seeking, thrill seeking)

_____

_____

Negative creative traits

_____

_____

The Berkeley studies

_____

_____

Biographical traits of creative people

_____

_____

Six ingredients of creativity (Barron, 1988)

_____

_____

_____

Tardiff and Sternberg's (1988) information processing characteristics (Table 4.7)

_____

_____

_____

Tannenbaum (2003) Star Model

_____

_____

Walberg's Characteristics of Eminence

_____

_____

Creativity Consciousness

_____

_____

Let's Think about It

1. Look back at the Sixteen Traits of Creative Individuals highlighted in this chapter. Review the adjectives associated with each in Table 4.2. Which FOUR do you feel relate the most to you? Identify and give examples of how you embody, exhibit, or exude these traits below

   a. Trait 1: _____

   _____

   b. Trait 2: _____

   _____

c. Trait 3: _____

_____

d. Trait 4: _____

_____

2. Now let's focus on Table 4.3 which lists seven "negative" traits of some creative individuals. Examine the adjectives and examples listed for each. Do any of these relate to you? Pick two that most typify your attitude, actions, behavior, or temperament and describe how these traits that are perceived to be negative could actually help you be more creative

a. Trait 1: _____

_____

_____

b. Trait 2: _____

_____

_____

Look at the "not so subtle" list of creative activities listed in Table 4.4. Think back to activities you have engaged in that you would use to demonstrate your sustained history of creative behavior. NOW, imagine you are applying for a job that required a resume line for you to document your experiences. Create your creativity resume below with examples of three recent creative behaviors and two bullet points for each as to how it enhanced or increased your own creativity

1. _____

• _____

• _____

2. _____

• _____

• _____

3. _____

• _____

• _____

3. In relation to creativity and eminence, look back at the theories presented in this chapter. With those explanations in mind, answer the question "Why are some people more creative than others?" In the space belowlist all the factors you can think of (from this chapter or your own experience and best guesses) that relate or are relevant

_____

_____

_____

_____

_____

Of everything you listed from above, which factors do you think are most important?

_____

_____

Least important?

_____

_____

4. What might teachers do to foster the development of the "important" factors? (DO NOT look at the last sentence of this chapter, just before the Summary.)

_____

_____

5. Think of three bizarre ideas for increasing the creativity of high school or college students—ideas that are guaranteed to get you FIRED if you tried to implement.

a. _____

b. _____

c. _____

6. What can YOU do to become a more creative person?

_____

_____

_____

7. Creative abilities and information processing traits mentioned in this chapter include:

**Originality   Analysis   Evaluation/Decision Making   Synthesis   Making Connections
Seeing in New Ways   Elaboration   Fluency   Flexibility   Logical Thinking   Able to Regress
Able to Predict Outcomes   Transformation   Intuition   Sensitivity to Problems
Able to Define Problems   Questions Norms   Visualization
Finds Order in Chaos   Analogical Thinking   Avoids Perceptual Sets**

   a. Draw a circle around the seven you believe are most important.

   b. Draw a square around the six you believe are least important.

   c. Underline darkly the five you believe YOU are best at.

   d. Be sure you understand all of these terms.

Thrill-Seeking Test

Many highly creative people are "thrill seekers" or "sensation seekers." How would you score on this short test of thrill seeking?

Indicate the degree to which each statement applies to you. Use the following scale:

1 = No
2 = To a small degree
3 = Average
4 = More than average
5 = Definitely

———   1. I would like to learn mountain-climbing.

———   2. I would like to get a pilot's license.

———   3. I would like to live and work in a foreign country.

———   4. I would like to be hypnotized.

———   5. I like a cold, brisk day.

———   6. I would like to try skydiving.

———   7. I like the nonsense forms and bright colors of modern art.

———   8. I usually jump right in a cold pool, instead of slowly getting used to it.

———   9. On vacation, I prefer camping to a good motel.

—————— 10. I would like to take up skiing.

—————— 11. I am a risk taker.

—————— 12. I avoid activities that are a little frightening.

—————— 13. I would take a college course that 50 percent flunk.

—————— 14. I enjoy a job with unforseen difficulties.

—————— 15. I like to explore new cities alone, even if I get lost.

Scoring: Add up your ratings. The following is a guideline for interpretation:

15–27	Low in thrill seeking
28–39	Below average
40–51	Average
52–62	Above average
63–75	High in thrill seeking

5 Creative Process

"I put my heart and soul into my work, and I have lost my mind in the process."

—*Vincent van Gogh*

Part of the creative process involves simply not thinking. Something magical happens in the pure act of being so wholly devoted to a single thing that it takes almost no conscious effort. Ideas come to life faster than you can even record them.

Like Van Gogh alludes to in this quote, the process of creating and thinking of solutions causes you to use so much of your mind that your mind doesn't even realize it is working. You produce creative idea after creative idea without it even being something you think hard about because you are so invested and caught up in the act of creating! Vincent Van Gogh supposedly saw everything with a cloudy yellow tint as a side effect of a medication called digitalis that he had to take to treat his epilepsy.

Apparently, this likely contributes to the unique yellow cloud surrounding the stars in his painting Starry Night. See, creative inspiration can come from seemingly nothing, from everyday occurrences, from out of nowhere.

As you will learn in this chapter, part of the creative process involves simply living your normal life and accidentally having spontaneous ideas. "Aha moments" occur randomly with no predictable source or reason. There is something about coming up with your own, unique ideas that brings a sort of pride and drive—once the ideas pop into your head, you naturally become so devoted to developing them that you cannot wait to bring them to fruition.

Van Gogh's process of creating this masterpiece did not involve stressing about a deadline or applying the perfect formula—it simply came into existence as Van Gogh poured his heart out through his paintbrush.

You will learn in this chapter how to apply this to your own creative process.

To give a fair chance to creativity is a matter of life and death for any society.

—Arnold Toynbee

Where Do Ideas Come from?

The topic of the *creative process* brings us to a core issue: *Where do ideas come from?* We saw glimpses and suggestions throughout Chapters 1, 2, and 4 in discussions of the creative person, process, product, and environment; mystical mental happenings; classical and contemporary theories; and descriptions of "the creative person."

The idea-combining—or *bisociation of ideas* (Koestler, 1964)—notion remains popular. No doubt, because combining ideas is a comprehendible and logical explanation of the creative process and creative products: Chocolate combined with peanut butter produced *Reese's Peanut Butter Cups*. Combining celebrity names to provide supercouple nicknames is prevalent, with examples of former flames that have since become extinguished (Brangelina or Bennifer), to those that are still "pop"ping such as Kimye and Balder. Or classic laws of the propagation of light plus the Lorentz transformation can produce new light propagation equations compatible with the principle of relativity (Einstein, 1961), if you are well prepared in this sort of thing.

Think about your Sonic happy-hour drink or choice or Starbucks order. How many flavor combinations can you think of? How many sound pretty good? (and this author recommends the Pumpkin Roll . . . an off-the-menu delight that combines Pumpkin Spice Latte with Cinnamon Dolce. It's delish!)

You may recall that Perkins' (1988) mentioned the "mindful direction" of "combinatorial explosions." Simonton (1988) said about the same thing using the terms *permutations* and *configurations* of ideas, based in experience and influenced by rules, conventions, and sensibility. Koestler's (1964) *bisociation of ideas* simply meant combining ideas.

Sometimes the new idea combination takes the form of an analogical relationship ("Hey, our problem is just like . . . "; "Now if you use that idea here we get . . . "; or "Look, let's just steal that advertising idea and . . .") or a sudden change in perception, in which a new meaning is added ("If you look at it this way you see . . ." or "Now if we turn the situation around we have . . .").

Under *mysterious mental happenings* in Chapter 1 we found that much about internal creative thinking and problem-solving remains a mystery even to creative people. We did learn that artists find ideas while sketching, writers find ideas while writing, and scientists find ideas while doing science—indicating that active involvement stimulates both the recall of relevant experiences and the creation of new possibilities.

As suggested in Kubie and Rugg's psychoanalytic approaches in Chapter 2, one's (unconscious, subconscious) storehouse of ideas, skills, and training logically interacts with a conscious problem to create new solutions. The role of "preconscious," "fringe conscious," or "off-conscious" activity is vague, no pun intended. It apparently varies in degree of awareness. It also seems important. Don't we all hatch new ideas while half-awake at night or early in the morning? We will see that *incubation* is a popular creative process that apparently involves such fringe-conscious activity.[1]

This chapter first will look at the creative process as a sometimes-conscious sequence of *steps* or *stages* through which the creative person proceeds in clarifying a problem, working on it, and producing a solution that resolves the difficulty. We will also distinguish between problem-finding and problem-solving as they pertain to creativity.

Second, we will examine the creative process as a mostly involuntary, relatively rapid change in perception. A stimulus–response conditioned reaction (of sorts). This mental transformation takes place when a new idea, meaning, implication, or solution suddenly is detected.

Third, we will look at other aspects of imagery and visualization and their role in creativity.

---

[1] Suggestion: When working on a project, keep a pad and pencil by your bed.

The topic of the creative process also encompasses the *techniques* and strategies that all creative people use, sometimes consciously and sometimes unconsciously, to produce the new idea combinations, analogical relationships, meanings, and transformations. Chapter 6 will focus on that most common and effective creative thinking technique, *analogical thinking*—seeing a connection between one situation and another, as when cockle burrs inspired engineer George De Mestral to create Velcro, or a cartoonist sees a connection between David and Goliath and steroid testing and writes, "Bad news David, the Philistines want to check you for steroids!". Creative thinking techniques are taught in creativity courses, books, and workshops.

Conscious, deliberate, organized, and surprisingly effective creativity techniques currently thrive in businesses and corporations. Virtually every part of such establishments depends on creative ideas, for example, in attracting quality personnel, effective management, developing new products, competing successfully, marketing and advertising, and more (see, for example, de Bono, 1992a; Higgins, 1994; Van Gundy, 1983).

www.CartoonStock.com

One Process or Many?

In discussing the complexity of creativity we noted that intelligent, creative people claim that the creative process is basically the same in art, science, business, and elsewhere. Other intelligent, creative people argue that there is no one creative process, and there may be as many creative processes as there are creative people. The truth depends upon which aspect of the creative process one looks at.

At a fairly global level, most new creations are combinations of previously unrelated ideas, and so one can view the creative process as combining Idea 1 with Idea 2 to produce novel Idea 3. Common creative techniques, particularly analogical thinking and modifying existing products and procedures, can be used by creative thinkers in any topic area to produce novel Idea 3.[2] Ellie the Elephant and the Scrub Daddy have put a smile on inventors faces (and money in their pocket!) There also is a similarity in the steps or stages through which an artist, scientist, business person, or other problem-solver proceeds in defining, clarifying, and solving a problem. However, despite commonalities in such global processes as combining ideas, using similar idea-finding techniques (e.g., looking for analogies), and proceeding through similar steps, there still are unique and idiosyncratic experiences, abilities, perceptions, thinking styles, and strategies that influence the creative processes of each creative person. Obviously, the particular area or media within which one creates—math, chemistry, room decorating, report planning, biology, drawing, architecture, poetry, music, theater, vacation planning, and so on—logically demands thinking with different concepts and different problem-solving techniques.

But with these differing problem-solving techniques in mind, Dillon (1982) noted that problems that are the most ripe for the fruits of creative labor might, require us to shake the whole apple tree instead of cherry picking for the best solution. Non-routine problems that are ill-defined, through perfectly primed for creativity, might challenge the traditional creative problem-solving process. With the previous analogy in mind, one might miss the proverbial forest for the (apple) trees if they can't see, understand, or appreciate a larger situation.

---

[2] Modifying the important attributes of an existing product is an effective and common idea-finding technique. It is discussed in Chapter 8 and is called *attribute listing*.

With that challenge in mind, Runco (1994) put out a book with a collection of perspectives on the difference between problem-finding and problem-solving, clearly distinguishing between the two. A prominent view on **problem solving** can be found in the work of Scandura (1977) who defined it as the creation and implementation of specific steps and sequences to result in the accomplishment of a goal state. Solving a problem requires both declarative knowledge about a field and procedural knowledge of how to put this knowledge into action. Getzels (1979) notes that "the way the problem is posed is the way the dilemma will be resolved" (p. 167) and identifies **problem-finding** as not only the capacity for *discovering problems* but also *inventing them*; a unique capability representing human intellect and insight. Runco and Nemiro (1994) agree, asserting that "the generation of problems, though related to ideation, is statistically and behaviorally distinct from the ideation used when solving problems" (pp. 236–237). A family of skills related to problem-finding is identified (Mumford, Mobley, Uhlman, Reiter-Palmon, & Doares, 1991; Reiter-Palmon, Mumford, O'Connor Boes, & Runco, 1997; Runco & Okuda, 1988), including distinctions between problem construction (actively defining the goals and applying a context for problem-solving effort), problem discovery (ability to define a workable task and identify resources necessary to fashion a solution), and problem identification (recognizing a problem exists).

Creative Process: Insight, Chance, or Hard Work?

Different opinions exist regarding whether creativity is "building on an initial insight" or whether it is the result of systematic planning and hard work—with sudden "insights" and chance discoveries playing no noticeable role.

The two views are not inconsistent. A creative problem solution may be born instantly in an "Aha!" (insight) experience, inspired perhaps by the chance encounter of a needed idea or solution. A creative product also may result from months or years of systematic planning, hard work, and trial-and-error experimentation—perhaps based on an earlier "Aha!" or insight that was a chance occurrence. For example, in Hollywood one busy street passes through a tunnel under a hill. The illusion of height created in the Harold Lloyd movie *Safety Last* was discovered by chance—in a sudden insight—when a fence was trimmed out of a picture taken from that hilltop (see attached picture). The movie scenes themselves, of course, required months of planning, development, hard work, and creative problem-solving.

"Do I think 'chance' plays a role in creativity? No, of course not. It's all hard work. I don't believe in taking chances." (From Safety Last!, starring Harold Lloyd. Copyright © 1923 by Harold Lloyd Trust. Reprinted by permission.)

Steps and Sequences

Solving a problem or "doing something creative" necessarily involves the three steps already casually mentioned—clarifying the problem, working on it, and finding a good solution. More formal sets of stages are elaborations of these.

For example, Torrance's (1988) definition of creativity that we saw in Chapter 1 describes a four-step process of:

1. Sensing a problem or gap in information
2. Forming ideas or hypotheses
3. Testing and modifying the hypotheses
4. Communicating the results.

John Dewey (1933), writing on the nature of thinking, compressed the Torrance steps into just two, with no apparent loss of information. First, there appears a state of doubt, perplexity, or mental difficulty in which the thinking originates, followed by an act of searching, hunting, or inquiring to find material that will resolve the doubt, and settle and dispose of the perplexity. It's also clear that the first two stages pertain to problem-finding and the latter two stages to problem-solving.

The Wallas Model

The best-known analysis of stages in the creative process was created by Graham Wallas in 1926. The fact that his model has survived nearly a century of scrutiny says something about the appeal of the model. There are four steps.

Preparation. Preparation includes just that—exploring and clarifying the situation; perhaps looking for the "real," underlying, or more general problem; thinking about requirements for a good solution; reviewing relevant data, ideas, and experiences; becoming acquainted with innuendos, implications, and perhaps unsuccessful solutions; itemizing available materials and resources, and so on. Synectics (Chapter 7) guru William J. J. Gordon (1961) called this stage "making the strange familiar," an important creative activity. Wallas emphasized its conscious and deliberate nature.

Incubation. The *Journal of Creative Behavior* devoted one entire issue (1979, Issue 1) to untangling the mysteries of incubation. With limited success. According to Wallas (1926), and as we saw in the theories of Kubie and Rugg (Chapter 4), incubation may best be viewed as a period of preconscious, fringe-conscious, off-conscious, or perhaps even unconscious mental activity that takes place while the thinker is (perhaps deliberately) jogging, watching TV, playing golf, eating pizza, walking along a lakeshore, or even sleeping. In Wallas' own words, "The incubation stage covers two different things, of which the first is the negative fact that during incubation we do not voluntarily or consciously think on a particular problem, and the second is the positive fact that a series of unconscious and involuntary (or foreconscious and forevoluntary) mental events may take place during that period . . . the period of abstention may be spent either in conscious mental work on other problems, or in relaxation from all conscious mental work."

Guilford (1979) suggested that incubation takes place during reflection, a pause in action, and that some people are simply more reflective than others. Gilhooly, Georgiou, Garrison, Reston, and Sirota (2012) were able to dispel the notion that during incubation individuals were engaging in intermittent conscious work.

Regardless, there is a preponderance of evidence in support of the benefits of incubation on creativity. A meta-analysis by Sio and Ormerod (2009) showed positive effect sizes across a multitude of studies in which incubation was employed before engaging in insight-based or divergent thinking tasks.

Illumination. The "Aha!" or "Eureka" experience. There is a sudden change in perception, a new idea combination, an insight, an inspiration, or a transformation that produces a solution that appears to meet the requirements or the problem. There is a good feeling, even excitement. So what are the elements that serve as the filaments to the lightbulb over your head? In shedding light on this phenomenon, Metcalfe and Wiebe (1987) describe **insight** as a major mental transition that is sudden in nature with explicit clarity as to the exact solution or essential features of the problem (that may have been out of awareness before). Building on that notion Hélie and Sun (2010) radiated an explicit–implicit interaction theory (EII) to explain insight, examining how explicit knowledge (that can readily access using attentional resources) combines with implicit knowledge (out-of-awareness information) to spark illumination. Runco (2006) expands upon this by stating "the use of preconscious or unconscious processes allows the individual to utilize different reasoning processes, that, by virtue of their being beyond conscious awareness, are able to value and explore those things that allow original thinking" (p. 109).

Verification. *Verification* is checking the solution, in case your Eureka turns out to be a vacuous idea. In the business world, verification of an illuminating idea usually requires extensive further analysis. In the arts, verification corresponds to executing the idea—writing the sentence, paragraph, or story or putting paint to the canvas. Ultimately, the entire purpose of this stage is to validate whether a solution is workable. If not, the cognitive spin cycle starts again! (hope you brought extra quarters).

Like other sets of stages, the Wallas stages resemble steps in the scientific method of stating the problem, proposing hypotheses, planning and conducting research, and evaluating the results.

Note also that the Wallas stages are not an invariant sequence. Some stages may be skipped, or the thinker may backtrack to an earlier stage. For example, the process of defining and clarifying the problem (preparation) often leads directly to a good, illuminating idea. Or if the verification confirms that the idea won't work or is not acceptable, the thinker will recycle back to the preparation or incubation stage. Furthermore, noted Wallas, it is common to be consciously preparing for one problem or verifying a solution to another while incubating still others.

While the Wallas model sits fresh in your consciousness, Norlander (1999) used the Wallas model to examine the effects of alcohol on creativity. He added a stage, a fifth step of ***restitution*** (Köski-Jannes, 1985), which is a resting or recovery stage necessary to avoid burnout.[3] After reviewing past work on creative writing, laboratory studies of word associations, divergent thinking, and associations to ink blots, Norlander separated the five stages into those requiring conscious feedback—preparation, some parts of illumination, and verification—and those not requiring conscious feedback—incubation, some parts of illumination, and restitution.

Norlander's (1999) research indicated that moderate alcohol consumption impaired or obstructed stages that require conscious feedback (preparation, some parts of illumination, and verification). Such processes require "learned, logical, analytical, conventional . . . and conscious activities" (p. 34). Some writers "stated specifically that they could not write under the influence of alcohol" (Norlander, 1999, p. 24). But moderate drinking apparently can "disinhibit" the unconscious stages (incubation, some parts of illumination, and restitution). With incubation, for example, "it may be an advantage if order and logic . . . remain in the background and . . . alcohol [may] contribute toward release of the thought-flow" (p. 35). Also, alcohol is believed by some to "accelerate the restitution process when under strain" (p. 38).

Under the heading "Popular Beliefs," Plucker and Dana (1999) also mentioned the "disinhibition hypothesis," the notion that alcohol is believed to strengthen creativity by reducing writer's block. They noted that many creative persons used and abused "alcohol and other drugs" (p. 607), for example, Ernest Hemingway, Edgar Allen Poe, Richard Burton, John Belushi, Janis Joplin, Charlie Parker, and Kurt Cobain. Noting the problem of little research, Plucker and Dana concluded that "creativity gains

---

[3] In light of the context of the Norlander (1999) study, *restitution* is NOT part of a 12-step program by which we atone for our creativity by "Blaming it on the Alcohol."

no positive benefit from drug [including alcohol] use. Long-term use . . . may have a detrimental effect on creative production" (p. 609). Kaufman, Kornilov, Bristol, Tan, and Grigorenko (2010) go on to note that the disinhibition hypothesis "seems to focus only on the first step of creative cognition, setting up the necessary prerequisites for the 'real' creative cognition that occurs in other brain regions." (p. 224) So for those who were hoping to "C" their creativity grow through the influence of illicit substances, might "B" "D"isappointed.

Feedback Loops and the Creative Process

Building on the theory of Wallas, Shaw (1989) purported a flowchart-style model, that added in feedback loops between the stages of preparation (immersion), incubation, and illumination (Figure 5.1). On the relevance of including these feedback loops and justification for their names, Shaw explains:

- "Arieti (1976) suggested that the processes of immersion (conscious) and incubation (unconscious) interplay with one another. Freud identified unconscious processes as primary and the conscious process as secondary. Arieti proposed the existence of a coupled process that he called tertiary, but can also be called the Arieti loop" (pp. 288–289)
- "Vinacke (1952) saw that coupling existed between the incubations and illuminations. This can be called the Vinacke loop" (p. 289)

And what of the other two boxes in the flowchart? Shaw writes that "the validation process is a major component of the human condition" (p. 289) and included aspects of explication (process of analyzing and developing an idea in detail) and creative synthesis, which looks at the idea, breakthrough, or product itself and whether we personally like it (self-validation) AND whether society will accept it (social validation). Shaw noted that there are "strong periodic couplings between the illumination and explication phases: Explanations lead to further illuminations. This can be called the Lalas loop (D. Lalas, personal communication, 1988). The coupling between the phases of explication and creative synthesis can be called the communication loop" (p. 289). Finally, the Rossman Loop is indicative of the entire feedback-validation process, and "if validation is accepted, the loop extends back into the knowledge or immersion phases" (p. 289).

In reaction to this model, Aldous (2007) purports that if you combine evidence that creativity involves pre-verbal and non-verbal processes, pro-conscious activity, and gut feelings onto the Shaw (1989) model, then a clear framework of creative problem-solving arises that reflects an interaction between visuospatial and linguistic brain circuits and between non-conscious and conscious thoughts and general intuition.

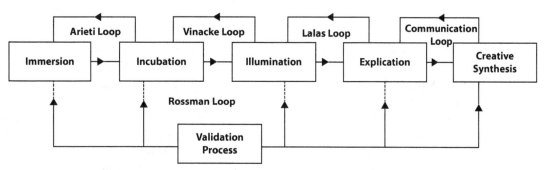

FIGURE 5.1. A model for the structure of the Heuristic process with feedback. Source: Shaw, M. P. (1989). The Eureka process: A structure for the creative experience in science and engineering. *Creativity Research Journal, 2,* 286–298.

An Information Processing Theory of Incubation

Developments in cognitive psychology suggest another way to interpret the less-than-conscious incubation process. *Levels of processing theory* focuses on the common human ability to consciously attend to one, and only one, main activity (such as talking, listening, watching, or thinking), yet conduct several other activities at the same time. For example, while talking you also can walk, chew gum, drive a car, or notice leaves rustling in the wind. These other activities are said to be processed at lower levels of consciousness.

More specifically, or more theoretically, familiar and expected activities and events are said to be "matched" against internal representations (or *schemas*) of these activities and events (e.g., Norman, 1976). If there is a match, these events are "accounted for," and further processing at a higher, conscious level is unnecessary. The events are dealt with completely at a fringe-conscious or even unconscious level. However, if something unexpected or novel occurs—stepping in dog stuff, having a food that isn't supposed to crunch come alive in our mouth (have you looked at the statistics about bugs in our potato chip bags!), or seeing a cow in the road (not uncommon here in Texas!) or a sloth in a tree (an exciting part of your author's visit to Costa Rica)—the matter cannot be handled at the lower, unconscious level. That is, the novel event does not match existing schemas; it therefore is passed to higher processing levels where, by definition, it receives one's full attention.

It is conceivable that incubation involves similar information processing activities. "Getting away from the problem" essentially means that one's high-level, conscious attention is directed toward other matters—other problems, watching TV, playing golf, eating pizza, and so on. However, perhaps one's fringe-conscious or unconscious processing activities occasionally review a particular problem and possible solutions. When something novel occurs—namely, a good solution—the matter instantly gets passed to higher levels of processing. It gets your full attention. Psychologically you experience it as a sudden "Eureka!" experience.

These levels of processing interpretation of incubation are similar to Kris' psychoanalytic description of creative thinking (Chapter 2): Preconscious primary process fantasy activity is followed by a "Eureka!" and conscious secondary process logical thinking.

The Creative Problem-Solving (CPS) Model

It is difficult to say enough about the extremely useful Creative Problem-Solving (CPS) model, a remarkable set of five (or six) stages. It is virtually guaranteed to help you solve or find ideas for any type of personal or professional problem. The strategy originally was formulated by Alex Osborn (1963), creator of brainstorming, founder of the Creative Education Foundation (CEF), and cofounder of Batten, Barton, Dursten, and Osborn, the New York advertising agency. Sidney Parnes, a bright and creative person who followed Osborn as President of CEF, invested nearly 40 years teaching creativity workshops, institutes, and college courses—and thinking about the creative process. His best shot at "What is the creative process?" and "How can we teach creativity?" is (you guessed it) the CPS model. Parnes' (1981) inspiring book *Magic of Your Mind* explains how using the CPS model can improve your life. (We'll touch on this in the last chapter of this book regarding self-actualization and unlocking your true creative potential.) Parnes' book and the CPS model are highly recommended.

Creativity leaders Treffinger, Isaksen, Firestien, and Dorval (Treffinger & Isaksen, 2004; Treffinger, Isaksen, & Dorval, 1994a, 1994b; Treffinger, Isaksen, & Firestien, 1982; Treffinger, Selby, & Isaksen, 2008) understand well the remarkable potential of this model as an effective and teachable creative problem-solving strategy. They also refined and redefined the use of the CPS model in some insightful and contemporary ways that will be described in this section. But first, we'll be "finding" ourselves looking at the original terms, tenants, steps, and stages of the original CPS model.

CPS: The Original Model

The model usually is presented as five steps. However, Parnes and Treffinger and colleagues also note a sixth step, a preliminary one—called *mess-finding*—which involves locating a challenge or problem to which to apply the model. The total six stages are *mess-finding, fact-finding, problem-finding, idea-finding, solution-finding* (idea evaluation), and *acceptance-finding* (idea implementation).

The CPS steps guide the creative process. They tell you what to do at each immediate step in order to eventually produce one or more creative, workable solutions. A unique feature is that each step first involves a **divergent** thinking phase in which one generates lots of ideas (facts, problem definitions, ideas, evaluation criteria, implementation strategies) and then a **convergent** phase in which only the most promising ideas are selected for further exploration. Figure 5.2 illustrates the divergent/convergent nature of each step. It's important here to differentiate between divergent and convergent thinking to truly understand how the process of this model works.

In the *Journal of Creative Behavior*, Parkhurst (1999) provides a good comparison of the two cognitive processes. He states that convergent thinking is the kind of thinking used to narrow down a range of ideas to a potential/plausible solution. In contrast, he identifies divergent thinking as a cognitive style that produces multiple responses, novel ideas, and unusual suggestions to a question. Though convergent thinking has been criticized for its potential to induce cognitive fixation (following a narrow path to arrive a single right answer), the appropriate and alternative use of both strategies are essential in the CPS model.

Mess-finding is elaborated in Inset 5.1. The next step—which would be the first step if you already have selected a problem—is *fact-finding*, which involves listing what you know about the problem or challenge. It includes "Visualizing . . . in your imagination everything you know about it" (Parnes, 1981, p. 133) or "Examining many details, looking at the Mess from many viewpoints" (Treffinger et al., 1994a, p. 19). The goal is "to help you explore all the information, impressions, observations, feelings, and questions that you have about a mess on which you've decided to work" (Isaksen & Treffinger, 1985). Parnes recommends *who, what, when, where, why,* and *how* questions:

Who is or should be involved?
What is or is not happening?
When does this or should this happen?
Where does or doesn't this occur?
Why does it or doesn't it happen?
How does it or doesn't it occur?

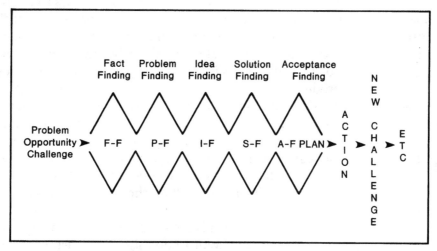

FIGURE 5.2. The creative problem-solving (CPS) model.

INSET 5.1
Discovering Problems and Challenges

One crucial stage in the CPS model takes place *before* the five steps of fact-finding, problem-finding, idea-finding, solution-finding, and acceptance-finding: finding a problem, opportunity, or challenge to which to apply this dynamite model. Instead of passively waiting for a problem to bang on the door and demand a creative solution, we can take a more active, high-initiative approach to improving our lives by looking for nuisances, challenges, or things that you would like to see happen—difficulties that seem to cry out "Help! Help! Get the CPS model, quick!"

To help you discover challenges and opportunities and generally increase your problem sensitivity, Parnes (1981) itemized a list of prodding questions, some of which are itemized below. Do these suggest topics for one-person CPS sessions? For improving your life?

What would you like to get out of life?
What are your goals, as yet unfilled?
What would you like to accomplish, to achieve?
What would you like to have?
What would you like to do?
What would you like to do better?
What would you like to happen?
In what ways are you inefficient?
What would you like to organize in a better way?
What ideas would you like to get going?
What relationship would you like to improve?
What would you like to get others to do?
What takes too long?
What is wasted?
What barriers or roadblocks exist?
What do you wish you had more time for?
What do you wish you had more money for?
What makes you angry, tense, or anxious?
What do you complain about?

As an example of the CPS model, let's say the problem is thinking of ways to improve our creative thinking and problem-solving in a classroom, a business organization, or our personal lives. An individual or group first would list all of the facts they could think of relating to training creative thinking and perhaps to the nature of creativity and creative abilities. The *who, what, when, where, why,* and *how* questions aid thinking in this step. The list of ideas is then convergently narrowed to a smaller number of facts that *might be* especially productive.

The second stage, *problem-finding*, involves listing alternative problem definitions (which should be familiar as we previewed this term as a family of skills involved in problem-finding). *One principle of creative problem-solving is that the definition of a problem will determine the nature of the solutions.* In this step, it helps to begin each statement with "In what ways might we (or I) . . ." **(IWWMW)**. For example, the IWWMW phrase can involve finding resources; good workbooks or other materials, problems to practice, as well as persons or consultants who will do the creativity training or suggest/teach ways to have people teach themselves.

It may help to ask what the *real* problem is: What is the main objective? What do you really want to accomplish? Also, in most cases asking "*Why* do I want to do this?" after each problem statement will lead to another statement that is more broad and general. For example, asking "Why do I want to find problems to practice on?" leads to the answer, "In order to strengthen creative attitudes and abilities," which suggests the broader problem statement "IWWMW strengthen creative attitudes and abilities?"

And asking "Why do I want to strengthen creative attitudes and abilities?" leads to the answer, "In order to improve creative potential and self-actualization," which in turn leads to the more general "IWWMW improve creative potential and self-actualization."

One or more of the most fruitful definitions is selected for the third stage, *idea-finding*. This is the divergent-thinking, brainstorming stage. Ideas are freely proposed, without criticism or evaluation, for each of the problem definitions accepted in the second stage.

The fourth stage, *solution finding*, should have been named *idea evaluation*. In three related steps, (1) criteria for evaluation are listed, (2) the ideas are evaluated, and (3) one or more of the best ideas are selected. In general, evaluation criteria might include:

> Will it work?
> Is it legal?
> Are the materials and technology available?
> Are the costs acceptable?
> Will the public accept it?
> Will higher-level administrators accept it?
> Would grandmother approve?[4]

Relating specifically to the problem of teaching creativity, some criteria might be: Will the strategy strengthen important creative abilities? Will it teach creative attitudes and awarenesses; that is, will it work? Will it cost too much? Will it take too long? Are materials available? Will others accept the idea? Will the students enjoy the experience? Will they cooperate? The list may be convergently reduced to the most relevant criteria. As Isaksen and Treffinger (1985) point out, the "criteria are used to screen, select, and support options for which you will eventually be developing a plan of action."

Sometimes, an evaluation matrix can be helpful, with possible solutions listed on the vertical axis and the criteria across the top (see Figure 5.3). Each idea is rated according to each criterion, perhaps on a 1 to 5 scale, with the ratings entered in the cells. The scores would be totaled to find the "best"

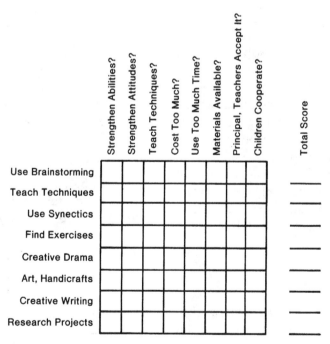

FIGURE 5.3. Example of an Evaluation Matrix. The problem was, "How can we teach creativity?" Each idea is rated on a 1 (*low*) to 5 (*high*) scale according to each criterion. Total scores are then tallied.

---

[4] Another list of evaluation criteria appears in the brainstorming section of Chapter 8.

idea(s). Parnes (1981) suggested that you also can evaluate ideas by taking the perspective of another person and imagining how the idea looks to them, or else visualizing others' reactions as you tell them about the idea.

Another evaluation device is to make a list of what is *good* and what is *bad* about each idea. This approach helps prevent prematurely discarding an idea that has some good qualities or prematurely accepting an idea that has some serious faults.

Finally, *acceptance-finding* (idea implementation) amounts to thinking of "ways to get the best ideas into action" (Parnes, 1981). It may involve creating an action plan, which is a plan containing specific steps to be taken and a timetable for taking them.

Treffinger (1995; Treffinger et al., 1994b) noted that acceptance finding will be helped by looking for **assisters and resisters**. Assisters are people ("key players"), essential resources, and the best times, places, and methods that will help implementing the solution. Resisters include contrary people, missing materials, ineffective methods, bad timing, bad locations, or other problems that will interfere with implementation. One might ask, "What difficulties could arise?" and "What is the worst thing that could happen?" These questions suggest ideas for responding to difficulties.

When selecting one or more of the best ideas at each of the CPS steps, Treffinger et al. (1982) recommended looking for **hits and hotspots**. Hits are ideas that strike the problem-solvers as important breakthroughs—directions to be pursued further. Hotspots are groups of related hits. Hits and hotspots clearly are leads to good solutions.

In his book *The Magic of Your Mind*, Parnes (1981) leads the reader through problem after problem with the goal of making the five steps habitual and automatic. That is, when encountering a problem, challenge, or opportunity one quickly would review relevant facts, identify various interpretations of the problem, generate solutions, evaluate the ideas, and speculate on how the solution(s) might be implemented and accepted.

In the classroom or corporation, Parnes' CPS stages may be used to guide a creative thinking session that (1) teaches an effective creative problem-solving strategy, (2) improves understanding of the creative process, (3) exposes learners to a rousing creative-thinking experience, and (4) solves a problem. However, in attempting to solve a problem, Parnes did state that people could use the five stages too rigidly (a source of contemporary criticism, which we will soon preview). Therefore, he stated that thinking processes in the CPS model could be in alignment with the star-shaped model you see in Figure 5.4, a variation that supports the notion that one may flexibly move (or star-hop) from any one step to any other. But there are other variations of this original model that have emerged, and we will deal with each of these sequentially.

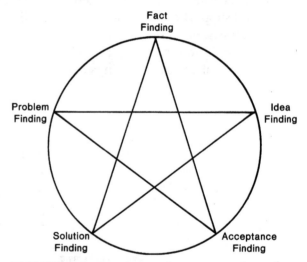

FIGURE 5.4. An alternative conception of the CPS model emphasizing that one may flexibly move from any stage to any other.

The Simplex Model

Instead of a star, Basadur (1992, 1994) shaped a circular model with three separate activities and eight sequential steps that resemble the CPS model. The activities are as follows:

1. In *Problem-Finding Activity* one discovers and clarifies important problems needing solving.
2. *Problem-Solving Activity* is developing imaginative solutions.
3. Finally, *Solution Implementation Activity* is executing one or more solutions.

The model is circular in the sense that "each implemented solution leads to new, useful problems" to be solved (Basadur, Runco, & Vega, 2000, p. 79).

Basadur, Runco, and Vega subdivided their Problem-Finding Activity into two steps of *Problem-Generating* and *Problem-Formulating*. They included two steps within each of the four stages. The now eight-step model, called *Simplex*, is summarized in these stages and steps:

Stage 1. Problem-Generating
1. Identifying the problem
2. Finding facts

Stage 2. Problem-Formulating
1. Defining the problem
2. Finding ideas

Stage 3. Problem-Solving
1. Evaluating and selecting ideas
2. Planning

Stage 4. Solution Implementation
1. Gaining acceptance ("selling the idea")
2. Taking action

Like the similar CPS model, Simplex provides a nice guide for systematically attacking, for example, a pesky corporate difficulty. In commenting on this model, Sousa, Monteiro, and Pellissier (2009) state that "in each step, there is a moment for active divergence, when individuals or groups produce as many ideas or options as they can find, in a supporting climate in which judgment is deferred to allow the perception of new relationships between facts" (p. 44). So circle the wagons gang, creativity doesn't have to be complex—instead this model makes it very simplex!

CPS: An Updated Model (Version 6.1)

Isaksen, Dorval, and Treffinger (2000, 2010) introduced substantial changes to the language used to describe the steps and sequences in the Creative Problem-Solving model. Labeling it version 6.1, this updated model is described by Treffinger et al. (2008) as containing "four components and eight different stages, portrayed in a circular rather than linear fashion, reflecting the reality that problem solvers enter and exit the process based on their own level of readiness and understanding of the problem situation" (p. 391). This circular approach is similar in structure (literally and conceptually) with the Simplex model and addresses concerns echoed by Buijs, Smulders, and van der Meer (2009) as to whether the Creative Problem-Solving model is actually linear (step by step). The new model is presented in Figure 5.5.

First of all, readers will notice the addition of a "Planning Your Approach" stage at the center of this new model, which includes Appraising Tasks and Designing Process aspects. As Treffinger et al. (2008) note, "Planning Your Approach functions as a management component, guiding problem solvers in analyzing and selecting process components and stages deliberately" (p. 391). The other three components, "Understanding the Challenge," "Generating Ideas," and "Preparing for Action" should look familiar, as though the language has changed, they still have ties to the original model. Mess-Finding, Fact-Finding, and Problem-Finding constitute "Understanding the Problem," which now has new identified stages related to "Constructing Opportunities," "Exploring Data," and "Framing Problems," respectively. In talking about these differences, Treffinger et al. (2008) state that "Constructing Opportunities involves generating broad, brief, and beneficial statements that help set the principal direction for problem-solving efforts. Exploring Data includes generating and answering questions that bring out key information, feelings, observations, impressions, and questions about the task. . . . Framing Problems involves seeking a specific or targeted question on which to focus subsequent efforts" (p. 392).

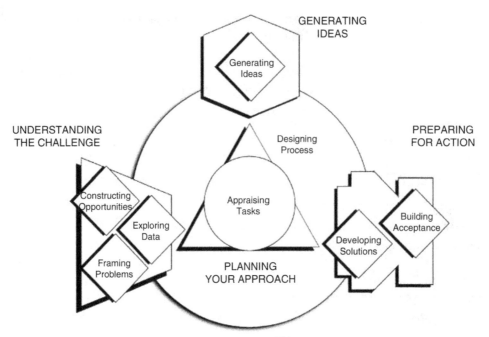

FIGURE 5.5. The creative problem-solving version 6.1™ framework © 2000. Creative Problem Solving Group and Center for Creative Learning; reproduced by permission.

The "Generating Ideas" component is still tied to the divergent thinking aspect of the original Idea-Finding stage of the original CPS model. Treffinger et al. (2008) postulates that "The Generating Ideas component and stage includes coming up with many varied or unusual options for responding to a problem" (p. 392).

Finally, the "Preparing for Action" component relates back to the original Solution-Finding and Acceptance-Finding stages of the CPS model, with new identified stages of "Developing Solutions" and "Building Acceptance" (respectively). In making decisions about what to do with the ideas that have been generated, "developing solutions involves analyzing, refining, or developing promising options" (p. 392). After that work has been done, Building Acceptance is where we "identify possible factors that may influence successful implementation of solutions. The aim is to help prepare solutions for improved acceptance and greater value" (p. 392).

So, whether you utilize the original model or subscribe more to the updated 6.1 version, it is clear that the Creative Problem-Solving method is well entrenched and established as a means of facilitating the creative process.

A Two-Stage Analysis

Stripped to its essentials, creating something in art, science, business, or any other area involves two fairly clear steps: the *big idea* stage and an *elaboration* stage. The big-idea stage is a period of fantasy in which the creative person looks for a new, exciting idea or problem solution. After the idea is found, perhaps using analogical thinking or some other creative thinking technique, the elaboration stage requires idea development and implementation.

Some (e.g., von Oech, 1983) assume that only the first stage requires imaginative, creative activity—idea combining, idea modifying, analogical thinking, projecting future needs, or other imagery and fantasy. When the creative idea is found, logical thinking activities of analyzing and sequential planning are needed to develop and implement the idea. Actually, continued creative thinking and problem-solving are needed for the elaboration and development stage as much as the initial fantasy stage needs them. Consider, for example, the elaboration and development of the plot for a novel, a research idea, a new teaching method, or a new consumer product. Considerable imagination and creative problem-solving are needed after the big idea is found.

The Creative Process as a Change in Perception

The process of creation frequently involves a dramatic and, usually instantaneous, change in perception. There suddenly is a new way of looking at something, a transformation, a relationship that was not there before. Tan, Teo, and Chye (2009) state, "the creative process is viewed as a change in perception, or seeing new idea combinations, new relationships, new meaning, or new applications that have NOT been perceived before" (p. 7). This phenomenon occurs whether the illumination is a simple modification of a cookie recipe, perhaps substituting mint candies for chocolate chips, or an unfathomably complex discovery in mathematics, physics, medicine, or astronomy.

One simple way to illustrate this sudden perceptual change is with visual puzzles such as the ambiguous illusions featured in next page. For example, look at Figure 5.6 and 5.7.

I'm all ears (of corn?) takes on all new meaning when you have a face made of fruits and vegetables (Figure 5.6). How many different sea animals can you see in Figure 5.7? Can you "spot" an animal that no one else "nose?" More importantly, has how you have processed the image you are looking at changed? Instead of top-down processing (from big picture to tiny details) what if you flipped the script and approach the stimuli from a bottom-up manner (feature analysis in which we use the tiny details to construct the big picture). We are quick to employ top-down processing in many tasks, including skimming textbook pages for the general gist and then forgetting (instantly) what we just read! It's neat when our perceptual processes can lead to sudden insight where we can see something that simply wasn't there before and where you might find yourself exclaiming, "Oh, there it is!" or "Now I see it!"

We do not understand this sudden perceptual change or transformation very well. It is the mental activity underlying the creative insight itself; it is the very birth of creative inspiration. In some cases, the perceptual transformation takes place while viewing or thinking about one or two objects or ideas, and then mentally modifying them, combining them, or otherwise detecting a new meaning or relationship. We already mentioned that one of Harold Lloyd's moviemakers experienced an abrupt perceptual change when a hilltop view of a Hollywood street suddenly was seen as an illusion of great height. A sudden transformation in verbal perception and meaning is illustrated by the bumper sticker, "My karma ran over my dogma." A writer may "see" an intriguing story take shape as the result of a visit to Kuwait and Baghdad. A product developer may "see" a new product, new use for a material, or new marketing possibilities while scrolling through their Facebook feed. Inventor De Mestral "saw" a new line of

FIGURES 5.6 AND 5.7. Ambiguous Illusions. These images by Arcimboldo present a "fresh" look at faces, but use fruit and fish to complete the profile. How many varieties of each can you find?

fastening devices while plucking cockleburrs from his hunting dog and thus "Velcro" was introduced (and became a staple of this author's 1980s shoe closet!) The perceptual change or transformation process appears to be partly, if not largely, involuntary.

One book entitled *Playful Perception* (Leff, 1984) seeks to teach creative thinking by helping the reader to perceive the environment in creative, entertaining, and unusual—make that *weird*—ways. Leff describes the use of *awareness plans*, essentially "procedures for perceiving and thinking about the world around us" (p. 4). Such plans are designed to stimulate "powers of attention and imagination . . . [to open] doorways to expanded awareness on a variety of fronts . . . [and] stimulate your insight and curiosity about your surroundings" (p. 7). Some exercises are simply for fun and fantasy.

You probably will not be able to resist trying some of the following exercises, Inset 5 (adapted from Leff, 1984):

INSET 5.2

Try seeing and thinking about everything around you as if it were alive.

(Is the light bulb a visitor from space? The space between your car seat and console a helpless, hungry creature . . . after all, it swallows everything from french fries, to loose change, to cell phones!)

Think of past and future reincarnations of things around you.
(In its next life, will that garbage be the next Wall-E?? We might be on the "Eve" of finding out!)

Think of alternative meanings and interpretations of common things and events.
(Is the clerk's "May I help you?" a religious invocation? A four-word poem? A secret password? Is a volleyball game a new dance?)

Reverse things, events, and causation from what you normally assume they are.
(Articles discarded into the attic may be seen as valuable treasures, expensive jewelry as junk. Bicycles cause kids feet to turn in circles.)

View the world from the perspective of an animal or an object.
(How does the big dog look to a visiting cat? What if you are the room you are in, and the things in the room are part of you?)

See everything as edible and imagine how it would taste.
Look at objects as the tops of things, and imagine what the underground portion looks like.

Visually search your environment for things that are beautiful or aesthetically interesting.

Look for things you normally would not notice.

Look for boring things, and then think of something interesting about them.

Imagine the likely past and future of different objects.

Think about cultural values implied by things in your environment.

Think about what you can learn from whatever you encounter.

Did you experience perceptual changes and transformations? Lots of imagination and fantasy?

If not, in the second edition of his "Creativity" anthology, Runco (2014) offers up several tactics that can be used to enhance our perceptual ability as it pertains to creativity. Among them are: shifting perspectives, in which an individual is asked to uproot themselves (mentally or physically) to break routines; turning the situation around (literally or figuratively), in which the focal point is changed; and deviation amplification, in which one examines the major impacts of minor adjustments or tweaks.

The Imagery–Creativity Connection

It seems evident that creativity takes place in the head or mind via the manipulation of mental images. The word *imagination* is a virtual synonym for *creativity* itself. Houtz and Patricola (1999) visualize imagery as "an individual's mental representations of real objects, scenes, events or symbols in the absence of the direct, external, observable, concrete experiencing (i.e., sensation) of the objects or events themselves" (p. 1). They go on to discuss how research on imagery and creativity fall into one of three categories: self-report studies of the visual imagery of creative individuals, use of imagery in problem-solving, and a correlation between our ability to generate images and scores on creative thinking tests. This contemporary slant is backed by historical figures such as Aristotle, who wrote, "The soul never thinks without a mental picture" (Yates, 1966, p. 32), implying that images supply the continuous connection between perception (input), thought (mental activity), and action (output).

But what exactly IS the connection? To review some historical notes relating to imagery, early behaviorist John B. Watson, the "father of behaviorism," denied the existence of imagery, calling it "a figment of the psychologist's terminology." To Watson, thinking was subvocal speech – silent motor activity in the throat – which is nicknamed "muscle twitchism." Behaviorist Skinner did not improve matters much. He proposed that one's behavior (response) was triggered by the environment (stimulus), and the consequences (reward) strengthens the tendency to act the same way again. Forget unobservable—hence unscientific—imagery and any other form of mental life. During the 1960s' transition to cognitive psychology, concessions to mental imagery took the form of implicit verbal responses and verbal associations, which behaviorists could live with. Meanwhile, earlier in the century and in the psychoanalytic ballpark, Freud proposed that *primary process* thinking, which we saw in Chapter 4, would occur during relaxation and includes dreams, reveries, free associations, and fantasies. Definitely closer to human creativity than a rat punching a bar to get fed.

It is quaint that the author of a major 1964 article, entitled "Imagery: The Return of the Ostracized" and published in the top-status *American Psychologist*, felt compelled to argue for the very existence of mental imagery. Holt's (1964) supporting evidence (other than in his own head) stemmed from published reports of hallucinations, neurological research, drug-induced imagery, and creativity studies. More positively, he categorized several types of images, many of which relate closely to creative imagery:

Thought images are faint, subjective representations without sensory input. They include memory images and imagination images; they may involve any sensory modality or be totally verbal.

Eidetic images are said to be greatly enhanced thought images of such vividness and clarity as to seem like actual perceptions. The person, particularly a child, may believe the images are real. Too much of this probably would land a person on lithium or in an institution.

Synesthesia, as we mentioned in Chapter 4, is cross-modal imagery, in which, for example, one may hear colors or taste shapes.

Hallucination is imagery related to a person's beliefs. It is perceived as part of reality, but in fact does not exist. The related paranormal hallucination is said to be the experience of a ghost or other religious, mystical, or supernatural visions. Can you think of specific circumstances in which hallucination is acceptable? Even praiseworthy?

Dream images. Hallucinations during sleep.

Hypnagogic and hypnopompic images are images of great clarity that appear in the drowsy state just before sleep (hypnagogic) or in the drowsy state while awakening (hypnopompic). These are times of fantasy and imagination related to those daily problems and challenges.

Highly creative individuals are most likely to cite *dream images*, *hypnagogic* and *hypnopompic images*, and conscious, purposeful *imagination images* (a subtype of thought images) as sources of creative ideas (Daniels-McGhee & Davis, 1994).

Historic anecdotes are unnecessary to convince readers of the reality of imagery. Nonetheless, the following classic examples illustrate some processes of constructing, taking apart, modifying, combining, and transforming mental imagery—in any sensory mode or across sensory modes (synesthesia)—into new ideas.

Said Beethoven:

> I carry my thoughts with me for a long time. . . . I shall not forget [a theme] even years later. I change many things, discard others, and try again and again until I am satisfied; then, in my head, I begin to elaborate the work. . . . It rises, it grows. I hear and see the image in front of me from every angle. (Hamburger, 1952, p. 194)

Beethoven's sound images had form and color.

We noted that creativity in writing can happen "between the pencil and the paper." William Wordsworth's imagery and writing did indeed interact during the writing process. Said Wordsworth, "A picture is not thought out and settled beforehand. While it is being done it changes as one's thoughts change" (Jeffrey, 1989, p. 83). Wordsworth defined a poet as a person with intensely vivid imagery plus the ability to communicate those images.

Artist Wassily Kandinsky expressed his experiences with a touch of synesthesia when he wrote that "the sound of colors is so definite that it would be hard to find anyone who would try to express bright yellow in the bass notes, or [a] dark lake in the treble" (Solso, 1991, p. 20). Guaranteed you have seen his concentric circles with squares painting that adorns art galleries (and dorm-room walls) all over the nation.

Robert Woodward (no relation to me), whose double-helix model of growth and reproduction won him a 1965 Nobel Prize, could visualize complex three-dimensional structures, the path of possible reactions within the structure, and possible transformations of that structure. Said Woodward, it is "the sensuous elements which play so large a role in my attraction to chemistry. I love the crystals, the beauty of their form—and their formation; liquids, dormant, distilling, sloshing, swirling; the fumes, the odors—good and bad; the rainbow of colors; the gleaming vessels of every size, shape, and purpose . . . [chemistry] would not exist for me without these physical, visual, tangible, sensuous things" (C. E. Woodward, 1989, p. 237).

Robert Woodward also noted, "chemical synthesis is entirely a creative activity in which art, design, imagination, and inspiration play a predominant role" (p. 233).

Kekule's account of his discovery of the benzene ring is an often-cited and particularly vivid description of the role of mental imagery in creative thinking and problem-solving:

> I turned my chair to the fire and dozed. Again the atoms were gamboling before my eyes. The smaller groups kept modestly in the back-ground. My mental eye, rendered more acute by visions of this kind, could now distinguish larger structures, of manifold conformation, long rows sometimes more closely fitted together, all twining and twisting in snake-like motion. But look! What was that? One of the snakes had seized hold of its tail and the form whirled mockingly before my eyes. As if by a flash of lightening I awoke. (Koestler, 1964, p. 118)

But the definitive word on the relationship between mental imagery and creativity could be found in a meta-analysis conducted by LeBoutillier and Marks (2003), who investigated evidence regarding both the individual differences approach (self-reported imagery against divergent thinking measures) and image generation approach (emergence of creativity through visualization of specific forms). Their findings concluded that the association between imagery and creativity is robust, with the strongest support that *vividness* (clarity) of the image experienced and *control* of the imagery process were the most important variables that drove the findings. With the findings in mind, they also noted that it would take (approximately) 100 studies with contrary evidence to be published to refute the statistical relationship between imagery and creativity. Pretty powerful stuff!

Imagery and the Creative Process

A key question is: What do creative persons *do* with mental imagery that is different. Note first that *involuntary* perceptual processes ("I see those McDonald's arches!") promote organization, constancy, and survival. *Voluntary* processes are less rigid; they can operate deliberately on the mental images stimulated by perceptions and memories ("Forget it, let's pick up some crackers, ham, Gouda, and Grey Poupon"). One possibility then, is that the creative individual has superior voluntary control over such processes as selective attention, recall, manipulation, and modification of mental images; generation of novel images ("How do we farm in the year 2050?"); and perhaps even cross-modal representation. The creative person more easily can modify a single mental image to create several novel possibilities (Flowers & Garbin, 1989).

According to Flowers and Garbin, creativity requires a certain "looseness" of perception, rather than tight organization and constancy, and an absence of perceptual rigidity. When one is dozing, dreaming, or on drugs, perceptual mechanisms that normally organize the world become "decoupled" from sensory input, providing opportunities for fantasy and innovation. The perceptual mechanisms essentially "run on their own." Note that "decoupling" is indeed more likely to occur during hypnogogic and hypnopompic states, periods of high creativity for many individuals. Said Kosslyn (1983), "One can create scenes that never existed or transform the commonplace into the extraordinary . . . [We can] imagine the world not merely as it is, but as it could be" (p. 91).

Of course, during wakeful periods of sobriety the ideas are evaluated, selected, and refined in accord with the second part of this chapter's two-stage analysis (elaboration of the big idea). Chapters 8 and 9, dealing with creativity techniques, will describe specifically how we can manipulate mental images.

Summary

The "creative process" topic deals with where ideas come from, as in Koestler's bisociation (idea combining) notion, analogical relationships, and changes in perception.

Problem-finding (discovering and inventing problems) is different than problem-solving and the way that the problem is posed will determine the approach necessary to solve it.

New ideas occur while one is creating. Fringe consciousness seems important. The creative process also includes steps and stages in creative problem-solving and conscious techniques for creative thinking.

Many global processes are common across different areas. However, the specific creative processes of each person are influenced by their experiences, abilities, styles, strategies, and problem requirements.

Insight, chance, and hard work all contribute to creative productivity. All have a role and are interrelated.

Three intuitively necessary stages are clarifying the problem, working on it, and finding a solution.

Torrance's definition of creativity included steps of sensing a problem, forming hypotheses, testing the hypotheses, and communicating the results.

Dewey reduced problem-solving to two steps: a state of perplexity followed by searching for a solution to resolve the difficulty.

The classic Wallas model included preparation, incubation, illumination, and verification. The stages do not necessarily occur in exactly that order.

Levels of Process theory suggests that incubation may involve fringe-conscious "low level" mental activity. If a good solution is encountered, it is passed to higher-conscious levels of processing. Eureka!

Hélie and Sun proposed of a model that explains how explicit and implicit knowledge interact to provide insight, or sudden illumination.

Adding a fifth step of restitution, Norlander concluded that alcohol affects only stages requiring feedback (preparation, part of illumination, verification) and not the other stages (incubation, part of illumination, restitution).

Kaufman examined disinhibition hypothesis regarding the influences of substances on creativity, but found no substantive relationship.

Shaw provided feedback (loops) to the Wallas model.

The CPS model included six steps of mess-finding, fact-finding, problem-finding, idea-finding, solution-finding (idea evaluation), and acceptance-finding (implementation). The first stage sometimes is ignored. Each step first involves a divergent-thinking phase (multiple possibilities), then a convergent-thinking (selecting possibilities) phase.

The CPS model guides the creative process. It represents both a creative process and an effective way to teach creative problem-solving.

Mess-finding is locating a problem to which to apply the CPS model.

Fact-finding is aided by asking who, what, when, where, why, and how questions.

Problem-finding involves listing IWWMW questions, looking for the "real" problem, and asking "Why?" after each problem statement.

Idea-finding requires deferred judgment, the main brainstorming principle.

Solution-finding includes listing evaluation criteria, evaluating the ideas, and selecting the best idea(s). An evaluation matrix may be used. One also can take another's perspective on the problem, or list what is good and what is bad about each idea.

Acceptance-finding results in an action plan.

Parnes recommends practicing the CPS model until the five steps become habitual and automatic. Said Parnes, if it helps, the steps can be used in any order.

Strongly resembling the CPS model, the Simplex model includes four stages (problem-generating, problem-formulating, problem-solving, solution implementation) with divergent and convergent thinking taking place at each stage.

Treffinger and colleagues proposed an update to the CPS model, with four components and eight stages, including preparing for action, understanding the problem (mess-finding, fact-finding, and problem-finding), generating ideas (idea-finding), and planning for action (solution-finding plus acceptance-finding).

Treffinger recommended looking for assisters and resisters. His convergent techniques included finding hits, seemingly important ideas, and hotspots, which are groups of related hits.

A two-stage analysis of creative problem-solving included a big-idea stage, followed by an elaboration stage. Creativity is involved in both stages.

Perceptual change or transformation is a mysterious but core process that underlies insight and creative inspiration. It can be demonstrated with visual puzzles, in which new meanings, transformations, and idea combinations suddenly are "seen."

Leff's book *Playful Perception* provides many exercises, or action plans, for perceiving the environment in new and creative ways.

Runco identified tactics to increase creative perception abilities, including shifting perspectives, turning the situation upside down, and deviation amplification.

Imagery and creativity have been studied in relation to what visualization skills do creative individuals possess, how imagery relates to standardized tests of creativity, and how imagery can aid problem-solving.

Imagery was ignored in classic behaviorism (Watson, Skinner). Creative imagery relates closely to Freud's primary process thinking.

When imagery was beginning to become legitimate (1960s), Holt differentiated thought images, eidetic images, synesthesia, hallucinations, dream images, and hypnagogic and hypnopompic images. Dream images, hypnagogic and hypnopompic images, and deliberate-imagination images (a type of thought image) are the ones most used by creative people.

Imagery was described by Beethoven, Wordsworth, Kandinsky, Einstein, Robert Woodward, and Kekule.

A meta-analysis by LeBoutillier and Marks confirmed the relationship between imagery and creativity.

Involuntary perceptual processes promote constancy and organization. Voluntary processes can underlie manipulation and modification of mental images. "Looseness of perception" and "decoupling" of perceptual mechanisms have been suggested.

Review Exercises

Creative Process

Self-Test: Key Concepts, Terms, and Names

Briefly define or explain each of these:

Koestler (1964) Biosociation of Ideas

_____

_____

Problem Solving vs. Problem Finding

_____

_____

Torrance's four-step process of creativity

1.

2.

3.

4.

Graham Wallas' four-step model of creativity

1.

2.

3.

4.

Feedback Loops & Creativity

_____

_____

Original CPS model

_____

_____

Mess-finding

_____

_____

Problem-Finding / IWWMW

_____

_____

Solution-finding

_____

_____

Acceptance-finding

_____

_____

Assisters and Resisters

_____

_____

Hits and Hot spots

_____

_____

Updated CPS Model – summarize the changes

_____

_____

Creative process as a change in perception

_____

_____

Imagery - creativity connection

_____

_____

Involuntary, voluntary perceptual processes in imagery

_____

_____

Let's Think about It

1. In your own creative productivity (even if it is just writing term papers), how much of the final product is due to *hard work*, one or more sudden "*insights*," or some *chance* note, even though some of you might give 110% on term papers, you only have 100% to allocate to the three categories listed below! happenings or discoveries?

   Hard work: _____percent

   Sudden Insights   _____percent

   Chance Discoveries   _____percent

2. Think about the last "Aha" or "Eureka" experience that you had related to solving a problem or generating an idea. Describe the nature of the insight that you gained. Can you apply Wallas' model to explain where your idea came from? What preparation was in place? Were you able to incubate before the illumination occurred? How did you verify the solution and put it into place? Depict or describe your mental transformation below (and if you haven't had a Eureka experience YET, describe how you could put the Wallas model into practice to achieve one!)

   Preparation:

   _____

   Incubation:

   _____

   Illumination:

   _____

   Verification:

   _____

3. Think of a REAL problem or challenge you have (e.g., not enough time; raising money for a study abroad trip to Europe; raising your grade-point average; learning to play the ukelele or speak Russian; job hunting; etc.).

Walk yourself through the CPS stages from the original model.

General Problem:

_____

4. Fact-finding: What do I know about the problem? What are some important facts? Ask yourself who, what, when, where, why, and how questions.

_____

_____

_____

_____

_____

Problem-finding: Think of different problem statements. What are some altenative ways of "framing" the problem? What is the REAL problem?" Again, it helps to begin each statement with "IWWMW."

IWWMW_____?

IWWMW_____?

IWWMW_____?

IWWMW_____?

IWWMW_____?

Idea-finding: Brainstorm ideas for one or two of your best problem statements.

Idea 1: _____

Idea 2: _____

Idea 3: _____

Idea 4: _____

Idea 5: _____

Solution-finding: Are there some good ideas? Do you need to create an evaluation matrix to help select your best idea(s)? Be sure to use good evaluation criteria.

Criteria 1: _____

Criteria 2: _____

Criteria 3: _____

Criteria 4: _____

Criteria 5: _____

5. Rate each idea from "1" (won't work or not acceptable) to "5" (extremely promising) according to each criteria. Add up the points. Most points wins.

Acceptance-finding: How can you get your best solution(s) into action?

Action Plan:

_____

_____

_____

Creative Perception Exercises.

6. Look at the prompts listed in Inset 5.2 that were adapted from Leff's (1984) notion of Playful Perception. Choose one from the list to answer below (or create one of your own):

_____

_____

_____

7. Generate statements that represent synesthesia or cross-modal imagery. (ex: I smell trouble if you can't complete this exercise!) Several corporations have tapped into these to advertise their products (i.e. Taste the Rainbow!). What can you come up with on your own?

_____

_____

_____

8. Holt (1964) identified hypnagogic and hypnopompic images or ideas as occuring before you go to bed or right before you truly wake up. Describe an instance (or instances) when your creative process was at work in either of these drowsy states. What connection did you make or idea did you come up with?

Hypnagogic (before sleep)

_____

Hypnopompic (before waking up)

_____

"I don't know anything with certainty, but seeing the stars makes me dream."

—*Vincent van Gogh*

The stars
How close they seem
The thought of them is blinding
Shining bright
Illuminating the night
Can I borrow them from the sky?
Could this be a dream?
Reach out and grab your fate
How can I create my own destiny?
When the music is daunting
Dancing on starlight
The canvas of painted stars
The anatomy of it all
Performing a play in the dark
A constellation connecting the lines
What else is out there?
More answers within the stars
Together as one
Solving all of my questions
Opening my eyes to see the stars in a new light
They shine for me in this fantasy
Dark stars gleaming
Teach me to shine
Metaphorically speaking, of course.

The poem embodies the main elements of analogical thinking, "borrowing" ideas from different domains for creative innovation. By stating how close that stars seem and wanting to borrow them for the night, this relates not only to the Van Gogh quote but also to the field of astronomy. And though paintings are representations of visual art, there are relationships in this poem to performance art, such as music, theater, and dance. Dancing on Starlight. Performing a play in the dark. The entirety of the poem was to convey the complex elements of analogical thinking, give new life to the elements in the chapter through a poetic view, and how they aid the creative process of the creative person.

And here it is that analogy comes in. . . . If the mind cannot solve its problem in terms dictated
by the situation itself, it will try to solve it in terms of some other but similar situation.

—*Brand Blanchard*

Importance of Analogical Thinking

One cannot overstate the importance of analogical and metaphorical thinking in creativity.[1] Welling (2007)
identified analogical thinking as one of the four mental operations essential to creativity. In defining analogical thinking, he states that "it implies the transposition of a conceptual structure from one habitual context
to another innovative context. The abstract relationship between the elements of one situation is similar to
those found in the innovative context" (p. 168). It is simply and absolutely true that many—perhaps the large
majority—of our creative ideas and problem solutions are born in analogical and metaphorical thinking. *When
we think analogically (or metaphorically), we take ideas (or words) from one context and apply them in a new
context*, producing the new idea combination, new transformation, new theoretical perspective, or more colorful literary passage. We "make a connection" between our current problem and a similar or related situation.

Analogical and metaphorical thinking is extremely common in all areas of creativity and creative
problem-solving. The phrases "was inspired by" and "is based upon" indicate that ideas for a specific
creation were suggested by or borrowed from another source by the particular composer, novelist, moviemaker, artist, architect, decorator, designer, scientist, engineer, new product developer, cartoonist,
business entrepreneur, or other creative person. Said historian Jacob Bronowski (1961), "The discoveries of science, the works of art, are explorations—more, are explosions—of [seeing] a hidden likeness."
Arthur Koestler (1964) observed that the creative thinker finds such metaphoric and analogical connections while other individuals do not.

As you become sensitive to the role of analogical thinking in creative innovation, you will see it continually. As preliminary examples, in art Edward Degas "borrowed" the beauty and grace of ballerinas, and
sometimes thoroughbred horses, for his famous painting style. Leonardo da Vinci reportedly wandered
Italian streets, sketchbook in hand, to find interesting faces for his painting The Last Supper. The inspiration behind Van Gogh's "Starry Night" (which in turn was the inspiration for the new textbook cover) has
been chronicled in the opening text of each of the chapters so far, with influences from physics, astronomy,
and psychology being analyzed. Throughout the history of art (and literature and moviemaking) ideas have
been taken from mythology, the Bible, historical events, news events—or somebody else's earlier work. Lone
Ranger creator Fran Striker kept stacks of western paperbacks handy, all filled with ideas for horse operas.

The brilliantly creative and successful Broadway musical *CATS (much maligned as a movie ... or is
that meow-ligned?!)* was "based on" *Old Possum's Book of Practical Cats*, a book of poems by T. S. Eliot.
The *CATS* playbill reads:

> Most of the poems comprising *Old Possum's Book of Practical Cats* have been set to music complete
> and in their originally published form. However, some of our lyrics, notably *The Marching Song of the
> Pollicle Dogs* and the story of *Grizzabella*, were discovered among the unpublished writings of Eliot.
> The prologue is based on ideas and incorporates lines from another unpublished poem entitled *Pollicle
> Dogs and Jellicle Cats*. Growltiger's aria is taken from an Italian translation of *Practical Cats*. *Memory*
> includes lines from and is suggested by *Rhapsody on a Windy Night*, and other poems of the *Prufrock*
> period. All other words in the show are taken from the Collected Poems.

Is analogical thinking important in high-level creative accomplishment?

Sometimes an analogical connection will burst into awareness suddenly and unpredictably. That is,
a sudden "insight" may be a matter of instantly "making a connection."

---

[1] In the creativity literature the distinction between *analogical* and *metaphorical* thinking is blurred—the terms are used almost
interchangeably. Officially, a metaphor is a verbal analogy, as in "crumbling expectations," a rich "fat cat," or Shakespeare's
"all the world is a stage." In analogical thinking in creativity, one transfers ideas (not colorful language) from one situation to
another, as you'll see when we look at the origins of velcro and other inventions.

Other times the creative person will deliberately and painstakingly search for suitable analogical relationships, as when a professional advertiser looks at magazines, billboards, or TV ads for a good strategy for promoting a client's product, or an architect searches his or her books and magazines for ideas for a creative home or building.

Is "Borrowing" Ideas Ethical?

In the following pages of examples, the reader will see that analogical and metaphorical thinking is exceedingly common in creative innovation. It is both an explanatory creative *process*; it also is a learnable creative thinking *technique*.

But where, one might ask, does stealing and plagiarism end and true originality begin? Young and idealistic creative persons may worry about this issue more than experienced and successful ones, who realize that (1) ideas come from somewhere and (2) the analogical use of ideas is common, effective, and usually quite legitimate, and seeing analogical and metaphorical connections is quite a creative thing to do.

> I am a thief . . . and I glory in it . . . I steal from the best where it happens to be—Plato, Picasso, Bertram Ross. . . . I think I know the value of what I steal and I treasure it for all time—not as a possession but as a heritage and a legacy.
>
> —*Martha Graham*

Martha Graham's comment from above—about the honest, legitimate, and creative stealing of ideas—seems right on target regarding the ethics of "borrowing" ideas. T. S. Eliot is reputed to have stated that "good writers borrow ideas, great writers steal them."

Using analogically related ideas as an idea source usually poses no ethical questions at all, as when:

Chemist Kekule used the circular snake as an analogical inspiration for the benzene ring.
Bohr used the solar system as a model for the structure of the atom.
Darwin found inspiration for his theory of natural selection in selective cattle breeding.

A fourth-grader says, "Hey, let's flip this classroom into a big top for parents' night!" (Presumably this child was either a show-off or "The Greatest Showman")

A moviemaker or writer of Broadway plays uses any number of historical events, Biblical events, fictional novels, or comic book characters for inspiration (e.g., *Jesus Christ Superstar, Evita, Wicked, Spiderman*).

A novelist, mystery writer, or playwright finds inspiration in real events, myths, news stories, or children's stories, as Truman Capote, Ernest Hemingway, Agatha Christie, Shakespeare, and many others have done.

Ideas come from somewhere. This fence-hurtling strategy was inspired by billiards. (Keystone Cops in "A Dash of Courage," 1916. Courtesy of PhotoFest.)

In the business and corporate world, borrowing and modifying other successful (e.g., marketing) strategies generally is good problem-solving. We will see many more examples of analogically, and ethically, "borrowing" ideas in later sections.

Of course, if you literally "lift" someone else's work, for example, a scientific theory or a contemporary musical composition, change a few details and then claim it for your own, that quite obviously is unethical, if not illegal as well. To avoid copyright infringement, one publisher of American folk tunes changed the title of *Happy Birthday* to "*Happy Bird Day*" and published exactly the original melody. Lyrics were changed to bird words.

There are, however, grey areas, as when a TV movie plot is based directly on, say, an Agatha Christie or other novel without crediting the source; an artist too closely copies the techniques and ideas of another; or 17 companies create their own version of the *Weed Eater*. One must reach one's own conclusions regarding the originality and ethics of creations that appear too directly influenced by a successful predecessor.

Analogical Thinking in Creative Innovation

Before we look at how analogical and metaphorical thinking is used to find new ideas, it is important to recall the two-stage model of the creative process described in Chapter 5. Stage 1 is the *Big Idea* stage in which the main idea for the artistic creation, invention, or problem solution is found. Stage 2 is the *Elaboration* stage in which the Big Idea is developed. In the following examples, analogical and metaphorical thinking takes places most clearly in the Big Idea stage—finding that new idea for a creative problem solution, composition, invention, theory, and so on. After the Big Idea is found, of course, it must be developed and implemented, which may or may not involve additional analogical thinking.

Music

Your author would not even hint that all music written by all composers is analogically borrowed from earlier melodies. Some compositions inexplicably pop into the heads of classic and contemporary composers, with roots somewhere in their immense mental store of musical experiences and potential musical combinations. Other compositions are the product of laboriously experimenting with ideas—manipulating, modifying, and revising until something good is created. However, there are many instances in which the Big Idea for a composition clearly is borrowed from an earlier piece, consciously and deliberately.

Franz Liszt composed 15 Hungarian Rhapsodies, cleverly titled "Hungarian Rhapsody Number 1," "Hungarian Rhapsody Number 2," "Hungarian Rhapsody Number 3," and so on. All 15 "were built upon traditional songs or dance airs of the romantic gypsies of Hungary" (Thompson, 1942, p. 90). Franz had good company. Peter Tchaikovsky based his *Marche Slav* on a folk tune, the same tune used by Cesar A. Cui for his *Orientale*, which accounts for the "striking similarity between this melody (*Orientale*)

and that of *Marche Slav*" (Thompson, 1942, p. 11). And more: "The waltzes of Brahms like those of Beethoven have for their inspiration the old German 'Landler' or peasant dance . . ." (Thompson, 1942, p. 38).

Aaron Copland's *Appalachian Spring* symphony was based upon a Shaker folk tune entitled *Simple Gifts*. However, to keep Copland's creative genius in its mystical perspective, in a 1984 television interview Copland mentioned that when music comes alive in his head, he has no choice but to find pencil and paper and start writing.

The Broadway musical *Sunday Afternoon in the Park with George* was inspired by Georges Seurat's famous painting *Sunday Afternoon on the Isle of La Grand Jatte* and Seurat's personal life.

In the popular music category, Gary's daughter Sonja Davis was one day playing Chopin's *Prelude in C Minor*. She stopped in mid-melody to announce, "Hey, this is Barry Manilow's '*Could It Be Magic*'!" A check of the Manilow album cover credited these composers, "Barry Manilow, Adrienne Anderson, and F. Chopin." But the magic quickly wore off for recent artists who have been charged with stealing the melody, hooks, or other inspiration from original source material. Some are "Shallow" claims (literally, as the Oscar-winning song by Lady Gaga is now being litigated) and yet others made "Joyful Noise" over a "Dark Horse" hit by Katy Perry (a claim that resulted in a "Firework" judgment against the pop star).

With Fireworks in mind, "God Save Us" from treason as we sing along to "My Country 'Tis of Thee" adopted by Samuel Francis Smith as a U.S. patriotic song from a melody taken from Symphony No. 3 by Muzio Clementi, who considered England his adopted country. I'm sure he'd demand a "queens ransom" if he found out that our country had taken the British National Anthem and made it our own until 1931. With our current national anthem in mind Francis Scot Key's *Star Spangled Banner*, is also set to the tune of an English drinking song—The Anacreontic Song—which in the context of today's society makes sense as there is plenty that "ales" us!

The Big Ideas for these and many other popular songs and classical pieces were borrowed from earlier, usually simpler tunes. This is not plagiarism; it is a common analogical creative thinking process used by uncommonly creative people.

Cartoons

Many newspaper cartoons, both political cartoons and cartoon-strip "funnies," are good examples of analogical thinking in creativity. While all cartoons are not necessarily inspired by related sources, many of them are. If you watch, the funniest cartoons usually are analogical in nature, with ideas from an unrelated context combined with a current political event or with regular cartoon-strip

characters. To the reader, the resulting combination produces a surprising and comical "Aha!" experience.

Note the several types of idea sources for the cartoons on this and the following pages—news events, political events and issues, children's stories, even the Bible. It is not unusual to see political and other cartoons based upon, for example: popular TV commercials (Can You Hear Me Now?); movies such as *Superman*, TV shows such as Game of Thrones (Hillary Clinton to Cersei Lannister); mythology such as *Dracula* (George W. Bush); or classic literature such as *Robin Hood*, *Dr. Jekyll and Mr. Hyde*, or the *Wizard of Oz*. Cartoon strips such as *Frank and Earnest*,

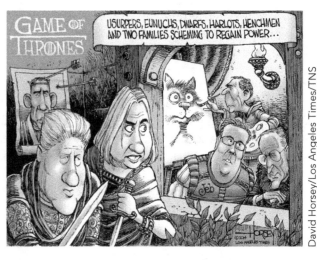

Zippy, and *The Wizard of Id* regularly incorporate current news and political events into their cartoons. A paper by Conners (2007) showed that allusions to sports, entertainment, TV, and literature were found in 27% of all political cartoons during the 2004 election cycle—the second highest percentage

Defying convention, defying gravity? All yellow brick roads lead to one conclusion as to how Gary Varvel "wickedly" used analogical thinking to relate the Emerald City of Oz with Washington D.C.

trailing only news and noteworthy events from the campaign trail itself (kissing babies, state fair photo ops, etc.). A sample of political cartoons from recent times are provided.

See how it works? Could you write a picnic episode, describing in battlefield terms the difficulties with ants and their allies the bees? Could you describe how to bake cookies using the language of a hospital operating room? Could you use the language of a cat stalking a mouse to describe a clever salesperson trying to sell someone an expensive color TV set? Try it.

If those exercises worked, perhaps you are ready for more. Think about the idea sources in the top section of Inset 6.1. Imagine how some of them might be used in either a political cartoon or a brief written satire involving the topics at the bottom of the page. Try a few. You probably will surprise yourself?

INSET 6.1
Imagine You Are a Cartoonist: Exercise in Analogical Thinking

Look at the serious topics and situations in the top section. Then look at the "scenarios"—children's stories, movies, commercials, and other scenarios—in the bottom section. See if you can create one or more original cartoons by metaphorically using the children's stories, movie characters, or other scenarios to portray (explain, criticize, laugh at) your serious topic or situation in the top section.

Sometimes there will be an easy fit; for example, just using the Coca Cola commercial "Coke is it'!" in connection with a drug problem. If you prefer, try a short written spoof like the Art Buchwald column, using the scenario language at the bottom to describe the situation at the top.

Situations in Which to Use Characters and Ideas

Summit talks between the U.S. President and the North Korean leader
Elon Musk Space X program
Auto-driving cars
Income disparity and revisions in Federal Income Tax that still favor the rich
Trade disparity with China
War Climate Change and human impact on our environment
Reliance on foreign oil
Opioid epidemic
Gun violence and school shootings
Other events?

Source of Characters and Ideas

Alice in Wonderland (Queen of Hearts, Mad Hatter, Mushroom that makes you grow)
Snow White (Seven dwarfs, Prince Charming, Wicked Queen, poisoned apple)
Cinderella (ugly stepsisters, wicked stepmother, magic coach)
Goldilocks and the Three Bears (too hot, too cold, JUST right)
Three Little Pigs and the Wolf (straw, wood, brick houses)
Robin Hood, who steals from the rich to give to the poor, and villain Sheriff of Nottingham
Star Wars characters (Kylo Ren, Rey, Luke Skywalker, Princess Leia, Darth Vader, Ben Kenobi, Yoda)
Lord of the Rings characters (Hobbits, wizards, one ring that unites us all!)
Sasquatch (Big Foot); Loch Ness Monster (Nessie)
Marvel Cinematic Universe (Thanos, Thor, Ant-Man, Iron Man, Black Widow) and "snap" judgments
Bible (Moses, Noah, Daniel in lion's den, Adam and Eve)
Ninth innings of close baseball game or fourth, and goal in the fourth quarter of a football game

Science and Invention

In chronicling the analogical process in the sciences, Dunbar (1995) identified three different types of analogical connections: *local* (a single characteristic is transferred from one experiment to another); regional (a series of relationships are transferred from one domain to another); and *long distance* (a connection is made where there wasn't one before). In all instances though Dunbar notes that finding and implementing an analogy IS considered a creative work.

With creative works in mind, the first known example of analogical transfer in the sciences, according to Holyoak and Thagard (1996), comes from an Ancient Roman architect and engineer named Vitruvius, who constructed theaters based on principles of how sound would best be perceived that derived from principles of how water waves travel. The reasoning process they depict is as follows: "voice is a flowing breath of air, perceptible to the hearing by contact. It moves in an endless number of circular rounds, like the innumerably increasing circular wave which appear when a stone is thrown into smooth water" (p. 11).

There are numerous other examples that aren't a stone's throw away conceptually from the Vitruvius example from above. William J. J. Gordon (1974b), champion of the analogical basis of creativity, described a number of instances of analogical thinking in science and invention depicted below.

Gutenberg (1398–1468), inventor of movable printing type, was not too crazy about hand-engraving an entire page of text on a single slab of smooth wood. The analogy of coin-making, in which plain discs are stamped by a coin punch, suggested separate metal letters that could be rearranged and reused. A wine press suggested his printing press.

In the 1850s, George B. Bissel grew tired of inefficiently gathering oil out of shallow wells with buckets or else sopping it up with blankets and wringing them out. He borrowed ideas from a brine pump at a salt plant to design a similar pump for raising oil. James Watt's steam engine was inspired by the jangling lid of his mother's tea kettle. The wife of Luigi Galvani placed a steel knife on a tin plate, accidentally touching a frog's leg that suddenly twitched. Galvani deduced that electricity had been created by the joining of two dissimilar metals and promptly invented the battery. His young son deduced that the leg was not yet dead and promptly smacked it with a cleaver.

Sir Marc Isambard Brunel wrestled with the problem of constructing underwater tunnels. He happened to observe a shipworm constructing a tube for itself as it moved forward through a timber, which suggested a short steel cylinder that could be pushed forward as tunnel work progressed. Were it not for that worm, New York's Holland and Lincoln tunnels would be filled with water today (but they are still filled with traffic regardless!)

Samuel Morse's first telegraph messages became weak after just a few miles. What hath God wrought?! (which was actually the first telegraph message ever sent). Stagecoach relay stations, where fresh horses were added, suggested relay stations at appropriate distances where more power could be added to the fading signal.

The development of Elias Howe's sewing machine was aided when Howe put the eye in the *point* of the needle, which was suggested by weaving shuttles. Howe's sewing machine principle was applied by the Singer Company to a leather stitching machine for making shoes.

Charles Darwin observed that animal breeders could selectively breed cattle for characteristics that improved the cattle's market value. This observation suggested that a similar process could happen in natural selection in nature, but so far Campbell's hasn't seen fit to look into canning or distributing primordial soup in grocery stores.

Eli Whitney developed his cotton gin after watching a pussycat trying to catch a chicken through a fence. The cat missed, coming up with a pawful of feathers. Hundreds of paws on his cotton gin reach through a tight fence and pull cotton away from the seeds.

Wine grapes, which ferment only when crushed, suggested to Louis Pasteur that human flesh would not putrefy unless an open wound allowed putrefying agents to get in. An experiment confirmed this novel idea, which advanced medical understanding of infections and the use of Band-Aids to prevent them.

George Westinghouse, after surviving a head-on train crash, learned of a Swiss rock drill that was powered by an air hose 3,000 feet from the compressor. He immediately designed the Westinghouse air brake. Scotsman Dunlop's first tire was not only inspired by the flexibility of a garden hose; it *was* a piece of garden hose wrapped around a wheel.

One autumn, George De Mestral walked with his hunting dog through a field that was booby-trapped with cockleburs, most of which ended up on the dog. During the extraction process he examined the structure of the burs and determined to replicate its ferocious cling in a commercial product. After hundreds of attempts and dollars and several years' work, he invented Velcro.

Charles Duryea, looking for a better way to squirt gas into engine cylinders, used the analogy of his wife's perfume atomizer to develop a spray injection carburetor. The Wright brothers needed to be able to turn their plane. The solution came from a buzzard who twisted the back of its wing slightly downward to increase air pressure in order to turn. Tying buzzards to each wing did not work, but movable wing flaps did. The Schick injector razor, invented by an army person, was inspired by the loading mechanism of the repeating rifle.

These are a handful of the many discoveries and inventions "inspired by" or "based upon" some analogically related object, process, or idea.

Literature, Moviemaking, TV, Broadway

Scholars in university English departments sometimes do source studies to identify the sources of ideas and inspirations underlying the works of noteworthy authors and playwrights. We will go right to the top by examining the idea sources of William Shakespeare. Table 6.1 presents a shortened version of a complete list of Shakespeare's plays and their idea sources that appear in the *World Book Encyclopedia*. The left column lists some of his better-known plays; the right column identifies the source from which

TABLE 6.1 Idea Sources of Shakespeare (Abridged from the *World Book Encyclopedia*)

PLAY	SOURCE
Taming of the Shrew	Taming of the Shrew (unknown English playwright)
Romeo and Juliet	Romeo and Juliet (poem by Arthur Brooke)
Merchant of Venice	Il Pecorone (short story by Giovanni Fiorentino)
Julius Caesar	A tragedy from Plutarch's Lives
Much Ado About Nothing	Orlando Furioso (comedy by Ludovico Ariosto)
Twelfth Night	Farwell to the Military Profession (short story by Barnabe Riche)
Hamlet	Hamlet (play by unknown English author) and Histories Tragiques (Francois Belleforest)
All's Well That Ends Well	The Palace of Pleasure (short story by unknown author)
Othello	Promos and Cassandra (play by George Whetstone)
King Lear	The Union of Two Noble and Illustrious Families of Lancaster and York (by Edward Hall, historian) and Holinshed's Chronicles (sixteenth-century history book)
Macbeth	Holinshed's Chronicles
Antony and Cleopatra	Plutarch's Lives

he apparently derived the characters, settings, and main plots. While the Big Idea for each play has been traced, the character development, dramatic conflicts and tension, humor, and so on are creative beyond description. It is the elaboration and development stage of creativity that appears to be the most mysterious and intriguing process and one that sets Shakespeare apart from mortal bards.[2]

Many movies, TV dramas, and Broadway plays continue to be inspired by or based upon recognizable events and idea sources. The following is a small sample.

From contemporary events: *All the President's Men* (from Watergate), *In Cold Blood* (a mid-west murder), *High Noon* (inspired by senate investigations of organized crime in Hollywood), *Killing Fields* (Cambodian holocaust), and according to some, James Cameron's *Aliens* is metaphorically related to the Vietnam war.

From history: *The Longest Day, From Here to Eternity, Tora! Tora! Tora!, Pearl Harbor, Voyage of the Damned, Saving Private Ryan, The Pianist, Darkest Hour, Dunkirk* (all from the Second World War); *Gone With the Wind, Red Badge of Courage* (Civil War); *I, Claudius; Cleopatra; Ben Hur; Salamis* (Roman, Egyptian, Greek history); *Les Miserables, A Tale of Two Cities,* and *Marie Antoinette* (French history).

From biographies: *Citizen Kane* (life of San Francisco newspaperman William Randolph Hearst); *El Cid* (legendary Spanish hero); *Edison, the Man; Patton; The Miracle Worker* (Helen Keller); *Elephant Man* (story of John Merrick); *Gandhi; Bird Man of Alcatraz; Three Faces of Eve; I'll Cry Tomorrow* (Lillian Roth); *When We Were Kings* (athletes); *Evita; Shine* (story of pianist David Helfgott), *Leadership in Turbulent Times* (Abraham Lincoln); *My Own Words* (Ruth Bader Ginsburg); and *Alexander Hamilton* by Ron Chernow, which served as the inspiration for Lin Manuel Miranda's sold-out Broadway adaptation, which people need a loan from the treasury department to get tickets. #notthrowingawaymyshot

From the Bible: *Ten Commandments; David the King; Jesus Christ, Superstar; Moses.*

From classic and contemporary literature: *Dr. Jekyll and Mr. Hyde, Ivanhoe, David Copperfield, Alice in Wonderland, Wizard of Oz, Jane Eyre, For Whom the Bell Tolls, To Kill a Mockingbird, Tale of Two Cities, Castaway* (Robinson Crusoe), *Spiderman series, Superman series, Batman series, Lord of the Rings series, Harry Potter series.*

From mythology, legend, supernatural: creature features, including *Love at First Bite, American Werewolf in London,* and *Teen Wolf* (both the Michael J. Fox movie AND the recent MTV adaptation); *Three Musketeers; Harry and the Hendersons* (Sasquatch, and HBO's *True Blood*).

What are some other movies, TV shows, or Broadway shows "inspired by" specific sources?

Architecture, Clothes Design

These two unrelated topics are lumped together because they both can make use of the same analogical strategy for finding ideas. Want to design a creative home? Ideas for a unique wardrobe? Try thinking about other countries and other times. Visit a museum, look at pictures in history books, or flip through encyclopedias. Do you think you could find a few hundred inspirations from Mexico, China, Holland, Greece, Ancient Egypt, Peru, Africa, Switzerland, America's pilgrims, Atlanta in 1855, Disneyland, the roaring 1920s, rural America, other places and times? Of course you could.

Professional designers have stacks of books and magazines filled with ideas waiting to be modified and applied. The castles at Disneyland and Disney World were inspired by the Neuschwanstein castle near Fussen, Germany. Frank Lloyd Wright used Viennese, Japanese, and Aztec designs in his architecture. Frank was reasonably successful.

---

[2] Example of "seeing a connection" in humor: Did you know that Shakespeare's mother was an Avon lady?

Analogical Thinking in Problem Solving

Unless you have a clearly convergent problem with one and only one correct answer (e.g., an arithmetic problem, "Where's my dog?" or "Whose picture is on the fifty?"), creativity can be involved in every step of problem-solving. The CPS model in Chapter 5 illustrated how creativity can help clarify a problem (fact-finding stage), define the problem (problem-finding), list solution alternatives (idea-finding), evaluate ideas (solution-finding), and implement the solution(s) (acceptance-finding). We'll have you apply this theory more in Chapter 8.

The most obvious use of analogical thinking in the CPS model is in the idea-finding process. Consider a problem such as "How can we get more parents to the school play?" One could find ideas by asking questions that stimulate analogical thinking, such as the ones listed below.

What else is like this?
What have others done?
What could we copy?
What has worked before?
What would professionals do?

Such questions elicit deliberate analogical thinking. Analogical ideas also will occur spontaneously—"Say, Benedict Arnold High School got free newspaper and radio advertising. John Wilkes Booth High held a raffle with the admission ticket—community businesses donated tons of prizes!"

Incidentally, two of the above five questions appear in Osborn's checklist "73 List Spurring Questions" (see Chapter 8). That checklist encourages analogical thinking for finding ideas and problem solutions.

With that in mind, Krumnack, Kühnberger, Schwering, and Besold (2013) examined analogical reasoning in invention and noted that "an analogy is usually considered as a structural mapping between a source (base) and a target domain. To establish an analogy, common substructure of the two domains are identified and mapped to each other" (p. 56). They continue, "analogies are usually NOT judged right or wrong, rather they can be more or less plausible, based on the degree of structural coherence that they exhibit" (p. 56). Building upon this, Gassmann and Zeschky (2008) stated that "analogies can be drawn in different settings and directions. In some cases, a solution is found in one industry and applied to solve a problem in a different industry" (p. 98). This is the example that they use when describing how the BMW corporation used joystick technology from the video game industry (non-automotive domain) to build their *iDrive* device, which reduced clutter on your dashboard (reducing knobs, dials, bells, and whistles) and helped them create the ultimate driving machine. Though this technology was far from new, (pardon my German) the analogical transfer brought Fehrvergnugen (and driving pleasure) to millions!

But the Creative Problem-Solving method isn't the only systematic approach to applying analogies to inventive problem-solving. A Russian inventor named Renrikh Saulovich Altshuller developed the *"Teorija Reschenija Izobretatel'skich Zadac"* method (shortened to TRIZ), which in English translates to "Theory of Inventive Problem-Solving." In building his theory, Altshuller scrutinized design patents from a myriad of industries to try and find common patterns and principles that could be prove useful in problem-solving. A guiding principle of this theory is that patterns of technical knowledge and product evolution are repeated across varying disciplines, field, and industries (Barry, Domb, & Slocum, 2010). In describing this unique feature of TRIZ, Orloff (2003) described this as "condensing the experience gathered from the best solutions into concrete rules" (p. 2) and using past successes to help guide current problem-solving. In TRIZ, the specific problem that you are trying to solve is abstracted to a higher level, in which you try and find commonalities or evidences in other domains as to how others have approached your problem before. Therefore, creativity (in this regard) is finding a solution that already exists and fashioning it to your own problem state. Applications of TRIZ to various STEM-based fields are numerous (Cascini & Rissone, 2004; Kim, Kim, Lee, Lim, & Moon, 2009; Yang & Chen, 2011).

Synectics Methods

The word *synectics* is from the Greek *syn*, meaning *together*, along with *-ectics*, which was arbitrarily selected (Prince, 1982). Synectics is "the joining together of different and apparently irrelevant elements" (Gordon & Poze, 1980a, 1980b). The synectics methods are conscious, analogy-based, and metaphor-based techniques for bringing together these different elements. The originator of the synectics methods is William J. J. Gordon, former school teacher, horse handler, salvage diver, ambulance driver, ski instructor, sailing schooner master, college lecturer, and pig breeder. The outcome of the pig project was "a lot of bone and not much bacon, but they were the fastest pigs in the East" (Alexander, 1978). Gordon and his colleagues hold more than 200 patents. Their creative writing, published in the *New Yorker* and *Atlantic Monthly*, won them an O. Henry Short Story Award and a Science Fiction Award. A few examples of synectics inventions are Pringles Potato Chips, a trash compactor, the electric knife, an early space suit closure device for NASA, a space feeding system, a space-saver Kleenex box, disposable diapers, a disposable baby bottle with formula, an ice cube maker, a jet marine engine, a Ford truck frame suspension system, an accelerated wound-healing system, operating table covers, Sunoco's dial-your-own-octane gas pump (now deceased), and the presumably similar automatic liquor dispenser.

Gordon's early experience with creative thinking groups helped him to identify analogical thinking strategies that creative people use spontaneously. He clarified these strategies, making them conscious and teachable in a form for adults (e.g., Gordon, 1961; Prince, 1968) and for children. Said Gordon (Gordon & Poze, 1980b), "Everyone, to some degree or another, consciously or unconsciously uses analogies to solve problems. The purpose of . . . synectics is to give you a way to use analogies that will make your problem-solving process more effective." In agreement, former synectics colleague George Prince (1968) observed that the procedures "help you think unhabitually." Gordon's workbooks and exercise books *Making It Strange* (Gordon, 1974a), *New Art of the Possible* (Gordon & Poze, 1980b), *Metaphorical Way of Learning and Knowing* (Gordon & Poze, 1971), *Teaching Is Listening* (Gordon & Poze, 1972a), and *Strange and Familiar* (Gordon & Poze, 1972b) give children first-hand experience with the fascinating synectics problem-solving methods of *direct analogy*, *personal analogy*, *fantasy analogy*, and *symbolic analogy*. Let's take a look at them one by one.

Direct Analogy

With the *direct analogy* method, the problem-solver is asked to think of ways that related problems have been solved. While analogies of any sort are welcome, those from nature are especially encouraged. How have animals, birds, flowers, insects, worms, snakes, and so on solved similar problems? Gordon and Poze (1980b), for example, speculate that civilization itself progressed when individuals made analogical connections—seeing that this situation is like that situation. Imagine a starving cave person unsuccessfully trying to spear fish with a sharp stick. There are fish all over the place, but the cave person cannot stab enough to feed family and friends. Cave person sees a small swarm of flies become entrapped in a spider's web. Aha! Cave person makes an analogical connection, dashes back to the group, dumps the neighbor out of a hammock, and uses the hammock to net fish by the dozens. Another primitive has trouble keeping his pants up, and a snake wrapped around a rock suggested the first belt (Gordon & Poze, 1972b). When his socks kept falling down, a little garter snake suggested a similar solution.

Gordon himself was part of an emergency group faced with removing a sunken ship that blocked the Tripoli harbor during the Second World War. An army colonel imagined his mother vigorously raking away at dirt lumps in her garden, which suggested blasting the offending ship to smithereens and then "raking" it level just as mother did. It worked.

In one synectics session, the problem was to package potato chips compactly, without breaking them, and to reduce shipping costs. Wet leaves—which pack snugly together without breaking—led to Pringles Potato Chips. Magnesium-impregnated bandages that sped up the healing of wounds came from the analogy of a broken electrical wire—one must restore transmission across the damaged gap (Gordon & Poze, 1980b).

Virtually any sort of problem can be attacked with the direct analogy method. For example, in a University of Wisconsin creativity workshop for retired people many expressed concern for their personal safety. With the direct analogy approach the problem became: How do animals, plants, birds, and so on protect themselves, and how can these ideas help the elderly?[3] The idea list included spray cans of skunk scent, slip-on fangs and claws, a compressed air can that screams when activated, a snake-faced mask that scares the bejeebers out of potential muggers, an electronic device that secretly "yells" for the police, traveling only in groups, and camouflage or disguises, for example, wearing a police uniform.

Personal Analogy

Imagine you are a dum-dum sucker. You are sitting quietly in a large jar with all of your assorted flavored friends on the counter of a doctor's office or hair salon. All of a sudden, a little boy peers in and with his grubby hands reaches in and grasps for you. How do you feel? What are your thoughts? You notice that the little boy's nose is running and he sniffles a lot (presumably why he was at the doctor?!). How do you feel about your immediate future?

With the *personal analogy* method, the thinker achieves new perspectives on a problem by imaginatively becoming part of that problem. What would you be like if you were a dazzling dinner for important friends? Or a really efficient floor mop? If you were a check-book or thumb drive, how could you avoid becoming lost? (side note, does anyone even write checks anymore?)

In one synectics problem-solving session, the group members (intelligent adults) imagined themselves to be rapidly multiplying viruses, tiny and crowded, in order to shed light on the problem of getting an accurate sample of oil-saturated rock from under a reservoir (Gordon, 1961). Said one person, "I feel I am a very successful virus. With the way these other guys feel, I can sit back and relax, enjoy life, and play a guitar. One is going to take care of reproducing and one killing. Why should I worry?" Responded another, "I resent his playing his guitar while I'm panicky!" The eventual solution stemmed from "calming the oil down by stroking it like a cat," which led to freezing the gooey sample with liquid nitrogen so it could be brought to the surface intact.

As we will see in Chapter 8, Einstein used the personal analogy method when he imagined himself on a speed-of-light trip through space, which contributed to his theory of relativity.

Imagining yourself to be a problem object or process should stimulate an inside view of the situation—and some new ideas while you are there. What would you be like if you were an extremely efficient racing bike? Leaf rake? Flashlight? Ski parka? Snow blower/remover?

Fantasy Analogy

With the *fantasy analogy* approach the problem-solver thinks of fantastic, far-fetched, perhaps ideal solutions that can lead to creative yet practical ideas. Gordon (1961) saw this method as a sort of Freudian wish fulfillment. In one of his sessions, the task was to invent an air-tight zipper for space suits. In response to the question, "How do we in our wildest fantasies desire the closure to operate?" (Gordon, 1961, p. 49), group members imagined two rows of insects clasping hands on command to draw the closure tight. This fantasy led to a workable device.

An almost tongue-in-cheek strategy that appears to be a variation of the fantasy analogy method was called the *Get Fired Technique*. As described by synectics thinker George Prince (1968), "The idea you develop must be so outrageous and such a violation of common sense and company policy that when you present it to your boss he will immediately fire you" (p. 73). In the example accompanying this quote the problem was to "Devise a liquid cake icing that will firm up when released from a can." The get-fired idea was: "I am going to hire out-of-work West Virginia coal miners—very small ones—and put one in each can. When the person presses the valve, the miner goes to work!" The craziness stimulates the playfulness that facilitates creative thinking (Prince, 1968).

---

[3] The author is indebted to Jean Romaniuk for suggesting this problem.

The fantasy analogy method includes looking for ideal or perfect solutions, such as asking how the problem can solve itself. Years ago some creative people probably asked: How can we make a carriage propel itself? How can we create a magic drain that will make bones and waste disappear? (Prince, 1982). Consider also: How can we make a refrigerator defrost itself? How can we create a fabric that eliminates ironing? How can we make an oven clean itself? How can we make a forgotten iron shut itself off? Plug-in engine diagnosers probably came from, "How can we make the motor tell us what's wrong?"

Teachers might pose such questions as: "How can we get the School Board to *want* to give us a new basketball floor? How can we get the hallways to keep themselves free of litter? How can we get delinquents to want to be honest citizens?" People in business can ask, "How can we make the product double its own sales?" "How can we have employees raise their own morale?" "What will the ideal kitchen (bathroom, family room, garage) be like in the future?" Will we even cook? Will all our recommended daily allowance of nutrients be downloadable?

This strategy of looking for perfect, fantastic solutions builds upon the time-tested problem-solving method of working backward from an ideal goal—thinking of what you ideally want, then figuring out how to reach that goal.

Symbolic Analogy

A fourth synectics technique is called *symbolic analogy*; other names are *compressed conflict* and *book titles*. Your dictionary will call them *oxymoron*. The strategy is to think of a two-word phrase or "book title" that seems self-contradictory, such as "careful haste" or "gentle toughness." The compressed conflict would relate to a particular problem and would stimulate ideas. For example, the phrase "careful haste" might be used by educators or fire fighters to stimulate ideas for quickly and safely evacuating a large school building. "Gentle toughness" might stimulate ideas for designing automobile tires, durable fabrics, or long-distance bicycles.

In one zany synectics session, the problem of designing an ice cube maker led to the problem restatement, "How [can we] make an ice tray disappear after ice is made." This definition suggested the analogy of a boy breaking a window—after which he disappears (Prince, 1968). Book titles for boy-breaks-window included *healthful destruction*, *right wrongness*, *intelligent mistake*, and *rational impetuousness*. Speculating on examples of rational impetuousness led to an electric eel, which rationally defends itself by impetuously shocking enemies, and from the eel to a material that would shrink at about 20 degrees—that is, after the water is frozen—and free the ice cubes, which are mechanically dumped.

Gordon and Poze (1980b) presented some practice problems to help you create and use paradoxes. For example: Imagine you have a littering problem in your school or company, even though there are plenty of trash barrels around. What are some book titles? What examples do the book titles suggest? Do the examples suggest some creative solutions?

An exercise from a synectics workbook, *Teaching Is Listening* by Gordon and Poze (1972a), includes a direct analogy, a personal analogy, and illustrates how a symbolic analogy can stimulate ideas:

1. What animal typifies your concept of freedom? (Direct analogy)

   _____

2. Put yourself in the place of the animal you have chosen. Be the thing! Describe what makes you feel and act with so much freedom. (Personal analogy)

   _____

   _____

   _____

3. Sum up your description of the animal you chose by listing the "free" and "unfree" parts of your animal life.

Free: _____

_____

Unfree: _____

_____

4. Express each of these parts of your life in a single word. Put together these two words and refine them into a poetic, compressed conflict phrase.

_____   _____

_____   _____

_____   _____

5. Circle the phrase you like best. Write an essay about freedom. Use any material you may have developed in this exercise.

Gordon's Equation Form of Synectics

In his book *The New Art of the Possible*, Gordon (1987) sought to teach the use of analogies in creative problem-solving by using an equation. The four steps take the form of an analogy that one might find in an intelligence test or thinking skills exercises:

$$\frac{\text{Step 1. Paradox}}{\text{Step 2. Analogue}} = \frac{\text{Step 4. (Equivalent)}}{\text{Step 3. Unique Function}}$$

As an example, let's consider a product improvement problem described by Gendrop (1996), who worked with Gordon. Step 1, the problem or issue (stated as a *paradox*) was that the more management encouraged product improvement ideas from sales people, the fewer ideas the salespeople submitted. The Step 2 *analogue* was quicksand. The Step 3 *unique function* was stated as "viscous material with a base molds to the body and creates a suction." The Step 4 *equivalent*—the relationship of the analogue to the paradox—was to give sales people a "solid base" that would encourage ideas instead of sales. To change the focus from sales to ideas, a solution was to release one sales person per month to work on product improvement.

Teaching Synectics Thinking

For students and adults, the synectics methods themselves can be material for lessons on (a) creative thinking techniques, (b) the nature of the creative process, and (c) the importance of analogical thinking in creativity. For students of all ages, including professional adults, Gordon and his colleagues have published workbooks and text books filled with exercises aimed at strengthening skills of analogical thinking and aimed at helping the reader understand the creative power of analogical thinking. The following are similar to exercises in Gordon (1974a), Gordon and Poze (1971, 1972a, 1972b, 1980b), Stanish (1977), and Davis (1996a).

What animal is like a bass fiddle? Why?

A hamburger is like a _____ because _____

How is a jar of paste like a school bell?

Which is stronger, a brick wall or a young tree? Why?

Which is heaviest, a boulder or a sad heart? Why?

What color is sadness? Why?

In what ways can coolness be seen?

In what ways can softness be heard?

What is another sound like a dog's bark?

How is life like a flashlight battery?

Which grows faster, your self-confidence or an oak tree?

What could have given a cave dweller the idea for a spear? What was the connection?

A parachute is like what animal? Why?

Why is a calendar like a mirror?

What would it be like to be inside a lemon?

If you were a pencil, how would it feel to get sharpened? To get chewed on? To get worn down to a stub?

When you are happy you are like a _____.

When you are busy you are like a _____.

How is someone who steals like a hungry shark?

How is vandalizing like sticking your finger in a light socket?

How is a friendly, helpful person like a hot fudge sundae?

How is a good education like a good dream?

How is an iceberg like a creative idea?

If a classroom were a lawn, what would the weeds be? How do the weeds affect the rest of the class?

If you doubt whether any of these analogical thinking and synectics strategies will work, there is current research supporting the use of this approach. A study by Gendrop (1996) showed that nurses who were trained in synectics enhanced their creative abilities. Aiamy and Haghani (2012) found that third-grade students who were taught science in a synectics framework had greater scores on divergent thinking tests and approached STEM-based problems more creatively. As Joyce, Weil, and Calhoun (2004) identified, the synectics approach can be utilized to make the familiar strange, or help students see old problems, ideas, or products in a new, more creative light. This *defamiliarization* aspect of synectics can break up rigid and regimented problem-solving techniques and give individuals a fresh lens or vantage point to view or visualize or revisit a problem state.

Analogical and metaphorical thinking lie at the core of much creativity. Furthermore, it may be possible to teach analogical thinking strategies, such as the synectics methods of direct analogy, personal analogy, fantasy analogy, and symbolic analogy, or to otherwise strengthen skills of analogical thinking through practice.

Summary

Most creative ideas are in some way born in analogical or metaphorical thinking. One sees a similarity or makes a connection between the present problem and a related situation. The credits "was inspired by" and "is based upon" imply an analogical or metaphoric source for the artistic, literary, scientific, or technological innovation.

The analogical connection may appear suddenly, as in an insight, or require a painstaking search.

Borrowing and transferring ideas usually is a genuine and legitimate creative process, not plagiarism. However, there are ambiguous cases.

Analogical and metaphorical thinking appear most obviously in the Big-Idea stage of the two-stage model described in Chapter 5.

Many classical and contemporary music composers have used existing tunes as the basis of their compositions (e.g., Tchaikovsky, Copland, Barry Manilow).

The seemingly funniest political cartoons and cartoon strips are analogically based upon popular movies, well-known TV advertisements, children's stories, news events, and other sources.

Dunbar identified three different types of analogical connections: local, regional, and long-distance.

Examples of analogical thinking in science and invention included Gutenberg's movable type and printing press, the battery, the steam engine, a strategy for building underwater tunnels, the cotton gin, and the air brake.

Shakespeare's Big Ideas apparently came from identifiable sources. Countless movies and TV shows have been "inspired by" contemporary and historical events, biographies, the Bible, classic and contemporary literature, mythology and legend, and in the case of *Moonlighting*, even holidays.

Ideas for architecture and clothes design may be borrowed from other countries and other times. Professional designers in many areas consult books and journals for ideas.

In problem-solving one can use analogical thinking to stimulate ideas by asking such questions as: What else is like this? What have others done? What could we copy?

Gassmann and Zeschky drove off with the idea that a solution in one industry can be applied to another.

TRIZ is a theory of inventive problem-solving that examines how patterns and principles that have been used to solve previous problems can be applied to current situations—creativity is just finding the link between what has been done and what needs to be done!

Synectics methods are deliberate analogical thinking techniques developed by William J. J. Gordon. He made some spontaneous (unconscious) techniques conscious and teachable.

With direct analogy, the thinker looks for ways that related problems have been solved, especially in nature.

With personal analogy one achieves new perspectives by becoming part of the problem.

Fantasy analogy is a wild wish-fulfillment approach, including looking for ideal or perfect solutions. Prince's "get fired" technique seems a variation of fantasy analogy.

Symbolic analogy is using two-word compressed conflicts to stimulate ideas.

In a 1987 book, Gordon recommended the use of a four-step equation for using analogical thinking in problem-solving: 1. Paradox, 2. Analogue, 3. Unique Function, and 4. Equivalent (the solution).

Teaching the synectics methods themselves helps the learner to understand creative thinking techniques, the nature of the creative process, and the importance of analogical thinking. Exercises may strengthen analogical thinking abilities.

Synectics is a process of making the familiar strange.

Analogical and metaphorical thinking are extremely important in creativity.

Review Exercises

Creative Inspiration and Analogical Thinking

Self-Test: Key Concepts, Terms, and Names

Briefly define, explain, or give examples of each of these.

Importance of Analogical thinking

_____

_____

Analogical thinking in creative innovation

_____

_____

Analogical thinking in problem solving

_____

_____

Triz Method

_____

_____

Direct analogy

_____

_____

Personal analogy

_____

_____

Fantasy analogy

_____

_____

Symbolic analogy

_____

_____

Synectics Methods (Gordon)

_____

_____

Let's Think about It

1. Lets ponder the question "Is Borrowing Ideas Ethical".

In the spaces below, write three reasons that you feel would compellingly support the use of analogical or metaphorical thinking in the act of creativity

a. _____

b. _____

c. _____

Now for the counter argument. Come up with three reasons why some individuals might argue that the borrowing or stealing of ideas should not be permitted.

d. _____

e. _____

f. _____

Finally, look at the arguments and counter-arguments you've developed. Which side do you take?

2. Look at the cartoon exercises in Inset 6.1. Glance through the first (serious) section, Situations in Which to Use Characters and Ideas. Find two or three you would like to parody. Then look through the second section, Source of Characters and Ideas, to find amusing ways to satirize the serious idea or problem.

Situation 1.

Cartoon idea.

_____

_____

_____

Situation 2.

Cartoon idea.

_____

_____

_____

Situation 3.

Cartoon idea.

_____

_____

_____

3. Now, pick one of the situations you identified and draw your cartoon in the space below:

(blank drawing box)

4. Use the direct analogy strategy to think of ideas for removing three inches of water from your basement floor. That is, ask "How do plants, animals, or other phenomena in nature move water from here to there?"

_____

_____

_____

5. Use the *personal analogy* method to help you think of ideas for encouraging elementary children to finish their cafeteria lunches—and not waste food. (E.g., ask "What would I be like if I were a lunch that was always 100 percent eaten?" Or "What would my attitude or personality be if I were a kid that always finished his or her lunch?" Or "What kind of cafeteria would I be if I STRONGLY encouraged kids to finish their lunches?")

_____

_____

_____

_____

6. Use the *fantasy analogy* method to think of ideas for improving school attendance ("What in my wildest imagination would make kids hate to miss school?")

_____

_____

_____

_____

7. How might you use the *symbolic analogy* "cheap luxury" to help you find ideas for taking a trip to Yellowstone Park with equally poor college friends?

_____

_____

_____

_____

8. You work for an advertising agency. Your boss wants you to come up with some GREAT advertising ideas (Magazine, Newspaper, TV, Internet, Social Media Applications) for *AT-Verisprin Mobile Technologies*, which just produced a new low- priced, super-fast cell phone with a gigantic memory, fantastic camera, and an unparalled 6G network. What would you call this phone? What would the tagline of the company or product be?

a. How would you use analogical thinking to find terrific ideas? That is, without outright stealing, how might you borrow, modify, or build on others successful advertising ideas to build your campaign?

_____

_____

_____

7 Creative Products

"If I am worth anything later, I am worth something now. For wheat is wheat, even if people think it is a grass in the beginning."

—*Vincent van Gogh*

We see Van Gogh's Starry Night as a product of creativity now, but in his lifetime he was considered mentally unstable. What constitutes a "creative product," and is the definition fluid?

One can easily argue that any result of the creative process, whether tangible or not, is a product.

While the process and the passion behind it are critical, the final product itself is the thing that sparks change.

Van Gogh believed that it doesn't matter if an idea or set of ideas is initially deemed ridiculous or misunderstood, for a product's worth is not diminished simply because no one currently acknowledges it. However, most believe that creativity is justified by "creative achievements . . . that are recognized by others" (Sordia, Martskvishvili, & Neubauer, 2019).

Van Gogh's paintings were not recognized as genius until long after his death, but the paintings themselves never changed—only people's perception of them. The products produced by people over time have varied widely in both type and purpose, as have their reception and recognition.

The definition of "creative product" may not be so straightforward.

Up until now, we have examined traits and characteristics of creative individuals, and explored models, steps, and sequences involved in the creative process, but ultimately, the "product" or end result of multiplicative efforts in these domains is the creative product itself. What is created. But that statement could just as easily be rephrased. Add some capital letters and italics for emphasis and in true Jeopardy fashion ask it in the form of a question. What *IS* created? Do you think Ken Jennings has a clue? This chapter will seek answers and explore conceptualizations to that question as we dive into the facets and features of the creative product, and how creations can be shaped, scrutinized, molded, and modified

Creative Product: A Definition

All Rhodes Lead to Creativity

In his influential article, Mel Rhodes (1961) wrote about creative products in this way. A creative product ". . . refers to (something) which has been communicated to other people in the form of *words*, *paint*, *clay*, *metal*, *stone*, *fabric*, or other material. When we speak of an original idea, we imply a degree of newness in the concept. When an idea become embodied into tangible form it is called a product . . . products are artifacts of thoughts" (p. 309). We'll come back to that word artifact as it pertains to creative products at the conclusion of the chapter, but we can explore examples of each of the domains that Rhodes alluded to as a way of putting creative products into perspective.

From a words standpoint, "Shall I compare thee to a Summer's Day? Thou art more lovely and more temperate" (Shakespeare, 2012). While it might be true that truer words were never spoken, and that many vows, proposals, PROMposals (and when did THAT become a thing), and wedding ceremonies are built around the classic sonnet 18, how does to stanza compare to the millions of others extant in literature anthologies. Is it a preeminent example of a creative product?

Creative Products Make an Impression(ist)?

A perspective on creative products from painting can be drawn from Claude Monet's Impressionist classic "Poppy Fields near Argenteuil," prominently displayed in the Musee d'Orsay in Paris. But versions of this painting can also be found held up with magnets on refrigerators or with thumbtacks in dorm rooms as you can buy a paint-by-numbers watercolor kit and try your own hand at this piece of art. Do those kits and subsequent attempts at recreating a masterpiece represent creative products?

One of the most famous actors to come out of the long-running Saturday Night Live sketch series isn't Will Ferrell or Bill Murray. Rather, it's another Bill. Mr. Bill to be precise, a clay figurine clown that was the brainchild of Walter Williams. Mr. Bill first appeared in 1976 and continuously faced peril at the hand of Mr. Hands. While many of you were not around in the mid-1970's, no doubt you have seen the exploits of Mr. Bill on YouTube or via some vicious .gif sent to you by the owner of a rival fantasy football team after the dismemberment of your squad. His blue jeans, red shirt, and classic open-mouthed expression live on in our "meme"ories, but is Mr. Bill creative? And what is his role in inspiring Kenny from South Park, and other cartoon characters (Wile E Coyote?) who met ominous and continuous fates.

Truth, Justice, and the Sumerian Way of Creativity

For metal and stone examples, look no further than the Sumerians. Glassner and Herron (2003) attribute the invention one of the earliest forms of communication (pictographs) to this ancient Mesopotamian civilization. Their efforts to draw pictures and images onto stone developed into a formal writing system called cuneiform. Early cuneiform artifacts fetch a pretty penny on the auction market. And with pennies in mind, the Sumerians were credited with being one of the very first users of the non-precious metal copper (Frankfort, 1928). They figured out how to extract and work with this material, developing early copper fabrication skills that allowed them to craft arrowheads, jugs, and other vessels from this metal. But, while their arrows might have been "on point," do you consider their contributions or products creative? Think about that next time you take a sip of your Moscow Mule from a copper cup.

Creativity Influencer

And from fabrication to fabrics, famous designer Gianni Versace once said, "Don't be into trends. Don't make fashion own you, but decide what you are, what you want to express by the way you dress and the way to live." We live in a day and time in which the fabrics we wear are influenced by influencers. People who portray a sense of style along with a glamorous lifestyle via social media platforms such as Instagram. Can their looks be considered creative? Is creativity in this sense based on the number of looks (views) or likes one gets on Facebook? What about all of the copycat trends this inspires.

Transitioning from paint, stone, clay, and fabrics back to the original "source material," Rhodes (1961) expands upon his view of the creative product, noting that "a system is needed for classifying products according to the scope of newness . . . theories such as relativity or electromagnetic waves or mechanical flight are of tremendous scope. From any one of those theories thousands of inventions may germinate. Therefore, **ideas in theory** are of higher order in the scale of creativity than **ideas for inventions**. After inventions appear, numerous innovations or new twists in design or structure are suggested by users. Thus, the idea for an invention is of higher order in the scale of creativity than an idea for an innovation to an existing invention. The significance of this suggestion to classify ideas by degree of newness is that it would place emphasis on higher mental processes rather than on dazzling objects" (p. 309).

And there you have it. The very first classification system in the sorting and ranking of products, ideas, inventions, and subsequent spin-offs. But this call to action caused others to weigh-in as well, prompting measures, models, and metrics about the nature of the creative product and the weighing of creative contributions that we will start to preview and profile.

Essential Characteristics of Creative Products

Let's start with MacKinnon's (1999) view of the creative product. He stated that "the starting point, indeed the bedrock of all studies of creativity, is an analysis of creative products, a determination of what it is that makes them different from more mundane products" (p. 125). So if creative products are indeed the bedrock of creativity studies, there have to be some terms that give us a firm foothold on exactly how this can be conceived. With that in mind, MacKinnon went on to state and formally identify what he thought were the five essential characteristics inherent to those products deemed creative.

New or Novel?

The first that he listed is *novelty* in that the product or idea is original. But MacKinnon went on to note that "novelty and originality need further specification. Within what frame of reference or range of experience is the product original . . . thus the creativeness of a product when judged in terms of novelty, originality, or statistical infrequence is always relative to a given population of products" (p. 126).

Creativity P-H Balanced?

This notion was picked up by Boden (1999), who in her discussion of novelty, makes a clear differentiation between psychological novelty (P-creative) and historical novelty (H-creative). She stated that a "P-creative idea is one that's new to the person who generated it. It doesn't matter how many times, if any, other people have that idea before" (p. 352). In contrast, a "H-creative idea is one that is P-creative AND has never occurred in history before" (p. 352). P-creative is always present in H-creative and H-creative supersedes P-creative. How many times have YOU had a great idea for a product invention only to find out that someone beat you to the punch (or patent)? That's the difference between P-creativity and H-creativity.

The inclusion of novelty in the describing creative products is (ironically) NOT novel. Over a half-century ago, Morgan (1953) demonstrated through an exhaustive search of variety of creativity definitions that the most common element in all of them *WAS* novelty. Stein (1953) builds upon this, by noting that:

"The creative work is a novel work that is accepted as tenable or useful or satisfying by a group in some point in time. . . . By "novel" I mean that the creative product did not exist previously in precisely the same form. . . . The extent to which a work is novel depends on the extent to which it deviates from the traditional or the status quo. This may well depend on the nature of the problem that is attacked, the fund of knowledge or experience that exists in the field at the time, and the characteristics of the creative individual and those of the individuals with whom he [or she] is communicating." (pp. 311–312)

Apt to be Adaptive

In defining the novelty aspects of the creative product, Stein also opens the door to MacKinnon's second identified characteristic: **adaptive** to reality. MacKinnon states that "mere novelty of a product does not, however, justify its being called creative. There is a second requirement, namely, that the product be adaptive to reality. In other words, it must serve to solve a problem, fit the needs of a given situation, or accomplish some recognizable goal" (p. 126).

In putting forth the standard definition of creativity that serves as a contemporary guide for many creativity theorists and researchers, Runco and Jaeger (2012) agree with MacKinnon and state that "originality is not alone sufficient for creativity. Original things must be *effective* to be creative. Like originality, effectiveness takes various forms. It may take the form of (and be labeled as) *usefulness, fit, or appropriateness*" (p. 92). With usefulness in mind, value Beghetto (2005) states that "creativity requires novelty and usefulness. Recognizing that creativity requires both attributes cannot be understated. Creativity often is viewed as simply that which is unique, out of the ordinary, bizarre, or even deviant. Without the additional criterion of usefulness, creativity quickly can become a euphemism for negative, undesirable traits" (p. 256)

So now we have three synonyms for the adaptive nature of the creative product. How many more can you think of that would serve to fulfill the tenants listed in the last sentence of MacKinnon's definition? List a few more here:

_____

_____

_____

Now look back at your list. Do you agree with the "value" of including aspects of usefulness, fit, effectiveness, and appropriateness into the conceptualization of creative products? Not all theorists do.

The CAT is out of the Bag

Weisberg (2015) weighs in on the "value" of usefulness in the definition of creativity, noting that nearly all theories or conceptualizations of creative products include mention of usefulness or a close correlate in their definition. However, he voices concern over this, with a chief complaint being that "value" is a subjective judgment contingent on aspects of ones' standing in the field, societal factors, or mere serendipity (right place, right time!). While not specifically mentioned, this seemingly might be in reaction to Amabile's (1982) Consensual Assessment Technique, which seeks to operationalize creative assessment methodologies. Amabile summarizes this viewpoint by stating that "a product or response is creative to the extent that appropriate observers independently agree it is creative. Appropriate observers are those familiar with the domain in which the product was created or the response articulated. Thus, creativity can be regarded as the quality of products or responses judged to be creative by appropriate observers, and it can also be regarded as the process by which something so judged is produced" (p. 1001).

For the fashion designer who was under the "Gunn" to create a dress that ultimately falls flat on the (project) Runway, they might disagree with (so-called) expert opinions on their creation. Maybe the trend is too new. Perhaps the hem-line is trending in that direction, but the field isn't ready for that yet (more on that in a minute). Even if they get the Klum and Doom phrase of "YOU'RE OUT" does that really mean what they fashioned isn't creative? That's why Weisberg (2015) includes as the second requirement of a creative product his notion of intentionality. In this view, any novel product is creative, regardless of whether it is ever of value to anyone.

Which one of these viewpoints regarding the inclusion of usefulness in the definition of creative products you "judge" to be the most correct? If put on the stand, where do you stand? It's "plaintiff" see that there are certainly differences, perhaps irreconcilable ones! Verdict? Perhaps it's a hung jury. Before we declare a mistrial, let's move on to the next characteristic MacKinnon identified, which is actually rooted in the last word of the Amabile (witness) statement.

Apt to be Adaptive

Did you look back up to see what it was? If so, you probably "produced" the answer. As MacKinnon states, "a third requirement that a fully creative product must meet is that the insightful reorganization which underlies it be sustained, evaluated, elaborated, developed, and communicated to other—in other words, the creative product must be ***produced***" (p. 126).

Rollo May's (1994) iconic quote that creativity is "bringing something new into being" certainly applies here. The end-state of an idea state that is now in an extant state. The genesis of creation. From the physical act of making or manu-facturing a model or prototype to the in-tellectual enactment of an idea or plan of action, the general gist is that the creative product now has taken a life of its own.

As Zhou, Wang, Song, and Wu (2017) state, "a novel idea may be just an initial thinking that is far from complete or a fresh thought for which the value is not yet known. Novel ideas are raw materials at early stages of development" (p. 1). Work MUST be done on these raw materials so that they are seen through to fruition. This creative product action was described by Dudek (1973) as a transformation of raw materials. "This means that the artist (sci-entist) selects, changes, fashions, the initial material by a process of will, of decision, into a final articulated form which, in the

Life, Life, Give My Creation Life!

end, has little resemblance to the raw material, and is finally detached from his personal motivations" (p. 3). It could be truly that where there is a will, there is a way (and means) to be creative.

The combined aspects of produced, adaptive to reality, and novel were what MacKinnon stressed were the absolute criteria for which a creative product should be judged, but also indicated that there are other additional criteria that should be considered. In his explanation of these two aspects, he states that "the more of them that are met, the more creative the product, for, though there may be many correct solutions to a problem, not all solutions are equally good" (p. 126). The word *good* provides a great segue to the first of the additional criterion MacKinnon listed.

The fourth criterion of a creative product is that it yields an ***aesthetically pleasing*** solution. The an-swer that the product yields can be described as both "true and beautiful" (p. 126). From a Bohemian perspective, it refers to an idyllic product that leads to a happy and peaceful resolution.

A Creative "Rite" of Passage?

To put this in perspective, let's flash back to 1913 Paris—a true Bohemian city in every sense of the word. Paris at the time was a European mecca for culture and art. Champagne flowed nightly on

Roger-Violet, Paris/Bridgeman Images

The Rite of Spring

the Champs-Elysees and citizens enjoyed and indulged in high fashion, succulent meals, and lavish stage productions from every medium, including opera and ballet. On May 29, 1913, a Russian composer named Igor Stravinsky debuted a new ballet called *The Rite of Spring*, a production that depicted a ceremony of sacrifice in which a young girl is chosen to dance until she dies to ensure next year's harvest would be a good one (truly a feel good story that can't be "beet"). Everything about this production challenged the audience; dissonant sounds and disjointed dance moves. Complex musical passages that featured both polyrhythms and polytonality meant that patrons were exposed to several rhythms at once simultaneously played in different keys. To say that that attendees were up in arms would be an understatement as the musical schemes and pagan themes brought some to blows! After the debut, Craft (1969) documents that Stravinsky wrote home noting that "things got as far as fighting." Hood (2017) depicts the scene that unfolded as riotous as "the un-balletic movements of the dancers and the unsettling dissonance of the music incited a riot, and the audience shouted insults and profanities at the ballet company" (p. 6). On the 100th year anniversary of this production, the BBC News (Hewett, 2013) ran an article that stated "of all the scandals of the history of art, none is so scandalous as the one that took place on the evening of 29 May 1913 in Paris at the premiere of Stravinsky's ballet "The Rite of Spring."

Shortly after its debut, you would presumably be hard pressed to find anyone who would agree that this was a creative product that had value. But why? Stravinsky was writing melodies that were novel, adapted to the art forms of both orchestral music and ballet, and were ultimately produced. But, in alignment with what MacKinnon states above, the work itself was not aesthetically pleasing to the contemporary tastes of the listeners at the time. To help explain this and align with MacKinnon's viewpoint, Jackson and Messick (1965) distinguished between external criteria of creative products (the tangible aspects—what can be seen, experienced, heard, etc.) and internal criteria (intangible elements) such as flow and harmony (presumably missing from The Rite of Spring!). They go as far as stating that "the first three criteria of creativeness . . . may possibly be the source of three types of aesthetic responses, which may be summarized by the key words *surprise, satisfaction, and stimulation*" (p. 318). Surprise is evoked when the individual has a "confrontation with an unusual object or event" (p. 317) that forces them to react to the experience. Satisfaction is equated to the "general condition of comfort" in which the creative product is judged to be "not only right, but just right" given the context in which it is embedded and in its final form is "complete or sufficient" (p. 317). Finally, stimulation refers to the "power to alter the viewer's conventional way of perceiving or thinking about his world" (p. 317). Jackson and Messick go on to state that this in not only in reference to the creative product itself but the new environment created by that product. This was the case with Stravinsky's work.

Today, *The Rite of Spring* is considered a classic, and as Hood (2017) went on to proclaim, "ushered in a new era of modernism" that forced listeners to reconcile and adapt to complex melodies and chord structures. Parts of it were even adapted for the Walt Disney animated feature "Fantasia" (1940) featuring prancing dinosaurs instead of pagan rituals. While Rite of Spring wouldn't have (at the time) qualified as aesthetically pleasing, it certainly would have received kudos and accolades for fulfilling the last aspect of a creative product identified by MacKinnon.

Transcending and Transforming Nature

In his identification of this aspect, MacKinnon states "the fifth and highest criterion for a creative product is seldom met since it requires that the product create new conditions of human existence, ***transcending and transforming*** the generally accepted experience of man by introducing new principles that defy tradition and radically change man's view of the world" (p. 126). Citing the astrological model of Copernicus as a bright shining star of an example, he states as to how this theory fundamentally changed how we view the world. Literally. There are many theories out in the creativity cosmos that are in alignment with this last aspect of MacKinnon's and examine how to evaluate the transcending and transforming nature of a creative product. But how do these essential characteristics line up with the criterion for evaluation? We're about to find out.

Evaluation of Creative Products

Interestingly enough, we can find precedent for our evaluation of creative product from the U.S. Patent office. Section 101 of the U.S. Patent Act sets for the general requirements of patent protection

> Whoever invents or discovers any new and useful process, machine, manufacture, or composition of matter, or any new and useful improvements thereof, may obtain a patent, subject to the conditions and requirements of this title. (35 U.S.C. § 101)

Now, while that casts a seemingly broad net, there are four requirements for a patent to be issued; some of which should be VERY familiar to you. They are:

- The invention must be *statutory*.
  Simply put, the subject matter of the patent must be patentable. You can't patent an abstract idea or naturally occurring phenomenon, such as the law of gravity. (Well, technically you could send the paperwork up, but the patent office will come down hard on you!)

- The invention must be *new*.
  This is clarified to mean that the invention was not known to the public or existed in print/media before the patent was filed. So when a contestant on Shark Tank tells Mr. Wonderful they haven't filed for a patent yet, you can't beat them to it as it has already been communicated to the word via the medium of television.

- The invention must be *useful*.
  This means that a specific purpose or use must be in the patent application.

- The invention must be *nonobvious*.
  This determination is made based on examining prior products and determining if the new invention differs. Is it a nonobvious improvement to what existed before (35 U.S.C. Section 103).

Neat to see the statues and stipulations for recognizing and rewarding entrepreneurial invention and innovation align with several of the essential characteristics we alluded to before. However, as useful as these four aspects might be for government officials and patent attorneys, they aren't nearly specific enough for the purpose of evaluating a creative product in its entirety. But fear not . . . the Oracle has foretold that we are about to journey into the Matrix; the Creative Product Analysis Matrix (CPAM) first proposed by Besemer and Treffinger (1981), then refined by Besemer and O'Quin (1986, 1987, 1999). Pass the blue pill! (or was it the red pill).

Creative Product Analysis Matrix (CPAM)

As described by Besemer and O'Quin (1999), the CPAM was "developed to help cultivate more careful observation of created products and to focus judges' attention on relevant attributes of products. The CPAM is a three-dimensional model of creativity in products, which hypothesizes *Novelty*, *Resolution*, and *Elaboration and Synthesis* as the three factors" (p. 287). Factor analysis led to subsequent revisions and a shortened Creative Product Semantic Scale (CPSS) used for product ratings, but the original CPAM structure remained the same, with the three main dimensions divided into several subscales (originally called attributes). Table 7.1 below shows the three dimensions and nine subscales, but we will take the time to describe each one by one:

Novelty

Besemer and Treffinger (1981) describe the first dimension of Novelty as "the extent of newness of the product in terms of the number and extent of new processes, new techniques, new materials, new concepts included, in terms of the newness of the product both in and out of the field, and in terms of the effects of the product on future creative products" (p. 163). You see a recurring theme in the conceptualization of this dimension? If so, it shouldn't be "new" to you . . . novelty has already been highlighted as an essential characteristic of a creative product, so it is of no surprise it is at the fore-front of the CPAM model.

Besemer and Treffinger did go on to clarify that newness can have several levels and that a product that is just new to an individual is not as creative as one that is new to an entire population.

As far as the subscales listed under novelty, *originality* is the first. With firsts in mind, this is one of the first times you will see these terms listed in a hierarchical fashion; with originality being an attribute of novelty. Here, originality specifically refers to the statistical uniqueness of the creative product, referring to a relative infrequency of its occurrence. Besemer and Treffinger (1981) went on to clarify that originality here specifically was in reference to "the degree of deviance from the normal incidence of occurrence of similar products in the population at hand" (p. 163). They also go on to note that this aspect of originality is the key aspect in establishing patentability, so how about that tie in from the way we started this section of the chapter off! Beyond that, if you were surprised to see *surprise* as the second subscale, you shouldn't be! Other theorists aside from Besemer and Treffinger have written about the surprise element of creative products. Bruner (1967) labelled the kind of novelty that produced a shock of recognition in observers as "effective surprise," and in his commentary about this theory, Dacey (1989) stated that surprise for CPAM rating purposes meant that "before any evaluation is made, the mind registers a sense of being startled or shock" (p. 155). This literally means that

TABLE 7.1 Creative Product Analysis Matrix (CPAM)

NOVELTY	RESOLUTION	ELABORATION AND SYNTHESIS
Subscales:	Subscales:	Subscales:
Original	Valuable	Well-crafted
Surprise	Logical	Organic
	Useful	Elegant
	Understandable	

Source: Besemer, S. P. (1998). Creative product analysis matrix: Testing the model structure and a comparison among products—Three novel chairs. *Creativity Research Journal, 11*(4), 333–346, Taylor & Francis. Reprinted by permission of the publisher. (Taylor & Francis, Ltd, http://www.tandfonline.com)

creative products must have shock value, right? Finally, in an earlier version of the CPAM, Besemer and Treffinger listed germinal as a third attribute (pertaining to the degree that a creative product could spawn other creative ideas), but apparently this attribute wasn't contagious enough to be passed along to the revised version of the model (cough, cough).

Resolution

Besemer and Treffinger (1981) stated that the second dimension of resolution "includes criteria which pertain to the correctness or rightness of the solution to the problematic situation" (p. 167). This definition was expanded to relate to the functionality and workableness of the product, and Besemer (1998) extended it to relate to "how well the product does what it is supposed to do" (p. 335). Under Resolution, there are four subscales listed.

The first subscale is not new and should be of no surprise. The inclusion of *value* harkens back to the essential characteristics of MacKinnon and one of the two main attributes that, according to general consensus, a creative product should possess. Value in the CPAM is described by Besemer and Treffinger (1981) as "the judged worth of the product" (p. 169), though they are quick to note that this judgment is subjective, depends on the context of the evaluation (individual, economic, social, etc.), and that "if judges are not aware of which sense of the word value is to be considered, reliability can suffer" (p. 170).

The second subscale is *logical*, defined by Besemer and O'Quin (1986) as "the extent to which the solution is consistent with the facts or the extent to which the product follows the rules of the game" (p. 167). However, the authors are quick to state that being logical doesn't make a product creative and (relative to the category of non-obviousness from above) a standalone product that was merely logical might cause a patent application to get rejected! However, Vulcans would certainly agree that this aspect of an idea is important to include (live long and prosper!).

The third subscale of *useful* relates to the product's clear and practical applications to the field. In the revised CPSS, terms such as effective-ineffective; functional-nonfunctional; operable-inoperable; and workable-unworkable are listed as ways to rate a product's usefulness. Obviously, products with prefix designations (in-, non-, and un-) aren't likely to fix any problems or be of any use!

Finally, the last subscale of *understandable* was adapted from the original attribute of expressive and is meant to signify whether the product is presented in a communicative, self-disclosing way that is "user friendly." Besemer and O'Quin (1986) state that this new term might be misconstrued in the matrix but did provide a definition that related to "the ability of the product to communicate its function or message to its user or observer . . . (or its) clearness of purpose" (p. 116). So with that said, are you clear on what is meant by the subscale *understandable* and the other subscales of the resolution dimension? If so, let's move on!

Elaboration and Synthesis

This final dimension is colloquially referred to as "style" and contains elements that reflect the level of a product's aesthetic appeal. In the original publication, Besemer and Treffinger (1981) described this dimension as referring to the "degree to which the product combines unlike elements into a refined, developed, and coherent whole" (p. 164). This was updated by Besemer and O'Quin (1986) to reflect the "stylistic attributes of the finished product" (p. 115). In describing this dimension, Besemer and Treffinger (1981) note that this category "refers to the degree of manipulation which has taken place in developing the solution" (p. 170).

The first subscale is *well-crafted*, which "relates to the amount of effort expended in production . . . and the care with which ideas are developed" (p. 171). Based on meticulous attention to minute details, this aspect relates to expert craftsmanship of which Bob Vila would be proud.

The second subscale of *organic* has nothing to do with getting down to the "nuts" and bolts of a product, but rather "refers to the extent to which a product has an organizational unity, comprehensiveness, or completeness about it" (p. 172). Just as Whole Foods is stocked with organic produce (that no one can afford!), organic in CPAM refers to the completed whole of a creative product and how its attributes all relate to a central theme or core concept.

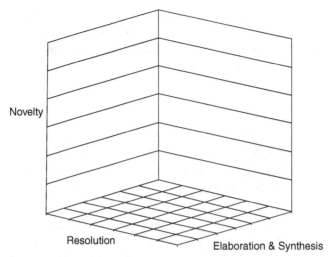

Novelty

Resolution

Elaboration & Synthesis

FIGURE 7.1 Creativity cubed? A visual look at the CPAM model

Creative Product Analysis Matrix: Testing the Model Structure and a Comparison Among Products - Three Novel Chairs, Susan P. Besemer, *Creativity Research Journal*, 11(4), pp. 333–346, 1998, Taylor & Francis. Reprinted by permission of the publisher. (Taylor & Francis, Ltd, http://www.tandfonline.com).

The last stylistic subscale of *elegance* was defined by Besemer and Treffinger (1981) as "the extent to which the product provides an understated or economical solution" (p. 173). Products identified as elegant are subtle and perhaps even simplistic. They aren't flashy or flamboyant, but rather low-key and layered. On a crowded shelf with similar products that have numerous bells and whistles, the elegant product still stands out based on the fact that it represents a refined yet reserved solution that is appealing both aesthetically and economically to consumers.

Now that you have been given a description of the three dimensions of the CPAM, Figure 7.1 above shows you a 3D view of how they all fit together.

Categorization of Creative Contributions

Big C versus Little c Creativity

"C"ategorizing the identification of creative products or impact of creative individuals by their transcending and transforming nature is at the "c"enter of the Big "C" vs. little "c" conceptualization of creativity. In defining the difference between these two aspects, Plucker and Beghetto (2003) summarize that *Big C* creativity focuses on domain-shifting ideas along with individuals who could be labeled as *prodigious, eminent* and are *renowned* for their works, contributions, or creative potential. In contrast, *little c* creativity is used to describe functional ideas along with individuals who could be labeled as *proficient, clever,* or *emergent.* Merrotsy (2013) summarized it like this: "Big-C Creativity is the kind of clear-cut, genius-level creativity that is reserved for the eminent and the great . . . little-c creativity refers to the everyday, common, or garden-variety creativity that may be found in most people" (p. 474). In this dichotomy, it appears to come down to differences in achieving eminence (Big C) and everyday activities (little c), but let's "see" what others have to say about this Big C versus little c distinction.

Little c Creativity

Starting small, we can turn to the work of Simonton (2013) who developed a "calculated" way to categorize creative contributions at the individual level. Ideas can be ranked as to their *personal probability,* which Simonton (2013) described as "the initial subjective likelihood that the idea would be generated by the given individual . . . the very first idea that comes to mind will have a higher probability than the very last idea" (p. 72). The second parameter he identified was the idea's *personal utility*—the degree to which it fulfills the "proportion of requirements that have been initially stipulated for an idea to be fully useful" (p. 72). Note, that usefulness or utility here is determined at the individual level. Finally, the last aspect identified was *personal obviousness*, which is a gauge as to how well the idea can be put into practice. With "trial and error" experimentation at the low end of the spectrum, "hunches" or "guesses" in the middle, and ideas with relative certainty at the upper end, this parameter provides a continuum of categorization as to whether the idea will work. To Simonton, little c creativity was more than the sum of these parts; it was a multiplicative relationship. He states that "an idea's little-c creativity is the three-fold product of its personal originality, utility, and surprisingness . . . (and) if any of the three attributes has a zero value, so will the resultant creativity be zero" (pp. 72–73).

Another three-part conceptualization of little c creativity was put forth by Craft (2001), who suggested a framework of LCC (the way she captured the term) consisting of *agents, processes,* and *domains*. These aspects individually and collectively provide "a 'frame' or perspective through which to both observe and also foster creativity. All are necessary parts of the whole" (p. 54). In describing the agents aspect, Craft states that "the term 'agent' implies activity undertaken by the person concerned . . . each individual plays out the LCC in a unique way, according to their talents, skills, and aspirations" (p. 55). Craft (2002) expanded upon this creative agency by saying that "little c creativity is driven by a particular 'mind-set' or attitude. Being creative means being inclined to be so, and being sensitive to opportunities in which to be so" (p. 57). The processes aspect of LCC "involves using one's imagination; not being satisfied with what already exists, but considering other possibilities, which may include ones we do not know about yet" (p. 55). Craft goes on to state the processes involved in LCC can range from unconscious to conscious thought and from gut-level instinct and intuition to formal and rational logical thinking. Finally, with regards to the last aspect of domain, Craft (2002) notes that "in acts of little c creativity there is no necessary reference to a field of experts, but rather to a spectrum of reference-points of non-expert peers, which provide the 'field' that scrutinizes the little c creative act" (p. 57). These individuals serve to guide, shape, foster, judge, influence, and perpetuate the little c creative act and the creative actions necessary to complete it. Completing her conceptualization of little c creativity, Craft (2002) postulates that "little c creativity describes an approach to life which is driven to find solutions and ways through all situations, an approach to life which in the vernacular may be labelled as 'can do'" (p. 57). So, just as Bobby Boucher shouted in the "Waterboy," with regards to little c creativity—YOU CAN DO IT!

From "can-do" attitude to "must-do" mindset, in her book *Everyday Creativity* Ruth Richards (2010) defines little c creativity as "human originality at work and leisure across the diverse activities of everyday life" (p. 190). In contrast to the conceptualization of Big C creativity (seemingly reserved for the elite), she goes on to state that "everyday creativity, by contrast, is for all of us. It is not only universal but necessary to our very survival as individuals and as species" (p. 190). It is through everyday creativity that we adapt to our ever-changing world and find unique and creative ways to fill niches, gaps, or voids with ideas that are practical and purposeful.

It's a Small World After All?

With the qualities of ideas in mind, Schilling (2005) literally diagrammed a notion of what she termed "small-world" network explanations of insight. The general principle of her network is that "cognitive insight occurs when an atypical association, forged through a random recombination or directed search, results in a 'shortcut' in an individual's network of representations . . . which can prompt a cascade of other connections" (p. 131). Kilgour (2007) related this concept to little c versus Big C ideation and stated that Schilling's network model "provides a basis by which connections of category elements based on their degree of atypicality can explain major versus minor contributions. Ideas that are the result of more distant, or atypical connections will result in more novel ideas than those that are the result of more typical connections, or part of the same category" (p. 19). This small-world network is layered within a larger social world, which helps us bridge the gap between little c and Big C creativity. In talking about the differences between the two, Kilgour (2007) went on to note that "a person may be making a creative connection that is a new combination at the individual level, but that is not new to society."

Therefore, little c creativity stops short of the societal breakthrough we'll talk about in the next section. However, before we go there, we would be remiss to dismiss the value of little c creativity. Using the wisdom of Horton, who famously said, "even though you can't see or hear them at all, a person's a person no matter how small," the same can be said of little c contributions. Though you can't hear them or see them, they are there. They have value to the creator and (collectively) have a large impact on everyday life. Doing things better makes the world a better place, even if it doesn't impact the domain.

Big C Creativity

On a larger scale, we can look at conceptualizations of how eminence is achieved in a domain through a three-pronged approach of Big C creativity, with a collection of three big names behind them.

Feldman, Csikszentmihalyi, and Gardner (1994) put forth a systems framework, identifying that Big C creativity emerges from the triangulation of aspects related to (1) *the individual*, and their skills, abilities, talents, and interests; (2) *the domain*, or the area in which they operate; and (3) *the field*, which includes those in a position to judge, rate, or recognize profound achievements, remarkable break-throughs, and highly creative accomplishments. We previewed this back in Chapter 2. Though we will now look at each individually, the DIFI (domain field interaction framework) holds that these operate dynamically in tandem and in accordance with each other.

Characteristics of the Individual

A historiometric approach has been used to study creative individuals who gained eminence in a field, correlating various characteristics with Big C creative output. These are exhaustive studies with analyses regarding how an individuals' personal statements revealed, behavior typified, demographics influenced, and life circumstances impacted their creative genius. To compile and chronicle evidence about the nature (and nurture) of creative geniuses, Simonton (1994) published a book entitled "*Greatness: Who Makes History and Why*" that chronicles many of these factors. Among his prominent findings were:

Heredity and DNA

Following the hereditary genius conceptualization of Galton (1869), who demonstrated (among other findings) a long lineage of eminent musicians in Bach's family tree, Simonton researched the notion as to whether genetics had an influence on creativity. Could DNA lead to Big C? While it certainly could be a factor, Simonton argued that there were three drawbacks to explaining eminence based solely on DNA evidence: (1) It diminishes the role of the environment, including tutelage and training experiences; (2) it underestimates the power of being born into an eminent family, and all the doors that having a certain "last name" opens; and (3) it neglects the impact of material resources (a.k.a. wealth) that can support and substantiate a creative lifestyle and career. Beyond these, Simonton went on to state that "at least part of what makes a person pre-eminent may be governed by events occurring *before his or her* birth. Psycho-biographers must document this birthright if they wish to explain an individual's greatness" (p. 49). Weiner (2016) states that "when it comes to creative genius, genes are part of the mix, but a relatively small part, somewhere between 10 and 20 percent" (p. 5). Therefore, while it could be true that some Big C individuals are "born-great," the vast majority require an extraordinary amount of circumstances to align for them to achieve at an extraordinary level (though if you are an aspiring athlete with a last name of Jordan, it doesn't initially hurt to have the moniker of the G.O.A.T. in a pick-up game of HORSE or in your quest to join the NBA).

Age and Experience

Analyzing classical musicians who achieved notoriety for their symphonies and other compositions, Simonton (1994) found evidence that with regards to notoriety "it is not a simple matter of chronological age or life experience that is the crucial factor" (p. 68). Rather, it is the amount of dedicated work and devoted study put in. Beghetto and Kaufman (2007) assert that "genius-level creators typically require 10 years of preparation in a domain of expertise to reach world-class expert-level status" (p. 60). Mozart might have written his first composition at age 4, but didn't pen his first masterpiece until the age of 12. Age of creator was also researched by Simonton (1997) who found that Big C contributions don't (generally) begin until the third decade of life, reach a peak at around the age of 40, and then gradually decline after that. So for all you 20-somethings out there reading this, though you haven't even begun to make your mark, if you haven't started preparing yet, the field has got a 10-year head start on you! It's not just the *deck* but the *decade* that's stacked against you!

Family Factors

Simonton (1994) noted three circumstances in one's home life or family environment that could impact Big C creativity: (1) ordinal position in family, (2) experience of traumatic events, and (3) family provision for mental stimulation (p. 144). With regards to the first aspect, in general, Simonton cites evidence as to the majority of Big C creators being first-born. Work by Roe (1972) showed that in the sciences, firstborns are cited more frequently in impactful literature and field-based journals, are judged more creative by experts in their field (more on that in a second), and claimed more Nobel Prize awards than their younger counterparts. *Early* birth order *could* be a factor (but we also offered up contrary opinions in Chapter 3, however those were dealing with everyday creativity, not the aspect of eminence). There are other early effects as well, specifically those related to *early adversity* in ones' life. Simonton (1994) states that "retrospective biographies of historic figures often reveal frequent hardships in childhood and adolescence" (p. 153). Would Marie Curie have won Nobel Prizes in Physics and Chemistry if she hadn't lost her mom in her teenage years? Would P. T. Barnum have developed "The Greatest Show on Earth" if his life wasn't a circus, being the sixth of 10 children and losing his father at an early age? Simonton (1994) states that "when we examine the general population, just two groups show orphan-hood rates similar to those of the eminent—juvenile delinquents and psychiatric patients" (p. 155). It does appear that some use these early experiences as a means to build mental resolve, which serves them well later in life. Finally, eminent creators were more likely to have early learning experiences, with home environments that were not just well off, but rich with stimulating materials. As Simonton (1994) states, "parents of future achievers . . . frequently adopt a rather active role in propelling their offspring to precocious accomplishments. In short, a stimulating home environment probably gives the child an early start on the expertise acquisition so essential to later success" (p. 158).

Taxonomy of Big C Creators

A second historiometric approach was supplied by Howard Gardner (2008), who profiled four "Extraordinary Minds" and the historical, social, psychological, and biographical factors of these individuals. Using Wolfgang Mozart, Sigmund Freud, Mahatma Gandhi, and Virginia Woolf as examples, Gardner's work bloomed into a taxonomy that is useful in classifying what he called the four forms of extraordinariness.

Gardner prefaced this by placing "relates to domain" on one end and "relates to other people" at the other, with "relates to self" the middle. This, therefore, forms a continuum by which eminent individuals can be classified as *Influencers, Introspectors, Makers, or Masters.*

We are all familiar with the term "Influencer" in today's society, but according to Gardner, Influencers have "as a primary goal the influencing of other individuals" (p. 12). Citing the political and pacifist leadership style of Gandhi as an example of someone who was able to inspire a nation into action (or inaction, as it might be) and become a figurehead for the Indian independence movement from Britain (perhaps the very first Brexit?). "Introspectors" have the primary concern of "exploring his or her inner life; daily experiences, potent needs and fears, and the operation of consciousness" (p. 12). Gardner placed Virginia Woolf in this category based not only on her published writings, but the diaries, letters, and other correspondence that she wrote that revealed her inner thoughts. Though introspectors may have indirect influence and live in their own world, their contributions are nonetheless powerful and can inspire people to action. Both influencers and introspectors fall on the "relates to people" side of the continuum.

Masters and Makers are at the opposite domain-oriented end of the scale. Masters are individuals who "gain complete mastery over one of more domains of accomplishment; his or her innovative occurs within established practices" (p. 11). These individuals serve as exemplars of excellence in their domain; the standard bearers by which all others are judged. Gardner listed Mozart, but also cited Rembrandt and others as examples. Makers "may have mastered existing domains, but he or she devotes energies to the creation of a new domain" (p. 12). Gardner cites Freud's development of the psychoanalytic domain as an example, but also references Jackson Pollock and the domain of abstract action painting as an example as well. Aside from these categorizations, Gardner also profiled characteristics that transcend the taxonomy—aspects of the individuals that help them achieve at the highest status and earn their position in the field.

The first characteristic of creatively eminent individuals is their adept ability to *frame the situation*. Gardner (2008) stated that in the face of setbacks, eminent individuals "reconstitute (the situation) as an opportunity from which they can draw lessons" (p. 122). They do not fear failure, but instead spin it as an opportunity to learn and improve. Framing, to Gardner, is "the capacity to construe experiences in a way that is positive, in a way that allows one to draw apt lessons and, thus, freshly energized, to proceed with one's life" (p. 149).

Second, what sets creatively eminent individuals apart is that they are highly skilled at *leveraging*. Leveraging "is the capacity of certain individuals to ignore areas of weakness" and, in effect, ask, "In which ways can I use my own strengths in order to gain a competitive advantage in the domain in which I work?" (p. 148).

At my university, I have my creativity students every semester take the CliftonStrengths[r] assessment, a tool that reveals your top five strengths out of a comprehensive list of 34. So often, we approach tasks from a deficit model—I need to get better at things I'm not good at. StrengthsQuest turns that upside down and instead focuses on things you do well and how you can integrate your strengths into everyday activities that will increase your productivity and potential. This is what Leveraging is all about. A list of the 34 strengths (by name) is provided in Table 7.2. If you want to know what they are, you'll need to take the assessment (perhaps you can "Woo" your boss, professor, or university administrator).

TABLE 7.2 StrengthsFinder

Achiever	Connectedness	Futuristic	Positivity
Activator	Consistency	Harmony	Relator
Adaptability	Context	Ideation	Responsibility
Analytical	Deliberative	Includer	Restorative
Arranger	Developer	Individualization	Self-assurance
Belief	Discipline	Input	Significance
Command	Empathy	Intellection	Strategic
Communication	Focus	Learner	Woo!
Competition		Maximizer	

Source: Gallup Organization.

Finally, it is appropriate to close this section with the last characteristic of *reflecting*. Gardner (2008) defines reflecting as "regular, conscious consideration of the events of daily life, in light of longer-term aspirations" (p. 146). Gardner also was quick to point out that, with relation to reflecting, that "it is important to monitor one's potential audiences—be they family, friends or peers, or those unknowns who will ultimately render judgments about inventions or writings. Lessons from exemplars are clear. Seek feedback and listen to what others are saying. Do not be overwhelmed; it is important not to jettison one's own critical faculties. But, especially during formative years, savor the careful feedback of individuals knowledgeable in the domain" (p. 147). Sage works from an eminent creativity theorist along with a perfect segue to aspects of the creative domain.

Characteristics of the Domain

The domain is the recognized area in which creativity occurs. Big C creators presumably have domain-specific skills, abilities, talents, or gifts that are noteworthy. Examples of domains can include literature (poetry, novels), the arts (dance, music, painting), or science (anything that ends in -ology). Piirto (2011) commented that "the formal study that is necessary to create within a domain cannot be short-circuited. Expertise is necessary . . . if you are interested in doing something, you should study it, preferably in a formal way. You're not going to invent a new car design without studying car design and know what has been done before, what didn't work, what worked, and where the car design field can be pushed" (p. 10).

"Pushing" that Piirto quote forward, in commenting on the role of the domain in Big C creativity, Csikszentmihalyi (1999) identified several salient aspects that will contribute to whether an idea or contribution is considered merely relevant or, in contrast, revolutionary. The first factor is the *level of development* the domain has achieved. We can equate this to terms akin to maturation (milestone developments), self-actualization (realization of potential), or advances that serve to fulfill or complete the domain. As Csikszentmihalyi states, "there is time when the system of a domain is so diffuse and loosely integrated that it is almost impossible to determine whether a novelty is or is not an improvement on the status quo" (p. 319). He goes on to note that "creativity (within a domain) is likely to be more difficult before a paradigmatic revolution" (p. 320).

Another factor brought up is that at any given point of time in history, *certain domains will attract more bright, young, creative minds* than others. Csikszentmihalyi (1999) points out that "the attraction of a domain depends on several variables: its centrality in the culture, the promise of new discoveries and opportunities that it presents, the intrinsic rewards accruing from working in the domain" (p. 320). What do you think are the domains that offer the most creative potential right now? We are engulfed in a technological revolution in which our society is evolving and adapting at a rapid rate. Which industry should a current college student focus on to have the biggest impact (or chance at Big C creativity) post-graduation?

The third aspect of the domain Csikszentmihalyi brought up is that of *accessibility*. We will expand upon this point later when we address aspects of the creative field, but he notes "sometimes rules and knowledge become the monopoly of a protective class or caste, and others are not admitted to it" (p. 320). OR, permitted to change it, which brings us to the last aspect of the domain. *Change factors.* He notes that "some domains are easier to change than others . . . dependent in part on how autonomous a domain is from the rest of the culture or social system that supports it" (p. 320). This last point of Csikszentmihalyi brings up an interesting point about the role of culture in Big C creativity. Culture most certainly impacts a domain and, as Csikszentmihalyi so aptly states, "creativity is the engine that drives cultural evolution" (p. 320).

Cultural Contributions to Big C Creativity

Culture is a rich term full of connotations and connections. If we define culture to be the knowledge, values, attitudes, and traditions that guide the behavior and beliefs of a group of people, you can certainly see how culture *could* influence creativity within any given domain. People have regional, racial, and religious differences. Practices reflect norms, which are established and accepted patterns of behavior. Therefore, what is the role of culture in defining creativity in a domain and does having a multicultural background influence or predict creative output?

Leung, Maddux, Galinsky, and Chiu (2008) defined multicultural experience as "direct or indirect experiences of encountering and interacting with the elements and/or members of foreign cultures" (p. 1) and went on to examine the role of multicultural experiences on creativity. Their research found four salient findings: (1) Multicultural experience increases creative performance; (2) the impact of multicultural experience on creativity is greatest when individuals are immersed in a foreign culture; (3) within a foreign culture individuals with higher levels of cultural awareness and cross-cultural competence will show a larger boost in creativity; and (4) the influence of multicultural experience on creativity is diminished in domains that rely on conventional knowledge and traditional thinking.

So, will going on a study abroad lead you to a creative breakthrough? What about streaming "An Idiot Abroad" on Netflix? Using the framework of Leung et al., Rich (2009) proposed another dichotomy, that of little m and Big M creativity. The **little m** can be construed as "mild forms of multicultural experience" (p. 156), such as spending a week (or so) abroad, or a single exposure to a foreign culture that was controlled, temporary, or fleeting. **Big M** multiculturalism is seen as being much more pervasive or profound—living in a foreign country, taking a new job with a diverse workforce, using a language to communicate that isn't your native tongue. Rich (2009) points out that although Leung et al. "focused the majority of their attention on little c creativity and Big M multicultural experience" (p. 156), their contributions to the understanding of the role of multiculturalism on creativity are as important as the cultural influences themselves.

Creative Artifacts versus Creative Products

Before we leave the aspect of culture and its role on creativity, it is important to mention the work of Glăveanu. In Chapter 4, we covered his theory in relation to the creative person, and how in response to Rhodes (1961) Four Ps theory he developed a new Five As framework by which a creative person could be labeled an "Actor." Here in this chapter, this is a perfect place to mention his view of the *creative product*, and his view on the limitations of that term. Glăveanu (2013) states that:

> products are often considered in isolation . . . from the processes leading up to them and the sociocultural context fostering their creation . . . when we analyze a product, we can measure its physical properties and/or notice whether it is considered creative or not by a group of judges, but this will not tell us anything about the origin and functions of the product in question. It is only when adopting a sociocultural epistemology that we are compelled to conclude about each and every creative outcome, for as minor as it may be, that it is equally a product of cultural participation and thus an artifact or cultural object. (p. 74)

Glăveanu (2011) expands upon this by mentioning that the term artifact "serves to underline the socio-cultural nature of every creation . . . artifacts are not made by individuals and exist only for individuals; they require communication, attribution of meaning, mediation between self and other, creator and members of the audience. Artifacts emerge and exist only in relation to other people and other artifacts, only in a cultural system" (p. 53).

We can use a quote by Weiner (2000) regarding this distinction to wrap up the domain-based aspects that influence Big C conceptualizations and transition to the characteristics of the field. Weiner (2000) states that "each creation comes into being, is understood, and is valued as part of a large web of relations of people, things, institutions and beliefs beyond that particular creation" (p. 254). The people, things, and institutions that Weiner reference are exactly who make up the field that will (ultimately) pass judgment on the Big C value of an idea, product, or artifact.

Characteristics of the Field

Up until now, we've examined person-centered factors and domain-specific characteristics that can lead to Big C breakthroughs. Check all those boxes and you are home free, right? As famous ESPN commentator Lee Corso might say, "Not so fast my friend!" You see, while all of those pieces might be in place, there is one more proverbial hoop to jump through or "boss level" to clear; the field itself. The field in this regard represents those who have the credentials and control to pass judgment on the relative worth of a creative idea or creative product. From positive declarations of "greatest thing since sliced bread, Ms. Baird!" to disdainful commentary such as "shouldn't quit your day job, Mr. Clean" the field has the power to elevate or decimate Big C potential.

Credentials

As Kaufman and Baer (2012) note, "when it comes to judging real-world creative products, few people look to divergent-thinking test scores, psychologist-defined scoring rubrics, or self-assessment checklists. They ask experts. Not everyone will agree with every expert opinion . . . yet there is no higher court of appeal" (pp. 83–84).

In commenting on the characteristics of expert judges, Galati (2015) states that "there are two important characteristics which must be taken into account; the person's experience and his or her expertise in the field. Experience can be defined as the acquisition and cumulative knowledge of reality, mechanisms, rules, and procedures related to a specific domain; expertise identifies a set of recognized, combined, and proven representations, knowledge, skills, and behavior in a given context" (p. 26). In a way, this serves as a de facto norm-referenced comparison; the relative standing of the creator "to whom" they are presenting their idea, invention, or innovation. As Kaufman and Baer (2012) note, the "According to whom?" question is a salient one, and, at the highest levels, the credentials of those who judge Bic C creations could consist of a pool of Nobel Prize, Fields Medal, or Pulitzer Prize winners. Yikes! You might want to stick your toe in first before jumping into that pool!

Control

The field is the gatekeepers who have the potential (in true Monty Python fashion) to dole out more than flesh wounds in declaring "None Shall Pass!" If the credentials represent norm-referenced status (individual compared to a group), the control the field wields is analogous to criterion-referenced standards. The proverbial bar that is set to determine whether an idea will be accepted into the community or adopted into practice.

With this bar in mind, Simonton (2017) points out that for a Big C idea to be accepted, the judgment of the field must be consensual (a.k.a. in agreement). This can be achieved through both top-down (apex predators making determinations that permeate throughout food chain) or bottom-up (a series of hurdles that one must clear to finish the race to eminence) fashions. As Simonton (2017) notes, "in many creative domains, the consensual evaluations will be arrayed into a hierarchy" (p. 10). An analogy that helps this make sense can be seen in our courtrooms (since we are talking about judgments, after all). Though some cases are so monumental in their nature they will find their way directly to the high or supreme courts, many must pass through a myriad of municipal courts before the judgments become statutes or law. Many times arguments are shot down, with little avenue or room for appeal based on the decision of a single judge, let alone an entire supreme court. As Jim Morrison sang, it is hard to "break on through to the other side" or kick down "The Doors" that might be blocking you. Finally, one final note about the aspect of control. Those who have it aren't keen to lose it. If a revolutionary idea comes through that challenges status quo or fundamentally disrupts the firm foundation in which a field has been based on, what do YOU think the reaction of those who achieved notoriety in an area will do with an idea that makes their thinking outdated (or worse) obsolete. Things that make you go Hmm. . . . . .

Bridgeman Images

None Shall Pass!

More C's to "C"onsider—Mini C and Pro C Distinctions

Beyond little c and Big C, Beghetto and Kaufman (2007) added "mini-c" creativity to the list, identifying it as "the novel and personally meaningful interpretation of experiences, actions, and events" (p. 73); a more personalized view of creative potential. At the smaller, micro, level, it can be conceived as "an interpretive and transformative process" (p. 73) that looks at the role of experience, cognition, and insight in the generation of larger, macro-level ideas. It not only adds in elements of individual meaning-making (first-wave constructivism) to the construction of creative products but also looks at how authentic and formative feedback can further someone's creative potential.

This Creativity Is JUST Right

Beghetto and Kaufman likened this to the "Goldilocks principle," explaining how if an individual is not supported in their creative pursuits, they can close themselves off to their creative potential. On the opposite end, if a student is given effusive praise for their emerging work but never provided any constructive criticism regarding areas for growth, the ceiling for their creative potential is capped. And of course, as the principle would imply, there is an appropriate balance; a "just right" mix of detailed yet demanding feedback from stakeholders (parents, educators, etc.) who recognize creative potential and provide both support and structure in building self-efficacy regarding creative potential. Using that frame of reference, the Table 7.3 shows how Beghetto and Kaufman differentiated between Big C, little c, and mini c creativity

Going Pro in Creativity?

Shortly thereafter, Kaufman and Beghetto (2009) added "Pro-C" to their model, "representing an individual's developmental and effortful progression beyond little-c (but that has not yet attained Big-C status)" (p. 5). This comes with the realization that there is a big gap between every-day and eminent creativity so the "Pro-C" distinction was inserted to allow for evidence of *expertise*. A highly trained chef may never get their 5-star Michelin rating, but still has perfected the art of cooking. Though they may never adorn cookbooks or have a brick-and-mortar restaurant in a major metropolitan city, they have perfected their craft none-the-less. BAM!

TABLE 7.3 Distinguishing Mini c from Big C and Little c

	BIG C	LITTLE C	MINI C
Scope	Breakthrough creativity that changes a field	Everyday creativity that may make a solid contribution	Intrapersonal creativity that is part of the learning process.
Example of a product	A painting by Van Gogh	A painting you create to give to a dear friend	A student's sketch pad with various combinations of light and shadow.
Example of a person	Bill Gates	A colleague	A high school art student
Assessment	Usually historiometric: examining impact or citations	Psychometric tests: Consensual Assessment Technique	Microgenetic methods
Experience	More than 10 years needed	Some level of schooling or general experience	Virtually none

Source: Beghetto, R. A., & Kaufman, J. C. (2007). Toward a broader conception of creativity: A case for "mini-c" creativity. *Psychology of Aesthetics, Creativity, and the Arts, 1(2),* 73–79.

Propulsion Model—Categorizing Creative Contributions

Kaufman and Beghetto (2009) conclude their Four-C conceptualization of creativity by pointing to an example of an existing theory that would fit into the Pro-C category—Sternberg's Propulsion Theory of Creative Contributions (1999), since expanded by Sternberg, Kaufman, and Pretz (2013).

Sternberg (1999) conceived the Propulsion Model to "distinguish types of creative contributions and systematically base the distinctions among these various types of contributions on a single unified spatial representation" (p. 86). This theory serves to classify the nature of creative contributions across different domains (formal body of knowledge) and various fields (social organization of the domain). Toward this goal, the term *propel* is purposeful as each contribution moves a field in some specific manner. Kaufman and Skidmore (2010) point out that this is a classification system as this "categorizes these contributions based on their relationship to the existing domain" (p. 378). Therefore, even if we don't have an understanding of quantum physics or abstract art, we can still understand how an individual contribution helped shape that domain and field as a whole. The eight creative contributions, with their definitions are illustrated in Figure 7.2 below:

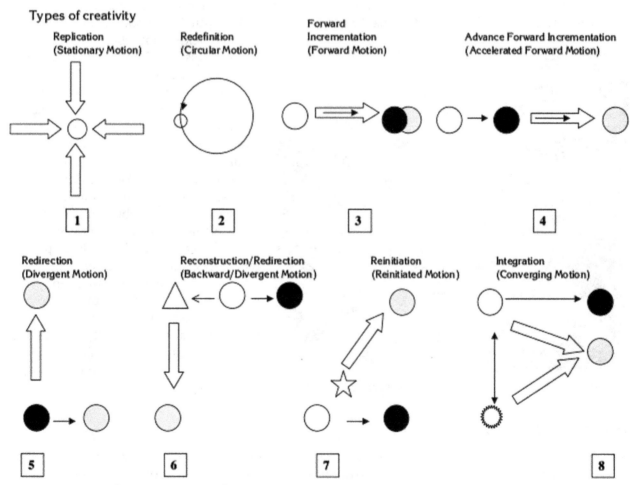

FIGURE 7.2. Eight creative contributions.

The Propulsion Model of Creative Contributions Applied to the Arts and Letters, Jean E. Pretz, James C. Kaufman, Robert J. Sternberg, *The Journal of Creative Behavior*, 2011, 35(2), pp. 75–101. Copyright © 2011 John Wiley and Sons. Permission conveyed through Copyright Clearance Center.

Replication

According to Sternberg (1999), this contribution is "an attempt to show the field is in the right place. The propulsion keeps the field where it is rather than moving it. This type of creativity is represented by stationary motion, as of a wheel that is moving but staying in place" (p. 88). Sternberg et al. (2002) go on to state that the goal of replication is "not to move a field forward so much as to establish that it is really where it is supposed to be" (p. 15).

They continue, "replications help ensure that an approach is robust and can generate a number and variety of works" (p. 18). This is no more evident than on the shelves of your local Barnes and Noble Bookseller. The success of *The Hunger Games* trilogy by Suzanne Collins inspired a great number of authors to crank out young adult novels featuring a hero or heroine in a fragmented dystopian society. If a formula works, sales are good, and people are happy, then why diverge from it . . . after all, do you really want to be "Divergent?!" (excuse my Erudite Candor in pointing out the similarities!).

Redefinition

Sternberg (1999) states that a redefinition "is an attempt to redefine where the field is. The current status . . . is seen from different points of view. The propulsion leads to circular motion, such that the creative work leads back to where the field is, but as viewed in a different way" (p. 88). Expanding upon this, Sternberg et al. (2002) state that "a redefinition in a conceptual space leads people to realize that the field is not where they thought. Work of this kind is judged to be creative to the extent that the redefinition of the field is different from the earlier definition (novelty) and to the extent that the redefinition is judged to be plausible or correct (quality)" (p. 23). Kaufman and Skidmore (2010) point out that there has been a redefinition regarding video games, in that they are no longer a stationary experience, but rather can involve elements of movement and even a "Wii" bit of "Fit"ness. Examples of redefinition given by Sternberg include artwork by both Lichtenstein and Warhol, who took mediums that were perceived to have little artistic value (comic books and cans, respectfully) and turned them into respectful and field-accepted art forms. Just thinking about it brings a tear to my eye!

Crying woman in the style of 60s comic books, pop art.

© Art Villone/Shutterstock.com

Forward Incrementation

Sternberg (1999) notes that this is the most common type of creative contribution. "It occurs when a piece of work takes the field at the point where it is and moves it forward from that point . . . in the direction work is already going. There is no change in the trajectory of the field. Work of this type is judged to be creative to the extent that it seems to move the field forward from where it is and to the extent that the movement appears to be correct or desirable" (p. 91). Driving this example is car manufacturer Toyota. In an article in the *New Yorker* magazine, Surowiecki (2008) describes Toyota's approach to innovation "as an incremental process, in which the goal is not to make huge, sudden leaps but, rather, to make things better on a daily basis." He points out that this principle is known by its

Japanese name *kaizen*, which translated literally means continuous improvement. So though it isn't a Rad reconceptualization, little changes to the dash, dials, or driving system of your Rav-4 could be construed as forward incrementation. Little changes that serve as a Pathfinder for other advances to come!

Advanced Forward Incrementation

With advances to come in mind, Sternberg et al. (2002) state that "advance forward incrementation occurs when an idea is ahead of its time. Although the field is moving in a certain direction, it is not yet ready to reach a given point. Someone has an idea that leads to the point not yet ready to be reached" (p. 43). Perhaps the value of the idea can't yet be understood, captured, or realized. We've already profiled *The Rite of Spring* at the beginning of this chapter as an examplar. But continuing with our automotive theme, true to the futurist tendencies of Tesla for which he named his car company, one could classify the ideas of Elon Musk (self-driving cars, SpaceX, tunnels beneath Los Angeles) as an example here as well (but on a scale from 1 to 100 on avoiding rush hour traffic, California drivers might rank Musk's idea a 105!)

What all of these first four categories have in common is that they can be labeled as *paradigm preserving*, as they leave the field where it is. But now we'll preview the four *paradigm-rejecting* contributions that move the field in a new direction from an existing or preexisting starting point.

Redirection

Sternberg (1999) defines redirection as "taking the field where it is at a given time but attempting to move in in a new direction" (p. 93). "One Direction" the music industry has been headed is digitalization. When is the last time you bought a CD? In fact, if you purchased any physical music at all, it was probably a vinyl record (perhaps an example of reconstruction, which we will preview next). Starting with early iterations (such as Napster) and continuing all the way through iTunes, the entire music industry has been revolutionized. Literally we have gone wireless, as we've gone from cord-based ear buds to Bluetooth-enabled EarPods that can now been seen protruding from the lobes of undergraduates everywhere. Same concept, but different domain with regards to on-demand entertainment. Be kind and rewind back to when there was a Blockbuster on every corner. Now, there is just one store left in the world (in Oregon!). Why? Netflix took advantage of 21st century technology and provided entertainment at your fingertips. People started "streaming" toward this service, abandoning DVD's and instead opting to "chill" on dates in dorm rooms. . . .

Reconstruction

Reconstruction, according to Sternberg et al. (2002), "suggests that at some point in time the field went off track" (p. 65). Therefore, ideas and creative contributions construed as reconstructive suggest that the field move back to a previous state and then advance in a different direction than where it initially headed. In contrast to the sound produced by digital music, "going retro" with vinyl records allows us to recapture music the way that it was meant to be experienced. Leight (2019) projects that vinyl records are set to outsell CDs for the first time since the mid-1980's! Prominent politicians can even base an entire platform on the notion that the direction our country needs to

The last Blockbuster store in America in Bend, OR.

be changed and that we need to get back to where we were before so that America can be "made great again." We'll see if America agrees in 2020. . . .

Reinitiation

Perhaps the most radical contribution, Sternberg (1999) defines reinitiation as a contribution that "suggests a field or subfield has reached an undesirable point or has exhausted itself moving in the direction that it is moving" (p. 94). But, instead of moving in a different direction, the contributor suggests that the field hit the "reset" button and started over. We now understand the truly global nature (and shape) of our globe. The world is round. But it wasn't too many centuries ago that the prevailing conceptualization was that the world was flat and that you could literally sail off the map. Pythagoras initially had the "theorem" of a spherical earth, but Magellan's circumnavigation in the early 17th century seemed to prove it. Publications such as Newton's *Principia* served to reinitiate our understanding, but don't tell that to the attendees of the annual "Flat Earth International Conference," which is now in its third year.

Integration

Finally, the last contribution is integration, in which two diverse domains are merged to create a new idea (Sternberg, Kaufman, & Pretz, 2001). Sternberg et al. (2002) integrated the following into the definition: "what formerly were viewed as distinct ideas now are viewed as related and capable of being unified. Integration is a key means by which progress is attained" (p. 87). The rise of smartphones is a prime example of integration, with functions usually provided by separate entities (calculators, calendars, cameras, and computers) now being merged into a singular (or is it "Cingular") device.

All of the applications (or apps) that smartphones provide are an excellent example of integration and serve as a great segue to our next two chapters on how to integrate creativity into two very creative applications, those of brainstorming and lateral thinking.

Summary

Mel Rhodes provided one of the first perspectives on the creative product, using terms such as *original* and *degree of newness* in his conceptualization.

MacKinnon defined the three essential characteristics of the creative product to be novelty, adaptive to reality, and produced.

Novelty can be related to statistical uniqueness.

Boden differentiated between P-creative (new to the creator) and H-creative (new to everyone) ideas.

Runco and Jaeger put forth a standard definition of creativity that included effectiveness as the second required criterion, which can be equated to usefulness, fit, or appropriateness.

Weisberg voiced concern that value-based aspects of the creative product include subjective judgments.

Dudek defined creativity as a transformation of raw materials into a creative product.

MacKinnon added *aesthetically pleasing* as an additional criterion of a creative product, reflecting the true and beautiful nature of the creation.

Stravinksy's *Rite of Spring* was NOT deemed to be aesthetically pleasing when it debuted, but is now conceived as a creative masterpiece.

The fifth criterion of a creative product MacKinnon identified is *transcending and transforming*, introducing new principles that radically change our view of the world.

U.S. patents are granted based on principles of creativity and require evidence of newness, usefulness, and non-obviousness.

Besemer and O'Quin introduced the Creative Product Analysis Matrix (CPAM) to evaluate creative products.

CPAM included dimensions of Novelty, Resolution, and Style.

Novelty in the CPAM model reflects subscales of *Originality* and *Surprise*.

Bruner conceived *effective surprise* to be a key component of novelty.

The Elaboration and Synthesis dimension of the CPAM relates to aspects of style, including whether a creative product is well-crafted (detailed), organic (complete), and elegant (subtle).

In categorizing creative contributions, Plucker and Beghetto distinguished between little c (everyday) and Big C (eminent) creativity.

Little c creativity refers to the personal factors of creativity

Craft put forth a model of LCC (little c creativity) that includes domains of agents, processes, and domains.

Richards asserted that little c creativity is essential for our survival.

Schilling distinguished between little c and Big C ideation, with Big C ideas being distinguished by more atypical associations.

Feldman, Ciskszentmihalyi, and Gardner developed a systems approach to explain Big C creativity that consisted of a triangular framework of the individual, the domain, and the field.

Simonton chronicled individual factors that contribute to Big C creativity, citing evidence from biological (nature) and environmental (nurture) factors.

Gardner distinguished between Influencers, Introspectors, Makers, or Masters based on the extent to which a creator related to people or related to the domain.

You can find (and utilize) your own creative strengths via StrengthsQuest.

Piirto defined the importance of the domain in defining creative contributions.

Csikszentmihlayi stated that the current state of the domain, its ability to attract young minds, and its accessibility to new ideas all relate to the creative potential in a domain.

Leung et al. looked at how multicultural experience in a domain can contribute to creativity.

Rich distinguished between little m and Big M multicultural factors.

Glăveanu prefers the term *artifacts* (over *product*) due to the sociocultural nature of that term.

Field-based factors involved in Big C decisions come down to gatekeepers who have both credentials and control of what is deemed creative.

Beghetto and Kaufman added mini C creativity to relate to the individual factors involved in the creative process and used Goldilocks Principle to explain how this aspect can be fostered.

Pro C creativity relates to expertise in a domain, even if Big C creative status is never attained.

Sternberg prosed a Propulsion Model of Creativity that could be used to explain and classify creative contributions across domains.

Paradigm-preserving aspects in the propulsion model include replication, redefinition, forward incrementation, and advanced forward incrementation.

Paradigm-rejecting aspects in the propulsion model include redirection, reconstruction, reinitiation, and integration.

Review Exercises

Creative Products

Self-Test: Key Concepts and Terms

Essential Characteristics of Creative Products

_____

_____

P-creative versus H-creative

_____

_____

Novelty

_____

_____

Usefulness

_____

_____

Dimensions of Creative Product Analysis Matrix (CPAM)

_____

_____

Little c creativity

_____

_____

Big C Creativity Characteristics of Individual

_____

_____

Big C Creativity Characteristics of Domain

_____

_____

Big C Creativity Characteristics of Field

_____

_____

Mini C and Pro C distinctions

_____

_____

Propulsion Model

_____

_____

Let's Think about It

1. Write down your best P-creative idea about a product you'd like to invent, writing down key terms or features of what your product is or will do here:

   _____

   _____

   _____

   Now, using the ideas, words, or phrases you listed above, do a quick patent search (http://books.google.com/advanced_patent_search) to see if anyone else has come up with it yet?

   Write down what you find:

   _____

How many patents exist related to your idea? If there are none, what are you waiting for!!

2. Out of all of the characteristics that MacKinnon listed, which one do YOU think most defines a product that is considered creative. Pick one characteristic from his list to remove and explain why it might be considered "nonessential"? Develop an "essential" characteristic to add in its place!

_____

_____

_____

_____

3. View an episode of ABC's Shark Tank (recent or rerun) and pick ONE of the featured products to review using Besemer's Creative Product Analysis Matrix (CPAM). Use the three dimensions and nine subscales to review and rate the relevant attributes of the product. Based on this description, would you invest? Why or why not?

Novelty

_____

_____

_____

Resolution

_____

_____

_____

Elaboration and Synthesis

_____

_____

_____

4. Pick and research a Big C individual from a field or domain of your choosing (well-known author or artist, a theorist you have seen pop up over and over and over again in your college coursework, etc.). What is it about their work, ideas, or contributions that was especially noteworthy? What factors helped them achieve eminence? List any personal, domain-specific, or field factors that you can find that could categorize their elevation to the Big C status.

Individual Factors

_____

_____

_____

Domain Factors

_____

_____

_____

Field Factors

_____

_____

_____

5. Look at Table 7.2. Out of the 34 themes listed, which 5 do you believe are personal or particular strengths of yours? How would you define them relative to creativity? How can you use or utilize them to increase your creative capacity?

_____

_____

_____

_____

_____

_____

_____

6. The propulsion model is a way to classify creative contributions. Using Figure 7.2 as a reference, can you generate a historical or modern example (from any domain or industry) that would fit the requirements of each of the following classifications:

Replication

_____

_____

Redefinition

_____

_____

Incrementation (Forward OR Advanced Forward)

_____

_____

Redirection

_____

_____

Reconstruction

_____

_____

Reinitiation

_____

_____

Integration

_____

_____

8 Creative Applications, Pt. 1—Brainstorming and Creative Problem Solving

Contributing Author – Hector Ramos to this part

"A great fire burns within me, but no one stops to warm themselves at it, and passers-by only see a wisp of smoke."

—Vincent van Gogh

Creativity is often described as an exclusive experience only talented individuals can do. But as a fire can be started just as simple as two sticks rubbing together, so can a development of creativity within someone arise.

We all have ideas we would like to bring about and make them successful, but sometimes discouragement arises when there is opposition and disapproval, and no one stops to hear it. We get discouraged when our ideas and aspirations are ruled out as "crazy" or "not worth it." But this is the very key to a motivated individual.

Everything and everyone can push you, but with your effort and ideas, there is no harder push-back. Discovery of oneself and the experience they want for themselves, I believe, ultimately set a succeeding and failing individual a part.

As long as the smoke dances out of an individual's mind, its evidence of attempt and creation, pay no mind to the individuals who pass you up, because there is, behind that smoke, a fire—a working idea that could hold a blazed potential.

It's much **easier to tame a wild idea** than invigorate one that has no life in the first place.

—Alex Osborn

"Corporate" Creativity

Generally the word "corporate" is most commonly associated with businesses, board rooms, and large companies. But in another context, corporate can mean something that is shared by the members of a group. This chapter will examine both meanings. Osborn (1953), the creator of the technique brainstorming, realized the importance of generating highly original ideas that could then be modified to better serve a certain corporate and industrial context.

According to poet Brewster Ghiselin (1952), "Production by a process of pure conscious calculation seems never to occur . . . many artists of great note or of little have described some considerable part of their invention as entirely spontaneous and involuntary" (p. 15). Undoubtedly true, as we saw in Chapter 3. However, writing about 1950 Ghiselin likely was unaware of creative thinking and problem solving techniques that were developing at the time—techniques now used deliberately and successfully in major corporations worldwide. At a scheduled time and place, techniques can help a person or group think of remarkably innovative ideas and solutions, without waiting for their Muses.

As noted by Smith (1998), idea-finding "techniques" can range from simple advice ("Hey, use your imagination for a change!") to time-consuming mechanical procedures, such as the Storyboarding or Idea Board methods (Higgins, 1994), described later.

If you feel analytical, VanGundy (1987a) classified creative thinking techniques as *individual* or *group* (a distinction often lost, as in brainstorming or synectics procedures that may be used alone or in a group); *verbal* or *silent* (many techniques require quietly writing ideas); *forced relationships* or *free association* (i.e., using techniques versus intuition); and using stimuli that are *related* or *unrelated* to the problem (i.e., working with the problem as given versus using random words or stimuli to prod new connections).

We will suggest another two-part distinction: *Personal* versus *standard* creative thinking techniques. Personal techniques are individual strategies that are developed and used by every creatively productive person. As we saw in Chapter 6, many people use analogical thinking as their pet personal technique for finding ideas. We will examine a few others. Standard techniques are strategies that are taught in many books (e.g., de Bono, 1992a; Higgins, 1994; Isaksen, Dorval, & Treffinger, 2010; Michalko, 2006; Osborn, 1963; Puccio, Mance, & Murdock, 2010; VanGundy, 1983, 1987a), courses, and workshops.

It is important to note that *in every case* the particular standard technique originated as some creative individual's personal technique for producing ideas and solving problems. Like the synectics methods, these strategies were made conscious, knowable, and teachable.

Personal Creative Thinking Techniques

Personal techniques are methods that are developed and used by all creative people, regardless of the subject or content of his or her creations. The topic lies at the core of such central questions as "Where do ideas come from?" and "What is the nature of internal creative processes?"

After you become sensitive to this notion of personal creative thinking techniques, you will see them continually. For example, while looking at a movie, TV show, paperback book, political cartoon, or new consumer product or while listening to a new hit tune, you may understand where the creative person found the idea. The particular innovation might be recognized as a "spin-off" or modification of an earlier idea, a combination of several familiar ideas, or the innovator may have analogically based the idea on a news event, a historical event, or an earlier melody, book, movie, and so on.

As an example in the science area, Einstein used what he called "mental experiments" to stimulate new perspectives and ideas. For example, in what seems to be a personal analogy, Einstein once imagined himself as a tiny being riding through space on a ray of light, which contributed to his general theory of relativity.

In art, we find recurrent subjects and styles with every creatively productive artist, reflecting his or her personal creative thinking techniques. Picasso, for example, deliberately disassembled faces and other elements and put them back together in more original arrangements. He also used analogical thinking, most obviously in his African, Harlequin, blue, and pink (rose) periods during which his paintings were "inspired by" particular themes.

Renoir is noted for his soft, pastel, frilly, and flowery female subjects and still-life. Paul Gauguin found ideas in South Pacific natives and settings, again and again. Georges Seurat used a "dot" painting style (pointillism), usually featuring people, water, and sailboats. Van Gogh's style—dashes instead of dots—was admitted to be influenced by his friend George Seurat. The unique style of Toulouse-Lautrec's heavily outlined, tall, and cartoonlike subjects in evening dress also is familiar. Maurice Utrillo used simple street scenes, devoid of humans.

Professional comedians also use personal creative-thinking techniques, both for their unique type of humor and for their original delivery style. As illustrated, more or less, at

All creative people personal styles and idea-finding techniques. This creative chap operates his handle with a distinctive creative flair. "I can do it with my left foot up, too," says Charlie. Source: Charlie Chaplin in "Modern Times," 1936. Courtesy of PhotoFest.

the outset of this chapter, one technique is to use funny malapropisms, a routine borrowed from comedian Norm Crosby (as were about one-third of the malapropisms). Don Rickles insults people, using the same insults again and again ("Shut up dummy, you're makin' a fool of yourself!").

Joan Rivers and Rodney Dangerfield both continually put themselves down. Rivers claims that when she was a child she was so ugly her father sent a picture of her to Ripley's *Believe it or Not*. They sent it back with a note "We don't believe it!" Dangerfield's most famous line is "I don't get no respect," always accompanied by sweating and straightening his tie. When he was born the doctor told his mother "I did everything I could, but he's gonna' be okay!" Said Dangerfield, "I had to share my sand box with two cats. They kept tryin' to cover me up! Once I called this girl for a date, she said 'Sure, come on over, there's nobody home.' So I went over an' nobody was home! Last week my psychiatrist said I was crazy. I told him I wanted a second opinion an' he said, 'Okay, I think you're ugly too!'"

Early movie comic Charlie Chaplin invented his still-imitated walk. He also combined comedy with sympathy and tenderness. Rival W. C. Fields made us laugh with sober surprises—"I love children, if they are properly cooked."

A new generation of women comics use the shock value of brash sex and earthy language for their laughs. Nope, no examples; see cable TV after 9:00 PM.

The *Star Wars* movies, which began in the 1970s and continue (9 episodes and subsequent spin-offs as of this writing), are among the most successful Hollywood movies ever. They were based partly upon an effective personal creative thinking technique used by moviemaker George Lucas. While writing the script for the original *Star Wars*, Lucas read books on mythology. Said Lucas in a *Time* magazine interview, "I wanted Star Wars to have an epic quality, and so I went back to the epics." Thus, we find a young man who must prove his manhood to himself and to his father; he rescues a fair maiden in distress; he has an older and wiser mentor (actually two, Ben Kenobi and Yoda); and he battles with a villain, Darth Vader. Many western movies have been built around the same epic principles.

Virtually all movies, novels, and short stories include surprising twists, along with plenty of deliberate fears, tension, and "dramatic conflict." The greater the dramatic conflict, the better the story (Striker, n.d.). Remember these techniques when you begin writing your short story or book.

Examples of personal creative thinking techniques probably are as endless as the number of highly visible creative people. Probably all are aware of most of their idea-finding techniques and their unique, creative styles.

Discovery-driven innovation happens when a fortuitous event is observed leading to an invention. A creative thinker would then turn that invention into an innovation. Some of the examples of such innovation include Alexander Fleming's invention of penicillin, Roy Plunkett's invention of Teflon (Tanner & Reisman, 2014), and Nicholas Terrett's invention of Viagra. Note that the ability to innovate from a serendipitous event was mainly in applying the insightful observation into a different context.

Encouraging Personal Creative Thinking Techniques

Three general suggestions to help students and others develop personal creative thinking techniques are these. First, as presented mainly in Chapters 5 and 6, this chapter, and Chapter 9, we can help students understand deliberate methods and techniques that are used by even extraordinarily creative people to generate ideas and creatively solve problems. We can help demystify creativity and help convince budding innovators that they also can build upon, modify, and combine existing ideas without feeling uncreative.

Second, the techniques presented can become "personal" creative thinking techniques that a person may adjust to fit his or her personal style of creative thinking. That is, analogical thinking strategies in Chapter 6 and the "standard" techniques in this chapter and Chapter 9 can become "personal" techniques—if they work for an individual and if they become habitual ways of finding ideas and solving problems.

The following are some recurrent guides and suggestions that can help build our repertoires of personal creative thinking techniques:

1. Consistent with analogical thinking, we can learn from successful styles or idea sources used by persons with similar types of problems, for example, in art, music, advertising, journalism, creative writing, speaking, theater, business, or science research.
2. Also analogical in nature, we can look for parallel problems and solutions, for example, in books in one's field, the Internet, history or travel books, encyclopedias, catalogs, the Yellow Pages, and the like. Do you need inspiration for a short story plot? Consult the front and inside pages of your newspaper. Agatha Christie found some mystery ideas this way.
3. We always can modify, combine, adapt, and improve present ideas.
4. We can prod our imaginations by asking "What would happen if . . . ?"
5. We can start with an "ideal" or "perfect" goal or solution—such as having the problem solve itself—and work backward to deduce what is required to reach that goal.
6. We can ask ourselves how the problem will be approached or solved 25, 100, or 200 years in the future. The Arthur Anderson School of the Future program in Oakland, California, has designed teaching and learning systems partly by speculating on how students will be educated 50 years in the future.

Third, personal creative thinking techniques are acquired in the course of doing creative things and reflecting on the creative work done. This can be done individually, in pairs through coaching, and in groups through facilitation. Therefore, it is important for students to become involved in creative activities. In school, these might include art, photography, creative writing, theater, journalism, physics labs, computer projects, or engaging in other challenges and activities that require creative thinking and problem solving. Two national school programs, *Odyssey of the Mind* (OM; https://www.odysseyofthemind.com/) and *Future problem solving* (FPS; https://www.fpspi.org), are designed to stimulate active creative problem solving (see Chapter 11; also Davis & Rimm, 2004).

In the corporation, practicing creativity can take innumerable forms, for example, thinking of and implementing ideas to increase efficiency, employee morale, or production; reduce waste, costs, and overhead; and design new products, processes, methods, procedures, marketing techniques, and automation systems. In the corporation, it can also be enlightening to hear about creativity and idea-finding techniques either from persons who are themselves creatively productive, or from creativity consultants acquainted with blocks to creativity and techniques for sparking new viewpoints, perceptions, analogies, and idea combinations.

In the schools, visiting creative thinking professionals, facilitators, or coaches can help students understand the creative processes of successful artists, writers, scientists, business entrepreneurs, or highly innovative companies.

Whether creativity is practiced in corporations or schools, the creative thinking methodology used could include problem identification (what is the root cause of the problem that needs attention?), ideation (what are the most original and useful ideas?), solution development (how can those ideas be developed into workable solutions?), and implementation (what is the best strategy to implement the solution?). Isaksen et al. (2010) explain how this Creative problem solving methodology can be used in the corporate and school arenas.

Standard Creative Thinking Techniques

There are several well-known methods for producing new ideas and new idea combinations that, as we mentioned, are taught in most university (McDonough & McDonough, 1987; Pappano, 2014) and professional creativity courses (Puccio & Cabra, 2010; Vernon, Hocking, & Tyler, 2016). The strategies also may be taught to high school students, middle school students, and even elementary students. It is important to emphasize that the techniques are intended to *supplement*—not replace—one's intuitive idea supply. When you have a sticky problem and run out of ideas, one or more of these techniques will help.

As an illustration of the usefulness of deliberate imagination-prodding methods, Davis (2004a, 2004c) used, as teaching devices, the brainstorming and reverse brainstorming procedures presented in this chapter, plus analogies (Chapter 6), visualization (Chapter 4), "What would happen if . . . ?" (this chapter), plus other empathy-stimulating activities in two character education books, an idea book for teachers plus a self-study workbook for students. The goal was to prompt students to think (creatively, futuristically) about and make commitments to positive values, to help them understand both the personal benefits of productive values and the life-damaging consequences of poor values. As some examples:

Brainstorming. "Why should we be honest? List all of the ideas you can think of." "What happens to people when they drop out of high school? Let's think of all the ideas we can." "How many ways can you think of to save electricity at home?" "What rights do ALL of us have—children, parents, teachers, store clerks, and everyone else?"

Reverse Brainstorming. "How many ways can we think of to show that we just are not to be trusted?" "How many ways can we think of to be unfriendly and to hurt the feelings of a new student in class (or in the neighborhood)?" "How many ways can we violate each other's rights?"

Analogical Thinking. "How is being rude to people like a flat tire on a bicycle?" "How is responsibility like a good wrist watch?" "How is a good education like a good dream?"

Visualization. "Imagine that you are a big, dumb, pushy bully . . . you see a smaller child and you yell, 'Hey stupid, is that your face or a pile of garbage?' . . . You laugh because you think you are funny . . . In class you turn to Maggie in the next seat and whisper, 'Hey Lanky, how come you're so tall an' skinny? Weather okay up there? Glad I ain't a toothpick like you!' [etc., etc.]."

What Would Happen If . . . ? "What would happen if everyone were a thief?" "If nobody were friendly to YOU?" "If nobody accepted responsibility for their bad behavior?" "If the school were vandalized every night?"

Intuitive and Deliberate Creativity

We should note the distinction between *intuitive* creativity and *deliberate* creativity. Intuitive creativity, as the name suggests, refers to the unpredictable inspirations that may or may not appear when and where you need them. There is nothing wrong with inspiration, intuition, and spontaneous creative thought; they solve problems and keep the topic of creativity interesting. Most creativity is spontaneous and intuitive, even if rooted in past, perhaps near-buried experiences.

With deliberate creativity a person or group consciously decides to sit down and creatively tackle a problem. They may use one or more techniques—most often brainstorming—to clarify the problem, perhaps redefine or broaden the problem, and think of new ideas, improvements, approaches, or other innovations.

Brainstorming

The label *brainstorming* has become a handy, descriptive, and loosely used household word. Many people use *brainstorming* simply to mean *creative thinking or coming up with ideas*. Many say they are "brainstorming" whenever they think of a new idea: "Hey, I had a brainstorm! I'm gonna' put *two* olives in my next martini!" "Hey, I brainstormed a couple a' slogans for our grasshopper jelly: 'Put the hop back into breakfast!', 'Get a jump on the day!', an' 'It'll get you ready to kick butt!' Whadaya' think?" (Sound of crickets chirping). Others also misuse the word "brainstorming" to push their own idea or to examine the next idea generated by the group.

Anyone interested in creative processes or creative problem solving should try "official" brainstorming, that is, brainstorming guided by the four simple rules described later in this section. Newcomers to brainstorming always are impressed by the surprising ideas and perceptions of others—ideas that in a group setting stimulate or "cross-fertilize" further ideas and viewpoints. That is, group members *hitch-hike* or *piggyback* on each other's ideas. Brainstorming undoubtedly is the most popular form of deliberate creativity, and is used regularly to prod flights of professional imagination. Corporate and business uses of brainstorming are without limit, for example, in developing new products, in improving existing products or processes, or in solving marketing, advertising, personnel, or management problems. In the classroom, a flexible teacher will schedule brainstorming sessions either for practice in creative thinking or for solving real problems, such as high absenteeism, messy school grounds, traffic safety, bicycle thefts, drug use, raising money, or selling play tickets.

Reasons for the popularity of brainstorming are not particularly mysterious:

It's intuitively appealing.
It's simple.
It's fun.
It's therapeutic.
It works.

The high *intuitive* appeal stems from the main hard-and-fast rule, the principle of *deferred judgment*—the seemingly self-evident notion is that either the positive evaluation of the idea or criticism will interfere with flexible idea production. The originator of brainstorming, Alex Osborn (1963), simply noted that one cannot be critical and creative at the same time. Makes sense. Deferred judgment produces the essential *creative atmosphere*. The principle of deferred judgment allows participants to generate different ideas before entering into the evaluation stage later on.

Brainstorming is *simple* because, again, the main rule is—no criticism or evaluation. No training is needed beyond a few minutes' clarification of the ground rules (below). Even young children can brainstorm real or imaginary problem, thereby exercising their creative abilities, learning attitudes and principles of effective thinking, and learning a creativity technique.

Regarding *fun*, professionals sometimes feel guilty about being paid for having such a swell time. New idea combinations are often humorous. Note that jokes, like other creative ideas, also are made of surprising idea combinations.

The *therapy* comes from the enjoyable session itself, from being asked for ideas (which is rare in many organizations), from the chance to speak up, kick around ideas and solve problems, and from satisfying often stifled needs to create and construct. Importantly, group members have ownership of the innovative ideas and, therefore, will work to see them implemented.

And it *works*, whether the goal is to stimulate imagination, flexibility, and creative attitudes as a training exercise—for children or professionals—or to solve some elusive corporate problem. For example, a Denver postmaster and 11 staff brainstormed the problem, "What can be done to reduce man-hour usage?" Some of the 121 ideas led to a saving of 12,666 work-hours in the following 9 weeks. A Pittsburgh department store, stuck with some chair-covering material, brainstormed "other uses" for the fabric, leading to advertising that sold the entire stock in a week. A brainstorming group at Heinz Foods spent just 1 hour on the problem, "How can we help increase the sales of products made at this factory?" They generated more and better ideas than a special committee had produced in 10 ordinary conferences. Reynolds Metals brainstormed some "new and more convenient ways to package a client's cornmeal mix." Some of the ideas were included in a prize-winning and sales-stimulating package. "Quality action teams" in 11 divisions at Federal Express successfully brainstormed ways to improve delivery promptness. AT&T used brainstorming to identify corporate strategies for the new millennium. A "professional excellence committee" at DuPont used brainstorming to identify important corporate problems and later brainstormed solutions (Higgins, 1994). Finally, the success of the New York Advertising agency Batten, Barton, Durstine, and Osborn—the late Alex Osborn's own organization—is good evidence for the effectiveness of brainstorming. Noted Higgins (1994), "Thousands of organizations have used brainstorming successfully...[it] remains a solid technique for generating creative ideas" (p. 121).

The four ground rules of brainstorming are uncomplicated:

1. *Criticism and premature evaluation are ruled out.* This is deferred judgment, which means, as delicately stated in *Imagination Express* (Davis & DiPego, 1973), "You don't want some crab knocking down people's ideas before they have a chance." Deferred judgment produces the receptive, encouraging creative atmosphere. The difference is reinforcement, not punishment, for innovative, perhaps even far-fetched ideas.
2. *Freewheeling is welcomed.* Said Osborn, the wilder the idea the better. You are more likely to find a creative idea by being wild first and "taming down" the idea second, rather than criticizing, evaluating, and editing as you go. In one of your author's classroom brainstorming sessions, someone suggested that a movie theater could be quickly emptied by collapsible seats that slide patrons out the front of the room. This freewheeler was followed immediately by the more practical idea of seats that fold down so that in an emergency patrons could rapidly exit by walking over them.
   Are wild ideas wasted? Well, yes. It is assumed that about 95% of the ideas will not merit further exploration. The other 5% may solve problems in imaginative and effective ways.
3. *Quantity is wanted.* This principle reflects the purpose of the brainstorming session—which is to produce a long list of ideas. The mathematically sensible rationale is that with a larger number of ideas there is a better chance of finding good ideas. Typically, ideas produced later in the session—after the quick-and-easy common ones are out—will be more imaginative.
4. *Combination and inspiration are sought.* This lengthens the idea list. Actually, during the session, thinkers will spontaneously hitchhike on each other's ideas, one idea inspiring a bunch more. Ideas therefore work as triggers to generate more ideas. Since group members generate a variety of ideas, they will also enjoy a variety of triggers to generate other ideas that go beyond the usual.

Group brainstorming provokes new perceptions, relationships, and ideas by others, who bring diverse backgrounds and experiences (Osborn, 1963; Siau, 1995; Taggar, 2001). Beyond finding ideas for the given problem, group members also may question old assumptions and/or suggest totally new approaches.

Taggar (2001) noted these three facilitative factors, or "Team Creativity-Relevant Processes" (TCRP):

1. *Inspirational motivation*: A group setting raises motivation and expectations. Members set high goals.
2. *Organization and coordination*: The group provides an organized setting, with systematic feedback and coordinated contributions.
3. *Individualized consideration*: Individual contributor's ideas and viewpoints are elicited and appreciated.

Taggar (2001) found that group productivity increased *exponentially* (!) with the number of highly creative people in the group—but only when these TCRPs were relatively high.

On the downside, unsuccessful thinking sessions can stem from such creativity-suppressing matters as:

1. Worry about being criticized or evaluated or laughed at
2. Low motivation or ability to generate ideas
3. Free riding and social loafing—letting others do the work.
4. "Production blocking" (Siau, 1995), because only one person can speak at a time (and some people don't shut up).

In order to overcome those factors you can use the defer judgment principle: engage the group with a warm-up activity to motivate them and overcome any fear of the process (1), explain well the participation guidelines (2), and use silent tools at first (3, 4), such as having them write down their ideas first.

Noted Taggar, the "overall creative performance of a group will depend upon the balance between creativity-enhancing behavior and creativity-stifling behavior" (p. 263).

Despite the relative simplicity of running a brainstorming session in an elementary, secondary, or college classroom, Taggar (2001) named complexities likely to occur in organizational settings. Specifically, the brainstorming problem can be "complex, varied, and multi-part" (p. 267), including, for example, identifying the problem, agreeing on how to approach the problem, producing some good ideas, producing an action plan, implementing the plan, evaluating the outcome—and perhaps modifying the problem solving and decision-making procedures for the future.

When a session is complex, brainstorming can be used to identify the points of the problem that need to be clarified and reach a consensus on the type of problem to be solved, the value sought in the ideas created, and a possible strategy to build a group solution.

Running a Brainstorming Session

It is comparatively simple to run a brainstorming session. The facilitator reviews the four ground rules, along with procedural details. For example, some groups keep a small bell in the center of the table to ding anyone who criticizes or even asks for justification for an idea ("Why did you suggest that?"). Some facilitators prefer to go around the table, letting each participant speak in turn, but allowing someone with a pressing idea to interrupt. It is best to write ideas on a whiteboard where they will be available for combination, modification, and non-duplication. Audio and video recorders also have been used.

The facilitator's role is straightforward. In addition to organizing the session, explaining the ground rules, and reviewing the problem, he or she occasionally asks, "What else can we think of?" Sometimes the facilitator serves mainly as place for participants to focus their attention and to share their ideas.

A more sophisticated facilitator may take suggestions from Osborn's CPS model (Chapter 5) and ask, "Well folks, what do we know about the problem?" (fact-finding) or "How else can we define, view, approach, or broaden the problem?" (problem-finding). Helping the group broaden the problem can be especially valuable. For example, instead of redesigning heating elements on an electric range the group can look for innovative ways to "heat food"; instead of building a better mouse trap the group can think of ways to "get rid of mice." We noted in Chapter 5 that asking "Why" after each problem definition produces increasingly more general problem statements.

In addition to the four main ground rules, Osborn (1963) suggested a few more procedures. Group size should be about 10 or 12. An ideal panel consists of a leader, an associate leader, about five regular members, and about five guests. Note, however, that one can brainstorm *alone* or with a 500-person group.

To increase the source and variety of ideas, members should be heterogeneous in training, experience, and gender. In most circumstances, rank should be roughly equal. Imagine the intimidating and stifling effect of Microsoft President Bill Gates sitting in on a managerial-level brainstorming session.

With serious problems (not "What can a clever chipmunk do while blind-folded?"), the problem should be circulated 48 hours in advance so that members can come in with ideas. A follow-up request for ideas may be circulated 48 hours after the session in order to salvage ideas that participants wish they would have thought of at the time.

During silent periods, if any, the leader may ask the quieter members for ideas, pull out some shirt-pocket ideas of his or her own that were prepared in advance, or else suggest a new way to look at the problem. The leader also can roll out Osborn's *idea-spurring questions* (described later), which Osborn frequently used in brainstorming sessions.

Incidentally, a critical pre-session consideration is whether to use a group to solve the problem in the first place. Even Osborn (1963) recognized that "Despite the many virtues of group brainstorming, individual ideation is usually more usable and can be just as productive."

Isaksen et al. (2010) suggest three key issues to consider before engaging in this methodology based on direct ownership or level of influence over the issue, high motivation to invest the effort, and the need for a creative approach.

Evaluating the Ideas

Assuming the group produces a nice, long list of ideas—some absurd, some wild and innovative, and others quite serious—what then? This group or another group can evaluate the ideas in any number of ways. Realistically, a few ideas sometimes simply will look darn good, and they probably are. This simplifies idea evaluation. However, if a potential solution may have messy complications or implications, it is possible to brainstorm criteria for evaluation and use a formal evaluation matrix as explained in Chapter 5. Some evaluation criteria can focus directly on those potential complications and implications. Some possible criteria are:

Will it work? Will it do the job? Does it improve present methods?
Are the materials available? Are needed personnel available?
Does it reduce costs? Eliminate unnecessary work? Increase production? Improve quality? Improve safety? Improve the use of manpower? Improve working conditions? Improve morale?
Does the idea really "grab" people? Do people ask, "Why didn't I think of that?"
Is it timely?
Is it a temporary or permanent solution?
Will it cost too much?
Is it too complicated? Is it simple and direct?
Is it suitable? Will others accept it (higher management, the public, our union, suppliers' unions, parents, the secretary, your mother)?
Is it legal?
Are there patent infringements?
Are we trying to swat a fly with dynamite?

When we select criteria we should consider a singular distinct issue at a time, phrase it in a positive form, and choose criteria that can be easily measured. In the classroom or corporation, using objective criteria for the evaluation process serves several purposes:

1. Using criteria helps us evaluate ideas systematically and, therefore, to solve a problem in a reasonable, mutually agreed upon way.
2. It helps children and adults learn to evaluate as part of the overall creative problem solving process.
3. It requires people to consider many aspects of a problem, including aspects that did not occur to anyone during the session.
4. In some cases, evaluation can help a group explore its own values relative to the problem at hand. For example, "How can we save money on our school bus training program?"
5. It allows groups to develop meaningful discussions and reach a consensus or at least common understanding on the most important value sought in a selection of ideas.
6. Finally, evaluation can prove that thinking of "silly" and "far-fetched" ideas truly can result in practical solutions to problems.

Variations on Brainstorming

There are dozens of variations on basic brainstorming. Some variations are slight and legitimate modifications of the brainstorming procedure. Other times the word *brainstorming* is used only because it's a familiar label, and the only commonality with Osborn's brainstorming is that the goal is to solve a problem.

Brainstorming variations follow—or should follow—brainstorming rules:

1. We don't criticize;
2. We can suggest wild and preposterous ideas (which may lead to other ideas);
3. We want lots of ideas; and
4. We can hitchhike (piggyback) on others' ideas (which will happen even without a rule).

Reverse Brainstorming is a powerful and fun variation. We find new ideas, viewpoints, and possibilities by turning the problem around: How can we increase costs? Increase waste? Run up the light bill? Increase employee dissatisfactions? Stimulate absenteeism? Increase drug use? Increase traffic or industrial accidents? Reduce sales? Increase complaints? Gain weight? Suppress creative thinking? Always, participants list what in reality is actually happening—which leads to positive solutions. Glasman (1989) called this procedure *Reversal-Dereversal*, with dereversal referring to correcting each identified deficiency.

With regular brainstorming you begin with a problem and try to find satisfactory solutions. With *Backward Brainstorming* you start with a satisfactory situation and look for potential problems. You "see what you can find wrong with it" (Higgins, 1994, p. 40).[1] One is reminded of a reputed comparison of American with Japanese design philosophy. American designers correct problems, as in regular brainstorming. Japanese designers seek improvements where there are no obvious problems, as in Backward Brainstorming.

With *Stop-and-Go Brainstorming*, short, 10-minute periods of unrestrained freewheeling are interrupted by brief idea evaluations. The evaluations help keep the group on target or help select profitable directions.

The *Phillips 66* procedure is used with medium-to-large audiences. After the problem is explained, small groups of six will brainstorm for six minutes. One person in each group records the ideas. After six minutes the person reports all or the best ideas to the larger group.

Let's call this nameless procedure *Complaint Brainstorming*. Hidden problems may be uncovered by asking customers, employees, or others to brainstorm (think of) complaints (Higgins, 1994; Skagen, 1991) or by asking employees or teachers to list stumbling blocks they have tripped over. Once identified, the problem likely can be corrected.

There are many varieties of *Brainwriting* and what we can call *Brain Drawing*. Generally, in all brainstorming methods the solution ideas should be visually available whenever possible—mainly to aid idea hitchhiking, but also to avoid duplications and help record the ideas. With brainwriting and brain drawing the visibility of accumulating ideas is even more important—most procedures specifically require and capitalize on idea hitchhiking.

In basic *brainwriting*, members of each small group write down an idea (solution, improvement, new direction), then pass the paper to the next person. This second person may (1) use the idea to simulate another idea and write the hitchhike on the paper, (2) modify the idea and write down the modification, or (3) write down a new idea. When the sheets circulate back to the original owner, ideas are discussed, perhaps summarized on a board, and probably evaluated.

In a modification of *brainwriting* intended for large groups, each person receives a paper divided into four columns. The person writes ideas in the first column, then circulates the paper to three

---

[1] Higgins (1994) and others (Creativity Group Techniques, 1984) call this procedure *Inverse Brainstorming*, which seems too easily confused with Reverse Brainstorming.

others, who—in turn—add their hitchhikes, modifications, or new ideas in the other three columns (Higgins, 1994).

With the *Take Five* procedure (Higgins, 1994; Thiagarajan, 1991) the leader describes and clarifies a problem to members of a medium-sized group. Allowed just two minutes, each participant creates a list of ideas. Then teams of five combine members' ideas into a single longer list. The teams rank ideas in importance. Together, all members create still another list containing only the best ideas—with a limit of 10 ideas. These are further discussed and evaluated.

With *Brainwriting Pool* (VanGundy, 1987a), developed by the Battelle Institute in Frankfort, Germany, six to eight people write down possible solutions to a problem. When finished (minimum of four ideas), they slide their paper to the center of the table and pick up another person's list of ideas, on which to hitch-hike with further ideas. Each person should hitchhike on at least one other person's list of ideas.

Mitsubishi Brainstorming (Higgins, 1994; Tatsuno, 1990) is a Japanese version of brainstorming/brainwriting that is designed to not publicly embarrass slower idea producers. Participants write ideas before sharing them. When comfortable, they volunteer to present their ideas aloud, allowing others to write down idea hitchhikes. Participants with few ideas at first thus can thus wait to read their own ideas and hitchhikes. After about an hour, the leader writes an "idea map" on the board, allowing everyone to see ideas and their interrelationships. They discuss and evaluate the ideas.

Brainwriting 6-3-5 (Higgins, 1994) also was created by the Battelle Institute. Given *one* problem, six (6) people each create three (3) columns on a piece of paper, then write one different solution at the top of each of the three columns. The initial total is thus 18 ideas. After five minutes, the person passes the paper to the next person, who hitchhikes and/or adds a new idea to each column. Papers are passed six (I think Higgins meant *five*) times to allow all participants to add ideas to all papers. The ideas are discussed and evaluated. Said Higgins, "This is a very productive effort . . . within 30 minutes the group can produce 108 ideas" (p. 129).

Higgins (1994) described *Mind Mapping* as an individual brainstorming procedure intended to organize, clarify, and help solve a complex problem. It asks for lots of ideas, including crazy ones, with criticism deferred. Procedure: Use a large piece of paper. Write down a problem in the center of the paper. Then brainstorm 5 or 10 major ideas related to the central problem. Write these ideas in a circle around the central problem with lines ("roads") connecting each major idea to the central problem. Then brainstorm sub-ideas related to each major idea, again connecting the sub-ideas to the major ideas with more "roads."

You should end up roughly with a top view of a tree: The trunk (main problem) sits in the middle, some large branches (major ideas) extend in every direction, and lots of smaller branches (sub-ideas) sprout from the large branches. According to Buzan (1983), mind mapping visually organizes a problem much like the brain organizes information.

The Japanese *Lotus Blossom* technique (Higgins, 1994; Tatsuno, 1990) is virtually identical to mind mapping, except that exactly eight major ideas for a problem (in the central stamen) each elicit exactly eight more sub-ideas (in the blossoms).

The extremely similar *Method 6-3-5* (J. Shah, personal communication, April 15, 2003) differs just slightly in procedure. No columns, and "5" refers to the number of exchanges, not minutes. Again there are six people. At the session outset, each person "writes down three rough solutions in the form of keywords . . . After *x* minutes each participant passes his/her list to the person next to him/her. Each participant then adds three further solutions or developments of the three previous ideas. The exchanges continue... through all participants (five exchanges)."

With Shah's (J. Shah, personal communication, April 15, 2003) *C-Sketch* (collaborative sketching), no verbal communication is allowed. After receiving the problem, each of five participants sketches a solution idea on a sketch pad. After x minutes, the person passes his or her sketch to the next person, who modifies the sketch or develops it further in any way he or she wishes. Part—but not all—of the previous sketch can be erased. Exchanges continue until all have responded to each sketch.

If you are in no rush, the *Idea Board* (Glasman, 1989; Higgins, 1994) strategy may be useful. A written problem is posted on a board. Participants write ideas on cards and post them under the problem. Cards are rearranged into meaningful columns. The ideas may be discussed informally or in discussion groups. One person is responsible for posting problems and deadlines and for giving feedback to everyone.

With the Battelle Institute *Gallery Method* (Higgins, 1994), after receiving the problem each group member takes 30 minutes to create a "gallery" of ideas on a board (or flip chart). Members then take five minutes to review each of the others' galleries and take notes. They return to their own gallery and add hitchhikes and new ideas. In a variation, members can add ideas to other persons' galleries. Ideas are summarized and distributed later.

If you really are in no rush, *Storyboarding* (Higgins, 1994) uses cards pinned on a board or wall so that the 8 to 12 members and a leader can see interconnections among problem components and specific ideas. The eventual visual storyboard display—a matrix with headings at the top of each column—is used with complex problems. In step 1 of storyboarding, the group is given a topic or problem. In step 2, the top left card (the first "header") is named a *Purpose* header, and the group brainstorms reasons for pursuing the topic, each of which is written on a card and pinned in a vertical column under the *Purpose* card. In step 3, the group brainstorms other headers—issues and solution directions that are pinned up as column headings. Then, in step 4, header by header, the group brainstorms ideas related to each heading. After a 30-minute break, group members think critically ("Why did we think of this?" "Is the idea essential?" "It is feasible?"). The group reorganizes cards on the storyboard as they evaluate.

The *NHK* method (Higgins, 1994; Tatsuno, 1990) also requires many steps. Participants are given a problem, then they write down five ideas, one per card. In groups of five, each person explains his or her ideas as others write down idea hitchhikes or more new ideas, also on separate cards. All cards are collected and sorted into meaningful stacks. Now groups of two or three participants examine one (or more) of the stacks of cards and brainstorm still more ideas stimulated by the ideas on the cards—also written on separate cards. Then each small group reorganizes its cards and reports the ideas to the larger group. The leader writes all ideas on a board. Finally, groups of 10 participants brainstorm further ideas to all ideas on the board—"one idea at a time" (Higgins, 1994, p. 150). They return home in a month or so.

The *SIL* method is a Battelle Institute strategy for recombining ideas into additional ideas. "SIL" is a German acronym that approximately translates "successive integration of problem elements" (Higgins, 1994, p. 160). Each group participant writes ideas for a problem. After two group members each read one idea aloud, other participants try to merge the two ideas into a single idea. A third member reads a single idea and others try to synthesize it with the previous idea. Und so weiter until a practical solution is found. Or until everyone goes out for a dünkel bier.

Electronic Brainstorming: Voice Messaging, Computers, and E-mail

Someone combined the concept of *brainstorming* with *modern electronics* to produce *electronic brainstorming*. It was bound to happen. A more general term is *Group Support Systems* (GSS). According to Siau (1995), GSS aids in (1) generating ideas or plans, (2) making decisions, (3) resolving conflicts (e.g., in viewpoints), and (4) seeking consensus (e.g., for executing ideas). Brainstorming falls mainly into category 1.

Electronic brainstorming seems to have the advantages (e.g., diverse member backgrounds, cross-fertilization of ideas) without the potential disadvantages mentioned earlier—worry about criticism, low motivation, and "production blocking" by yackety-yak participants (Siau, 1995).

Note that brainstorming with *voice messaging* (audio) and *e-mail* (text and graphics) eliminates the problem of getting a group together at a given time and place. Voice messaging and e-mail also allow virtually any number of persons to participate. And you can pick the brains of experts in Moscow, Saudi Arabia, Tahiti, or Panguitch, Utah.

According to some researchers (Nunamaker, Briggs, & Mittleman, 1995; Valacich, Dennis, & Connolly, 1994), electronic brainstorming groups generate more ideas per person than face-to-face groups. However, Ziegler, Diehl, and Zijlstra (2000) concluded that "firm conclusions cannot be drawn" (p. 144).

For completeness, we should note that Siau (1995) named three types of GSS conferences that solve the space problem, but not the time one. Synchronous video systems, telephone conferences, and inter-active computer conferences allow persons at distant locations to participate in the same brainstorming session, but all must be available simultaneously.

A myriad of companies have sprung up on the Internet offering services related to brainstorming and mind mapping. Companies such as miro.com, stormz, mindmeister provide free and paid services to help groups tap into group creativity. Dennis and Williams (2003) give an analysis of the benefits of electronic brainstorming, including greater anonymity and synergy. However, some electronic brainstorming groups experience greater social loafing. Other advantages of electronic brainstorming is adding an asynchronous dimension, connecting people from different nations and cultures, and tapping into a variety of visual and audio stimuli that can help trigger ideas.

Computer Programs

The following computer programs are not strictly labeled *brainstorming*. However, the programs generate alternatives, idea combinations, and mind-prodding suggestions, and some teach problem solving steps (Higgins, 1994). Close enough.

With *Idea-Fisher* (Brody, 1990) you click on one of several thousand questions in the three categories of *orientation—clarification, modification,* or *evaluation*. Idea-Fisher quickly spits out answers from its 60,000 words and phrases and 650,000 idea associations.

Ideagen (McCune, 1992) leads the thinker through problem solving steps. Ideagen also supplies *random* phrases to prod the problem solver's imagination, that is, to force new solution alternatives and approaches. In Chapter 9, we will see de Bono's (1992a) similar Random Input and Random Word techniques— both designed to stimulate utterly new viewpoints on a problem.

Idea Generator (Mattimore, 1990) also walks the thinker through problem solving steps. It prods the person to consider all aspects of the problem. As promised by its name, it also generates ideas.

Like Ideagen and de Bono's Random Input/Random Word, *ThoughtPath* (Klein, 2000) uses unusual-to-bizarre "mind triggers" (Higgins, 1994, p. 72) to elicit unusual ideas and problem approaches. In Higgins' example, "link an elephant with an oil well, then determine how this association might give clues to solving your problem" (p. 72). ThoughtPath also presents problem solving steps.

The *Invention Machine* (Hall, 1990) presents questions to help the thinker define an engineering or scientific problem. It can draw from its stored 1,250 types of engineering problems, 1,230 physical or chemical scientific effects, and 2,000 "of the world's most innovative inventions" (Higgins, 1992a, p. 72).

Is the reader surprised by the use of electronics, computers, and software programs in creative problem solving? Probably not.

Other innovation software includes Remesh, Innovation Central, Rever Continuous Improvement, Crowdcity Idea Management, Confluence, NanoNotion, Vanilla, Nectir Idea Management, Mindmeister, Aha! and Stormz. (capterra.com)

Cautions About Brainstorming

In 1963, Osborn offered a number of cautions about brainstorming. His warnings likely apply to electronic brainstorming as well as to traditional 12-person groups in Room 251 at 10:30 AM. His main admonition was simply that brainstorming is not a cure-all for every person or organization needing effective solutions for difficult problems. Brainstorming may fail to provide the creative breakthroughs that were anticipated.

Osborn suggested three reasons for some disappointments. First, the organizers and members may not be following the recommended procedures. Second, they may have unrealistically expected miracles in the first place. Third, some individuals can be more creative alone than when in groups. Again, all deliberate creativity techniques should supplement, not replace, an individual's intuitive, original thinking.

Attribute Listing

Brainstorming is a general thinking strategy that mainly requires creative attitudes and a creative atmosphere. Attribute listing is a more specific technique for generating new ideas that, in fact, can be used within a brainstorming session. Robert Crawford (1978) is the designer of attribute listing, and in 1931 at the University of Nebraska taught probably the very first creativity course. He argued that "Each time we take a [creative] step we do it by changing an attribute or quality of something, or else by applying that same quality or attribute to some other thing." Attribute listing is therefore both a *theory* of the creative process and a practical creative thinking *technique*. Following Crawford's definition, there are two forms of attribute listing: (1) *attribute modifying* and (2) *attribute transferring*. Either strategy may be used individually or in a group.

Attribute Modifying

With attribute modifying, the thinker lists main attributes (characteristics, dimensions, parts) of the problem object or process and then thinks of ideas for improving each attribute. For example, a group might invent new types of candy bars or breakfast cereals by first identifying important attributes (e.g., size, shape, flavor, ingredients, color, texture, packaging, nutritional value, audience, product name) on the blackboard, and then listing specific ideas under each main attribute. Particularly good combinations may be picked out of the lists of ideas. Inset 8.1 includes three exercises from *Imagination Express* (Davis & DiPego, 1973) intended to teach attribute listing to upper elementary and junior high school students. Attribute listing is taught in design engineering courses under the name *substitution method*; you "substitute" different sizes, shapes, colors, materials, and so on.

Do creative people really use this technique? Fran Striker, Professor of English at the University of Buffalo, used attribute listing for a couple of decades to help generate radio and TV plots for his *Lone Ranger* series. Striker used the attributes of *characters*, *objectives*, *obstacles*, and *outcomes* in a diagram similar to the first exercise (breakfast cereals) in Inset 8.1. As examples from his unpublished college text *Creative Writing Workbook* (Striker, n.d.), in the first column he listed ideas for *characters*—for example, a playboy, scientist, nurse, king, and gravedigger. Some *objectives* included obtaining love, wealth, or honor; escaping from captivity, fear, or persecution; or getting revenge against an arsonist, slanderer, or the community. A sample of *obstacles*—needed for dramatic conflict and emotion—included being pitted against beauty, power, or the law; being blind, despised, or stupid; a lack of courage, loyalty, or tact; or being held to a contract, tradition, or promise. Finally, a list of ideas to stimulate possible *outcomes* included espionage, disguise, persuasion, wits, or the sacrifice of pride, wealth, or life. Even with Striker's paltry sample of 42 ideas per column, the possible story combinations are virtually endless.

Striker also kept a stack of western paperbacks in the corner of his office that he mined for ideas when additional inspiration was needed.

Striker's (n.d.) *Creative Writing Workbook* and college course included lessons in introducing the preliminary situation (time, place, characters, atmosphere, initial incident), how to create conflict and emotion,[2] how to develop a central story purpose, 10 experienced explanations why your story can be rejected, and more.

---

[2] Consistent with the checklist method described later, Striker (n.d.) included a checklist of 45 emotions that a creative writer might use.

INSET 8.1
The Attribute Listing Method*

Some breakfast cereals are shaped like tiny little letter Os. Let's invent some new breakfast cereals by thinking of some different *shapes, flavors, colors,* and *sizes.* These are four *qualities* of breakfast cereals, right? Be imaginative.

SHAPES	*FLAVORS*	*COLORS*	*SIZES*
_____	_____	_____	_____
_____	_____	_____	_____
_____	_____	_____	_____
_____	_____	_____	_____
_____	_____	_____	_____
_____	_____	_____	_____
_____	_____	_____	_____

Suppose you were a toy manufacturer with a warehouse full of unsold skateboards. The problem is to change one (or more) parts or qualities of the skateboards to make them really different so they'll once again sell like crazy and make you another million $$$. List some parts or qualities of the skateboards, and then think of ideas for changing these parts. Be creative.

Part or quality   #1_____   #2_____   #3_____   #4_____

Changes:

_____	_____	_____	_____
_____	_____	_____	_____
_____	_____	_____	_____
_____	_____	_____	_____
_____	_____	_____	_____

What are some *qualities* of

a. a doorbell? _____

b. a bicycle basket?_____

c. a Band-Aid? _____

d. a piece of sandpaper? _____

e. a paperweight? _____

f. a rose? _____

g. an umbrella _____

h. a potholder? _____

i. a cocker spaniel? _____

*From *Imagination Express,* © 1973 DOK Publishers. Reprinted by permission.

In sympathy with beginners, he wrote, "Take heart! Every great writer was once an amateur . . . The great bulk of their writing . . . is distinctly mediocre in quality—and their early work is generally drivel."[3]

Attribute modifying may be used with any sort of problem in which the attributes, dimensions, or parts are identifiable. For example, the problem of reducing absenteeism in the corporation could be reduced to dimensions of "sources of unpleasantness" in the company; "characteristics of employees who frequently stay home"; "types of inducements, rewards, or threats that might reduce absenteeism"; and others. Advertising strategists might examine dimensions of advertising appeals, for example, with suggestions that the product will "make life more comfortable or enjoyable," "improve the buyer's social standing," "demonstrate the buyer's good taste," "make the buyer appear more energetic and healthy," "make the buyer more sexually attractive," and so on.

Any type of product improvement or new product development problem is a natural for attribute listing. New lines of refrigerators are created by modifying attributes of sizes, shapes, colors, door arrangements, shelf designs, appearance, materials, dispensers, butter and veggie keepers, or other modifications, uses, or functions (e.g., cooling wine, playing music).

Attribute Transferring

Attribute transferring is another name for analogical thinking, which we covered in Chapter 6. When Fran Striker lifted a plot, character, or "new angle" from one of his westerns and modified it to fit a Lone Ranger episode, he was transferring an attribute to a new creation. As described in Chapter 6, to stimulate attribute transferring—or analogical thinking—one can ask: What else is like this? What have others done? Where could we find an idea? What could we copy? What has worked before? What would professionals do?, and so on.

For example, in a classroom or exhibition hall some truly imaginative and memorable displays could be created by borrowing attributes (ideas) from a circus; Disney characters; MacDonald's; a Harry Potter, Lord of the Rings, or Star Wars movie; China; the Aztecs; a football game; the old west; and so on.

Barron (1988) made a strong statement about creative thinking that seems to justify Crawford's enthusiasm for attribute listing as a core creative processes:

> . . . the ability to change things . . . is central to the creative process. New forms do not come from nothing, not for us humans at any rate; they come from prior forms, through mutations, whether unsought or invited. In a fundamental sense, there are no theories of creation; there are only accounts of the development of new forms from earlier forms. (p. 83)

At any age level or with any learners, the two attribute listing strategies provide material for a good lesson in "where ideas come from" and in using an effective creative thinking technique, one used by many—Crawford and Barron might say *all*—creatively productive people.

Morphological Synthesis

Higgins (1994), VanGundy (1983), and others call this procedure "Morphological Analysis." So did I until I received a long and polite letter from Myron Allen about 1975 explaining exactly why his procedure is correctly named *Morphological Synthesis*, not "Morphological Analysis." Something to do with combining (synthesizing) ideas into an innovative whole, rather than analyzing component parts.

Morphological Synthesis (Allen, 1962, 1968) basically is an extension of the attribute-modifying procedure. Here, specific ideas for one attribute or dimension of a problem are listed along one axis of a matrix. Ideas for a second attribute are listed along the other axis. Lots of new idea combinations are

---

[3] Fran Striker had a subtle sense of humor. In Spanish, his Indian companion's name, *Tonto*, means "stupid." Tonto's name for the Long Ranger, *Kemo Sabe*, doesn't mean anything. But *quien no sabe* translates "[one] who knows not"—a know-nothing. ("C'mon, Stupid, after 'em!" "I'm coming, you Know-Nothing!") This joke continued for years, right under our monolingual noses.

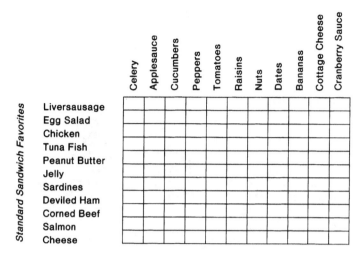

New Companions to Add Zest

Standard Sandwich Favorites	Celery	Applesauce	Cucumbers	Peppers	Tomatoes	Raisins	Nuts	Dates	Bananas	Cottage Cheese	Cranberry Sauce
Liversausage											
Egg Salad											
Chicken											
Tuna Fish											
Peanut Butter											
Jelly											
Sardines											
Deviled Ham											
Corned Beef											
Salmon											
Cheese											

Ratings of Various Spreads

	Choices				
Flavor	1st	2nd	3rd	4th	5th
Super Goober (Peanut Butter/Cranberry)	17	2	1	0	4
Charlie's Aunt (Tuna and Applesauce)	3	16	2	2	1
Irish Eyes are Smiling (Corned Beef and Cottage Cheese)	0	0	16	2	6
Cackleberry Whiz (Hard-Boiled Eggs/Cheese Whiz)	1	3	2	14	4
Hawaiian Eye (Cream Cheese and Pineapple)	3	3	3	6	9

(Six girls had squeamish stomachs and did not participate.)

FIGURE 8.1 A Morphological Sandwich

A sixth-grade Milwaukee class used the morphological synthesis method to generate 121 zany ideas for creative sandwiches. Can you find a tasty combination? A revolting one? (Davis & DiPego, 1973)

in the cells of the matrix. One sixth-grade Milwaukee class used the technique to invent new sandwich ideas (Figure 8.1). The kids had a swell time designing the new sandwich spreads, many of which are not too revolting. They also learned that they are capable of thinking of clever new ideas and that, if needed, this "checkerboard method" (Davis & DiPego, 1973) can help them find ideas. Note that with a third dimension, for example, 10 types of bread, we would have a three-dimensional cube containing 1,210 (11 × 11 × 10) idea combinations.

The morphological synthesis method may be used with a half-dozen-or-so dimensions by listing ideas in columns and, if you wish, cutting the columns into vertical strips. Each strip would slide up or down; new idea combinations would be created by reading horizontally (Fabun, 1968). With the strategy used by Fran Striker to generate *Lone Ranger* plots, four dimensions were used. If Striker systematically examined each and every one of his hundreds of possible combinations, we would call his method *morphological synthesis*, as Shallcross (1981) did, rather than *attribute listing*. The methods are similar.

Earlier in this chapter, we mentioned two books for teaching character and values, both of which use creativity techniques to stimulate students to think about their own character and values. Each section of *Character Education: Activities and Exercises for Developing Positive Attitudes and Behavior* (Davis, 2004a) covered one category of values, namely, honesty and trustworthiness, rights of others, manners, school and work habits, energy and the environment, and personal development (e.g., responsibility, compassion,

Roof inspector Gilbert Gluefinger used the morphological synthesis technique to find ideas for getting to the building top. "The combination of 'climb' and 'wall' produced this solution," observes the regretful inspector. "Maybe I should have tried 'ride' and 'elevator'." Source: From Safety Last!, Starring Harold Lloyd. Copyright © 1923 by Harold Lloyd Trust. Reprinted by permission.

valuing health, valuing respect, caring for animals). *A separate morphological synthesis chart was used to help generate exercises for each section.* For example, types of honesty and trustworthiness were listed on one axis (not cheating, not stealing, not shoplifting, not lying, returning things, keeping promises, not vandalizing), and idea-finding techniques appeared along the other (brainstorming, reverse brainstorming, analogical thinking, visualization, taking another perspective, "What would happen if . . . ?"). The half-dozen morphological synthesis charts helped generate hundreds of ideas for thought-provoking exercises.

Of course, *Character Education* included other material, such as introductory chapters, a quick summary of moral education theory, a *Values Bill of Rights*, crossword and word search puzzles, values quizzes, and more. However, ideas for exercises came directly from a series of morphological synthesis charts. The strategy produced more ideas than your author could use; I stopped writing when the book seemed long enough.

How about a little practice with the morphological synthesis method? Look back at the sandwich makings in Figure 8.1. Can you substitute a few more exotic entries into the vertical and horizontal axes, add a "bread" dimension, and create some spit-inducing (or is it "mouth-watering") combinations? You might try using two ideas from the vertical axis with one from the horizontal axis. How about corned beef with green peppers on rye? Sliced turkey with a little deviled ham and celery on cracked wheat? Liver sausage with tomatoes and walnuts on pumpernickel? Peanut butter with sardines and ginger root on white? Well, three out of four isn't bad.

TABLE 8.1 Osborn's (1963) 73 Idea-Spurring Questions

Put to other uses? New ways to use as is? Other uses if modified?
Adapt? What else is like this? What other idea does this suggest? Does past offer parallel? What could I copy? Whom could I emulate?
Modify? New twist? Change meaning, color, motion, sound, odor, form, shape? Other changes?
Magnify? What to add? More time? Greater frequency? Stronger? Higher? Longer? Thicker? Extra value? Plus ingredient? Duplicate? Multiply? Exaggerate?
Minify? What to subtract? Smaller? Condensed? Miniature? Lower? Shorter? Lighter? Omit? Streamline? Split up? Understate?
Substitute? Who else instead? What else instead? Other ingredient? Other material? Other process? Other power? Other place? Other approach? Other tone of voice?
Rearrange? Interchange components? Other pattern? Other layout? Other sequence? Transpose cause and effect? Change pace? Change schedule?
Reverse? Transpose positive and negative? How about opposites? Turn it backward? Turn it upside down? Reverse roles? Change shoes? Turn tables? Turn other cheek?
Combine? How about a blend, an alloy, an assortment, an ensemble? Combine units? Combine purposes? Combine appeals? Combine ideas?

Idea Checklists

Sometimes, one can find an idea checklist that suggests solutions for your problem. A checklist may directly suggest ideas and solutions, or else items on the list may indirectly stimulate combinations beyond what actually appears on the list. As some examples, the Yellow Pages of a phone book may be used as a direct checklist for problems like "Who can fix the TV?" or "Where can I get a haircut?" A high school counselor might use the Yellow Pages for ideas on career counseling—"Look over these 10,000 occupations, Chris, maybe you can find a few interesting career possibilities." A department store or cheese store catalog or a jewelry store advertisement can be an idea checklist for a gift-giving problem. Wandering through a grocery store, department store, gift shop, or florist shop also amounts to reviewing "idea checklists" for creative meals, clothes, gifts, or centerpieces. A trip through the Yellow Pages or a department store catalog also might suggest product markets or applications for a new process or material.

Some idea checklists have been designed especially for creative problem solving. These lists indirectly push the imagination into new idea combinations and new analogical solutions. The best known of these is Osborn's (1963) *73 idea-spurring questions* (Table 8.1). Simplified versions of Osborn's checklist have appeared in creativity workbooks for children, for example, *Hippogriff Feathers* (Stanish, 1981) and *The Hearthstone Traveler* (Stanish, 1988). The children's version sometimes is called the SCAMPER technique (e.g., Westberg, 1996), an acronym for *S*ubstitute, *C*ombine, *A*dapt, *M*odify/*M*agnify/*M*inify, *P*ut to other uses, *E*liminate, and *R*everse/*R*earrange. As you wander through Osborn's list, ask yourself how a hamburger, TV, suitcase, soda pop product, or other object or process could be improved. The ideas will appear almost involuntarily.

In a creative engineering class at MIT, John Arnold (Mason, 1960) developed a shortlist of self-questions aimed at improving critical engineering features of commercial products (Table 8.2). Think about a bicycle or a proper upright vacuum cleaner as you look through his list.

VanGundy (1983) assembled a three-section checklist of "idea stimulators" based on "the principle of provocation" (presumably drawing from de Bono's provocation techniques, described in Chapter 9). The principle is that randomly selected words (or objects) can provoke colorful ideas and new viewpoints for a problem. Sometimes, a solution idea may be two or three steps removed from the initial stimulus phrase or word.

TABLE 8.2 Arnold's Checklist for Improving Engineering Features

Can we increase the function? Can we make the product do more things?
Can we get a higher performance level? Make the product last longer? More reliable? More accurate? Safer? More convenient to use? Easier to repair and maintain?
Can we lower the cost? Eliminate excess parts? Substitute cheaper materials? Design to reduce hand labor or achieve complete automation?
Increase the salability? Improve the appearance of the product? Improve the package? Improve its point of sale?

While Osborn's checklist did not say *Look stupid*, it did say *Reverse, Turn it backward,* and *Put to other uses.* "I just invented the horse-hair beard!" exclaimed Max Harp. Copyright by Universal City Studios, Inc. Courtesy of Universal Studios Publishing Rights. All rights reserved. Source: Harpo Marx in "Horse Feathers", 1932. Courtesy of Universal Studios Licensing LLC.

The top section of Table 8.3 contains a sample of VanGundy's "Try to" phrases. In VanGundy's example, if your neighbor's barking dog keeps you awake, you peruse the "Try to" list and perhaps speculate on *Seal it. Seal it* suggests *closing off, securing,* or *attaching.* You might consider sound insulation, ear plugs, *securing* an agreement from the neighbors to keep their dog quiet, or *attaching* a siren to your house that blasts when the dog barks.

The middle section of Table 8.3 contains one-word "Make it" stimulators for changing or improving a situation. Again using VanGundy's barking dog, you might freely associate to *Concave* and think of *hollow, curved,* and *reflective.* You decide the neighbor's promise to keep the dog quiet was a *hollow* gesture, and stronger measures are required. *Concave* suggests an electronic dish that immediately magnifies the bark to throw it back at the neighbors. *Reflective* suggests recording the bark and playing it under the sleeping neighbors' bedroom window at 4:00 AM.

You'll feel better just thinking of such ideas.

A checklist of "Think of" idea stimulators appears in the bottom section of Table 8.3. The objects in the list may inspire a new idea or approach to a problem. Let's apply it to the barking dog. Perusing the list, *Sardine cans* suggest placing nasty odors (perhaps only offensive to dogs) on your property line so the dog will keep its distance. *Superman* suggests a "get tough" approach—perhaps calling the police daily until the yapping is resolved. *Camels* are larger animals, which suggests borrowing a bigger and meaner dog that barks back. *Gyroscopes* are self-correcting devices. Perhaps the problem could be defined more broadly as "How can we make the dog want to stop barking?" Offer to pay for pet training lessons?

TABLE 8.3 Samples of "Try to," "Make it," and "Think of" Idea Stimulators
(Based on VanGundy, 1983)

Try to:		
Build it up	Compress it	Constrain it
Cushion it	Do it backwards	Enlarge it
Float it	Force it	Jiggle it
Loosen it	Mix it	Modify it
Multiply it	Push it	Rearrange it
Seal it	Shake it	Split it
Sprinkle it	Stack it	Suspend it
Tear it down	Tilt it	Turn it inside out
Understate it	Use a different medium	Use substitutions
Make it:		
Adjustable	Breathe	Complex
Concealed	Concave	Dirty
Disposable	Explode	Flimsy
Futuristic	Heavy	Hover
Invisible	Light	Nostalgic
Pop up	Reciprocate	Repetitious
Revolve	Romantic	Simple
Sleek	Slippery	Swivel
Timid	Transparent	Zigzag
Think of:		
Aerosol sprays	Balloons	Camels
Compost heaps	Contact lenses	Conveyor belts
Corsets	Disappearing ink	Earthquakes
Ejection seats	Gyroscopes	Mercury
Pogo sticks	Pole vaulting	Popcorn
Sardine cans	Scuba diving	Shutters
Sir Lancelot	Spider webs	Superman
Tea kettles	Telescopes	Time machines
Turtles	Waffle irons	X-rays

Checklist of Idea Stimulators

In 108 *Ways to Get a Bright Idea*, VanGundy (1983) listed—I forgot how many— strategies to help you become a more creative thinker and problem solver. The following are a few of his favorite questions that could provoke new ideas and problem solutions.

> *What is the principle underlying the problem?* When you find the underlying, broader problem, you open up lots more ideas. You don't want to just "prevent the dog from barking." A broader problem is how to "create silence." (We will see this strategy again in Chapter 9.)
>
> *What assumptions are you making about the problem?* Assumptions can be constraining. If you examine your assumptions, you may discover you're working on the wrong problem.
>
> *What seems to be most essential to consider with this problem?*
>
> *What is least important?*
>
> *Why is this a problem?*
>
> *Can you redefine the problem?* Said VanGundy (1983), "a well-defined problem is a solved problem. . . . As information is added, the problem becomes more structured . . . [and] it becomes relatively clear how to proceed" (p. 104).
>
> *Can you work backwards from a perhaps ideal solution?* This is a well-known engineering strategy.
>
> *Can you ask "What if …?"*
>
> *Can you use analogies?* What else is like this? Where can we borrow ideas?
>
> *Can you try to become the problem?* You get new viewpoints when you imagine that you yourself are the barking dog, the unused waste basket in the school hallway, or the herd of moles destroying your front lawn.
>
> *Can you visualize the problem?* Be a right-brain thinker while working on a problem. Relax and visualize the whole, interrelated problem situation.

Techniques and Active Ingredients

In an otherwise clearly written article, Smith (1998) presented a "formulary" and an "armamentarium" of creative thinking techniques. We'll call it a *checklist*. He examined 172 techniques, many of which appear in this book, and identified 50 "devices" or "active ingredients," which are the underlying mental mechanisms. By now, most of these mental devices should not surprise you. Some of Smith's most frequently occurring mental devices are:

> *Abstracting.* Viewing a problem in broader, more general terms.
>
> *Anonymity.* Ensuring that ideas are presented anonymously, to reduce inhibition.
>
> *Block removal.* Eliminating mental barriers to idea flow.
>
> *Bootstrapping.* Analyzing current ideas to produce further possibilities.
>
> *Boundary stretching.* Examining excessive values of problem factors.
>
> *Challenge assumptions.* Disputing given premises or principles in order to overcome habits.
>
> *Change of perspective.* Considering others' viewpoints.
>
> *Checklists.* Using idea checklists.
>
> *Combining.* Merging elements and aspects of the situation.
>
> *Concrete stimuli.* Using pictures or physical objects to spur thinking.
>
> *Decomposing.* Analyzing parts, attributes, and means to ends.
>
> *Deferred evaluation.* No criticism during idea generation to reduce inhibitions.
>
> *Display.* Making ideas visible (as in the various brainwriting and pin-card procedures).
>
> *Enhancement.* Improving current ideas.
>
> *Fantasizing.* Using imagination to briefly discard constraints of reality.
>
> *Force fit.* Examining previously unrelated ideas together.
>
> *Goal focus.* Breaking the task into sub-problems.

Goal setting. Establishing deadlines or quotas for motivational effect.

Group interaction. Hitchhiking on others' ideas.

Mental stimulation. Mentally creating images or scenarios.

Nominal group. Silently producing ideas; group members often do not interact.

Nondisclosure. Avoiding habitual responses by not clearly presenting the problem at the session outset.

Relationship search. Seeking connections or relationships among "things."

Remote stimuli. Using pictures or physical objects unrelated to the problem to spur thinking.

Using analogies. Searching for mechanisms or parts that are somehow similar to the given problem.

For further brainstorming and other idea-finding techniques, see *101 Creative Problem Solving Techniques* (Higgins, 1994), *108 Ways to Get a Bright Idea* (VanGundy, 1983), and *Serious Creativity* (de Bono, 1992a).

Summary

Success in today's organizations depends on creative problem solving.

Poet Ghiselin acknowledged that creativity in art is largely spontaneous and involuntary.

VanGundy classified creativity techniques as individual or group, verbal or silent, forced relationships or free association, and using stimuli that are related or unrelated to the problem.

Personal creative thinking techniques are idea-finding strategies that all creatively productive people use. Most involve analogical thinking.

Einstein used "mental experiments" to stimulate new perceptions and ideas.

Artists develop pet topics and styles that lead to their creative products. Ideas for art have been derived from the Bible, mythology, and historical events.

Comedians also use unique sources for their humor, for example, insults and self-criticism.

To develop personal idea-finding techniques, understand the techniques that others use. Standard procedures and techniques, such as analogical thinking and other techniques described in Chapters 5, 6, this chapter, and Chapter 9—if they work for you—can become personal techniques.

Additional techniques include asking, "What would happen if . . . ?," working backward from the goal, or speculating on how the problem will be solved in the future.

Other recommendations are to become involved in creative activities and to invite creative professionals and consultants to discuss creativity techniques. Creative persons serve as models.

Standard creative thinking techniques are taught in university and professional creativity courses. They also can be learned by elementary and secondary students. Davis used creativity techniques to prod students to think about their character and values.

Techniques involve deliberate creativity, which contrasts with intuitive creativity.

The term "brainstorming" is used loosely. True brainstorming is guided by Osborn's four basic ground rules: no criticism (deferred judgment), wild "freewheeling," quantity is wanted, and combination and improvement are desired.

Group members bring diverse backgrounds and experiences, and they hitchhike on each other's ideas. It is used in corporate settings. It also is used in classrooms as an exercise and for solving real problems. Brainstorming is intuitively appealing, simple, fun, therapeutic, and it works.

In brainstorming sessions, Taggar noted facilitative factors of raised motivation, an organized setting, and appreciation for contributors' ideas. Creativity-suppressing factors included worry about criticism, low motivation, "free riding," and somebody talking too much. In corporate settings, brainstorming problems can be complicated (e.g., identifying the problem and implementing an action plan).

The leader organizes the session, reviews the ground rules and procedural details, and explains the problem. He or she may ask for problem facts or alternative problem definitions. Group members should vary in backgrounds and training to stimulate different viewpoints; they should be equal in status to reduce inhibitions.

An important decision is whether or not to use a brainstorming group in the first place.

Some ideas simply may stand out, or evaluation criteria and an evaluation matrix may be used. Evaluation teaches people to evaluate as part of the creative process and to look at many problem components. Evaluation may help clarify the group's values and can prove that silly ideas may suggest productive ones.

Variations include Reverse Brainstorming (make the problem worse), Backward Brainstorming (find problems), Stop-and-Go Brainstorming, the Phillips 66 procedure, and Complaint Brainstorming.

Brainwriting requires writing or drawing ideas. Mind mapping can clarify a complex problem. With basic brainwriting, members circulate written ideas around the table for additional hitchhikes. With Take Five, teams of five rank ideas in importance; their best ideas are then ranked by the whole group. With Brainwriting Pool, group members around a table randomly select each other's idea lists from the center of the table for further hitchhikes.

In Mitsubishi Brainstorming, members can delay reading their ideas aloud to avoid embarrassment. With Brainwriting 6-3-5 and Method 6-3-5, six people begin with three ideas for a problem that are circulated for hitchhikes and new ideas. C-Sketch is almost identical except sketched solutions are circulated, and speaking is forbidden.

Using an Idea Board, a posted problem elicits solutions that are posted under it. With storyboarding, posted column headings (e.g., "Purpose" plus main issues and solution directions) each elicit ideas that are posted under the suitable "header." In the NHK method, members write five ideas on separate cards; hitchhikes and more hitchhikes also are written on separate cards; all ideas are written on a board, which stimulates even more hitchhikes.

In the Gallery Method, each member creates a "gallery" of ideas for a problem, which stimulates hitchhikes by other members. With the SIL method members successively merge their ideas into a single solution.

Electronic Brainstorming, a form of Group Support Systems (GSS), claims typical brainstorming advantages of diverse member backgrounds and cross-fertilization of ideas (hitchhiking, piggybacking). With voice messaging and e-mail, any number of experts worldwide can participate, and at their convenience (no space and time problems). With synchronous video systems, telephone conferences, and interactive computer conferences, distant members must be available at the same time.

Some researchers (not all) find that electronic brainstorming produces more ideas per person than regular brainstorming sessions.

Several computer programs (IdeaFisher, Ideagen, Idea Generator, MindLink, StormZ, and Invention Machine) lead thinkers through problem solving steps and generate mind-prodding ideas and problem approaches.

Herrmann's whole brain approach amounted to building a creativity group composed of people each of whom is strong in a particular ability—which agrees with Osborn's emphasis on heterogeneity of brainstorming group membership.

Osborn cautioned us that brainstorming is not a miracle cure-all, particularly if recommended procedures are not followed. Some folks are more creative alone.

Crawford's attribute listing included attribute modifying and attribute transferring (analogical thinking). Fran Striker used a form of attribute listing to generate plots for Lone Ranger episodes. Crawford and Barron agreed that modifying existing ideas is a core creative process.

Morphological synthesis amounts to attribute listing in a matrix form. One normally would use two or three dimensions, but six or more are possible. Your author used morphological synthesis charts to help generate hundreds of exercises for a character education book. The technique suggests large numbers of ideas.

The Yellow Pages or catalogs can serve as idea checklists. Osborn's 73 idea-spurring questions were deliberately designed to stimulate creative thinking. Arnold aimed his idea checklist at improving engineering features.

VanGundy's three-section checklist presents provocative "Try to," "Make it," and "Think of" idea stimulators. VanGundy also itemized a checklist of questions that can provoke new ideas and problem solutions.

Smith reviewed 172 creativity techniques and identified core "devices," such as viewing a problem in broader terms, using idea checklists, and using pictures/objects to spur thinking.

Review Exercises

Techniques of Creative Thinking: Increasing Your Idea-Finding Capability

Self-Test: Key Concepts, Terms, and Names

Briefly define or explain each of these:

Spontaneous and involuntary (Ghiselin) _____

_____

Personal creative thinking techniques _____

_____

Brainstorming _____

_____

Deferred judgment _____

_____

"Team Creativity-Relevant Processes" _____

_____

Production Blocking _____

_____

Reverse Brainstorming_____

_____

Backward Brainstorming _____

_____

Stop-and-go Brainstorming _____

_____

Phillips 66 technique _____

_____

Mind Mapping _____

_____

Mitsubishi Brainstorming _____

_____

C-Sketch _____

_____

Idea Board _____

_____

Advantages of electronic brainstorming (e.g., via e-mail) _____

_____

Attribute Modifying _____

_____

Attribute Transferring _____

_____

Morphological Synthesis _____

_____

Idea checklists _____

_____

Osborn's 73 Idea Spurring Questions _____

_____

"Try to," "Make it," and "Think of" _____

_____

Let's Think about It

1. Brainstorming. You are an executive for Tombstone Pizza, Inc. You just brought home a Mexican Pizza, and the wheels started spinning. "Mexico isn't the only place with unique groceries," you think to yourself. Think of other countries (or locations, such as western U.S.) that might suggest new and exciting pizza combinations, and then suggest some of the ingredients that would represent that country.

   Name of your first pizza invention (include country or area) _____

   _____

   Possible ingredients _____

   _____

   Second pizza _____

   _____

   Possible ingredients _____

   _____

   Third pizza _____

   _____

   Possible ingredients _____

   _____

2. Let's try REVERSE Brainstorming. Imagine there is a burglary problem in your neighborhood. Think of all the ideas you can to make the problem WORSE. That is, what can you do to attract burglars and make it easy for them to break in and steal your stuff?

   _____

   _____

   _____

   _____

   Do these ideas give you a few suggestions for reducing break-ins?

   _____

   _____

   _____

3. Let's try BACKWARD Brainstorming. Imagine your favorite restaurant. Think of all the problems you can with this restaurant. That is, think of how it might be improved still further.

_____

_____

_____

_____

4. Imagine you are a short-story writer, perhaps aspiring to write TV scripts. Let's use attribute listing to generate story ideas. Be imaginative.

In the first column below, list interesting *characters*. They can be real characters in today's news; mythological or Biblical characters; characters with magical abilities; perhaps stereotyped characters from mysteries, romances, adventure stories, westerns, science fiction; and so on. Include some important *objects* (powerful, valuable, magical) in this list and, if you wish, an *animal* or two.

In the second column, list some *goals* (objectives)—things that story characters might want to possess, achieve, become, prevent, have happen, get revenge against, cure, and so on.

In the third column, list some *obstacles*, such as being blind, poor, or gullible; personality weaknesses; bureaucratic barriers; lack of power; traditions; weather; isolation; and so on.

Finally, list some *outcomes* (solutions), perhaps stemming from cunning, courage, espionage, persistence, prayer, wits, changing one's mind, or sacrificing something one values.

Characters	Goals	Obstacles	Outcomes
_____	_____	_____	_____
_____	_____	_____	_____
_____	_____	_____	_____
_____	_____	_____	_____
_____	_____	_____	_____
_____	_____	_____	_____
_____	_____	_____	_____
_____	_____	_____	_____

Now pick three or four ideas from the *Characters* column and one or two ideas each from the *Goals*, *Obstacles*, and *Outcomes* columns, and sketch an outline of your creative TV episode.

_____

_____

_____

_____

_____

5. Look at Osborn's "73 idea-spurring questions" in Table 8.1 (p. 165). Look around the room or in your pocket, purse, or backpack for some relatively simple consumer product (perhaps the backpack itself). Use the "questions" in the list to think of ways the product might be changed or improved.

Object: _____

Ideas for improvement:

_____

_____

_____

_____

_____

_____

6. What's "good" about the concept of "creativity techniques"?

_____

_____

_____

_____

What's "bad" about "creativity techniques"?

_____

_____

_____

7. Think about recent movies, books, breakfast cereals, Broadway shows, inventions, political cartoons, or new consumer products you have seen lately. Where do you think the idea might have come from? That is, can you think of a technique or source of inspiration the innovator might have used to create the idea?

Innovation 1:_____

Likely Source or Technique: _____

Innovation 2:_____

Likely Source or Technique: _____

Innovation 3:_____

Likely Source or Technique: _____

Can you think of situations in which no obvious source of inspiration or "technique" was used to produce the idea?

8. Going back to the Morphological Sandwich presented in Figure 8.1, what new deli item did you come up with? If you didn't generate one do it now. Take one item from the vertical list and one from the horizontal list and combine them together. Give you sandwich a name that everyone is sure to remember !

Creativity Applications, Pt. 2—Lateral Thinking and Six Thinking Hats

9

Contributing Author: Hector Ramos

"The painter of the future will be a colorist in a way that no one else has before."

—Vincent van Gogh

Black, blue, yellow hue
The Starry night swirls "adieu"
Red, white, not in sight
Some colors just aren't right
Flow, Flow, with Van Gogh
Brushes stroking a mental show
Red, white, green black . . .
Switching colors just like hats
When used wisely
And concisely
Your work of art
Will show up nicely

This original poem was inspired by Edward de Bono's "six hats." It parallels the colors used of a painter, Van Gogh, with the colors of de Bono's "six hats." In the *Starry Night* portrait, Van Gogh paints with black, blue, and yellow colors. Together, they produce his most renowned work of art. And in the same way, when different color thinking "hats" are used wisely, the result will be just like a work of art.

De Bono on Creativity

> Mr. Churchill sat down next to lady Astor at dinner one day. She turned to him and said. "Mr Churchill, if I was married to you I should put poison in your coffee." Mr Churchill turned to her and said: "Madam, if I was married to you . . . I should drink the coffee."
>
> A flock of sheep was moving slowly down a country lane which was bounded by high banks. A motorist in a hurry came up behind the flock and urged the shepherd to move his sheep to the side so that the car could drive through. The shepherd refused since he could not be sure of keeping all the sheep out of the way of the car in such a narrow lane. Instead he reversed the situation. He told the car to stop and then quietly turned the flock round and drove it back past the stationary car.
>
> In Aesop's fable the water in the jug was at too low level for the bird to drink. The bird was thinking of taking water out of the jug but instead he thought of putting something in. So he dropped pebbles into the jug until the level of water rose high enough to drink.
>
> Traditional thinking is concerned with recognizing standard situations and applying standard solutions. . . . In a changing world . . . there is a need for the "what-can-be" type of thinking . . . to bring about new things that have not yet existed.
>
> Everyone has the right to doubt everything as often as he pleases and the duty to do it at least once. No way of looking at things is too sacred to be reconsidered. No way of doing things is beyond improvement

> *—Edward de Bono*

Edward de Bono has written over **60** books on thinking, mainly creative thinking, and translated into 43 languages. He was a Rhodes Scholar at Oxford, and held appointments at Oxford, Cambridge, and Harvard, which included medical research, and the University of London, facts mentioned in every book. He also runs a training franchise with **300** certified trainers in **72** countries. De Bono's thinking systems include training in Lateral Thinking, Six Thinking Hats, and Simplicity.[1]

He credits his medical experience with aiding his understanding of brain functions, which is curious since he studied "circulation, respiration, ion control, kidney functions, hormones, etc." (de Bono, 1992b, p. 28). As two more serious and important points, first, he noted that the brain will organize even bizarre verbal or visual input—for example, from some of his lateral thinking techniques—into more-or-less sensible patterns and sequences. Second, he emphasized the brain's normal tendency to form habits, expectations, and patterns that prevent thinking of new ideas and problem solutions.[2]

De Bono sees combating such interfering expectations and mental patterns as the core purpose of his lateral thinking techniques. Many of his techniques require the individual or group to work from often outlandish statements—which can lead to highly imaginative, yet workable problem solutions. Sometimes.

De Bono has an impressive track record. He personally takes credit for the *Neighborhood Watch* idea. Peter Ueberroth, using lateral thinking techniques learned from de Bono, in 1984 saved the International Olympics from ending due to financial difficulties. De Bono's clients include many of the leading corporations in the world, including IBM (which taught his Six Thinking Hats strategy to 40,000 employees worldwide), Boeing, 3M, GM, Kraft, Nestle, Du Pont, Prudential, and Shell Oil.

---

[1] www.debono.com

[2] In introductory psychology courses, these habit-based brain functions are called *mental sets* and *perceptual sets*.

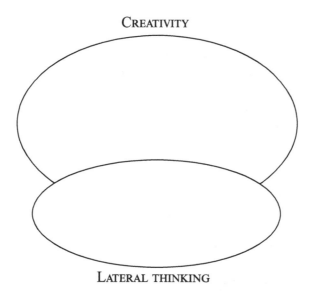

FIGURE 9.1 Relationship between creativity and lateral thinking.

Lateral Thinking

De Bono's popular concept of *lateral thinking* commonly is taken to exactly mean *creativity*. However, de Bono describes them as overlapping (Figure 9.1). As we will see in the discussion of *Six Thinking Hats*—a book title and a major lateral thinking strategy—problem-solvers examine information, explore feasibility, criticize, and review progress. Such thinking falls outside of narrower conceptions of *creativity*. At the same time, much creativity—for example, from intuition or in art or literature—lies outside of de Bono's lateral thinking. In his writing, de Bono himself regularly uses the term *creativity*.

Consider de Bono's time-honored metaphor: Instead of digging a hole deeper (i.e., examining familiar paths and solutions), we should creatively dig the hole in a different place. With vertical thinking, we build on a given position with logical, selective, and sequential steps. But "lateral thinking is generative" (de Bono, 1970, p. 12). We move sideways "to find other approaches and other alternatives" (de Bono, 1992a, p. 52) and "different perceptions and different concepts" (p. 53). Lateral thinking, he emphasizes, is not linear, sequential, logical, or based on "old structures, old patterns, old concepts, and old perceptions" (p. 17).

According to his proud spot in the *Concise Oxford Dictionary*, Edward de Bono's *lateral thinking* seeks "to solve problems by unorthodox or apparently illogical methods."

In de Bono's (1992a) amusing example, Granny is trying to knit, but little Susan upsets her by playing with the ball of yarn. One parent suggests putting Susan in the playpen. The other suggests putting Granny in the playpen. And even though we can (dirty) dance around the issue, the fact remains that regardless of who is in the playpen, NOBODY puts Baby in a corner.

He differentiates *lateral thinking* from *creativity* mainly by criticizing the often "hit-or-miss" (de Bono, 1992a, p. 39), "craziness-based" (p. 38), "scatter-gun" (p. 39), and "simply suspending judgment" approaches of creativity, particularly in brainstorming, which he frequently insults. Said de Bono, the "wide and confused meaning" (p. 55) of *creativity* includes elements of *new* and *value*. In contrast, "lateral thinking is concerned with changing [our] concepts and perceptions" (p. 55) and includes specific, more focused techniques. Lateral thinking "is practical and makes a difference" (de Bono, p. 77). As mentioned earlier, de Bono freely uses the word *creativity*. He titled a 1992 book *Serious Creativity*, not "Serious Lateral Thinking."

Six Thinking Hats

After his 1970 *Lateral Thinking* book, another de Bono creativity sensation was *Six Thinking Hats* (de Bono, 1986). The simple-but-enlightening message is to clarify and control six common roles that people play when solving problems or thinking creatively.

Briefly, the six hat method designates a time for groups or individuals to consider the given information; generate creative ideas; be optimistic; grouch and criticize; toss out hunches, feelings, and guesses; and summarize where they are. Usually, but not necessarily, at the leader's direction the group members put on a different colored hat and think differently. They don't continue to grouse, grumble, and complain; they don't get lost in minor diversions; and they don't worry about voicing feelings and hunches. Participants must look beyond their own favorite position. Cooperative exploration replaces time-wasting adversarial thinking. This exploration together happens through parallel thinking as participants do at all times the same type of thinking (de Bono, 1986).[3] Game-like thinking sessions become productive. Said de Bono (1992a), "At last there is a way of breaking free from the traditional argument system" (p. 81).

The description and purpose of the Six Thinking Hats are summarized in Table 9.1. Study the table—it's important and valuable. Briefly, wearing the white hat individuals or group members discover and review information about a problem. The green hat signals that it's time to be creative—members freely generate new possibilities, alternatives, and approaches. The optimistic yellow hat asks for benefits,

TABLE 9.1 Six Thinking Hats

HAT	MNEMONIC	CONCERN/PURPOSE	EXAMPLES OF CONCERNS
White	"White paper" (informative, neutral)	Getting information, new data	What information do we have? What information do we need? How can we get information?
Green	"Vegetation, rich growth" (generating ideas, possibilities)	Positive creative effort	We need ideas for this. Is there a different approach? Are there other explanations?
Yellow	"Sunshine" (optimism, positive view)	Looks for benefits, feasibility, how something *can* be done	A new benefit would be. . . . It would work if we. . . . It would raise morale. . . .
Black	"Stern, black-robed judge" (critical judgment)	Identifies mistakes, illegalities, unworkability, unprofitability	Against regulations That didn't work before. We are unable to do that.
Red	"Fire and warm" (feelings, emotions, hunches, intuition)	Expressing feelings, emotions, etc.	This is how I feel. . . . My intuition says that we. . . . My gut feeling is. . . .
Blue	"Sky" (an overview; thinking about current thinking)	Suggests next thinking step, using other hats, summaries, conclusions, decisions	Let's summarize our views. Let's try green (yellow, black, etc.) hat thinking. . . . Let's think about priorities. . . .

Source: Based on de Bono (1985); de Bono, E. (1992a). *Serious creativity.* New York, NY: Advanced Practical Thinking Training.

---

[3] Parallel Thinking http://www.debonogroup.com/parallel_thinking.php

feasibility, and other positive inputs. With the black hat members can bring up objective negative elements into the discussion. They can assess the risk by comparing to previous experience or suggest faults in a design. The intention of black hat thinking is to separate feelings and opinions from facts. The red hat allows expressing emotions and "gut feelings" ("Hey, that direction looks mighty promising!"). This is usually done with one word and not taking as a venting opportunity for group members. The blue hat normally is worn only by the leader to facilitate the hat process as the hats could follow a predetermined sequence. These facilitators also review ideas and sum up progress ("Putting on my blue hat, this is what we have so far . . . "), or suggest a different hat ("Let's do some more green hat thinking about Cathy's approach"). Hats may be used more than once. For instance, black hat thinking may reveal flaws that need to be addressed with green hat thinking. Green hat thinking may need to be explored through the benefit-related yellow hat thinking. White hat thinking may take place at different times as the facilitator senses the need to review further information that the use of other hats helped uncover.

Of course, some group members are better at one kind of thinking than another. We have critical Ebenezer Scrooges, new-idea Thomas Edisons, and optimistic Cinderellas and Pinocchios. It should be clear that with the six hat method, when members switch hats they also switch their thinking. Scrooge might look for benefits and feasibility (yellow hat), Cinderella and Pinocchio look for faults, short-comings, and unworkability (black hat), or Edison raises his eyebrows and shares feelings, emotions, and hunches regarding an idea or concept (red hat).

The typical and logical sequence is:

White hat: *Information*. What do we know? What information do we need?
Green hat: *Ideas and alternatives*. Are there other approaches? Explanations?
Yellow hat: *Optimism*. What are some benefits? Is this feasible? How is it valuable?
Black hat: *Critical judgment*. Is this a mistake? Is it legal? Is it profitable?
Red hat: *Intuition and feelings*. I feel this is better than that. That scares me.
Blue hat: *Overview*. This is what we have so far. . . . Okay, we've decided to. . . .

Even if the order is not fixed, the facilitators guide the conversation. Usually, the group leader asks for thinking wearing a particular hat ("Let's put on our black hats. Will this idea work? Anything illegal? Immoral? Unethical?"). Or the facilitator may introduce yellow hat thinking to explore the benefits of some ideas generated.

According to de Bono, "normal discussion" can take place both before and after the group thinks under a given hat. Using the Six Thinking Hats creates an enjoyable game-like atmosphere, and, more importantly, the thinking session stays on target.

Six Thinking Hats allows groups to move from ego-centered arguments to directing attention to six ways of thinking about a subject.

De Bono emphasizes the importance of role playing as participants agree to use certain rules. This process disarms them from their traditional approach of personally advocating for an idea to engaging in a group effort that is constructive in nature.

Six Thinking Hats has been used in schools not only to help math students improve their creative thinking skills (Farajallah & Saidam, 2018) but also to teach students in critical thinking and problem-solving (Kivunja, 2015), creative thinking (Kaur, 2017), and creative writing (Majid & AL-Tarawneh, 2015). Six Thinking Hats has also been used to improve managerial decision-making (Aithal & Kumar, 2017) and increase the speed of brainstorming (Göçmen & Coşkun, 2019).

Lateral Thinking Strategies

The specific strategies in de Bono's 30 to 55 books cannot be adequately summarized in one chapter. I recommend his 338-page *Serious Creativity* (de Bono, 1992a), which reviews lateral thinking in general, Six Thinking Hats, lots of remarkable lateral thinking techniques, and more. To truly master lateral thinking, he recommends his training course.

While the six hat technique controls the orderliness and productivity of a personal or, more often, group thinking session, de Bono's lateral thinking techniques aim mostly at green hat thinking—finding new ideas, approaches, alternatives, viewpoints, and solutions. If done properly, his lateral thinking techniques absolutely force departures from habitual thinking and perceiving.

Underlying concepts. One important preliminary idea—and lateral thinking technique—is acknowledging the distinction between thinking of specific solution *ideas* for a problem versus looking for a more general underlying *concept*. Sometimes, we suggest ideas and solutions for the problem as given; sometimes we search for and elaborate on the underlying concept. We might ask, "What concept underlies this idea?" or "What is the broader concept here?". In Chapters 6 and 8 we mentioned searching for broader, underlying problems, perhaps by repeatedly asking "Why?"

For example, instead of finding specific ideas to improve snow blowers, we might explore concepts of "keeping sidewalks free of snow" or "preventing slipping and falling, regardless of snow." Clearly, looking at underlying concepts broadens the problem and leads to a wider variety of approaches and ideas. Sometimes, underlying concepts will suggest still broader underlying concepts, such as, in this example, "preventing snowfalls" (perhaps with an awning).

As we will see later, the *Concept Fan* technique requires working back and forth between ideas and their underlying concepts to find additional specific ideas, additional underlying concepts, and even more general concepts.

Fixed Points. Another preliminary, important, and related notion is de Bono's *fixed point.* The initial problem as given is a fixed point from which ideas flow. Or an underlying concept can be the fixed point that suggests new directions, ideas, or further underlying concepts.

Creative Pause

One of de Bono's core procedures, the first described in *Serious Creativity* (de Bono, 1992a), is the Creative Pause. It's just that. One pauses to make a creative effort. A person or group pays deliberate attention to some element or detail, perhaps one that typically is overlooked. A creative pause implies motivation—the person or group intends to be creative. "We need to think about this," "Are there other possibilities here?" With a creative pause, thinkers notice things—new possibilities, new routes, new lines of thought. Said de Bono (1992a), "The pause is a way of building up a creative attitude" (p. 90).

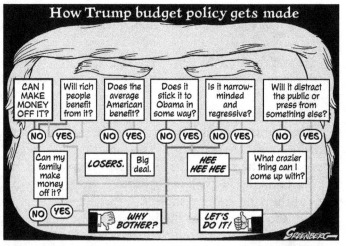

Asking "Why?" Source: Joe Heller, © 2003 Green Bay Press Gazette. Reprinted by permission.

Focus

De Bono's emphasis on Focus—"a very powerful creative tool" (de Bono, 1992a, p. 91)—takes many forms. For example, instead of trying to find ways to improve a common and well-designed item, it may be easier and more effective to switch one's focus to something less noticed. In de Bono's example, while Black and Decker designers focused on improving their power tools, an outside inventor shifted focus and designed the practical Black and Decker Workmate work table. He made millions.

One principle is thus to seek out unnoticed, perhaps unusual, focus points. Once a focus area is identified, it may be attacked as a problem needing creative ideas. Focusing, and altering our focus, can become a valuable habit, particularly in yellow hat (optimism) and green hat (idea generation) thinking.

Focus may be *general* or *specific*. General area focus is simply defining the area in which we want ideas, for example, in the area of retail stores, cell phones, or Internet use. A general area focus may be wide (cell phones) or narrower (the use of cell phones by teenagers). Having a specific focus—or purpose—is more common. We may wish to review or improve a situation, solve a specific problem, accomplish a task, explore "idea-sensitive points" (spots where a small change can make a big difference), explore opportunities (e.g., more and more Minnesota snow birds like warmer winters), or just pursue a whim, which is essentially a no-reason-at-all creative focus.

A broad focus may be broken into simpler, multiple, perhaps overlapping foci. For example, a general focus on improving customer relations may be broken into such specific foci as: How can we improve the pleasantness of customer service? How can we avoid wasting customers' time? How can we make the store appear more customer-friendly? How can we give customers pleasant surprises?

Said de Bono, the focus habit especially benefits persons who normally think creatively only when faced with a definite problem.

You may have deduced accurately that creative pause and focus are closely related. One pauses to focus on creative possibilities. Both require a comparatively simple mental adjustment. Let's pause and think about implications of the creative pause and focus.

Creative Challenge

The creative challenge simply asks whether the current way is the best way. We can creatively challenge any operation or action—which quickly stimulates alternatives. Is this the only way to look at this situation? Why are we doing it this way? Are there other ways to do this? What is the underlying concept? What are we assuming? What are crucial features? What should be avoided? Aren't there other types of containers?

Creative challenge is not criticism or dislike, but a valuable exploration of possibilities.

Alternatives

Of course, a search for alternatives underlies most forms of creative thinking. De Bono (1992a) observed that when things go well we tend not to look for alternatives and improvements—even though there are better or more profitable ways to accomplish a task. He named this the *continuity of neglect*.

The search for alternatives is aided by the three procedures already described: creative pause, focus, and creative challenge. All other lateral thinking techniques are strategies for finding sometimes highly imaginative ideas.

Concept Fan

The Concept Fan is an organized search for alternatives. In a three-level fan, the given problem suggests a mid-level general approach to solutions. Each mid-level approach leads to a larger number of specific ideas for that approach. One works back and forth. That is, mid-level concepts suggest specific ideas, and the specific ideas suggest additional mid-level concepts, and so on. When diagrammed we have a concept fan.

In de Bono's (modified) example, the main problem was a water shortage. Three intermediate general directions were to (1) reduce consumption, (2) increase the water supply, and (3) do without water. Specific ideas for (1) were (a) discourage use of water, (b) reduce wasting water, and (c) public education. Specific ideas for (2) were (a) find new sources, (b) recycle water, and (c) (again) reduce wasting water. Specific ideas for (3) were (a) recycle water, (b) use substitutes for water, and (c) avoid the need to use water.

A fourth level for this concept fan could be created, for example, by speculating on ways to discourage the use of water (1a), for example, charge more for water, publish names of heavy users, and add a harmless smell to the water.

Concepts

As we have seen, identifying underlying concepts will suggest new ideas and approaches to solutions. The more general concept thus becomes a new "fixed point" for generating alternatives or still other underlying concepts (as in the concept fan, discussed above). De Bono (1992a) identified *purpose* concepts ("What is the purpose here?"), *mechanism* concepts ("How does this gadget operate to achieve its effect?"), and *value* concepts ("Why is this useful or valuable?"). The three types of questions will help identify underlying (purpose, mechanism, value) concepts.

Creative people, said de Bono, continually and habitually think back and forth between ideas and concepts.

Stepping Stones and Other Provocations

De Bono's "Stepping Stone" label is misleading. It suggests a clear path—stepping stones—that leads without effort to some nice problem solutions at the end of the garden path. Hardly true. Said de Bono (1992a), a stepping stone provocation "turns the problem inside out and puts things in a way that demands new thinking" (p. 194); "you should have no idea where the provocation might lead" (p. 169); "a provocation seeks to take our perceptions away from their usual direction" (p. 149); and "the more of a fantasy it is, the more provocative will be the provocation" (p. 175).

He also noted that 40% of provocations should lead nowhere.

De Bono describes four stepping stone provocative techniques, or just "Po" (provocative operation). A *reversal* provocation is just that. With de Bono's example, Po, "the telephone rings all the time and falls silent when there is a call" (p. 170). The subsequent thinking noted that the continual ring confirms that the phone is working, which suggested a small red light on the phone.

As an *exaggeration* stepping stone, de Bono (1992a) himself suggested "police have six eyes" in response to the problem of inadequate police to patrol New York City streets. This suggested that "individuals act as extra eyes and ears for the police" (p. 172) and eventually led to Neighborhood Watch programs.

A *distortion* stepping stone also is just that—some part of the problem is greatly distorted. Po: Students examine each other. This led to—as an exam question—asking students to create exam questions and explain why they proposed their questions.

Finally, *wishful thinking* also is self-defining. With a problem of downtown parking congestion, de Bono suggested: Po—cars should limit their own parking time. As one solution, if you leave your headlights on you need not pay the parking meter—you are certain not to park long.

Escape

Escape is another de Bono provocative technique, and a comparatively simple one. With escape, we just "escape" from what we take for granted. By upsetting normal procedures, we necessarily produce creative ideas. In de Bono's example, Po—restaurants do not provide silverware and plates (which we take for granted). His idea: Since you must take your own—and leave them at the restaurant—you could impress clients by using special plates displaying your company logo.

Random Word or Random Input

The Random Word/Random Input technique is a sixth provocative strategy, one described as "very powerful but seems totally illogical" (de Bono, 1992a, p. 177). Essentially, we randomly select a word and combine it with the situation. The strategy resembles chance events triggering new discoveries, many of which were noted in Chapter 6 (e.g., Westinghouse heard about the Swiss air-powered rock drill and promptly invented the air brake).

There are several random-word methods. For example, de Bono carried with him a list of 60 randomly selected words (occasionally renewed). He would look at the second hand on his watch, then select the word corresponding to the number of seconds. This random word is combined with the problem situation to suggest ideas. Or using a dictionary one might think of a page number (e.g., 579) and a word number (e.g., 21), then open to page 579 and find word number 21. (If it is not a noun, proceed down the page to the first noun.) Or close your eyes and touch a spot on a newspaper or book page—that's your random word.

The random-word method, which extends to random objects, is most suitable to "wide-open" types of thinking. In de Bono's examples, "cigarette Po traffic light," suggested a red band near the butt-end of cigarettes to prevent smoking into the most harmful zone. "Office copiers Po nose" suggested that specific copier malfunctions could emit specific smells.

The Random Word/Random Input procedure is particularly helpful when you don't know where to start, when you run out of ideas, or when you would like an additional line of thinking. Do you recall, in Chapter 8, combining an elephant with an oil well, and then thinking of how this association might help solve your problem? Same idea.

Stratals

A Stratal, another term coined by de Bono, and one of his two "sensitizing" techniques, begins with five or six different phrases, statements, or observations that relate to a particular area. Perusal of the stratal may suggest new ideas and idea combinations. To prevent selecting phrases that reflect one's current ideas, stratal lines can be picked blindly from a bag.

For example, a stratal for making cruise ships and cruises more appealing might include these statements:

As de Bono promised, this budding musician received surprising inspiration from the random words *floor*, *piano*, *nose*, and *shoe*. "But it would be easier if you didn't keep time on my face!" he complained. (Max Linder, Courtesy of PhotoFest.)

> Young couples rarely take cruises.
> Clientele don't wish to repeat the same cruise.
> Cruises are famous for gourmet food and overeating.
> Cruise ships sail to attractive locations.
> Cruise ships generally look alike.
> Cruise ships offer evening entertainment.

This stratal may suggest: Reducing prices for young couples; allowing young couples to sail free if they bring two or more parents; improved entertainment for children; adding younger generation attractions (discos, athletic opportunities, exotic ports and beaches);[4] offering shows that appeal to all or different ages; painting/decorating the ship to appeal to younger and older people; painting the ship so the cruise line will be recognized five miles away; sailing to exotic and historically fascinating places; and offering gourmet but low-calorie, smaller-portion dinners and desserts.

---

[4] Your author would note that obsolete is an anagram for obese lot!

Filament Technique

The Filament Technique, the second sensitizing technique, resembles stratals. We first list probably four to six normal one-word (or two-word) requirements for the problem situation. Then—ignoring the original problem context—we list four or five brief examples of each of the requirements ("filaments"). For example, in designing or improving mass transit stations we might consider:

FAST: No time wasted, no waiting, expedited, high speed
PLEASANT SURROUNDS: Nice wallpaper, attractive exterior, attractive interior, floral displays, relaxing
CONVENIENT: Close to home, easy parking, no hiking, hassle-free
CHEAP: Low cost, low overhead, low wages, low upkeep, high gas mileage
SAFE: No risk to people, no accidents, easy escapes, police presence, safe for children

Finally, we review the "parallel filaments"; select one item from each of several strands, and try to assemble these into a new idea for the initial problem. With designing/improving mass transit stations, the filaments *expedited, attractive exterior, hassle-free, low wages,* and *police presence* suggest an extra-attractive rural mass transit station with ticket machines (not ticket sellers) that accept money or credit cards, and with obvious video monitors and alarm buttons to deter crime. The filament *no time wasted, floral displays, close to home, low-cost,* and *safe for children* suggests an interesting indoor garden and an inexpensive, safe, and fun entertainment area for young children.

Specific Situations

De Bono (1992a) named 13 "specific situations"—think of them as problem situations—that need ideas or solutions.

1. *Problems.* Usually a difficulty you must remove.
2. *Tasks.* Something you voluntarily wish to do.
3. *Improvement.* Refining or bettering something already in operation.
4. *Opportunity.* A change in circumstances that may present opportunities, for example, a new low-cost material or strong growth in international travel.
5. *Invention.* General, for example, "something for the kitchen," or specific, for example, "a new drawer-closing mechanism."
6. *Design.* Creating something with a specified outcome.
7. *Stagnant Situations.* No recent creativity or new ideas.
8. *Greenfield Thinking.* Don't know where to begin.
9. *Projects.* Tasks requiring competence.
10. *Conflict.* Bargaining or negotiating, with conflicting interests.
11. *Futuristic thinking.* Extending present trends, anticipating new developments.
12. *Strategy.* A complex process involving most other situations, for example, "problems, opportunities, tasks, futures, and conflict . . . which are put together in a design process" (de Bono, 1992a, p. 205).
13. *Planning.* Finding better ideas.

Many of the 13 "specific situations" are similar, and distinctions seem to depend on one's choice of wording or other minor matters. Small wonder that de Bono noted that most types of lateral thinking techniques are useful with most "specific situations."

Nonetheless, de Bono (1992a) named which lateral thinking techniques seem best suited for each of the 13 problem situations. It would be tedious—and a highly forgettable waste of space—to walk through each of the 13 problem situations and indicate exactly which of the 14 lateral thinking techniques de Bono believes to be best suited for each. Besides, he's probably changed his mind.

But these are some general trends:

All 13 specific problem situations require finding alternatives, which is aided by the creative pause, focus, and creative challenge ("Aren't there better ways to do this?"). De Bono adores his six provocation (Po) techniques. He recommends the stepping stone techniques of Reversal, Exaggeration, Distortion, and Wishful Thinking plus Escape and Random Input/Word whenever one needs truly unique ideas, views, or starting points, as in Stagnant Situations, Greenfield Thinking, and most of the other specific situations.

Logically, the creative pause is recommended with conflict (bargaining, negotiating), a situation often requiring delicate diplomacy.

If the reader's head isn't sufficiently boggled with problem situations and lateral thinking techniques, de Bono (1992a) also identified three "basic types of thinking" (p. 193):

1. *Achievement Thinking (Reach)*, which "covers problems, tasks, projects, negotiation, conflicts, and so on" (p. 193).
2. *Improvement Thinking (Change)*, as described on our list (item 3).
3. *Greenfield Thinking (Start)*, as described on our list (item 8).

We noted that most lateral thinking strategies are useful with most of the 13 problem situations. De Bono (1992a) especially recommended challenge and his provocative techniques for all three basic types of thinking.

Teaching Thinking Skills to Children

Creativity and thinking skills are related in that creativity may be considered one complex type of thinking skill. Furthermore, most other thinking skills contribute to effective creative thinking and problem-solving. The general topic of thinking skills includes, for example, Bloom's (1974) classic *application, analysis, synthesis,* and *evaluation*; probing reasons, evidence, implications, and consequences (Paul et al., 1989); critical thinking as evaluating (Swartz & Perkins, 1990); critical thinking as problem-solving (e.g., Budmen, 1967); cause–effect relationships; identifying underlying assumptions; recognizing contradictory statements; many types of ethical and moral thinking (Davis, 2004a, 2004c; Lipman, 1991); Feuerstein's (1980) Instrumental Enrichment strategies for reducing impulsivity and promoting analyzing, comparing, planning, and using logical evidence; persisting, thinking flexibly, striving for accuracy, asking questions, imagining, and thinking independently (Costa, 2003); and a bunch more. In Davis and Rimm (2004) 10 tables list approximately 450 teachable thinking skills.

Probably all 450 contribute to thinking creatively, solving problems, and finding ideas and approaches for de Bono's (1992a) 13 specific situations.

CoRT Thinking Skills Program

Davis and Rimm (2004) also briefly described de Bono's (1973, 1983, 1985a, 1986) *CoRT* (Cognitive Research Trust) *Thinking Skills Program,* a "delightful set of materials for the direct teaching of thinking as a skill" (p. 260). Consider the following magazine excerpt:

The place is Maracaibo, second largest city in Venezuela. There is a meeting of about 20 people (doctors, parents, government officials) to discuss the setting up of a new medical clinic. For three hours, the arguments flow back and forth—in the usual fashion.

Suddenly, a 10-year-old boy who has been sitting quietly at the back of the room because his mother could not leave him alone at home approaches the table.

He suggests to the group that they "do an AGO (set the objectives), followed by an APC (outline alternatives), and then an FIP (set priorities) and, of course, an OPV (analyze other people's views). In a short while, there is a plan of action.

That 10-year-old had participated in the routine thinking skills program that is now mandated by law in all Venezuelan schools (de Bono, 1985a).

According to de Bono (1985a), the CoRT thinking program requires little or no teacher training and is enjoyable for both students and teachers. The 50 skills are taught in a "direct" fashion—students understand the value of each skill and why, when, and how it should be used.

As just one example of the 50 skills, the PMI technique (Pluses, Minuses, Interesting points) teaches evaluation. Students learn that suggestions, proposals, ideas, activities, and probably anything else can be evaluated intelligently by looking at the good points (P), bad points (M), and points that are just interesting (I). Students learn principles behind PMI, and they practice the technique. For PMI, five principles explain that:

By using the PMI approach we will not quickly reject an idea that initially looks bad.
We also will not too quickly adopt an attractive-looking idea that contains overlooked disadvantages.
Some ideas are neither good nor bad, just relevant and interesting. They may lead to other ideas.
Without using a PMI, our emotions may interfere with good judgment.
With a PMI you judge an idea after it is explored, not before.

In a University of Wisconsin College for Kids program, small groups of fifth graders did PMIs on "being gifted." They discovered that others also had social problems, and they better appreciated their intellectual gifts.

Many of do Bono's 50 thinking skills involve complex thinking strategies that require the use of previously learned skills. For example, *Planning* requires subskills of Consider All Factors (CAF) and itemizing Aims, Goals, and Objectives (AGO).

Each lesson typically includes these six sections:

1. *Introduction.* The introduction defines and explains the skill. For example, with *Consider All Factors* (CAF) students learn that with all decisions and choices there will be many factors to consider. If they leave out some factors, their choice may be wrong. Also, they can look for factors that other people have left out of their thinking.
2. *Example.* The skill is applied to a sample problem. For instance, in London a recent law required all new buildings to provide basement parking. They did not consider that basement parking would encourage driving to work and thus increase traffic congestion.
3. *Practice.* Four or five practice problems give students experience with each thinking skill. For example: What factors are involved in choosing a hair style? What factors would you consider when interviewing a potential teacher?
4. *Process.* In a class discussion, students consider such matters as: When should we consider all factors? Is it easy to leave out important factors? What happens when others leave out important factors? Should we consider all factors or just important ones?
5. *Principles.* Usually five principles present reasons for and advantages of using the skill.
6. *Project.* These are additional practice problems.

The CoRT thinking skills are not tied to a particular subject matter. Thinking is taught as an independent subject, and as a conscious and deliberate skill. Many of the CoRT thinking skills are summarized briefly in Inset 9.1.

INSET 9.1
De Bono's (1973) CoRT Thinking Skills

In *Teach Your Child How to Think* (de Bono, 1992b), de Bono included seven important thinking skills from his CoRT (Cognitive Research Trust; de Bono, 1973) thinking skills program. Children learn the value of each skill and when, why, and how it should be used. The first seven thinking skills in the list below appear in *Teach Your Child How to Think*. The remainder of the list describes some of de Bono's other 50 CoRT thinking skills. Which do you think are the most valuable for creative thinking? For thinking generally?

From *Teach Your Child How to Think*

Thinking of good points (Pluses), bad points (Minuses), and interesting points (I) when evaluating ideas (PMI). Considering All Factors (CAF) when making choices or decisions.

Thinking of many Alternatives, Possibilities, and Choices (APC), for example, in interpreting causes or in considering alternative actions.

Thinking of short-, medium-, and long-term consequences of actions (C&S; "S" means Sequel, which may be ignored).

Seeing Other's Points of View (OPV), which exist because other people may consider different factors, see different consequences, or have different objectives or priorities.

Thinking about Aims, Goals, and Objectives (AGO), including other people's goals.

Learning to prioritize by considering what is First in Priority (FIP), for example, relevant factors, objectives, and consequences.

Other CoRT Thinking Skills

Planning, which includes considering all factors and itemizing goals and objectives.

Decision-making, which requires considering the factors involved, objectives, priorities, consequences, and possible alternatives.

Making selections according to your needs and requirements, that is, according to "best fit."

Organizing by analyzing what needs to be done, what is being done, and what is to be done next. You may need to consider all factors and think of alternatives.

Focusing on different aspects of a situation. That is, know when you are analyzing, considering factors, thinking of consequences, and so on.

Concluding a thinking project, perhaps with ideas, answers to a question, a problem solution, an action—or conceding an inability to solve the problem.

Recognizing opinions versus facts as two types of evidence.

Recognizing evidence that is weak, strong, or key.

Being right by referring to facts, authority, and so on.

Supporting an argument by using value-laden words, such as right, proper, fair, or sincere versus ridiculous, dishonest, devious, or stupid.

Being wrong in an argument because of exaggerating, making factual mistakes, or by having prejudiced ideas. Challenging existing ways of doing things as a means of stimulating new ideas.

Improving things by identifying faults and thinking of ways to remove them.

Solving problems by thinking about solution requirements.

Recognizing information that is given versus information that has been omitted but needed. Recognizing contradictory information, which can lead to false conclusions.

Recognizing guesses based on good information ("small guesses," for example, the sun will rise tomorrow) versus guesses based on little information ("big guesses," for example, the final score of tomorrow's basketball game).

Distinguishing between ordinary emotions (e.g., fear, anger, love, sorrow) and those relating to one's view of oneself (ego-emotions, for example, pride, power, insecurity).

Understanding that values determine thinking, judgments, choices, and actions.

Realizing that each of us has things we value highly, and things that are of little value to us.

And more.

TABLE 9.2 Teaeach Your Child How to Think

Six Thinking Hats + CoRT Skills + Lateral Thinking + More	De Bono's (1992b) *Teach Your Child How to Think* combines (1) Six Thinking Hats, (2) parts of his remarkable CoRT thinking program, (3) other aspects of lateral thinking, such as Provocation (Po), and (4) many other enlightening and excellent principles for good thinking. Parents are asked to simplify the book's principles for young children. Older children can read the book themselves. De Bono rightly notes that "there is no upper age limit . . . the methods and techniques are as suitable for adults as for children" (p. 31).
Modesty Disabled	De Bono (1992b) also included other crucial introductory matters. For example, his entire third chapter is entitled *Note about the Author*, and in 8½ pages, he elaborates on his accomplishments listed at the outset of this chapter and more. The summary emphasizes that "It is possible that Dr. de Bono is the best person with the background, credentials, and experience to write this book" (p. 29).[5]
PMI, CAF, APC, C&S, OPV, AGO, FIP, PDQ	Drawing from his *CoRT Thinking Skills Program*, de Bono (1992b) included these seven thinking skills in *Teach Your Child How to Think*: Think of good points (Pluses), bad points (Minuses), and points that are just interesting (PMI); Consider All Factors (CAF); think about Alternatives, Possibilities, and Choices (APC); think about Consequences (C&S); consider Other People's Views (OPV); consider Aims, Goals, and Objectives (AGO); and consider what is First in Important Priorities (FIP). These and many other CoRT thinking skills are itemized in Inset 9.1.
Values	In addition to CoRT thinking skills, de Bono (1992b) presents and simplifies other important thinking skills. For example, a chapter on *values* discusses the values of farmers versus those arguing for big highways across farmland. One exercise asks the reader to consider the comparative values among cats, dogs, mice, and people.
Focus Relates to Purpose	Another chapter explains *focus* and *purpose*, which resembles the CoRT AGO and FIP. The topic also resembles de Bono's (1992a) strong emphasis on focus as a lateral thinking technique. Here, one's focus should relate to one's purpose. An exercise asks: To help find a friend's lost dog, what should you focus on?
TO/LOPSO/ GO	TO/LOPOSO/GO is a "very simple five-stage general-purpose thinking structure" (de Bono, 1992b, p. 230).
TO	Briefly, TO asks: Where are we going (to)? What is the objective? TO suggests using AGO.
LO	LO, from *look*, asks what information is available and needed. LO suggests using CAF and OPV.
PO	PO, from *possible ideas*, asks for green hat thinking. Alternatives? Hypotheses?
SO	SO, from "so what do we have?," essentially asks for idea evaluation. De Bono suggests using an FIP to line up priorities, which are evaluated with PMI, C&S, and OPV.
GO	GO means action—go forward: "Where do we go now?" "How do we implement this?"

---

[5] "In the universe" is implied.

TO/LOPOSO/GO, like de Bono's six hats and 50 thinking skills, might well improve children's and adults' thinking and problem-solving. (Remember the Maracaibo story?)

Still other chapters in *Teach Your Child How to Think* review such thinking and creative problem-solving concepts as:

Finding a broader idea (which is the concept strategy described earlier)
Generating lots of alternatives when solving a problem
Truth (the way things are) versus creativity (the way things could be)
Truth value (e.g., of information received)
Reasoning, critical thinking, and logic
Hypotheses and speculation
Creative attitudes
Scientific (analytic) thinking and business (speculative) thinking
Lateral thinking ("You may need to move laterally to try new ideas," p. 186)

Provocation and "Po," including Reversal, Escape, Wishful Thinking, Random Word, plus "Outrageous" ("anything at all you wish to set up as a provocation. Po: "Cars are made of spaghetti"; p. 197).

Plus many more thinking concepts and lots of reviews and exercises to illustrate and teach skills and values of effective thinking and creative problem-solving.[6]

Summary

This chapter is about the creative problem-solving ideas and strategies of Edward de Bono, particularly as summarized in his 1970 *Lateral Thinking*, 1985 *Six Thinking Hats*, and 1992 *Teach Your Child How to Think*.

His thinking strategies aim at overcoming expectations and mental patterns that interfere with creativity.

The term *lateral thinking* commonly means creativity. According to de Bono they overlap. His famous metaphor includes moving laterally; digging a hole somewhere else.

He criticizes other creativity techniques, particularly brainstorming, for encouraging craziness and suspending (deferring) judgment. Lateral thinking changes our concepts and perceptions.

Six Thinking Hats, a lateral thinking technique, includes examining information (white hat), thinking of ideas (green hat), positively exploring feasibility (yellow hat), finding fault (black hat), expressing feelings (yellow hat), and reviewing progress (blue hat). The strategy keeps the group on target.

Lateral thinking strategy includes looking for broader underlying concepts. It also includes "fixed points," for example, the initial problem or a broader concept from which to associate ideas.

Creative Pause means slowing down—pausing—to make a creative effort.

Focus includes seeking unusual areas in which to find ideas. Focus may be general or specific. Creative pause and focus are related.

Creative Challenge refers to habitually looking for better ideas and improvements. ("How else can we do this?")

Alternatives, and searching for them, underlies most creative thinking, including lateral thinking.

A Concept Fan diagram summarizes the initial problem, intermediate general ideas, and specific ideas related to each general idea. One works back and forth among general and specific ideas.

Regarding broader underlying concepts, de Bono identified purpose, mechanism, and value concepts.

Four Stepping Stone provocative techniques include reversal, exaggeration, distortion, and wishful thinking provocations.

Random Words and Random Objects also can provoke highly unusual solution ideas.

---

[6] On the downside, the curious absence of an index is frustrating.

With the Escape provocative procedure, one departs from what we take for granted. "Po" (Provocative operation) is de Bono's abbreviation for any of the six provocative techniques.

With the Stratal technique, one creates and reviews a half-dozen statements or observations related to a situation. They suggest ideas.

With the Filament technique, one lists a half-dozen one-word requirements for a problem situation, then four or five brief examples of each. Then one selects one item from each of several strands, which when combined suggests ideas and approaches.

De Bono listed 13 "specific situations" (problem types), for example, problems, improvements, opportunities, stagnant situations, conflict, and planning. He described which lateral thinking techniques are most suitable for each situation. Finding Alternatives, Creative Pause, Focus, and Creative Challenge are suited for all 13.

Also, Provocative (Po) techniques ensure unique ideas.

Apart from the 13, three "basic types of thinking" are Achievement (e.g., problems, tasks, projects), Improvement, and Greenfield (not knowing where to begin) Thinking.

Creativity is part of the more general topic of thinking skills, but all thinking skills probably aid creative thinking.

Based on 50 principles, the remarkable CoRT (Cognitive Research Trust) programs teach children to think.

De Bono's *Teach Your Child to Think* taught seven CoRT principles, ideas from *Six Thinking Hats*, provocation techniques, and other ideas related to thinking and solving problems (e.g., different values, relating focus to purpose).

TO/LOPOSO/GO is a five-step thinking strategy that includes asking where one is going and what information is needed, green hat thinking, idea evaluation, and taking action.

Review Exercises

Lateral Thinking and Six Thinking Hats: Edward de Bono

Self-Test: Key Concepts and Terms

1. *Briefly define or explain each of these:*

Lateral thinking _____

_____

White hat thinking _____

Green hat thinking _____

Yellow hat thinking _____

Black hat thinking _____

Red hat thinking _____

Blue hat thinking _____

Underlying concepts _____

_____

Fixed points _____

_____

Creative Pause _____

_____

Focus _____

_____

Creative Challenge _____

_____

_____

Concept Fan _____

_____

Four Provocative Techniques / Stepping Stones _____

_____

Reversal provocation _____

Exaggeration _____

Distortion _____

Escape _____

Random Word _____

Stratals _____

_____

Filament Technique _____

_____

Specific situations _____

_____

Achievement Thinking (Reach) _____

Improvement Thinking (Change) _____

Greenfield Thinking (Start) _____

CoRT thinking skills _____

PMI _____

CAF _____

AGO _____

FIP _____

OPV _____

C&S _____

TO/LOPOSO/GO _____

_____

Let's Think about It

1. Consider the problem of not having enough study time. Put on each of the six hats and write down an idea or two wearing that hat.

    White _____

    Green _____

    Yellow _____

    Black _____

    Red _____

    Blue _____

2. What do you see as advantages or disadvantages of de Bono's Six Thinking Hats strategy?

    _____

    _____

    _____

    _____

3. Think about the problem of insufficient money for school and entertainment. Use one or more of the Provocative (Po) techniques (Reversal, Exaggeration, Distortion, Wishful Thinking, Escape, Random Word) to find ideas for this problem.

    _____

    _____

    _____

4. Pick either the problem of insufficient study time or insufficient money. Run through the TO/ LOPOSO/GO procedure for solutions.

    _____

    _____

    _____

    _____

Does it work? Why or why not? Are you still too busy and too broke? (Dang!)

_____

_____

10 Creativity Assessment

"I don't know anything with certainty, but seeing the stars makes me dream."

—*Vincent van Gogh*

As we take a look at creativity assessment I would like you to keep in mind the point of what is presented. For example, astronomy education has taken on van Gogh's paintings to ask questions and seek appropriate evidence, revising, and so on just to become more open to learning regardless of their close or distant relevance. That is the point.

As creativity is being assessed, there is no right or wrong, there is infinite space between relevance and irrelevance, and in the end there is simply self-approving acceptance to what was and is being created or analyzed. Anyone can be creative, and although testing and games question the level an individual stands on the scale, the stress that everyone can be creative and can come up with creative innovations, is a very real thing.

In 1950, J. P. Guilford spearheaded the scientific research of creativity with his landmark address to the American Psychological Association. Citing a relative lack of creativity citations in professional journals, Guilford's podium speech served as a platform to purport creativity as a psychological construct (say that three times fast!). Plucker (2001) provides a perspective that debates Guilford's speech as the sole spark that provided a sudden combustion of "serious" interest in the field, but nonetheless, it *did* provide an impetus for the psychometric interest in this construct to grow.

Psychometrics

What is psychometrics? Jones and Thissen (2006) identify psychometrics as a branch of psychology concerned with psychological measurements and highlight how this field of study has early origins in the testing for individual differences (i.e., quantifying how humans differ from each other on measureable traits). Tying both psychometrics and individual differences back to the assessment of creativity, Guilford (1950) pointed out that a lot of the early research on creativity dealt with examining characteristics that produced eminent creators; the Big C creativity we discussed in Chapter 7. But what about the little guys? (literally). Sternberg and Lubart (1999) point out that from a psychometric standpoint "highly creative people are rare and difficult to study in the psychological laboratory" and that, according to Guilford (1950), "the rarity of these individuals had limited research on creativity" (p. 6). Therefore, Guilford's call to action included developing everyday means to study creativity in common individuals with authentic tasks that could be completed quickly and compiled efficiently (i.e., paper and pencil test). Though Plucker and Renzulli (1999) point out that psychometric approaches date from well before Guilford's address, they also state that his speech served as the "formal starting date of scientific creativity research" (p. 36). The modern movement of psychometrics in creativity had officially begun!

Testing, Testing, 1, 2, 3

From the middle of the twentieth century to the early twenty-first century, we've seen a seismic shift in the importance psychometrics has added to the understanding of creativity. Plucker and Renzulli (1999) note that "practically all current work on creativity is based upon methodologies that either are psychometric in nature or were developed in response to perceived weaknesses of creativity measurement. As such, the psychometric studies of creativity conducted in the past few decades form the foundation of current understandings of creativity" (p. 35). With foundations in mind, Plucker, Makel, and Qian (2019) identify that "psychometric methods in creativity research are typically grouped into four types of investigations; creative processes, personality and behavioral correlates of creativity, characteristics of creative products, and attributes of creativity-fostering environments" (p. 45). While we will look at all of these areas, we will start with the one that, in the truest sense of the word, is the most traditionally ascribed to assessment—the creativity test—and highlight three more-or-less accepted strategies for evaluating creative potential:

1. Inventories that evaluate creative personality traits and dispositions,
2. Inventories that evaluate actual past involvement in creative activities, and
3. Divergent thinking tests, which evaluate the production of creative responses to given problems.

However, before we start "testing," it's important to provide some perspective on traditional uses of creativity tests and some issues involved with creativity measurement.

Uses of Creativity Tests

Some of the uses of creativity tests include identifying creatively gifted children for gifted programs, research, and counseling.

Identifying Creatively Gifted Children. The most extensive use of creativity tests is for selecting creatively gifted students for participation in programs for the gifted and talented (Kim, 2006). State directors, district G/T teacher-coordinators, and other program planners (teachers, school board members, parents) are becoming more and more aware that high intelligence is just one type of giftedness. In his Manifesto, Torrance (2002) asserted that if we only use metrics of IQ and standardized tests in selection, we would eliminate 70% of the top 20% of creative students from consideration. Eventually, students who are creatively gifted probably will make the most valuable contributions to society, and certainly deserve the frog-kissing, prince-becoming benefits of G/T programs.

Selecting creative children requires some index of creativeness, which often means creativity test scores, hopefully supplemented with teacher, parent, peer, or self-ratings of creativeness plus enthusiasm for the program.

Research. A second important use of creativity tests is for research into the nature of creativity and creative people. Creativity tests typically are used in two ways.

First, researchers may need to identify creative children or adults in order to compare them, their backgrounds, or their task performance with "regular" (control) children or adults. If the researcher wishes to explore whether creative persons are more likely to have certain personality traits, motivations, abilities, cognitive styles, behavior patterns, career choices, histories, low anxiety, a cat, an imaginary playmate, or a belief in flying saucers, the experimenter first must locate the creative subjects.

The second research use of creativity tests is to evaluate any beneficial effect of some educational or creativity training experience, for example, a gifted program that focuses on training problem-solving and creativity.

Incidentally, sometimes the most effective way to evaluate creativity training effects is *not* with a published creativity test—which may not measure what was taught (more on that in a second)—but with an original questionnaire that asks: Was the experience worthwhile? Do you believe you are more creative as a result of the program? Did you enjoy the experience? Are you more likely to engage in creative activities as a result of the experience? Such an inventory usually will produce more direct and relevant results than a published test that asks participants, for example, to list unusual uses for a tin bucket.

Counseling. The third use of creativity testing is in counseling and guidance. A counselor or school psychologist in the elementary or secondary school may want more information about a student who is referred because of apathy, underachievement, uncooperativeness, disruptiveness, or other personal or education problems. For example, a creative child who is independent, curious, artistic, risk-taking, and who has high energy and a good sense of humor may not be "well-rounded" and may have few friends (Millar, 1995; Torrance, 1981a). Furthermore, he or she may have an aversion to routine, rigid, authoritarian classrooms—resulting in a refusal to complete work, becoming aggressive or a class clown, feigning illness to stay home, or other maladaptive behavior. Information regarding creativeness will help the counselor diagnose the problems.

Issues in Measuring Creativity

Measuring Traits versus Predicting Eminence

Attitudes regarding our ability to evaluate creativity differ dramatically. On one hand, educators committed to fostering creativity and giftedness agree that students with creative potential can and should be *identified*. On the other hand, critics hold the opinion that true creativity cannot be *measured* with currently available creativity tests (Callahan, 1991).

One reason for pessimism lies in the complexity and many forms of creativity, for example, the many kinds of needed personality traits, motivations, and intellectual abilities; the distinction between self-actualized and special talent creativity; the required combination of training, experience, available knowledge, and an environment that rewards a particular type of creative thinking (e.g., Morelock & Feldman, 2003); the role of non-rational factors such as fantasy, illogical thinking, and sometimes a touch of psychopathology; and the two biggest "ifs" of all, chance and opportunity. As a sample of mystery in creativity thinking, we noted in Chapter 1 that composers hear symphonies in their heads. A comparable process happens with writers—as Ernest Hemingway once said, "The stuff comes alive and turns crazy on ya'" (Bass, 1968). The reader also may recall remarkable speculations on the roles of one's muses, psychical capabilities, the libido, primordial archetypes, and accessing a universal mind.

We review this sample of complexity and mystery to remind ourselves that trying to measure "creativity" with paper-and-pencil tests oversimplifies highly complicated phenomena. These complexities and more limit the ability of creativity tests to measure creative capability or productivity.

A second reason for pessimism is partly semantic, centered on whether we define *creativity* as (1) possessing personality traits, relevant abilities, or experience in creative thinking versus (2) having achieved creative eminence. With the first definition, there seems little doubt that children and adolescents identified by teachers, parents, or creativity tests as possessing strong creative cognitive and affective traits will—on average—behave more creatively than a random sample of students. For example, their products and achievements will be evaluated as more creative and they will pursue more creative interests, careers, and hobbies (e.g., Davis, 1975, 1989a; Davis & Rimm, 1982; Okuda, Runco, & Berger, 1991; Torrance, 1981a, 1988; Torrance & Safter, 1989).

But can we predict great creative eminence? As we conceded at the beginning of this chapter, it has not been done yet.

By way of comparison, our esteemed intelligence tests do not predict professional eminence one whit better. Among Lewis Terman's 1,528 gifted children, nearly all of whom scored above IQ 140 (some above 180), *not even one* reached the eminence of an Einstein, Picasso, or Howard Hughes (Golman, 1980). In fact, one person who was tested and did not qualify in Terman's screening was William Schockley, who went on to co-invent the transistor and earn a Nobel Prize—he out-achieved all 1,528 people who met Terman's IQ criterion of genius. To quote Dean Keith Simonton (1997; see also Simonton, 2003), "Rather than become a gifted child, he became a famous scientist instead" (p. 340).

Reliability and Validity in Creativity Assessment

The two criteria that are used to judge the psychometric properties of any instrument of assessment are reliability and validity. These are the standard-bearers whose presence gives us confidence in the interpretation of our results (or whose absence gives us pause).

Reliability

Drost (2011) defines reliability as "the extent to which measurements are repeatable—when different persons perform the measurements, on different occasions, under different conditions, with supposedly alternative instruments which measure the same thing" (p. 106). That's a lot of requirements related to reliability! Boiling this definition down to a single synonym, Bollen (1989) equates reliability to *consistency*. Nunnally (1978) describes it as *stability*, or how the same results should be obtained despite variances in measurement techniques or testing conditions. With testing conditions in mind, think about the last time you took a quiz in class. What variables were in play that could have influenced your results? Time of day, motivation level, preparedness (wait, you mean that studying could improve my grade?!). If you had taken the exact same quiz again, would your results have been the same? What about a different version of the quiz in which the actual questions were different but they covered the exact same material? How would your two scores have compared? Finally, what if the teaching assistant had graded it instead of the professor? How close would those marks line up? As Dross (2011) points out, "because reliability is a consistency of measurement over a variety of conditions, the most common used technique to estimate reliability is with a measure of association, often termed reliability coefficient" (p. 108). An efficient explanation of what a coefficient is now follows.

A correlation coefficient can tell you the magnitude (strength) and direction (positive or negative) that two variables are related. The scale runs from positive 1 to negative 1. A zero represents no relationship. High positive numbers (0.9 and above) mean that they have a strong positive relationship. Lower numbers (0.6–0.8) pertain to a moderate relationship. Even lower than that (0.4–0.6) represents a mild or moderate relationship, bad for creativity testing (and presumably your dating life!) Negative numbers means there is an indirect relationship (as one goes up the other goes down). While beer drinking before the night of a classroom exam might be negatively correlated with academic achievement in that class, what impact would alcohol have on creativity test performance? I'll leave that IRB submission to someone else. Point being, the decimal points DO matter in pointing to the consistency of a creativity test as "the reliability coefficient is the correlation between two variables which measure the same thing" (p. 108). There are several types of reliability that can be used to determine the consistency of creativity test results.

Reliability Types

Test–Retest Reliability

There are several types of reliability. Specific to the first example from above, we can correlate scores on a second administration of a test with the scores from the first administration (*test–retest reliability*). As Drost (2011) defines, "test-retest reliability refers to the stability of a test from one measurement session to another. The procedure is to administer the test to a group of respondents and then administer the same test to the same respondents at a later date" (p. 108). But, while this is relatively straightforward, it does come with some rather obvious sources of error. What potential problems do you see in getting the exact same score twice on the exact same quiz. How many of you after a test go home and immediately look up the answers for questions you were unsure of? Do you think that gain of memory (or knowledge) might help you should you see that question again? Also, what if, after getting a bad grade on the first quiz, you devoted yourself to learning the material more? Those gains in knowledge, skills, or abilities could also influence how you do the second go-round. Finally, how soon the second quiz is given (time-related factors) will also influence consistency of your two scores.

Alternate Forms Reliability

Beyond that, with the second example in mind, we can evaluate how well scores on different forms of a test correlate with each other (*alternate forms reliability*). Alternative forms reliability involves creating two "separate but equal" versions of the same assessment. The number of items, responses processes, depth of content, and administration aspects are the same, but the actual questions themselves are different. Prominent examples of alternate forms instruments exist in the domain of creativity testing. Torrance (1966a) has two different forms of his classic Torrance Tests of Creative Thinking (TTCT) that we will highlight later in this chapter. An early test review by Holland (1968) showed alternate forms reliability coefficients for the TTCT exceeding 0.7.

Interrater and Internal Consistency Reliability

Finally, with the third example in mind, we can evaluate the degree to which different raters of creative people (or products) are consistent with each other (*interrater reliability*). We also can evaluate whether all items on a creativity test measure the same trait (*internal consistency reliability*). Interrater and internal consistency reliabilities can be very high, sometimes in the 0.9s (e.g., Davis, 1975; Torrance, 1990a, 1990b). Just as the 1990s were a "Nirvana" for the creativity of grunge music, being in the 0.9s bodes well for the stability of scores on creativity testing. But what prevents us from achieving that perfect 1.00 mark (and wouldn't it be nice if 1.00 was the standard-bearer for college GPA?!)

Interfering with the consistency of our results is a pesky little thing called error. Error is anything that can inflate or deflate (looking at you, Tom Brady!) scores in an unpredictable manner. Later in this chapter, you'll see evidence of different types of creativity tests that have response processes that vary from drawing, to making up scenarios, to listening to audio recordings. Do you think how creativity is assessed will influence creativity scores? Based on your drawing ability, if your example of a visual masterpiece is a stick-figure with all its appendages, how do you think your score will compare to someone who had formal art lessons (or experienced "The Joy of Painting" by practicing along with Bob Ross). Error associated with measurement here might mean that your creativity score will go down based on the requirements of the test while the other person might see their score soar. In painting, Bob Ross was famous for saying, "we don't make mistakes, just happy little accidents." Well, in the world of psychometrics, we call these happy little accidents error, and they can have a big impact over the interpretation of results.

Reducing Error

To ensure consistency of scores and the ability of all participants to "ace" their creativity test, your author recommends an A.C.E. approach regarding reducing errors associated with reliability related to administration, context, and the examinees themselves. From an administration standpoint, avoid the dreaded "Three Es." Don't provide examples, elaborate beyond what is on the printed page, or emphasize any one word or phrase on the instructions. From a context standpoint, make sure you control the environmental effects as much as possible. When possible, testing should be done in the same room, or location. Also, try and simulate the original testing conditions (time of day, etc.). Many of you would agree that your creativity fluctuates based on the time of day. Morning people might struggle with a late-afternoon creativity test. Night owls certainly might not give a "hoot" for a creativity test in the early a.m. Which brings us to the last aspect about ensuring consistency—reducing error effects from the examinees themselves. The two most common aspects that can reduce stability of scores in human subjects are related to fatigue and motivation. The temporal time of when a test was given also relates to the temporal lobe of the human brain and fatigue factors. Ensuring that your examinees are motivated also ensures peak performance, though don't incentivize the first test and then on the retest remove that reinforcement. Consistency and accuracy of results might follow. With accuracy in mind, that brings us to the next key factor in testing: validity.

Validity

Drost (2011) defines validity as being concerned with whether researchers are "measuring what they intended to measure" (p. 114). Heaton (1975) went a step further and defined it as "the extent to which it measures what it is supposed to measure *and nothing else*" (p. 153). Brualdi (1999) equates the process of validation to accumulating empirical data to construct logical arguments that support the inferences made from test results. To summarize validity, the word *accurate* seems (well) accurate! And this accuracy, for psychometrics, is imperative. A reliable test can be inaccurate. Think about it . . . you can consistently measure something in an inaccurate way.

If I was a baseball scout looking for the next great hitting or pitching phenom, I could track how many sunflower seeds a particular player ate over nine innings. Based on the seeds I see scattered through the dugout, I would assume that the results would be pretty consistent from game to game (no seeds of doubt, if you will). But, that has NOTHING to do with on-the-field performance. It's a consistent metric applied in an inaccurate way. Same goes for creativity testing. We want to ensure that the results derived from creativity tests are true and accurate and represent one's TRUE creativity (instead of something else that isn't related). With that in mind, there are four types of validity related to creativity testing.

Validity Types

Construct Validity

Drost (2011) refers to *construct validity* as "how well you translated or transformed a concept, idea, or behavior—that is a construct—into a functioning and operating reality" (p. 116). Construct validity is essential and relates to the question, "Is this test TRULY measuring creativity?" This is at the center of the debate for a lot of creativity tests that rely on measures of divergent thinking. As Plucker and Renzulli (1999) state, "divergent thinking tests requires individuals to produce several responses to a specific prompt, in sharp contrast to most standardized tests of achievement that require one correct answer. This emphasis upon fluency . . . is seen as a key component of creative processes" (p. 39). Key component could be rephrased as key construct. As you will see later, fluency, ideational fluency, or ideation factor heavily into divergent thinking tests. But does fluency wholly and completely capture the entire domain of creativity? It's one of the key constructs that Michael and Wright (1989) identify as being associated with creativity. The observe that "among the most commonly cited constructs are those originally proposed by Guilford in his structure-of-intellect (SOI) model. They include fluency, originality, flexibility, and elaboration in divergent thinking" (p. 35), all of which we will cover later. But precedent doesn't necessarily preclude prediction.

Mayer (1999) points out that "critics argue that divergent-thinking tests do not really measure or predict creative thinking, are too task specific, and have added little to cognitive theory or educational practice" (p. 454). Regarding the TTCT, Zeng, Proctor, and Salvendy (2011) assert that "a majority of criticism has been directed towards its construct validity. It is not yet clear exactly what or how many dimensions of creativity is measured by the TTCT" (p. 30). And as Kim (2006) reports, studies on the TTCT have shown conflicting reports regarding its dimensionality, citing evidence from Abernathy Tannehill (1998) that "subscores of the TTCT may not measure independent constructs" (p. 7). However, positive support for the construct validity of creativity tests was put forth by Fleenor and Taylor (1994), who found strong construct validity for both the CPI Creativity Scale and the MBTI Creativity Index (both self-report measures of creativity). All of these instruments will be profiled in this chapter. We'll let you take a look at their constructs and make up your own mind as to their construct validity.

Face Validity

With taking a look in mind, a validity type that is literally akin to "judging a book by its cover" is the aspect of *face validity*, the second type of validity. Drost (2011) describes face validity as "a subjective judgment on the operationalism of a construct" (p. 116). While seen as a weak form of construct validity, if I handed you a coloring book instead of a test booklet and told you I would be assessing your creativity, you probably wouldn't be convinced as to the validity of what was about to take place. In fact, you might turn "brick red" in the face over this "razzmatazz" I called a creativity test and storm out while "screaming green" from the top of your lungs that I was cray-cray(ola?)[1]

Content Validity

Bollen (1989) defines content validity as "a qualitative type of validity where the domain of the concept is made clear and the analyst judges whether the measures fully represent the domain" (p. 185). Therefore, according to Drost (2011), the burden of the researcher and test developer is to establish content validity by "selecting indicators that thoroughly cover its domain and dimensions" (p. 118). Creativity tests are full of indicators. Indicators such as fluency, flexibility, originality, and elaboration are standards of many creativity tests. But do these indicators represent the entire domain of creativity as a whole?

Tests can fall short of establishing content validity if they have *content underrepresentation* or *content irrelevancy*. So, if Dr. Olaf gives his Arenndelle University students a test over the four seasons, but the quiz was only over (you guessed it) summer, then that is underrepresentation. The test didn't adequately cover all aspects of the domain it was meant to represent. And what about Dr. Dillamond at Shiz University. If his Chemistry final included Physics questions about (defying the) laws of gravity, then you might never bring his students down from their anger over the content irrelevancy of those items, as they had nothing to do with the domain they were being tested over. He certainly wouldn't be the most "Popular" professor. Michael and Wright (1989) propose that "if a teacher is interested in bringing about the manifestation of creative behaviors, the steps that would be taken to realize content validity would parallel those associated with the evaluation of the nature and amounts of learning that have taken place in almost any instructional unit" (p. 42). They equated content validity to a grid-like layout in which learning objectives (rows) were overlaid with cognitive activity associated with those objectives (columns). Anything outside that grid is irrelevant. Overemphasis of one section of the grid is

---

[1] Yes, those are all real Crayola crayon names!

underrepresentation. Regarding whether creativity tests adequately sample the full spectrum of creative behaviors, Yamamoto (1966) states that it "seems difficult to claim that the universe of creative behavior, as broadly conceived, is fairly and thoroughly sampled by available measures" (p. 195).

Criterion-Related Validity

The last validity type we will preview is *criterion-related validity*. Drost (2011) defines this type as "the degree of correspondence between a test measure and one or more external referents" (p. 118). One of the largest ways that criterion-related validity has been established is correlating scores on a creativity test with some other measure (criterion) of creativity. This can be convergent in nature, which is simply a correlation between scores on a new creativity test and scores on another creativity test. As Drost (2011) states, this process tests for "convergence across different measures or manipulations of the same thing" (p. 119). You would expect scores on two creativity tests to converge together and the correlation of scores forms a validity coefficient that can be used to make this determination. Surely this is the case, right? Well, Clapham (2004) compared scores of the Torrance Test of Creative Thinking (TTCT) with scores on two creativity interest inventories, Davis's How Do You Think? and Raudsepp's How Creative Are You? The resulting correlation coefficients were weak (ranging from 0.05 to 0.25) suggesting that there is "very little convergent validity between the creative interest (inventories) and the TTCT scores" (p. 834). Hocevar (1981) also notes that "the correlations of divergent thinking with other measures of creativity have been inconsistent with some investigators finding a positive relationship . . . and other investigators no relationship. Further, in studies where significant positive correlations have been reported, the correlation is seldom higher than 0.3" (p. 462). However, could it be that due to the complexities of creativity mentioned earlier, differences between test content and criterion content prevent high-validity coefficients? For example, should the number of unusual uses that you list for an automobile tire and a button—two items used in divergent thinking creativity tests (Wallach & Kogan, 1965)—correlate extremely highly with your score on a creative lifestyle checklist? Or with your art teacher's rating of your creativeness? It simply might be hard to substantiate.

Another type of criterion-related validity is predictive, where the scores on the creativity test are compared against future events our outcomes (criterion) meant to symbolize as creative achievement or accomplishment. For example, some outside validating criteria might be ratings of the creativeness of student art, writing, and invention samples (Davis, 1975; Davis & Rimm, 1982; Davis & Subkoviak, 1978), and teacher ratings of student creativeness (Rimm, 1976, 1983). In validating the TTCT, Torrance and Safter (1989) used as validating criteria the number of high school creative achievements, number of post–high school creative achievements, scores on a creative lifestyle checklist, ratings of individuals' highest creative achievements, and ratings of the creativeness of one's future career image. Cramond, Matthews-Morgan, Bandalos, and Zuo (2005) reported a predictive validity coefficient as high as 0.63 from a longitudinal study of elementary school students and their resulting creative achievements. However, as Zeng et al. (2011) observe, "Given the weaknesses previously discussed, there is little surprise that the predictive validity of existing divergent thinking inventories has been criticized" (p. 33). Citing evidence from Sternberg and Lubart (1996), Zeng et al. go on to state that "longitudinal studies showed that the correlations between creative abilities as measured by DT tests and prediction of later creative achievements typically range from 0.2 to 0.3" (p. 33).

Plucker and Runco (1998) believe that "many possible reasons for weak predictive validity coefficients represent weaknesses in methodology more than weaknesses in psychometric creativity research" (p. 37). In addition, Michael and Wright (1989) note that "several limiting of modifying circumstances arise in conjunction with the meaningful interpretation of validity coefficients . . . probably the most important concern in the realization of predictive validity is that of identifying a truly satisfactory relevant criterion measure . . . creative behaviors are likely to be multidimensional, complex, and difficult to define in operational terms" (p. 43).

Outside Validating Criteria

On a scale of 0 to 1, most creativity test validity coefficients are between 0.4 and 0.5. Many are lower. A few creativity test developers claim higher-validity coefficients. For comparison, most psychological tests (e.g., of motivation or anxiety) show validity coefficients around 0.60 to 0.70. Does this mean we should abandon creativity testing? If so, the chapter would end right here! But take heart, as despite the negativity, no negative correlations were reported and that is a cause for optimism!

Optimism about Identifying Creative Persons

Whew! We had a lot of issues to cover. But with those out of the way, based on your author's experience in developing creativity tests (Davis, 1975; Davis & Rimm, 1982), Torrance's 22-year longitudinal study of his divergent thinking tests (e.g., Torrance & Safter, 1989), and a host of other studies that validate the use of inventories that assess creative personality traits, inventories that assess biographical information about creative activities, and tests of divergent thinking (all reviewed later in this chapter)—and despite complexity problems, critic's pessimism, and measurement problems—many creativity tests are on-target, moderately valid, and helpful within certain limitations.

One limitation is *false negatives*—the failure of a test to identify a truly creative person due to a Grand Canyon of difference between test content and the individual's particular form of creativeness. We call these Type II errors. *False positives*, the identification of uncreative persons as highly creative, are not likely—although some (perhaps many) tests can be faked by shrewd test-takers. These are known as Type I errors. For example, when instructed to do so, college students deliberately produced high scores on an inventory assessing creative personality characteristics (Ironson & Davis, 1979).

Typically, a high creativity test score means that the student probably has good creative potential and/or creative experience. Such creative potential or talent may have been invisible due to student reticence or to a classroom that did not ask for creative ideas.

Solution: Two Criteria of Creativity

Because of limitations in reliability and validity, creativity test results must be used cautiously and preferably in combination with other information regarding students' creativeness. If creativity tests, ratings, or nominations are used, it is best to use *at least two* such criteria. For example, scores on a divergent thinking test may be used along with scores on a personality/biographical inventory, or else scores on either type of creativity test may be used together with teacher (or parent) ratings of creativeness. If a student scores high on two criteria, we can be comfortable in naming that student as having creative potential.

In contrast, if a student scores average or below average on a single criterion, such as one creativity test (e.g., listing unusual uses for an automobile tire and a button), it could be—and often is—a great error to accept that mediocre score as a true measure of creative capability. As we will see in Chapter 11, it is common in the field of gifted education to use a multidimensional approach to identification, that is, to use many selection criteria. Within the creativity area, we also should use several identification criteria.

High IQ as an Indicator of Creative Potential

Early research by Barron (1969), MacKinnon (1961, 1978a, 1978b), Getzels and Jackson (1962), and Wallach and Kogan (1965) confirmed our common sense suspicion that creativity and intelligence are different yet related. One visible difference lies in the role of personality and motivation characteristics. No one claims that a person's level of intelligence level depends heavily on personality and motivational traits, but many know absolutely that creative productivity does. You may recall Sternberg's (1988;

Chapter 4) three-facet model of creativity in which two factors were cognitive style and personality/motivation and the third factor was *intelligence*.

Getzels and Jackson (1962) made the important observation that their high-intelligence students were capable of thinking creatively—but they were not disposed to do so. Perhaps they were conventional by habit, insecure about being different, or just not motivated to think creatively because creativity was not encouraged or rewarded. The Getzels and Jackson conclusion underscores the key role of attitudinal, personality, and motivational characteristics, with *creativity consciousness* at the forefront.

We already have seen the Barron and MacKinnon *threshold* concept (MacKinnon, 1978a; Chapter 4), which states that a minimum IQ of about 120 is needed for noteworthy creative accomplishment.

There is little question that intelligence and creativity are different, but important to the present argument, they also are related. We know from research by Catharine Cox (1926), the Goertzels (Goertzel, Goertzel, & Goertzel, 1978), Walberg (Walberg, Williams, & Zeiser, 2003), and Simonton (2003)—again, along with our intuitions—that high intelligence is a requisite trait among creatively eminent men and women.

An implication is that young people with high intelligence have a unique potential for creative productivity. Therefore, high intelligence is a good clue for identifying creative potential.

Formal Identification: Inventories and Tests

As mentioned earlier, we will examine three categories of creativity tests: *creative personality inventories*, inventories that evaluate *past creative activities*, and *divergent thinking tests*. Personality inventories evaluate the kinds of attitudes, personality dispositions, and motivational characteristics described in Chapter 4, and sometimes interests and biographical information. Evaluations of past creative activities and involvement are just that—assessments of student involvement in creative art, writing, theater, science projects, inventions, collections, and other home, school, or community projects reflecting initiative and imagination.

Verbal versus Nonverbal

Divergent thinking tests evaluate a sample of cognitive abilities, but ignore personality and background information, although these undoubtedly affect test performance. Most (not all) *verbal* divergent thinking tests ask students to list as many ideas as they can for an open-ended problem or question, such as the century-old "List unusual uses for a brick" problem. *Nonverbal* (figural, drawing) divergent thinking tests ask the test-taker to add to (embellish) the given simple figures. Verbal and nonverbal tests typically are scored at least for *ideational fluency* (total number of relevant ideas) and *originality* (uniqueness or statistical rarity of each idea). However, as we will see, two nonverbal divergent thinking batteries are scored for 18 and 11 creative abilities, "strengths," and personality dispositions.

Creative Personality Inventories

Scales for Rating the Behavioral Characteristics of Superior Students

A shining example of on-target efficiency is Renzulli's (Renzulli, Smith, White, Callahan, & Hartman, 2001) 10-item creativity rating scale from his Scales for Rating the Behavioral Characteristics of Superior Students (Table 10.1). A teacher who knows an elementary or secondary student well can use the scale to rate the student's creativeness. The scale evaluates important, intuitively appealing, and empirically confirmed traits of creative children, adolescents, and adults. Its contents square well with other descriptions of the creative personality.

TABLE 10.1 Scale for Rating Characteristics of Creative Students

	1	2	3	4
1. Displays a great deal of curiosity about many things; is constantly asking questions about anything and everything.	_____	_____	_____	_____
2. Generates a large number of ideas or solutions to problems and questions; often offers unusual ("way out"), unique, clever responses.	_____	_____	_____	_____
3. Is uninhibited in expressions of opinion; is sometimes radical and spirited in disagreement; is tenacious.	_____	_____	_____	_____
4. Is a high risk-taker; is adventurous and speculative.	_____	_____	_____	_____
5. Displays a good deal of intellectual playfulness; fantasizes; imagines ("I wonder what would happen if"); manipulates ideas (i.e., changes, elaborates upon them); is often concerned with adapting, improving and modifying institutions, objects, and systems.	_____	_____	_____	_____
6. Displays a keen sense of humor and sees humor in situations that may not appear to be humorous to others.	_____	_____	_____	_____
7. Is usually aware of his impulses and more open to the irrational in himself (freer expression of feminine interest for boys, greater-than-usual amount of independence for girls); shows emotional sensitivity.	_____	_____	_____	_____
8. Is sensitive to beauty; attends to aesthetic characteristics of things.	_____	_____	_____	_____
9. Is nonconforming; accepts disorder; is not interested in details; is individualistic; does not fear being different.	_____	_____	_____	_____
10. Criticizes constructively; is unwilling to accept authoritarian pronouncements without critical examination.	_____	_____	_____	_____

Source: Reproduced by permission of Joseph Renzulli.

How Do You Think?

The How Do You Think? (HDYT) test (Davis, 1975, 1991a; Davis & Subkoviak, 1978) evaluates such traits as independence, confidence, risk-taking, energy, adventurousness, curiosity, reflectiveness, humor, playfulness, liking for complexity, artistic interests, creative interests and activities, as well as belief in ESP and flying saucers. HDYT includes 100 items in a five-point rating-scale, "No" to "Definitely."

HDYT has shown reasonably good psychometric properties (e.g., Runco, Okuda, & Thurston, 1988; Schuldberg, 1993). Internal reliability, for example, virtually always is above 0.90. The inventory originally was validated against actual creative products (art, writing, inventions) required for a college creativity class ($r = 0.42$; Davis, 1975). With an experimental and a control group, Davis and Bull (1978) demonstrated that HDYT scores were significantly higher as a result of taking a college creativity course, which is evidence of construct validity. Moss (1991) found a correlation of 0.53 between HDYT scores and the Myers–Briggs Type Inventory measure of *intuition*.

Runco et al. (1988) used HDYT scores as the "outside" criterion for validating nine divergent thinking measures. Correlations ranged from 0.14 to 0.45 between HDYT scores and the divergent thinking scores. Runco, Okuda, and Hwang (1987) found that HDYT scores were correlated with success in a math and science program for gifted and talented high school students, even when ability scores (PSAT-Math) were controlled. Runco (1999a) noted that the HDYT has "good predictive validity" (p. 758). Runco, Okuda, and Hwang concluded that HDYT, along with PSAT-Math, could be used to select students for gifted programs.

HDYT seems to work well with high school and middle school students, although middle school students may need a word or two defined (Lees-Haley & Swords, 1981). One study successfully used HDYT with 61 gifted 9-to-12-year-old children, showing correlations of 0.42 and 0.59 with their Creative Behavior Inventory (Lees-Haley & Sutton, 1982), a checklist of creative activities. Lees-Haley and Sutton recommended the HDYT for identifying creative elementary children because it worked and because the children found it "interesting, engaging, and stimulating."

Based on decades of experience of observing HDYT performance, your author's conclusion is this: It works surprisingly well!

Group Inventory for Finding Talent: The GIFFI Tests

There have been several spin-offs from HDYT. The Group Inventory for Finding Interests II (GIFFI II; Davis & Rimm, 1980, 1982) is a high school inventory built of 60 items from the HDYT, again in a five-point rating scale format. GIFFI II has been validated with urban, suburban, and rural students in many ethnic groups and at all socioeconomic levels. The original validity criterion was teacher ratings of student creativity plus ratings of the creativeness of students' short stories. The median validity coefficient was 0.45. Sample items from GIFFI II, and therefore HDYT, appear in Table 10.2. GIFFI II produces a total creativity score plus five subscale scores: *confidence, challenge-inventiveness, imagination, creative arts and writing*, and *many interests*.

TABLE 10.2 Sample Items from GIFFI II

ITEM	TRAIT
I have a very good sense of humor.	Humor
I have done a lot of creative writing.	Creative Activity
I enjoy thinking of new and better ways of doing things.	Originality
I tend to become childishly involved with simple things.	Playfulness, Curiosity
I am quite original and imaginative.	Self-rating of Creativity
I am very curious.	Curiosity
I have had many hobbies.	Wide Interests, Many Hobbies
I have been active in photography or filmmaking.	Creative Activity
I am able to work intensely on a project for many hours.	Energy, Commitment
I would like to learn mountain climbing.	Adventurousness, Risk-Taking
I have a great many interests.	Wide Interests
I have participated in theatrical productions.	Creative Activity
I am artistic.	Artistic
I am a risk-taker.	Risk-Taking

The Group Inventory for Finding Interests I (GIFFI I) for middle school students is a combination of (simplified) items from HDYT plus items from Rimm's elementary-level Group Inventory for Finding Creative Talent (GIFT; Davis & Rimm, 1982; Rimm & Davis, 1979, 1983). As with GIFFI II, GIFFI I also includes 60 items with five-point rating scales, and it also produces a total creativity score plus scores on the same five subscales.

Group Inventory for Finding Creative Talent: GIFT

The Group Inventory for Finding Creative Talent (GIFT; Rimm, 1976; Rimm & Davis, 1980) includes three forms, Primary for grades 1 and 2, Elementary for grades 3 and 4, and Upper Elementary for grades 5 and 6. The inventories are relatively brief, just 32, 34, and 33 yes-no items, respectively, with 25 items common to all three levels. The main difference between forms is the size of the print.

The GIFT inventories primarily assess independence, flexibility, curiosity, perseverance (energy), breadth of interests, and past creative activities (e.g., "I ask a lot of questions," "I like to paint pictures"). Along with a total score, three subscale scores are *imagination, independence,* and *many interests.*

The GIFT tests have been used with children who are White, Black, Spanish surnamed, high SES, low SES, urban, suburban, rural, immigrant, learning disabled, gifted, Israeli, French, Australian, and Chinese (Rimm & Davis, 1976, 1980). Internal reliability figures, using data from several studies, for the primary, elementary, and upper elementary forms were 0.80, 0.86, and 0.88, respectively. Frequently, the validation research conducted by others was more favorable than our own, which testifies not only to the value and virtues of GIFT but also to our unquestionable honesty as well. Validity coefficients usually range from about 0.25 to 0.45, sometimes lower and sometimes higher.

Preschool and Kindergarten Interest Descriptor

Preschool? Yes indeed, the creative traits are there and can be evaluated with high reliability and good validity. PRIDE is the Preschool and Kindergarten Interest Descriptor. (The acronym PRIDE does not fit its title too well, but it sounds better than PKID.) PRIDE may be used with children age 3 to 6. It consists of 55-point rating scale items ("No" to "Definitely"), and it measures the same kinds of traits assessed by GIFT, the two GIFFI tests, HDYT, and other creativity inventories—"many interests, curiosity, independence, perseverance, imagination, playfulness, humor, and originality" (Rimm, 1983).

An internal consistency reliability of 0.92 was reported. Like GIFT, validity was established by correlating PRIDE scores with scores derived by combining (preschool) teacher ratings of creativeness with experimenter ratings of the creativeness of children's pictures and short stories. With three samples of children, three validity coefficients were 0.38, 0.50, and 0.32. As with GIFT and the GIFFI tests, there are subscale scores (*many interests, independence-perseverance, imagination playfulness, originality*) that may prove useful.

Creativity Attitude Survey

Schaefer (1971) developed a creativity inventory for grades 4 to 6 entitled the Creativity Attitude Survey (CAS). The CAS includes 32 yes-no items and seems to measure many of the same traits evaluated by HDYT, GIFT, and the GIFFIs: confidence in one's own ideas and imagination, appreciation of fantasy and wild ideas, humor, an interest in art and writing, a desire for novelty, and an attraction to the abstract and magical. The manual reported internal consistency reliabilities of 0.75 and 0.81 and a five-week test–retest reliability of 0.61. Adequate.

Evidence for validity was provided by research with 31 fifth-grade children who participated in a creativity training program for 1 hour per week for 14 weeks. Their CAS scores improved significantly from pre-test to post-test while the scores of students in two control groups did not. Twenty months later, children who received the creativity training still scored higher on the CAS than did the others.

A second validity study in primarily African American and Puerto Rican American schools with 321 experimental and 366 control children replicated the earlier project: Post-test CAS scores for the trained children were significantly higher than for control children. Finally, 17 students who were nominated by a fifth-grade language arts teacher as having shown "concrete evidence of creativity" scored higher on the CAS than 18 other students who were judged equally bright. One reviewer (McKee, 1985) noted that although the CAS has not been widely adopted, it could be used for evaluating the success of programs designed to teach creative thinking in elementary-age children.

Test author Schaefer (1970) concluded that "Favorable changes in attitudes toward creativity seem to be a primary effect of creativity training programs, and these attitudinal changes seem to be relatively resistant to extinction over time." Read this statement again. The quote mirrors one main point of this entire volume.

Creativity Self-Report Scale

Feldhusen, Denny, and Condon (1965) created an unpublished inventory, the Creativity Self-Report Scale, consisting of 67 phrases considered by Torrance (1965) to describe the "behaviors and attributes" of creative persons. If you can find Torrance's book, the test is available. Junior or senior high school students simply check which of the phrases "is true of you." A sample of the 67 items appears in Table 10.3. A danger is that a "yea sayer" can check all of the items and receive a top score.

TABLE 10.3 A Sample of Creativity Self-Report Scale Items

Not bothered by mess or disorder	Sometimes stubborn
Like adventure	Persistent
Like things which are mysterious	Willing to take risks
Full of energy	Sometimes sloppy
Like working with ideas	Sometimes act without planning
Full of curiosity	Question authority and rules
Like to be independent	Open-minded
Have some odd habits	Enjoy taking things apart
Get lost in a problem	Cannot write fast enough to keep up with thoughts
Like complicated ideas	Sometimes question or disagree
Ask many questions	with statements made by the teacher
Like to hear other people's ideas	Stick with a project to completion
Act childish or silly sometimes	Seen by some students as being different
A self-starter	Look for new ways of doing things
Self-confident	Not afraid of being thought to be "different"
Good sense of humor	
See beauty in some things	

Source: Feldhusen, J. F., Denny, T., & Condon, C. F. (1965). *Manual for the creativity self-report scale.* Unpublished manuscript, Purdue University, West Lafayette, IN.

Adjective Check List

The Adjective Check List (ACL; Gough & Heilbrun, 1965) is a one-page test containing 300 adjectives from *absent-minded* to *zany*. It is used for personality assessment and psychometric research. The test-maker simply marks those adjectives that apply to him or her. It may be scored for 37 characteristics—for example, needs for achievement, dominance, nurturance, autonomy, masculinity, femininity, and personality adjustment (Consulting Psychologists Press, 1988). The ACL manual does not include a scoring key for creativity. However, Harrison Gough (1979) himself developed and validated a 30-item creativity scale.

The scale is easily scored. As shown in Table 10.4, 18 items are positive indicators of creativity and 12 are negative indicators. One simply subtracts the number of negative indicators endorsed from the number of positive indicators endorsed. If you enjoy checking test items and happen to endorse all 30, your score of 6 would be compared to the scores of others.

Zhou and Oldham (2001) asked 68 college students in a management class to find creative solutions for 16 different personnel problems. Judges rated the creativeness of their solutions. Zhou and Oldham evaluated the creativeness of the students by asking them to indicate which of Gough's (1979) 19 (not all 30, curiously) adjectives in his ACL creativity scale described them. Note that the authors "examined the direct contribution of creative personality to individuals' creativity" (p. 155). They followed Gough's scoring method, subtracting the number of negative items endorsed from the number of positive items endorsed. Sure enough, students who scored higher on their version of Gough's ACL creativity scale produced ideas that were significantly more creative than lower-scoring students.

TABLE 10.4 Gough's (1979) Scoring Key for the *Adjective Check List*

POSITIVE ITEMS		NEGATIVE ITEMS	
Capable	Interests wide	Affected	Honest
Clever	Inventive	Cautious	Interests Narrow
Confident	Original	Commonplace	Mannerly
Egotistical	Reflective	Conservative	Sincere
Humorous	Resourceful	Conventional	Submissive
Individualistic	Self-confident	Dissatisfied	Suspicious
Informal	Sexy		
Insightful	Snobbish		
Intelligent	Unconventional		

Score: 18 (positive items) minus 12 (negative items). (No correction for number of items checked.)

Barron–Welsh Art Scale

Many lists of characteristics of creative people will include "attraction to complexity" or "preference for complexity and asymmetry," characteristics that in part were born in the research of George Welsh and Frank Barron with their Barron–Welsh Art Scale (Welsh & Barron, 1963). The test is unlike other creative personality inventories. In fact, it's not an inventory at all, but it does evaluate attraction to complexity, asymmetry, and ambiguity. The test is a set of 80 abstract line drawings, some simple and balanced and others complex and asymmetrical. Test-takers simply mark (+ or −) which of the drawings

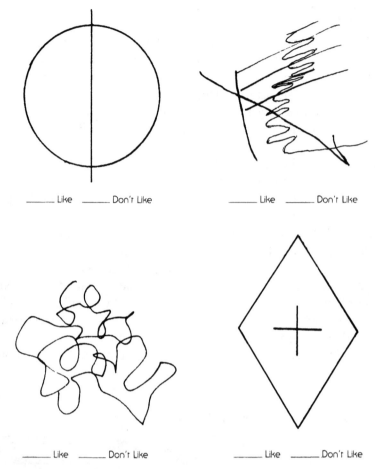

_____ Like   _____ Don't Like   _____ Like   _____ Don't Like

_____ Like   _____ Don't Like   _____ Like   _____ Don't Like

FIGURE 10.1 Patterns similar to those in the *Barron–Welsh Art Scale*. Are you simple and balanced? Or complex and smudgy?

they like and which they do not like. Artists and people who are more creative tend to like the complex and asymmetrical drawings and do not like the simple and balanced ones. Some patterns similar to those in the Art Scale appear in Figure 10.1.

There is a correct answer for each of 60 of the items; the other 20 are "fillers." One's creativity score is the total number of correct answers (0–60). With adults the test is quite good, but it has not been widely used in the schools.[2] The *Barron–Welsh Art Scale* may or may not be useful below college level.

One Inventory with Three Creative Attitude Scales

Basadur, Taggar, and Pringle (1999) reduced an unnamed 136-item inventory to its best 44 items. Both the long and short inventories measure "attitudes toward creativity, divergent thinking, and new ideas" (p. 78). Both inventories are comprised of three attitude scales named (1) *Valuing New Ideas*, (2) *Belief That Creativity Is Not Only for a Select Few*, and (3) *Not Feeling Too Busy for New Ideas*. Each item is rated from "1" ("strongly disagree") to "9" ("strongly agree"). Both the 136-item and 44-item inventories appear in their entirety in Basadur et al. Sample items from the 44-item scale appear in Table 10.5.

---

[2] Translation: Your author does not know of any studies using this test with elementary or secondary students.

TABLE 10.5 Creative Attitude Scales

Valuing New Ideas
18. Old problems can be solved with new ideas.
25. You shouldn't prejudge your new ideas.
40. We'll get left behind unless we spend some time on new ideas.
41. We really need creative people.
Belief That Creativity Is Not Only for Select Few
21. Creative people wear unique glasses. (R)
23. Outsiders have the best ideas. (R)
27. Creative people are flaky. (R)
28. Creative people are not responsible. (R)
Not Feeling Too Busy for New Ideas
2. I don't have much time for thinking up wild ideas, I'm too busy just getting my job done. (R)
13. The business environment doesn't encourage the use of creativity. (R)
33. If everyone is thinking, then no one is doing. (R)
39. New ideas almost always take too much time. (R)

Source: From Basadur et al. (1999).
"(R)" indicates reverse scoring—agreement is a "1," disagreement is a "9."

Kirton Adaptation–Innovation Inventory

A final personality-related inventory is the British Kirton Adaptation–Innovation Inventory (KAI; Kirton, 1976, 1987). It differs from other creativity inventories in that it measures *style* of creative problem-solving and *level*. The KAI evaluates two styles that are assumed to be ends of a continuum.

Adaptors tend to accept the problem as defined and generate ideas designed to "do things better" (Mudd, 1995). They are more likely to use conventional solutions. Adaptors are described as resourceful, efficient, organized, conscientious, and dependable, but also bureaucratic, close-minded, and dogmatic (e.g., Kwang & Rodrigues, 2002).

Innovators, at the other end of the continuum, solve problems by trying new approaches. They may redefine the problem and break previously perceived restraints in order to "do things differently." Innovators are described as original, energetic, individualistic, spontaneous, insightful, and a creative loner, but sometimes impractical, abrasive, and creators of confusion (e.g., Kwang & Rodrigues, 2002). According to Kirton (1976), innovators access a larger cognitive domain than adaptors do.

Puccio, Treffinger, and Talbot (1995) administered a slight modification of the KAI to 59 British workers from an iron foundry and 81 from a research and development organization. Sure enough, a more adaptive style was related to products "that fulfilled their intended purposes or functions . . . followed accepted and understood rules associated with the job . . . and had clear practical applications" (p. 167). The products were "logical, adequate, well-crafted, and useful" (p. 157). An innovative style was highly related to products described as "new or unusual . . . caught the attention of others . . . [and] helped others view their work in new and different ways" (p. 167). These products were said to be "original, attractive, transformational, and expressive" (p. 157).

Mudd (1995) noted that "Adaptors and innovators do not readily get on, especially if they are extreme scorers. Middle scorers . . . do not easily reach the heights of adaptation or innovation as do extreme scorers . . . but they more easily act as "bridges," forming the consensus group and getting the best out of clashing extreme scorers" (p. 242).

According to Hammerschmidt (1996), extreme adaptors and innovators just don't speak the same language. KAI scores range from 32 to 160, with an American mean of 95—and an average organizational work group difference of just 5 KAI points will cause communication problems. As validity evidence, Hammerschmidt compared four-person *planning* groups (more rule-bound and requiring more conventional thinking) versus *implementation* groups (less structured and requiring less conformity). When adaptors and innovators were assigned to work groups consistent with their KAI preference, the group was more successful.

The KAI showed an internal consistency reliability of 0.86—indicating that all test items generally measure the same thing, namely, traits relating to adaptation versus innovation tendencies (Mudd, 1995). Comparing KAI scores with divergent thinking scores, Gelade (1995) confirmed that, sure enough, innovators produced more original ideas and a greater number of ideas.

While the KAI seems designed for adults—for example, in business, administration, and management—it apparently can be used with middle-school students (Selby, Treffinger, Isaksen, & Powers, 1993).

Cautions in Using Personality Information to Identify Creative Students

As perhaps an obvious caution, despite recurring commonalities in personality traits, not all creative students will show all traits. Creative students differ dramatically from each other. Some are high achievers whose creativity takes socially valued artistic and scientific forms. Other creative students will be more unconventional in appearance and behavior, and may even be rebellious and antiestablishment—unwilling to tolerate a bureaucracy perceived as inflexible and irrelevant to their problems or to world problems. Many creative students will be energetic, outgoing, confident, and comical—our classic theater types. Others, perhaps artistic, poetic, or scientific-minded students, will be introverted, anxious, and socially withdrawn.

In rating or nominating students as creative, some teachers will not recognize characteristics of creativity. They might favor the dutiful and conforming "teacher pleasers" over the sometimes unconventional, overactive students who may think oddly, dress oddly, ignore rules and conventions, ask too many questions, do poor work when not interested, or be radical or defiant.

Some energetic creative students will be perceived by teachers as having attention deficit hyperactivity disorder (ADHD; Cramond, 1994; Leroux & Levitt-Perlman, 2000; Zentall, Moon, Hall, & Grskovic, 2001). Because of the similarity of symptoms of ADHD and the creative personality, some teachers are more likely to recommend consulting a physician about medication than to nominate an active child as creative.

A minor caution in identifying creative secondary school students is the existence of a few *pseudo-creatives*, pretentious students who feign creativeness by dressing and acting the way they believe eccentric creative people are supposed to dress and act.

Nonetheless, a teacher, counselor, school psychologist, or parent who is aware of personality and biographical indicators of creativeness can capitalize on the information to formally or informally identify creative potential in children and adolescents.

Assessing Past Creative Activities

Creativity tests are incomplete. As we have seen, personality inventories such as Renzulli's Scale for Rating Characteristics of Creative Students, How Do You Think?, and others measure character and motivational traits related to creativeness. Divergent thinking tests evaluate abilities related to producing lots of imaginative ideas. But information about students' *actual* creative activities and behaviors reflects traits and abilities underlying both types of tests, plus whatever other abilities, thinking styles, experiences, predispositions, and parental and environmental influences have led to their real creative behavior.

Therefore, a credible—but little used—way to locate creative students or adults is to examine students' past and present creative activities (e.g., Bull & Davis, 1980; Holland, 1961; Lees-Haley, 1978; Okuda et al., 1991; Plucker, 1999). Face validity is high. For example, Holland identified high school students who were creatively talented in art or science by soliciting their history of creative activities. *He concluded that past creative achievement is the single best predictor of future creative achievement.*

Does the elementary child have unusually wide interests, unique hobbies, strange collections? Perhaps dinosaurs, magic, Egyptology, ventriloquism, or a collection of animal bones? Does the child have unusual experience or talent in art, poetry, creative writing, handicrafts, building things, music, dance, computers, or a science area? Perhaps you know a "dinosaur kid," a "photography kid," or a child who knows more about Picasso, Gandhi, Russian cosmonauts, DNA, hostas, or the insides of computers than do the teachers.

Maybe the child or adolescent is a theater kid or had an imaginary playmate.

Renzulli's Action Information. Renzulli's concept of *Action Information* is used to help select energetic, creative students for participation in gifted education programs (Renzulli, 1994; Renzulli & Reis, 1997, 2003). Action information reflects creative behaviors and creative personality traits—energy, imagination, resourcefulness, high interest, the works—which teachers can use to help identify creative students. Renzulli and Reis assembled many examples of the kinds of behaviors exhibited by creative children and adolescents. Part of their list appears back in Table 4.5. Students who show these or similar behaviors are good candidates for having potential for present and future creative work.

Consensual Assessment Method. With Amabile's (1983) *consensual assessment* strategy teachers deliberately elicit samples of creative work from students. Groups of teachers then informally evaluate the creativeness of the products. In one study (Hennessey & Amabile, 1988), 5-to-10-year-old children made up a story, in about 10 minutes, to fit a wordless picture book adventure of a boy and his dog at a pond. Three teachers rated the stories on *creativity, how well they liked the story, novelty, imagination, logic, emotion, grammar, detail, vocabulary,* and *"straightforwardness."* Interrater reliability was remarkably high, indicating that the teachers' implicit theories of creativity were quite in agreement.

Detroit Public Schools Creativity Scales. The Detroit Public Schools Creativity Scales (Parke & Byrnes, 1984) use a process similar to Amabile's consensual assessment. In this case, however, community experts in a subject area evaluate the creativeness of music compositions, music performances, dance, art, short story and novel writing, drama, poetry, or speeches. One problem might be locating and recruiting experts in each area.

Note that evaluating actual creative products and behaviors, as in the informal methods described by Renzulli, Amabile, and Parke and Byrnes, reflects the way talent and capability are recognized in the real world (Borland, 1997).

Creative Activities Inventories

Several inventories and checklists were designed specifically to assess past creative activities.

Creative Activities Check List. Okuda et al. (1991) used the Creative Activities Check List (CACL), adapted from Hocevar (1980), as an outside criterion for validating their test of students' ability to find problems. Their version of the CACL included 50 creative activities in five domains. Each item began with "How many times have you . . . ?" and upper elementary students were asked to respond (1) never, (2) once or twice, (3) three to five times, or (4) six or more times. The five domains were *art* (e.g., painted an original picture), *crafts* (e.g., designed a craft out of wood), *literature* (e.g., wrote a poem or short story), *mathematics* (e.g., applied math in an original way to solve a practical problem), and *public performance* (e.g., choreographed a dance). Students were instructed to think only of activities outside of school—not class projects or homework. Subscale internal reliabilities ranged from 0.71 to 0.91 and for the total scale, 0.91. Problem-finding scores correlated between 0.38 and 0.58—validity coefficients—with CACL subscores and total score. Concluded Runco (1987), creative activities questionnaires such as CACL have "more than adequate psychometric properties" (p. 121).

SPCA. With their Statement of Past Creative Activities (SPCA) inventory, Bull and Davis (1980) asked college students to "List any creative activities (artistic, literary, technical, or scientific) in which you are or have been engaged in the past two to three years." The creativity scores derived from the SPCA showed moderately good correlations with other criteria of creativity, for example, 0.41 with scores on the *How Do You Think?* inventory (Davis, 1975) and 0.40 with an original measure of "internal sensation seeking" (which evaluated, for example, desire for fantasy/daydreaming and vividness of imagery), created by Bull.

Creative Behavior Inventory. Lees-Haley's (1978) Creative Behavior Inventory includes a checklist of creative behaviors along with an open-ended question that, together, assess past creative performance. Higher scores would reflect, for example, having written a play, choreographed a dance, published a poem, acted in a movie, or created a scientific theory. The inventory has been used successfully with both middle school (Lees-Haley & Swords, 1981) and elementary students (Lees-Haley & Sutton, 1982).

Things Done on Your Own. In the last three pages of his *Guiding Creative Talent*, Torrance (1962) presented a checklist of 100 creative activities entitled Things Done on Your Own. The checklist evaluates children's creative activities in "language arts, science, social studies, art, and other fields" (p. 251). Students were asked to "Indicate which ones you have done during this school term . . . Include only the things you have done on your own, not the things you have been assigned or made to do" (p. 251). Look again at Table 4.4, which includes a sample of Torrance's 100 creative biographical activities.

Original Self-Report Inventories. In addition to published checklists and open-ended assessments of creative activities, it would not be difficult to create an original self-report inventory for either students or parents to complete. As an example, the following simply asks about a student's past or present strong interests or hobbies:

> Describe any hobbies, collections, or strong interests that you [your child may] have had. For example, have you [has your child] been really interested in reptiles, writing poetry or stories, magic tricks, theater, computers, Ancient Athens or Rome, dinosaurs, unusual collections, art, creating or building things, handicrafts, music, or space travel or other science area? Other hobbies or strong interests? If so, list them.

Most likely, a few statements reflecting outstanding creative involvement and creative potential will float to the top.

A relationship between past, present, and future creativity is not surprising. Therefore, reports of past and current creative activities—determined with open-ended questions or structured checklists—should be highly valid and useful ways to identify creative children and youth.

Divergent Thinking Tests

Torrance Tests of Creative Thinking

By far the most popular creativity tests of any kind are the Torrance Tests of Creative Thinking (TTCT; Torrance, 1966a). Torrance inadvertently may have led others to believe that his tests measure creativity, all creativity, and nothing but creativity, but he did not delude himself. In his original technical manual, Torrance (1966b) wrote:

> Since a person can behave creatively in an almost infinite number of ways, in the opinion of the author it would be ridiculous even to try to develop a comprehensive battery of tests of creative thinking that would sample any kind of universe of creative thinking abilities. The author does not believe that anyone can now specify the number and range of test tasks necessary to give a complete or even an adequate assessment of a person's potentialities for creative behavior. He does believe that the sets of test tasks assembled in the [Torrance Tests] sample a rather wide range of the abilities in such a universe. (p. 23)

The Torrance tests were 10 years in development, have the most complete administration and scoring guides and norms, have a longitudinal validation history (e.g., Torrance, 1984a, 1988; Torrance & Goff, 1989; Torrance & Safter, 1989; Yamada & Tam, 1996), have been translated into 34 languages, and have recent scoring guides and norms (Torrance, 1990a, 1990b).[3] They have generated well over 1,000 published research studies. In 1984, Torrance reported that about 150,000 children and adults took the tests each year. Because the tests are so well known and widely used, we will describe this battery in more detail than others.

The Torrance tests originated in the 1950s and 1960s from Torrance's Minnesota Tests of Creative Thinking, which themselves were based upon Guilford's Structure of Intellect creativity tests (described later). During their 10 years of development, Torrance firmed up administration and scoring procedures, assembled normative data, gathered reliability and validity data, and put it all into four test booklets, four administration and scoring manuals for the Verbal Forms A and B and Figural Forms A and B, and a norms and technical manual. All subtests are timed, with either a 5- or 10-minute limit.

The verbal tests may be group-administered from fourth grade through graduate school but are individually administered from kindergarten through the third grade. The figural (nonverbal) tests may be group-administered from kindergarten through graduate school. According to Torrance (1977), the figural tests—which draw less from middle-class verbal skills—are more culturally fair.

The verbal test, Thinking Creatively with Words, is built of seven subtests or "activities." The first three subtests evolve around a curious picture (imagine an elf with pointed ears and pointed shoes looking at his or her reflection in a stream). Torrance feels that the ability to ask questions (sense problems, detect gaps in information) is an important creative ability. In fact, it is part of his definition of creativity (Torrance, 1977, 1988; see Chapter 1). Therefore, the first activity, asking, requires the test-taker to list all of the questions he or she can think of about the events in the picture, questions that cannot be answered by simply looking at the picture (e.g., are the ears pointed?). The second subtest, Guessing Causes, asks the test-taker to list possible causes of the events shown in the picture. The third activity, Guessing Consequences, asks for a list of consequences of the events taking place in the drawing.

The fourth verbal subtest, Product Improvement, includes a sketch of a stuffed monkey (or elephant). The examinee lists all of the improvements he or she can think of that would make the stuffed animal more fun to play with. A fifth subtest, Unusual Uses, asks the taker to list uses for cardboard boxes (or tin cans). The related sixth subtest, Unusual Questions, again focuses upon question asking: List all of the questions you can about cardboard boxes (or tin cans).

The final, seventh verbal subtest, Just Suppose, is an old creativity favorite—the "what would happen if . . . ?" question. In this case, the unlikely event is clouds with strings attached to them, or in the other test form, clouds so low you could only see people's feet. What would happen? Would you wear anything but shoes?

There are just three nonverbal or figural subtests in Thinking Creatively with Pictures. In all three cases, an incomplete or abstract sketch is presented and the examinee is asked to complete the drawing—making the picture into something meaningful and imaginative. The first subtest, Picture Construction, presents a sausage-shaped (or egg-shaped) form that is used as the basis for an imaginative drawing. The second subtest, Picture Completion, presents the test-taker with 10 simple, abstract shapes similar to those in Figure 10.2 that he or she completes and labels. Finally, the third figural activity, Circles, includes two pages of circles (or parallel lines) that the test-taker incorporates into meaningful, and perhaps clever drawings.

The subtests of the Torrance tests, verbal and figural, are scored for *fluency, flexibility, originality,* and *elaboration.* These are considered basic creative abilities, as well as dimensions of the scoring. A newer, streamlined scoring scheme for the Figural Forms A and B, which produces 18 creativity scores, will be described later.

The fluency score is simply a count of ideas listed or drawings completed, after duplications and irrelevant entries (e.g., copying instructions or reciting Mary Had a Little Lamb) are excluded.

---

[3] The American publisher, Scholastic Testing Service, distributes only an English Language version of the Torrance Tests.

Originality scores are based upon *statistical infrequency* norms. That is, each idea is listed in a table in the scoring guide where it is awarded 0, 1, or 2 points depending upon how infrequently (rarely) that idea was listed by subjects on whom the test was normed. Scoring for originality is not as simple as scoring for fluency. Because some ideas will be ambiguous or not in the scoring guide, the test scorer must make a judgment as to the degree of "creative strength" shown by the ambiguous idea and, therefore, the number of points to award. For example, using a cardboard box for a dog house is not original, but what about using it for a house for a pet anteater or pet Martian?

Torrance Tests of Creative Thinking

The *Torrance Tests of Creative Thinking* (Torrance, 1966) measure creative abilities of fluency (number of ideas), *flexibility* (number of different types or categories of ideas), *originality* (uniqueness), and *elaboration* (number of embellishments). Exercises similar to Torrance's subtests are presented below. Spend a few minutes on each one. Are you fluent? Flexible? Original? Are you elaborate?

Directions: Make a meaningful picture out of each of the nonsense forms below. Try to be original. Give each one a name.

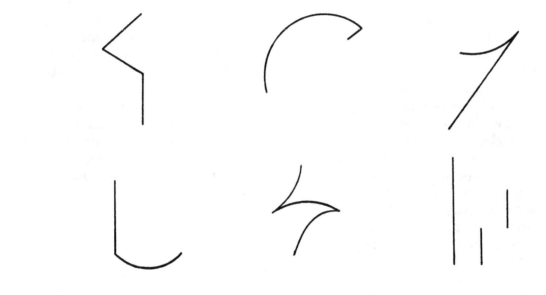

Directions: List as many unusual uses as you can for discarded rubber tires.

_____   _____
_____   _____
_____   _____
_____   _____
_____   _____
_____   _____
_____   _____
_____   _____

(For additional space use inside back cover of book.)

FIGURE 10.2 Torrance tests of creative thinking.

Flexibility refers to the number of different categories of ideas or the number of different approaches one takes to a problem. For example, if Roberta Rutt's list of tin can uses includes "put buttons in it, put pennies in it, put bottle caps in it, put nails in it, put washers in it, put feather in it, etc.," Roberta would have a very low flexibility score. In scoring the Torrance tests, as the scorer looks up the originality weight he or she also will find a number indicating the flexibility category. The number of different flexibility categories is the flexibility score for that subtest.

The figural tests may be scored for elaboration by counting the number of details beyond the basic picture. These are details that are added to the figure itself, its boundaries, and/or to the surrounding space (e.g., additional ideas, decorations, emotional expressions, color, shading). *Title originality*, on a 0 to 3 scale, is an optional *verbal* score that may be derived from figural Activity 1, Picture Construction, and Activity 2, Picture Completion. Bonus points (2–25) are awarded for Activity 3, Circles (or Parallel Lines), if the clever person combines two or more circles into a single picture. These points are added to the figural originality score.

The norms and technical manuals (Torrance, 1974, 1990b) report interscorer reliabilities (correlations) as high as 0.99 (for fluency) and almost always above 0.90. Test–retest reliabilities are in the moderate 0.6 to 0.8 range, with a few lower and many higher. The test–retest reliability figures are undoubtedly depressed by Torrance's peculiar procedure of using Form A for the first administration and Form B for the later administration, which muddles test–retest reliability with alternate forms reliability.

Validating creativity tests is not an easy chore, for reasons cited earlier. Much of Torrance's validation work, in fact, has been of the construct validity type—demonstrating that high scorers on the Torrance tests show characteristics commonly associated with creativity. One study indicated that high scorers on the Torrance tests had reputations for producing wild or silly ideas, their drawings were described as highly original, and they tended to be humorous and playful (Torrance, 1974). Another study showed that high scorers were rated high in humor and gave ink blot responses traditionally associated with imagination and creativity—responses were unconventional, fanciful, and included human movement and color (Weisberg & Springer, 1961). Fleming and Weintraub (1962) found a significant inverse relationship between creativity scores and rigidity scores. Still other studies showed Torrance test scores to be significantly correlated with the originality of imaginative stories (Yamamoto, 1963); involvement in creative activities and hobbies (art, drama, literature, music; Cropley, 1971, 1972); preferences for creative and unconventional careers (Torrance & Dauw, 1965); and teacher nominations of, for example, "Who thinks of the most unusual, wild, or fantastic ideas?" (Torrance, 1974).

Research that provides the best evidence of a relationship between Torrance test scores and real-life creative achievement comes from two longitudinal studies, one involving high school students tested in 1959 and followed up 7 and 12 years later (i.e., in 1966 and 1971), and another involving elementary school students tested in 1958 (and for five subsequent years) and followed up 22 years later (i.e., in 1980; Torrance, 1988). Though Torrance passed away in 2003, Cramond et al. (2005) continued his investigation with a 40-year follow-up, and Runco, Millar, Acar, and Cramond (2010) recently reported on the 50-year follow-up! That's a half-century of data, so as you can imagine, the findings must have been impactful. And they were. Compared with low Torrance test scorers, high scorers reported a larger *quantity* of creative achievements, higher *quality* of their creative achievements, and a higher level of *creative motivation* (career aspirations). For example, the "publicly recognized and acknowledged creative achievements" included such items as patents and inventions; plays or music compositions that were performed publicly; art awards; founding a business, journal, or professional organization; developing an innovative technique in medicine, science, business, teaching, and so on. Torrance (1984a, p. 4) reported that after 22 years, as young adults

> . . . the creatively gifted group excelled a high IQ group on the quality of their highest creative achievements, their high school creative achievements, the number of creative lifestyle achievements, and the creativity of their future career images. They also tended to excel the IQ gifted group on number of post-high school creative achievements but the difference fell short of statistical significance. The doubly gifted group [high creativity, high IQ] equaled but did not excel the creatively gifted group on all five of the criteria of young adult creative achievement.

Interestingly, the difference in creative achievements and motivations between high and low creatives increased over time—while the highs got higher, the lows did not change. Cramond et al. (2005) found that "IQ, fluency, and originality scores obtained in childhood were the best test predictors of quantity of creative achievement. . . . The best test predictors of quality of creative achievements were IQ, flexibility, originality, and the creativity index" (p. 287). They noted that the TTCT scores also explained 23% of the variance in creative production—noteworthy not only based on this accounting for nearly a quarter of the difference but also across half-a-century! Runco et al. (2010) took the results a bit "beyond" the scope of the original study and found that three indicators—Love of Work, Tolerance of Mistakes, and Minority of One—were positively correlated with achievement. Those three indicators sound like a great life mantra to me! ***Streamlined Scoring.*** Torrance confessed that, despite generally satisfactory reliability and validity evidence and proven usefulness in education, "many users have made two major criticism: The scoring is too time-consuming and the tests assess only the divergent production abilities and do not tap the essence of creativity" (Torrance & Ball, 1984, p. 5).

Torrance's (Torrance & Ball, 1984) *streamlined* scoring system, for the figural tests only, was designed to (1) streamline the scoring (surprise!) and (2) assess other dimensions of creativity beyond the divergent thinking abilities of fluency, flexibility, originality, and elaboration. The new system, nine years in development, retains the *fluency* measure essentially "as is" (which was easy to score in the first place), expedites the scoring of *originality* and *elaboration*, and adds two easily scored dimensions called *abstractness of titles* and *resistance to premature closure*. Also added were no less than 13 "creative strengths."

To be as brief as possible, the five scoring dimensions of fluency, originality, elaboration, abstractness of titles, and resistance to premature closure are considered *norm-referenced*, which means that the number of points earned are relative to the norm group. (Actually, fluency is not scored relative to a norm group.) The other 13 creative strengths are *criterion-referenced*, which means that the criterion (the creative strength) either appears in the person's test or it does not. The total 18 scores are:

1. *Fluency*, as in the original scoring guides, is a count of relevant, non-duplicated ideas. If two or more figures are combined, credit still is given for the number of figures used.
2. *Originality* is the score after non-original ideas, listed in tables, are eliminated.
3. One *elaboration* point is given for adding decorations, color, shading, each major variation of design, and each elaboration of the title beyond minimal labeling.
4. *Abstractness of titles* is scored from 0 to 3 points according to degree of abstractness; for example, a 3-point idea involves "the ability to capture the essence of the information involved, to know what is important . . . [and] enables the viewer to see the picture more deeply and richly" (Torrance & Ball, 1984, p. 19).
5. *Resistance to premature closure* earns 0 to 2 points depending upon the degree to which the test-taker (prematurely) closes the incomplete figure, "cutting off chances for more powerful original images" (p. 22).

Turning to the list of creative strengths, in general one plus sign ("+") is awarded if one or two instances of the creative strength occur (in the entire test booklet); two plus signs ("++") are given if three or more instances occur.

1. *Emotional expressiveness* is the communication of feelings or emotions (sad, happy, angry, scared, lost) in either the drawing or the title.
2. *Storytelling articulateness* is including enough detail to put the picture in context and tell a story.
3. *Movement or action* is scored if it appears in the title or the picture (e.g., running, flying, dancing, swimming).
4. *Expressiveness of titles* is scored if emotion and feeling are shown in the title (e.g., "lonely," "ambitious").
5. *Synthesis of incomplete figures*, a rare occurrence, is the combination of two or more figures in the Picture Completion subtest.

6. *Synthesis of lines or circles* is the tendency to combine two or more circles or sets of lines, which is "an important indicator of a creative disposition or thinking ability" (Torrance & Ball, 1984, p. 34).

7. *Unusual visualization* is the tendency to present ideas or objects from a novel visual perspective, for example from underneath, on top, or in a cutaway view.

8. *Internal visualization* is the tendency to visualize the internal workings of things, for example, body parts seen through clothing, the internal parts of a machine, or ants in an anthill.

9. *Extending or breaking boundaries* may occur by lengthening some lines in the Parallel Lines subtest (e.g., to make a table), dividing a pair of lines for different aspects of a picture, or by adding depth perception with circles.

10. *Humor*—puns, word play, exaggeration, absurdity—may appear in the figures or in the titles.

11. *Richness of imagery* is scored if the drawing "shows variety, vividness, liveliness, and intensity . . . has freshness . . . and provides delight for the tired scorer" (p. 41), for example, a pair of cat eyes, an alligator, or a surfer.

12. *Colorfulness of imagery* "is defined as exciting in its appeal to the sense of taste, touch, smell, feel, sight, etc." (p. 44), for example, a whale ride, banana store, ghost, or toothache.

13. *Fantasy* is reflected in fairytale episodes or characters from fables, science fiction, or other fantasy literature; also original fantasy, such as talking rain drops or a parachute hat creation.

A comparison of the original scoring of fluency, originality, and elaboration with the new stream-lined scoring showed very high agreement (correlation coefficients of 0.92, 0.94, and 0.92, respectively; Torrance & Ball, 1984). The streamlined scoring test manual presents extensive validity coefficients (correlations between scores and criteria of creativity) for all 18 measures for students in grades 3 through 12, derived from the longitudinal data mentioned earlier plus other research, that range mostly between 0.3 and 0.6.

Based on his intuition and validity data, Torrance (1990b) noted that "The [total] number of criterion-referenced indicators has elements in common with the right hemisphere style of thinking, creative personality characteristics, an innovative style of management, creative motivation, and Rorschach [ink blot] movement and originality" (p. 11).

Finally, in addition to the five norm-referenced and 13 criterion-referenced figural creativity scores, one may compute a *Creativity Index*—an overall creativity score munched into one number. It's handy for research (e.g., Saeki, Fan, & Van Dusen, 1991). The computation becomes easy with practice. For each test-taker, one first records all 18 (5 + 13) raw scores, including the number of +'s and the number of ++'s, on Torrance's *Streamlined Scoring Sheet* (Torrance, Ball, & Safter, 1992). Then for each of the five norm-referenced raw scores (fluency, originality, elaboration, abstractness of titles, and resistance to premature closure), and for each student, you look up the corresponding five standard scores in Torrance's (1990b) *Norms-Technical Manual*, which you also record on the *Streamlined Scoring Sheet*. A student's Creativity Index is the *average* of his or her five standard scores, plus the *sum* of the 13 criterion-referenced "creative strengths" ("+" counts one point, "++" is two points). Easy as pie.

On one hand, changing the scoring system from 4 to 18 scores somehow loses the flavor of "stream-lining." On the other, the new scoring system, with practice, is indeed expedient and supplies rich and useful information. The reader interested in further details regarding scoring and validation should see Torrance and Ball (1984) and Torrance (1974, 1990a, 1990b).

Research Suggestions for Program Evaluation. As a first suggestion, if a research design for evaluating a training program includes both a *before* and an *after* measure of creativeness using two different test forms, such as Form A and Form B of the Torrance tests, give half of the subjects Form A and half Form B as a pretest. Each subject would take the other form as the posttest. This strategy controls for the possibility that the two test forms may not be exactly equivalent. That is, average scores on Form A (or Form B) might tend to run higher, regardless of intervening training. It would not be sensible or accurate to provide objective test evidence that (1) the gifted and talented program depressed student creativity (because students happened to take the difficult form as a posttest) or (2) the program was wildly successful in teaching creativity (because students took the easy form as a posttest).

As a second suggestion, in evaluating program success a control group (comparable subjects who do not receive the training) is recommended so that a logical person can conclude that improvement from pretest to posttest truly is due to the creativity training and not due to having taken the creative test once before.

Both errors are common.

Creativity and School Achievement. Creative traits such as unconventionality and independence, sometimes mixed with a little resistance to domination and indifference to rules and conventions, surely can work against school achievement. However, other traits and abilities of creative students are definite assets in school: flexibility, curiosity and inquisitiveness, perceptiveness and the ability to see relationships, resourcefulness, high energy and enthusiasm, confidence, inner-directedness, an experimental attitude, intuitive thinking, open-mindedness, and verbal creativity, generally. Torrance (1974) reported correlations roughly in the range of 0.35 to 0.45 between verbal creativity scores and scores on standardized achievement tests (reading, language, arithmetic), with intelligence held constant. Figural creativity scores showed lower correlations (0.16–0.25) with achievement. Torrance noted that correlations between creativity scores and achievement will be lower when children are taught by authority, and higher when taught in creative ways such as using discovery, experimentation, and the like.

Importantly, summarizing the results of many studies, Torrance reported the median correlation between figural creativity and intelligence as 0.06 and between verbal creativity and intelligence as 0.21. These figures indicate that creative abilities and abilities measured by intelligence tests are not the same, especially with nonverbal creativity.

Test for Creative Thinking–Drawing Production (TCT-DP)

About 1986 Klaus Urban and Hans Jellen in Hannover, Germany, first published a few articles describing their Test for Creative Thinking–Drawing Production (TCT-DP). An updated manual is dated 1993 (Urban & Jellen, 1993). The TCT-DP resembles Torrance's figural tests, but the appearance and scoring are unique.

Form A is comprised of a single 6-inch square frame within which are five so-called figural fragments: a 90-degree angle, a half-circle, a squiggly line, a dot, and a short dotted line. Outside the square frame lies a sixth fragment, a small square with one open side. Form B is identical except the figural fragments are arranged differently. The test can be used with single subjects or groups "between 5 and 95 years of age." Administration requires 15 minutes or less. After considerable practice, scoring is said to require one to two minutes.

One 1990 evaluation of the factor structure and other psychometric features of the TCT-DP led the highly impressed Polish researchers to recommend that the test be normed and used as an official screening instrument in Poland for identifying gifted and creative students (Urban, 1993).

As for instructions, the administrator reads clearly and slowly:

> In front of you is an incomplete drawing. The artist who started it was interrupted before he or she actually knew what should become of it. You are asked to continue with this incomplete drawing. *You are allowed to draw whatever you wish*! You can't draw anything wrong. Everything you put on the paper is correct. When you finish your drawing, please, give me a sign, so that I can take it. . . . Just begin your drawing and don't worry about the time, . . . But we don't have a whole hour to complete this drawing.

As each student finishes the administrator records the time, which is 1 of 11 scoring dimensions: The TCT-DP is scored for:

1. *Continuations*: Any use, continuation, or extension of the six given figural fragments.
2. *Completion*: Any additions, completions, complements, or supplements made to the used, continued, or extended figural fragments.
3. *New elements*: Any new figure, symbol, or element.
4. *Connections made with a line*: Any connection between one figural fragment or figure and another.

5. *Connections made to produce a theme*: Any figure contributing to a compositional theme or "gestalt."
6. *Boundary breaking that is fragment dependent*: Any use, continuation, or extension of the "small open square" located outside the square frame.
7. *Boundary breaking that is fragment independent*: Drawing extensions, figures, and/or elements that break the boundary or lie outside the large square frame, but are independent from the small open square.
8. *Perspective*: Any breaking away from two-dimensionality.
9. *Humor and affectivity*: Any drawing that elicits a humorous response or shows affection, emotion, or strong expressive power.
10. *Unconventionality*: (a) Any manipulation of the material; (b) any surrealistic, fictional, and/or abstract elements or drawings; (c) any usage of symbols or signs; or (d) unconventional figures.
11. *Speed*: If the drawing accumulates at least 25 points from the first 10 categories, up to 6 more points are awarded for speed. For example, 6 points are awarded if one finishes under two minutes, but no points if one takes longer than 12 minutes.

Each dimension earns 0 to 6 points, except *Unconventionality*, which earns 0 to 12 points. The possible total score is thus 0 to 72 points. Points are added together to produce a total score, with no transformations.

The authors claim that the TCT-DP is different and superior to existing divergent thinking tests. However, there is a great similarity to several aspects of the streamlined scoring of the Torrance tests—of which Urban and Jellen may have been unaware when they built the TCT-DP. Specifically, both tests award points for unconventionality (Torrance's fantasy), humor (same in both), affectivity (Torrance's emotional expressiveness), connections made with a line (Torrance's synthesis of lines or circles), producing a theme (Torrance's storytelling articulateness), boundary breaking (same in both), and perhaps more.

It is difficult to determine whether the TCT-DP will produce more useful and important information than will the Torrance figural tests with streamlined scoring.

The Guilford Tests

Some problem-sensitive readers may have wondered why Guilford's (1967, 1977) *Structure of Intellect* (SOI) model did not appear in Chapters 1 or 2 with other theories of creativity. Answer: It was saved until now. Guilford created a three-dimensional cube—a theory of intelligence—which was intended to describe anything anyone could ever do with his or her brain. Figure 10.3 presents the 1988 (and final) edition of the SOI cube, with its three dimensions of *contents*, *products*, and *operations*. This newest version is known only to the readers of his five-page 1988 article or this chapter. In its original form (Guilford, 1967), 4 types of contents combined with 6 products and 5 operations to produce 120 cells ($4 \times 6 \times 5 = 120$). Most people who write about Guilford's model stopped here—with "120 SOI abilities" forever ossified in their frontal lobes. In fact, Guilford (1977) extended the model by subdividing the "figural" content into *visual content* and *auditory content*, creating 150 cells. Shortly before his death he also subdivided the "memory" operation into *memory retention* (long-term memory) and *memory recording* (short-term memory)—producing no fewer than 180 cells (Guilford, 1988).

Our limited space will not permit a complete description of the SOI model (which makes tedious reading anyway). Briefly, each of the 180 cells of the model is interpreted to be a unique cognitive ability. This approach stands in sharp contrast to the two IQ scores of the WISC-III or the four scores of the *Stanford–Binet Intelligence Scale, Fourth Edition*. J. Paul Guilford invested about three decades creating tests that measure each one of those 180 abilities.

The darkened slab of the model in Figure 10.3 includes the operations of *divergent production*. Tests that measure a few of these 30 abilities (6 products $\times$ 5 contents) are marketed as tests of creativity. For example, *Word Fluency* is a four-minute test that requires the examinee to produce a list of words containing a specified letter or letters (e.g., R_M). In the SOI cube, this is divergent production of symbolic units, or DSU. The *Expressional Fluency* test, divergent production of semantic systems

CONTENT

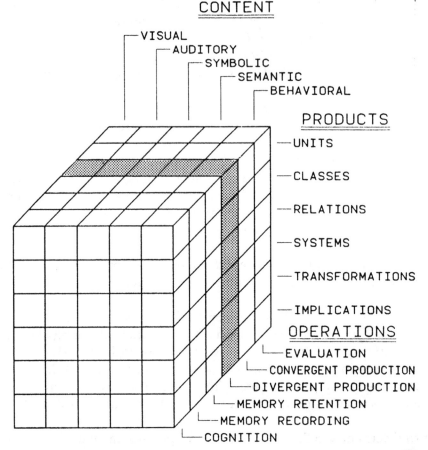

FIGURE 10.3 The Revised Structure of Intellect Model. X-Ray examination confirmed that Guilford's cerebral cortex looked exactly like this. Source: Reprinted by permission of *Educational and Psychological Measurement.*

(DMS), allows eight minutes to verbally express an idea using a given first letter for each word (e.g., E___R___L___P). Other fluency tests include *Ideational Fluency* and *Associational Fluency*; there also are *Consequences* ("What would happen if . . . ?") and *Alternate Uses* tests.

In addition to the divergent production abilities (the darkened slab), Guilford (1986) explained how *transformations* (a *product*; can you find the transformations slab in Figure 10.3?) also are important creative abilities. For example, a scientist might be strong in cognition of visual transformations (CVT); a cartoonist strong in cognition of semantic transformations (CMT); and the creativity of scientists, inventors, and decorators will involve the evaluation of visual or semantic transformations (EVT, EMT; Guilford, 1986).

One cell in the 1967 SOI model is the divergent production of figural transformations (DFT)—combining the divergent production operation with the transformation product. One test of DFT may be familiar—matchstick problems. For example, given the six squares in Figure 10.4, one problem is to remove three matchsticks and leave four squares; another problem is to remove four matchsticks and leave three squares. See Guilford (1967, 1977, 1986) for descriptions of the many, many other specific SOI tests.

On the downside, regarding Guilford's 120, 150, or 180 abilities—and as attractively worded by Guastello, Bzdawka, Guastello, and Rieke (1992)—while Guilford's model suggests an interesting explanation for the nature of thought, the SOI model "may be criticized for having fractured intellectual functioning into too narrowly defined units relative to what human faculties are actually engaged in ordinary intellectual endeavors" (pp. 260–261).

FIGURE 10.4 Matchstick problem measuring the divergent production of figural transformations (DFT). Try removing three matches to leave four squares; four matches to leave three squares. Do not leave excess, dangling matches.

Incidentally, for some years Meeker (1969, 1978; Meeker & Meeker, 1986) has used groups of the Guilford tests in a diagnostic-remediation approach to teaching reading, math, writing, and creativity. Specific weaknesses are diagnosed with the *SOI-Learning Abilities* test, which then are remediated with equally specific exercises (Meeker, Meeker, & Roid, 1985). More recently, Meeker created SOI Model Schools, which include an SOI curriculum (Staff, 1995). Currently more information SOI can be found online at http://www.soisystems.com.

Wallach and Kogan Tests

The Wallach and Kogan (1965) creativity tests are not published in the sense that you could buy a box of 25 for 20 or 30 dollars. The deal is much better. The tests appear in their entirety in *Modes of Thinking in Young Children*, complete with administration and scoring directions. Educators or researchers can use the tests without charge.

The Wallach and Kogan test administration procedure is unique and well known on two counts. First, a relaxed, game-like atmosphere is established. Second, the tests are untimed. The purpose of these two manipulations is to remove the pressured, test-like atmosphere that characterizes intelligence testing. According to Wallach and Kogan, these game-like and untimed conditions reduce the influence of intelligence upon the creativity scores to about zero.

There are five tests. Each test is scored for *fluency*, the total number of ideas listed, and *uniqueness*, the number of ideas that are not given by any other person in the testing group. Obviously, the uniqueness score will depend upon group size—with only 5 or 10 test-takers, uniqueness scores will be much higher than with 100 or 500 students. The Wallach and Kogan sample consisted of 151 fifth-grade children.

This is not to say it is a children's test battery. The tests worked very well with a group of 37 college students (Bartlett & Davis, 1974). Fluency and uniqueness scores correlated 0.33 and 0.35 with overall ratings of the creativeness of art and writing products and ideas for inventions and creative teaching methods.

With the Instances test, students list instances or examples of each of four class concepts. For example, "Name all of the *round* things you can think of." Ditto for "things . . . that will make a noise," "square things," and "things . . . that move on wheels."

Alternate Uses is, of course, our old friend, the Unusual Uses, test. In eight questions, subjects were to "Tell me the different ways you could use a newspaper (knife, automobile tire, cork, shoe, button, key, and chair)." The Similarities test asks the person to "Tell me all the ways in which a potato and a carrot (cat and mouse, train and tractor, milk and meat, grocery store and a restaurant, etc.) are alike."

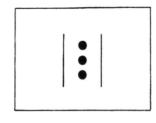
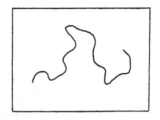

Pattern   Line

FIGURE 10.5 Items similar to those in the Wallach and Kogan (1965) Pattern Meanings and Line Meanings tests.

Two similar tests use visual materials. With Pattern Meanings, subjects list possible meanings or interpretations of eight abstract visual designs: "Tell me all of the things you think this could be." With Line Meanings, subjects list interpretations of line drawings, some squiggly and abstract, others simple. One, in fact, is a straight line. Drawings similar to those in Pattern Meanings and Line Meanings appear in Figure 10.5.

Getzels and Jackson Tests

As with the Wallach and Kogan tests, the Getzels and Jackson (1962) tests are published only in the authors' book, *Creativity and Intelligence*. Four of the subsets appear in their entirety, complete with administration and scoring directions. The fifth is copyrighted by others. The four tests again appear to be available for general use without charge.

The Word Association Test presents the person with a list of 25 words, each of which has multiple meanings (e.g., *arm*, *duck*, *bolt*, *punch*, and *tender*). Fifteen minutes are allowed to list as many meanings as possible. The creativity score is the total number of *different* meanings listed (e.g., *arm of chair* and *arm of sofa* would receive just 1 point, not 2).

The Uses Test asks the person to (what else?) list as many different uses as he or she can for five objects (bricks, pencils, paper clips, toothpicks, a sheet of paper). Again, 15 minutes are allowed. The test is scored for the *number of different uses* for an object and for the relative *uniqueness* of the uses. The test-taker receives a uniqueness point for each idea listed by less than one-fifth of the group of responders. The number of different uses is added to the number of unique uses to produce a total Uses Test score.

Hidden Shapes, the copyrighted test, consists of 18 simple geometric figures, each of which is accompanied by four complex figures. The problem is to identify which complex figure contains the simple figure. The test is supposed to measure "critical exactness" or "critical practicality," which is "predictive of individual and creative work thoroughly done" (Cattell, 1955). A full three-and-a-half minutes are allowed.

We should note that some versions of this type of test are called *hidden figures* or *embedded figures* tests, and are interpreted to reflect a cognitive style of *analytic* (or *field-independent*) thinking versus *global* (or *field-dependent*) thinking (see Witkin, Moore, Goodenough, & Cox, 1977).

The Fables Test consists of four fables whose last lines are missing. The test-taker is allowed 30 minutes to supply a (a) moralistic, (b) humorous, and (c) sad ending for each fable. For example:

A grasshopper, that had merrily sung all summer, was almost perishing with hunger in the winter, so she went to see some ants that lived near, and asked them to lend her a little of the food they had put by.

"You shall certainly be paid before this time of year comes again," she said.

"What did you do all the summer?" asked they.

"Why, all day long, and all night long too, I sang, if you please," answered the grasshopper.

"Oh, you sang, did you?" said the ants. . . .

The answers are scored for *appropriateness* (is it really moralistic, humorous, or sad?) and *relatedness* (does the ending logically follow from the given material?). Appropriateness and relatedness scores are added together for a total *Fables* score.

Finally, with the Make-up Problems test students are given four paragraphs, each of which contains numerical statements about (1) building a swimming pool, (2) doing a science experiment, (3) earning money at odd jobs, and (4) conducting a survey of apartment rental rates. Students are allowed approximately 30 minutes to make up as many mathematical problems as they can with the given information. Each problem is scored for the number of *elements* (pieces of numerical information) and number of *operations* (addition, subtraction, multiplication, division). Again, the two scores are added together for a total Make-Up Problems score.

The Getzels and Jackson Make-Up Problems test has been used as a test of mathematical creativity.

Thinking Creatively in Action and Movement

Torrance's (1981b) Thinking Creatively in Action and Movement (TCAM) is a preschool measure of creative potential. The tests grew out of Torrance's observations of the ways in which preschool children in daycare centers expressed their creativeness. Said Torrance, these tests of creativity in movement are developmentally appropriate to preschoolers and "sample the kinds of creativity that are important in the lives of such children . . . [and the tests] make sense to them."

The first subtest, How Many Ways?, asks children to "think up as many ways as you can to walk or run" between tape markers on each side of the room. The experimenter records the ideas, which are later scored for *fluency* (number of ideas) and *originality* (according to a scoring guide and influenced by judgments of creative strength, with 0–3 points per idea). The second activity is Can You Move Like . . . ?, for example, a tree in the wind and assorted animals, totaling six situations. It is scored in one category, *imagination*, which is rated as the student performs each of the six movements. Activity 3, What Other Ways?, requires a large supply of paper cups and one waste basket. The test administrator asks the child how many ways he or she can put a paper cup in the wastebasket. A little-known fact is that Michael Jordan got his start by taking this test. The fourth and final subtest is What Can You Do With a Paper Cup?, a children's form of the Unusual Uses test. Both Activities 3 and 4 are scored for fluency and originality, as with Activity 1. Extra credit (up to 4 points) is given for "unusual flourishes and choreographing executed by some children." The student winds up with a total fluency, total originality, and an imagination score.

The tests are basically untimed, although the tester is urged to record the time required for each subtest—usually between 10 and 30 minutes. Scores on the tests appear to have no racial, gender, or socioeconomic bias and are relatively unrelated to previous preschool attendance or measures of intelligence. They can be used with handicapped groups such as emotionally disturbed students and deaf students (Torrance, 1981b).

Torrance (1981b) reported interscorer reliabilities of 0.99 for fluency and around 0.96 for originality. He also reported a high test–retest reliability coefficient of 0.84 for the overall test, with subtest test–retest reliabilities from 0.58 to 0.79.

Regarding validity, Torrance again noted the difficulty of finding a suitable criterion against which to validate the tests. Several studies produced significant correlations between TCAM scores and criteria associated with creativeness. For example, TCAM fluency and originality scores were correlated 0.44 and 0.42, respectively, with children's Knock-Knock joke humor. Knock Knock. (Who's There?) Ithsmus. (Ithsmus who?) Ithsmus be about the best data Torrance could find, under the circumstances.

However, on the negative and eyebrow-raising side, Tegano, Moran, and Godwin (1986) found significant correlations between TCAM fluency scores and IQ scores, suggesting that TCAM performance is not independent of intelligence. Incidentally, the users' comments reported in the TCAM manual suggest that the test helps improve teachers' creativity consciousness and helps them recognize specific creative children: "What a splendid tool this is. . . . The staff . . . were so awakened, saying such things as 'Why I never saw that in (name) before!' or 'Why I never paid attention to that before!' or 'Oh! Look what I have missed!' or 'I'm going to have a whole new way of teaching now!'"

Sounds and Images, Onomatopoeia and Images

Thinking Creatively with Sounds and Words (Torrance, Khatena, & Cunnington, 1973) takes the form of two long-playing records that include the two tests Sounds and Images and Onomatopoeia and Images. They are not "divergent thinking tests" in the strict sense that a test-taker will brashly list every idea he or she can think of. However, the test-taker does think up and write down ideas that are scored for originality. The tests fit best in this divergent thinking category.

The Sounds and Images test presents four abstract sounds. After each sound, the test-taker is given a few seconds to describe on the score sheet the mental images stimulated by that sound. The set of four sounds is presented three times under the assumption that the associations will become more and more original with repetition. They usually do. Each of the 12 responses receives between 0 and 4 originality points, based upon the norms in the scoring guide. We saw this *statistical infrequency* scoring procedure in our discussion of the Torrance tests.

The Onomatopoeia and Images test is similar, except that 10 image-stimulating onomatopoeic words (e.g., *zoom*, *boom*, *fizzy*, and *moan*) are used instead of four sounds. Again, the 10 words are presented three times, and 0 to 4 points are awarded for each answer according to tabled norms.

There are two forms of Sounds and Images and two forms of Onomatopoeia and Images. The forms differ only in the specific abstract sounds or onomatopoeic words used. Also, the tests are available in an adult form and a children's form. The introductory narratives of the children's forms are simpler.

The authors present extensive reliability and validity information for the two tests. Considering both tests, interscorer reliabilities ranged from 0.88 to 0.99. Alternate forms reliability ranged from a disturbingly low 0.36, reflecting poor consistency and low accuracy, to 0.92. Validity criteria varied and so did the validity coefficients, usually between 0.13 and 0.45. Correlations between Onomatopoeia and Images and measures of intelligence were close to zero.

Apart from its use as a test, *Sounds and Images* makes a good imagination-stimulating creativity exercise, which is what it was created for in the first place (Torrance et al., 1973).

Other Creativity Tests

If one wished to scour the literature for old, unpublished, or obscure tests—perhaps for a particular subject area or purpose—some lists that include an astonishing variety of instruments appear in Dacey (1989), Davis (1971, 1973, 1989b), Kaltsoonis (1971, 1972), and Kaltsoonis and Honeywell (1980).

As some examples, one unique creativity test is the Percept Generic Test. The administrator repeatedly presents a picture at ever-shorter exposure times until the original is quite unrecognizable (Smith & Carlsson, 1987). We are advised that creative people more quickly break away from the dominant ("correct") perception and construct an imaginative, subjective interpretation. The Judging Criteria Instrument (Eichenberger, 1978) is used by peers or oneself to evaluate creativity in a physics class, using rating scales that evaluate fluency, flexibility, originality, elaboration, usefulness, social acceptance, and worth to science. A Test of Musical Divergent Production evaluates fluency, flexibility, originality, and elaboration, along with quality, with instrumental music students (Gorder, 1980). A Life Experience Inventory is said to identify creative electrical engineers (Michael & Colson, 1979). The Creative Processes Rating Scales is an apparently easy-to-use instrument for evaluating sixth-grade children's creativity in the visual arts (Kulp & Tarter, 1986). Torrance worked on the inventories What Kind of Person Are You? and Something About Myself (Khatena & Torrance, 1976). Still other creativity tests measure empathy with story characters, creative writing, preference for polygons, and motor creativity. There are many math creativity tests, a chemistry creativity test, an "experiential curiosity measure," a pun test, an ingenuity test, and more.

Runco (1999a) assembled a list of old and new creativity tests, inventories, and rating scales (many of which are reviewed in this chapter) in 14 categories. Using his labels, familiar categories included Biographical Inventories, Personality, Activity Checklists, Preferences and Attitudes, and Divergent Thinking and Problem-Solving. Less familiar are Runco's categories of, for example, Work and Educational Environment, Projective and Perception Measures, and a potpourri "Domain-Specific Measures" category that included musical creativity, poetry writing, inventiveness, evaluating performance in technical personnel, a preconscious activity scale, an anagram test, and a pun test.

A survey of recent literature—particularly in the *Journal of Creative Behavior*, the *Creativity Research Journal*, and computer searches of ERIC and PsychLit—will turn up still more creativity tests. Speaking from experience, it seems that many newcomers to the creativity field experience an overwhelming urge to develop a creativity test.

Recommendations

Your author's first recommendation would be, when possible, to evaluate students' backgrounds of creative activities and current demonstrations of creative motivation and interest. Several evaluation forms and strategies were mentioned earlier; especially noteworthy were Torrance's (1965) 100-item Things Done on Your Own checklist and Renzulli's (1994; Renzulli & Reis, 1997, 2003) concept of *action information*. With a little imagination, the reader can create an original form, perhaps with inspiration from the Torrance and Renzulli methods. A person's record of creative activities and behavior logically seems the most reliable and valid indicator of future creative behavior.

Regarding divergent thinking and personality/biographical types of creativity tests, both work reasonably well—given such built-in limitations as the inherent complexity of creativity and evaluating just part of human creativity (a sample of creative personality traits or creative abilities). As a practical matter, personality/biographical inventories usually can be administered and scored more quickly and efficiently than divergent thinking tests.

Among personality/biographical inventories, Renzulli's creativity rating scale, the *How Do You Think, GIFT, GIFFI I and II*, and Schaefer's *Creativity Attitude Survey* show high internal reliability and good track records for predicting student creativeness.

As for divergent thinking tests, the Torrance tests must remain at the top of the list, due to their careful 10-year development, longitudinal validation studies, and recently revised norms. The more efficient newcomer, Jellen and Urban's *Test for Creative Thinking-Divergent Production*, seems promising. If cost is an issue, the Getzels and Jackson and Wallach and Kogan tests are available in their respective books, have good development histories, and seem available without charge.

As a final reminder, the challenge is to *identify* creative children and youth. Tests and inventories that attempt to *measure* creative abilities and personality dispositions are just one way to identify creative youngsters. An awareness of creative characteristics, creative abilities, and especially students' backgrounds of creative activities can help teachers and others identify creative students with accuracy and validity—perhaps without using tests or inventories at all.

Summary

Guilford started a creative revolution by inciting colleagues to action to scientifically study creativity.

Psychometrics is a field concerned with psychological measurements.

Evaluating creative potential can be done through creative personality inventories, past creative achievements, or divergent thinking tests.

Uses of creativity tests range from identifying gifted and talented students in schools to research on a college campus or counseling in a professional setting. We can identify students who, on average, will behave more creatively by measuring creative personality traits and abilities and assessing backgrounds of creative activities. We cannot beat the very long odds of predicting creative eminence, but neither can intelligence tests.

There are issues in creativity assessment related to aspects of reliability and validity.

Reliability is equated to consistency or stability of scores. Test–retest reliability involves giving the same test twice and comparing the scores. Alternate Forms reliability involves generating two "separate but equal" forms of a test.

Interrater reliability tries to reduce the subjectivity of scoring of creativity and increase consistency of scores from two or more judges.

The degree of reliability can be computed with coefficients that represent the magnitude and direction of how two scores are related. Strong correlations are 0.9 and above.

Validity relates to the accuracy of test scores.

Construct validity answers the key question, "Are we measuring what we intend to measure?"

Content validity relates to how accurate a test covers the entirety of a domain. If a test is too narrow, it has content underrepresentation. If a test includes items that are extraneous to a domain, it has content irrelevance.

Criterion-related validity is the correlation of a creativity test with an external reference of creativity. Convergent validity involves the correlation of two creativity tests together. Predictive validity examines how well scores on a creativity test will predict a future outcome on an activity or achievement related to creativity.

Face validity is simply based on whether the test looks good.

Despite problems, creativity tests are moderately valid and helpful.

One problem is false negatives, when a test misses a creative person. False positives refer mainly to faking an undeserved high creativity score.

For accurate identification, two criteria of creativity are recommended, for example, a creativity test plus teacher or parent nominations.

Creativity is related to intelligence. Therefore, high IQ suggests creative potential.

Three types of measurement instruments are inventories that evaluate creative personality characteristics, inventories, or checklists of past creative activities, and divergent thinking tests.

Among creative personality inventories, Renzulli's 10-item creativity scale from his Scales for Rating the Behavioral Characteristics of Superior Students has high face and empirical validity.

Davis's 100-item How Do You Think? test shows high reliability and good validity as a general creative personality/motivation inventory. Spin-offs from HDYT include GIFFI I and II. The elementary-level GIFT and the preschool PRIDE also evaluate creative personality traits and behaviors.

Schaefer's Creativity Attitude Survey resembles the GIFT and GIFFI creative attitude/personality inventories. Schaefer concluded that training results in favorable attitudes toward creativity.

Feldhusen and others devised the Creativity Self-Report Scale—67 descriptive phrases prepared by Torrance—as a checklist of creative behaviors and characteristics.

Gough built a creativity scale for the Gough and Heilbrun Adjective Check List.

With the Barron–Welsh Art Scale one indicates which of 80 abstract drawings one likes or does not like. It evaluates preference for complexity and asymmetry.

Basadur et al.'s three-part inventory assesses valuing new ideas, believing that creativity is important for everyone, and not feeling too busy for creativity.

The Kirton Adaptation-Innovation Inventory identifies two styles of problem-solvers: conventional-thinking adaptors and more creative, but perhaps abrasive, innovators. They may not get along.

One caution is that not all creative students will show all creative personality traits, which is not surprising. Also, teachers may favor dutiful "teacher pleasers," or else suspect ADHD and recommend medical treatment for energetic creative children.

Self-reports of creative activities seem a self-evident and valid way to locate creative students or adults.

Renzulli's action information reflects creative behaviors and personality traits and may be used for identification.

With Amabile's consensual assessment method, teachers elicit and then evaluate samples of creative work.

The Detroit Public Schools Creativity Scales uses community experts to evaluate creative products and performances.

Runco and friends used a Creative Activities Check List, 50 activities in the five domains of art, crafts, literature, math, and public performance, as a creativity validating criterion.

The Statement of Past Creative Activities by Bull and Davis also evaluated creative involvement.

Lees-Haley devised a checklist, the Creative Behavior Inventory, to evaluate students' past creative activities.

Torrance's Things Done on Your Own is another checklist of 100 creative activities.

One also can create an original self-report inventory to assess students' past or present strong creative interests and hobbies.

The Torrance Tests of Creative Thinking are the best known and most carefully developed and evaluated divergent thinking battery. They stem from his earlier Minnesota Tests of Creative thinking and include Verbal Forms A and B (seven subtests) and Figural Forms A and B (three subtests). They traditionally are scored for fluency, flexibility, originality, and, for the figural tests, elaboration. Torrance evaluated construct validity and, in three long-term studies, criterion-related validity, using real-life creative achievements.

Cramond et al. and Runco et al. extended the analysis of Torrance's longitudinal data "beyond" the original scope of the project.

Torrance and Ball in 1984 created the streamlined scoring system for the figural tests, which expedites scoring and produces 18 scores. The 18 scores may be combined into a single Creativity Index.

The German-born Test for Creative Thinking-Drawing Production is a figural test consisting of a 6-inch frame plus six "figural fragments." The TCT-DP evaluates 11 creative abilities and personality dispositions, is administered in about 15 minutes, and may be scored in under two minutes (maybe).

The 1988 version of Guilford's Structure of Intellect includes 180 cells. His creativity tests stem from the divergent thinking (operation) part of the model and, to a lesser degree, from the transformation (product) slab. Meeker uses the SOI model and her SOI-Learning Abilities test in a diagnostic-remediation fashion.

Wallach and Kogan administered their tests in an untimed and game-like atmosphere. The battery includes verbal and nonverbal subtests that are scored for fluency and uniqueness.

The Getzels and Jackson tests also include verbal and nonverbal subtests. Their unique Fables Test requires a moralistic, humorous, and sad ending for each of four fables. Their Make-Up Problems test has been used to measure mathematical creativity.

Torrance's Thinking Creatively in Action and Movement is a preschool measure of creative potential. Three subtests ask for different kinds of movements, actions, or pantomimes; a fourth asks for unusual uses for paper cups.

Thinking Creatively with Sounds and Words includes two tests Sounds and Images and Onomatopoeia and Images. With Sounds and Images, test-takers write down mental images stimulated by four abstract sounds. Onomatopoeia and Images is similar, except that the stimuli are words.

With searching, a reader could locate many additional creativity tests, perhaps for specific purposes such as evaluating creative potential in math, art, music, physics, or writing.

Your author recommends evaluating students' past and present creative activities. Divergent thinking and personality tests also work reasonably well.

The challenge is to identify creative potential. Tests and inventories represent just one avenue.

Review Exercises

Assessing Creative Potential: Issues, Biographical Information, Tests

Self-Test: Key Concepts, Terms, and Names

Briefly define or explain each of these:

Three current uses for creativity tests _____

_____

Formal and informal creativity evaluations _____

_____

Predicting creative eminence _____

_____

Construct validity _____

_____

Criterion-related validity _____

_____

Face validity _____

_____

Reliability (any type) _____

_____

Creative personality inventories _____

_____

Scale for Rating Characteristics of Creative Students (from SRBCSS) _____

_____

Barron–Welsh Art Scale _____

_____

Adaptors and innovators _____

_____

Creative activities inventories and checklists _____

_____

Action information _____

_____

Consensual assessment method _____

_____

Divergent thinking tests _____

_____

Torrance Tests of Creative Thinking _____

_____

Fluency _____

Flexibility _____

Originality _____

Elaboration _____

Streamlined scoring of the Torrance tests _____

_____

Torrance's Creativity Index _____

_____

Test for Creative Thinking-Drawing Production _____

_____

Structure of Intellect Model _____

_____

Thinking Creatively in Action and Movement _____

_____

Thinking Creatively with Sounds and Words _____

_____

Which is Which?

Let's classify each of the following tests, test batteries, or procedures according to whether they are classified in this book as (1) a creative personality inventory, (2) an evaluation of past creative activities, or (3) a divergent thinking test.

Place a "P" in the space before each inventory that mainly measures creative *personality/motivation* traits.

Place a "CA" in the space before each procedure or inventory that measures *actual creative activities.*

Place a "DT" in the space before each *divergent thinking* test.

Also, can you identify which tests were devised by creativity leader Paul Torrance? Place a "T" after the name of test, inventory, or procedure that Paul Torrance developed.

——— How Do You Think?

——— Things Done on Your Own

——— Wallach and Kogan tests

——— Kirton Adaptation-Innovation Inventory

——— Action information

——— GIFFI I and II, GIFT, PRIDE

——— Torrance Tests of Creative Thinking

——— Adjective Check List

——— Getzels and Jackson tests

——— Thinking Creatively in Action and Movement

———   Thinking Creatively with Sounds and Words (Sounds and Images, Onomatopoeia and Images)

———   Guilford Structure of Intellect tests

———   Scales for Rating the Characteristics of Creative Students (from SRBCSS)

———   Barron-Welsh Art Scale

———   Creativity Attitude Survey

Let's Think about It

1. According to the text, why is testing for creative potential a difficult challenge?

_____

_____

_____

Can you add to these ideas—why do YOU think it is difficult to measure a person's creative capability?

_____

_____

_____

2. Do you think creative personality inventories, reports of past creative activities, and divergent thinking tests will identify the same creative students? Yes? No? Partly? Sometimes? Explain or comment.

_____

_____

_____

3. Imagine that the Gifted and Talented Committee of a local school district has asked YOU to help them identify creative *elementary* school children for their gifted program. Based on what you have read in this chapter and Chapter 5 (personality traits, abilities, biographical factors), what would you recommend?

_____

_____

_____

4. Imagine that Megacorporation wishes to award $1,000 scholarships to the 10 most creative persons in your previous *high school*. How would you help your old high school identify strong candidates? What would you recommend? (Creativity tests? Accomplishments? Activities? Awards won? Teacher nominations? Some combination?)

_____

_____

_____

5. Now imagine that the local Chapter of *Americans against Change and Progress* wants to give *Rigidity Awards* to the 10 most unimaginative, rigid-thinking, tradition-oriented, and conforming students in your former high school. How might these students be identified? (Under no circumstances should you give humorous answers to this question!!)

_____

_____

_____

Creativity in Education

Contributing Author: Joyce Juntune

"In my view, I am often immensely rich, not in money, but (although just now perhaps not all the time) rich because I have found my metier, something I can devote myself to heart and soul and that gives inspiration and meaning to my life."

—*Vincent van Gogh*

Many people believe that creativity is a necessary but insufficient component of high intelligence to activate creativity, that creativity is a complex factor in its relationship to giftedness (Van Tassel-Baska, J.) But creativity is an outlet for anyone who wants to express something, whether that be an idea or an emotion. Anyone can develop this skill.

While intelligence is the act of apprehending something (OED), creativity is the ability to come up with new ideas by connecting existing concepts (Tanner Christensen.) There is no limit, there is simply discoverable value.

This discovery can be found anywhere and in any vocation—As a restaurant owner and the creation of his meals, the preparation and presentation; a lawyer and their chosen path to defend an accused individual—this is the value that creativity has in any line of work and field. As long as there is passion and pursuit, creativity can be used in any calling.

Joyce Junetune

"21st Century Classrooms and Creativity"

As education focuses on twenty-first-century learning, creativity has taken on new importance in the schools. It is listed as one of the top critical skills for students heading into the future labor market. Sawyer (2019) clarifies the difference between the current learning of facts as "shallow knowledge" and the focus on creative knowledge that he calls "deep knowledge." Shallow knowledge is the precursor to deep knowledge. Deep, creative knowledge brings understanding to shallow knowledge. These two kinds of knowledge work together so students are able to master the content as they increase their creative thinking ability.

Teachers can infuse creative thinking into all of the content areas by asking students to think more deeply about the content or to use the content to think in new and different ways. A classroom that nurtures creativity is a classroom where questions are valued (Starko, 2014). Using curiosity-spurring questions such as: "What do you wonder about____?, What questions do you have about ____ to which you do not know the answer?" build curiosity and a sense of wonderment. Asking students to solve a math problem three different ways or generating seven to eight ways a concept you are studying is like a common object, (How is a desert ecosystem like a fork?) are examples of ways to nurture creativity in the classroom.

Many schools have set aside time for students to explore topics of interest through *Genius Hour* (McNair, 2017). As students engage in projects that have meaning for them, they ignite their curiosity and put in use creative thinking and problem-solving strategies. These projects involve creative thinking at many levels—from the spark that begins the exploration to ways to present their final project to an authentic audience in a meaningful and relevant way.

Teachers might use learning stations to build curiosity about a topic as well as a way to practice learned skills in a new setting. Learning stations are places where students can work independently or with a partner to observe, test ideas, develop models, or obtain information to be used to further learning. The stations can be used in a rotation or as a self-contained learning activity (Keeley, 2018).

Preschool through higher education have embraced the use of Makerspaces (Peterson & Scharber, 2018; Truitt & Ku, 2018) as a means for sparking innovative thinking by involving students in hands-on learning (Hira & Hynes, 2018). The use of Makerspaces for learning was initially part of the engineering programs in K-12 classrooms within the STEM focus (Martinez & Stager, 2019). It has since become common to see Makerspaces in many classrooms (Halverson & Sheridan, 2014) and schools (Kurti, Kurti, & Fleming, 2014). Makerspaces can be related to the content lessons or be used as independent learning experiences.

A recent creative approach to learning is *Visible Learning* (Hattie & Yates, 2014). Hattie's focus is on learning versus teaching even though the purpose of teaching IS learning. He is concerned that learning becomes visible—that teachers can view learning through the eyes of their students. Creative thinking is one of the strategies students can use to move from "not knowing" to "knowing." A part of being a creative thinker is the ability to be comfortable with "not knowing." It involves high levels of uncertainty. Hattie (2014) identifies this "not knowing" space as an important component of successful learning. Making learning visible requires creative thinking on the part of the teacher as they design ways to engage students in the process of learning through the use of music, relationships, chunking, gestures, and so on.

Dual Code Theory (DCT) combines elements of creativity into the learning process through the use of mental images and text (Sadowski & Paivio, 2013). DCT examines the two separate systems for coding our experience—textual (verbal) and images (verbal). The use of two coding systems helps the student gain a more complete understanding of what they are learning than the use of one coding system. Unfortunately, many schools focus only on the words or text, ignoring the power of mental images. Research conducted in schools with high numbers of students from poverty found that students raised in poverty had higher levels of ability in image thinking than textual thinking (Juntune, Kaya, & Tyrrell, 2017). Using the power of image thinking and encouraging students to create multiple images, Ramos (2017) documented how using *Mindsketching* (Juntune & 120 Creative Corner, 1987) in the classroom resulted in heightened student engagement in the learning process. Creative thinking and successful learning go hand in hand for all students, but especially those living in poverty (Juntune et al., 2017).

The Workshop Model is a teaching structure that challenges students to be creative and take responsibility for their own learning. The model was developed by Lucy Calkins and Carmen Farina as a way to teach writing (Calkins, 1986). Later it was used to teach reading (Calkins, 2015). Currently, teachers use the Workshop Model across the curriculum to build student engagement in learning and increase understanding. The Workshop Model has four parts for learning: (1) opening or introduction to the learning, (2) a mini-lesson taught by the teacher, (3) student work time, and (4) a time for reflection and debriefing. The largest amount of time is spent in the student work time. Students work in small groups or pairs and are encouraged to experiment, try different approaches to the task, and ask questions to clarify their understanding.

This is especially important based on research by Herrington, Reeves, & Oliver (2005) which showed "for many students, the traditional didactic lecture, when applied as the primary instructional method, fails to provide opportunities for integrating knowledge. Lecture may lead to memorization of factual information but often do not succeed well in eliciting comprehension of complex concepts." Or for utilization of creativity.

Closely aligned with the Workshop Model approach is Problem-based Learning (PBL). Both are designed to build student inquiry, both allow time for messy learning, both are student-centered, both encourage learning reflection, and both pursue student-driven inquiry. PBL students learn by actively engaging in real-world meaningful projects. They gain knowledge and skills by investigating and responding to an authentic and complex problem or challenge (Kim, Belland & Axelrod, 2019). PBL started in the medical and pre-professional schools, but has since moved into all areas of higher education as well as into K-12 classrooms (McConnell, Parker, & Eberhardt, 2017; Whitlock, 2019).

In a meta-analysis of over 30 studies over a 20 year period featuring over 12,000 students in nearly 200 schools, Chen and Yang (2019) found that the implementation of project based learning into the curriculum had a significant and profound effect on student achievement. These positive results were seen across many different demographic (age, grade, gender) and domain specific (subject matter) variables.

A great resource for bringing creative thinking into the classroom is TED-Ed: *Lessons Worth Sharing* (http://ed.ted.com). It is a branch of the popular TED Talks but is especially designed for educators. On this website educators will find videos, lessons from teachers around the world, and ways to customize lessons for any classroom setting.

Creativity in Gifted Education

At present, every state in the United States has enacted legislation that (a) recognizes that gifted students exist; (b) acknowledges that they have special needs, which usually are not met in regular educational programs; and (c) recommends or requires differentiated educational services for them. Gifted programs also exist across Canada. Furthermore, with an incomplete list, Davis, Rimm, and Seigle (2011) listed 44 countries from Australia and Austria to the Ukraine and Wales that offer advanced or accelerated educational programs for gifted students.

Creativity plays a key role in all aspects of gifted education—defining "giftedness," formulating goals and objectives of a program, identifying gifted and talented students, and planning acceleration and enrichment activities that enhance students' creative potential.

The two fundamental aims of G/T programs are to help individual students develop their high potential and to provide society with educated professionals who are creative leaders and problem-solvers.

Definitions of Giftedness

Defining *gifted and talented* is important because the definition adopted by a school district will determine who is selected for the special services and training. There is continual danger that one's definition, and consequent identification methods, will discriminate against such special populations as poor, minority, handicapped, underachieving, and even female gifted students.

Five Categories of Definitions

As an introduction to the definition problem, Stankowski (1978) outlined five categories of definitions of "gifts" and "talents." All but the first currently are used in various programs to guide the identification process.

First, *after-the-fact* definitions emphasize established prominence in one of the professions. The "gifted" are those who have shown consistently outstanding achievements, usually creative ones.

Second, *IQ* definitions set a cutoff point on the IQ scale. "Gifted" students are those scoring at or above the cutoff, for example, an IQ score of 120 or 130. Note that such a shortsighted definition can—and often does—excludes highly creative students.

Third, *percentage* definitions set a fixed proportion of the school (or district) as "gifted," based on IQ scores, grades, or teacher recommendations. The percentage may be a restrictive 3% to 5% or a more generous 15% to 20%, as in Renzulli's (Renzulli & Reis, 1997, 2003) Schoolwide Enrichment Model (SEM; described later).

Fourth, *talent* definitions focus on students who are outstanding in art, music, math, science, or other specific aesthetic or academic areas.

Finally, *creativity* definitions emphasize creative abilities and talents, as reflected in creativity test scores, teachers' nominations, or ratings of creative products.

U.S. Office of Education Definitions

The first federal definition for gifted was developed in 1972. It came from the Marland (1972) Report.

Gifted and talented children are those identified by professionally qualified persons who by virtue of outstanding abilities are capable of high performance. These are children who require differentiated educational programs and services beyond those normally provided by the regular school program in order to realize their contribution to self and society.

Children capable of high performance include those with demonstrated achievement and/or potential ability in any of the following areas:

1. General intellectual aptitude
2. Specific academic aptitude
3. Creative or productive thinking
4. Leadership ability
5. Visual and performing arts

This definition was modified in 1978 by the U.S. Office of Education to read:

> [The gifted and talented are] children and, whenever applicable, youth who are identified at the preschool, elementary, or secondary level as possessing demonstrated or potential abilities that give evidence of high performance capability in areas such as *intellectual, creative, specific academic* or *leadership* ability or in the *performing and visual arts*, and who by reason thereof require services or activities not ordinarily provided by the school (U.S. Congress, Educational Amendment of 1978 [P.L. 95-561, IX (A)]).

Note that the definition recognizes not only high general intelligence but also gifts in specific academic areas, creativity, leadership, and the arts. It is considered a "multiple-talent" definition. Note also that by including "demonstrated or *potential* abilities" the definition includes underachievers, whose abilities may not be demonstrated in actual high-quality performances.

The next federal definition came in 1988 when Congress passed the Jacob K. Javits Gifted and Talented Students Education Act (P.L. 100-297).

The term *gifted and talented student* means children and youth who:

1. Give evidence of *higher performance capability* in such areas as intellectual, creative, artistic, or leadership capacity or in specific academic fields, and who
2. Require services or activities *not ordinarily provided by the schools* in order to develop such capabilities fully.

In 1991, a group of psychologists, parents, and educators met in Columbus, Ohio. The sought to redefine giftedness in terms of the inner experience of the individual. This definition is known as *asynchronous development.*

> Giftedness is **asynchronous development** in which advanced cognitive abilities and heightened intensity combine to create inner experiences and awareness that are qualitatively different from the norm. This asynchrony increases with higher intellectual capacity. The uniqueness of the gifted renders them particularly vulnerable and requires modifications in parenting, teaching and counseling in order for them to develop optimally. (The Columbus Group, 1991, 2013)

Renzulli's Three-Ring Definition

Joseph Renzulli's *three-ring definition* of giftedness also is well-known and widely accepted. Renzulli (1977; Renzulli & Reis, 1997, 2003) has argued that people who truly make creative contributions to society—that is, truly gifted and talented persons—possess three characteristics: They have high *creativity*, high *task commitment* (motivation), and at least above-average (though not necessarily outstanding) *ability* (intelligence; Figure 11.1). It has been a common mistake among people who endorse Renzulli's three-ring definition to *select* for gifted and talented programs only those children who appear to be strong in all three characteristics—creativity, motivation, and intelligence. In fact, as we will see in the identification section, Renzulli and Reis (1997, 2003) recommend a much different, highly flexible, and generous five-step identification strategy. Furthermore, motivation and creativity in the three-ring model "are considered developmental objectives that we attempt to produce in the target population" (Renzulli & Reis, 1991, p. 114).

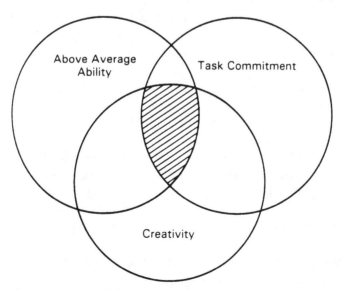

FIGURE 11.1 Renzulli's three-ring model.
Source: Reprinted by permission of J. S. Renzulli.

Characteristics of Gifted Students

While high creativity is one characteristic that is important in selecting students for G/T programs, intellectual giftedness typically is valued even more. Apart from its appearance in high IQ scores and high grades, intellectual giftedness also can be seen informally in precocious language skills, including an advanced vocabulary, superior comprehension, and very logical thinking processes. Also common among the intellectually gifted are early reading, writing, math, music, and art skills, along with advanced interests and very wide interests. There also are many common affective traits, such as high motivation and persistence; confidence, low anxiety, better self-concepts, and an internal locus of evaluation; plus higher levels of moral thinking, due to a strong empathy ability and good sense. Superior humor is also common.

Due to their ability, creativity, independence, and motivation, gifted students prefer to learn in less structured, more flexible ways—independent study and projects (Davis et al., 2011; Silverman, 2013)

We should mention the Terman studies, since so many lists of characteristics of gifted and talented students are based on his and his colleagues' long-term research (e.g., Terman & Oden, 1947). In the 1920s, Lewis Terman (1925) and others used the *Stanford–Binet Intelligence Scale*, which Terman developed, to identify 1,528 boys and girls with IQ scores of 140 and above—the top 1%. The personal and professional activities of these people were studied and followed up in a series of interviews and mailings for the next 60 years.

In contrast to the prevailing beliefs at the time about gifted as social misfits and physically weak, Terman actually found that "the average member of our group is a slightly better physical specimen than the average child." They were superior in all academic areas. They also were more trustworthy, better adjusted, and emotionally stable in their youth and adulthood, as evidenced by lower rates of mental illness and suicide. Many had successful careers (Shurkin, 1992). For example, Ancel Keys made the covers of *Time* and *LIFE* by discovering and popularizing the connection between high cholesterol and health problems. He also invented WWII K-Rations, the high-nutrition, pocket-size meals for soldiers. "K" stands for Keys.

Identification of Gifted Students

Space will not permit a detailed discussion of test scores, nomination forms, and matrix systems used in identification or the problems and delicate issues of deciding who is and who is not "gifted and talented" (see Davis et al., 2011). Identification methods are, or should be, related to program definitions of giftedness and program content and goals. Selection should include both objective scores (tests, grades) and subjective nominations and ratings (Hunsaker, Odoardi, & Smith, 2012; Johnsen, 2018).

Creative talent is one criteria for selection, based on teacher ratings of creativeness, creativity test scores, and perhaps ratings of creative products. For accurate identification, as we noted in Chapter 10, teachers should use two criteria of creativity. A student who scores high on both is extremely likely to be identified correctly as creative.

Regrettably, many state governments and school districts ignore creativity altogether in favor of high grades and IQ scores plus teacher ratings of academic potential—despite the fact that motivated creative students are the most likely to make innovative contributions to society. As one too-common occurrence, an unimaginative and unmotivated student with an IQ score of 130 (the cutoff score) may be stamped "gifted" and admitted automatically to a G/T program, but an enthusiastic and creative youth with an IQ of only 129 will be stamped "not gifted" and excluded. Said Torrance (1984a), "The use of intelligence tests to identify gifted students misses about 70% of those who are equally gifted on creativity criteria."

Bureaucracies are not particularly famous for flexibility, fairness, or agreeing with your author's totally sensible concern for creative talent.

The following is an unelaborated list of identification methods, which are used by school screening committees singly and in every conceivable combination.

- Intelligence test scores
- Achievement test scores
- Overall grades or grades in specific areas
- Teacher nominations (informal or using rating scales)
- Creativity test scores
- Nominations by parents, peers, or self
- Product evaluations

As we saw in the section on percentage definitions of giftedness, some programs will select a restrictive 3% to 5%, while others will use a talent pool approach—"cast a wide net"—and identify 15% to 20%. The philosophy is: When in doubt, admit.

Within a wide-net approach, Renzulli and Reis (1991) outlined a five-step selection strategy using *all* of the above criteria. First, students who score above the 92nd percentile on intelligence or achievement tests are admitted automatically. Second, teachers nominate additional students who display creativity, motivation, unusual interests or talents, or areas of superior performance. Third, "alternate pathways" such as parent nominations, peer nominations, self-nominations, or creativity test scores are brought to the screening committee for review. Fourth, to avoid biases of current teachers, nominations by past teachers are solicited. Finally, *action information* (remember action information?) reflecting high enthusiasm about a project is used by teachers or students themselves for nomination and selection into the program.

Goals and Curricula of Programs for the Gifted

Many lists itemize the *needs* of students who are gifted and talented. These logically translate into the *goals* and *curricula* of G/T programs (see Davis et al., 2011). An abbreviated overview of curriculum for the gifted includes:

1. *Maximum achievement in basic skills*, including learning at an appropriate level and pace, and based on needs rather than grade-level appropriateness.
2. *Content beyond the prescribed curriculum*, related to broad-based issues, abstract ideas, theories, and problems that stimulate reflective, evaluative, critical, and creative thinking. These may require materials and resources beyond the designated grade level.
3. *Exposure to a variety of fields of study*, including new disciplines and new occupations.
4. *Student-selected content* based on interests and needs, including in-depth studies of self-selected topics.
5. *Experience in creative thinking and problem-solving*, including futuristic thinking.
6. *Development of thinking skills*, such as independent and self-directed study skills, library skills, and research/scientific skills; critical thinking in the sense of evaluating biases, credibility, logic, and consistency; decision-making, planning, organizing, analyzing, synthesizing, and evaluating.
7. *Development of self-awareness and self-understanding* regarding one's capabilities, interests, and needs; appreciating individual differences; and relating to other gifted students.
8. *Development of motivation*, including independent and self-directed thinking and work, plus increased achievement motivation that includes high-level educational and career aspirations.

All acceleration and enrichment activities should be planned with these types of objectives in mind. Although it is essential for learning experiences to be enjoyable, they should not be "fun and games" or busywork designed to keep students occupied.

Acceleration, Differentiation, and Enrichment Alternatives

Acceleration

A handy way to differentiate *acceleration* from *enrichment* in gifted education programs is to define *acceleration* as any strategy that results in advanced placement or credit. *Enrichment* includes strategies that extend beyond standard grade-level work, but do not result in advanced placement or credit (i.e., anything else). A great resource that pulls together the research on the effects of acceleration is *A Nation Empowered,* Vols. 1 and 2 (Assouline et al., 2015). http://www.accelerationinstitute.org

Some popular acceleration strategies are:

1. Early admission to kindergarten or first grade
2. Grade skipping ("full acceleration")
3. Subject skipping ("partial acceleration")
4. Early admission to junior or senior high school
5. Credit by examination
6. Advanced Placement courses in high school
7. College courses while in high school
8. College correspondence courses in high school
9. Early admission to college (early high school graduation)
10. Telescoping, for example, four years of high school into three

The best-known example of accelerating bright secondary students into college-level mathematics courses is the Study of Mathematically Precocious Youth (SMPY) program. SMPY was born at Johns Hopkins University in 1971, brainchild of Julian Stanley. Primarily seventh-grade boys and girls were identified as mathematically precocious (top 1%) based on their *Scholastic Aptitude Test-Mathematics* scores (Lupkowski-Shoplik, Benbow, Assouline, & Brody, 2003).

The students participated in fast-paced summer math programs at Johns Hopkins, usually covering one to two years of high school algebra and geometry in three weeks, because, said Stanley, they were working, not sleeping. In addition, they were counseled regarding the suitability of a smorgasbord of acceleration options: They may attend college part-time, earn college credit by taking Advanced Placement classes, skip a grade, collapse two or more years of math into one, or enter college early, perhaps by skipping high school graduation. The results, said Stanley and Benbow (1986), are an increased zest for learning, enhanced feelings of self-worth, reduced egotism due to the humbling effects of working with intellectual peers, far better preparation for college, better fellowship opportunities, and the opportunity to enter a professional career at an earlier age.

The SMPY model evolved into the nationwide summer Talent Search program, which uses the newer Scholastic Assessment Test (SAT-I) and the ACT Assessment to identify precocious students. Talent Search provides suitable coursework for both mathematically and verbally talented seventh-grade students (Lupkowski-Shoplik et al., 2003). Recently, an elementary talent search was initiated to locate (who else?) academically precocious elementary students. For identification, the elementary talent search uses, for example, the Educational Testing Service PLUS Academic Abilities Assessment and the American College Testing EXPLORE. A variety of acceleration and enrichment opportunities are made available, for example, grade skipping, testing out of future classes, taking advanced classes, individualized instruction, academic contests and Olympiads, independent projects, and enrichment classes.

Most acceleration strategies do not "teach creativity" directly in the same sense that this book teaches creative attitudes, techniques, and an understanding of the topic of creativity. However, by advancing students' knowledge in a subject matter field we indirectly enable them to think creatively in that area and prepare them to make creative discoveries and innovations. They have advanced information with which to be creative.

Differentiation of Curriculum and Instruction

Kaplan

Whether students are in a classroom with multiple abilities or in a classroom for gifted students, the teacher is expected to differentiate the curriculum and instruction for the gifted students. Kaplan (2018) describes the necessity to differentiate by bringing depth and complexity to the curriculum. Depth and complexity strategies serve as tools to generalize study within and across disciplines. Some of the depth strategies include examining: patterns in the content, the big ideas overarching the content being studied, the language used within specific disciplines of study, ethical issues, and so on. Complexity strategies includes such things as: examining a field of study over time, looking more closely into differing points of view, studying the multiple factors impacting the content/situation/action, and so on. Kaplan stresses that this approach to learning is related to critical thinking, creative thinking, problem-solving, and logical thinking.

Tomlinson

Tomlinson (2017, 2018) looks at differentiation as a way to respond to student differences in readiness, interest, and learning profile (which includes their learning style, culture, gender, and intellectual preferences). Her approach focuses on ways to differentiate the content, process, and product. Content includes the "what" the students need and want to learn. Process includes "how" they go about that learning process and come to own the learning—"make it their own" (Sousa & Tomlinson, 2018, p. 107). Product is about the outcome of the learning. What they do with what they have learned to show evidence of understanding. She maintains that "highly effective teachers teach students first, then content" (Tomlinson, 2017, p. 39). She also stresses the importance of engaging students in critical and creative thinking as part of the differentiation process.

Menus

A popular approach for classroom teachers charged with differentiating the curriculum and instruction for the various levels of learners in the classroom is to use menus. Menus are designed to provide teachers and students with an array of choices. Renzulli's (2018) approach to menus for the classroom includes combining Received Knowledge (content) with Analyzed Knowledge (process) and Applied and Created Knowledge (Application) as the main "ingredients." The interaction of these three types of knowledge, plus the type of instructional technique chosen, will result in a choice of products for the student to do as their learning output. He proposed a knowledge menu, an instructional strategies menu, and a student activities menu.

Westphal (2017a, 2017b) has written books for almost every subject and every grade level with easy-to-use activity choices for students. Westphal's purpose is to provide teachers with an avenue for implementing student-centered learning based on choice. The activities are designed to guide the student in making a decision as to which product to develop after studying a major concept or unit. She provides specific guidelines for each product as well as guidelines for assessing the products.

Tiered Assignments

The tiered approach looks at differentiation as a learning ladder (Roberts & Inman, 2015). The goal of tiered instruction is continuous progress for all students. There are various tiers of learning that increase in difficulty and complexity as a student progresses up the learning ladder. Pre-assessment enables the teacher to place each student at the most appropriate tier for his or her level of readiness and interest. Students progress through the tiers at different paces. Therefore, students studying the same concepts are learning by different routes. Roberts and Inman (2015) give examples of how to tier assignments through a combination of levels of the content, the thinking processes, and the learning outcome products.

Enrichment: Grouping Plans

Many school districts offer enrichment activities within some type of *grouping* structure. For example, the most common grouping plan is the *pull-out* program. Elementary students are "pulled out" of their regular classes two or three hours per week to participate in enrichment activities guided by a G/T teacher-coordinator. If the students must be transported to a resource room elsewhere in the district, it is called a *resource room* plan, which is virtually identical in operation to a pull-out program.

A common criticism of pull-out (and resource-room) programs is that they are a part-time solution to a full-time problem.

With *cluster grouping*, usually 5 to 10 gifted, say, fourth-graders are "clustered" together in one class, along with regular students and an enthusiastic teacher who has the interest and experience to work with these students and is trained in gifted education. The cluster students work on independent research projects or advanced academic subjects individually or in small groups. The teacher is responsible for differentiating the curriculum and instruction to meet the needs of students in the cluster (Gentry, 2018).

Some schools will create *special classes* for gifted students within a particular grade level or age range. In addition to covering prescribed grade-level objectives, a variety of enrichment, personal development, and skill development experiences—including creative skills—are planned.

Many schools *mainstream* their gifted students, leaving it to individual teachers to provide suitable activities for the G/T student in their classes. In some cases, mainstreaming is a default arrangement—the school simply has no other plan for gifted students. Or perhaps the school district surrendered to the anti-tracking, anti-grouping bandwagon of the 1980s and canceled all gifted programs.

Some large cities have *special elementary and middle schools* for the gifted, to which students from throughout the school district are bused daily. A similar large-city option is magnet high schools in which an entire high school attracts students interested or gifted in, for example, math and science, the performing arts, business, technical skills, or trade skills (MacFarlene, 2018).

With the *school-within-a-school* plan, gifted students from around the district not only attend some classes with regular students (e.g., physical education, study hall, manual arts, home economics) but also attend special classes taught by teachers acquainted with gifted education.

Enrichment Activities

The following are enrichment activities that may be planned within most or all of the grouping options described above. All seek to strengthen creative thinking and problem-solving skills along with improving academic competence.

With *library research projects* students pursue answers to a specific problem, such as "Why and how was the Great Wall of China built?" The final product need not be a neatly written report. It could be a more creative demonstration of some activity or skill, a student-made video or slide show, a TV news report, a mini-play, or a newspaper column.

There are virtually limitless types of art, theater, and scientific research projects, all of which require creative thinking and problem-solving.

Some teachers effectively use *learning centers*, either teacher-made or commercial, to engage gifted students in art, math, science, social studies, creative writing, music, or language-learning projects. The Station Rotation blended learning model (Truitt & Ku, 2018) can be used to give students an opportunity to differentiate learning experiences by blending teacher-directed learning, online learning, and small group learning.

Field trips acquaint students with cultural or scientific topics and with career possibilities. Field trips are valuable for all students; gifted students should have specific problems to solve or questions to be answered.

Some colleges and universities sponsor *Saturday programs* and *summer programs.* These typically take the form of mini-courses in art, theater, biology, TV production, limnology, and so on and are taught by college graduate students or faculty. There is much creative involvement. Your author recommends you check out the Youth Adventure Program based at Texas A&M in College Station as an example of an enrichment program for highly precocious adolescents who are driven by career exploration (http://yap.tamu.edu).

A *mentorship* traditionally involves an extended relationship between a student and a community professional. The student learns the activities, responsibilities, problems, attitudes, and lifestyle associated with the career. While normally a high school plan, mentorships are becoming a popular elementary-level enrichment alternative for gifted students (Clasen & Clasen, 2003).

Many schools use the *Future Problem Solving http://www.fpspi.org* program as an enrichment activity. A team of students (in an upper elementary, middle school, or high school division) are registered with the National Future Problem Solving (FPS) program. Each FPS season, student teams are given the opportunity to research and engage in five topics representing issues in the strands of Business and Industry, Social and Political, and Science and Technology. These topics provide the basis for both the Problem-Solving Performance and Scenario-Writing competitions. Topics have included such issues as educational disparities, food loss and waste, identity theft, sleep patterns, living in poverty, gamification, and drones. Each problem is solved with the following Six-Stage Creative Problem Solving (CPS) model. The model duplicates almost exactly the CPS model described in Chapter 5. Educators do not have to be involved in the competitions to benefit from this program. FPS offers several classroom guides and educational resources teachers can use to build creative problem skills in elementary and secondary classrooms.

1. Students research information related to the general future-oriented topic. Specific articles are provided; students also search out books, magazines, or other sources, and perhaps visit agencies and interview experts.
2. They brainstorm 20 possible problems related to the situation and select one underlying problem they feel is central to the situation.
3. They brainstorm solutions for this problem.
4. They brainstorm evaluation criteria and then, using their five best criteria, evaluate ideas using an evaluation matrix of the type described in Chapter 5. Their 10 most promising solutions are rank-ordered.
5. Finally, their best solution is described carefully in a few paragraphs.

The team's work for steps 2 to 5 is sent to the state FPS office for evaluation and feedback. Based on the quality of the third problem, the top 10% of the teams are invited to participate in a state FPS bowl, the winner of which is sent to the National FPS competition.

Overall, the FPS experience develops creativity, analytical and critical thinking, research skills, speaking and writing skills, and teamwork and interpersonal skills.

Like FPS, *Odyssey of the Mind* (OM; formerly Olympics of the Mind) http://www.odysseyofthemind.com is a national program designed to foster creative development. A team of seven (five players, two alternates) registers with the state OM committee in an elementary, middle school, or high school division. The OM Association provides each team with detailed directions for preparing *long-term problems* that they will work on usually in weekly meetings throughout the school year. For example, with the *Chameleon* problem the team creates and drives a vehicle that changes appearance to fit three different settings. The driver also must blend in. With *Center Stage* the team creates a humorous performance based on a selection from a list of classical literature. The team creates a stage set and choreographs a dance. A concluding epilogue includes a character from a different selection on the list. With *It's a Snap*, using only balsa wood and glue and no other fasteners, the team builds components of a structure that must interlock. The structure must stay together when lifted from any piece of wood. It must support as much weight as possible—before being crushed in the OM competition.

In the OM competitions, students also solve on-the-spot short-term problems, both in practice and in competition (e.g., "List all of the giants you can think of"). Creative, sometimes off-the-wall, answers received three points (e.g., "Eddie Murphy is a giant of comedy," "Cheerios are giant wheels to an ant"), common answers receive one point. Within each state there are regional competitions, the winners of which participate in annual state competitions. State winners compete in an annual world OM competition.

In addition to the FPS and OM programs, there are other national programs and competitions that stimulate creative thinking, academic excellence, or both, for example, the Junior Great Books program and the United States Academic Decathlon. For a remarkable list of academic competitions at all grade levels, see Karnes and Riley (1996).

Enrichment Triad Model

Probably the best known curriculum guide is the *Enrichment Triad Model* (Renzulli & Reis, 1997, 2003). The "triad model" can be used with students of any age and in any grouping arrangement. There are three more-or-less sequential but interactive stages (Figure 11.2). With Type I enrichment, General Exploratory Activities, students are exposed to topics that are not a normal part of the school curriculum. Type I enrichment may involve a well-stocked resource center (books, magazines, other media) and field trips to meet creative and productive professionals. One purpose of Type I enrichment is to help students find a later independent project (Type III enrichment).

The purpose of Type II enrichment, Group Training Activities, is to "promote general and specific skills—thinking and feeling processes" (Renzulli & Reis, 1985)—in the four categories of:

1. *Cognitive and affective thinking*, including creative thinking, problem-solving, decision-making, critical and logical thinking, and affective processes such as appreciating and valuing.
2. *How-to-learn skills*, such as listening, observing, perceiving, reading, note-taking, outlining, interviewing and surveying, and analyzing and organizing data.
3. *Advanced research skills and reference materials* that prepare the students for Type III investigations, including using the library, information retrieval systems, and community resources.
4. *Written, oral, and visual communication skills* that will be directed toward maximizing the impact of students' products.

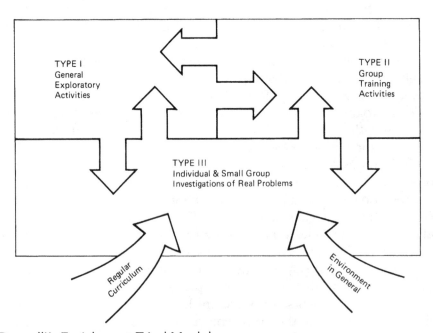

FIGURE 11.2 Renzulli's Enrichment Triad Model.

Source: From Renzulli, J. S. (1977). *The Enrichment Triad Model: A guide for developing defensible programs for the gifted and talented.* Mansfield Center, CT: Creative Learning Press. Reprinted by permission.

Type III enrichment, Individual and Small Group Investigations of Real Problems, is exactly that. The young person becomes an actual researcher or artist dealing with a real problem in an artistic, scientific, literary, business, or other area. Students should be producers of knowledge, not merely consumers or reproducers.

It is important for students to (a) produce a product and (b) have an audience for their products. The teacher may need a lively imagination to help locate or create audiences for students' Type III products.

Schoolwide Enrichment Model

The Enrichment Triad Model is incorporated into Renzulli's broader *Schoolwide Enrichment Model* (SEM; Renzulli, 1994; Renzulli & Reis, 1997, 2003; Reis & Renzulli, 2018). There are a few central characteristics of the SEM plus an even one billion minor details. First, unlike traditional G/T plans that identify about 5% of the students for participation, the SEM identifies 15% to 20% of the school population for a *talent pool*. Identification is flexible and designed to include students, not exclude them.

Second, talent pool students, and occasionally non-talent pool students, who show or develop high creativity and motivation (i.e., they display *action information*) revolve into a resource room to carry out their projects under the direction of a resource teacher. When the projects are completed, students revolve back out.

Third, it is called the *Schoolwide Enrichment Model* because it is intended to be "schoolwide." Both regular teachers and resource teachers bring Type I exploratory activities plus Type II creativity, thinking, research, learning-to-learn, and communication skills into the regular classroom for all children. The SEM thus tries to help all students. The approach also reduces criticisms of elitism, the most common of which is: Wouldn't that G/T activity be good for all students? (The answer often is "yes.")

To clarify how to implement and run a Schoolwide Enrichment plan, Renzulli (1994; Renzulli & Reis, 1997, 2003) elaborated on the billion details pertaining to the history of SEM; underlying theory, issues, supportive research, identification forms and strategies, parent communications, planning forms for everything (some of which ensure that the staff work gets done); learning style assessments; ideas for implementing Types I, II, and III enrichment; lists of specific topics in art, science, language, and so on; lists of specific thinking skills to be fostered; strategies for curriculum compacting (to "buy time"); suggestions for project evaluation; and much more.

Feldhusen's Three-Stage Enrichment Model

Feldhusen's *three-stage enrichment model* (Moon et at., 2009; Feldhusen & Kolloff, 1986), known also as the Purdue Three-Stage model, provides tenants on G/T student identification and G/T teacher selection and training and then focuses on the curriculum and instruction aspects in the classroom, centered on three types or stages of instructional activities that are intended to foster creative development.

Stage I focuses upon *enhancing divergent and convergent thinking abilities*. Corresponding instructional activities include relatively short-term, teacher-led exercises mainly in creative thinking but also in logical and critical thinking. For example, creativity exercises include unusual uses, product improvement, and "What would happen if . . . ?" problems. Other thinking skills include exercises in analysis, logic, critical thinking, evaluation, and question asking.

Stage 2 requires *more complex creative and problem-solving activities* that may extend over a longer period of time and, importantly, require less teacher direction and more student initiative. Students learn and practice creative thinking techniques such as brainstorming and the synectics methods and work through systematic problem-solving models such as the CPS and FPS models.

Stage 3 activities aim at strengthening *independent learning abilities* and developing the ability to apply knowledge to real life problems. Said Feldhusen and Kolloff (1981), "Stage 3 projects should challenge gifted youngsters to define and clarify a problem, gather data from books and other resources, interpret findings, and develop creative ways to communicate their results."

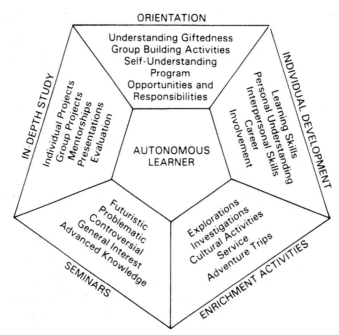

FIGURE 11.3 Autonomous learner model (Betts, 1985).

Other Curriculum Models

The three models summarized above—Renzulli's triad and SEM models and Feldhusen's three-stage model—focus on creative development as a main program goal. There are many more models that guide G/T program and curriculum planning. All of these include creative development either directly, as in group creativity exercises, or indirectly, as when students work on independent projects.

The *Autonomous Learner Model* (ALM; Betts & Kercher, 1999), like Renzulli's SEM, is an overall program plan. The ALM includes five steps of (1) orienting students and parents to giftedness and program opportunities, (2) individual development of learning skills and interpersonal skills, (3) enrichment activities, including investigations of high-interest problems and "adventure trips" (e.g., studying geology in the Grand Canyon), (4) seminars in which students research and present topics, and (5) in-depth long-term research projects. These five steps are slightly elaborated in Figure 11.3.

In gifted education, most teachers and program planners are creativity-conscious. The goal of developing student creativity runs throughout definitions of giftedness, statements of program goals, selection criteria, acceleration and enrichment curriculum plans, and program evaluation.

Summary

Creativity is a twenty-first-century skill that should be developed in all classrooms and in all content areas. Creative thinking is also a valued aspect of most gifted programs.

Creativity is central to all aspects of gifted education—definitions, goals and objectives, identification, and acceleration and enrichment activities.

One's definition of giftedness determines who gets the special services. There is no consensus in defining "gifted" versus "talented"; some use the terms interchangeably, others do not. There is no special term for the extremely gifted child.

There have been a series of federal definitions of giftedness. The definitions include the five categories of general intellectual ability, specific academic talent, creativity, leadership, and ability in the performing and visual arts in defining giftedness. They also focus on a student's potential to perform rather than exhibited performance. The Columbus definition points to the inner experience of being gifted.

Renzulli's three-ring definition includes high creativity, high motivation (task commitment), and at least above-average ability—characteristics of people who make creative contributions to society.

Intellectually gifted students are developmentally advanced in many areas. They also tend to show high motivation, confidence, humor, and higher moral thinking. These traits appeared in Terman's classic research.

Identification methods should be related to program definitions of giftedness and program content and goals. Both objective and subjective information should be used. The overuse of IQ scores discriminates against creative students.

There are many identification methods, including ability scores, achievement scores, creativity test scores, product evaluations, and nominations by teachers, parents, peers, and students themselves. The Renzulli and Reis five-step identification strategy uses all of these and action information.

Goals of G/T education include: maximum achievement, content beyond the regular curriculum, exposure to a variety of fields, student-selected content, creative thinking and problem solving, thinking skills, self-awareness and self-understanding, and the development of motivation and self-directedness.

Acceleration strategies, as defined here, result in advanced placement or credit. In Julian Stanley's SMPY, mathematically precocious seventh-grade students participate in fast-paced summer math programs. Talent search programs accommodate both mathematically and verbally precocious students. An elementary-level talent search recently was begun.

Enrichment plans include pull-out (resource-room) programs, cluster grouping, special classes, mainstreaming, special elementary schools, magnet high schools, and school-within-a-school plans.

Enrichment activities can include library, art, theater, or science projects, learning centers, field trips, Saturday and summer programs, mentorships, or participation in Future Problem Solving, Odyssey of the Mind, or other competitive programs.

Program models structure the enrichment activities.

Renzulli's Enrichment Triad Model includes general exploratory activities (Type I enrichment), group training activities (Type II), and individual or small group research projects (Type III).

The Triad model expands into the Schoolwide Enrichment Model, which includes the talent pool concept—identifying 15% to 20% of the students within the participation. When a student shows or develops high motivation and creativity, the student revolves into a resource room to work on an independent (Type III) project. Regular and G/T teachers do Types I and II activities in the regular classroom.

Feldhusen's *three-stage enrichment* (a.k.a the Pudue Three-Stage Model) outlines three levels of creativity training: basic exercises to strengthen divergent and convergent thinking abilities, more complex creative activities such as learning creativity techniques, and involvement in independent projects.

Betts' Autonomous Learner Model is an overall program plan that includes the five steps of orientation, individual development of learning and interpersonal skills, enrichment activities, seminars, and in-depth long-term research projects.

Review Exercises

Creativity in Education

Self-Test: Key Concepts, Terms, and Names

Briefly define or explain each of these:

After-the-fact definitions _____

_____

IQ definition _____

_____

Percentage definitions _____

_____

Talent definitions _____

_____

Creativity definitions _____

_____

Three ring definition (Renzulli) _____

_____

Talent pool _____

_____

Acceleration _____

_____

Telescoping _____

_____

SMPY _____

_____

SAT-I _____

_____

Talent search _____

_____

Enrichment _____

_____

Pull-out programs _____

_____

Cluster grouping _____

_____

Mainstreaming _____

_____

School-within-a-School _____

_____

Mentorships _____

_____

FPS _____

_____

Odyssey of the Mind _____

_____

Enrichment Triad Model _____

_____

Schoolwide Enrichment Model _____

_____

Types I, II, and III Enrichment _____

_____

Feldhusen's Three-Stage Model _____

_____

Autonomous Learner Model (Betts) _____

_____

Let's Think about It

1. How do you think the topic of creativity can be developed at various levels in the school?

   Preschool/Kindergarten _____

   _____

   Elementary _____

   _____

   Middle School _____

   _____

   High School _____

   _____

2. Which definition of "giftedness" do you think is the most useful?

   _____

   Why? _____

   _____

   _____

3. Compare the various federal definitions of giftedness and the Columbus definition. Where do you see similarities and differences?

4. Look over the eight "Goals and Curricula" in this chapter. Rank order them according to which you feel should be most important, second most important, etc., in the education of gifted and talented students.

First in importance: _____

Second: _____

Third: _____

Fourth: _____

Fifth: _____

Sixth: _____

Seventh: _____

Last: _____

5. Let's think like a cranky, negativistic person who is critical of everything—including gifted education. Think of one thing WRONG (e.g., somehow unfair, troublesome, inconvenient, expensive, bad for the student's social life, bad for his or her education) related to each of these *acceleration* methods.

a. Early admission to kindergarten or first grade

_____

b. Grade skipping

_____

c. Subject skipping

_____

d. Early admission to junior or senior high school

_____

e. Credit by examination

_____

f. College courses while in high school

_____

g. Early admission to college

_____

h. Telescoping

_____

6. Describe the relationship among these concepts: _Enrichment Triad Model, Talent Pool,_ and _School-wide Enrichment Model._

_____

_____

_____

_____

_____

7. Put yourself into the position of a parent with a gifted child. How would you want them identified? What type of curriculum would you want them to engage in? Which instructional strategies do you feel would be best to foster and nature their advanced abilities? Put your thoughts here!

12 Creativity Is Forever: Unlocking Your Creative Potential

"What am I in the eyes of most people—a nonentity, an eccentric, or an unpleasant person—somebody who has no position in society and will never have; in short, the lowest of the low. All right, then—even if that were absolutely true, then I should one day like to show by my work what such an eccentric, such a nobody, has in his heart. That is my ambition, based less on resentment than on love in spite of everything, based more on a feeling of serenity than on passion. Though I am often in the depths of misery, there is still calmness, pure harmony and music inside me. I see paintings or drawings in the poorest cottages, in the dirtiest corners. And my mind is driven towards these things with an irresistible momentum."

—*Vincent van Gogh*

Vincent Van Gogh is one of the greatest examples of a creative person. From this quote we can see into the mind of Van Gogh, his creative characteristics and mind resulting in more than just his artwork. The first part of the quote is inspiring because Van Gogh can recognize his talent, what he is capable of, and the potential for what he can become. Self-actualization, according to Humanistic psychologists Abraham Maslow and Carl Rodgers, is one of the most important aspects of a creative person and in the concepts of creativity. Despite the blocks and barriers in his life, his ambition and love for what he does remains. Creativity is important because it affects not only how you see your own personal growth but also how you see the world around you. In the second part of the quote, Van Gogh is explaining how everyday experiences with a free creative mind-set allow a new perspective. As discussed by Kaufman and Gregoire (2016) in their book "Wired to Create," this is an example of a Crystallizing Experience, where "Ultimately, the individual and the activity become one and the same." Van Gogh's words match his art; he is bold, dramatic, expressive of emotions, and never afraid to go with the flow with his imagination.

Vincent Van Gogh, almost 130 years after his death, still stands as an inspiration to many as his creative works and mind challenge many over the course of time showing us that maybe creativity really is forever and has a forever impact.

Educating for Creative Thinking and Problem-Solving

Fresh off Chapter 11, where we looked at Creativity in Education and the systematic and scholastic approach to delivering creativity to a classroom or cohort, we will now turn our focus to the individual: Unlocking your OWN creative potential. To do this, we have divided this chapter into four main parts. We first will look at some issues and considerations that relate to strengthening individual skills, abilities, and predispositions for creative thinking—beginning with the core questions "Can creativity be taught?" The matter is not simple nor does it elicit quick agreement. Second, we will review concepts, ideas, and assumptions related to teaching for creative growth that appeared in every previous chapter. Third, we will look at ways to self-actualize YOUR true creative potential. Finally, we will describe five core goals of creativity training plus strategies for achieving them.

1. Issues
2. Earlier Chapters
3. Self-Actualization
4. Five Core Goals

Issues in Creativity Training

This section will look at these issues:

- Can creativity be taught?
- Individual differences in responsiveness to creativity training
- Individual differences in motivation to create
- The importance of a creative climate
- Must creativity be taught within a content area?

Can Creativity Be Taught?

A frequent question that is asked is, "Can creativity be taught? Or are you born with it?" Sometimes the issue is raised in a negative form—"I don't think you can teach creativity," followed by the inevitable rationale, "You either have it or you don't!"

Of course, there are tremendous individual differences in innate creative abilities and in affective dispositions toward creativity, just as there are wide variations in every other mental and physical characteristic. In addressing the question, "Can creativity be taught?" Roeper and Ruff (2016) state that "we cannot teach the passion of an inspiration, not the intuitive quality of creativity. We cannot teach the instinctive impulse leading to a creative thought, much less can we arrange for the conflict in the unconscious, which is the source of creativity, according to Freud" (p. 225). Realistically, no amount of the most carefully orchestrated creativity training can mold an average person into a Leonardo DaVinci, Marie Curie, Thomas Edison, William Shakespeare, Walt Disney, Booker T. Washington, or Orson Welles. Such people are born with a special combination of high intelligence, creative ability, extraordinary drive, and a strong sense of vision and destiny. Their drive leads them to acquire a great depth of knowledge and experience in their chosen fields.

However, it also is absolutely true that every individual can raise his or her creative skill, creative productivity, and creative living to a higher level. An irrefutable argument for the trainability of creativity is simply that, with interest and effort, all of us can make better use of the creative abilities we were born with.

What does creativity guru Paul Torrance (1995) say about whether creativity can be taught?

> I know that it is possible to teach children to think creatively and that it can be done in a variety of ways. I have done it. I have seen my wife do it; I have seen other excellent teachers do it. I have seen

children who had seemed previously to be "non thinkers" learn to think creatively, and I have seen them continuing for years thereafter to think creatively. I have seen, heard, and otherwise experienced their creativity. Their parents have told me that they saw it happening. Many of the children, now adults, say that it happened. I also know that these things would not have happened by chance because I have seen them not happen to multitudes of their peers. (p. 269)

Torrance (1995) itemized 142 studies describing efforts to "teach creativity" with divergent thinking exercises, training in the Creative Problem Solving (CPS) model, training in creative art or writing, establishing a creative climate, or using various creativity training workbooks or programs. Success rates (Torrance Test scores, creative products, creative self-perceptions) were good. "Massive evidence" was the phrase Torrance (1987b) used to describe the overall results of these efforts to teach creative thinking. CPS, FPS, and OM especially were recommended.

Individual Differences in Responsiveness to Creativity Training

Just as there are immense individual differences in cognitive abilities and affective predispositions for creativity, there also are individual differences in *receptiveness* to creativity training, that is, receptiveness to adopting the required creativity consciousness and other attitudinal predispositions toward thinking creatively and doing things creatively. Some children and adults respond quickly and positively to such training. They learn that, yes indeed, they can imagine, visualize, create, and solve problems better than they expected—the capability was there all along, they just never tried to use it. Others seem impervious to creativity training, due to some combinations of disinterest, rigidity, insecurity, conformity, or other traits and barriers that are incompatible with creative thinking and behavior.

Your authors taught undergraduate and graduate courses in creative thinking that had two purposes. First was the academic goal of transmitting a body of knowledge about issues, theories, characteristics, processes, tests, and techniques of creativity, along with strategies for teaching for creative growth. The second purpose was to help students become more creatively productive by raising their creativity consciousness, explaining how others use creativity techniques, and motivating them to use their creative abilities. One of our studies showed that, *on average*, students who completed the course improved in their affective creative traits—creative attitudes, predispositions, and self-ratings of creativity—significantly more than students who had registered for but had not yet taken the course (Davis & Bull, 1978).

However, there always were substantial differences in the degree to which students' creative potential was affected by the exposure. Some students registered for the course, met the requirements, but remained untouched by the potentially life-changing principles and concepts. Other students experienced changes in their self-perceptions of creativeness and their actual creative output; they discovered capabilities they did not know they had. The foreword for each of the chapters of this textbook is written by students pursuing creative studies at the university level. Beyond the pages of this textbook, one student wrote her first and potentially publishable children's book as a direct result of the class; another invented an educational game that was sold to Fisher Price Toys; and another began writing poetry, and lots of it, for the very first time. Two memorable testimonials were, "Now I understand my own creativity better," and "Now I'm able to stretch my brain to think about and apply concepts in ways I had never thought of before"

There are wide differences then, in responsiveness to creativity training. Teachers of creativity should be prepared for these differences, and perhaps ready to work a little harder with low-receptivity students.

Individual Differences in Motivation to Create

There also are large differences in motivation for creativity. As we noted in Chapters 1 and 4, a high energy level is a common characteristic of creative people. Related traits are high levels of curiosity, adventurousness, spontaneity, and risk-taking, plus wide and perhaps novel interests and hobbies. For creative eminence, Torrance's (1987a) "blazing drive" seems to energize the creative productivity.

Motivation theorists Berlyne (1961) and Farley (1986) assume that the high level of "arousal-seeking" common among creative people is governed by the reticular activating system (RAS) in the brain stem. According to this theory, creative and adventurous activities are sought out in order to raise an uncomfortably low level of RAS activity to a higher, more optimal state.

There is not much we can do about students' reticular activating systems. However, the RAS hypothesis does not prevent a teacher from working to elevate students' interest in creative thinking, while concurrently exercising creative skills and abilities and engaging students in artistic, scientific, and other entrepreneurial work.

Creative Atmosphere

We do not need a long discussion of the critical importance of a receptive and reinforcing creative atmosphere. Carl Rogers (1962) called it *psychological safety*; in brainstorming it is *deferred judgment*. We saw in Chapter 3 that if creative ideas are not reinforced—or worse, if they are blocked, criticized, or squelched—normal children and adults simply will not produce creative ideas in those unreceptive circumstances. Starko (1995) identified several salient aspects of a classroom climate that cultivates a creative atmosphere, including: rewarding creative ideas, encouraging risks, imagining other viewpoints, and allowing for mistakes. One of our five main goals of creativity training will be fostering creativity consciousness and creative attitudes. These require a creative atmosphere.

Must Creativity Be Taught within a Content Area?

Effective creativity training may be content free or it may be embedded within a content area.

Content free creativity instruction can be seen through Maslow's (1954) *self-actualized creativity*. This viewpoint includes the mentally healthy tendency to approach all aspects of one's life—personal, professional, avocational—in a creative fashion. It is a general content, a free form of creativeness. As we noted earlier, many successful creativity courses, programs, workshops, and educational workbooks try to teach a general creativeness by strengthening creativity consciousness and other creative attitudes, as well as by exercising creative abilities and teaching creativity techniques, perhaps including the CPS model. These efforts help the learner to understand creativity and to approach personal, academic, and professional problems in a more creative fashion. The approach is sensible, common, and effective. It is not tied to a particular subject or content. We will profile self-actualization further in this chapter later on.

On the other hand, Maslow's *special talent creativity* refers to an obviously outstanding creative talent or gift in art, literature, music, theater, science, business, or other area. Special talent creativity presumes some mastery of that area, and the greater the sophistication the more likely are creative contributions. Snow (1986), for example, wrote that "Creativity . . . is an accomplishment born of intensive study, long reflection, persistence, and interest . . . A rich store of knowledge in a field is required as a base for idea production" (p. 1033). Baer (2016) provides an interesting perspective. He writes "think about how students learn other kinds of things. If we want students to learn calculus, world history, and biology, we don't assume some general kind of study will help them learn all three. We understand that these are different domains, that each requires domain-specific instruction and study, and there is little reason to expect much transfer among them. Ditto for creative-thinking skills" (p. 15). Dow and Mayer (2004) found evidence of domain specificity in their investigation of creativity training, with previous experience in a domain mitigating or masking the effectiveness of instruction.

As for teaching special talent creativity, the two goals are strengthening creative thinking and problem-solving attitudes and skills while concurrently guiding students in mastering content and technical skills in the particular area. With the typical independent projects approach, students are given (or find) a high-interest project or problem. They proceed to clarify it, consider various approaches, find a main solution or resolution, and then create or prepare the project or problem for presentation. Throughout, students identify and resolve numerous subproblems; they evaluate their methods and results; they acquire content knowledge and develop technical skills; and they develop content-related creative problem-solving skills and abilities. The independent projects strategy fits Maslow's category of special talent creativity very well.

As the reader might guess, special talent creativity may be strengthened while teaching a general, self-actualized type of creativeness, and vice versa. For example, within a primarily content-free creativity session students might brainstorm a science-, history- or math-related problem or they might do creative writing, creative dramatics, or art activities. Conversely, creative projects in a subject area (special talent creativity) are very likely to help develop general creative abilities and attitudes (self-actualized creativity) that extend beyond the specific topic at hand.

However, the (frequent) argument that "you can't teach creativity in the abstract because you have to have something to be creative with" sounds logical but makes little sense. Every creativity course, program, and technique, in addition to this book tries to teach a general creativeness, which can be applied in many specific situations.

This Book So Far

In our first 11 chapters we have seen many concepts and principles related to becoming a more imaginative, flexible, creative thinker.

Chapters 1 and 2

The definitions and theories in Chapters 1 and 2 increase our understanding of creativity and creative ideas, which contributes to creativity consciousness. The emphasis of many definitions is on *combining* ideas implicitly justifying the use of deliberate creativity techniques, which basically force new idea combinations. The ancient learning theory concept of strengthening behavior through reinforcement definitely applies to creativity: Children (and adults) will do what they are rewarded for doing, including thinking creatively. In Plato's words, "What is valued in one's country is what will be cultivated."

Chapter 3

Chapter 3 looked at blocks and barriers that prevent us from thinking and behaving more creatively. We reviewed the effects of habit and learning, rules and traditions, perceptual blocks, cultural blocks (especially conformity and the cultural mores themselves), emotional blocks, and even resource barriers. We noted that creativity expert von Oech recommended a "whack on the side of the head" to jolt us out of our mental blocks—habits and attitudes relating to finding one right answer; being logical, practical, and correct; avoiding ambiguity, play, and foolishness; and assuming "I'm not creative!" The chapter ended with a list of statements that squelch creative thinking—the idea squelchers.

Chapter 4

Chapter 4 described personality and biographical characteristics of creative people. We normally do not speak of "teaching personality traits." However, it may be sensible to cultivate in students these kinds of creative thinking traits, habits, and behaviors: confidence, independence, willingness to take a risk, open-mindedness, curiosity and wide interests, humor and playfulness, taking time to incubate and create, and the number one trait—creativity consciousness.

As we noted in Chapter 4, the main difference between people who *have* creative abilities and those who *use* their creative potential lies in affective traits that predispose some people to think and behave in creative ways.

Research in creative eminence reinforced the importance of high motivation—Torrance's "blazing drive." The Bloom and Sosniak (1981; Bloom, 1985; Sosniak, 2003) research and writing stressed the critical role of parents—and other supportive "communities of practice" (Sosniak, 2003)—in the early development of talent in musical, academic, and athletic areas.

Chapter 5

Chapter 5 looked at the creative process, first as a change in perception—"seeing" new meanings, relationships, combinations, and transformations. A teacher can use optical illusions and visual puzzles to illustrate how—with a little effort—one always can "see different things" and find more ideas. Chapter 5 also looked at creative problem-solving as sets of stages. The stages of the remarkable CPS model will almost always help the thinker (or group) produce creative and workable problem solutions.

Chapter 6

An inspirational source of creativity is analogical thinking. Most of the personal creative thinking techniques described in Chapter 8 involve seeing a connection between the problem at hand and the solution to another situation, or transferring ideas from one situation to another. Try the analogical thinking exercises within this chapter (Inset 6.2). Show students how it works. Practice the clever synectics variations (direct analogy, personal analogy, fantasy analogy, compressed conflicts) and the analogical thinking exercises at the end of the chapter. Combined with the techniques of Chapters 8 and 9, you and your students will feel that you better understand how creative people think, and are better able to produce new idea combinations and problem solutions on demand.

Chapter 7

The results of creative thinking are evident in creative products, which were profiled in Chapter 7. Aspects of novelty, adaptiveness, usefulness, and aesthetics combine together to produce something that can be deemed to be creative. The Creative Product Analysis Matrix (CPAM) of O'Quin and Besemer (1999) was presented as a way of judging creative products, with special "style" points for organic, well-crafted, and elegant *artifacts* (a term put forth by Glaveneu to capture the cultural aspect of creativity) Types of creative contributions were also profiled, with little c (everyday) and Big C (eminent) categorization being compared and contrasted, with room for micro-C (individual level) and Pro-C (expertise) distinctions. The Propulsion model of Sternberg (1999) incrementally advanced our understanding of the paradigm-shifting nature of creativity on a field.

Chapter 8

When it comes to teaching creativity, the techniques described in Chapter 8 represent teachable ways that honest-to-goodness creative people use to find creative idea combinations. Brainstorming and its many spin-offs, including various brainwriting and electronic brainstorming procedures, plus attribute listing, morphological synthesis, and idea checklists all were derived from creatively productive people. Most of these techniques are finding their way into elementary and secondary classrooms via workbooks (e.g., Stanish, 1981, 1988) and teachers who wish to help students understand where creative ideas sometimes come from.

Chapter 9

Edward de Bono explained numerous dynamics of creative thinking and blocks to creative problem-solving. His techniques were all designed to overcome habits and blocks and produce new insights and idea combinations. The Six Hats concept described roles people play in group thinking, and a strategy for staying on target. Students also will be surprised and delighted with the creative results of some de Bono techniques, for example, the simple creative pause and creative challenge, along with a search for alternatives, search for broader underlying concepts, and the provocative techniques. The 13 types of problem situations also can be enlightening.

Chapter 10

Chapter 10 on assessing creative potential presented precious little related to improving creativeness. An examination of the underlying assumptions regarding what is being evaluated—usually personality traits, divergent thinking abilities, or experience with creative activities—should help students' understanding of creativity. Guilford (1967, 1986) suggested that to strengthen creative abilities we might give students exercises similar to the tests that measure the particular abilities. Meeker (Meeker & Meeker, 1986; Staff, 1995) uses approximately this strategy not only to teach creativity, but reading, writing, and math also. The same strategy would apply to teaching the content of attitude/personality inventories.

Chapter 11

Chapter 11 was the education chapter. A main goal of most program models and enrichment and acceleration strategies is to strengthen creative thinking and problem solving skills and abilities. For example, the Future Problem Solving and Odyssey of the Mind programs were designed entirely to foster creative development. Renzulli's Type II Enrichment includes creativity training (exercises, techniques), and his Type III Enrichment highlights creative involvement in individual research projects. The Feldhusen and Kolloff three-stage model explains that creativity training should begin with basic divergent thinking exercises, progress to more advanced creativity techniques and problem-solving strategies, and finally include independent problems and projects.

This Chapter

This chapter seeks to increase your creativity consciousness by stressing the importance of creativity, both to yourself as a self-actualizing person and to society. Nothing can be more important to life satisfaction (yours) than becoming self-actualized: becoming what you are capable of becoming, being an independent, forward-growing, fully functioning, and mentally healthy individual. So what are we waiting for? Let's get started!

Self-Actualization and Creativity

One of the most profoundly important concepts in the field of creativity is the relationship between creativity and self-actualization. Humanistic psychologists Abraham Maslow and Carl Rogers describe *self-actualization* as using all of one's talents to become what one is capable of becoming—actualizing one's potential. Further, the self-actualizing person is mentally healthy, self-accepting, forward growing, fully functioning, democratic minded, and more. In Maslow's (1954) words, self-actualization "refers to our desire for self-fulfillment, namely, to the tendency for a person to become actualized in what he or she is potentially . . . the desire to become more and more what one is, to become everything that one is capable of becoming . . . what one can be, one must be." After 14 years of thought, Maslow (1968) added, "We are dealing with a fundamental characteristic, inherent in human nature, a potentiality given to all or most human beings at birth, which most often is lost or buried or inhibited as the person gets enculturated" (p. 138). Maslow further observed that self-actualization includes an ever-increasing move toward unity, integration, and synergy within the person. Look carefully at Maslow's description of self-actualized people in Inset 12.1. After careful consideration, you may agree that few things in life are more important than one's self-actualization.

Rogers (1962) tied self-actualization to creativity with these words: "The mainspring of creativity appears to be the same tendency which we discover so deeply as the curative force in psychotherapy—one's tendency to actualize oneself, to become one's potentialities . . . the urge to expand, extend, develop, mature—the tendency to express and activate all of the capabilities of the organism" (pp. 65–66). In a scientifically cautious statement, Maslow (1971) similarly noted "the concept of creativeness and the concept of the healthy, self-actualizing, fully human person seem to be coming closer and closer together, and may turn out to be the same thing" (p. 57).

INSET 12.1
Maslow's 15 Characteristics of Self-Actualized People

According to Maslow, self-actualized people:

- Perceive reality more accurately and objectively. They are not threatened by the unknown, and tolerate and even like ambiguity.
- Are spontaneous, natural, and genuine.
- Are problem-centered, not self-centered or egotistical. They have a philosophy of life and probably a mission in life.
- Can concentrate intensely. They need more privacy and solitude than do others.
- Are independent, self-sufficient, and autonomous. They have less need for popularity or praise.
- Have the capacity to appreciate again and again simple and commonplace experiences. They have a zest for living and an ability to handle stress.
- Have (and are aware of) their rich, lively, and intensely enjoyable "peak experiences"—moments of intense enjoyment.
- Have a high sense of humor, which tends to be thoughtful, philosophical, and constructive (not destructive).
- Form strong friendship ties with relatively few people, yet are capable of greater love.
- Accept themselves, others, and human nature.
- Are strongly ethical and moral in individual (not necessarily conventional) ways. They are benevolent and altruistic.
- Are democratic and unprejudiced in the deepest possible sense. They have deep feelings of brotherhood with all mankind.
- Enjoy the work in achieving a goal as much as the goal itself. They are patient, for the most part.
- Are capable of detachment from their culture, and can objectively compare cultures. They can take or leave conventions.
- Are creative, original, and inventive, with a fresh, naive, simple, and direct way of looking at life. They tend to do most things creatively, but do not necessarily possess great talent.

Is it important to develop your self-actualized creativity?

To add further credibility to this paramount relationship, Clark Moustakis (1967), another early humanistic psychologist, wrote, "It is this experience of expressing and actualizing one's individual identity in an integrated form in communication and with one's self, with nature, and with other persons that I call creative." Finally, a definitive study was conducted by Runco, Ebersole, and Mraz (1991) who found strong empirical support for the theories of Maslow by linking self-assessment measures of creativity to indices of self-actualization.

Creativeness is not identical to mentally healthy *self-actualization*; however, it is an important component. Further, the more you come to define *creativity* as a lifestyle—a way of living and perceiving—the greater is the overlap. Creativity clearly is more than producing zany ideas in art, science, business, and on divergent thinking tests.

Popular Use of "Self-Actualization and Creativity"

In recent decades the bond between self-actualization and creative development has caught on to the point where the relationship is both a semantic trend and virtually a given. For example, Moyer and Wallace (1995) argued that the role of education is not to foster compliance, but to develop the self-actualization that springs from individuality and creative growth. Weiner (1992) stressed a mentor's role in heightening students' anticipation, expectations, individuality, and value—and creativity and self-actualization. Weaver (1990) described techniques to increase the "growth"—job-satisfaction, life-satisfaction, creativity, and self-actualization—of university faculty. (We need it!) Under the umbrella of *aging individuals*, radio-journalist Goldman (1991) described her "late bloomers" program that fosters lifelong learning—and self-esteem, self-actualization, and creativity. Kastenbaum (1991) noted that for many senior citizens, creativity and self-actualization continue into later years—they remain open to new experiences, have healthy creative attitudes, and engage in creative activities.

The self-actualization approach has been named a *growth* theory of creativity (e.g., Treffinger, Isaksen, & Firestien, 1982), since one grows—or should grow—in self-actualization and creativity. This growth label is important as it aligns with the motivational theory of Dweck who distinguishes between growth and fixed mindsets in approaching tasks and in assessing one's own ability. Specific to creativity, Dweck, Chiu, and Hong (1995) would identify those who believe that their creativity is nonmalleable and nothing they do will change their ability as having a fixed mindset. They view their ability as fixed and no amount of training or practice will increase their level of performance. In contrast, those with a growth mindset truly believe that "practice makes perfect" and that creativity is a set of skills that can be incrementally increased. Karwowski (2014) was able to substantiate that growth mindset and creative self-concept were strongly correlated. O'Connor, Nemeth, and Akutsu (2013) found that those with a growth mindset (incremental view of their creative abilities) demonstrated enhanced creative problem-solving skills.

Flow, Entrepreneurship, and Self-Actualization

Csikszentmihalyi's (1990b) best-selling book *Flow* tries to describe solutions for nothing less than our search for happiness. "Flow" is involving oneself with an activity to such an extent that nothing else seems to matter—*the experience itself is intensely enjoyable*. Activities that consistently produce flow, noted Csikszentmihalyi, are sports, games, art, and hobbies. Further, experts such as artists, athletes, musicians, chess masters, or surgeons experience flow because they are doing exactly what they want to do. The essence is captured by Hooker and Csikszentmihalyi (2003) who describe flow as a "state of consciousness in which people feel completely involved in an activity to the point that they lose track of time and lose awareness of self, place, and all other details irrelevant to the immediate task at hand. It is what the athlete feels at the top of his game—deep concentration and a vibrant sense of master and coordination. It is how totally involved an artist becomes with what becomes manifest on her canvas— colors, tones, and figures fitting together to give shape to her emerging vision . . . in other words, it is deep engagement and pure enjoyment of an activity for its own sake" (p. 220). It sounds disarmingly simple. He also emphasized personal dedication, experiencing exhilaration from taking control of our lives, and the "direct control of experience—the ability to derive moment-by-moment enjoyment from everything we do." According to Gardner's (1993) interpretation, "those 'in flow'" . . . feel that they have been fully alive, totally realized, and involved in a 'peak experience'" (pp. 25–26). Does flow relate directly to Maslow's self-actualization or creativity? Perhaps; Cseh, Phillips, and Pearson (2015) found two interesting results related to flow: (1) the presence of flow increased affect (positive feelings) during a creativity task; but (2) the presence of flow did NOT impact actual performance in the creativity task. Their analysis of this was that "flow may therefore motivate perseverance towards eventual excellence rather than provide direct cognitive enhancement" (p. 281).

There is also literature on *entrepreneurship* with main points that seem identical to Csikszentmihalyi's *flow*. For example, Solomon and Winslow (1988) define an entrepreneur as "one who starts and is successful in a venture and/or project that leads to profit (monetary or personal) or benefits society." Rather than great wealth, entrepreneurs described the best thing about being an entrepreneur as, for example, "Freedom to test my ideas and the pleasure of seeing the fruits of my labor," and "Being in complete control of my professional and personal life." They defined *success* as "Doing what I like to do," "Having control over my own destiny," "Being happy with myself, doing things I enjoy," and "Seeing my baby live and grow." Does entrepreneurship resemble Csikszentmihalyi's flow experience? Tomasino (2007) answers this rhetorical question through this finding that "entrepreneurial decision and action is informed by an unusually high degree of both creativity and intuition. Research has identified a distinct psychophysiological state that appears to facilitate creativity and receptivity to intuitive insight. This state, termed *psychophysiological coherence*, is naturally activated during the experience of sustained positive emotions" (p. 1). So it appears that there is a coherent connection between body, mind, flow, creativity, and entrepreneurship.

Research Relating Self-Actualization and Creativity

This psychophysiological connection that Tomasino brought up provides a great segue. The relationship between creativity, on one hand, and mentally healthy, and forward-growing self-actualization, on the other, has lent itself nicely to empirical research. The obvious research question is: Does the relationship exist or not?

As background, the main measure of Maslow's self-actualization has been Shostrom's (1963) Personal Orientation Inventory (POI) and slightly newer Personal Orientation Dimensions (POD; Shostrom, 1975).[1] Crandall, McCoun, and Robb (1988) described a shortened version—just 15 items—of the POI entitled the Short Inventory of Self-Actualization (SI). Buckmaster created the 80-item college-level Reflections on Self and Environment (ROSE) inventory (Buckmaster & Davis, 1985). For younger students, Schatz and Buckmaster (1984) built the 62-item Reflections on Self by Youth (ROSY). Both the ROSE and the ROSY inventories were based directly on Maslow's 15 characteristics described in Inset 12.1, and both used a rating-scale format.

Now Maslow's (1970) best-known concept is his motivational or "need" hierarchy. Beginning at the bottom, seven levels include *physiological* needs, *safety* needs, *love and belonging* needs, needs for *esteem*, needs to *know and understand, aesthetic* needs, and at the top, needs for *self-actualization*. According to Maslow, lower level needs must be met before one addresses higher levels of needs. The Maslowian Scale (Lewis, 1993) is a brief, 12-question test based on this hierarchy that produces a total score reflecting movement toward self-actualization.

Turning to the research, college students' scores on the ROSE measure of self-actualization (Buckmaster & Davis, 1985) were compared with their scores on a shortened version of the creativity inventory How Do You Think? (HDYT; Davis, 1975, 1991a; described in Chapter 10), which measures personality and biographical characteristics of creative people. The statistical correlation between scores on the two inventories was a whopping .73 (on a scale of 0–1.0). Almost every individual who scored high in self-actualization also scored high in creativity and vice versa, despite the fact that the inventories were constructed based on two supposedly different sets of concepts and literature. Also with college students, Runco et al. (1991) found that intercorrelations between subscales of the HDYT (Davis & Subkoviak, 1978) and the Short Inventory of Self-Actualization again showed good relationships between creativity and self-actualization. The *energetic originality* and *arousal and risk-taking* subscales were the best predictors of SI scores (rs = 0.42 and 0.46, respectively).

Research with 302 grade 4, 5, and 6 students who took the ROSY focused on test item interrelationships and clusters (Schatz & Buckmaster, 1984). One main cluster was entitled *perceptions*, with items relating to perceptions of oneself as creative (e.g., "I have a good imagination," "I like to try new and different things," and "I am creative, I can think of many new or unusual ideas"). Importantly, other test items in this same cluster reflected other components of self-actualization (e.g., "I am fair to everyone when I work and play," "I speak my opinions without worrying about being right or wrong," and "I can laugh at myself"). The authors concluded their research with the ROSY, "further confirms the relationship between self-actualization and creativity." And we are talking about 9- to 11-year old children.

Lewis, Karnes, and Knight (1995) administered the ROSY, the Maslowian Scale, and the Piers-Harris Children's Self-Concept Scale, basically a measure of healthy personality adjustment,

---

[1] The POI was considered by Maslow himself to be a sensible test of self-actualization. It has nothing to do with Hawaiian dining.

to 368 high IQ students in grades 4 through 12. Everything was related to everything. Scores on the ROSY and the hierarchy-based Maslowian Scale correlated 0.51. ROSY and the Piers-Harris correlated 0.43, meaning that the higher their ROSY self-actualization scores, the better were their Piers-Harris self-concept scores.

Earlier, Yonge (1975) had reviewed research showing positive correlations between scores on the POI and various measures of creativity, for example, scores on a creativity scale for the Adjective Check List (Chapter 10). Damm (1970) concluded that it helps to be smart, too. While measures of creativity and intelligence each were related to self-actualization scores, the highest levels of self-actualization were reached by his high school students who were both creative and intelligent.

This sample of research confirms that creativity and self-actualization are indeed related. But, the next section complicates the issue.

Self-Actualized Creativity and Special Talent Creativity

It may or may not have occurred to the thoughtful reader that many world-class creative people have been extraordinarily neurotic—not at all self-actualized in the mentally healthy sense. History is full of neurotic creative geniuses. The names of Vincent van Gogh and Edgar Allen Poe come to mind, and perhaps Beethoven, Mozart, Howard Hughes, Judy Garland, John Belushi, Janis Joplin, and introvert Yves St. Laurent. (Can you think of others?)

The solution to this apparent dilemma lies in Maslow's (1954) perceptive distinction between *self-actualized* versus *special talent* creative people. By now you should understand the notion of a general, self-actualized creativeness. In contrast, special talent creative people—by definition—possess an extraordinary creative talent in art, literature, music, theater, science, business, or other area. These people could be well-adjusted and live reasonably happy, self-actualized existences. Or they might be neurotic and miserable in their personal, professional, and social lives. As we saw in Chapter 4, a long-standing and continuing literature relates high creativity to psychopathology (e.g., Barron, 1969; Kaufman, 2001; Richards, 1990; Richards et al., 1988), for example, among entrepreneurs (Solomon & Winslow, 1988), regular college students (Schuldberg, 1990), and most notably artists and writers, especially poets (Ludwig, 1995).

There are two important implications of distinguishing between self-actualized and special talent creativity: (1) Living and thinking creatively without having a specific great talent and (2) the core role of personality and affective traits in creativity. We will look briefly at each.

One Can Be Creative Without a Great Creative Talent

The first implication of the distinction between self-actualized and special talent creativity is tucked into Maslow's last item in Inset 12.1. Under no circumstances should the reader stop and look at the last item in Inset 12.1. Self-actualized creative people are mentally healthy and live full and productive lives; it is a general form of creativeness. Such people tend to approach all aspects of their lives in a flexible, creative fashion. They do not necessarily have an outstanding creative talent in a specific area, for example, one that makes them famous and probably rich. *You need not possess exceptional artistic, literary, scientific, or entrepreneurial talent to consider yourself a creative person and live a creative life.* It is unfortunate that the word *creativity* is associated too strongly with the possession of extraordinary, distinguished, and highly visible talent.

Emphasis on Personality and Affective Traits

The second implication is the built-in emphasis on the importance of affective and personality traits—attitudes, motivations, and conscious dispositions to think creatively. *Affective traits, not basic intelligence, mark the difference between people who do or do not use their capabilities in a creative way.* We have argued that creativity is a lifestyle, a way of living, a way of perceiving the world, and a way of growing.

Living creatively is developing your talents, learning to use your abilities, and striving to become what you are capable of becoming. Being creative is exploring new ideas, new places, and new activities. Being creative is developing sensitivity to problems of others and problems of humankind. Consider Maslow's list in Inset 12.1. Is this what life is—or should be—about?

The humanistic, self-actualization approach to creativity does not focus only on developing one's creative abilities and creative processes. From this theoretical viewpoint, one's creative abilities and processes are by-products of a larger, more important growth in self-actualization.

Look back at Chapter 4. Most of the creative personality characteristics described in that chapter—for example, independence, adventurousness, curiosity, humor, perceptiveness, open-mindedness—mesh nicely with Maslow's description of self-actualization and with Csikszentmihalyi's *flow*.

Self-Actualized and Special-Talent Creativity: Two Continua

While Maslow identified the two types—self-actualized and special-talent creativity—it seems more logical that each of the two traits lies on an independent continuum. As illustrated on the horizontal axis of Figure 12.1, any given person will be low to high in Maslow's general, *self-actualized creativity*. As we have seen, a person high in this trait takes a creative approach to most aspects of life; it is a way of living, growing, and perceiving one's world, as well as a way of thinking and solving problems. Such a person is mentally healthy, self-accepting, and grows toward self-realization. As represented on the vertical axis of Figure 12.1, a person also may be low to high in recognized creative productivity, Maslow's *special talent creativity*. By definition, a person high in this dimension has achieved recognition for socially judged creative achievement, for example, in art, science, or business. He or she may or may not be mentally healthy in the self-actualization sense.

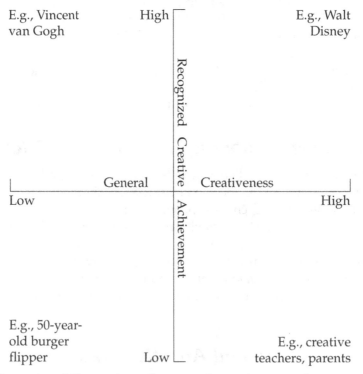

FIGURE 12.1 Two-dimensional illustration of personal creativeness. A person may be low to high in general creativeness, which is a lifestyle and a thinking style (Maslow's self-actualized creativity), and low to high in recognized creative achievement (Maslow's special-talent creativity).

This broad conception of creativity acknowledges the obvious—that many people think and act creatively, some in just a few areas, some in all areas of their lives, and a handful achieve recognition and eminence. This view also acknowledges the truism that everyone has an opportunity to live a more creative life and become a more fulfilled and creatively productive person. The word *creative* must not be restricted only to persons who have achieved creative eminence, as is claimed by some (Chapter 7).

Creativity Consciousness and Creative Attitudes

We turn now to the first of five recommendations for teaching creativity. A focus on *raising creativity consciousness* and teaching creative attitudes will be followed by suggestions for *developing a metacognitive understanding of creativity, strengthening creative abilities, teaching creativity techniques,* and *involving students in creative activities.*

Increasing creativity consciousness and creative attitudes is the single most important component of teaching for creative growth. Every creative person is aware of creativity and his or her own creativeness. The single best item on adult creativity inventories is the question "Are you creative?" Creative people make conscious decisions: "Today I'm going to think creatively and do some creative work!"

Ironically, creativity consciousness is both the most important aspect of becoming more creatively productive, yet also the easiest to teach. Creativity consciousness will be a natural outgrowth of virtually any type of creativity exercises and activities, such as reading this book.

Creativity consciousness and creative attitudes include:

- An awareness of the importance of creativity for personal development (self-actualization), and for solving personal and professional problems
- An appreciation of the role of creative ideas and creative people in the history of civilization—which may be seen as a history of creative innovation in every field
- An awareness of barriers to creativity—habits, traditions, rules, policies, and particularly social expectations and conformity pressures
- A receptiveness to the novel, unconventional, even zany and farfetched ideas of others
- A predisposition to think creatively, play with ideas, and become involved in creative activities
- A willingness to take creative risks, make mistakes, and even fail

Every college course in creativity and every professional workshop stresses creativity consciousness, appropriate creative attitudes, and removing barriers to creative thinking and behavior. Regardless of whether innate abilities can be changed, by changing attitudes and awareness in a more creative direction we stimulate people to use the creative abilities that they already have. Most creativity courses and workshops stress the nature of creativity and creative persons, and all encourage learners to approach personal, academic, and professional problems in a more creative fashion. This approach to teaching creativity is sensible, common, and effective (e.g., Davis & Bull, 1978; de Bono, 1992a; Edwards, 1968; Parnes, 1978, 1981; Smith, 1985; Stanish, 1979, 1981, 1988; Torrance, 1987b, 1995; von Oech, 1983, 1986). The general approach is characteristic of teaching *brainstorming* and the *Creative Problem Solving* (CPS) model of the Creative Education Foundation (Chapters 5 and 8).

On the other hand, a goal might well be to strengthen creative thinking and problem-solving skills as they relate directly to a specific subject such as creative writing, photography, theater, botany, architecture, astronomy, or dinosaurs. With the typical independent projects approach, students are given (or find) a project or problem and proceed to clarify it, consider various approaches, settle on a project or problem definition, research it, process it, and prepare a project report or problem solution. Throughout, students identify and resolve numerous subproblems, evaluate their methods and results, acquire knowledge, develop technical skills in the content area, and strengthen their creative abilities and skills.

Note that the concept of a creative atmosphere, mentioned earlier, fits in exactly here. A creative atmosphere rewards creative thinking and helps it become habitual. It includes Rogers' concept of psychological safety, the deferred judgment concept of brainstorming, and good old-fashioned reinforcement theory.

The reader may wish to look again at the *idea squelchers* in Chapter 3. This is what a creative atmosphere and a creative person are not. Increasing creativity consciousness and fostering favorable attitudes toward creative thinking is truly item number 1 in becoming a more creative person and helping others to develop and use their creative potential.

Metacognitive Understanding of Creativity

Metacognition is thinking about thinking—or in this case, thinking about *creative* thinking. The predisposition to think creatively will take a giant step forward if a person knows more about the topic. A major purpose of this book is to expand the reader's metacognitive understanding of creative thinking. An increased understanding of creativity will help raise creativity consciousness, demystify creativity, and convince readers that given their present abilities they are perfectly capable—with interest and effort—of hatching creative ideas and producing creative things.

Lessons on creativity can include such topics and principles as:

- The importance of creativity to everyone and to society. Improved creative thinking and problem-solving can help everyone live a more interesting, enjoyable, and successful life
- Social pressures and personal rigidity that block or squelch creativity
- The nature of creative ideas as modifications of existing ideas, new combinations of ideas, and products of analogical thinking
- Biographies, personality characteristics, and cognitive abilities and styles of creative people
- How creative people must play with possibilities, take risks—and sometimes make mistakes and even fail
- How creative people use deliberate techniques, especially analogical thinking, to extend their intuition and spontaneous imaginations
- What is measured by creativity tests, such as the *Torrance Tests of Creative Thinking*, for example, the meaning of fluency, flexibility, originality, elaboration, resistance to premature closure, breaking boundaries, fantasy, emotional expressiveness, synthesis of figures, and unusual visualization
- The nature of the creative process, as represented in the Wallas (1926) stages and the CPS model. The creative process also can be viewed as a "change in perception" or mental transformation. Visual puzzles, optical illusions, and even *Far Side* cartoons illustrate this sudden "seeing" of new ideas, new meanings, new combinations, and new modifications. Creativity techniques also illustrate conscious idea-finding processes.
- Definitions and theories of creativity
- How creative people use their talents, not waste them

Exercising Creative Abilities

This section will take a little longer.

In Chapter 4 we itemized abilities that logically underlie creativity, each with a brief definition. It is a common and reasonable strategy to try to strengthen creative abilities through practice and exercise, the same way we strengthen skills of reading, typing, solving chemistry problems, and shooting baskets. We will look at some of these abilities (listed in Table 12.1) and itemize a few exercises, strategies, or materials that aim at strengthening that ability.

Fluency, Flexibility, Originality, and Elaboration. You should recognize these as the original four abilities measured by the Torrance Tests of Creative Thinking (Chapter 10). Many creativity exercises and workbooks use open-ended, think-of-all-you-can divergent thinking problems to try to improve these abilities. Note that such exercises intrinsically raise creativity consciousness and teach creative

TABLE 12.1 Some Creative Abilities That Can Be Exercised

General Creative Abilities	
Fluency	Imagination
Flexibility	Analogical Thinking
Originality	Analysis
Elaboration	Synthesis
Resisting Premature Closure	Evaluation
Problem Sensitivity	Transformation
Problem Defining	Predicting Outcomes
Visualization	Logical Thinking
Creative Abilities Particularly Relevant to Art and Writing	
Emotional Expressiveness	Breaking or Extending Boundaries
Movement and Action	Humor
Synthesizing Figures	Colorfulness in Imagery
Internal or Unusual Perspective	Fantasy

attitudes—valuing creativity, thinking creatively, and being receptive to innovative ideas of others. Variations can be used to teach constructive values—honesty, manners, promptness, valuing education, neatness, energy conservation, and so on—while strengthening creative abilities (Davis, 2004a, 2004b; 2004c; see final six exercises).

The "*What would happen if . . . ?*" divergent thinking exercise is an old standby. It appears in workbooks for children (e.g., Stanish, 1977) and books for teaching creativity and futuristic thinking (e.g., Shallcross, 1981; Torrance, Williams, Torrance, & Horng, 1978). You can create problems that relate to classroom content, character education, business or economics, or virtually anything else. As some examples, "What would happen . . . ?":

If we did not have arithmetic?
If all WiFi in the world disconnected?
If the British had won the Revolutionary War?
If people with blond hair were not allowed in hotels or restaurants and could not vote?
If the only musical instruments were drums?
If people could not solve problems and create?
If Edison had become a plumber and did not invent light bulbs?
If the Wright brothers stuck to bicycles?
If there were no corn grown in Nebraska or potatoes in Idaho?
If global warming was a reality and Miami Beach became the North Pole?
If everyone looked exactly alike?
If union wages were cut in half? If teacher pay was tripled? (or vice-versa)
If our main raw materials (wood, steel, cotton) became unavailable?
If there were no gravity in this room?
If you had an eye in the back of your head?
If no one told the truth?
If everyone wasted school supplies?

Another traditional divergent thinking problem is asking learners to think of *unusual uses* for any common object, for example, discarded tires, ping pong balls, a tea cup, a tennis racquet, a chair, a piece of chalk, a clothes pin, a wink, a new material, a new product, or a new process. Again, it is easy to make up additional problems.

Product improvement problems ask students to think of ways to change or improve a familiar object, such as a bath tub, Cracker Jacks, Jell-O, a drinking fountain, a bicycle, or a television set. With character education problems one asks how to improve student helpfulness, honesty, courtesy, promptness, or pro-school attitudes. Product improvement exercises can deal with business matters, such as thinking of ways to improve management efficiency, sales, hiring practices, morale, or product quality.

Design problems are similar to product improvement problems. For example, designing a bathtub is about the same as thinking of improvements for a bathtub. Other design problems can ask students to design a dog walking machine, a new trash collection procedure, a safer traffic intersection, a cat petter, an airplane for animals, a burglary-prevention system, a theft-proof computer, or children who are never late.

There are virtually unlimited numbers of open-ended questions and problems that would exercise the learner's fluency, flexibility, originality, and elaboration abilities. Some exercises try to focus on just one or another of these four abilities. For example, *fluency* is exercised by asking students to list things that are round, square, sweet, sour, blue, white, made of metal, made of wood, long and slender, short and stubby, smell good, taste bad, or have sharp edges. Some *flexibility* exercises try to have students look at things from different perspectives, for example:

How does this room look to a tidy housekeeper? A hungry mouse? An alien from outer space?

How does an old wooden chair look to a tired person? A termite? An antique collector?

How does a train station look to a train? To a duck flying overhead? To a Muggle who can't find platform 9¾?

How does a highway look to a tire? To a crow? To a lost pilot?

How does a salad bar look to a nine-year-old? A teenager? A college student? A vegetarian? A carnivore? The elderly?

Elaboration exercises require the learner to build upon a basic idea, for example, developing the dog walking or cat petting machine or the new bathtub in specific detail—measurements, materials, costs. Or writing a story built upon a specified theme, for example, a fish who cannot swim, a child with no hair, or a town with no rules or laws, or developing the marketing or morale-improvement plan to the last detail.

Fluency, flexibility, originality, and elaboration abilities also can be exercised with relatively complex brainstorming-type problems. Some problems ask for *solutions*, for example:

How can we make school more interesting?

How can the lunch menu be improved?

How can bicycle theft be eliminated?

How can the school (or home or business) electric bill be reduced?

How can we prevent the best teachers from quitting?

What can we do for a parent on his or her birthday for less than 10 dollars?

How can our company benefit from the increasing numbers of retired persons and help them at the same time?

Other problems ask for *explanations*, for example:

The grass behind a Wyoming billboard is extra lush and green. Why?

The principal unexpectedly cancels gym classes for 2 weeks. What are some explanations?

Ten paintings were discovered missing from the art gallery on Monday morning, but there was no sign of a break-in. How could they have disappeared?

Sales suddenly dropped 30%. What are some explanations?

Note that these latter exercises involve presenting students with incompleteness, ambiguities, and paradoxes, all of which raise tension and motivate students to look for new combinations and relationships.

We have mentioned that it is possible to teach constructive attitudes and values while strengthening fluency, flexibility, originality, and elaboration. You also had a chance to flex your creativity muscles via the "What Would Happen If . . ." exercises and statements covered in the previous pages. Students also can work on such *brainstorming* problems as:

Why is it good to be honest?
Think of ways to show respect to the elderly.
Think of ways to show friendliness in the classroom.
How many different safety rules can you think of?

Or with *reverse brainstorming*. In describing reverse brainstorming, Hagen, Bernard, and Grube (2016) identified it as a "scenario in which an individual or group is asked to identify the opposite and/or reverse solution to a particular problem; instead of asking how to fix a problem, participants are asked about how they might make it worse . . . this process leverages negative energy to spark creativity" (p. 86).

Channel your inner Trunchbull and think of new ways to be unpleasant to new students.
How can we pollute our waters more? Add more trash to our landfills?
How might we waste lots and lots of electricity in our school building or company?
How can we avoid thinking creatively?

Exercises for strengthening fluency, flexibility, originality, and elaboration were created by Stanish (1979) and others before the development of Torrance's 18 "streamlined" creativity scores and Urban and Jellen's 11 test scores, both of which represent creative abilities. Both scoring systems also suggest drawing or writing activities that could strengthen underlying creative abilities while teaching elementary principles of creative thinking.

In Torrance's Picture Completion test, *resistance to premature closure* is the too-early closing of an "open" part of a figure, which prevents one from using the figure in more unique ways. This test itself, or a similar activity, could serve as a creative drawing exercise in which students are expressly advised "Now don't close the figure with another line, because closing the figure can stop you from finding unusual ideas for the figure." The general principle is: Don't grab the first idea that comes along; don't jump to conclusions; keep your mind open to more possibilities.

Emotional expressiveness, which Jellen and Urban called *affectivity*, also can be encouraged in the Picture Completion test or in creative writing assignments. Many students will not think of adding features of gaiety, gloom, or disappointment to a picture, short story, or poem.

Movement and action can be encouraged in drawing or writing as a route to greater originality and interest.

Synthesis of incomplete figures and *synthesis of lines and circles* also are legitimate rule-breakers that rarely occur to test takers. Students can be urged to: "Go ahead and combine two or three figures (circles, pairs of line) if you wish. Nobody said you had to make a single picture out of each little drawing. Your picture probably will show more imagination if you combine some of the figures. Think of lots of possibilities." Students should try to look at any challenge from a broader perspective, one with more possibilities than originally assumed. Can they think about bending or breaking formalized drawing or writing rules? Channel your inner Salvadore Dali and maybe through this mind melding you can truly get the clock melting experience. With that in "mind" lets move on to visualization and perspective taking.

Internal visualization, unusual visualization, and *unusual perspective* are the tendencies to visualize something from the inside, top, bottom, or other unusual perspective, or to imagine a two-dimensional picture as three-dimensional. Such visualization and perspective-taking can be encouraged, just as with other suggestions. "You could draw (or write about) something as if you were inside, as if you were looking at it from underneath or on top, or from some other viewpoint. How would it look to a soaring eagle or to a burrowing mouse, or to a curious cat or sly fox? Can you find some different ideas for strange ways to see something?"

Extending or breaking boundaries can be encouraged. "The pair of lines don't have to belong together—you can split them into different parts of the picture." "Sure, you can draw beyond the frame. Nobody said you had to draw only on the inside of the frame." "You don't have to write about normal people. Give them strange powers. Invent some new kinds of people. Turn something upside down or backwards. Maybe Gwendolyn guinea pig can talk or go for a bike ride." Looking at things differently is a solid principle of creative thinking.

Humor also may be encouraged. To anticipate "But how do I draw something funny?" the teacher can suggest that students draw something absurd (like a combination animal) or exaggerate something, like the size of ears, teeth, a chin, a nose, or a smile. Add ideas from *Star Wars* or *Snow White*. Cartoonists do these things regularly.

Colorfulness of imagery refers to drawings that appeal to other senses. "Can you make your drawing (or writing assignment) appeal to our sense of taste? Touch? Smell? Feel? What would be some ideas?"

Fantasy is just that. "If you can't think of an idea, how about including characters from a fairy tale, Lord of The Rings., or Harry Potter? Or what about other imaginary features? Remember *Green Eggs and Ham*? Can you put arms and legs on something? Make things in your picture talk or sing? It's your drawing—your sailboat can sing or dance on the lake if you want it to. Although students may follow the teacher's suggestions too closely (and draw a dancing sailboat), they at least are learning to look for possibilities beyond the givens and assumptions.

Strengthening Other Creative Abilities

Sensitivity to Problems, Problem Finding. Exercises aimed at strengthening problem sensitivity should have the learners find problems, detect difficulties, or detect missing information. One type of exercise aimed at increasing problem sensitivity has students *ask questions* about an ambiguous situation or even a common object. What questions could you ask about clouds? Computers? The sun? The ocean? Weather? The competitor's products? Increasing creative thinking? A variation would begin with "What don't we know about . . . ?" Question asking also may be placed in a fictitious television interview context (Myers & Torrance, 1964): What three questions might you ask a dictator who has been driven from office? The mother of eight children just named "Mother of the Year"? (presumably NOT Octomom). A bus driver who refused to stop working after winning a fifty-million dollar lottery?

Problem Defining. Problem defining exercises would evolve around:

1. Identifying the *real* problem and simplifying and clarifying the problem, for example: "What is the real problem here?" "What are we trying to do?" "What is it that really needs attention?"
2. Isolating important aspects of a problem, for example: "What are the important parts of this problem?" "What should we focus on?"
3. Identifying subproblems, for example: "What problems are related to this main problem?" Can we solve them? What problems will we have if we try this solution?
4. Proposing alternative problem definitions, for example: "How else can we define the problem?" "How else can we look at this?" "How else might we cope with this difficulty?" The "In What Ways Might We . . . ?" strategy of the CPS model (Chapter 5) aimed at finding additional problem definitions.
5. Defining a problem more broadly to open new possibilities, for example: Why is this a problem?" "Why do we need to take care of this?" "Is there a bigger (underlying, more general) problem here?"

Visualization and Imagination. Many exercises stimulate visualization and imagination. Two books, *Put Your Mother on the Ceiling* (Mille, 1973) and *Scamper* (Eberle, 1995), assume that imagination can be strengthened with exercise. With both books, the listeners relax, shut their eyes, and visualize the colorful narrations read by a teacher or parent.

For example: "Now put a light bulb in each hand, hold your hands straight out to the side, pretend that your light bulbs are jet engines and run down the street for a take off! . . . Zoom over town and look down. . . . Zoom away and look at the mountains . . . the ocean. . . . When you are over your house let loose the light bulbs and have them zip away into space. . . . Open your parachute . . . As you float down look all around you. . . . Touch your feet down. . . . Go tell people you are home. . . . Nothing is very hard to do . . . if you use your imagination" (Eberle, 1995, p. 46).

Developed by Eberle (1971, 1996), the SCAMPER method involves checklisting techniques to spur ideas and spawn creativity. Each of the letters in the acrostic stands for an action that one can take to turn a stale idea into something fresh. Serrat (2017) presents them as follows:

- Substitute—(e.g., new materials, different people)
- Combine (e.g., mix, integrate, or conjoin elements)
- Adapt (e.g., analogical reasoning as you beg, borrow, or steal ideas from another domain)
- Magnify/Modify (e.g., increase size or scale, change shape, alter attributes)
- Put to other uses (e.g., extend purpose or practicality of idea beyond what is intended)
- Eliminate (e.g., remove elements, reduce components, simplify complexity)
- Rearrange/Reverse (e.g., sequence things differently, change the order, interchange parts or pieces)

How could you use the SCAMPER technique to build a better mousetrap? Or, from the rodent's perspective, avoid getting snared but still get the goods (or gouda).

Analogical Thinking. Exercises for practicing analogical thinking appear in Chapter 6. Stanish's (1977) Sunflowering and Gordon's (1974a) Making it Strange are loaded with exercises in analogical thinking.

Analysis, Synthesis, Evaluation. These, of course, are higher-level thinking skills in Bloom's taxonomy of educational objectives. Exercises include asking students to *analyze* components, relationships, hypotheses, patterns, and causes and effects; *synthesize* parts into plans, theories, generalizations, designs, and compositions; and *evaluate* the accuracy, value, efficiency, or utility of alternative ideas or courses of action.

De Bono's (1992b) PMI evaluation strategy asks children to think of what is good about an idea (*pluses*), *bad* about an idea, and simply *interesting*. The PMI strategy prevents the premature acceptance or rejection of an idea. Students also can learn to use an evaluation matrix, as described in Chapter 6, which emphasizes using several evaluation criteria. Parnes (1981) recommended evaluating a problem solution by looking at it from other people's perspectives.

Transformation. Transformation abilities are related to visualization, imagination, and creativity in general. Students can practice making mental transformations with complex visual puzzles of the type shown in Chapter 5. What else can they see in the picture? People differ vastly in their ability to "see" other meanings and perceptions suggesting that many need practice with this particular ability. Sounds, such as crumpling paper, also elicit meanings and transformations.

Predicting Outcomes. Predicting outcomes is related to evaluation abilities in the sense that evaluating problem solutions amounts to predicting their utility. Also, exercises of the "What would happen if . . . ?" variety give students practice at predicting outcomes. It's a form of futuristic thinking.

Logical Thinking. Logical thinking is underrated as a central creative ability. Logical thinking is involved in clarifying the problem, figuring out solution requirements, relating proposed ideas to solution requirements, and implementing the solution. There seem to be few exercises designed to strengthen logical thinking abilities, other than syllogistic reasoning ("all A is B, all B is C, therefore all A is C") and related problems such as "If Tom is taller than Giselle, and Giselle dresses better than Dennis Rodman, who is the best golfer (or G.O.A.T. if you will)?"

An early workbook by Myers and Torrance (1966) included exercises in logic that could serve as models for similar teacher-constructed activities. For example, explain why each of the following is *true* or *false*:

If something is beautiful, it has to be valuable.
Joe has one sister, but three brothers-in-law.
An object has color or else it has no colour.
Joe, a strict vegetarian, prefers fish to beef.
The twins rode into town by themselves, with Chuck in the middle.

The headlights of the oncoming car blinded its driver, causing him to run off the road.

Diamonds are more expensive than pearls; therefore, pearls are more expensive than rubies.

The workbooks published by Critical Thinking Press and Software, especially those by Anita Harnadek and Howard and Sandra Black supply hundreds of exercises in logical thinking. For example, "What might Kitty do to convince her parents that she's old enough to start choosing some of her own clothes?" and "What might Kitty's parents do to convince her that she isn't old enough to start choosing some of her own clothes?" (Harnadek, 1979). Other problems include, for example, predicting how a folded paper with holes punched in it will look when unfolded (Black & Black, 1984).

The list of creative abilities in this section appears central to creative thinking, and we have described some exercises that may help strengthen them. Of course, it is not an exhaustive list. As noted in Chapter 4, it would be extremely difficult to identify a cognitive ability or style that is *not* in some way involved in the complex requirements of creative thinking. The takeaway here is that these CAN be taught (see Schlichter, 1997). Tardif and Sternberg (1988) described as important creative abilities *decision making, independence of judgment, coping with novelty, ability to escape perceptual sets, ability to find order in chaos, aesthetic ability* (taste and judgment), and *versatility*. Many of these resemble the present creative abilities or the personality characteristics described in Chapter 4.

Creative Thinking Techniques

We have devoted considerable space to *techniques* of creative thinking in Chapters 8 and 9. Teaching students to use such techniques not only provides them with strategies for generating ideas, but helps them to also understand the nature of creative ideas and creative processes used by others. Children's versions of the techniques are found in Davis and DiPego (1973), Stanish (1977, 1981, 1988), Gordon (1974a), and Gordon and Poze (1972a, 1972b).

As a caution, it is not easy for adults or children to quickly adopt an unfamiliar thinking or problem-solving method. Nonetheless, creative people do use such techniques, consciously or unconsciously, and the techniques work. Personally, your author found ideas for the more-or-less amusing dialogues of this book by creating checklists of well-known children's stories (Alice in Wonderland, Cinderella, Harry Potter), famous people and comedians (Sigmund Freud, Woody Allen, Barbara Walters, Don Rickles, Rodney Dangerfield, Norm Crosby), and myths and legends (Frankenstein, the devil, an oracle), and using these as analogical inspiration. Success was mixed. As mentioned earlier, the morphological synthesis technique helped generate hundreds of exercises that use creativity procedures (brainstorming, analogical thinking, "What would happen if . . . ?" visualization) to help students understand values and character—constructive and self-destructive (Davis, 2004a, 2004c).

Involvement in Creative Activities

Leonardo DaVinci did not become a great painter by practicing shuffleboard, nor did Hemingway spend much time on juggling skills. The strongest and most logically sound recommendation for strengthening creativity is to involve yourself or your students in activities that intrinsically require creative thinking and problem-solving. It is virtually assured that creative attitudes, abilities, and skills will be strengthened in the course of actual creative involvement.

If a teacher is creativity conscious, most classroom activities can be modified to elicit creative thinking, for example, with creative questioning. What would happen if nobody could spell or if nobody could read? If only children, but not adults, could read or if nobody could do arithmetic? If cashiers could not do arithmetic, and they had no cash registers, could they sell things? How? What would have happened if Columbus did not discover America? If the British won the Civil War? If Thomas Jefferson did not buy the Louisiana Territory from France? If nobody knew anything at all about people and traditions in other countries? What would the world be like if ice didn't float? If there were no trees or wood? If (when) we run out of oil and gas? If people had no fingers? If California became the South Pole?

What would the world be like if there had been no energetic, creative people? In art? In music? In math? In science? In engineering? In inventing? In manufacturing? In government? With interest and effort, the reader can think of endless ways to stretch the imaginations of children and adolescents. The *Future Problem Solving* and *Odyssey of the Mind* programs, as described in Chapter 11, were designed to promote creative thinking through involvement.

In addition to reviewing a few issues pertaining to "teaching creativity," along with contributions from earlier chapters, the main focus of this chapter was on self-actualizing your own creative potential. Towards that lofty goal, we provided an overview of five core objectives of creativity training and their related strategies that can help you get there. As for which approach or combination of approaches produces the greatest gains the most quickly and efficiently, the variety of ages, abilities, interests, and needs of particular students—along with a virtual absence of relevant research—make it impossible to specify an all-around ideal recipe. Your authors recommend a confluence approach . . . using *all* of the goals/ activities in approximately the order they were presented. Students need to be aware of creativity and acquire attitudes that predispose them to thinking creatively; they need to metacognitively understand creative people and creative thinking; their creative abilities and skills should be exercised; they should learn brainstorming and other idea-finding techniques; and they definitely should be involved in activities that require creative thinking and problem-solving.

Very little in your own personal development or in the education of your children or students is as critical as strengthening creative potential. Creative self-actualization should not be left to chance, as (just as the title of this textbook suggests) Creativity IS Forever

Summary

Education for creativity is important.

There is massive evidence for the teachability of creativity, said Torrance.

There are individual differences in responsiveness to creativity training.

Differences in motivation to create—arousal-seeking tendencies—are thought to be governed by the brain's reticular activating system.

The psychological safety (Rogers) of a receptive and reinforcing creative atmosphere is essential.

Starko identified elements of a classroom climate that is conducive to creativity, including rewarding ideas, encouraging risks, and allowing for mistakes.

Maslow distinguished between self-actualized creativity (content free) and special talent creativity (domain specific gift, talent, or ability).

Baer provided evidence of the necessity of specified instruction for the cultivation of specific creativity skills

Earlier chapters made the following contributions to the teaching of creativity.

Chapters 1 and 2 looked at definitions, theories, and approaches, which can increase one's understanding of creativity.

Chapter 3 reviewed blocks and barriers to creativity, including von Oech's 10 mental blocks and idea squelchers.

Chapter 4 reviewed characteristics of creative people, including eminent ones, many of which can be reinforced or otherwise cultivated.

Chapter 5 illustrated perceptual change as a process, discussed the effective CPS model, and noted how some eminent persons have used imagery in their creative thinking.

Chapter 6 covered the most common and useful creative thinking process/technique of all, analogical thinking.

Chapter 7 looked at conceptualizations of creative contributions and categorizations of creative products.

Chapter 8 described brainstorming, brainwriting and related techniques, plus electronic brainstorming, attribute listing, morphological synthesis, and idea checklists—all useful strategies devised and used by creative persons.

Chapter 9 reviewed de Bono's six hats and other lateral thinking idea-finding procedures, including his provocative techniques, plus ideas for teaching children to think.

Chapter 10 reviewed creativity tests, which included creative personality inventories, assessment of past creative activities, and divergent thinking tests, all of which increase our understanding of creative persons and creative abilities. Test items may be used as creativity exercises.

Chapter 11 summarized G/T program models and enrichment and acceleration strategies that feature creative development as a main goal.

This chapter presented issues and suggestions for improving cognitive development, stressed the importance of creativity to the (self-actualized) individual, and emphasized five main points (goals, strategies) related to increasing creative potential.

Self-actualization is developing your talents to become what you are capable of becoming. It includes being mentally healthy, forward growing, and more. Creativity and self-actualization are intimately related, perhaps identical, say humanists Carl Rogers, Abraham Maslow, and Clark Moustakis.

Popular usage assumes a relationship between creativity and self-actualization. Csikszentmihalyi's *flow* and the topic of entrepreneurship both relate to self-actualization and creativity.

Measures of self-actualization include the POI, the POD, the shorter SI (based on the POI), the ROSE, the ROSY, and the Maslowian Scale. Research with these instruments supports a fairly strong relationship between self-actualization and measures of creativity.

The self-actualized creative person approaches all aspects of life in a creative fashion. The special talent creative person has a great creative talent, but may or may not be self-actualized in the mentally healthy sense.

Five main points (goals, strategies) related to increasing creative potential are as follows:

First, we should increase students' creativity consciousness and creative attitudes, especially an appreciation for creative ideas and a predisposition to think creatively.

Second, we should help students metacognitively understand the topic of creativity, such as the importance of creativity, blocks and barriers, nature of creative ideas, creative characteristics, techniques, rationale of tests, ways to view the creative process, CPS model, definitions and theories.

Third, we should help strengthen creative abilities. Many divergent thinking types of exercises and brainstorming problems have been suggested for strengthening fluency, flexibility, originality, and elaboration. The newer Torrance and Urban and Jellen scoring systems suggest exercises for resisting premature closure and, at least in drawing and writing, combining figures, breaking boundaries, and adding emotional expressiveness, movement and action, unusual perspectives, and humor.

The fourth main goal of creativity training is teaching creative thinking techniques.

Fifth, we should involve students in creative thinking and problem-solving activities.

Creativity training might proceed in the sequence in which the five points were presented.

Educating for creativity is important as CREATIVITY IS FOREVER

Review Exercises

Creativity is Forever: Unlocking your creative potential

Self-Test: Key Concepts and Terms

Briefly define or explain each of these:

Can creativity be taught? _____

_____

Responsiveness/receptiveness to creativity training _____

_____

Motivation to create _____

_____

Creative atmosphere _____

_____

Content-free creativity training _____

_____

Self-Actualization _____

_____

Flow _____

_____

Special talent Creativity _____

_____

Creativity consciousness _____

_____

Creative attitudes _____

_____

Metacognition _____

_____

Let's Think about It

1. You are a parent of a three-year-old and a six-year-old. Based on your experience, intuition, or material from this book, how might you stimulate flexible thinking, creativity, problem solving, and good character (e.g., honesty, respecting others' rights) for each child?

   Three-year-old_____

   _____

   _____

   _____

   Six-year-old _____

   _____

   _____

   _____

2. Which chapter in this book has helped you the most in understanding "creativity"? Explain.

   _____

   _____

   _____

3. Some people have argued that "creativity" must be taught within a subject area. How does the author use the relationship between self-actualized and special talent creativity to help resolve the issue?

   _____

   _____

   _____

4. A key part of creativity training is *involving* students in projects and activities that require creative thinking.

    a. What are some projects and activities that might strengthen a general, *self-actualized* type of creativeness (with either elementary or secondary students)?

_____

_____

_____

    b. What are some projects and activities that might strengthen *special talent creativity* (with either elementary or secondary students)?

_____

_____

_____

5. Either in schools or a business setting, how can we:

    a. Raise creativity consciousness?

_____

_____

_____

    b. Help people overcome blocks and barriers?

_____

_____

_____

    c. Develop creative personality traits?

_____

_____

_____

d. Develop a habit of "mentally transforming" objects, ideas, or processes into creative variations?

_____

_____

_____

e. Help people think more analogically; that is, help them draw ideas from other sources or see connections between "this problem" and a related situation?

_____

_____

_____

f. Motivate people to use creativity techniques when they are stuck for ideas?

_____

_____

_____

g. Improve understanding of creativity?

_____

_____

_____

h. Exercise and strengthen important creative abilities?

_____

_____

_____

6. Use the following elaboration exercises in reference a university setting

_____

a. *Generate solutions* for how we can make college more accessible?

_____

_____

_____

b. *Explain why* undergraduate degrees have lost occupational value over the years related to the "inflation of education"? (needing a master's degree to do a job that a bachelor's degree traditionally would suffice for)

_____

_____

_____

c. *Reverse brainstorm* ways to decrease your tuition bill each semester!

_____

_____

_____

7. As presented in the chapter, use the SCAMPER method to come up with a creative way to get rid of unwanted rodents or creepy crawlies (insects and arachnids)? What are traditional pest control methods? How can you use SCAMPER to come up with new ideas?

SUBSTITUTE:

COMBINE

ADAPT:

MAGNIFY/MODIFY:

PUT TO OTHER USES:

ELIMINATE:

REARRANGE/REVERSE:

8. How has this book increased YOUR creative potential and/or your creative outlook on life?

_____

_____

_____

_____

If your answer is "It hasn't!" explain why not. (Hints: "I am already quite creative, thank you." "I have a rigid personality and no imagination." "I'm just interested in football." "I prefer to be a conformer." "I didn't know I was supposed to learn to be more creative." "I could be more creative if I wanted, but it's too much like work." "I just needed a "C" in this class." "I KNOW without a doubt that creativity absolutely cannot be taught or learned—particularly by me.")

_____

_____

_____

9. Think of some problems or challenges in your life, or some things you would like to do better.

a. _____

b. _____

c. _____

d. _____

Think of one or two creative solutions for each problem/challenge/goal.

a. _____

_____

b. _____

_____

c. _____

_____

d. _____

_____

References

Abernathy Tannehill, R. L. (1998). An analysis of selected creativity tests administered to students affiliated with the Cherokee tribe. *Dissertation Abstracts International, 58*(7-a), 2526. (UMI No. 9801472)

Aiamy, M., & Haghani, F. (2012). The effect of synectics & brainstorming on 3rd grade students' development of creative thinking on science. *Procedia—Social and Behavioral Sciences, 47*, 610–613.

Aithal, P. S., & Kumar, P. M. (2017). Ideal analysis for decision making in critical situations through Six Thinking Hats method. *International Journal of Applied Engineering and Management Letters, 1*(2), 1–9.

Albert, R. S. (1990). Identity, experiences, and career choice among the exceptionally gifted and eminent. In M. A. Runco & R. S. Albert (Eds.), *Theories of creativity.* Newberry Park, CA: Sage.

Aldous, C. R. (2007). Creativity, problem solving and innovative science: Insights from history, cognitive psychology and neuroscience. *International Education Journal, 8*(2), 176–186.

Alexander, T. (1978). Inventing by the madness method. In G. A. Davis & J. A. Scott (Eds.), *Training creative thinking.* Melbourne, FL: Krieger.

Allen, M. S. (1962). *Morphological creativity.* Englewood Cliffs, NJ: Prentice-Hall.

Allen, M. S. (1966). *Psycho-dynamic synthesis.* West Nyack, NY: Parker.

Amabile, T. M. (1982). Social psychology of creativity: A consensual assessment technique. *Journal of Personality and Social Psychology, 43*, 997–1013.

Amabile, T. M. (1983). *Social psychology of creativity.* New York, NY: Springer-Verlag.

Amabile, T. M. (1987). The motivation to create. In S. G. Isaksen (Ed.), *Frontiers of creativity research: Beyond the basics* (pp. 223–254). Buffalo, NY: Bearly.

Amabile, T. M. (1988). A model of organizational innovation. In B. M. Staw & L. L. Cummings (Eds.), *Research in organizational behavior* (Vol. 10, pp. 123–167). Greenwich, CT: JAI.

Amabile, T. M. (2012). Componential theory of creativity. *Harvard Business School, 12*(96), 1–10.

Amabile, T. M., & Mueller, J. S. (2008). Studying creativity, its processes, and its antecedents: An exploration of the componential theory of creativity. In J. Zhou & C. E. Shalley (Eds.), *Handbook of organizational creativity* (pp. 33–64). New York, NY: Lawrence Erlbaum.

Ambrose, D. (1995). Creatively intelligent post-industrial organizations and intellectually impaired bureaucracies. *Journal of Creative Behavior, 29*, 1–15.

Ambrose, D. (1996). Turtle soup: Establishing innovation-friendly conditions for school reform. *Journal of Creative Behavior, 30*, 25–38.

Amsterdam. (12 July 2016). https://www.vangoghmuseum.nl/en/news-and-press/press-releases/van-goghs-illness-ear-and-suicide-explored-in-depth-for-the-first-time?v=1. Accessed 13 October 2019.

Andreasen, N. C. (2011). A journey into chaos: Creativity and the unconscious. *Mens Sana Monographs, 9*(1), 42.

Andreason, N. C. (1978). Creativity and psychiatric illness. *Psychiatric Annals, 8*, 113–119.

Andreason, N. C. (1987). Creativity and mental illness: Prevalence rates in writers and their first-degree relatives. *American Journal of Psychiatry, 144*, 1288–1292.

Andreason, N. C., & Canter, A. (1974). The creative writer: Psychiatric symptoms and family history. *Comprehensive Psychiatry, 15*, 123–131.

Andreason, R. N., & Glick, I. D. (1988). Bipolar affective disorder and creativity: Implications and clinical management. *Comprehensive Psychiatry, 29*, 207–216.

Arieti, S. (1976). *Creativity: The magic synthesis.* New York, NY: Basic Books.

Arons, M. (1992). Creativity, Humanistic psychology and the American Zeitgeist. *The Humanistic Psychologist, 20*(2–3), 158–174.

Assouline, S. G.; Assouline, S. G.; Colangelo, N.; Gross, M. U. M.; Templeton Foundation, Connie Belin & Jacqueline, N; Blank International Center for Gifted Education and Talent Development; & National Association for Gifted Children (U.S.). (2015). *A nation empowered: Evidence trumps the excuses holding back America's brightest students.* Iowa City, IA: Connie Belin & Jacqueline N. Blank International Center for Gifted Education and Talent Development, University of Iowa.

Averill, J. R. (1999). Individual differences in emotional creativity: Structure and correlates. *Journal of Personality, 67,* 331–371.

Averill, J. R. (2005). Emotions as mediators and as products of creative activity. In J. C. Kaufman & J. Baer (Eds.), *Creativity across domains: Faces of the muse* (pp. 225–243). Mahwah, NJ: Erlbaum.

Averill, J. R. (2009). Emotional creativity: Toward "spiritualizing the passions." In S. J. Lopez & C. R. Snyder (Eds.), *Oxford handbook of positive psychology* (p. 249). Oxford, England: Oxford University Press.

Averill, J. R., & Thomas-Knowles, C. (1991). Emotional creativity. In K. T. Strongman (Ed.), *International review of studies on emotion* (Vol. 1, pp. 269–299). London, England: Wiley.

Baer, J. (1997). *Creative teachers, creative students.* Boston, MA: Allyn & Bacon.

Baer, J. (2008). Gender differences in creativity. *The Journal of Creative Behavior, 42,* 75–102.

Baer, J. (2016). Creativity doesn't develop in a vacuum. *New Directions for Child and Adolescent Development, 2016*(151), 9–20.

Barron, F. (1955). The disposition toward originality. *Journal of Abnormal and Social Psychology, 51,* 478–485.

Barron, F. (1961). Creative vision and expression in writing and painting. In D. W. MacKinnon (Ed.), *The creative person* (pp. 237–251). Berkeley, CA: Institute of Personality Assessment Research, University of California.

Barron, F. (1965). The psychology of creativity. In F. Barron, W. C. Dement, W. Edwards, et al., (Eds.), *New directions in psychology II.* New York, NY: Holt.

Barron, F. (1968). *Creativity and personal freedom.* Princeton, NJ: Van Nostrand.

Barron, F. (1969). *Creative person and creative process.* New York, NY: Holt.

Barron, F. (1978). An eye more fantastical. In G. A. Davis & J. A. Scott (Eds.), *Training creative thinking* (pp. 181–193). Melbourne, FL: Krieger.

Barron, F. (1988). Putting creativity to work. In R. J. Sternberg (Ed.), *The nature of creativity* (pp. 76–98). New York, NY: Cambridge University Press.

Barry, K., Domb, E., & Slocum, M. S. (2010). TRIZ—What is TRIZ. *The TRIZ Journal,* 603–632. Retrieved from http://triz-journal.com/archives/what_is_triz/

Bartlett, M. M., & Davis, G. A. (1974). Do the Wallach and Kogan tests predict real creative behavior? *Perceptual and Motor Skills, 39,* 730.

Basadur, M. (1992). Managing creativity: A Japanese model. *Academy of Management Executive, 6*(2), 29–42.

Basadur, M. (1994). *Simplexfi: A flight to creativity.* Buffalo, NY: Creative Education Foundation.

Basadur, M., Runco, M. A., & Vega, L. A. (2000). Understanding how creative thinking skills, attitudes and behaviors work together: A causal process model. *Journal of Creative Behavior, 34,* 77–100.

Basadur, M., Taggar, S., & Pringle, P. (1999). Improving the measurement of divergent thinking attitudes in organizations. *Journal of Creative Behavior, 33,* 75–111.

Bass, S. (1968). *Why man creates* (16 mm film). Oakland, CA: Kaiser Aluminum.

Batey, M., & Furnham, A. (2010). Creativity, intelligence and personality: A critical review of the scattered literature. *Genetic, Social, and General Psychology Monographs, 132,* 355–429.

Beghetto, R. A. (2005, September). Does assessment kill student creativity? *The Educational Forum, 69*(3), 254–263.

Beghetto, R. A., & Kaufman, J. C. (2007). Toward a broader conception of creativity: A case for "mini-c" creativity. *Psychology of Aesthetics, Creativity, and the Arts, 1,* 73–79.

Begley, S. (1993, June 28). The puzzle of genius. *Newsweek,* pp. 46–51.

Bem, S. L. (1974). The measurement of psychological androgyny. *Journal of consulting and Clinical Psychology, 42,* 155–162.

Bem, S. L. (1981). *Bem sex-role inventory: Professional manual.* Palo Alto, CA: Consulting Psychologists Press.

Berlyne, D. E. (1961). *Conflict, arousal, and curiosity.* New York, NY: McGraw-Hill.

Besemer, S. P. (1998). Creative product analysis matrix: Testing the model structure and a comparison among products—Three novel chairs. *Creativity Research Journal, 11*(4), 333–346.

Besemer, S. P., & O'Quin, K. (1986). Analyzing creative products: Refinement and test of a judging instrument. *The Journal of Creative Behavior, 20*(2), 115–126.

Besemer, S. P., & O'Quin, K. (1987). Creative product analysis: Testing a model by developing a judging instrument. In S. G. Isaksen (Ed.), *Frontiers of creativity research: Beyond the basics* (pp. 341–357). Buffalo, NY: Bearly.

Besemer, S. P., & O'Quin, K. (1999). Confirming the three-factor creative product analysis matrix model in an American sample. *Creativity Research Journal, 12*(4), 287–296.

Besemer, S. P., & Treffinger, D. H. (1981). Analysis of creative products: Review and synthesis. *Journal of Creative Behavior, 15*(3), 158–178.

Betts, G. (1991). Autonomous learner model. In N. Colangelo & G. A. Davis (Eds.), *Handbook of gifted education* (pp. 142–153). Needham Heights, MA: Allyn and Bacon.

Betts, G. T., & Kercher, J. K. (1999). *Autonomous learner model: Optimizing ability.* Greeley, CO: Alps Publishing.

Biondi, A. M. (1980). About the small cage habit. *Journal of Creative Behavior, 2,* 75–76.

Black, H., & Black, S. (1984). *Building thinking skills.* Pacific Grove, CA: Thinking Skills Press and Software.

Black, H., & Black, S. (1988). *Building thinking skills.* Pacific Grove, CA: Critical Thinking Press and Software.

Bloom, B. S. (1985). *Developing talent in young people.* New York, NY: Ballantine Books.

Bloom, B. S. (Ed.). (1974). *Taxonomy of educational objectives.* New York, NY: McKay.

Bloom, B. S., & Sosniak, L. A. (1981). Talent development vs. schooling. *Educational Leadership, 39,* 86–94.

Boden, M. A. (1999). Computer models of creativity. In R. J. Sternberg (Ed.), *Handbook of creativity* (pp. 351–372). New York, NY: Cambridge University Press.

Bollen, K. A. (1989). *Structural equations with latent variables.* New York, NY: John Wiley.

Borland, J. (1997). Evaluating gifted programs. In N. Colangelo & G. A. Davis (Eds.), *Handbook of gifted education* (2nd ed., pp. 253–266). Boston, MA: Allyn & Bacon.

Briskman, L. (1980). Creative product and creative process in science and art. *Inquiry, 23,* 83–106.

Brittain, W. L., & Beitel, K. R. (1961). A study of some tests of creativity in relationship to performance in the visual arts. *Studies in Art Education, 2,* 54–65.

Brockes, E. (2005, September). *Return of the time lord.* Retrieved from https://www.theguardian.com/science/2005/sep/27/scienceandnature.highereducationprofile

Brody, E. W. (1990, Winter). Software reviews: IdeaFisher 3.0. *Public Relations Review,* 67–68.

Bronowski, J. (1961). *Science and human values.* London, England: Hutchinson.

Brualdi, A. (1999). Traditional and modern concepts of validity. *ERIC/AE Digest.* Retrieved from https://eric.ed.gov/?id=ED435714

Bruner, J. S. (1967). *On knowing: Essays for the left hand.* New York, NY: Atheneum.

Buckmaster, L. R., & Davis, G. A. (1985). ROSE: A measure of self-actualization and its relationship to creativity. *Journal of Creative Behavior, 19,* 30–37.

Budmen, K. O. (1967). What do you think, Teacher? Critical thinking, a partnership in learning. *Peabody Journal of Education, 45,* 2–5.

Buijs, J., Smulders, F., & van der Meer, H. (2009). Towards a more realistic creative problem solving approach. *Creativity and Innovation Management, 18*(4), 286–298.

Bull, K. S., & Davis, G. A. (1980). Evaluating creative potential using the statement of past creative activities. *Journal of Creative Behavior, 14,* 249–257.

Bull, K. S., & Davis, G. A. (1982). Inventory for appraising adult creativity. *Contemporary Educational Psychology, 7*(1), 1–8.

Buzan, T. (1983). *Use both sides of your brain.* New York, NY: Dutton.

Calkins, L. (1986). *The art of teaching writing.* Portsmouth, NH: Heinemann.

Calkins, L. M. (2015). *A guide to the reading workshop, primary grades.* Portsmouth, NH: Heinemann.

Callahan, C. M. (1991). The assessment of creativity. In N. Colangelo & G. A. Davis (Eds.), *Handbook of gifted education* (pp. 219–235). Boston, MA: Allyn & Bacon.

Campbell, D. T. (1960). Blind variation and selective retention in creative thought as in other knowledge processes. *Psychological Review, 67,* 380–400.

Canfield, D. (1952). How flint and fire started and grew. In B. Ghiselin (Ed.), *The creative process.* New York, NY: Mentor.

Cascini, G., & Rissone, P. (2004). Plastics design: Integrating TRIZ creativity and semantic knowledge portals. *Journal of Engineering Design, 15*(4), 405–424.

Cattell, R. B. (1955). *Handbook for the objective-analysis test battery.* Champaign, IL: Institute for Personality and Ability Testing.

Chan, D. W., & Chan, L. (1999). British teachers' views of creativity. *Creativity Research Journal, 12,* 185–195.

Chase, W. I. (1985). Review of the *Torrance Tests of Creative Thinking*. In J. Mitchell (Ed.), *Ninth mental measurements yearbook* (Vol. 2). Lincoln, NE: Buros Institute of Mental Measurement.

Chen, C. H., & Yang, Y. C. (2019). Revisiting the effects of project-based learning on students' academic achievement: A meta-analysis investigating moderators. *Educational Research Review, 26,* 71–81.

Christensen, T. (2013). The relationship between creativity and intelligence. *Creative Something.* https://creativesomething.net/post/41103661291/the-relationship-between-creativity-and

Clapham, M. M. (2004). The convergent validity of the Torrance Tests of Creative Thinking and creativity interest inventories. *Educational and Psychological Measurement, 64*(5), 828–841.

Clark, C. H. (1958). *Brainstorming.* Garden City, NY: Doubleday.

Clasen, D. R. (Ed.). (1985). *Teaching for thinking: Creativity in the classroom.* Madison: University of Wisconsin-Extension.

Clasen, D. R., & Clasen, R. E. (2003). Mentoring the gifted and talented. In N. Colangelo & G. A. Davis (Eds.), *Handbook of gifted education* (3rd ed., pp. 254–267). Boston, MA: Allyn & Bacon.

Cocteau, J. (1952). The process of inspiration. In B. Ghiselin (Ed.), *The creative process.* New York, NY: Mentor.

Columbus Group. (1991, July). *Unpublished transcript of the meeting of the Columbus Group.* Columbus, OH: Author.

Columbus Group. (2013). *Off the charts: Asynchrony and the gifted child.* Unionville, NY: Royal Fireworks Press.

Conners, J. L. (2007). Popular culture in political cartoons: Analyzing cartoonist approaches. *PS: Political Science & Politics, 40*(2), 261–265.

Consulting Psychologists Press. (1988). *CPP catalog.* Palo Alto, CA: Author.

Conti, R., Coon, H., & Amabile, T. M. (1996). Evidence to support the componential model of creativity: Secondary analyses of three studies. *Creativity Research Journal, 9,* 385–389.

Cooper, L. (Trans.), Hamilton, E., & Cairns, H. (Eds.). (1961). *The collected dialogues of Plato.* Princeton, NJ: Princeton University Press.

Costa, A. L. (2003). In the habit of skillful thinking. In N. Colangelo & G. A. Davis (Eds.), *Handbook of gifted education* (3rd ed., pp. 325–344). Boston, MA: Allyn & Bacon.

Cox, C. M. (1926). *Genetic studies of genius. Volume II: The early mental traits of three hundred geniuses.* Stanford, CA: Stanford University Press.

Cox, J., Daniel, N., & Boston, B. A. (1985). *Educating able learners: Programs and promising practices.* Austin: University of Texas Press.

Craft, A. (2001). Little c creativity. In A. Craft, B. Jeffrey, & M. Leibling (Eds.), *Creativity in education* (pp. 45–61). London, England: Continuum.

Craft, A. (2002). *Creativity and early years education: A lifewide foundation.* London, England: A&C Black.

Cramond, B. (1994). Attention-deficit hyperactivity disorder and creativity—what is the connection? *Journal of Creative Behavior, 28,* 193–210.

Cramond, B., Matthews-Morgan, J., Bandalos, D., & Zuo, L. (2005). A report on the 40-year follow-up of the Torrance Tests of Creative Thinking. *Gifted Child Quarterly, 49,* 283–356.

Crandall, R., McCown, D. A., & Robb, Z. (1988). The effects of assertiveness training on self-actualization. *Small Group Behavior, 19,* 134–145.

Crawford, R. P. (1978). The techniques of creative thinking. In G. A. Davis & J. A. Scott (Eds.), *Training creative thinking* (pp. 52–57). Melbourne, FL: Krieger.

Creativity Group Techniques. (1984, September). *Small Business Report,* 52–57.

Cropley, A. J. (1971). Some Canadian creativity research. *Journal of Research and Development in Education, 4*(3), 113–115.

Cropley, A. J. (1972). A five-year longitudinal study of the validity of creativity tests. *Developmental Psychology, 6,* 119–124.

Cseh, G. M., Phillips, L. H., & Pearson, D. G. (2015). Flow, affect and visual creativity. *Cognition and Emotion, 29*(2), 281–291.

Csikszentmihalyi, M. (1988). Society, culture, and person: A systems view of creativity. In R. J. Sternberg (Ed.), *The nature of creativity* (pp. 325–339). New York, NY: Cambridge University Press.

Csikszentmihalyi, M. (1990a). The domain of creativity. In M. A. Runco & R. S. Albert (Eds.), *Theories of creativity* (pp. 190–212). Newbury Park, CA: Sage.

Csikszentmihalyi, M. (1990b). *Flow: The psychology of optimal experience.* New York, NY: Harper & Row.

Csikszentmihalyi, M. (1999). *Implications of a systems perspective for the study of creativity.* In R. J. Sternberg (Ed.), *Handbook of human creativity* (pp. 313–338). New York, NY: Cambridge University Press.

Dacey, J. S. (1989). *Fundamentals of creative thinking.* Lexington, MA: Lexington Books.

Dacey, J. S., Lennon, K., & Fiore, L. B. (1998). *Understanding creativity: The interplay of biological, psychological, and social factors* (1st ed.). San Francisco, CA: Jossey-Bass.

Damm, V. J. (1970). Creativity and intelligence: Research implications for equal emphasis in high school. *Exceptional Children, 36*, 565–570.

Daniels-McGhee, S., & Davis, G. A. (1994). The imagery-creativity connection. *Journal of Creative Behavior, 28*, 151–176.

Davis, G. A. (1971). Instruments useful in studying creative behavior and creative talent, Part II: Noncommercially available instruments. *Journal of Creative Behavior, 5*, 162–165.

Davis, G. A. (1973). *Psychology of problem solving.* New York, NY: Basic Books.

Davis, G. A. (1975). In frumious pursuit of the creative person. *Journal of Creative Behavior, 9*, 75–87.

Davis, G. A. (1989a). Objectives and activities for teaching creative thinking. *Gifted Child Quarterly, 33*, 81–84.

Davis, G. A. (1989b). Testing for creative potential. *Contemporary Educational Psychology, 14*, 257–274.

Davis, G. A. (1991a). *How do you think: Administration and technical manual.* Cross Plains, WI: Westwood.

Davis, G. A. (1991b). Teaching creative thinking. In N. Colangelo & G. A. Davis (Eds.), *Handbook of gifted education.* Boston, MA: Allyn & Bacon.

Davis, G. A. (1992). On Walberg's human capital model of learning, creativity, and eminence. *Creativity Research Journal, 5*, 341–343.

Davis, G. A. (1994, April). Discussant. In H. J. Walberg (Chair), *Notable American women: Childhood contexts and psychological traits.* Symposium conducted at the meeting of the American Educational Research Association, New Orleans, LA.

Davis, G. A. (1995). Portrait of the creative person. *Educational Forum, 12*, 205–212.

Davis, G. A. (1999). Barriers to creativity and creative attitudes. In M. A. Runco & S. R. Pritzker (Eds.), *Encyclopedia of creativity* (pp. 165–174). San Diego, CA: Academic Press.

Davis, G. A. (2003). Identifying creative students, teaching for creative growth. In N. Colangelo & G. A. Davis (Eds.), *Handbook of gifted education* (3rd ed., pp. 311–324). Boston, MA: Allyn & Bacon.

Davis, G. A. (2004). *Creativity is forever.* Dubuque, IA: Kendall Hunt.

Davis, G. A. (2004a). *Character education: Activities and exercises for developing positive attitudes and behavior* (2nd ed.). Unionville, NY: Royal Fireworks.

Davis, G. A. (2004b). *Values are forever: Self-guided activities in character education* (2nd ed.). Unionville, NY: Royal Fireworks.

Davis, G. A., & Belcher, T. L. (1971). How shall creativity be measured? Torrance Tests, RAT, Alpha Biographical, and IQ. *Journal of Creative Behavior, 3*, 153–161.

Davis, G. A., & Bull, K. S. (1978). Strengthening affective components of creativity in a college course. *Journal of Educational Psychology, 70*, 833–836.

Davis, G. A., & DiPego, G. (1973). *Imagination Express: Saturday subway ride.* Buffalo, NY: DOK.

Davis, G. A., & Rimm, S. (1980). *Group inventory for finding interests. II.* Watertown, WI: Educational Assessment Service.

Davis, G. A., & Rimm, S. (1982). Group inventory for finding interests (GIFFI) I and II: Instruments for identifying creative potential in the junior and senior high school. *Journal of Creative Behavior, 16*, 50–57.

Davis, G. A., & Rimm, S. B. (2004). *Education of the gifted and talented* (5th ed.). Boston, MA: Allyn & Bacon.

Davis, G. A., & Subkoviak, M. J. (1978). Multidimensional analysis of a personality-based test of creative potential. *Journal of Educational Measurement, 12*, 37–43.

Davis, G. A., Helfert, C. J., & Shapiro, G. R. (1973). Let's be an ice cream machine!: Creative dramatics. *Journal of Creative Behavior, 7*, 37–48.

Davis, G. A., Kogan, N., & Soliman, A. (1999). The Qatar creativity conference: Research and recommendations for school, family, and society. *Journal of Creative Behavior, 33*, 151–166.

Davis, G. A., Peterson, J. M., & Farley, F. H. (1973). Attitudes, motivation, sensation seeking, and belief in ESP as predictors of real creative behavior. *Journal of Creative Behavior, 7*, 31–39.

Davis, G. A., Rimm, S. B., & Seigle, D. (2011). *Education of the gifted and talented.* Boston, MA: Pearson.

de Bono, E. (1970). *Lateral thinking.* New York, NY: Harper & Row.

de Bono, E. (1973). *CoRT thinking.* Elmsford, NY: Pergamon.

de Bono, E. (1983). The direct teaching of thinking as a skill. *Phi Delta Kappan, 64*, 703–708.

de Bono, E. (1985a, September). Partnerships of the mind: Teaching society to think. *ProEducation*, 56–58.

de Bono, E. (1985b). *Six thinking hats.* New York, NY: Little, Brown.

de Bono, E. (1986). *CoRT thinking skills program.* Oxford, England: Pergamon Press.

de Bono, E. (1991). *Six action shoes.* New York, NY: HarperBusiness.

de Bono, E. (1992a). *Serious creativity*. New York, NY: Advanced Practical Thinking Training.

de Bono, E. (1992b). *Teach your child to think*. New York, NY: Penguin.

de Vries, R. E., de Vries, A., & Feij, J. A. (2009). Sensation seeking, risk-taking, and the HEXACO model of personality. *Personality and Individual Differences, 47*(6), 536–540.

DeMille, R. (1955). *Put your mother on the ceiling*. New York, NY: Viking/Compass.

Dennis, A. R., & Williams, M. L. (2003). Electronic brainstorming: Theory, research, and future directions. In P. B. Paulus & B. A. Nijstad (Eds.), *Group creativity: Innovation through collaboration* (pp. 160–178). New York, NY: Oxford University Press.

Dewey, J. (1933). *How we think*. Lexington, MA: D. C. Heath.

Dillon, J. T. (1982). Problem finding and solving. *The Journal of Creative Behavior, 16*(2), 97–111.

Domino, G. (1970). Identification of potentially creative persons from the *Adjective Check List. Journal of Consulting and Clinical Psychology, 35*, 48–51.

Dow, G. T., & Mayer, R. E. (2004). Teaching students to solve insight problems: Evidence for domain specificity in creativity training. *Creativity Research Journal, 16*(4), 389–398.

Drost, E. A. (2011). Validity and reliability in social science research. *Education Research and Perspectives, 38*(1), 105.

Drucker, P. (1989). *The new realities*. New York, NY: Harper and Row.

Dudek, S. Z. (1973). *Creativity in young children—attitude or ability*. Paper presented at the Annual Meeting of the American Psychological Association (81st, Montreal, August 27–31, 1973).

Dunbar, K. (1995). How scientists really reason: Scientific reasoning in real-world laboratories. In R. J. Sternberg & J. E. Davidson (Eds.), *The nature of insight* (pp. 365–395). Cambridge, MA: MIT Press.

Dweck, C. S., Chiu, C. Y., & Hong, Y. Y. (1995). Implicit theories and their role in judgments and reactions: A word from two perspectives. *Psychological Inquiry, 6*(4), 267–285.

Eberle, B., & Stanish, B. (1985). *CPS for kids*. Carthage, IL: Good Apple.

Eberle, P. (1971). *Scamper*. Buffalo, NY: DOK.

Edwards, M. O. (1968). A survey of problem solving courses. *Journal of Creative Behavior, 2*, 33–51.

Eichenberger, R. J. (1978). Creativity measurement through use of judgment criteria in physics. *Educational and Psychological Measurement, 38*, 221–227.

Einstein, A. (1952). Letter to Jacque Hadamard. In B. Ghiselin (Ed.), *The creative process* (pp. 43–44). Berkeley: University of California Press.

Einstein, A. (1961). *Relativity: The special and the general theory*. New York, NY: Crown.

Eisenman, R. (1964). Birth order and artistic creativity. *Journal of Individual Psychology, 20*, 183–185.

Eisenman, R., & Schussel, N. R. (1970). Creativity, birth order, and preference for symmetry. *Journal of Consulting and Clinical Psychology, 34*(2), 275.

Epstein, R. (1991). Skinner, creativity, and the problem of spontaneous behavior. *Psychological Science, 2*(6), 362–370.

Fabun, D. (1968). *You and creativity*. New York, NY: Macmillan.

Farajallah, A. K. M., & Saidam, S. M. (2018). The impact of employing the "Six Thinking Hats" strategy on the development of creative thinking skills and trends towards mathematics among sixth grade high-achieving students in mathematics. *Journal of Teaching and Teacher Education, 6*(02), 107–117.

Farley, F. H. (1986, May). The big T in personality. *Psychology Today*, 47–52.

Feist, G. J. (1998). A meta-analysis of personality in scientific and artistic creativity. *Personality and Social Psychology Review, 2*, 290–309.

Fekken, G. C. (1985). Review of *Creativity Assessment Packet*. In D. Keyser & R. Sweetland (Eds.), *Test critiques* (Vol. V). Kansas City, MO: Testing Corporation of America.

Feldhusen, J. F. (1995). Creativity: A knowledge base, metacognitive skills, and personality factors. *Journal of Creative Behavior, 29*, 255–268.

Feldhusen, J. F., & Kolloff, P. B. (1981). In R. E. Clasen, B. Robinson, D. R. Clasen, & G. Libster (Eds.), *Programming for the gifted, talented and creative: Models and methods*. Madison: University of Wisconsin-Extension.

Feldhusen, J. F., & Kolloff, P. B. (1986). The Purdue three-stage enrichment model for gifted education at the elementary level. In J. S. Renzulli (Ed.), *Systems and models for developing programs for the gifted and talented*. Mansfield Center, CT: Creative Learning Press.

Feldhusen, J. F., Denny, T., & Condon, C. F. (1965). *Manual for the creativity self-report scale*. Unpublished manuscript, Purdue University, West Lafayette, IN.

Feldman, D. H. (1994). *Beyond universals in cognitive development* (2nd ed.). Norwood, NJ: Ablex.

Feldman, D. H., Csikszentmihalyi, M., & Gardner, H. (1994). *Changing the world: A framework for the study of creativity.* Westport, CT: Praeger.

Feuerstein, R. (1980). *Instrumental enrichment.* Washington, DC: Curriculum Development Associates.

Finke, R. A., Ward, T. B., & Smith, S. M. (1992). *Creative cognition: Theory, research and application.* Cambridge, MA: MIT Press.

Flach, F. (1990). Disorders of the pathways involved in the creative process. *Creativity Research Journal, 3,* 158–165.

Fleenor, J., & Taylor, S. (2004). The assessment of creativity. In J. Thomas (Ed.), *Comprehensive Handbook of Psychological Assessment (Vol. 4): Industrial and Organizational Assessment.* New York, NY: John Wiley.

Fleming, E. S., & Weintraub, S. (1962). Attitudinal rigidity as a measure of creativity in gifted children. *Journal of Educational Psychology, 53,* 81–85.

Florida, R. (2002). *The rise of the creative class* (Vol. 9). New York, NY: Basic Books.

Flower, L., & Hayes, J. R. (1984). Images, plans, and prose. *Written Communication, 1*(1), 120–160.

Flowers, J. H., & Garbin, C. P. (1989). Creativity and perception. In J. A. Glover, R. R. Ronning, & C. R. Reynolds (Eds.), *Handbook of creativity* (pp. 147–162). New York, NY: Plenum Press.

Folmer, P. (1975). Creativity: The search for a definition. *Educational Media International, 2,* 2–7.

Frankfort, H. (1928). Sumerians, Semites, and the origin of copper-working. *The Antiquaries Journal, 8*(2), 217–235.

Freeman, J., Butcher, H. J., & Christie, T. (1968). *Creativity: A selective review of research.* London, England: Society for Research into Higher Education Ltd.

Freud, S. (1975). Creative writers and daydreaming. In A. Rothenberg & C. R. Hausman (Eds.), *The creativity question.* Durham, NC: Duke University Press.

Freud, S. (1976). Creative writers and day-dreaming (1908). In A. Rothenberg & C. R. Hausman (Eds.), *The creativity question* (pp. 48–54). Durham, NC: Duke University Press.

Galati, F. (2015). Complexity of judgment: What makes possible the convergence of expert and nonexpert ratings in assessing creativity. *Creativity Research Journal, 27*(1), 24–30.

Galton, F. (1869). *Hereditary genius: An inquiry into its laws and consequences* (Vol. 27). New York, NY: Macmillan.

Galton, F. (1876). A theory of heredity. *Journal of the Anthropological Institute of Great Britain and Ireland, 5,* 329–348.

Gardner, H. (1983). *Frames of mind: The theory of multiple intelligences.* New York, NY: Basic Books.

Gardner, H. (1993). *Creating minds.* New York, NY: Basic Books.

Gardner, H. (1999). Are there additional intelligences? The case for naturalist, spiritual, and existential intelligences. In J. Kane (Ed.), *Education, information and transformation* (pp. 111–131). Englewood Cliffs, NJ: Prentice Hall.

Gardner, H. (2011). *Creating minds: An anatomy of creativity seen through the lives of Freud, Einstein, Picasso, Stravinsky, Eliot, Graham, and Ghandi.* New York, NY: Basic Civitas Books.

Gardner, H. E. (2008). *Extraordinary minds: Portraits of 4 exceptional individuals and an examination of our own extraordinariness.* New York, NY: Basic Books.

Gassmann, O., & Zeschky, M. (2008). Opening up the solution space: The role of analogical thinking for breakthrough product innovation. *Creativity and Innovation Management, 17*(2), 97–106.

Gelade, G. (1995). Creative style and divergent production. *Journal of Creative Behavior, 29,* 36–53.

Gendrop, S. C. (1996). Effect of an intervention in synectics on the creative thinking of nurses. *Creativity Research Journal, 9*(1), 11–19.

Gentry, M. (2018). Cluster grouping. In C. M. Callahan & H. L. Hertberg-Davis (Eds.), *Fundamentals of gifted education: Considering multiple perspectives* (2nd ed., pp. 213–224). New York, NY: Routledge.

Getzels, J. W. (1979). Problem finding: A theoretical note. *Cognitive Science, 3*(2), 167–172.

Getzels, J. W., & Csikszentmihalyi, M. (1976). *The creative vision.* New York, NY: Wiley.

Getzels, J. W., & Jackson, P. W. (1962). *Creativity and intelligence.* New York, NY: Wiley.

Ghiselin, B. (Ed.). (1952). *The creative process.* New York, NY: Mentor.

Gilhooly, K. J., Georgiou, G. J., Garrison, J., Reston, J. D., & Sirota, M. (2012). Don't wait to incubate: Immediate versus delayed incubation in divergent thinking. *Memory & Cognition, 40,* 966–975.

Gilmore, M. (2014, April). *George R. R. Martin: The Rolling Stone Interview.* Retrieved from https://www.rollingstone.com/culture/culture-news/george-r-r-martin-the-rolling-stone-interview-242487/

Glasman, E. (1989, March). Creative problem solving. *Supervisory Management,* 17–18.

Glassner, J. J., & Herron, D. M. (2003). *The invention of cuneiform: Writing in Sumer.* Baltimore, MD: Johns Hopkins University Press.

Glǎveanu, V. P. (2011). Creativity as cultural participation. *Journal for the Theory of Social Behaviour, 41*, 48–67.

Glǎveanu, V. P. (2013). Rewriting the language of creativity: The Five A's framework. *Review of General Psychology, 17*(1), 69–81.

Göçmen, Ö., & Coşkun, H. (2019). The effects of the Six Thinking Hats and speed on creativity in brainstorming. *Thinking Skills and Creativity, 31*, 284–295.

Goertzel, M. G., Goertzel, V., & Goertzel, T. G. (1978). *300 eminent personalities.* San Francisco, CA: Jossey-Bass.

Goldman, C. (1991). Late bloomers: Growing older or still growing? *Generations, 15*(2), 41–48.

Golman, D. (1980, February). 1528 little geniuses and how they grew. *Psychology Today*, 28–53.

Gorder, W. D. (1980). Divergent production abilities as constructs of musical creativity. *Journal of Research in Music Education, 28*(1), 38–42.

Gordon, W. J. J. (1961). *Synectics.* New York, NY: Harper & Row.

Gordon, W. J. J. (1974a). *Making it strange* (Books 1–4). New York, NY: Harper & Row.

Gordon, W. J. J. (1974b). Some source material in discovery by analogy. *Journal of Creative Behavior, 8*, 239–257.

Gordon, W. J. J. (1987). *The new art of the possible: The basic course in synectics.* Cambridge, MA: SES Associates.

Gordon, W. J. J., & Poze, T. (1971). *Metaphorical way of learning and knowing.* Cambridge, MA: SES Associates.

Gordon, W. J. J., & Poze, T. (1972a). *Teaching is listening.* Cambridge, MA: SES Associates.

Gordon, W. J. J., & Poze, T. (1972b). *Strange and familiar.* Cambridge, MA: SES Associates.

Gordon, W. J. J., & Poze, T. (1980a). SES synectics and gifted education today. *Gifted Child Quarterly, 24*, 147–151.

Gordon, W. J. J., & Poze, T. (1980b). *The new art of the possible.* Cambridge, MA: Porpoise Books.

Gough, H. G. (1979). A creative personality scale for the Adjective Check List. *Journal of Personality and Social Psychology, 37*, 1398–1405.

Gough, H. G., & Heilbrun, A. B., Jr. (1965). *The Adjective Check List manual.* Palo Alto, CA: Consulting Psychologists Press.

Griggs, S., & Dunn, R. (1984). Selected case studies of the learning style preferences of gifted students. *Gifted Child Quarterly, 28*, 115–119.

Gruber, H. E. (1988). The evolving systems approach to creative work. *Creativity Research Journal, 1*(1), 27–51.

Guastello, S. J. (2009). Creativity and personality. In T. Rickards, M. A. Runco, & S. Moger (Eds.), *The Routledge companion to creativity* (pp. 267–278). New York, NY: Routledge/Taylor & Francis.

Guastello, S. J., Bzdawka, A., Guastello, D. D., & Rieke, M. L. (1992). Cognitive abilities and creative behaviors: CAB-5 and consequences. *Journal of Creative Behavior, 26*, 260–267.

Guilford, J. P. (1950). Creativity. *American Psychologist, 5*, 444–454.

Guilford, J. P. (1967). *The nature of human intelligence.* New York, NY: McGraw-Hill. (Creativity tests available from Consulting Psychologists Press, Palo Alto, CA.)

Guilford, J. P. (1977). *Way beyond the IQ.* Buffalo, NY: Creative Education Foundation.

Guilford, J. P. (1979). Some incubated thoughts on incubation. *Journal of Creative Behavior, 13*, 1–8.

Guilford, J. P. (1986). *Creative talents: Their nature, uses, and development.* Buffalo, NY: Bearly.

Guilford, J. P. (1988). Some changes in the structure-of-intellect model. *Educational and Psychological Measurement, 48*, 1–4.

Hadamard, J. (1945). *An essay on the psychology of invention in the mathematical field.* New York, NY: Dover.

Hagen, M., Bernard, A., & Grube, E. (2016). Do it all wrong! Using reverse-brainstorming to generate ideas, improve discussions, and move students to action. *Management Teaching Review, 1*(2), 85–90.

Hall, L. (1990, September). Can you picture that? *Training and Development Journal*, 79–81.

Hall, S. (1996). *Critical dialogues in cultural studies.* London, England: Routledge.

Halverson, E. R., & Sheridan, K. M. (2014). The maker movement in education. *Harvard Educational Review, 84*(4), 495–504.

Hamburger, M., (Ed. and Trans.). (1952). *Beethoven: Letters and journals and conversations.* New York, NY: Pantheon.

Hammerschmidt, P. K. (1996). The Kirton Adaption Innovation Inventory and group problem solving success rates. *Journal of Creative Behavior, 30*, 61–74.

Hasirci, D., & Demirkan, H. (2003). Creativity in learning environments: The case of two sixth grade art rooms. *Journal of Creative Behavior, 37*, 17–41.

Hattie, J., & Yates, G. (2014). *Visible learning and the science of how we learn*. New York, NY: Routledge.

Hélie, S., & Sun, R. (2010). Incubation, insight, and creative problem solving: A unified theory and a connectionist model. *Psychological Review, 117*(3), 994.

Helman, I. B., & Larson, S. G. (1980). *Now what do I do?* Buffalo, NY: DOK.

Hennessey, B. A., & Amabile, T. M. (1988). Story-telling: A method for assessing children's creativity. *Journal of Creative Behavior, 22*, 235–246.

Herrington, J., Reeves, T. C., & Oliver, R. (2005). Online learning as information delivery: Digital myopia. Journal of Interactive Learning Research, 16(4), 353–367.

Hetherington, E. M., & Parke, R. D. (1979). *Child psychology: A contemporary viewpoint*. New York, NY: McGraw-Hill.

Hewett, I. (2013, May 29). "Did the Rite of Spring really spark a riot?" *BBC News Magazine*. Retrieved from http://www.bbc.com/news/magazine-22691267

Higgins, J. M. (1994). *101 creative problem solving techniques*. Winter Park, FL: New Management.

Hilgard, E. R., Atkinson, R. L., & Atkinson, R. C. (1979). *Introduction to psychology* (7th ed.). New York, NY: Harcourt.

Hira, A., & Hynes, M. (2018). People, means, and activities: A conceptual framework for realizing the educational potential of makerspaces. *Education Research International*, 1–10. doi:10.1155/2018/6923617

Hittner, J. B., & Daniels, J. R. (2002). Gender-role orientation, creative accomplishments and cognitive styles. *Journal of Creative Behavior, 36*, 62–75.

Hocevar, D. (1980). Intelligence, divergent thinking, and creativity. *Intelligence, 4*, 25–40.

Hocevar, D. (1981). Measurement of creativity: Review and critique. *Journal of Personality Assessment, 45*(5), 450–464.

Hoffman, R. M., & Borders, L. D. (2001). Twenty-five years after the Bem Sex-Role Inventory: A reassessment and new issues regarding classification variability. *Measurement and Evaluation in Counseling and Development, 34*, 39–55.

Holland, J. L. (1961). Creative and academic performance among talented adolescents. *Journal of Educational Psychology, 52*, 136–147.

Holland, J. L. (1968). Test reviews. *Journal of Counseling Psychology, 15*(3), 297.

Holt, R. R. (1964). Imagery: The return of the ostracized. *American Psychologist, 19*, 254–264.

Holyoak, K. J., & Thagard, P. (1996). *Mental leaps: Analogy in creative thought*. Cambridge, MA: MIT Press.

Hood, R. (2017). The shadow's symphony: Archetypal awakening in Igor Stravinsky's *The Rite of Spring*. *Criterion: A Journal of Literary Criticism, 10*(2), 4.

Hooker, C., & Csikszentmihalyi, M. (2003). Flow, creativity, and shared leadership. In C. L. Pearce & J. A. Conger (Eds.), *Shared leadership: Reframing the hows and whys of leadership* (pp. 217–234). Thousand Oaks, CA: Sage.

Hospers, J. (1985). Artistic creativity. *The Journal of Aesthetics and Art Criticism, 43*(3), 243–255.

Houtz, J. C., & Patricola, C. (1999). Imagery. In M. A. Runco, M. A. Pritzker, S. R. Pritzker, & S. Pritzker (Eds.), *Encyclopedia of creativity* (Vol. 2, pp. 1–11). New York, NY: Elsevier.

Hunsaker, S., Odoardi, R. H., & Smith, E. V. (2012). Stages of gifted identification. In S. L. Hunsaker (Ed.), *Identification: The theory and practice of identifying students for gifted and talented education services* (pp. 197–215). Waco, TX: Prufrock Press.

Hyatt, K. S. (1992). Creativity through intrapersonal communication dialog. *Journal of Creative Behavior, 26*, 65–71.

Ironson, G., & Davis, G. A. (1979). Faking high or low creativity scores on the Adjective Check List. *Journal of Creative Behavior, 13*, 139–145.

Isaksen, S. G. (1987). Introduction: An orientation to the frontiers of creativity research. In S. G. Isaksen (Ed.), *Frontiers of creativity research: Beyond the basics* (pp. 1–26). Buffalo, NY: Bearly.

Isaksen, S. G., & Treffinger, D. J. (1985). *Creative problem solving: The basic course*. Buffalo, NY: Bearly.

Isaksen, S. G., Dorval, K. B., & Treffinger, D. J. (2000). *Creative approaches to problem solving: A framework for change*. Dubuque, IA: Kendall Hunt.

Isaksen, S. G., Dorval, K. B., & Treffinger, D. J. (2010). *Creative approaches to problem solving: A framework for innovation and change*. Thousand Oaks, CA: Sage.

Jackson, P. W., & Messick, S. (1965). The person, the product, and the response: Conceptual problems in the assessment of creativity. *Journal of Personality, 33*, 309–329.

Jamison, K. (1989). Mood disorders and patterns of creativity in British writers and artists. *Psychiatry, 52*, 125–134.

Jamison, K. R. (1993). *Touched with fire*. New York, NY: Free Press.

Jeffery, L. R. (1989). Reading and rewriting poetry: William Wordsworth. In D. B. Wallace & H. E. Gruber (Eds.), *Creative people at work: Twelve cognitive case studies*. New York, NY: Oxford University Press.

Johnsen, S. K. (2018). Evaluating the effectiveness of identification procedures. In S. K. Johnsen (Ed.), *Identifying gifted students: A practical guide* (3rd ed., pp. 151–160). Waco, TX: Prufrock Press.

Jones, G., & McFadzean, E. S. (1997). "How can Reboredo foster creativity in her current employees and nurture creative individuals who join the company in the future?", Case commentary. *Harvard Business Review, 75*(5), 50–51.

Jones, L. V., & Thissen, D. (2006). A history and overview of psychometrics. In C. R. Rao & S. Sinharay (Eds.), *Handbook of statistics* (Vol. 26, pp. 1–27). Amsterdam, Netherlands: Elsevier.

Joyce, B., Weil, M., & Calhoun, E. (2004). *Models of teaching* (7th ed.). New York, NY: Allyn & Bacon; Pearson Education.

Jung, C. G. (1933). *Psychological types*. New York, NY: Harcourt.

Jung, C. G. (1959). *The archetypes and the collective unconscious: Collected works*. New York, NY: Pantheon.

Jung, C. G. (1976). On the relation of analytic psychology to poetic art. In A. Rothenberg & C. R. Hausman (Eds.), *The creativity question* (pp. 120–126). Durham, NC: Duke University Press.

Juntune, J. E. (Producer), & 120 Creative Corner (Director). (1987). *Mindsketching: Sketching techniques to improve the power of visualization in learning and retention* [Video]. Circle Pines, MN: 120 Creative Corner.

Juntune, J. E., Kaya, F., & Tyrrell, S. (2017). Finding and serving gifted students raised in poverty. *Tempo, 38*(1), 6–11.

Kaltsoonis, B. (1971). Instruments useful in studying creative behavior and creative talents: Part I. Commercially available instruments. *Journal of Creative Behavior, 5*, 117–126.

Kaltsoonis, B. (1972). Additional instruments useful in studying creative behavior and creative talents: Part III. Noncommercially available instruments. *Journal of Creative Behavior, 6*, 268–274.

Kaltsoonis, B., & Honeywell, L. (1980). Additional instruments useful in studying creative behavior and creative talent: Part IV. Noncommercially available instruments. *Journal of Creative Behavior, 14*, 56–67.

Kang, C. (1989). *Gender differences in Korean children's responses to the Torrance Tests of Creative Thinking from first to sixth grade*. Unpublished MS thesis, University of Wisconsin, Madison.

Kanter, R. M. (1989). *When giants learn to dance*. New York, NY: Simon & Schuster.

Kaplan, S. N. (2018). Differentiating with depth and complexity. In C. M. Callahan & H. L. Hertberg-Davis (Eds.), *Fundamentals of gifted education: Considering multiple perspectives* (2nd ed., pp. 270–278). New York, NY: Routledge.

Karnes, F. A., & Riley, T. L. (1996). *Competition: Maximizing your abilities*. Waco, TX: Purfrock Press.

Karwowski, M. (2014). Creative mindsets: Measurement, correlates, consequences. *Psychology of Aesthetics, Creativity, and the Arts, 8*(1), 62.

Kashdan, T. B., & Silvia, P. (2009). Curiosity and interest: The benefits of thriving on novelty and challenge. In C. R. Snyder & S. J. Lopez (Eds.), *Oxford Handbook of Positive Psychology* (2nd ed., pp. 367–374). Oxford, England: Oxford University Press.

Kastenbaum, R. (1991). The creative impulse: Why it won't just quit. *Generations, 15*(2), 7–12.

Katz, A. N. (1980). Do left-handers tend to be more creative? *Journal of Creative Behavior, 14*, 271.

Kaufman, A. B., Kornilov, S. A., Bristol, A. S., Tan, M., & Grigorenko, E. L. (2010). The neurobiological foundation of creative cognition. In *The Cambridge handbook of creativity* (p. 216). Cambridge, England: Cambridge University Press.

Kaufman, J. C. (2001). The Sylvia Plath effect: Mental illness in eminent creative writers. *Journal of Creative Behavior, 35*, 37–50.

Kaufman, J. C., & Baer, J. (2012). Beyond new and appropriate: Who decides what is creative? *Creativity Research Journal, 24*(1), 83–91.

Kaufman, J. C., & Beghetto, R. A. (2009). Beyond big and little: The four c model of creativity. *Review of General Psychology, 13*(1), 1–12.

Kaufman, J. C., & Sternberg, R. J. (Eds.). (2010). *The Cambridge handbook of creativity*. Cambridge, England: Cambridge University Press.

Kaufman, J., & Skidmore, L. (2010). Taking the propulsion model of creative contributions into the 21st century. *Psychologie in Österreich, 5*, 378–381.

Kaufman, S. B., & Gregoire, C. (2016). *Wired to create: Unraveling the mysteries of the creative mind*. New York, NY: Penguin.

Kaur, M. (2017). Six Thinking Hats: An instructional strategy for developing creative thinking. *International Journal of Research in Social Sciences, 7*(10), 520–528.

Keating, D. P. (1980). Four faces of creativity: The continuing plight of the intellectually underserved. *Gifted Child Quarterly, 24,* 56–61.

Keeley, P. (2018). Using formative assessment probes to develop elementary learning stations. *Science & Children, 55*(9), 28–31.

Khaleefa, O. H., Erdos, G., & Ashria, I. H. (1996a). Creativity in an indigenous Afro-Arab Islamic culture: The case of Sudan. *Journal of Creative Behavior, 30,* 268–282.

Khaleefa, O. H., Erdos, G., & Ashria, I. H. (1996b). Gender and creativity in an Afro-Arab Islamic culture: The case of Sudan. *Journal of Creative Behavior, 30,* 52–60.

Khatena, J., & Torrance, E. P. (1976). *Manual for Khatena-Torrance Creative Perceptions Inventory.* Chicago, IL: Stoelting.

Kilgour, M. (2007). Big C versus little c creative findings: Domain-specific knowledge combination effects on the eminence of creative contributions. In S. Karkulehto & K. Laine (Eds.), *Call for Creative Futures Conference Proceedings* (pp. 15–35). Pori, Finland: University of Oulu, Department of Art and Anthropology.

Kim, J., Kim, D., Lee, Y., Lim, W., & Moon, I. (2009). Application of TRIZ creativity intensification approach to chemical process safety. *Journal of Loss Prevention in the Process Industries, 22*(6), 1039–1043.

Kim, K. H. (2005). Can only intelligent people be creative? *Journal of Secondary Gifted Education, 16,* 57–66.

Kim, K. H. (2006). Can we trust creativity tests? A review of the Torrance Tests of Creative Thinking (TTCT). *Creativity Research Journal, 18*(1), 3–14.

Kim, N., Belland, B. R., & Axelrod, D. (2019). Scaffolding for optimal challenge in K–12 problem-based learning. *Interdisciplinary Journal of Problem-Based Learning, 13*(1). doi:10.7771/1541-5015.1712

Kipling, R. (1952). Working tools. In B. Ghiselin (Ed.), *The creative process.* New York, NY: Mentor.

Kirton, M. J. (1976). Adaptors and innovators: A description and measure. *Journal of Applied Psychology, 61,* 622–629.

Kirton, M. J. (1987). *Kirton adaption-innovation manual* (2nd ed.). Hatfield, England: Occupational Research Center.

Kivunja, C. (2015). Using de Bono's Six Thinking Hats model to teach critical thinking and problem solving skills essential for success in the 21st-century economy. *Creative Education, 6*(03), 380.

Klein, E. E. (2000). Idea Generation Decision Tools: A Comparative Study. *AMCIS 2000 Proceedings,* 186.

Koestler, A. (1964). *The act of creation.* London, England: Hutchinson.

Kolloff, P. B., & Feldhusen, J. F. (1984). The effects of enrichment on self-concept and creative thinking. *Gifted Child Quarterly, 28,* 53–57.

Koski-Jänness, A. (1985). Alcohol and literary creativity—the Finnish experience. *Journal of Creative Behavior, 19,* 120–136.

Kosslyn, S. M. (1983). *Ghosts in the mind's machine.* New York, NY: Norton.

Kozbelt, A., Beghetto, R., & Runco, M. (2010). Theories of creativity. In J. Kaufman & R. Sternberg (Eds.), *The Cambridge handbook of creativity* (Cambridge Handbooks in Psychology, pp. 20–47). Cambridge, England: Cambridge University Press.

Krippner, S., & Murphy, G. (1976). Extrasensory perception and creativity. In A. Rothenberg & C. R. Hausman (Eds.), *The creativity question* (pp. 262–267). Durham, NC: Duke University Press.

Kris, E. (1976). On preconscious mental processes. In A. Rothenberg & C. R. Hausman (Eds.), *The creativity question* (pp. 135–143). Durham, NC: Duke University Press.

Krumnack, U., Kühnberger, K. U., Schwering, A., & Besold, T. R. (2013). Analogies and analogical reasoning in invention. In *Encyclopedia of creativity, invention, innovation, and entrepreneurship* (pp. 56–62). New York, NY: Springer.

Kubie, L. S. (1958). *Neurotic distortion of the creative process.* Lawrence: University of Kansas Press.

Kulp, M., & Tarter, B. J. (1986). The creative processes rating scale. *Creative Child and Adult Quarterly, 11,* 166–173.

Kurti, R. S., Kurti, D. L., & Fleming, L. (2014). The philosophy of educational makerspaces, *Teacher Librarian, 41*(5), 8–11.

Kwang, N. A., & Rodrigues, D. (2002). A big-five personality profile of the adaptor and innovator. *Journal of Creative Behavior, 36,* 254–268.

Land, G., & Jarman, B. (1993). *Breakpoint and beyond: Mastering the future–today.* New York, NY: HarperCollins.

Lawlor, T. M. (2013). Astronomy exercises for the artist: van Gogh the observer. *Astronomy Education Review, 12*(1), 0202.

LeBoutillier, N., & Marks, D. F. (2003). Mental imagery and creativity: A meta-analytic review study. *British Journal of Psychology, 94*(1), 29–44.

Lees-Haley, P. R. (1978). *Creative behavior inventory.* Huntsville, AL: Basic Research, Inc.

Lees-Haley, P. R., & Sutton, J. (1982). An extension of Davis' How Do You Think test to elementary school students. *Roeper Review, 4*(3), 43.

Lees-Haley, P. R., & Swords, M. (1981). A validation study of Davis' How Do You Think (HDYT) test with middle school students. *Journal for the Education of the Gifted, 4*(2), 144–146.

Leff, H. L. (1984). *Playful perception.* Burlington, VT: Waterfront Books.

Leight, E. (2019). Vinyl is poised to outsell CDs for the first time since 1986. *Rolling Stone.* Retrieved from https://www.rollingstone.com/music/music-news/vinyl-cds-revenue-growth-riaa-880959/

Leroux, J. A., & Levitt-Perlman, M. (2000). The gifted child with attention deficit disorder: An identification and intervention challenge. *Roeper Review, 22,* 171–176.

Leuner, H. (1973). Kreativität and "bewusstseinsveränderug." *Confinia Psychiatrica, 16,* 141–158.

Leung, A. K. Y., Maddux, W. W., Galinsky, A. D., & Chiu, C. Y. (2008). Multicultural experience enhances creativity: The when and how. *American Psychologist, 63*(3), 169.

Leveque, L. C. (2011). *Breakthrough creativity: Achieving top performance using the eight creative talents.* London, England: Nicholas Brealey.

Lewis, J. D. (1993). Self-actualization in junior high students: A pilot study. *Psychological Reports, 73,* 639–642.

Lewis, J. D. (1994). Self-actualization in gifted children. *Psychological Reports, 74,* 767–770.

Lewis, J. D., Karnes, F. A., & Knight, H. V. (1995). A study of self-actualization and self-concept in intellectually gifted students. *Psychology in the Schools, 32,* 52–61.

Lim, W., & Plucker, J. A. (2001). Creativity through a lens of social responsibility: Implicit theories of creativity with Korean samples. *Journal of Creative Behavior, 35*(2), 115–130.

Lindauer, M. S. (1998). Interdisciplinarity, the psychology of art, and creativity: An introduction. *Creativity Research Journal, 11*(1), 1–10.

Lipman, M. (1991). *Thinking in education.* New York, NY: Cambridge University Press.

Lombroso, C. (1895). *The man of genius.* London, England: Scribners.

Lowell, A. (1952). The process of making poetry. In B. Ghiselin (Ed.), *The creative process.* New York, NY: Mentor.

Lowes, J. L. (1927). *The road to Xanadu.* Boston, MA: Houghton Mifflin.

Lubetzky, O. (2019). Vincent van Gogh: The impact of events in his early life on his artwork. *Journal of Prenatal & Perinatal Psychology & Health, 33*(4), 314–324.

Ludwig, A. M. (1994). Mental illness and creative activity in female writers. *American Journal of Psychiatry, 151,* 1650–1656.

Ludwig, A. M. (1995). *The price of greatness.* New York, NY: Guilford Press.

Lupkowski-Shoplik, A., Benbow, C. P., Assouline, S. G., & Brody, L. E. (2003). Talent searches: Meeting the needs of academically talented youth. In N. Colangelo & G. A. Davis (Eds.), *Handbook of gifted education* (3rd ed.). Boston, MA: Allyn & Bacon.

MacFarlene, B. (Ed.). (2018). *Specialized schools for high-ability learners.* Waco, TX: Prufrock Press.

MacKinnon, D. W. (1961). Creativity in architects. In D. W. MacKinnon (Ed.), *The creative person.* Berkeley, CA: Institute of Personality Assessment and Research, University of California.

MacKinnon, D. W. (1976). Architects, personality types, and creativity. In A. Rothenberg & C. R. Hausman (Eds.), *The creativity question.* Durham, NC: Duke University Press.

MacKinnon, D. W. (1978a). Educating for creativity: A modern myth? In G. A. Davis & J. A. Scott (Eds.), *Training creative thinking.* Melbourne, FL: Krieger.

MacKinnon, D. W. (1978b). *In search of human effectiveness: Identifying and developing creativity.* Buffalo, NY: Creative Education Foundation.

MacKinnon, D. W. (1999). The creative product. In M. Joyce & S. Isaksen (Eds.), *An introduction to creativity* (2nd ed.; pp. 125–127). Acton, MA: Copley.

Majaro, S. (1988). *The creative gap: Managing ideas for profit.* London, England: Lonman.

Majid, A. K., & AL-Tarawneh, N. S. (2015). The effect of using the Six Thinking Hats method on the development of EFL female eleventh-grade students' writing skill in Southern Al-Mazar Directorate of Education. *International Journal of Arts and Humanities, 1*(4), 24–37.

Maltzman, I. (1960). On the training of originality. *Psychological Review, 67,* 229–242.

Marland, S. J. (1972). *Education of the gifted and talented. Report to the Congress of the United States by the U.S. Commissioner of Education.* Washington, DC: U.S. Government Printing Office.

Martindale, C. (July, 1975). What makes a person different? *Psychology Today,* 44–50.

Martinez, S. L., & Stager, G. (2019). *Invent to learn: Making, tinkering, and engineering in the classroom* (2nd ed.). Torrance, CA: Constructing Modern Knowledge Press.

Martinsen, Ø. L. (2011). The creative personality: A synthesis and development of the creative person profile. *Creativity Research Journal, 23*(3), 185–202.

Maslow, A. H. (1954). *Motivation and personality.* New York, NY: Harper.

Maslow, A. H. (1968). *Toward a psychology of being* (2nd ed.). Princeton, NJ: Van Nostrand.

Maslow, A. H. (1970). *Motivation and personality* (2nd ed.). New York, NY: Harper & Row.

Maslow, A. H. (1971). *The farther reaches of human nature.* New York, NY: Viking Press.

Mason, J. G. (1960). *How to be a more creative executive.* New York, NY: McGraw-Hill.

Mattimore, B. W. (1990). Mind blasters: Software to shatter brain block. *Success,* 46–47.

May, R. (1959). The nature of creativity. In H. H. Anderson (Ed.), *Creativity and its cultivation* (pp. 55–68). New York, NY: Harper & Row.

May, R. (1994). *The courage to create.* New York, NY: W. W. Norton.

McConnell, T. J., Parker, J., & Eberhardt, J. (2017). *Problem-based learning in the earth and space science classroom K-12.* Arlington, VA: NSTA Press.

McCune, J. C. (1992, July/August). Creativity catalysts. *Success,* 50.

McDonough, P., & McDonough, B. (1987). A survey of American colleges and universities on the conducting of formal courses in creativity. *Journal of Creative Behavior, 21*(4), 271–282.

McKee, M. G. (1985). Review of Creativity Attitude Survey. In D. Keyser & R. Sweetland (Eds.), *Test critiques* (Vol. V). Kansas City, MO: Testing Corporation of America.

McNair, A. (2017). *Genius hour.* Waco, TX: Prufrock Press.

Mednick, M. T., & Andrews, F. M. (1967). Creative thinking and level of intelligence. *Journal of Creative Behavior, 1,* 428–431.

Mednick, S. A. (1962). The associative basis of the creative process. *Psychological Review, 69,* 220–232.

Mednick, S. A. (1967). *Remote associates test.* Boston, MA: Houghton Mifflin.

Meeker, M. (1969). *The structure of intellect: Its use and interpretation.* Columbus, OH: Merrill.

Meeker, M. (1978). Nondiscriminatory testing procedures to assess giftedness in Black, Chicano, Navajo and Anglo children. In A. Baldwin, G. Gear, & L. Lucito (Eds.), *Educational planning for the gifted.* Reston, VA: Council for Exceptional Children.

Meeker, M., & Meeker, R. (1986). The SOI system for gifted education. In J. S. Renzulli (Ed.), *Systems and models for developing programs for the gifted and talented* (pp. 194–215). Mansfield Center, CT: Creative Learning Press.

Meeker, M., Meeker, R., & Roid, G. (1985). Structure-of-intellect learning abilities test (SOI-LA). Los Angeles, CA: Western Psychological Services.

Menaker, E. (1996). *Separation, will and creativity: The wisdom of Otto Rank.* London, England: Jason Aronson.

Merrotsy, P. (2013). A note on big-C Creativity and little-c creativity. *Creativity Research Journal, 25*(4), 474–476.

Metcalfe, J., & Wiebe, D. (1987). Intuition in insight and noninsight problem solving. *Memory & Cognition, 15*(3), 238–246.

Michael, W. B., & Colson, K. R. (1979). The development and validation of a life experience inventory for the identification of creative electrical engineers. *Educational and Psychological Measurement, 39,* 463–470.

Michael, W. B., & Wright, C. R. (1989). Psychometric issues in the assessment of creativity. In *Handbook of creativity* (pp. 33–52). Boston, MA: Springer.

Michalko, M. (2006). *Thinkertoys: A handbook of creative-thinking techniques* (revised ed.). Berkeley, CA: Ten Speed Press.

Millar, G. W. (1995). *The creativity man: An authorized biography.* Norwood, NJ: Ablex.

Moon, S. M., Kolloff, P., Robinson, A., Dixon, F., & Feldhusen, J. (2009). The Purdue Three-Stage Model. In J. S. Renzulli, E. J. Gubbins, K. S. McMillen, R. D. Eckert, & C. A. Little (Eds.), *Systems & models for developing programs for the gifted and talented* (2nd ed., pp. 289–321). Waco, TX: Prufrock Press.

Morelock, M. J., & Feldman, D. H. (1997). High IQ children, extreme precocity, and savant syndrome. In N. Colangelo & G. A. Davis (Eds.), *Handbook of gifted education* (2nd ed., pp. 439–459). Boston, MA: Allyn & Bacon.

Morelock, M. J., & Feldman, D. H. (2003). Extreme precocity: Prodigies, savants, and children of extraordinarily high IQ. In N. Colangelo & G. A. Davis (Eds.), *Handbook of gifted education* (3rd ed., pp. 455–469). Boston, MA: Allyn & Bacon.

Morgan, D. N. (1953). Creativity today: A constructive analytic review of certain philosophical and psychological work. *The Journal of Aesthetics and Art Criticism, 12*(1), 1–24.

Moss, M. A. (1991). *The meaning and measurement of Jung's construct of intuition: Intuition and creativity.* Unpublished doctoral dissertation, University of Wisconsin, Madison.

Moustakis, C. E. (1967). *Creativity and conformity.* Princeton, NJ: Van Nostrand.

Moyer, J., & Wallace, D. (1995). Issues in education: Nurturing the creative majority of our schools— A response. *Childhood Education, 72*(1), 34–35.

Mozart, W. A. (1952). A letter. In B. Ghiselin (Ed.), *The creative process.* New York, NY: Mentor.

Mudd, S. (1995). Suggestive parallels between Kirton's A-I theory of creative style and Koestler's bisociative theory of the creative act. *Journal of Creative Behavior, 29*, 240–254.

Mumford, M. D., Mobley, M. I., Uhlman, C. E., Reiter-Palmon, R., & Doares, L. M. (1991). Process analytic models of creative capacities. *Creativity Research Journal, 4*, 91–122.

Murphy, G. (1963). Creativity and its relation to extrasensory perception. *Journal of the American Society for Psychical Research, 57*, 203–204.

Mushens, J. (2015). *Get started in writing young adult fiction.* London, England: John Murray Press.

Myers, R. E., & Torrance, E. P. (1966). *Plots, puzzles and ploys.* Boston, MA: Ginn.

Newell, A., Shaw, J. C., & Simon, H. A. (1962). In H. E. Gruber, G. Terrell, & M. Wertheimer (Eds.), *Contemporary approaches to creative thinking* (pp. 63–119). New York, NY: Atherton.

Nicholls, J. G. (1972). Creativity in a person who will never produce anything original and useful: The concept of creativity as a normally distributed trait. *American Psychologist, 27*, 717–727.

Nietzsche, F. (1952). Composition of Thus Spoke Zarathustra. In B. Ghiselin (Ed.), *The creative process.* New York, NY: Mentor.

Niu, W., & Sternberg, R. J. (2002). Contemporary studies on the concept of creativity: The east and the west. *Journal of Creative Behavior, 36*, 269–288.

Norlander, T. (1999). Inebriation and inspiration? A review of the research on alcohol and creativity. *Journal of Creative Behavior, 33*, 22–44.

Norlander, T., Erixon, A., & Archer, T. (2000). Psychological androgyny and creativity: Dynamics of gender-role and personality traits. *Social Behavior and Personality, 28*, 423–436.

Norman, D. A. (1976). *Memory and attention: An introduction to human information processing* (2nd ed.). New York, NY: Wiley.

Nunamaker, J., Applegate, L. M., & Konsynski, B. R. (1987). Facilitating group creativity: Experience with a group decision support system. *Journal of Management Information Systems, 3*, 5–19.

Nunamaker, L., Briggs, R. W., & Mittleman, D. (1995). Electronic meeting systems: Ten years of lessons learned. In D. Coleman & R. Khanna (Eds.), *Groupware: Technology and applications* (pp. 149–193). Englewood Cliffs, NJ: Prentice-Hall.

Nunnally, J. C. (1978). *Psychometric theory.* New York, NY: McGraw-Hill.

O'Connor, A. J., Nemeth, C. J., & Akutsu, S. (2013). Consequences of beliefs about the malleability of creativity. *Creativity Research Journal, 25*(2), 155–162.

O'Quin, K., & Besemer, S. P. (1989). The development, reliability, and validity of the revised creative product semantic scale. *Creativity Research Journal, 2*(4), 267–278.

O'Quin, K., & Derks, P. (1997). Humor and creativity: A review of the empirical literature. *Creativity Research Handbook, 1*, 223–252.

Okuda, S. M., Runco, M. A., & Berger, D. E. (1991). Creativity and the finding and solving of real-world problems. *Journal of Psychoeducational Assessment, 9*, 45–53.

Orloff, M. (2003). *Inventive thinking through TRIZ: A practical guide.* Berlin, Germany: Springer.

Osborn, A. F. (1953). *Applied imagination.* New York, NY: Charles Scribner.

Osborn, A. F. (1963). *Applied imagination* (3rd ed.). New York, NY: Scribners.

Pappano, L. (2014, February 5). Learning to think outside the box. *The New York Times.* Retrieved from https://www.nytimes.com/2014/02/09/education/edlife/creativity-becomes-an-academic-discipline.html

Parke, B. N., & Byrnes, P. (1984). Toward objectifying the measurement of creativity. *Roeper Review, 6*, 216–218.

Parkhurst, H. B. (1999). Confusion, lack of consensus, and the definition of creativity as a construct. *The Journal of Creative Behavior, 33*(1), 1–21.

Parnes, S. J. (1961). Effects of extended effort in creative problem solving. *Journal of Educational Psychology, 53,* 117–122.

Parnes, S. J. (1978). Can creativity be increased? In G. A. Davis & J. A. Scott (Eds.), *Training creative thinking* (pp. 270–275). Melbourne, FL: Krieger.

Parnes, S. J. (1981). *Magic of your mind.* Buffalo, NY: Bearly.

Parnes, S. J., Noller, R. B., & Biondi, A. M. (1976). *Creative action book.* New York, NY: Scribners.

Paul, R., Binker, A. J. A., Martin, D., Vetrano, C., & Kreklau, H. (1989). *Critical thinking handbook: A guide for remodeling lesson plans in language arts, social studies, and science* (6th–9th grades). Rohnert Park, CA: Sonoma State University, Center for Critical Thinking and Moral Critique.

Perkins, D. A. (1988). The possibility of invention. In R. J. Sternberg (Ed.), *The nature of creativity: Contemporary psychological perspectives* (pp. 362–385). New York, NY: Cambridge University Press.

Perry, D. (1993). *Backtalk: Women writers speak out.* New Brunswick, NJ: Rutgers University Press.

Peters, T. (1992). *Liberation management.* New York, NY: Knopf.

Peterson, J. M., & Lansky, L. M. (1980). Success in architecture: Handedness and/or visual thinking. *Perceptual and Motor Skills, 50,* 1139–1143.

Peterson, L., & Scharber, C. (2018). Learning about makerspaces: Professional development with K-12 in-service educators. *Journal of Digital Learning in Teacher Education, 34*(1), 43–52. doi:10.1080/2153297 4.2017.1387833

Petkus, E., Jr. (1994). Ninja secrets of creativity. *Journal of Creative Behavior, 28,* 133–140.

Piaget, J. (1970). Piaget's theory. In P. H. Mussen (Ed.), *Handbook of child psychology* (3rd ed., Vol. 1, pp. 703–732). New York, NY: Wiley.

Piechowski, M. (2003). Emotional and spiritual giftedness. In N. Colangelo & G. A. Davis (Eds.), *Handbook of gifted education* (3rd ed., pp. 285–306). Boston, MA: Allyn and Bacon.

Piechowski, M. M. (1997). Emotional giftedness: The measure of intrapersonal intelligence. In N. Colangelo & G. A. Davis (Eds.), *Handbook of gifted education* (2nd ed., pp. 366–381). Boston, MA: Allyn & Bacon.

Piers, E. V., & Kirchner, E. P. (1971). Productivity and uniqueness in continued word association as a function of subject creativity and stimulus properties. *Journal of Personality, 39*(2), 264–276.

Piers, E. V., Daniels, J. M., & Quackenbush, J. F. (1960). The identification of creativity in adolescents. *Journal of Educational Psychology, 51,* 346–351.

Piirto, J. (2011). Creativity for 21st-century skills. In *Creativity for 21st-century skills* (pp. 1–12). Rotterdam, Netherlands: Sense Publishers.

Plucker, J. A. (2001). Introduction to the special issue: Commemorating Guilford's 1950 presidential address. *Creativity Research Journal, 13*(3–4), 247.

Plucker, J. A., & Beghetto, R. A. (2003). Why not be creative when we enhance creativity? In J. H. Borland (Ed.), Rethinking gifted education (pp. 215–226). New York, NY: Teachers College Press.

Plucker, J. A., & Renzulli, J. S. (1999). Psychometric approaches to the study of human creativity. In R. J. Sternberg (Ed.), *Handbook of creativity* (pp. 35–61). Cambridge, England: Cambridge University Press.

Plucker, J. A., & Runco, M. A. (1998). The death of creativity measurement has been greatly exaggerated: Current issues, recent advances, and future directions creativity assessment. *Roeper Review, 21,* 36–39.

Plucker, J. A., Beghetto, R. A., & Dow, G. T. (2010). Why isn't creativity more important to educational psychologists? Potentials, pitfalls, and future directions in creativity research. *Educational Psychologist, 39,* 83–96.

Plucker, J. A., Makel, M. C., & Qian, M. (2019). Assessment of creativity. In *The Cambridge handbook of creativity* (2nd ed., pp. 44–68). Cambridge, England: Cambridge University Press.

Poincaré, J. H. (1952). Mathematical creation. In B. Ghiselin (Ed.), *The creative process.* New York, NY: Mentor.

Porshe, J. D. (1955, October). *Creative ability: Its role in the search for new products.* Paper presented at the Special Conference on Managing Product Research and Development, American Management Association, New York, NY.

Post, F. (1994). Creativity and psychopathology: A study of 291 would-famous men. *British Journal of Psychiatry, 165,* 22–34.

Preston, J. H. (1952). A conversation with Gertrude Stein. In B. Ghiselin (Ed.), *The creative process.* New York, NY: Mentor.

Prince, G. (1968). The operational mechanism of synectics. *Journal of Creative Behavior, 2,* 1–13.

Prince, G. (1982). Synectics. In S. A. Olsen (Ed.), *Group planning and problem solving methods in engineering.* New York, NY: Wiley.

Pryor, K. W., Haag, R., & O'Reilly, J. (1969). The creative porpoise: Training for novel behavior. *Journal of the Experimental Analysis of Behavior, 12,* 653–661.

Puccio, G. J., & Cabra, J. F. (2010). Organizational creativity: A systems approach. In J. C. Kaufman & R. J. Sternberg (Eds.), *The Cambridge handbook of creativity* (pp. 145–173). Cambridge, England: Cambridge University Press.

Puccio, G. J., Mance, M., & Murdock, M. C. (2010). *Creative leadership: Skills that drive change.* Thousand Oaks, CA: Sage.

Puccio, G. J., Treffinger, D. J., & Talbot, R. J. (1995). Exploratory examination of relationships between creativity styles and creative products. *Creativity Research Journal, 8,* 157–172.

Ramos, S. J. (2017). Building academic literacy of gifted children from poverty using mindsketching: Research to practice. *Tempo, 38*(1), 21–25.

Ramos-Ford, V., & Gardner, H. (1997). Giftedness from a multiple intelligences perspective. In N. Colangelo & G. A. Davis (Eds.), *Handbook of gifted education* (2nd ed., pp. 54–66). Boston, MA: Allyn & Bacon.

Rank, O. (1932). *Art and artist.* New York, NY: Knopf.

Rank, O. (1945). *Will therapy, truth, and reality.* New York, NY: Knopf.

Read, G. M. (1955). *Profile of human materials.* Paper presented at the Centennial Symposium on Modern Engineering. University of Pennsylvania, Philadelphia, PA.

Reis, S. M., & Burns, D. E. (1987). A schoolwide enrichment team invites you to read about methods for promoting community and faculty involvement in a gifted educational program. *Gifted Child Today, 49*(2), 27–32.

Reis, S. M., & Renzulli, J. S. (2018). The School-wide Enrichment Model: A focus on student creative productivity, strengths, and interests. In C. M. Callahan & H. L. Hertberg-Davis (Eds.), *Fundamentals of gifted education: Considering multiple perspectives* (2nd ed., pp. 252–278). New York, NY: Routledge.

Reiter-Palmon, R., Mumford, M. D., O'Connor Boes, J., & Runco, M. A. (1997). Problem construction and creativity: The role of ability, cue consistency, and active processing. *Creativity Research Journal, 10,* 9–23.

Renzulli, J. S. (1977). *Enrichment triad model.* Mansfield, CT: Creative Learning Press.

Renzulli, J. S. (1983, September/October). Rating the behavioral characteristics of superior students. *G/C/T,* 30–35.

Renzulli, J. S. (1994). *Schools for talent development: A practical plan for total school improvement.* Mansfield Center, CT: Creative Learning Press.

Renzulli, J. S. (2003). Conceptions of giftedness and its relationship to the development of social capital. In N. Colangelo & G. A. Davis (Eds.), *Handbook of gifted education* (3rd ed., pp. 75–87). Boston, MA: Allyn & Bacon.

Renzulli, J. S. (2018). The multiple menu model: A guide for developing gifted differentiated curriculum and instruction. In C. M. Callahan & H. L. Hertberg-Davis (Eds.), *Fundamentals of gifted education: Considering multiple perspectives* (2nd ed., pp. 252–278). New York, NY: Routledge.

Renzulli, J. S., & Reis, S. M. (1997). *Schoolwide enrichment model: A how-to guide for educational excellence* (2nd ed.). Mansfield Center, CT: Creative Learning Press.

Renzulli, J. S., & Reis, S. M. (2003). The schoolwide enrichment model: Developing creative and productive giftedness. In N. Colangelo & G. A. Davis (Eds.), *Handbook of gifted education* (3rd ed., pp. 184–203). Boston, MA: Allyn & Bacon.

Renzulli, J. S., Smith, L., White, A., Callahan, C., & Hartman, R. (2001). *Scales for rating the behavioral characteristics of superior students* (Rev. ed., Manual and nine rating scales). Mansfield Center, CT: Creative Learning Press.

Rhodes, M. (1961). An analysis of creativity. *The Phi Delta Kappan, 42*(7), 305–310.

Rhodes, M. (1987). An analysis of creativity. In S. G. Isaksen (Ed.), *Frontiers of creativity research: Beyond the basics* (pp. 216–222). Buffalo, NY: Bearly.

Rich, G. J. (2009). Big C, little c, Big M, little m. *American Psychologist, 64,* 155–156.

Richards, R. (2010). Everyday creativity: Process and way of life—Four key issues. In J. C. Kaufman & R. J. Sternberg (Eds.), *The Cambridge handbook of creativity* (pp. 189–215). New York, NY: Cambridge University Press.

Richards, R. L. (1981). Relationships between creativity and psychopathology: An evaluation and interpretation of the evidence. *Genetic Psychology Monographs, 103,* 261–324.

Richards, R. L. (1990). Everyday creativity, eminent creativity, and health. *Creativity Research Journal, 3,* 300–326.

Richards, R. L., Kinney, D. K., Lunde, I., Benet, M., & Merzel, A. P. C. (1988). Creativity in manic-depressives, cyclothymes, their normal relatives, and control subjects. *Journal of Abnormal Psychology, 97,* 281–288.

Rimm, S. B. (1976). *GIFT: Group inventory for finding creative talent*. Watertown, WI: Educational Assessment Service.

Rimm, S. B. (1983). *Preschool and kindergarten interest descriptor*. Watertown, WI: Educational Assessment Service.

Rimm, S. B., & Davis, G. A. (1976). GIFT: An instrument for the identification of creativity. *Journal of Creative Behavior, 10*, 178–182.

Rimm, S. B., & Davis, G. A. (1979). *Group inventory for finding interests. I*. Watertown, WI: Educational Assessment Service.

Rimm, S. B., & Davis, G. A. (1980). Five years of international research with GIFT: An instrument for the identification of creativity. *Journal of Creative Behavior, 14*, 35–46.

Rimm, S. B., & Davis, G. A. (1983, September/October). Identifying creativity, Part II. *G/C/T*, 19–23.

Roberts, J. L., & Inman, T. F. (2015). *Strategies for differentiating instruction: Best practices for the classroom* (3rd ed.). Waco, TX: Prufrock Press.

Robinson, K. (2006). *Sir Ken Robinson: Do schools kill creativity?* TED Ideas Worth Spreading. Retrieved from http://temoa.tec.mx/node/1595

Robinson, K. (2006, February). Ken Robinson: How school kills creativity [Video file]. Retrieved from http://www.ted.com/talks/ken_robinson_says_schools_kill_creativity.html

Roe, A. (1972). Patterns of productivity in scientists. *Science, 176*, 940–941.

Roeper, G. A., & Ruff, M. (2016). Learning and creativity. *Roeper Review, 38*(4), 222–227.

Rogers, C. R. (1962). Toward a theory of creativity. In S. J. Parnes & H. F. Harding (Eds.), *A source book for creative thinking* (pp. 63–72). New York, NY: Scribners.

Rothenberg, A., & Hausman, C. R. (Eds.). (1975). *The creativity question*. Durham, NC: Duke University Press.

Rubenson, D. L. (1991). Creativity, economics, and baseball. *Creativity Research Journal, 4*, 205–209.

Rubenson, D. L., & Runco, M. A. (1992). The economics of creativity, and the psychology of economics: Arejoinder. *New Ideas in Psychology, 10*, 173–178.

Rudowicz, E., & Hui, A. (1997). The creative personality: Hong Kong perspective. *Journal of Social Behavior and Personality, 12*, 139–148.

Rugg, H. (1963). *Imagination: An inquiry into the sources and conditions that stimulate creativity*. New York, NY: Harper & Row.

Runco, M. A. (1987). The generality of creative performance in gifted and nongifted children. *Gifted Child Quarterly, 31*, 121–125.

Runco, M. A. (1990). Implicit theories and ideational creativity. In M. A. Runco & R. S. Albert (Eds.), *Theories of creativity* (pp. 234–252). Newbury Park, CA: Sage.

Runco, M. A. (1998). Suicide and creativity: The case of Sylvia Plath. *Death Studies, 22*, 637–654.

Runco, M. A. (1999a). Appendix II: Test of creativity. In M. A. Runco & S. R. Pritzker (Eds.), *Encyclopedia of creativity*. San Diego, CA: Academic Press.

Runco, M. A. (1999b). Implicit theories. In M. A. Runco & S. R. Pritzker (Eds.), *Encyclopedia of creativity*. San Diego, CA: Academic Press.

Runco, M. A. (2006). *Reasoning and personal creativity*. In J. C. Kaufman & J. Baer (Eds.), *Knowledge and reason in cognitive development* (pp. 99–116). Cambridge, England: Cambridge University Press.

Runco, M. A. (2014). *Creativity: Theories and themes: Research, development, and practice* (2nd ed.). San Diego, CA: Elsevier Academic.

Runco, M. A. (Ed.). (1994). *Problem finding, problem solving, and creativity*. Santa Barbara, CA: Greenwood.

Runco, M. A., & Albert, R. S. (Eds.). (1990). *Theories of creativity*. Newbury Park, CA: Sage.

Runco, M. A., & Jaeger, G. J. (2012). The standard definition of creativity. *Creativity Research Journal, 24*(1), 92–96.

Runco, M. A., & Nemiro, J. (1994). Problem finding, creativity, and giftedness. *Roeper Review, 16*(4), 235–241.

Runco, M. A., & Okuda, S. M. (1988). Problem discovery, divergent thinking, and the creative process. *Journal of Youth and Adolescence, 17*(3), 211–220.

Runco, M. A., Ebersole, P., & Mraz, W. (1991). Creativity and self-actualization. *Journal of Social Behavior and Personality, 6*(5), 161–167.

Runco, M. A., Johnson, D. J., & Bear, P. K. (1993). Parents' and teachers' implicit theories of children's creativity. *Child Study Journal, 23*, 91–113.

Runco, M. A., Millar, G., Acar, S., & Cramond, B. (2010). Torrance tests of creative thinking as predictors of personal and public achievement: A fifty-year follow-up. *Creativity Research Journal, 22*(4), 361–368.

Runco, M. A., Okuda, S. M., & Hwang, S. R. (1987). *Creativity, extracurricular activity, and divergent thinking as predictors of mathematics and science performance by talented students.* (Eric Document ED279523)

Runco, M. A., Okuda, S. M., & Thurston, B. J. (1988). Psychometric properties of four systems for scoring divergent thinking tests. *Journal of Psychoeducational Assessment, 5,* 149–156.

Sadowski, M., & Paivio, A. (2013). *Imagery and text: A dual coding theory of reading and writing* (2nd ed.). New York, NY: Routledge.

Saeki, N., Fan, X., & Van Dusen, L. (2001). A comparative study of creative thinking of American and Japanese college students. *Journal of Creative Behavior, 35,* 24–36.

Santrock, J. W. (1996). *Child development* (7th ed.). Dubuque, IA: Brown & Benchmark.

Sawyer, K. (2019). *The creative classroom: Innovative teaching for 21st-century learners.* New York, NY: Teachers College Press.

Saxon, J. A., Treffinger, D. J., Young, G. C., & Wittig, C. V. (2003). Camp invention: A creative, inquiry-based summer enrichment program for elementary students. *Journal of Creative Behavior, 37,* 64–74.

Scandura, J.M. (1977). Problem Solving. New York: Academic Press

Schaefer, C. E. (1969). Imaginary companions and creative adolescents. *Developmental Psychology, 1,* 747–749.

Schaefer, C. E. (1970). *Biographical Inventory–Creativity.* San Diego, CA: Educational and Industrial Testing Service.

Schaefer, C. E. (1971). *Creativity attitude survey.* Jacksonville, IL: Psychologists & Educators, Inc.

Schatz, E. M., & Buckmaster, L. R. (1984). Development of an instrument to measure self-actualizing grown in preadolescents. *Journal of Creative Behavior, 18,* 263–272.

Schiever, S. W., & Maker, C. J. (1997). Enrichment and acceleration: An overview and new directions. In N. Colangelo & G. A. Davis (Eds.), *Handbook of gifted education* (2nd ed., pp. 113–125). Boston, MA: Allyn & Bacon.

Schilling, M. A. (2005). A "small-world" network model of cognitive insight. *Creativity Research Journal, 17*(2–3), 131–154.

Schlichter, C. (1997). Talents unlimited model in programs for gifted students. In N. Colangelo & G. A. Davis (Eds.), *Handbook of gifted education* (2nd ed., pp. 318–334). Boston, MA: Allyn & Bacon.

Schmidhuber, J. (2006). Developmental robotics, optimal artificial curiosity, creativity, music, and the fine arts. *Connection Science, 18,* 173–187.

Schoemaker, P. J. H., & van der Heijden, C. A. J. M. (1992, May–June). Integrating scenarios into strategic planning at Royal Dutch Shell. *Planning Review,* 41–46.

Schubert, D. S. P., Wagner, M. D., & Schubert, H. J. P. (1977). Family constellation and creativity: Firstborn predominance among classical music composers. *Journal of Psychology, 95,* 147–149.

Schuldberg, D. (1990). Schizotypal and hypomanic traits, creativity, and psychological health. *Creativity Research Journal, 13,* 219–232.

Schuldberg, D. (1993). Personal resourcefulness: Positive aspects of functioning in high-risk research. *Psychiatry, 56,* 137–152.

Schuldberg, D., French, C., Stone, B. L., & Heberle, J. (1988). Creativity and schizotypal traits: Creativity test scores and perceptual aberration, magical ideation, and impulsive nonconformity. *Journal of Nervous and Mental Disease, 176,* 648–657.

Seidel, G. J. (1962). *The crisis in creativity.* Notre Dame, IN: University of Notre Dame Press.

Selby, E. C., Treffinger, D. F., Isaksen, S. G., & Powers, S. V. (1993). Use of the Kirton Adaption-Innovation Inventory with middle school students. *Journal of Creative Behavior, 27,* 223–235.

Senge, P., Cambron-McCabe, N., Lucas, T., Smith, B., Dutton, J., & Kleiner, A. (2000). *Schools that learn.* New York, NY: Doubleday.

Serrat, O. (2017). The SCAMPER technique. In O. Serrat (Ed.), *Knowledge solutions* (pp. 311–314). Singapore: Springer.

Shakespeare, W. (2012). Sonnet 18. In S. Greenblatt (Ed.), *The Norton anthology of English literature* (9th ed.; pp. 1172–1173). New York, NY: Norton.

Shallcross, D. J. (1981). *Teaching creative behavior.* Englewood Cliffs, NJ: Prentice-Hall.

Shaw, M. P. (1989). The eureka process: A structure for the creative experience in science and engineering. *Creativity Research Journal, 2,* 286–298.

Sheerer, M. (1963). Problem solving. *Scientific American, 208*(4), 118–128.

Shelley, M. W., Gavarni, P., Von, H. T., Schiller, F. A., Spottiswoode, R., & Henry Colburn and Richard Bentley (Firm). (1831). *Frankenstein, or, The modern Prometheus*. London, England: Henry Colburn and Richard Bentley.

Shields, S. (1989). *Creativity of radio announcers*. Unpublished Doctoral Dissertation, University of Wisconsin, Madison.

Shobe, E. R., Ross, N. M., & Fleck, J. I. (2009). Influence of handedness and bilateral eye movements on creativity. *Brain and Cognition, 71*(3), 204–214.

Shostrum, E. L. (1963). *Personal orientation inventory*. San Diego, CA: Educational and Industrial Testing Service.

Shostrum, E. L. (1975). *Personal orientation dimensions*. San Diego, CA: Educational and Industrial Testing Service.

Shurkin, J. (1992). *Terman's kids: The groundbreaking study of how the gifted grow up*. Boston, MA: Little-Brown.

Siau, K. L. (1995). Group creativity and technology. *Journal of Creative Behavior, 29*, 201–216.

Silverman, L. K. (2013). *Giftedness 101*. New York, NY: Springer.

Silvia, P. J. (2008a). Another look at creativity and intelligence: Exploring higher-order models and probable confounds. *Personality and Individual Differences, 44*(4), 1012–1021.

Silvia, P. J. (2008b). Creativity and intelligence revisited: A latent variable analysis of Wallach and Kogan. *Creativity Research Journal, 20*(1), 34–39.

Silvia, P. J., & Kaufman, J. C. (2010). Creativity and mental illness. In J. C. Kaufman & R. J. Sternberg (Eds.), *The Cambridge handbook of creativity* (pp. 381–394). Cambridge, England: Cambridge University Press.

Silvia, P. J., Beaty, R. E., Nussbaum, E. C., Eddington, K. M., Levin-Aspenson, H., & Kwapil, T. R. (2014). Everyday creativity in daily life: An experience-sampling study of "little c" creativity. *Psychology of Aesthetics, Creativity, and the Arts, 8*(2), 183.

Simberg, A. S. (1978). Blocks to creative thinking. In G. A. Davis & J. A. Scott (Eds.), *Training creative thinking*. Melbourne, FL: Krieger.

Simonton, D. K. (1988a). Creativity, leadership, and chance. In R. J. Sternberg (Ed.), *The nature of creativity: Contemporary psychological perspectives* (pp. 386–426). New York, NY: Cambridge University Press.

Simonton, D. K. (1988b). *Scientific Genius: A psychology of science*. Cambridge, England: Cambridge University Press.

Simonton, D. K. (1990). History, chemistry, psychology, and genius: An intellectual autobiography of histrionomy. In M. A. Runco & R. S. Albert (Eds.), *Theories of creativity*. Newbury Park, CA: Sage.

Simonton, D. K. (1994). *Greatness: Who makes history and why*. New York, NY: Guilford Press.

Simonton, D. K. (1997). When does giftedness becomes genius? And when not? In N. Colangelo & G. A. Davis (Eds.), *Handbook of gifted education* (3rd ed., pp. 358–370). Boston, MA: Allyn & Bacon.

Simonton, D. K. (2010). Creativity in highly eminent individuals. In J. C. Kaufman & R. J. Sternberg (Eds.), *The Cambridge handbook of creativity* (pp. 174–188). Cambridge, England: Cambridge University Press.

Simonton, D. K. (2013). What is a creative idea? Little-c versus Big-C creativity. *Handbook of Research on Creativity, 2*, 69–83.

Simonton, D. K. (2017). Big-C versus little-c creativity: Definitions, implications, and inherent educational contradictions. In *Creative contradictions in education* (pp. 3–19). New York, NY: Springer.

Sio, U. N., & Ormerod, T. C. (2009). Does incubation enhance problem solving? A metaanalytic review. *Psychological Bulletin, 135*, 94–120.

Skagen, A. (1991, October). Creativity tools: Versatile problem solvers that can double as fun and games. *Supervisory Management*, 1–2.

Skinner, B. F. (1971). *Beyond freedom and dignity*. New York, NY: Knopf.

Skinner, B. F. (1972). *Cumulative record: A selection of papers* (3rd ed.). Englewood Cliffs, NJ: Prentice-Hall.

Skura, M. (1980). Creativity: Transgressing the limits of consciousness. *Daedalus, 109*(2), 127–146.

Smith, E. (1985, September 30). Are you creative? *Business Week*, pp. 80–84.

Smith, G. F. (1998). Idea-generation techniques: A formulary of active ingredients. *Journal of Creative Behavior, 32*, 107–133.

Smith, G. J. W., & Carlsson, I. (1987). A new creativity test. *Journal of Creative Behavior, 21*, 7–14.

Smith, J. M. (1966). *Setting conditions for creative teaching in the elementary school*. Boston, MA: Allyn & Bacon.

Snow, R. E. (1986). Individual differences and the design of educational programs. *American Psychologist, 41*, 1029–1039.

Solomon, G. T., & Winslow, E. K. (1988). Toward a descriptive profile of the entrepreneur. *Journal of Creative Behavior, 22,* 162–171.

Solomon, G. T., & Winslow, E. K. (1993). Entrepreneurs: Architects of innovation, paradigm pioneers and change. *Journal of Creative Behavior, 27,* 75–88.

Solso, R. L. (1991). *Cognitive psychology.* Boston, MA: Allyn & Bacon.

Somers, J. V., & Yawkey, T. D. (1984). Imaginary play companions: Contributions of creativity and intellectual abilities of young children. *Journal of Creative Behavior, 18,* 77–89.

Sordia, N., Martskvishvili, K., & Neubauer, A. (2019). From creative potential to creative achievements: Do emotional traits foster creativity? *Swiss Journal of Psychology, 78*(3–4), 115–123.

Sosniak, L. A. (2003). Developing talent: Time, talent, and context. In N. Colangelo & G. A. Davis (Eds.), *Handbook of gifted education* (3rd ed., pp. 247–253). Boston, MA: Allyn & Bacon.

Sousa, D. A., & Tomlinson, C. A. (2018). *Differentiation and the brain* (2nd ed.). Bloomington, IN: Solution Tree Press.

Sousa, F., Monteiro, I. P., & Pellissier, R. (2009). Creativity and problem solving in the development of organizational innovation. *Projectics/Proyéctica/Projectique, 3,* 41–53.

Springer, S. P., & Deutsch, G. (1985). *Left brain, right brain* (2nd ed.). New York, NY: Freeman.

Staats, A. W. (1968). *Learning, language, and cognition.* New York, NY: Holt.

Staff. (1995). The SOI model school. *SOI News, 17*(2), 4–7.

Stanish, B. (1977). *Sunflowing.* Carthage, IL: Good Apple.

Stanish, B. (1979). *I believe in unicorns.* Carthage, IL: Good Apple.

Stanish, B. (1981). *Hippogriff feathers.* Carthage, IL: Good Apple.

Stanish, B. (1988). *Lessons from the hearthstone traveler.* Carthage, IL: Good Apple.

Stankowski, W. M. (1978). Definition. In R. E. Clasen & B. Robinson (Eds.), *Simple gifts.* Madison: University of Wisconsin-Extension.

Stanley, J. C., & Benbow, C. P. (1986). Youths who reason exceptionally well mathematically. In R. J. Sternberg & J. Davidson (Eds.), *Conceptions of giftedness.* New York, NY: Cambridge University Press.

Stariha, W. E., & Walberg, H. J. (1995). Childhood precursors of women's artistic eminence. *Journal of Creative Behavior, 29,* 269–282.

Starko, A. J. (1995). *Creativity in the classroom.* White Plains, NY: Longman.

Starko, A. J. (2014). *Creativity in the classroom* (5th ed.). New York, NY: Routledge.

Stamm, J. (1971). Vincent Van Gogh: Identity crisis and creativity. *American Imago, 28*(4), 363–372.

Stein, M. I. (1953). Creativity and culture. *Journal of Psychology, 36,* 311–322.

Sternberg, R. J. (1988a). A three-facet model of creativity. In R. J. Sternberg (Ed.), *The nature of creativity* (pp. 125–147). New York, NY: Cambridge University Press.

Sternberg, R. J. (1997). A triarchic view of giftedness: Theory and practice. In N. Colangelo & G. A. Davis (Eds.), *Handbook of gifted education* (2nd ed., pp. 43–53). Boston, MA: Allyn & Bacon.

Sternberg, R. J. (1999). A propulsion model of types of creative contributions. *Review of General Psychology, 3*(2), 83–100.

Sternberg, R. J. (2003). Wisdom, intelligence, and creativity synthesized. Cambridge University Press.

Sternberg, R. J. (2006). The nature of creativity. *Creativity Research Journal, 18*(1), 87–98.

Sternberg, R. J. (2012). The assessment of creativity: An investment-based approach. *Creativity Research Journal, 24*(1), 3–12.

Sternberg, R. J. (Ed.). (1988b). *The nature of creativity.* New York, NY: Cambridge University Press.

Sternberg, R. J., & Lubart, T. I. (1990, September). *The creative mind: An investment theory of creativity.* Paper presented at the meeting of the American Psychological Association, Boston, MA.

Sternberg, R. J., & Lubart, T. I. (1992). Buy low and sell high: An investment approach to creativity. *Current Directions in Psychological Science, 1,* 1–5.

Sternberg, R. J., & Lubart, T. I. (1995). *Defying the crowd: Cultivating creativity in a culture of conformity.* New York, NY: Free Press.

Sternberg, R. J., & Lubart, T. I. (1996). Investing in creativity. *American Psychologist, 51,* 677–682.

Sternberg, R. J., & Lubart, T. I. (1999) The concept of creativity: Prospects and paradigms. In R. J. Sternberg (Ed.), *Handbook of creativity* (pp. 3–16). New York, NY: Cambridge University Press.

Sternberg, R. J., Kaufman, J. C., & Pretz, J. E. (2013). *The creativity conundrum: A propulsion model of kinds of creative contributions.* New York, NY: Psychology Press.

Stravinsky, I., & Craft, R. (1969). *Retrospectives and conclusions.* New York, NY: A. A. Knopf.

Striker, F. (n.d.). *Creative writing workbook and the morphological approach to plotting.* Unpublished manuscript, University of Buffalo.

Strom, R. D., & Strom, P. S. (2002). Changing the rules: Education for creative thinking. *Journal of Creative Behavior, 36,* 183–200.

Subotnik, R. (1988). Factors from the structure of intellect model associated with gifted adolescents' problem finding in science: Research with Westinghouse science talent search winners. *Journal of Creative Behavior, 22,* 42–54.

Sulloway, F. J. (1999). Birth order. In M. A. Runco & S. R. Pritzker (Eds.), *Encyclopedia of creativity* (Vol. 1, pp. 189–202). New York, NY: Academic Press.

Surowiecki, J. (2008, May 12). The open secret of success. *The New Yorker.* Retrieved from http://www .newyorker.com/talk/financial/2008/05/12/080512ta_talk_surowiecki

Swartz, R. J., & Perkins, D. N. (1990). *Teaching thinking: Issues and approaches.* Pacific Grove, CA: Critical Thinking Books and Software.

Szobiová, E. (2008). Birth order, sibling constellation, creativity and personality dimensions of adolescents. *Studia Psychologica, 50*(4), 371.

Taggar, S. (2001). Group composition, creative synergy, and group performance. *Journal of Creative Behavior, 35,* 261–282.

Tan, O. S., Teo, C. T., & Chye, S. (2009). Problems and creativity. *Problem-Based Learning and Creativity,* 1–14.

Tannenbaum, A. J. (1997). The meaning and making of giftedness. In N. Colangelo & G. A. Davis (Eds.), *Handbook of gifted education* (2nd ed., pp. 27–42). Boston, MA: Allyn & Bacon.

Tannenbaum, A. J. (2003). Nature and nurture of giftedness. In N. Colangelo & G. A. Davis (Eds.), *Handbook of gifted education* (3rd ed., pp. 45–59). Boston, MA: Allyn & Bacon.

Tanner, D., & Reisman, F. K. (2014). *Creativity as a bridge between education and industry: Fostering new innovations.* North Charleston, SC: CreateSpace.

Tapscott, D., & Caston, A. (1993). *Paradigm shift: The new promise of information technology.* New York, NY: McGraw-Hill.

Tardif, T. Z., & Sternberg, R. J. (1988). What do we know about creativity? In R. J. Sternberg (Ed.), *The nature of creativity* (pp. 429–440). New York, NY: Cambridge University Press.

Tatsuno, S. M. (1990). *Creativity in Japan: From imitators to world-class innovators.* New York, NY: Harper & Row.

Taylor, C. W. (1986). Cultivating simultaneous student growth in both multiple creative talents and knowledge. In J. S. Renzulli (Ed.), *Systems and models for developing programs for the gifted and talented* (pp. 307–350). Mansfield Center, CT: Creative Learning Press.

Taylor, C. W. (1988). Various approaches to and definitions of creativity. In R. J. Sternberg (Ed.), *The nature of creativity* (pp. 99–121). New York, NY: Cambridge University Press.

Taylor, G. J. (1994). The alexithymia construct: Conceptualization, validation, and relationship with basic dimensions of personality. *New Trends in Experimental & Clinical Psychiatry, 10*(2), 61–74.

Tegano, D. W., Moran, J. D., & Godwin, L. J. (1986). Cross-validation of two creativity tests designed for preschool children. *Early Childhood Research Quarterly, 1,* 387–396.

Terman, L. M. (1925). *Genetic studies of genius: Volume I. Mental and physical traits of a thousand gifted children.* Stanford, CA: Stanford University Press.

Terman, L. M., & Oden, M. H. (1947). *Genetic studies of genius: Volume 4: The gifted child grows up.* Stanford, CA: Stanford University Press.

Thagard, P. (1997). Coherent and creative conceptual combinations. In T. B. Ward, S. M. Smith, & J. Viad (Eds.), *Creative thought: An investigation of conceptual structures and processes.* Washington, DC. American Psychological Association.

Thalbourne, M. A. (1991). The psychology of mystical experience. *Exceptional Human Experience, 9,* 168–186.

Thalbourne, M. A. (2000). Transliminality and creativity. *Journal of Creativity Behavior, 34,* 193–202.

Thalbourne, M. A., Bartemucci, L., Delin, P. S., Fox, B., & Nofi, O. (1997). Transliminality: Its nature and correlates. *Journal of the American Society for Psychical Research, 91,* 305–331.

Thiagarajan, S. (1991, February). Take five for better brainstorming. *Training & Development Journal,* 37–42.

Thompson, J. (1942). *John Thompson's modern course for the piano* (Fifth-grade book). Cincinnati, OH: Willis Music.

Tomasino, D. (2007). The psychophysiological basis of creativity and intuition: Accessing "the zone" of entrepreneurship. *International Journal of Entrepreneurship & Small Business, 4*(5), 528–542.

Tomlinson, C. A. (2017). *How to differentiate instruction in academically diverse classrooms.* Alexandria, VA: ASCD.

Tomlinson, C. A. (2018). Differentiated instruction. In C. M. Callahan & H. L. Hertberg-Davis (Eds.), *Fundamentals of gifted education: Considering multiple perspectives* (2nd ed., pp. 279–292). New York, NY: Routledge.

Torrance, E. P. (1962). *Guiding creative talent.* Englewood Cliffs, NJ: Prentice-Hall.

Torrance, E. P. (1965). *Rewarding creative behavior.* Englewood Cliffs, NJ: Prentice-Hall.

Torrance, E. P. (1966a). *Torrance tests of creative thinking.* Bensenville, IL: Scholastic Testing Service.

Torrance, E. P. (1966b). *Torrance tests of creative thinking, norms-technical manual.* Bensenville, IL: Scholastic Testing Service.

Torrance, E. P. (1968). A longitudinal examination of the fourth-grade slump in creativity. *Gifted Child Quarterly, 12,* 195–199.

Torrance, E. P. (1974). *Norms and technical manual: Torrance tests of creative thinking* (Revised ed.). Bensenville, IL: Scholastic Testing Service.

Torrance, E. P. (1977). *Creativity in the classroom.* Washington, DC: National Education Association.

Torrance, E. P. (1979). *The search for satori and creativity.* Buffalo, NY: Creative Education Foundation.

Torrance, E. P. (1981a). Non-test ways of identifying the creatively gifted. In J. C. Gowan, J. Khatena, & E. P. Torrance (Eds.), *Creativity: Its educational implications* (2nd ed., pp. 165–170). Dubuque, IA: Kendall/ Hunt.

Torrance, E. P. (1981b). *Thinking creatively in action and movement.* Bensenville, IL: Scholastic Testing Service.

Torrance, E. P. (1984). Some products of twenty-five years of creativity research. *Educational Perspectives, 22*(3), 3–8.

Torrance, E. P. (1987a). *The blazing drive: The creative personality.* Buffalo, NY: Bearly.

Torrance, E. P. (1987b). Teaching for creativity. In S. G. Isaksen (Ed.), *Frontiers of creativity research: Beyond the basics* (pp. 189–215). Buffalo, NY: Bearly.

Torrance, E. P. (1988). The nature of creativity as manifest in its testing. In R. W. Sternberg (Ed.), *The nature of creativity.* New York, NY: Cambridge University Press.

Torrance, E. P. (1990a). *Torrance tests of creative thinking: Manual for scoring and interpreting results. Verbal, forms A and B.* Bensenville, IL: Scholastic Testing Service.

Torrance, E. P. (1990b). *Torrance tests of creative thinking: Norms-technical manual. Figural (streamlined) forms A and B.* Bensenville, IL: Scholastic Testing Service.

Torrance, E. P. (1995). *Why fly? A philosophy of creativity.* Norwood, NJ: Ablex.

Torrance, E. P., & Ball, O. E. (1984). *Torrance tests of creative thinking: Streamlined (revised) manual, figural A and B.* Bensenville, IL: Scholastic Testing Service.

Torrance, E. P., & Dauw, D. C. (1965). Aspirations and dreams of three groups of creatively gifted high school seniors and a comparable unselected group. *Gifted Child Quarterly, 9,* 177–182.

Torrance, E. P., & Goff, K. (1989). A quiet revolution. *Journal of Creative Behavior, 23,* 136–145.

Torrance, E. P., & Myers, R. E. (1970). *Creative learning and teaching.* New York, NY: Dodd, Mead.

Torrance, E. P., & Safter, H. T. (1989). The long range predictive validity of the Just Suppose test. *Journal of Creative Behavior, 23,* 219–223.

Torrance, E. P., Khatena, J., & Cunnington, B. F. (1973). *Thinking creatively with sounds and words.* Bensenville, IL: Scholastic Testing Service.

Torrance, E. P., Williams, S. E., Torrance, J. P., & Horng, R. (1978). *Handbook for training future problem-solving teams.* Athens, GA: Georgia Studies of Creative Behavior, University of Georgia.

Torrane, E. P., Ball, O. E., & Safter, H. T. (1992). *Torrance tests of creative thinking: Streamlined scoring guide Figural A and B.* Bensenville, IL: Scholastic Testing Service.

Treffinger, D. J. (1985). Review of the *Torrance Tests of Creative Thinking.* In J. Mitchell (Ed.), *Ninth mental measurements yearbook* (Vol. 2, pp. 1632–1634). Lincoln, NE: Buros Institute of Mental Measurement.

Treffinger, D. J. (1995). Creative problem solving: Overview and educational implications. *Educational Psychology Review, 7,* 301–312.

Treffinger, D. J., & Isaksen, S. G. (in press). Creative problem solving: History, development, and implications for gifted education and talent development. *Gifted Child Quarterly.*

Treffinger, D. J., Isaksen, S. G., & Dorval, K. B. (1994a). *Creative problem solving: An introduction* (Revised ed.). Sarasota, FL: Center for Creative Learning.

Treffinger, D. J., Isaksen, S. G., & Dorval, K. B. (1994b). Creative problem solving: An overview. In M. A. Runco (Ed.), *Problem finding, problem solving, and creativity* (pp. 223–236). Norwood, NJ: Ablex.

Treffinger, D. J., Isaksen, S. G., & Firestien, R. L. (1982). *Handbook of creative learning* (Vol 1). Sarasota, FL: Center for Creative Learning.

Treffinger, D. J., Selby, E. C., & Isaksen, S. G. (2008). Understanding individual problem-solving style: A key to learning and applying creative problem solving. *Learning and Individual Differences, 18*(4), 390–401.

Truitt, A. A., & Ku, H. Y. (2018). A case study of third grade students' perceptions of the Station Rotation blended learning model in the United States. *Educational Media International, 55*(2), 153–169.

Unsworth, K. (2001). Unpacking creativity. *Academy of Management Review, 26*(2), 289–297.

Urban, K. K. (1993). *Test for creative thinking-drawing production (TCT-DP): Design and empirical studies.* Hannover, Germany: University of Hannover.

Urban, K. K., & Jellen, H. G. (1993). *Test for creative thinking–drawing production* (manual). Hannover, Germany: University of Hannover.

Valacich, J. W., Dennis, A. R., & Connolly, T. (1994). Idea generation in computer-based groups: A new ending to an old story. *Organizational Behavior and Human Decision Processes, 57*, 448–467.

Van Gogh Museum. (n.d.). Van Gogh's Illness, Ear and Suicide Explored in Depth for the First Time. Amsterdam, Netherlands: Author.

van Gogh, V. (1952). Letter to Anton Ridder van Rappard. In B. Ghiselin (Ed.), *The creative process.* New York, NY: Mentor.

Van Gundy, A. B. (1983). *108 ways to get a bright idea and increase your creative potential.* Englewood Cliffs, NJ: Prentice-Hall.

Van Gundy, A. B. (1987a). *Creative problem solving.* New York, NY: Quorum Books.

Van Gundy, A. B. (1987b). Organizational creativity and innovation. In S. G. Isaksen (Ed.), *Frontiers of creativity research* (pp. 358–379). New York, NY: Bearly.

Van Tassel-Baska, J. (2004). Creativity as an elusive factor in giftedness. *Update Magazine.* College of William and Mary School of Education.

Vernon, D., Hocking, I., & Tyler, T. C. (2016). An evidence-based review of creative problem-solving tools: A practitioner's resource. *Human Resource Development Review, 15*(2), 230–259.

Vernon, P. E. (1970). *Creativity.* Harmondsworth, UK: Methuen.

Vinacke, W. F. (1952). *The psychology of thinking.* New York, NY: McGraw-Hill.

von Károlyi, C., Ramos-Ford, V., & Gardner, H. (2003). Multiple intelligences: A perspective on giftedness. In N. Colangelo & G. A. Davis (Eds.), *Handbook of gifted education* (3rd ed., pp. 100–112). Boston, MA: Allyn & Bacon.

Von Oech, R. (1983). *A whack on the side of the head.* New York, NY: Warner Communications.

Von Oech, R. (1986). *A kick in the seat of the pants.* New York, NY: Harper & Row.

Walberg, H. A. (1988). Creativity and talent as learning. In R. W. Sternberg (Ed.), *The nature of creativity* (pp. 340–361). New York, NY: Cambridge University Press.

Walberg, H. J. (1994). Introduction. In H. J. Walberg (Chair), *Notable American women: Childhood contexts and psychological traits.* Symposium conducted at the meeting of the American Educational Research Association, New Orleans, LA.

Walberg, H. J., & Stariha, W. E. (1992). Productive human capital: Learning, creativity, and eminence. *Creativity Research Journal, 5*, 323–340.

Walberg, H. J., & Zeiser, S. (1997). Productivity, accomplishment, and eminence. In N. Colangelo & G. A. Davis (Eds.), *Handbook of gifted education* (2nd ed., pp. 328–334). Boston, MA: Allyn & Bacon.

Walberg, H. J., Williams, D. B., & Zeiser, S. (2003). Talent, accomplishment, and eminence. In N. Colangelo & G. A. Davis (Eds.), *Handbook of gifted education* (3rd ed., pp. 350–357). Boston, MA: Allyn & Bacon.

Walberg, H. J., Zhang, G., Cummings, C., Fillipelli, L. A., Freeman, K. A., Haller, E. P., et al. (1996). Childhood traits and experiences of eminent women. *Creativity Research Journal, 9*, 97–102.

Walker, A. M., Koestner, R., & Hum, A. (1995). Personality correlates of depressive style in autobiographies of creative achievers. *Journal of Creative Behavior, 29*, 75–96.

Wallach, M. A., & Kogan, N. (1965). *Modes of thinking in young children.* New York, NY: Holt.

Wallas, G. (1926). *The art of thought.* New York, NY: Harcourt.

Ward, T., Smith, S., & Finke, R. (1996). Creative cognition. In R. Sternberg (Ed.), *Handbook of creativity* (pp. 189–212). Cambridge, England: Cambridge University Press.

Warren, T. F. (1974). How to squelch ideas. In G. A. Davis & T. F. Warren (Eds.), *Psychology of education: New looks.* Lexington, MA: Heath.

Way, B. (1967). *Development through drama.* London, England: Longman.

Weaver, R. L. (1990). Faculty dynamation: Guided empowerment. *Innovative Higher Education, 14*(2), 93–105.

Weiner, D. A. (1992). Mentors highlight the essence. *Gifted Child Today, 15*(3), 23–25.

Weiner, E. (2016). *The geography of genius: A search for the world's most creative places from ancient Athens to Silicon Valley.* New York, NY: Simon and Schuster.

Weiner, R. P. (2000). *Creativity and beyond: Cultures, values, and change.* Albany, NY: State University of New York Press.

Weisberg, P. S., & Springer, K. J. (1961). Environmental factors in creative function. *Archives of General Psychiatry, 5,* 554–564.

Weisberg, R. W. (2015). On the usefulness of "value" in the definition of creativity. *Creativity Research Journal, 27*(2), 111–124.

Welling, H. (2007). Four mental operations in creative cognition: The importance of abstraction. *Creativity Research Journal, 19*(2–3), 163–177.

Welsh, G. S., & Barron, F. (1963). *The Barron-Welsh art scale.* Palo Alto, CA: Consulting Psychologists Press.

Wertheimer, M. (1959). *Productive thinking.* New York, NY: Harper & Brothers.

Westberg, K. L. (1996). The effects of teaching students how to invent. *Journal of Creative Behavior, 30,* 249–267.

Westphal, L. (2017a). *Differentiating instruction with menus: Math (grades 6–8)* (2nd ed.). Waco, TX: Prufrock Press.

Westphal, L. (2017b). *Differentiating instruction with menus: Science (grades 6–8)* (2nd ed.). Waco, TX: Prufrock Press.

Whitlock, A. M. (2019). Elementary school entrepreneurs. *Interdisciplinary Journal of Problem-Based Learning, 13*(1). doi:10.7771/1541-5015.1780

Winslow, E. K., & Solomon, G. T. (1989). Further development of a descriptive profile of entrepreneurs. *Journal of Creative Behavior, 23,* 149–161.

Witkin, H. A., Moore, C. A., Goodenough, D. R., & Cox, P. W. (1977). Field-dependent and field-independent cognitive styles and their educational implications. *Review of Educational Research, 47,* 1–64.

Woodman, R. W., & Schoenfeldt, L. A. (1990). An interactionist model of creative behavior. *Journal of Creative Behavior, 24,* 270–290.

Woodward, C. E. (1989). Art and elegance in the synthesis of organic compounds: Robert Burns Woodward. In D. B. Wallace & H. E. Gruber (Eds.), *Creative people at work: Twelve cognitive case studies* (pp. 227–254). New York, NY: Oxford University Press.

Yamada, H., & Tam, A. Y. (1996). Prediction study of adult creative achievement: Torrance's longitudinal study of creativity revisited. *Journal of Creative Behavior, 30,* 144–149.

Yamamoto, K. (1963). Creative writing and school achievement. *School and Society, 91,* 307–308.

Yamamoto, K. (1966). Do creativity tests really measure creativity? *Theory Into Practice, 5*(4), 194–197.

Yang, C. J., & Chen, J. L. (2011). Accelerating preliminary eco-innovation design for products that integrates case-based reasoning and TRIZ method. *Journal of Cleaner Production, 19*(9–10), 998–1006.

Yates, F. A. (1966). *The art of memory.* Chicago, IL: University of Chicago Press.

Yonge, G. D. (1975). Time experiences, self-actualizing values and creativity. *Journal of Personality Assessment, 39,* 601–606.

Yue, X. D., & Rudowicz, E. (2002). Perception of the most creative Chinese by undergraduates in Beijing, Guangzhou, Hong Kong, and Taipei. *Journal of Creative Behavior, 36,* 88–104.

Zeng, L., Proctor, R. W., & Salvendy, G. (2011). Can traditional divergent thinking tests be trusted in measuring and predicting real-world creativity? *Creativity Research Journal, 23*(1), 24–37.

Zentall, S. S., Moon, S. M., Hall, A. M., & Grskovic, J. A. (2001). Learning and motivational characteristics of boys with AD/HD and/or giftedness. *Exceptional Children, 67,* 499–519.

Zervos, C. (1952). Conversation with Picasso. In B. Ghiselin (Ed.), *The creative process.* New York, NY: Mentor.

Zhou, J., & Oldham, G. R. (2001). Enhancing creative performance: Effects of expected developmental assessment strategies and creative personality. *Journal of Creative Behavior, 35,* 151–167.

Zhou, J., Wang, X. M., Song, L. J., & Wu, J. (2017). Is it new? Personal and contextual influences on perceptions of novelty and creativity. *Journal of Applied Psychology, 102*(2), 180.

Ziegler, R., Diehl, M., & Zijlstra, G. (2000). Idea production in nominal and virtual groups: Does computer-mediated communication improve groups brainstorming? *Group Processes & Intergroup Relations, 3,* 141–158.

Zuckerman, M. (1975). *A manual and research report of the sensation seeking scale* (ETS Test Collection). Princeton, NJ: Educational Testing Service.

Name Index

A

Acar, S., 247
Aiamy, M., 136
Aithal, P. S., 209
Akutsu, S., 297
Albert, R. S., 64
Alcott, L. M., 58
Alexander, T., 132
Allen, M. S., 188
Allen, W., 308
AL-Tarawneh, N. S., 209
Amabile, T. M., 3, 27, 33, 65, 146, 147, 243, 258
Ambrose, D., 41
Anderson, A., 125
Andreason, N. C., 71
Andreason, R. N., 72
Andrews, F. M., 24
Archer, T., 65
Arieti, S., 3, 99
Arnold, J., 192
Arons, M., 26
Ashria, I. H., 45
Assouline, G., 274
Atkinson, R. C., 74
Atkinson, R. L., 74
Autry, G., 58
Averill, J. R., 46, 69
Axelrod, D., 269

B

Baer, J., 5, 44, 159, 292, 309
Ball, O. E., 248, 249, 259
Bandalos, D., 232
Barron, F., 3, 9, 63, 64, 66, 67, 70, 76, 188, 233–234, 258, 299
Barry, K., 125
Barrymore, E., 80
Bartemucci, L., 67
Bartlett, M. M., 253
Basadur, M., 104–105, 240, 258
Bass, S., 228
Batey, M., 3
Bear, P. K., 31, 64
Beethoven, L. V., 11, 77, 79, 110, 113
Beghetto, R. A., 3, 23, 146, 152, 155, 160–161, 165
Begley, S., 63
Belcher, T. L., 24
Belland, B. R., 269
Belushi, J., 98, 299
Bem, S. L., 26, 65

Benbow, C. P., 274
Benet, M., 299
Berger, D. E., 77, 228
Berlyne, D. E., 292
Bernard, A., 305
Besemer, S. P., 9, 149–150, 294
Besold, T. R., 131
Bethune, M. M., 80
Betts, G. T., 280–281
Binker, A. J. A., 215
Biondi, A. M., 48
Bissel, G. B., 128
Black, H., 308
Black, S., 308
Blanchard, B., 122
Bloom, B. S., 81–82, 85, 215, 293, 307
Boden, M. A., 145, 164
Bogen, G., 3
Bogen, J., 3
Bollen, K. A., 228, 231
Briggs, R. W., 185
Briskman, L., 8
Bristol, A. S., 99
Brody, E. W., 185
Brody, L. E., 274
Bronowski, J., 122
Brualdi, A., 230
Brunel, M. I., 128
Bruner, J. S., 150, 164
Buchwald, A., 127
Buckmaster, L. R., 298
Budmen, K. O., 215
Buijs, J., 105
Bull, K. S., 64, 83, 235, 243–244, 258, 291, 301
Burton, R., 98
Butcher, H. J., 3
Buzan, T., 183
Byrnes, P., 243
Bzdawka, D., 252

C

Cabra, J. F., 177
Calkins, L. M., 269
Callahan, C. M., 227, 234
Campbell, D. T., 29
Cantor, A., 72
Capote, T., 123
Carlsson, I., 256
Carson, R., 80
Caruso, E., 58
Caston, A., 41

Cattell, R. B., 254
Chan, D. W., 31
Chan, L., 31
Chaplin, C., 175
Chen, J. L., 131
Chiu, C. Y., 158, 297
Chopin, F., 125
Christie, A., 123–124, 176
Christie, T., 3
Churchill, W., 58
Chye, S., 107
Clark, C. H., 48
Clasen, D. R., 277
Clasen, R. E., 277
Clinton, H., 126
Cobain, K., 98
Cocteau, J., 11
Coşkun, H., 209
Coleridge, S., 13
Colson, K. R., 256
Columbus, C., 271, 308
Columbus Group, 271
Condon, C. F., 238
Conners, J. L., 126
Connolly, T., 185
Conti, R., 27
Coon, H., 27
Copland, A., 124
Costa, A. L., 215
Cox, C., 234
Cox, P. W., 254
Craft, A., 148, 153
Cramond, B., 232, 242, 247–248, 259
Crandall, R., 298
Crawford, R., 186, 188, 196
Cropley, A. J., 247
Crosby, N., 175, 308
Cseh, G. M., 297
Csikszentmihalyi, M., 3–4, 10, 27–28, 31, 33, 77, 79, 85, 154, 157, 297, 300, 310
Cui, C. A., 124
Cunnington, B. F., 256
Curie, M., 155, 290

D

Dacey, J. S., 47, 67, 76, 150, 256
Dali, S., 305
Damm, V. J., 299
Dana, 98
Dangerfield, R., 175, 308
Daniels, J. R., 65

Daniels-McGhee, S., 77, 110
Darwin, C., 80, 123
Dauw, D. C., 247
Da Vinci, L., 59,75, 79, 122, 290,
    308
Davis, G. A., 24, 24, 44, 64–65, 67–
    68, 71, 77, 79, 83, 110, 125,
    135, 176–177, 179, 186, 189,
    195, 215, 228–229, 232–233,
    235–237, 244, 253, 256, 258,
    269, 272–273, 291, 298, 301,
    303, 308
de Bono, E., 42, 47, 49, 174, 185,
    191, 195, 205–220, 301, 307,
    310
Degas, E., 122
Delin, P. S., 67
De Mestral, G., 95, 107, 129
deMille, R., 306
Demirkan, H., 4
Dennis, A. R., 185
Denny, T., 238
Derks, P., 66
Deutsch, G., 75
de Vries, A., 66
de Vries, R. E., 66
Dewey, J., 97, 111
Dickens, C., 58, 79
Diehl, M., 185
Dillon, J. T., 95
DiPego, G., 179, 186, 189
Disney, W., 148, 290
Doares, L. M., 96
Domb, E., 131
Domino, G., 69
Dorval, K. B., 6, 100, 105, 174
Dow, G. T., 3, 292
Drost, E. A., 228–232
Dunbar, K., 128, 137
Duncan, I., 58
Duryea, C., 129
Dweck, C. S., 297

E

Eberhardt, J., 269
Eberle, P., 306–307
Ebersole, P., 296
Edison, T., 47–48, 58, 290, 303
Edwards, M. O., 83, 301
Eichenberger, R. J., 256
Einstein, A., 3,11, 14, 28, 58, 77, 94,
    113, 133, 174, 195, 228
Eisenman, R., 75
Eliot, T. S., 3, 28, 122–123
Epstein, R., 22
Erdos, G., 45
Erixon, A., 65

F

Fabun, D., 7, 9, 66, 189
Fan, X., 249
Farajallah, A. K. M., 209

Farley, F. H., 65, 292
Feij, J. A., 66
Feist, G. J., 64, 84
Feldhusen, J. F., 238, 258, 279–281,
    295
Feldman, D. H., 79, 82, 85, 154, 165,
    227
Fields, W. C., 175
Finke, R. A., 25
Fiore, L. B., 47
Firestien, R. L., 100, 297
Fischer, B., 82
Fleming, E. S., 247
Fleming, L., 268
Florida, R., 45, 50
Flower, L., 77
Flowers, J. H., 43, 111
Ford, H., 58
Fox, B., 67
Frankfort, H., 144
Franklin, B., 59, 75
Freeman, J., 3
French, C., 67, 71
Freud, S., 2, 3, 5, 9, 20–21, 23, 28,
    33, 66, 99, 109, 112, 133,
    155–156, 290, 308
Furnham, A., 3

G

Galati, F., 159
Galileo, 79
Galinsky, A. D., 158
Galton, F., 74, 154
Galvani, L., 128
Gandhi, M., 3, 28, 130, 155, 243
Garbin, C. P., 43, 111
Gardner, H., 3–5, 10, 20, 28–31, 33,
    64, 79, 85, 154–157, 165, 297
Garland, J., 299
Garrison, J., 97
Gassmann, O., 131, 137
Gates, B., 180
Gauguin, P., 175
Gelade, G., 242
Gendrop, S. C., 135–136
Gentry, M., 276
Georgiou, G. J., 97
Gershwin, G., 58
Getzels, J. W., 59, 77, 96, 233–234,
    254–255, 257, 259
Ghiselin, B., 3, 40, 174
Gilhooly, K. J., 97
Glasman, E., 182, 184
Glassner, J. J., 144
Glăveanu, V. P., 59, 158, 165
Glick, I. D., 72
Gluefinger, G., 190
Göçmen, Ö., 209
Godwin, L. J., 255
Goertzel, M. G., 234
Goertzel, T. G., 234
Goertzel, V., 234

Goethe, J. W., 5, 79
Goff, K., 245
Goldman, C., 297
Goodenough, D. R., 254
Gorder, W. D., 256
Gordon, W. J. J., 26, 43, 47, 49, 97,
    128, 132–135, 137, 307–308
Gough, H. G., 64, 239, 258
Graham, M., 3, 28, 97
Gregoire, C., 68
Grigorenko, E. L., 99
Grskovic, J. A., 242
Grube, E., 305
Gruber, H. E., 43
Guastello, D., 252
Guastello, S. J., 4, 252
Guilford, J. P., 8, 77, 97, 226, 231,
    245, 251–253, 257, 259, 295
Gundy, Van, 10, 42, 45–47, 49–50,
    95, 174, 183, 188, 191–195,
    197
Gutenberg, J., 128, 137

H

Haag, R., 22
Hagen, M., 305
Haghani, F., 136
Hall, A. M., 242
Hall, L., 185
Hall, S., 41–42
Halverson, E. R., 268
Hamburger, M., 110
Hammerschmidt, P. K., 242
Harnadek, A., 308
Hartman, R., 234
Hasirci, D., 4
Hattie, J., 268
Hausman, C. R., 3, 20
Hayes, J. R., 77
Heberle, J., 67
Heilbrun, A. B., Jr., 239
Helfert, C. J., 67
Hélie, S., 98, 112
Hemingway, E., 98, 123, 228
Henie, S., 80
Hennessey, B. A., 9, 243
Herbig, M. P., 71, 79, 81
Herrmann, W. E., 196
Herron, D. M., 144
Hetherington, E. M., 75
Hewett, I., 148
Higgins, J. M., 95, 174, 179,
    182–185, 188, 195
Hira, A., 268
Hittner, J. B., 65
Hocking, I., 177
Holland, J. L., 229, 243
Holt, R. R., 109, 113
Holyoak, K. J., 128
Honeywell, L., 256
Hong, Y. Y., 297
Hooker, C., 297

Horng, R., 303
Hospers, J., 68
Houtz, J. C., 109
Howe, E., 128–129
Hughes, H., 59, 228, 299
Hui, A., 32
Hum, A., 71
Hunsaker, S., 272
Hynes, M., 268

I

Ideagen, 185, 196
Inman, T. F., 275
Ironson, G., 233
Isaksen, S. G., 6, 9, 100–101, 103, 105, 174, 177, 181, 242, 297

J

Jackson, M., 80
Jackson, P. W., 59, 72, 80, 148, 156, 233, 234, 254
Jaeger, G. J., 8, 65, 146, 164
Jamison, K. R., 71, 72
Jefferson, T., 59, 308
Jellen, H. G., 250–251, 257, 305, 310
Johnsen, S. K., 272
Johnson, D. J., 31, 64
Jones, G., 42
Jones, L. V., 226
Joplin, J., 98, 299
Jung, C., 5–6, 10, 20
Juntune, J. E., 268

K

Kaltsoonis, B., 256
Kandinsky, W., 110, 113
Kang, C., 44
Kaplan, S. N., 275
Karnes, F. A., 278, 298
Karwowski, M., 297
Kashdan, T. B., 66
Käski-Jannes, A., 98
Kastenbaum, R., 297
Katz, A. N., 76
Kaufman, A. B., 99, 112
Kaufman, J. C., 3, 68, 72, 99, 112, 155, 159–162, 164–165, 289, 299
Kaufman, S. B., 68
Kaur, M., 209
Kaya, F., 268
Keeley, P., 268
Kekule, F. A., 110, 113, 123
Keller, H., 80, 130
Kercher, J. K., 280
Keys, A., 272
Khaleefa, O. H., 45
Khatena, J., 256
Kilgour, M., 153–154
Kim, D., 131
Kim, J., 131
Kim, K. H., 63, 227, 231

Kim, N., 269
Kipling, R., 13–14, 77
Kirchner, E. P., 24
Kirton, M. J., 241, 258
Kivunja, C., 209
Knight, H. V., 298
Koestler, A., 7, 13, 23, 94, 110–111, 122
Koestner, R., 71
Kogan, N., 59–60, 232–233, 253–254, 257, 259
Kolloff, P. B., 279, 295
Kornilov, S. A., 99
Kosslyn, S. M., 111
Kozbelt, A., 23
Kreklau, H., 215
Kris, E., 21, 33, 100
Krumnack, U., 131
Ku, H. Y., 268, 276
Kubie, L. S., 23–24, 33, 94, 97
Kühnberger, K. U., 131
Kulp, M., 256
Kumar, P. M., 209
Kurti, D. L., 268
Kurti, R. S., 268
Kwang, N. A., 241

L

Lansky, L. M., 76
LeBoutillier, N., 110, 113
Lee, Y., 131
Lees-Haley, P. R., 236, 243–244, 258
Leff, H. L., 108, 112
Lennon, K., 47
Leroux, J. A., 242
Leung, A. K. Y., 158
Leveque, L. C., 6
Levitt-Perlman, M., 242
Lewis, J. D., 298
Lim, W., 31, 64, 131
Lincoln, A., 58, 79, 128, 130
Lipman, M., 215
Liszt, F., 124
Lloyd, H., 96, 130
Lombroso, C., 3–5, 13
London, J., 72
Lowell, A., 11, 14
Lowes, J. L., 13
Lubart, T. I., 20, 29, 226, 232
Lubetzky, O., 57
Lucas, G., 175
Ludwig, A. M., 11, 72, 79, 299
Lunde, I., 299
Lupkowski-Shoplik, A., 274
Luther, M., 79

M

MacFarlene, B., 276
MacKinnon, D. W., 63–64, 67, 70, 84, 145–149, 151, 164, 233–234
Maddux, W. W., 158

Majid, A. K., 209
Makel, M. C., 226
Maltzman, I., 22, 33
Mance, M., 174
Manilow, B., 125, 137
Marks, D. F., 110, 113
Marland, S. J., 270
Martindale, C., 67
Martinez, S. L., 268
Martinsen, Ø. L., 64
Maslow, A., 25–26, 33, 59, 71, 289, 292–293, 295–300, 309–310
Mason, J. G., 8, 191
Matthews-Morgan, J., 232
Mattimore, B. W., 185
Mayer, R. E., 231, 292
McConnell, T. J., 269
McCoun, D. A., 298
McCune, J. C., 185
McDonough, B., 177
McDonough, P., 177
McFadzean, E. S., 42
McNair, A., 268
Mednick, M. T., 24
Mednick, S. A., 24
Meeker, M., 253, 295
Meeker, R., 253, 295
Menaker, E., 5
Merrotsy, P., 152
Merzel, A. P. C., 299
Messick, S., 148
Metcalfe, J., 98
Michael, W. B., 234
Michalko, M., 174
Michelangelo, 75
Millar, G. W., 64, 223, 247
Mittleman, D., 185
Mobley, M. I., 96
Monet, C., 185
Moon, I., 131
Moon, S. M., 242, 279
Moore, C. A., 254
Morelock, M. J., 82, 227
Morgan, D. N., 145
Morse, S., 128
Moses, Grandma, 80
Moustakis, C., 296, 310
Moyer, J., 296
Mozart, W. A., 3, 10, 11, 13, 77, 79, 82, 155, 156, 299
Mraz, W., 296
Mudd, S., 7, 241–242
Mumford, M. D., 96
Murdock, M. C., 174
Murray, 9
Myers, R. E., 306, 307

N

Neitzsche, F., 3
Nemeth, C. J., 297
Nemiro, J., 96
Newell, A., 8

Nicholls, J. G., 3
Nietsche, F., 14
Niu, W., 32, 45
Norlander, T., 65, 98, 112
Norman, D. A., 100
Nunamaker, L., 185
Nunnally, J. C., 228

O
O'Connor, A. J., 297
O'Connor Boes, J., 96
Oden, M. H., 272
Odoardi, R. H., 272
Okuda, S. M., 77, 96, 228, 235–236, 243
Oldham, G. R., 243
O'Quin, K., 9, 66, 150–151, 164, 294
O'Reilly, J., 22
Ormerod, T. C., 97
Osborn, A. F., 6, 100, 131, 174, 178–182, 185–186, 191–192, 195–197

P
Paivio, A., 268
Pappano, L., 177
Parke, B. N., 243
Parke, R. D., 75
Parker, C., 98
Parker, J., 269
Parkhurst, H. B., 101
Parnes, S. J., 6, 83, 100–102, 104, 112, 301, 307
Pasteur, L., 58, 128
Patricola, C., 109
Paul, R., 215
Pavlov, I., 21, 24
Pearson, D. G., 297
Perkins, D. A., 7, 9, 13, 29, 94, 215
Perkins, D. N., 215
Peters, T., 41
Peterson, J. M., 65, 76
Peterson, L., 268
Phillips, L. H., 297
Piaget, J., 40, 44
Picasso, P., 3. 10, 13, 28, 58, 123, 175, 228, 243
Piechowski, M. M., 68
Piers, E. V., 24
Piirto, J., 157, 165
Plath, S., 72
Plato, 3, 6, 293
Plucker, J. A., 3, 31–32, 34, 64, 98, 152, 165, 222, 230, 232, 243
Poe, E. A., 77, 299
Poincaré, J. H., 11, 13
Pollock, J., 72, 156
Porshe, J. D., 7
Post, F., 72
Potter, H., 12
Powers, S. V., 242

Poze, T., 132, 134–135, 308
Preston, J. H., 11
Pretz, J. E., 161, 164
Prince, G., 48, 127, 132–134, 137
Pringle, P., 240
Proctor, R. W., 231
Pryor, K. W., 22
Puccio, G. J., 174, 177, 241

Q
Qian, M., 226

R
Ramos, S. J., 268
Ramos-Ford, V., 28
Rank, O., 5, 13, 20, 59
Read, G. M., 7
Reis, S. M., 72, 74, 84, 176, 243, 257, 270–271, 273, 278–279, 281
Reisman, F. K., 176
Reiter-Palmon, R., 96
Rembrandt, 79, 156
Remote Associates Test (RAT), 24, 33
Renoir, A., 175
Renzulli, J. S., 64, 69, 72, 74, 84, 226, 230, 234–235, 242–243, 257–258, 270–271, 273, 275, 278–281, 295
Reston, J. D., 97
Rhodes, M., 4, 8, 9, 13, 45, 50, 144, 145, 158, 164, 206
Rich, G. J., 158, 165
Richards, R. L., 71, 153, 165, 299
Rickles, D., 175, 308
Rieke, M. L., 252
Riley, T. L., 278
Rimm, S. B., 44, 64, 68, 96, 176, 215, 228, 232–233, 236–237, 269
Rivers, J., 175
Robb, Z., 298
Roberts, J. L., 275
Robinson, K., 9, 41, 49, 130
Rodrigues, D., 241
Roe, A., 155
Roeper, G. A., 290
Rogers, C. R., 7, 9, 25–26, 33, 58, 66, 292, 295, 301, 309–310
Rogers, W., 58
Roid, G., 253
Roosevelt, E., 80
Rothenberg, A., 3, 20
Rubenson, D. L., 29
Rubinstein, H., 80
Rudowicz, E., 32
Ruff, M., 290
Rugg, H., 24, 33, 94, 97
Runco, M. A., 3, 8, 23, 29, 31–32, 34, 43, 59, 64–65, 71, 77, 96, 98, 105, 109, 112, 146, 164,

228, 232, 235–236, 243, 247–248, 256, 258–259, 296, 298

S
Sadowski, M., 268
Saeki, N., 249
Safter, H. T., 228, 232–233, 245, 249
Saidam, S. M., 209
Salvendy, G., 231
Sawyer, K., 32, 268
Schaefer, C. E., 72, 237–238, 257–258
Scharber, C., 268
Schatz, E. M., 298
Schawlow, A., 65
Schilling, M. A., 153, 165
Schlichter, C., 308
Schmidhuber, J., 66
Schockley, W., 228
Schoenfeldt, L. A., 30
Schubert, D. S. P., 74–75
Schubert, H. J. P., 74–75
Schuldberg, D., 67, 71, 235, 299
Schussel, N. R., 75
Schwering, A., 131
Seidel, G. J., 6
Seigle, D., 269
Selby, E. C., 100, 242
Serrat, O., 307
Seurat, G., 125, 175
Shah, J., 183
Shakespeare, W., 22, 122–123, 129, 137, 290
Shallcross, D. J., 189, 303
Shaw, J. C., 8
Shaw, M. P., 99, 112
Sheerer, M., 43
Shelley, Mary, 12
Sheridan, K. M., 268
Shields, S., 71
Shostrom, E. L., 298
Shulz, C., 10
Shurkin, J., 272
Siau, K. L., 179–180, 184–185
Silverman, L. K., 272
Silvia, P. J., 60, 63, 66, 72
Simberg, A. S., 44, 46
Simon, H. A., 8
Simonton, D. K., 3–4, 10, 13, 29, 33–34, 63–65, 74–75, 79, 82–85, 94, 152–155, 159, 165, 228, 234
Sio, U. N., 97
Sirota, M., 97
Skagen, A., 182
Skinner, B. F., 3, 21–22, 24, 30, 33, 109, 112
Skuka, M., 24
Slocum, M. S., 131
Smith, E., 301

Smith, E. V., 272
Smith, G. F., 174, 194, 197
Smith, G. J. W., 256
Smith, J. M., 69
Smith, L., 234
Smith, S. F., 125
Smith, S. M., 25, 27
Smulders, F., 105
Snow, R. E., 292
Solomon, G. T., 64, 70–71, 297, 299
Somers, J. V., 72
Song, L. J., 147
Sosniak, L. A., 79, 81–82, 85, 293
Sousa, D. A., 275
Sousa, F., 105
Springer, K. J., 247
Springer, S. P., 75
St. Laurent, Y., 71, 299
Staats, A., 23, 33
Stager, G., 268
Stamm, J., 57
Stanish, B., 135, 191, 301, 303, 305, 307–308
Stankowski, W. M., 270
Stanley, J. C., 274, 281
Stariha, W. E., 29, 64, 79
Starko, A. J., 268, 292, 309
Stein, G., 11, 14
Stein, M. I., 145
Sternberg, R. J., 3–4, 20, 26–27, 29, 32–34, 45, 64–65, 67, 78, 161–165, 226, 232–233, 294, 308
Stone, B. L., 67, 71
Stravinsky, I., 3, 28, 148
Striker, F., 122, 175, 186, 188–189, 196
Subkoviak, M. J., 64, 67, 232, 235, 298
Subotnik, R., 77
Sulloway, F. J., 75
Sun, R., 98, 112
Surowiecki, J., 162
Sutton, J., 236, 244
Swartz, R. J., 215
Swords, M., 236, 244
Szobiová, E., 75

T
Taggar, S., 179–180, 195, 240
Talbot, R. J., 241
Tam, A. Y., 245
Tan, M., 99
Tan, O. S., 107
Tannenbaum, A., 79, 82, 85
Tanner, D., 176
Tapscott, D., 41
Tardif, T. Z., 3–4, 64–65, 78, 308
Tarter, B. J., 256

Tatsuno, S. M., 183–184
Taylor, C. W., 4, 7, 65
Taylor, G. J., 65, 231
Tegano, D. W., 255
Teo, C. T., 107
Terman, L. M., 74, 228, 272, 281
Thagard, P., 7, 128
Thalbourne, M. A., 67, 84
Thiagarajan, S., 183
Thissen, D., 226
Thompson, J., 124
Thurston, B. J., 235
Tolstoy, L., 58
Tomasino, D., 297–298
Tomlinson, C. A., 275
Torrance, E. P., 3, 4, 6, 13, 44, 50, 64, 67, 69, 72, 83–84, 97, 111, 223, 228–229, 232–233, 238, 244–251, 255–259, 272, 290–291, 293, 301–303, 305–307, 309, 310
Torrance, J. P., 303
Toynbee, A., 94
Treffinger, D. F., 241
Treffinger, D. H., 149–152
Treffinger, D. J., 6, 100–101, 103–106, 112, 149–152, 241–242, 297
Truitt, A. A., 268, 276
Twain, M., 58, 67
Tyler, T. C., 177
Tyrrell, S., 268

U
Ueberroth, P., 206
Uhlman, C. E., 96
Unsworth, K., 2
Urban, K. K., 250–251, 257, 305, 310

V
Valacich, J. W., 185
Van der Meer, H., 105
Van Dusen, L., 251
Van Gogh, V., 1, 3, 10, 13, 19, 28, 39, 57, 72, 93, 121–122, 143, 173, 175, 205, 221, 267, 289, 299
Van Gundy, A. B., 10, 42, 45–47, 49–50, 95, 174, 183, 188, 191–195, 197
Vega, L. A., 105
Vernon, D., 177
Vernon, P. E., 67
Vetrano, C., 215
Vinacke, W. F., 99
Von Braun, W., 58
Von Károlyi, C., 28
Von Oech, R., 40, 47–48, 50, 68, 106, 293, 301

W
Wagner, M. D., 74
Walberg, H. J., 29, 60, 63–64, 71, 79–81, 85, 234
Walker, A. M., 71
Wallace, D., 296
Wallach, M. A., 59–60, 232–233, 253–254, 257, 259
Wallas, G., 6, 13, 30, 97–99, 111–112, 302
Walters, B., 308
Wang, X. M., 147
Ward, T. B., 25
Warren, T. F., 48
Watson, J. B., 109
Watson, T., 48
Watt, J., 128
Weaver, R. L., 297
Weiner, D. A., 296
Weiner, E., 154
Weiner, R. P., 158
Weintraub, S., 247
Weisberg, P. S., 247
Weisberg, R. W., 146–147, 247
Welles, O., 59, 67, 290
Welling, H., 122
Welsh, G. S., 66, 239
Wertheimer, M., 40
Westberg, K. L., 191
Westinghouse, G., 129, 212
Westphal, L., 275
White, A., 234, 237
Whitlock, A. M., 269
Whitney, Eli, 128
Wiebe, D., 98
Williams, D. B., 63, 234
Williams, M. L., 185
Williams, S. E., 303
Winslow, E. K., 64, 70–71, 297, 299
Witkin, H. A., 254
Woodman, R. W., 30–31
Woodward, C. E., 110
Woodward, R., 110, 113
Woolf, V., 55–56, 72
Woolworth, F. W., 58
Wordsworth, W., 3, 110, 113
Wright, C. R., 231–232
Wright, F. L., 129
Wright, O., 58
Wright, W., 58
Wu, J., 147

Y
Yamada, H., 245
Yamamoto, K., 232, 247
Yang, C. J., 131
Yates, F. A., 109
Yates, G., 268
Yawkey, T. D., 72

Yonge, G. D., 299
Yue, X. D., 32

Z

Zaharias, B. D., 80

Zeiser, S., 60, 63, 79, 234
Zeng, L., 231–232
Zentall, S. S., 242
Zervos, C., 10
Zeschky, M., 131, 137

Zhou, J., 147, 239
Ziegler, R., 185
Zijlstra, G., 185
Zuo, L., 232

Subject Index

Note: Page number followed by *n* indicate notes

A

Abilities, in creative person, 58–59, 76–78
Acceleration, 274–278
Acceptance-finding, 104
Achievement Thinking, 215
Action Information, 243, 273
Adaptive, 146
Adaptors, 241
Adjective Check List (ACL), 70, 239
Advanced research skills, 278
Affective thinking, 278
After-the-fact, definitions of, 270
Alternate forms reliability, 229
Alternatives, search for, 211
Ambiguity, attraction to, 66–67
Ambiguous thinking, 47
Analogical thinking, 47, 95, 177, 307
  in architecture, 130
  in Broadway, 129–130
  in cartoons, 125–130
  in clothes design, 130
  in creative innovation, 124
  defined, 77
  ethics and, 123–124
  importance of, 122
  in literature, 129–130
  in moviemaking, 129–130
  in music, 124–125
  in problem-solving, 131
  in science and invention, 128–129
  synectics methods in, 132
    direct analogy, 132–133
    fantasy analogy, 133–134
    Gordon's equation form of, 135
    personal analogy, 133
    symbolic analogy, 134–135
    teaching synectics thinking, 135–136
  in TV, 129–130
Analogies
  direct, 132–133
  fantasy, 133–134
  personal, 133
  symbolic, 134–135
Analysis, 77, 307
Architecture, analogical thinking in, 130
Arousal seeking, 65
Art, mysterious mental happenings in, 10–11
Artistic, aesthetic interests, 67–68

Assisters, 104
Associational fluency, 76
Asynchronous development, 271
Attribute listing, 95*n*, 186–188, 189
Attribute modifying, 186–188
Attribute transferring, 188
Autonomous Learner Model (ALM), 280
Avoid Ambiguity, 47

B

Backward Brainstorming, 182
Barriers. *See also* Blocks
  to creativity, 39–49
  formalization, 42
  habit as, 40–41
  learning as, 40–41
  procedural, 42
  resource, 47
  social/political, 45
Barron–Welsh Art Scale, 60, 239–240
Be Practical, 47
Behaviorist theories
  Maltzman, Irving, 22
  Skinner, Burrhus F., 22
  Staats, Arthur, 23
Bem Sex-Role Inventory, 65
Berkeley studies, 70
Big C creativity, 152
  cultural contributions to, 157–158
  versus little C creativity, 152
  taxonomy of, 155–157
Big idea stage, 106, 124
Biographical characteristics in creative person, 58–59, 72–74
Biographical traits, 58–59
Birth-order effects, 74
Bisociation of ideas theory, 7, 94
Blocks
  cultural, 44–45
  emotional, 46
  perceptual, 42–43
Brain Drawing, 182
Brainstorming, 177, 178–180, 301
  backward, 182
  cautions about, 185–186
  complaint, 182
  electronic, 184–185
  evaluating ideas, 181
  group, 179
  inverse, 182*n*
  Mitsubishi, 183

  reverse, 177, 182
  running session, 180–181
  Stop-and-Go, 182
  variations on, 182–184
Brainwriting, 183
Brainwriting 6-3-5, 183
Brainwriting Pool, 183
Breaking boundaries, 249, 306
Broadway, analogical thinking in, 129–130

C

California Psychological Inventory, 70
Cartoons, analogical thinking in, 125–127
CATS (Broadway musical), 122
Chameleon problem, 277
Chance-configuration theory, 29
Checklist of idea stimulators, 194
Children, teaching thinking skills to, 215–219
Clothes design, analogical thinking in, 130
Cluster grouping, 276
Co-Incidence theory, 82
Cognitive abilities, 58
Cognitive style, 26–27, 59
Cognitive theories
  creative cognition, 25
  Kubie, Lawrence, 23–24
  Mednick, Sarnoff, 24
  Rugg, Harold, 24
Cognitive thinking, 278
Colorfulness of imagery, 249, 306
Combining ideas, creative process, 7–8
Communities of practice, 81–82
Complaint brainstorming, 182
Complexity, attraction to, 66–67
Component-based theories of creativity, 26
  Csikszentmihalyi, Mihalhyi, 27–28
  domain-relevant skills, creativity relevant processes, task motivation, and environment, 27
  intelligence, cognitive style, personality/motivation, 26–27
Computer programs for brainstorming, 185
Concentration, 78
Concept Fan technique, 210
Consensual Assessment Method, 243

Consensual Assessment Technique, 146
Consequences, predicting, 77
Construct validity, 230–231
Contemporary theories of
  chance-configuration theory, 29
  comment, 33
  implicit theories of creativity, 31–32
  Interactionist Model of Creative
    Behavior, 30–31
  interdisciplinarity, 32
  investment theory of creativity, 29–30
  person, domain, and field, 28–29
Content validity, 231–232
Control, 159
Convergent thinking, 279
CoRT (Cognitive Research Trust)
  Thinking Skills Program,
  217–218
  thinking skills program, 215–216
Creating minds, 28
Creative abilities, 76–78, 302–306
  strengthening other, 306–308
Creative activities
  assessing past, 242–243
  inventories, 243–244
  involvement in, 308–309
Creative Activities Check List (CACL),
  243
Creative attitudes, 301–302
Creative Behavior Inventory, 244
Creative Challenge, 211
Creative cognition, 25
Creative innovation, analogical
  thinking in, 124
Creative pause, 210
Creative person, 4–6, 57–84
  abilities of, 58–59, 76–78
  Berkeley studies, 70
  biographical characteristics of,
    58–59, 72–74
  creativity and intelligence in,
    59–63
  cultivating more creative personality,
    83–84
  eminence and, 79
  Jung, Carl, 5–6
  Lombroso, Cesare, 4–5
  mental disturbance and, 71–72
  negative creative traits in, 69–70
  Otto Rank, 5
  personality traits in, 58–59, 64–69
  similarities and differences in, 59
Creative personality
  cultivating more, 83–84
  inventories, 224–242
Creative potential, high IQ as
  indicator of, 233–234
Creative press, 9–10
Creative Problem Solving (CPS)
  model, 6, 100–106, 131, 301

original model, 101–104
simplex model, 104–105
updated model (version 6.1),
  105–106
Creative process, 6–8, 93–111
  as change in perception, 107–109
  combining ideas, 7–8
  Creative Problem Solving (CPS)
    model in, 6, 100–106, 131
  feedback loops and, 99–100
  imagery and, 109–111
  insight in, 96
  number of, 95–96
  sources of ideas in, 94–95
  steps and sequences in, 97
  Torrance, E. Paul, 6
  two-stage analysis, 106
  Wallas, Graham, 6
  Wallas model, 97–99
Creative Processes Rating Scales, 256
Creative Product Analysis Matrix
  (CPAM), 150–152
Creative Product Semantic Scale
  (CPSS), 9
Creative products, 8–9
  categorization of, 152
  creative artifacts versus, 158
  Creative Product Analysis Matrix,
    150–152
  definition, 144–145
  essential characteristics of, 145–149
  evaluation of, 149
  little C creativity, 152–160
  propulsion model, 161–164
Creative students, personality
  information to identify, 242
Creative thinking
  educating for, 290
  personal, 174–176
    encouraging, 176–177
  standard techniques, 177
  techniques, 308
Creative traits, negative, 69–70
Creativeness, awareness of, 64
Creativity, 2–3
  all Rhodes lead to, 144
  barriers to, 39–49
  complexity of, 95
  in creative person, 59–63
  definitions of, 4
  deliberate, 174–175
  early effects on, 155
  eminence and, 79
  entrepreneurship, 297–298
  flow, 297–298
  forced, 174
  in gifted education, 267–280
  implicit theories of, 31–32
  intelligence and, 59–60
  Interactionist Model of, 30–31
  intuitive, 177–178

investment theory of, 29–30
makers mark on, 155
mental disturbance and, 71–72
metacognitive understanding of, 302
popular use of, 296–297
research relating, 298–299
and school achievement, 250
self-actualization, 70, 295–296
special-talent, 59, 83
two criteria of, 233
Creativity approaches
  behaviorist
    Maltzman, Irving, 22
    Staats, Arthur, 23
    Skinner, Burrhus F., 22
  cognitive
    creative cognition, 25
    Kubie, Lawrence, 23–24
    Mednick, Sarnoff, 24
    Rugg, Harold, 24
  component-based theories of, 26
    chance-configuration theory, 29
    Csikszentmihalyi, Mihalhyi,
      27–28
    domain-relevant skills, creativity
      relevant processes, task
      motivation, and environment, 27
    intelligence, cognitive style,
      personality/motivation, 26–27
    person, domain, and field, 28–29
  contemporary theories of
    comment, 33
    implicit theories of creativity,
      31–32
    Interactionist Model of Creative
      Behavior, 30–31
    interdisciplinarity, 32
    investment theory of creativity,
      29–30
  humanistic, 25–26
  psychoanalytic
    Freud, Sigmund, 20–21
    Kris, Ernst, 21
  theoretical, 20
Creativity assessment
  assessing past creative activities,
    242–244
  creative personality inventories,
    234–242
  divergent thinking tests, 244–246
  formal identification, 234
  high IQ as indicator of, 233–234
  issues in measuring, 227–228
  psychometrics, 226
  recommendations, 257
  Torrance Tests of Creative Thinking,
    246–233
  uses of, 226–227
Creativity Attitude Survey (CAS),
  237–238
  one inventory with three, 240–241

Creativity connection, imagery and, 109–111
Creativity consciousness, 65, 83, 301–302
Creativity influencer, 145
Creativity-relevant processes, 27
Creativity Self-Report Scale, 238
Creativity tests, uses of, 256–257
Creativity training, issues in, 290
    creative atmosphere, 292
    individual differences in motivation to create, 291–292
    in responsiveness to, 291
    teaching, 290–291
        within content area, 292–293
Credentials, 159
Criterion-referenced, 248
Criterion-related validity, 232
    C-Sketch, 183
Csikszentmihalyi, Mihalhyi, 27–28
Cultural blocks, 44–45
Curiosity, 66
Curriculum, differentiation of, 275

D

Defamiliarization, 136
Deferred judgment, 9, 178
Deliberate creativity, 177–178
Design problems, 304
Detroit Public Schools Creativity Scales, 243
Developmental considerations, 83
Direct analogy, 132–133
Disinhibition hypothesis, 98–99
Distortion Stepping Stone, 212
Divergent thinking, 39, 101, 279
    tests, 234, 244–246
DNA, 154
Domain
    characteristics of, 157
    relevant skills, 27
Don't Be Foolish, 48
Double-helix model, 110
Dream images, 110
Dual Code Theory (DCT), 268
Dynamic dimensions, 79

E

E-mail, 184–185
Education, 83
Eidetic images, 109
Elaboration, 151–152, 302
    exercises, 304
    stage, 106, 124
Electronic brainstorming, 184–185
Elegance, 152
Embedded figures test, 254
Eminence
    classic characteristics of, 79–81
    creativity and, 79
Emotional blocks, 46

Emotional expressiveness, 248, 305
Emotional giftedness, 67
Enrichment, 274
    activities in, 276–278
Enrichment Triad Model, 278–280
Escape, 212
Ethical trait, 69
Ethics
    analogical thinking and, 123–124
    of borrowing ideas, 123–124
Evaluation, 77, 307
Exaggeration Stepping Stone, 212
Expressiveness of titles, 248
Extending boundaries, 249, 306

F

Face validity, 231
Fact-finding, 101, 102
False negatives, 233
False positives, 233
Fantasy, 36, 225, 282
    analogy, 133–134
    attraction to, 66–67
    thinking, 47
Feedback loops and creative process, 99–100
Field, characteristics of, 158–159
Field trips, 276
Filament Technique, 214
Fixed points, 210
Flexibility, 77, 302
Fluency, 76, 302
Focus, 210–211
Follow the Rules, 47
Foolish thinking, 47
Forced creativity, 174
Formalization barrier, 42
Four Ps
    creative person, 4–6
    creative press, 9–10
    creative process, 6–8
    creative product, 8–9
    creativity, 2–3
        definitions of, 4
Fourth-grade slump, 44
Freewheeling, 179
Freud, Sigmund, psychoanalytic theories, 20–21
Functional fixedness, 42
Future Problem Solving (FPS) program, 176, 277

G

Gallery Method, 184
Get Fired Technique, 133
Getzels and Jackson tests, 254–255
Gifted students
    acceleration differentiation, and enrichment alternatives, 274–278
    characteristics of, 272

goals and curricula of programs for, 273
    identification of, 272–273
Giftedness
    definitions of, 269–271
    emotional, 67
Goldilocks principle, 160
Greenfield Thinking, 214
Group brainstorming, 179
Group Inventory for Finding Creative Talent, 237
Group Inventory for Finding Interests (GIFFI), 236–237
Group Support Systems (GSS), 184
Grouping plans, 276
Guilford tests, 251–253

H

Habit, as barrier to creative thinking and innovation, 40–41
Hallucination, 109
Handedness, 74–76
Heredity, 154
Hidden figures test, 254
High energy, 65
Historiometric approach, 154
How Do You Think? (HDYT) creativity test, 67, 71, 235–236
How-to-learn skills, 278
Humanistic theories, 25–26
Humor, 66, 249, 306
Hypnagogic images, 110
Hypnopompic images, 110

I

Idea Board, 184
Idea checklists, 191–195
Idea-finding process, 103, 131
Idea-Fisher, 185
Idea-spurring questions, 191, 191–192
Idea squelchers, 48–49
Idea stimulators, checklist of, 191–192
Ideagen, 185
Ideas
    borrowing, 123–124
    sources of, 94–95
Ideational fluency, 76
Illumination, 98
I'm Not Creative, 48
Imagery
    creative process and, 111
    creativity connection, 109–111
Imagination, 109, 306–307
Implementation groups, 242
Implicit theories of creativity, 31–32
Improvement Thinking, 215
Incomplete figures, synthesis of, 248
Incubation, 97, 99
    information processing theory of, 100

Independence, 64
Independent learning abilities, 279
Information processing theory of
     incubation, 100
Information processing traits, 78
Innovators, 241
Insight in creative process, 96
Instruction, differentiation of, 275
Intelligence, 26, 59–63, 83
     creativity and, 59–63
Interactionist Model of Creative
     Behavior, 30–31
Interdisciplinarity, 32
Internal consistency reliability,
     229–230
Internal visualization, 249, 305
Interrater reliability, 229
Intrinsic task motivation, 27
Intuition, 78
Intuitive creativity, 177–178
Intuitiveness, 68
Invention, analogical thinking in,
     128–129
Invention Machine, 185
Inverse Brainstorming, 182*n*
Investment theory of creativity,
     29–30
It's a Snap, 277

J

Japanese Lotus Blossom technique,
     183
Judging Criteria Instrument, 256
Jung, Carl, 5–6
Junior Great Books program, 278

K

Kirton Adaptation–Innovation
     Inventory (KAI),
     217–218Koestler, Arthur, 7–8
Kris, Ernst, psychoanalytic theories, 21
Kubie, Lawrence, cognitive theories,
     23–24

L

Lateral thinking, 207
     strategies, 209–214
Learning, 59
     as barrier to creative thinking and
          innovation, 40–41
     centers, 276
Leveraging, 156
Library research projects, 276
Lines and circles, synthesis of, 301
Literature
     analogical thinking in, 129–130
     mysterious mental happenings in,
          10–13
Little C creativity (LCC), 152
Logical thinking, 78, 307

Lombroso, Cesare, 4–5
Long-term problems, 277
Lyrical thinking, 47

M

Magical ideation, 71
Mainstream, 276
Maltzman, Irving, behaviorist theories,
     22
Measuring traits and abilities versus
     predicting creative eminence,
     227–228
Mednick, Sarnoff, cognitive theories, 24
Mental blocks to creative thinking, 47
Mental disorder, 83
Mental disturbance
     creative person and, 71–72
     creativity and, 71–72
Mental set, 42, 206*n*
Mentorship, 277
Mess-finding, 101
Metacognition, 302
Method 6-3-5, 183
Mind Mapping, 183
Mindlink, 196
Minnesota Multiphasic Personality
     Inventory (MMPI), 70, 71
Mitsubishi Brainstorming, 183
Morphological synthesis, 188–191
Movement and action, 305
Moviemaking, analogical thinking in,
     129–130
Multiple-talent, definition, 270
Multiplicative notion, 82
Music, 124–125
     analogical thinking in, 124–125
     mysterious mental happenings in, 10
Myers-Briggs Type Indicator, 70
Mysterious mental happenings, 2, 10,
     94
     in art, 10
     in literature, 11–13
     in music, 10–11
     in science, 10
Mythical thinking, 47

N

Negative creative traits, 69–70
Negative traits in creative person, 69–70
Neighborhood Watch idea, 206
NHK method, 184
Nonconformists, 44*n*
Norm-referenced, 248
Novelty, 150–151
     attraction to, 66–67

O

Odyssey of the Mind (OM) program,
     176, 277
Onomatopoeia and Images test, 256

Open-mindedness, 68
Oral communication skills, 278
Organic, definition, 151
Original model, CPS, 101–104
Original self-report inventories, 244
Originality, 65, 77, 302–303
Outcomes, predicting, 77
Outside Validating criteria, 233
Overexcitability, 68

P

Paranormal hallucination, 109
Past creative activities, 234
Percentage, definitions of, 270
Percept Generic Test, 256
Perception, creative process as change
     in, 107–108
Perceptiveness, 68, 78
Perceptual aberration, 71
Perceptual blocks, 42–43
Perceptual set, 42, 206*n*
Perkins, David, 7
Permutations, 94
Personal analogy, 132
Personal creative thinking techniques,
     174–177
Personal obviousness, 153
Personal probability, 152
Personality, 83
Personality traits, 58–59, 64–69
     in creative person, 64–69
Personality/motivation dimension, 27
Phillips 66 procedure, 182
Planning groups, 242
Play Is Frivolous, 48
Poetic thinking, 47
Predicting outcomes, 307
Preparation, 97
Preschool and Kindergarten Interest
     Descriptor, 237
PRIDE scores, 237
Primary process thinking, 109
Problem-based Learning (PBL), 269
Problem finding, 96, 306
Problem solving
     analogical thinking in, 131
     educating for, 290
Procedural barriers, 42
Product improvement problems, 304
Program evaluation, research
     suggestions for, 249–250
Propulsion model, 161–164
     forward incrementation, 162–163
     advanced, 163
     integration, 164
     reconstruction, 163
     redefinition, 162
     redirection, 163
     reinitiation, 164
     replication, 162
Psychoanalytic theories

Freud, Sigmund, 20–21
Kris, Ernst, 21
Psychological safety, 9
Psychological type, 5
Psychometrics, 226
Pull-out program, 276

Q

Questions, idea-spurring, 181

R

Random Input, 212–213
Random Word, 212–213
Rank, Otto, 5
Reference materials, 278
Reflecting, 157
Regress, ability to, 78
Reliability
    in creativity assessment, 228–230
    reducing error, 230
    types, 229–230
Remote Associates Test (RAT), 24
Resistance to premature closure, 305
Resisters, 104
Resolution, 150
Resource barriers, 47
Resource room plan, 276
Restitution, 98
Reversal-Dereversal, 182
Reversal provocation, 212
Reverse Brainstorming, 177, 182, 305
Richness of imagery, 249
The Right Answer, 47
Risk-taking, 64
The Rite of Spring, 148
Rugg, Harold, cognitive theories, 24
Rules, 41–42

S

Saturday programs, 276–277
SCAMPER technique, 191, 307
School-within-a-school plan, 276
Schoolwide Enrichment Model, 279
Science
    analogical thinking in, 128–129
    mysterious mental happenings in, 11
Self-actualization
    and creativity, 83, 295–296
    entrepreneurship, 297–298
    flow, 297–298
    growth in, 26
    popular use of, 296–297
    research relating, 298–299
Self-actualized creativity, 300–301
    emphasis on personality and
        affective traits, 299–300
Self-actualized person, Maslow's 15
    characteristics of, 25
Sensation seeking, 65
Sensation Seeking Scale, 65

Sensitivity to Problems, 77, 300
Short-term problems, 277
SIL method, 184
Simplex model, CPS, 104–105
Six Thinking Hats, 208–209
Skinner, Burrhus F., behaviorist
        theories, 22
Social conscience, 9
Social/political barriers, 45
SOI-Learning Abilities test, 253
Solution finding, 101
Sounds and Images test, 256
Special talent creativity, 59, 83, 292
Speculative thinking, 47
Staats, Arthur, behaviorist theories, 23
Standard creative thinking techniques,
        177–178
Stanford-Binet Intelligence Scale, 251
Star model, 79
Statement of Past Creative Activities
        (SPCA) inventory, 244
Static dimensions, 79
Status hierarchy, 42
Stepping Stone provocation, 212, 215
Stop-and-Go Brainstorming, 182
Storyboarding, 184
Storytelling articulateness, 248
Stratals, 213
Streamlined scoring system, 248
Structure of Intellect (SOI) model, 251
Study of Mathematically Precocious
        Youth (SMPY) program, 274
Summer programs, 276–277
Surreal thinking, 47
Symbolic analogy, 134–135
Symbolic thinking, 47
Synectics
    in analogical thinking, 132–136
    Gordon's Equation Form of, 135
    teaching, 135–136
Synesthesia, 109
Synthesis, 77, 151–152, 305
    of incomplete figures, 248
    of lines or circles, 249
Synthetic thinking, 77

T

Take Five procedure, 183
Talent, definitions of, 270
Ten-Year Rule, 155
*Teorija Reschednija Izobretatel'skich
        Zadac* (TRIZ) method, 131
Test for Creative Thinking–Drawing
        Production (TCT-DP),
        250–251
Test–retest reliability, 229
That's Not Logical, 47
That's Not My Area, 48
Things done on your own, 244
Thinking. *See also* Analogical thinking;
        Creative thinking

affective, 278
ambiguous, 47
analogical, 307
cognitive, 278
convergent, 279
divergent, 47, 97, 279
fantasy, 47
foolish, 47
logical, 78
lyrical, 47
mythical, 47
poetic, 47
primary process, 109
speculative, 47
surreal, 47
symbolic, 47
synectics, 132
synthetic, 77
teaching skills in, to children,
        215–219
visual, 47
wishful, 212
Thinking Creatively in Action and
        Movement (TCAM), 255
Thoroughness, 85
Thought images, 109
Three-ring definition of giftedness,
        271
Three-stage enrichment model, 279
Threshold concept, 59–63
Thrill-seeking, 65
To Err Is Wrong, 47–48
Torrance, E. Paul, 6
Torrance Tests of Creative Thinking
        (TTCT), 229, 246–250, 302
    divergent thinking tests, 244–246
Traditions, 41–42
Transcending nature, 149
Transformation, 77, 307
Transforming nature, 149
Transliminality, 67
Traumatic events, 83
Triarchic model of creativity, 26
TV, analogical thinking in, 129–130
Two-stage analysis, 106

U

United States Academic Decathlon,
        278
Unusual perspective, 305
Unusual visualization, 249, 305
Updated model (version 6.1), CPS,
        105–106

V

Validity
    in creativity assessment, 230–233
    types, 230–233
Verbal versus nonverbal divergent
        thinking tests, 234
Verification, 98

Visible Learning, 268
Visionary type, 5
Visual communication skills, 278
Visual thinking, 47
Visualization, 77, 177, 307
Voice messaging, 184–185

W

Wallach and Kogan tests, 253–254
Wallas, Graham, 6
Wallas model, 97–99
Well-crafted, 151
What if? questions, 47

What Would Happen If . . . ?, 176, 303
Wishful thinking, 212
Word Fluency, 251–252
Workshop Model, 269
Written communication skills, 278